Corporate Social Responsibility in a Globalizing World

Why do corporations increasingly engage in good deeds that do not immediately help their bottom line, and what are the consequences of these activities? This volume examines these questions by drawing on historical documents, interviews, qualitative case comparison, fieldwork, multiple regression, time-series analysis, and multidimensional scaling, among others. Informed by neoinstitutionalism and political economy approaches, the authors examine how global and local dimensions of contemporary corporate social responsibility (CSR) intersect with each other. Their rigorous empirical analyses produce insights into the historical roots of suspicions concerning cross-societal economic actors, why and how global CSR frameworks evolved into current forms, how conceptions of CSR vary across societies, what motivates corporations to participate in CSR frameworks, what impacts such participation might have on corporate reputation and actual practices, whether CSR activities shield corporations from targeting by boycott campaigns or invite more criticism, and what alternative responses corporations might have to buying into CSR principles.

KIYOTERU TSUTSUI is Associate Professor in the Department of Sociology and Director of the Human Rights Initiative at the University of Michigan, Ann Arbor. His research focuses on global diffusion of human rights and its impact on local politics. He has conducted cross-national quantitative analyses on how human rights ideas and institutions expanded globally and impacted local politics, and qualitative case studies on the impact of global human rights on minority rights activism and discourse around World War II in Japan. In addition to government practices and activism by civil society actors, his recent research examines corporate behavior around social responsibility initiatives. His research has been funded by the National Science Foundation, National Endowment for the Humanities, Social Science Research Council, Center for Global Partnership, and other foundations, and his work has appeared in *American Sociological Review, American Journal of Sociology, Social Forces, Social Problems*, and other social science journals.

ALWYN LIM is an assistant professor of sociology at the University of Southern California with research interests in globalization, organizations, and institutions. His research examines the moral regulation of the global economy, in which global actors attempt to shape the institutions that govern macro society-economy relationships. Currently, his research examines the convergence of state and non-state actors around the global corporate responsibility movement. He is also developing further research on globalization and early nation-state formation that examines international agreements and treaties in the late nineteenth and early twentieth centuries. His work has appeared in the *American Sociological Review* and the *Annual Review of Law and Social Science*. He received his PhD from the University of Michigan, Ann Arbor, in 2012.

Business and Public Policy

Series Editor:

ASEEM PRAKASH, University of Washington

Series Board:

Vinod K. Aggarwal, University of California, Berkeley
Tanja A. Börzel, Freie Universität Berlin
David Coen, University College London
Peter Gourevitch, University of California, San Diego
Neil Gunningham, The Australian National University
Witold J. Henisz, University of Pennsylvania
Adrienne Héritier, European University Institute
Chung-in Moon, Yonsei University
Sarah A. Soule, Stanford University
David Vogel, University of California, Berkeley

This series aims to play a pioneering role in shaping the emerging field of business and public policy. *Business and Public Policy* focuses on two central questions. First, how does public policy influence business strategy, operations, organization, and governance, and with what consequences for both business and society? Second, how do businesses themselves influence policy institutions, policy processes, and other policy actors and with what outcomes?

Other books in the series:

TIMOTHY WERNER, *Public Forces and Private Politics in American Big Business*
HEVINA S. DASHWOOD, *The Rise of Global Corporate Social Responsibility: Mining and the Spread of Global Norms*
LLEWELYN HUGHES, *Globalizing Oil: Firms and Oil Market Governance in France, Japan, and the United States*
EDWARD T. WALKER, *Grassroots for Hire: Public Affairs Consultants in American Democracy*
CHRISTIAN R. THAUER, *The Managerial Sources of Corporate Social Responsibility: The Spread of Global Standards*

Corporate Social Responsibility in a Globalizing World

Edited by
KIYOTERU TSUTSUI AND ALWYN LIM

CAMBRIDGE
UNIVERSITY PRESS

University Printing House, Cambridge CB2 8BS, United Kingdom

Cambridge University Press is part of the University of Cambridge.

It furthers the University's mission by disseminating knowledge in the pursuit of education, learning and research at the highest international levels of excellence.

www.cambridge.org
Information on this title: www.cambridge.org/9781107098596

© Cambridge University Press 2015

This publication is in copyright. Subject to statutory exception and to the provisions of relevant collective licensing agreements, no reproduction of any part may take place without the written permission of Cambridge University Press.

First published 2015

A catalogue record for this publication is available from the British Library.

Library of Congress Cataloguing in Publication data
Corporate social responsibility in a globalizing world / edited by Kiyoteru Tsutsui and Alwyn Lim.
    pages   cm. – (Business and public policy)
ISBN 978-1-107-09859-6 (hardback)
1. Social responsibility of business.   I. Tsutsui, Kiyoteru.   II. Lim, Alwyn.
HD60.C69136   2015
658.4′08–dc23
                                                                           2014048021

ISBN 978-1-107-09859-6 Hardback

Cambridge University Press has no responsibility for the persistence or accuracy of URLs for external or third-party internet websites referred to in this publication, and does not guarantee that any content on such websites is, or will remain, accurate or appropriate.

For Aya, Julia, and Erin – Kiyoteru Tsutsui
For my family – Alwyn Lim

Contents

Figures	*page* xii
Tables	xiv
Notes on contributors	xvi
Acknowledgments	xxiii

1 The social regulation of the economy in the global context   1
ALWYN LIM AND KIYOTERU TSUTSUI

Part I   Legitimation and contestation in global corporate social responsibility   25

2 Legitimating the transnational corporation in a stateless world society   27
JOHN W. MEYER, SHAWN M. POPE, AND ANDREW ISAACSON

3 Corporate social responsibility and the evolving standards regime: regulatory and political dynamics   73
PETER UTTING

4 Explaining the rise of national corporate social responsibility: the role of global frameworks, world culture, and corporate interests   107
DANIEL KINDERMAN

Part II   Social construction and field formation in global corporate social responsibility   147

5 Corporations, conflict minerals, and corporate social responsibility   149
VIRGINIA HAUFLER

6	The institutionalization of supply chain corporate social responsibility: field formation in comparative context JENNIFER BAIR AND FLORENCE PALPACUER	181
7	Sustainability discourse and capitalist variety: a comparative institutional analysis KLAUS WEBER AND SARA B. SODERSTROM	218

Part III Corporations' reaction to global corporate social responsibility pressures — 249

8	Why firms participate in the global corporate social responsibility initiatives, 2000–2010 SHAWN M. POPE	251
9	Why do companies join the United Nations Global Compact? The case of Japanese signatories SATOSHI MIURA AND KAORU KURUSU	286
10	Global corporate resistance to public pressures: corporate stakeholder mobilization in the United States, Norway, Germany, and France EDWARD T. WALKER	321

Part IV The impact of global corporate social responsibility pressures on corporate social responsibility outcomes — 363

11	Is greenness in the eye of the beholder? Corporate social responsibility frameworks and the environmental performance of US firms ION BOGDAN VASI	365
12	The mobility of industries and the limits of corporate social responsibility: labor codes of conduct in Indonesian factories TIM BARTLEY AND DOUG KINCAID	393

13 Good firms, good targets: the relationship among
    corporate social responsibility, reputation, and activist
    targeting   430
    BRAYDEN G KING AND MARY-HUNTER
    MCDONNELL

14 Conclusion: corporate social responsibility as social
    regulation   455
    ASEEM PRAKASH

Index   473

Figures

1.1	Corporate social responsibility in the context of the social regulation of the economy	*page* 7
2.1a	Cumulative number of international nongovernmental associations (INGOs), 1900–2009	34
2.1b	Regional averages of tertiary students per capita, 1900–2000	35
2.1c	International human rights instruments: cumulative number of rights, freedoms, and entitlements declared over time	35
2.2	Number of multinational corporations, 1850–2000	37
2.3	Number of *New York Times* articles using the terms "multinational company" or "global company"	40
2.4	Articles referencing corporate social responsibility in trade journals and magazines/newspapers over time, 1970–2007	45
2.5	Corporate social responsibility initiatives, 1970–2010	47
2.6	Corporate membership in three major global corporate social responsibility initiatives, 2000–2010.	48
2.7	Dissertation and thesis abstracts with the phrases "corporate social responsibility" or "business ethics," 2000–2011	55
2.8	Cumulative number of corporate social responsibility rankings from 1995 to 2011	57
4.1	Counts of national corporate social responsibility associations, 1960–2010	119
4.2	The rise of national corporate social responsibility associations in Africa	123
4.3	The rise of national corporate social responsibility associations in Asia	124
4.4	The rise of national corporate social responsibility associations in Europe	124

List of figures

4.5	The rise of national of corporate social responsibility associations in North America	125
4.6	The rise of national corporate social responsibility associations in South America	125
4.7	National corporate social responsibility associations and corporate membership in the United Nations Global Compact	126
4.8	National corporate social responsibility associations and United Nations Global Compact national networks	127
4.9	National corporate social responsibility associations and companies reporting according to the Global Reporting Initiative	128
4.10	National corporate social responsibility associations and companies' participation in the Carbon Disclosure Project	129
4.11	International nongovernmental organization memberships in countries with and without national corporate social responsibility associations	134
4.12	Membership in international nongovernmental organizations and national corporate social responsibility	135
7.1	Nonmetric multidimensional scaling of country distances	241
7.2	Tree diagram of country clustering	241
8.1	Number of worldwide members of global corporate social responsibility initiatives by year	255
9.1	The number of United Nations Global Compact signatories in Japan, 2001–2013	296
12.1	Indonesian exports of textiles, yarn, and clothing to developed countries	403

Tables

3.1	Contemporary UN–business regulation (selected initiatives)	page 76
3.2	The expanding arena of civil regulation (selected initiatives)	85
4.1	Establishment dates of national corporate social responsibility associations in different countries	120
4.2	The average (mean) establishment date of national corporate social responsibility associations on six continents	126
4.3	Correlation coefficients for national corporate social responsibility and global actors and initiatives	136
5.1	Primary governance institutions for conflict minerals, 2003–2013	164
6.1	Organizations interviewed	190
6.2	Organizations in supply chain corporate social responsibility field	202
6.3	Comparison of codes	204
7.1	Country institutional profiles	225
7.2	Document sample	228
7.3	Concepts frequently associated with sustainability	229
7.4	Occurrence matrix of sustainability concepts across countries	232
7.5	Illustrative quotes from the analyzed news sources	236
8.1	Univariate statistics	268
8.2	Univariate statistics and correlation matrix	269
8.3	Fixed effects logistic regressions of participation in the Global Compact, Global Reporting Initiative, and Carbon Disclosure Project, 2000–2010	270
9.1	Framework of corporate motives and reasons for adopting voluntary initiatives	299

List of tables

9.2	The basic orientations of United Nations Global Compact signatories in Japan	310
10.1	Corporate grassroots practices in four nations	331
11.1	Means, standard deviations, and sources of variables used in the regression analyses	375
11.2	Corporate social responsibility initiatives and actual environmental pollution: toxic scores, 2007 (Tobit regressions)	377
11.3	Corporate social responsibility initiatives and change in actual environmental pollution: toxic scores change, 2002–2005 (Tobit regressions)	379
11.4	Corporate social responsibility initiatives and perceived EP: iRatings eco-value scores, 2007 (OLS regressions)	382
12.1	Employment of textile, apparel, and footwear production workers across provinces, 2000–2008	405
12.2	Logistic regression analysis of failure of Indonesian textile, apparel, and footwear firms, 2000–2008	408
12.3	Regression analyses of unstable/contingent employment in unionized textile, apparel, and footwear firms in Indonesia	412
13.1	Descriptive statistics and correlation matrix	443
13.2	Probit regressions predicting the likelihood of being boycotted, 1990–2005	446

Notes on contributors

JENNIFER BAIR

Jennifer Bair (PhD Duke) is a comparative sociologist who works at the intersection of economic sociology and the political economy of development. Among her research interests is the development and enforcement of labor standards in global industries, including the role of public and private organizations and other stakeholders in shaping debates and policies regarding labor compliance. She is the editor of *Frontiers of Commodity Chains Research* (2008) and the co-editor of *Free Trade and Uneven Development* (2002) and *Workers' Rights and Labor Compliance in Global Supply Chains: Is a Social Label the Answer?* (2013). She has conducted field research in Mexico, Honduras, the Dominican Republic, and Nicaragua. Her publications include articles in the journals *World Development*, *Social Problems*, *Global Networks*, *Economy and Society*, and *Signs*.

TIM BARTLEY

Tim Bartley is an associate professor of sociology at The Ohio State University. His research focuses on transnational governance and rule-making projects, especially those concerned with global labor and environmental conditions. He is writing a book that compares the implementation of fair labor and sustainable forestry standards in Indonesia and China. His previous work has been published in the *American Sociological Review*, *American Journal of Sociology*, *Social Forces*, *Social Problems*, the *Annual Review of Law & Social Science*, and other outlets. He is co-editor of *Regulation & Governance*, an international, interdisciplinary journal. He received his PhD from the University of Arizona.

VIRGINIA HAUFLER

Virginia Haufler is an associate professor in the Department of Government and Politics at the University of Maryland and is affiliated with the Center for International Development and Conflict Management. Her research focuses on the changing nature of governance in the global political economy, especially the role of transnational corporations. She is currently examining how transnational regulation of the private sector is being used to address issues of conflict and corruption. As Director of the Global Communities Living-Learning Program, she introduces students to both scholarship and experience regarding globalization. She has been a scholar at the University of California, Irvine; the University of Southern California; and the Carnegie Endowment for International Peace. She has served on the boards of nonprofit organizations and has been a consultant to government and international organizations.

ANDREW ISAACSON

Andrew Isaacson is a PhD candidate in sociology at Stanford University. He received his BS in sociology at Iowa State University. His dissertation is on roommate living among adults.

DOUG KINCAID

Doug Kincaid is a senior research associate at Greenwald & Associates in Washington, DC. His research focuses on issues surrounding retirement and investment behavior. He received his MA in sociology from Indiana University.

DANIEL KINDERMAN

Daniel Kinderman's research focuses on the politics of business in advanced capitalism. Current article projects include the struggles over European Union nonfinancial reporting regulation, German employers' neoliberal think-tanks, the relationship between corporate social responsibility and domestic economic liberalization, and the impact of firms' membership in sustainability organizations on their sustainability performance. He is also working on a book project that derives from his dissertation. His publications include articles in *Socio-Economic Review*, *Journal of Common Market Studies*, and *Review of International Political Economy*. He has been a visiting scholar at the Max Planck Institute for the Study of Societies in Cologne and at the Social Science Research Center (WZB) in Berlin; he is currently an assistant professor in the Department of Political Science and International Relations at the University of Delaware. He received his PhD from Cornell in 2011.

BRAYDEN G KING

Brayden G King is an associate professor of management at the Kellogg School of Management at Northwestern University. His research focuses on how social movement activists influence corporate social responsibility, organizational change, and legislative policy making. He has published articles in the *American Journal of Sociology*, *American Sociological Review*, *Administrative Science Quarterly*, *Organization Science*, and numerous other academic journals. He is currently a senior editor at *Organization Science*.

KAORU KURUSU

Kaoru Kurusu is Professor in International Relations at Kobe University, Japan. Her current research interests include human security, Japan's diplomacy in the United Nations, and theories of international relations. She studied at the Graduate School of Arts and Sciences, the University of Tokyo, and earned her PhD from Osaka University. Her publications in the English language include "Japan as an Active Agent for Global Norms"(trans. by R. Kersten) *Asia-Pacific Review* 18-2 (2011); "Japan's Struggle for UN Membership, 1955," in M. Iokibe et al., eds., *Japanese Diplomacy in the 1950s* (2008); "In Search of More Proactive International Role: the Political Dynamism behind Human Security in Japan," in W. Tow et al., eds., *New Approaches to Human Security in the Asia-Pacific* (2013).

MARY-HUNTER MCDONNELL

Mary-Hunter ("Mae") McDonnell is an assistant professor of Strategy, Economics, and Public Policy at Georgetown University's McDonough School of Business. She has a PhD in management and organizations from the Kellogg School of Management and a JD from Harvard Law School. Her work explores the political interactions between corporations and their myriad stakeholders. In particular, she is interested in how a company's sociopolitical embeddedness shapes its corporate social activity and nonmarket strategy. Her work additionally sheds light on the mechanisms that stakeholders use to enforce social norms for corporations and to punish corporate transgressions.

JOHN W. MEYER

John W. Meyer is Professor of Sociology Emeritus at Stanford. He has contributed to organizational theory, comparative sociology, and the sociology of education, developing lines of institutional theory. He has studied the impacts of global society on national states and societies (some papers are collected in *Weltkultur: Wie die westlichen Prinzipien die Welt durchdringen* [2005]; a more extensive set is in Kruecken and Drori, eds., *World Society: The Writings of John W. Meyer* [2009]). He now is involved in research on the world human rights regime, world curricula in mass and higher education, and the widespread expansion of formal organization.

SATOSHI MIURA

Satoshi Miura is a professor of international relations at the Graduate School of Law, Nagoya University. He has been a visiting scholar at the Institute of International Studies, the University of California, Berkeley; a senior fellow at the Ralph Bunche Institute for International Studies, the City University of New York; and a researcher in residence at the PRME Secretariat, UN Global Compact Office. He has written on heterarchy in world politics and transnational governance networks, particularly the UN Global Compact and UN-Supported Principles for Responsible Management Education (PRME), as well as on distributed innovation of norms. He is now examining the evolution of the UN Global Compact.

FLORENCE PALPACUER

Florence Palpacuer is a professor of management studies at the University of Montpellier, France, where she is responsible for a master program in organizational management and sustainable development and for a research program funded by the French National Research Agency on Governance of Enterprises, Organizations, and Sustainable Development (2010–2014). A former consultant at the International Labour Organization in Geneva, she has participated in various international research networks on global value chains, financialization, and their implications for employment and work conditions. Her recent research is on the rise of new resistance movements both in global value chains and in multinational corporations in France. She has published 15 international articles and book contributions on these issues. Her two co-authored books, published in French, promote a critical management perspective on the social consequences of globalization.

SHAWN M. POPE

Shawn M. Pope is a PhD candidate in the sociology department at Stanford University. His dissertation (in progress) examines the rise, diffusion, and entrenchment of global corporate social responsibility initiatives. He has served as a four-year assistant on the Advisory Panel of Investment Responsibility at the Stanford Endowment, spent three years as an investment banker on Wall Street, earned the Chartered Financial Analyst designation, and received a certificate in International Business Practice from the University of Cambridge International Examinations.

ASEEM PRAKASH

Aseem Prakash is Professor of Political Science, the Walker Family Professor for the Arts and Sciences, and the Director, Center for Environmental Politics at University of Washington, Seattle. He is the co-editor of *Journal of Policy Analysis and Management* and the associate editor of *Business & Society*. He is the author of *Greening the Firm* (Cambridge University Press 2000), and the co-author of *The Voluntary Environmentalists* (Cambridge University Press 2006). His recent co-edited books include *Voluntary Regulation of NGOs and Nonprofits: An Accountability Club Framework* (Cambridge University Press 2010), *Advocacy Organizations and Collective Action* (Cambridge University Press 2010), and *Voluntary Programs: A Club Theory Perspective* (2009). He serves as the vice president of the International Studies Association for 2014–2015.

SARA B. SODERSTROM

Sara B. Soderstrom is an assistant professor in organizational studies and program in the environment at the University of Michigan. She studies how individuals within organizations mobilize others, develop coalitions, and access key decision makers when they are trying to implement sustainability initiatives. Further, she studies individual and organizational responses to the ambiguity and uncertainty that surrounds sustainability, such as making sense of emergent issues, prioritizing and agenda setting, and balancing multiple goals. She completed her PhD at the Kellogg School of Management, Northwestern University. Prior to obtaining her PhD, Sara worked as a consultant at McKinsey & Company and led a business transformation team at The Auto Club Group. Sara holds MSE degrees in chemical and environmental engineering and a BSE degree in chemical engineering from the University of Michigan.

PETER UTTING

Peter Utting is Deputy Director, United Nations Research Institute for Social Development (UNRISD), where he coordinates international research projects on issues related to corporate social responsibility, the role of non-state actors in business regulation, social and solidarity economy, and social dimensions of the green economy. With a PhD specializing in the sociology of development, he has published extensively on sustainable development and social change in the global South and on the changing contours of international development policy. His recent edited volumes include *Corporate Social Responsibility and Regulatory Governance: Towards Inclusive Development?* (co-editor J. L. Marques; 2010), *Business Regulation and Non-State Actors: Whose Standards? Whose Development?* (co-editors D. Reed and A. Mukherjee-Reed; 2012), and *Social and Solidarity Economy: Beyond the Fringe* (forthcoming).

ION BOGDAN VASI

Ion Bogdan Vasi is an assistant professor at the University of Iowa in the Department of Sociology. His research examines how social movements contribute to organizational change, industry creation, and policy making. He has published articles in the *American Sociological Review, American Journal of Sociology, Social Forces, Mobilization*, and other journals; he is the author of *Winds of Change* (2011). He recently began projects on the adoption of solar photovoltaic and electric vehicle technologies in the United States.

EDWARD T. WALKER

Edward T. Walker is Associate Professor, Vice Chair, and Director of Undergraduate Studies in the Department of Sociology at the University of California, Los Angeles. His scholarly interests include organizations, social movements, political sociology, the nonprofit sector, and the politics of business. He is author of *Grassroots for Hire: Public Affairs Consultants in American Democracy* (Cambridge University Press 2014) and co-editor (with Caroline W. Lee and Michael McQuarrie) of *Democratizing Inequalities: Dilemmas of the New Public Participation* (forthcoming). His work appears in such venues as the *American Sociological Review, American Journal of Sociology, Social*

Problems, and *Public Opinion Quarterly* and has been funded by the National Science Foundation, the American Sociological Association, and the Robert Wood Johnson Foundation, among other sources.

KLAUS WEBER

Klaus Weber is an associate professor of management and organizations at the Kellogg School of Management at Northwestern University. His research uses cultural and institutional analysis to understand globalization, the environmental movement, and corporate social responsibility. He has studied these issues in the context of health care and biotechnology firms and in alternative agriculture and food production.

Acknowledgments

This volume is a result of two conferences on corporate social responsibility held at the University of Michigan, Ann Arbor, in 2010 and at the International House of Japan in Tokyo, in 2012. Most of the contributors to this volume participated in the two conferences, and presentations and comments by other participants also helped enhance our understanding of globalization and corporate social responsibility enormously. Among them, our special thanks go to Sarah Soule, Emi Sugawara, and Jim Walsh for providing us with extra help in making this volume possible even after (and before) the conferences. We would also like to thank Jerry Davis, Shin Furuya, Jonas Haertle, David Hess, Maureen Kilgour, Tom Lyon, Chris Marquis, Mark Mizruchi, Sandra Waddock, and Marina Whitman for their contributions at the conference in Michigan. We would like to extend our special thanks to the contributors to this volume who worked tirelessly over our two conferences and beyond. We are especially grateful to John Meyer, Aseem Prakash, Satoshi Miura, and Kaoru Kurusu for their support and guidance in putting the conference and edited volume together. We would also like to thank John Haslam and Carrie Parkinson at Cambridge University Press, as well as our anonymous reviewers, for their generosity and patience in seeing this volume through to its completion.

This volume would not have been possible without generous funding by the Japan Foundation Center for Global Partnership (CGP). The CGP enabled us to organize the two conferences and work on this volume, and we are deeply indebted to Tomoki Akazawa and Carolyn Fisher at CGP for working with us from the early stages of the project to the finish line. We also benefited greatly from the funding by the Department of Sociology, the Center for Japanese Studies, the International Institute, the Interdisciplinary Committee on Organizational Studies, and the Ross School of Business, all at the University of Michigan. This work was also supported by the National Research Foundation of Korea Grant funded by the Korean Government (NRF-2013S1A3A2055081).

1 | *The social regulation of the economy in the global context*

ALWYN LIM AND KIYOTERU TSUTSUI

The global expansion of corporate social responsibility (CSR) in recent decades has been spectacular. Although much debate continues on the content and efficacy of CSR, the notion that corporations are accountable for the social and environmental consequences of their activities has become widely accepted in the worlds of business, government, and civil society. Global CSR frameworks such as the United Nations Global Compact (UNGC) and the Global Reporting Initiative (GRI) include thousands of business participants across multiple countries and industries and attract wide support from governments and civil society organizations. Corresponding to the rising global profile of CSR, scholarly attention to CSR has grown tremendously (Haufler 2001; Hoffman 2001; Hoffman and Ventresca 2002; Vogel 2005; Prakash and Potoski 2006; May, Cheney, and Roper 2007; Potoski and Prakash 2009; Soule 2009; Smith et al. 2010; Utting and Marques 2010; Crouch and Maclean 2011; Lindgreen et al. 2012). Building on this literature, this volume examines two key issues in contemporary CSR activities.

The first is the global nature of contemporary CSR efforts. Many CSR debates and activities today assume that CSR entails global problems that require global solutions. Through what historical and institutional processes have we come to accept this global approach to CSR? How did different actors engage in the politics of legitimation and contestation in the evolution of CSR in international society? How have global and national forces combined to construct specific fields of CSR, such as cross-national supply chains, sustainability, and conflict minerals?

Second, the global expansion of CSR ideas and practices exerts considerable pressure on corporations to take a position. What factors shape their reaction to this growing call for CSR action? Why have some corporations joined the global CSR movement while others have resisted or rejected it? If corporations participate in this CSR movement, do they gain anything from their efforts, or do they become targets of further criticism? What impact do these global pressures ultimately have on actual CSR outcomes?

This volume addresses these questions using rich historical data, innovative discourse analysis, in-depth interviews, and sophisticated quantitative methods. In this chapter, we discuss our perspective on CSR as social regulation of the economy, present the analytical framework that guides all the chapters, and summarize the research presented in this volume.

Corporate social responsibility as social regulation of the economy

In this section, we introduce our perspective on the emergence and impact of CSR. We see the essence of contemporary CSR as the social regulation of the economy, which involves attempts by various actors to interpret, guide, and control economic processes that increasingly span national boundaries. A case in point is the emergence of global CSR frameworks. The process began in the early 1970s, when government representatives deliberated an international Code of Conduct for Transnational Corporations (Sagafi-Nejad 2008) amid other similar efforts such as the OECD Guidelines for Multinational Enterprises. Efforts to institutionalize the Code of Conduct as a legally binding UN initiative, however, were unsuccessful because the governments of developed countries subsequently defeated those efforts. Nevertheless, those early efforts in international forums like the UN set the precedent for future CSR frameworks with a global scope (Kell and Levin 2003; Kell 2005). From the 1970s on, other international organizations introduced variants of global CSR frameworks, such as the 1976 OECD Guidelines for Multinational Enterprises, the 1977 International Labour Organization (ILO) Tripartite Declaration, the 1999 Global Sullivan Principles, and the 2003 UN Norms on the Responsibilities of Transnational Corporations. Because of the difficulty all international organizations faced in adopting legally binding frameworks and implementing them, most contemporary CSR frameworks rely on voluntary commitment by corporations and naming-and-shaming efforts by civil society (see chapters in Part I for details of this history). Thus, rather than binding laws, social pressures have been the driving force in contemporary CSR developments.

Our view of CSR contrasts most directly with previous research that highlights internal firm characteristics to understand why corporations engage with CSR. Since corporate practices are the central focus of CSR, it is not surprising that many scholars emphasize internal firm characteristics in their analyses (Carroll 1991). Many such studies seek to link firms' financial performance and CSR adoption (see Pava and Krausz 1995 and Margolis and Walsh 2003 for excellent surveys of these studies). Although this internalist approach to CSR highlights important factors that shape individual corporations' CSR practices, exclusive focus on internal characteristics could mask the role of broader environmental factors in CSR politics. Although some scholars may view CSR as a new means for individual corporations to incorporate externalities into their decision-making process, this approach does not address why CSR became part of such calculations at the firm level. Indeed, recent research reveals that internal firm factors such as financial performance are only weakly correlated with CSR practices (Margolis and Walsh 2003). The lack of a "market for virtue" (Vogel 2005) also substantially weakens the oft-touted argument that CSR practices can be financially beneficial for corporations. Furthermore, a simple aggregation of corporate actions fails to explain the institutionalization of CSR in the form of voluntary frameworks (Sikkink 1986; Bartley 2007; Sagafi-Nejad 2008; Lim and Tsutsui 2012). Although internal firm factors are undoubtedly critical in understanding why individual corporations choose to engage with CSR, they may be less adequate for explaining patterns of CSR engagement across corporations, industries, and countries.

If internal firm factors cannot fully account for the emergence and impact of CSR, what alternative explanations can aid in understanding contemporary developments such as the prevalence of voluntary CSR frameworks? We argue that CSR developed as a result of efforts by various social actors to monitor and control the consequences of corporate and economic activities. We posit that external pressures exerted by trade and investment relationships, government actions, social movement activism, and taken-for-granted models of appropriate organizational behavior work at both global and national levels to push corporations to engage in, co-opt, or react against CSR activities. This approach has a theoretical and empirical basis in various long-standing traditions in social science research that see economic activities as embedded in social structures.

Based on historical and anthropological evidence and political-economic developments in early twentieth-century Europe, Polanyi (1944) argued that economic practices were embedded in social arrangements, particularly government actions that created the conditions for economic activities to flourish. Polanyi noted that it was political actions, not merely capitalist expansion, that established international free trade or the international gold standard. These government actions resulted in economic consequences that threatened existing social arrangements, thus prompting severe domestic reactions. This notion of embeddedness was also influential in sociological (Granovetter 1985; Krippner 2001) and political science (Ruggie 1982, 2003) perspectives on the social bases of economic and organizational practices. In particular, neo-institutionalism in organizational studies (Meyer and Rowan 1977; DiMaggio and Powell 1983; Brunsson 2002) argues that "control" over organizational practices stems from wider institutional sources and highlights external factors such as the coercive role played by powerful organizations, the mimetic effect of organizations conforming to taken-for-granted ideas, and the normative influence of professional organizations. Faced with these external pressures, organizations often forgo internal efficiency considerations and adopt practices that make them appear legitimate to their external constituents in the organizational field. Since the 1980s, the stakeholder perspective in management studies (Freeman 1984, 1994, 1999; Post, Preston, and Sachs 2002) has also theorized beyond firm-level conceptions of CSR by situating corporations' CSR practices in the context of relationships with their stakeholders. Here, it is external actors that directly affect or are affected by the firm's activities that participate in regulating corporate behavior. In management studies, the stakeholder perspective is discussed only within a narrow "shareholder versus stakeholder" debate (see Walsh 2005 for an extensive discussion on this point), but we also see the perspective as the starting point for including many other external influences, including norms, government action, and social movements, into the analysis of corporate engagement with CSR.

Therefore, our central argument is that CSR developments can be more fully accounted for by viewing CSR as a core component of the social regulation of the economy, whether that regulation stems from government policies, taken-for-granted organizational models, or stakeholders of the corporation. We posit that CSR research should devote more attention to situating corporations' CSR practices within this wider global, social, and political context in which corporations operate. This would enable us to more adequately explain many features of contemporary global CSR, such as its emergence, norms, frameworks, and impact on corporations. With this approach in mind, we now explain the more specific analytical framework that we derive from applying the social regulation perspective to the study of CSR.

Analytical framework of this volume

The analytical framework we employ emphasizes two themes that integrate the different chapters of the volume. Our first theme focuses attention on the institutional and economic contexts in which corporations operate – the broader external contexts that encourage or hinder the emergence and impact of global CSR. Our second core theme highlights how global and national dynamics shape CSR ideas and practices differently and how developments in CSR may congeal at the transnational level and yet differ regionally or nationally in their local impact.

First, we make a distinction between two broad sets of factors that are salient in corporations' external environments: institutional and economic factors. On the one hand, there are social-institutional factors such as the impact of norms, taken-for-granted notions of appropriate behavior, and established patterns of rules and meanings on organizational behavior. Sociological approaches such as organizational neo-institutionalism (Meyer and Rowan 1977; Powell and DiMaggio 1991) and world society theory (Meyer et al. 1997; Meyer 2000) emphasize these factors. On the other hand, we cannot ignore political-economic factors such as patterns of economic transactions, configurations of power and conflict dynamics among economic actors, and the intersection of state and corporate interests. These factors play a central role in world-system theory (Wallerstein 1979) and varieties of capitalism approaches (Hall and Soskice 2001).

Second, we give equal weight to the global level of analysis and national determinants of CSR. Although national boundaries and domestic factors serve as important constraints on organizational behavior, we argue that factors at the global and transnational level, especially in the post-World War II era (Meyer 2010), are also powerful shapers of CSR developments. Thus, we make a second set of analytical distinctions, this time regarding how factors at separate levels of analyses may impact the development of CSR ideas and practices. On the one hand, there are factors that operate at the domestic, nation-state level that push organizational action in specific directions, most notably factors associated with domestic business environments and the extent of state coordination or intervention in the national economy (Vogel 1989, 2005; Hall and Soskice 2001). On the other hand, we also emphasize the autonomy of global factors in shaping domestic organizational behavior, whether it is the power of global norms and institutions (Meyer et al. 1997) or economic transactions and dependence relations that span national borders (Wallerstein 1979).

In sum, we argue that studies of contemporary CSR ideas and practices require an analytical framework that enables them to examine institutional and economic contexts at both national and global levels. Our framework reflects recent scholarship that analyzes global governance and corporate responsibility concerns in these multicausal and multilevel contexts (Flohr et al. 2010; Dashwood 2012). Figure 1.1 summarizes some of the key factors in each of the four domains of the analytical framework that we derive by crossing the two contextual dimensions (institutional/economic, global/domestic) that encompass many contemporary developments in CSR. We note that this framework is a heuristic device and that, in reality, all those factors are often closely intertwined.

A growing body of research on CSR has recognized these various contextual factors as salient for explaining the ascendancy of the contemporary CSR movement across various countries. For social-institutional factors operating at the global level, Delmas and Montiel (2008) examine the diffusion of voluntary international management standards in the chemical industry over 113 countries and find that the level of international nongovernmental organizational (INGO) activity in a country, but not trade-related factors, puts pressure on chemical firms to adopt the International Organization for Standardization (ISO) 14001 standards. In their study of cross-national CSR adoption in ninety-nine countries, Lim and Tsutsui (2012) also find that countries' nongovernmental links encourage corporations in those countries to adopt frameworks like the UNGC and GRI but that corporate commitment to CSR is ceremonial in

	Social-Institutional Factors	Political-Economic Factors
Global Level	Normative pressures Global norms International organizations (IGOs/INGOs) Transnational social movements Global CSR frameworks International treaties Regional networks and collaborations World society theory	Foreign economic penetration Cross-national economic transactions Arm's-length/short-term vs. embedded/long-term relationships Economic dependence Race-to-the-bottom vs. ratcheting up Trade, foreign investment, debt World-system theory
Domestic Level	Cognitive receptivity Rationalization of business environment Predominance of rules, standard operational procedures Reduction of organizational uncertainty Transparency vs. corruption Democracy, human development Organizational institutionalism	National economic system Government orientation to economic planning Liberal vs. coordinated economies Government-business relationships Coercion vs. collusion between state and business actors Varieties of capitalism

Figure 1.1 Corporate social responsibility in the context of the social regulation of the economy

developed countries and more substantive in developing countries. Hirschland (2006) surveys the role that non-state actors like businesses and NGOs play in shaping global public policy and finds that these non-state groups are increasingly active in world business forums, global CSR policy circles, and socially responsible investment networks, thus resulting in the construction of many transnational CSR initiatives and code-making and monitoring regimes. Likewise, Segerlund (2010) examines the emergence and subsequent development of global CSR in a variety of intergovernmental settings and finds that NGOs were crucial entrepreneurs in constructing transnational standards for corporate behavior, mainly through multistakeholder processes that involve voluntary agreements established between NGOs and transnational corporations. This line of research demonstrates that social-institutional factors at the global level shape the emergence of global CSR frameworks as well as its diffusion across the globe.

Political-economic factors at the global level are also prominent in explaining CSR developments. Mosley and Uno (2007) study the impact of economic globalization on collective labor rights in developing countries and find that, whereas foreign investment inflows seem to encourage worker rights, trade competition has the opposite effect. Examining the impact of trade relations between countries, Prakash and Potoski's (2006) study of 108 countries finds that specific bilateral trade linkages encourage the adoption of ISO 14001 standards. Greenhill, Mosley, and Prakash (2009) find similar results in their analysis of the trade-based diffusion of labor rights in ninety developing countries. In research on global supply chains, Esbenshade (2004); Ngai (2005); Locke, Amengual, and Mangla (2009); and Fransen (2012) reveal how labor and factory violations by firms' suppliers in overseas locations prompted industry attempts to institute voluntary factory-monitoring regimes, although those regimes have not been entirely successful in addressing further criticisms. Bartley (2007) examines the role of political conflict and contestation between states, NGOs, and corporations in the often-compromised construction of transnational private regulation initiatives in the apparel and forestry industries after specific controversies in those industries in the 1980s and 1990s. Clearly, these global-level political-economic factors circumscribe the expansion of global CSR.

At the domestic level, social and institutional factors in specific countries' business environments can have powerful effects on shaping businesses' cognitive receptivity to CSR practices. Once institutionalized, standard rules and procedures allow corporations to tackle CSR concerns with appropriate responses to organizational uncertainty on a routine, taken-for-granted basis (Howard-Grenville and Hoffman 2003; Howard-Grenville 2006; Campbell 2006, 2007). Galaskiewicz's (1991, 1997) classic studies of corporate philanthropy in the Twin Cities of Minneapolis-Saint Paul find that business leaders' ties with the local community and local nonprofit organizations facilitated the institutionalization of corporate public service activity, leading to greater corporate prosocial actions (cf. Marquis, Glynn, and Davis 2007). In his study of the American chemical and petroleum industries, Hoffman (1999, 2001) finds that, partly due to growing pressure from environmental activists, firms based in the United States began in the 1980s to cooperate with the government to develop norms to signal their social responsibility, thus leading subsequently to more proactive and strategic forms of environmental management in the 1990s. Delmas and Terlaak (2002) compare the institutional structures of four developed countries and find that negotiated agreements between regulators and firms to voluntarily reduce pollution are more likely to be implemented in environments where regulators are able to commit to regulatory continuity. These processes operate in countries in which a culture of consensual policy making exists, especially in France, the Netherlands, and Germany, but not in the United States, which is characterized by a greater degree of fragmentation and open access in policy making. Kollman and Prakash (2002) examine variations among the adoption of global environmental management systems in the United Kingdom, the United States, and Germany. Focusing on the ISO 14001 and the European Union's Environmental Management and Audit Scheme, they find that varying corporate perceptions and responses to these standards were largely shaped by domestic factors, such as how leading firms promoted and disseminated information about those schemes, as well as varying domestic stakeholder responses. In contrast to the United Kingdom and Germany, in the United States, the lack of promotion, as well as lukewarm responses from government and environmental groups, resulted in lower rates of adoption of the ISO 14001 standard. In a similar study, Delmas (2002) finds that cultural elements in European countries, such as the quality of relationships between industry and government agencies, encouraged more corporations to adopt ISO 14001, whereas in the United States adoption was slower due to a lack of cooperation between those institutions. These studies point to how local social and institutional environments shape corporate CSR activities.

On domestic political-economic factors, scholars have examined the impact of different national economic systems and government orientations to economic activity. Matten and Moon (2008) compare American and European corporate approaches to CSR, arguing that more explicit, strategic, and voluntary CSR practices stem from economic systems like the United States where neoliberal government policies promote weaker social solidarity and welfare institutions. Building on Matten and Moon's argument, Jackson and Apostolakou (2010) compare the CSR policies of European firms in different national economic systems and find that CSR practices in liberal economies substitute for more institutionalized forms of stakeholder participation, whereas CSR in coordinated economies takes more implicit forms. Kinderman's (2012) study of Business in the Community, a leading business-led CSR coalition in the United Kingdom, shows how the development of CSR in the United Kingdom was coterminous with the evolution of neoliberal government policies, with members of the British business elite employing CSR to preempt or decrease further government regulation. Marens (2012) reaches similar conclusions in his study of the evolution of CSR in the United States, finding that business claims to social responsibility developed as a result of the weakening of American organized labor and trade unions and the rise of free market liberalism after World War II.

Integrating these four core factors but emphasizing some factors more than others, the chapters in this volume seek to explain the rise of the global CSR movement and its consequences for corporations and CSR outcomes. The authors employ the theories, concepts, and tools of social science disciplines such as sociology, political science, and management and organizations to focus on empirical analyses with reliable and replicable data. We do not start from strong normative positions on CSR; we do not see it as an inherently positive force in the contemporary world nor as an evil plot advanced by capitalists. As discussed earlier, CSR emerged through certain historical processes, and its impact should vary across different social and economic contexts. Thus, to understand the emergence, diffusion, and consequences of CSR, researchers would benefit greatly from social scientific methods that enable them to systematically examine the cross-national historical processes and social and economic contexts in which the CSR developments took place. The contributors to this volume employ various methods ranging from in-depth interviews and historical analysis to multidimensional scaling and longitudinal multivariate regression. We now briefly introduce the chapters.

Four parts of the volume

Contributions to this volume are organized into four main parts that examine (I) the history and current state of efforts to address CSR concerns, (II) global and transnational mechanisms of CSR field

The social regulation of the economy in the global context 11

formation, (III) varied corporate responses to growing global pressures to address CSR, and (IV) the impact of global pressures on actual CSR outcomes. Parts I and II address the first key issue, discussed at the outset, of the emergence and global spread of CSR, and Parts III and IV examine the second core issue of corporations' response to growing pressures to take CSR seriously. Although each chapter emphasizes different aspects of the contrast between institutional and political-economy factors and the interaction between global and local levels identified in Figure 1.1, the importance of integrating all these factors in empirical analyses is evident throughout the volume. Finally, a concluding chapter comments on the research presented in this volume and maps future directions in global CSR research.

Part I: Legitimation and contestation in global corporate social responsibility

Part I examines the broader historical context in which CSR evolved and traces the development of global CSR ideas, their legitimation as organizational practice, the contested status of their institutionalized forms, and their relationship with contemporaneous national CSR activities.

In Chapter 2, John W. Meyer, Shawn M. Pope, and Andrew Isaacson chart the evolution of global CSR concerns by examining the legitimation of the transnational corporation in the post-World War II era. Despite growing cross-national interactions, international society in this era lacks a strong central authority that could lend legitimacy to various international actors. Even so, intergovernmental organizations and INGOs gained legitimate standing in international society as entities for the public good. Transnational corporations, on the other hand, lacked public standing as legitimate actors in international society. This, they argue, is a problem that plagued cross-societal economic actors throughout history. With the growing economic might of transnational corporations, however, the legitimacy problem intensified in the past few decades. Consequently, corporations have been pressed by transnational social movements critical of neoliberal economic models to transform themselves into "good citizens." CSR emerged in this context as an attractive approach for corporations (and also for some civil society actors), and many have committed to global CSR norms in order to earn the "good citizens" label.

Complementing the social-institutional approach of Meyer et al., Chapter 3 by Peter Utting lays more emphasis on political-economy factors. He takes stock of existing multistakeholder CSR initiatives, including various global CSR frameworks, and examines the recent rise of civil regulation efforts around CSR and the potentials and challenges that organizational actors face in making them effective. He finds that the rise of the late-twentieth-century CSR agenda was largely accompanied by significant variations in regulatory approaches and outcomes challenging previous assumptions about the unidirectional shift from "hard" to "soft" regulation in global CSR and the inherent "progressive" trajectory of CSR norms and practices. He explains these variations by examining factors associated with the political economy of regulatory change – power relations, contestation, coalitions, and alliances – in case studies of the Roundtables on Sustainable Palm Oil and Responsible Soy, Fairtrade International, the UNGC, and the OECD Guidelines for Multinational Enterprises. Utting also offers a sobering picture that, despite the rapid growth of global CSR initiatives, only a tiny portion of all the major corporations in the world are members of these global initiatives.

In Chapter 4, Daniel Kinderman examines the extent to which global CSR frameworks shape national-level CSR organizations – business groups at the national level that address social or environmental causes. Those domestic CSR organizations are often rooted in national traditions, institutions, and cultures that vary across countries. He finds that national CSR associations were already successfully consolidated in several countries in the 1970s and 1980s and were relatively autonomous from global CSR frameworks that struggled to be institutionalized during the same time period. From a political economy perspective, it is not surprising that corporations would engage more with domestic business-led CSR organizations than alternative global frameworks over which they have less control. However, Kinderman also finds that the establishment of national CSR associations is strongly correlated with country memberships in INGOs. This suggests an important global-domestic dynamic whereby global nongovernmental linkages may have first encouraged the growth of national CSR associations before pushing CSR concerns up to the level of global CSR frameworks.

Part II: Social construction and field formation in global corporate social responsibility

Building on the analyses of macro-historical processes in Part I, Part II examines the formation of specific subfields of global CSR in the areas of conflict minerals, supply chain CSR, and sustainability.

In Chapter 5, Virginia Haufler examines institutional variation in the transnational regulation of corporations that deal in "conflict commodities," precious materials whose international trade is directly related to regional and national conflict. Her study includes a detailed historical account of field construction surrounding conflict commodities and asks why global efforts to address conflict commodities shifted from a single regulatory institution to multiple regulatory initiatives that combine public and private efforts. Haufler argues that state power, institutional competition, transnational activism, and industry structure were prominent factors that led to a single institution regulating the diamond industry (the Kimberly Process) in the early period (1998–2006) but that produced multiple subsequent initiatives for other conflict minerals as these factors changed in the later period (2006–2012). Although all these factors help to explain institutional variation, Haufler's chapter shows that industry consensus and industry structure were more important for the earlier field formation of conflict diamonds because the transnational diamond trade was dominated by more visible firms that were susceptible to activist targeting. Institutional competition and state power, on the other hand, were more salient for the subsequent regulation of other conflict minerals. In this later period, several initiatives developed, leading powerful states to "forum shop" and activist organizations to partition their attention across multiple industry-led initiatives.

In Chapter 6, Jennifer Bair and Florence Palpacuer examine the development and diffusion of supply chain CSR – a field-in-formation that focuses on multinational corporations' accountability for the actions of their overseas subsidiaries and subcontractors. To account for the development of supply chain CSR over two decades, they compare various explanations of institutional development with an emphasis on the varieties of capitalism perspective. Their research finds two phases in the evolution of supply chain CSR: an early period of field emergence leading to the establishment of multistakeholder initiatives (1989–1999) and a later period of field population and development dominated by business-led CSR initiatives (1999–present). In the first period, the emergence of supply chain CSR reflected an institutional context that shaped the role of business in society and the relationship of the private sector to other social actors. This led to different trajectories of supply chain CSR in the United States and Europe. In the second period, supply chain CSR reflected corporate responses to civil society groups' growing concern about the private governance model, with large retailers from both the United States and Europe creating business-led CSR initiatives.

In Chapter 7, Klaus Weber and Sara B. Soderstrom examine "sustainability" as a cultural category that is often ambiguously defined by practitioners and scholars. They investigate its implicit theorization in public discourse and the degree of consensus about the concept in the national media of six countries, linking differences and similarities in discourse to the institutional diversity of national political economies. Although they find evidence for a core global repertoire of concepts around sustainability, their analyses also reveal wide country-level variation in the extensiveness and content of the public understanding of sustainability, which they attribute to specific domestic processes rather than broad dimensions of capitalist variety. They conclude by reflecting on how cross-national differences in the understanding of sustainability may hinder global-level policy coordination despite consensus around common sustainability themes.

Part III: Corporations' reaction to global corporate social responsibility pressures

Part III examines how corporations react to global CSR pressures. Parts I and II established that global CSR initiatives have expanded exponentially in the past few decades and exert a great deal of pressure on corporations to engage with them. Whereas some corporations engaged proactively in establishing CSR initiatives, the vast majority of corporations respond reactively to CSR pressures. The chapters in Part III examine the diverse spectrum of corporate reactions, including joining the CSR movement by becoming members of some of the CSR initiatives, resisting the pressures by not participating in those initiatives, and finding an alternative approach to deal with CSR pressures.

In Chapter 8, Shawn M. Pope examines the various motives for and external pressures on companies that participate in global CSR frameworks, examining data on roughly 500 leading transnational corporations. He discusses two prevalent approaches to explaining CSR adoption: functional explanations that link CSR adoption to corporations' purposive action (e.g., through cost-benefit calculations, reputation management, or responses to social movement pressure) and institutional explanations that emphasize the appropriateness and legitimacy pressures of CSR adoption regardless of its utility (e.g., through corporate participation in world business forums or the impact of national and world institutional environments). His fixed-effects models find broad support for institutional factors pushing CSR participation.

Complementing Pope's large-N quantitative analyses, Chapter 9 by Satoshi Miura and Kaoru Kurusu employs in-depth interview data on Japanese corporate signatories to the UNGC to examine the organizational motives for CSR framework participation and the perceived impact of participation on corporate signatories. They focus on the importance of meanings that member corporations attribute to their participation in the Global Compact. Using a signaling approach that distinguishes between possible motivations on inward-external and reactive-proactive dimensions, their analysis finds that, although Japanese corporations often have multiple motives for participating in the Global Compact, the proportion of new corporate signatories with outward and reactive orientations to CSR has increased over time, suggesting increasingly stronger external pressures on Japanese corporations to signal their commitment to CSR.

In Chapter 10, Edward T. Walker examines an alternative response by corporations: corporate resistance to external CSR pressure in the form of firm-sponsored pro-corporate advocacy efforts in civil society. He compares corporate grassroots mobilization efforts in the United States, Norway, Germany, and France by examining how political regime types shape the scale of the interest group system and the channels of corporate influence in politics. He finds that statist systems without corporatist bargaining, such as France, are least likely to facilitate corporate mobilization, whereas liberal polities like the United States have an exceptionally high amount of corporate grassroots campaigning. By engaging in these corporate grassroots activities, corporations are proactively countering CSR pressures, demonstrating their "good citizen" side, and discouraging support for tighter governmental regulations. His comparative analysis reveals that the state–society relationship in a country shapes the ways in which corporations engage in grassroots activism as well as CSR efforts.

Part IV: The impact of global corporate social responsibility pressures on corporate social responsibility outcomes

In Part IV, the focus turns to the consequences of global CSR pressures on corporations' practices. The ultimate goal of global CSR movements is to reform corporate behavior and improve corporate practices on the ground. Recognizing this, the chapters in Part IV analyze those factors that lead to varied practical CSR outcomes.

In Chapter 11, Ion Bogdan Vasi examines this question in the area of environmentalism. He conducts quantitative analyses of an original dataset of large US firms' participation in various global and national CSR initiatives to determine the perceived and real impact of those initiatives on firms' environmental performance. He finds that industry analysts are more likely to perceive firms that adopt one or more CSR initiatives as "green" corporations. However, his analyses also reveal that actual superior environmental performance is only associated with firms that participate in the Global Compact framework or that employ GRI standards. He suggests that these frameworks lead to better corporate environmental performance than others because of their links to a broad coalition of economic and nongovernmental actors, reporting requirements, and provision of stakeholder support services.

Chapter 12 by Tim Bartley and Doug Kincaid examines the impact of CSR initiatives on labor issues. Their analysis on apparel, textile, and footwear industries in Indonesia finds major contradictions between voluntary labor standards for global supply chains and their practice "on the ground." Using longitudinal, firm-level, quantitative data, as well as qualitative interview data, they find that corporate commitment to labor standards fails to address capital mobility and employment stability in those industries and that dominant modes of trade undermine the practical application of those standards. Their study shows that even when brands and retailers engage in subcontractor monitoring to improve factory conditions, companies' demand for short production deadlines at low cost countervails any actual or potential CSR improvements for their suppliers and subcontractors. They suggest that CSR based on risk management may be less successful in translating standards into practices than a "patient capital" approach that supports improvements in domestic sociopolitical conditions that are favorable to collective action. This approach requires strong buyer commitments to stabilizing orders and bearing upswings in cost in order to reap future rewards in productivity or price premiums.

In Chapter 13, Brayden G King and Mary Hunter-McDonnell turn their attention to how corporate CSR activities might shape a different outcome: targeting by consumer and activist movements. They examine if corporations' engagement with CSR activities shield them from criticisms (halo effect) or invite even greater scrutiny (liability effect). Analyzing data on consumer boycotts against US firms from 1990 to 2005, they find that firms that create a more reputable and socially responsible image are more vulnerable to activist targeting through both formal and informal means, indicating a liability effect. They argue that firms that build strong CSR reputations also increase expectations on their actual behavior and that activists target highly visible firms to draw public attention to their causes.

In the concluding chapter to the volume, Aseem Prakash reviews the preceding studies and draws together common themes to suggest future directions for global CSR research. He emphasizes the social regulation theme of CSR, noting its current status as a contested global norm and thus its openness to capture by various political actors and institutions. Prakash suggests that future research should account for how CSR programs form part of an expanding "regulatory tool kit" for global governance, one that moves beyond rigid "states versus markets" debates that impose unrealistic standards for the performance of CSR programs. Based on these observations, Prakash suggests that, in order to explain the growing diversity in global CSR's dimensions, obligations, logics, and levels of application, CSR research should continue to assess the strengths and limitations of CSR programs while keeping in mind that they are imperfect governance tools.

Conclusion

CSR, seen in its global context, is the consequence of a multifaceted and often contrasting mix of processes that we have termed the "social regulation of the economy." Following this perspective, three core ideas have emerged from the research contained in this volume. First, many central CSR concerns, issues, and frameworks are now conceptualized and managed at the global and transnational level (Hirschland 2006; Segerlund 2010; Smith et al. 2010; Crouch and Maclean 2011; Lim and Tsutsui 2012), thus making it essential for scholars to understand both the regulation of corporations' cross-national practices as well as the international frameworks that impact corporations' domestic practices. Many existing and emerging CSR frameworks today surfaced specifically to manage CSR concerns that span national boundaries. Furthermore, the rapid expansion of CSR ideas and practices across countries has been possible because of the substantive affinity of CSR with other global progressive norms, such as ideas of human rights and environmental protection. On the one hand, there is a surprising consolidation of CSR norms at the global level, seen in the level of support for global CSR frameworks by international organizations. On the other, this broad consensus on the importance of corporations' social and environmental practices may also mask regional differences in CSR concerns, gaps in the implementation of CSR practices, and issues of power and contestation in CSR field formation.

Second, many of the factors that shape the form, content, direction, and efficacy of CSR norms have multicausal origins and are subject to multilevel dynamics. By placing CSR ideas and practices in their various social and political contexts, this volume has explicitly recognized that both social-institutional and political-economic factors have powerful effects in shaping corporations' conceptual understanding of and practical approaches to CSR. Thus, scholars attending to the emergence, consolidation, and impact of global CSR have the task of examining both institutional and economic factors. Furthermore, the research presented in this volume has also gone beyond simple global-domestic dichotomies to demonstrate how factors at both levels of analysis interact to produce given CSR outcomes, whether it is the final shape that a global CSR initiative takes or the implementation of global CSR frameworks "on the ground."

Third, our approach to CSR has also emphasized the theories, concepts, and methodologies of social science fields such as sociology, political science, and management and organizations. Many previous approaches to CSR adopt a normative paradigm that recommends CSR ideas and practices in relation to factors that are internal to the corporation. Although internal firm factors will undoubtedly remain significant in understanding future directions in CSR, the current momentum in CSR scholarship, reflected in the studies included in this volume, has demonstrated the efficacy of examining CSR as an organizational practice shaped by social, historical, and political processes external to corporations. The authors in this volume have also introduced concepts such as legitimation, contestation, social construction, and field formation into the lexicon of CSR analysis while employing a diversity of research methodologies including quantitative analysis, multidimensional scaling, interviews with CSR practitioners, field research, and historical analysis.

The diversity of areas of CSR concern, accompanied by pressing needs for comprehensive global CSR solutions, suggests that the global CSR field will encompass much organizational and institutional dynamism in the near future. Given the evolution of other global regimes, such as global human rights and environmental institutions, that have seen the consolidation of progressive and rationalized rules at the transnational level, we believe that global CSR frameworks – their construction, elaboration, and implementation – will continue to be the prime locus of legitimation and contestation among actors seeking a social regulation of the global economy. Our hope is that the research presented in this volume will contribute to concretizing the parameters of this continuing dialogue.

References

Bartley, Tim. 2007. "Institutional Emergence in an Era of Globalization: The Rise of Transnational Private Regulation of Labor and Environmental Conditions." *American Journal of Sociology* 113: 297–351.

Brunsson, Nils. 2002. *The Organization of Hypocrisy: Talk, Decisions and Actions in Organizations*. Chichester, UK: Wiley & Sons.

Campbell, John L. 2006. "Institutional Analysis and the Paradox of Corporate Social Responsibility." *American Behavioral Scientist* 49:925–938.

Campbell, John L. 2006. "Why Would Corporations Behave in Socially Responsible Ways? An Institutional Theory of Corporate Social Responsibility." *Academy of Management Review* 32: 946–967.

Carroll, Archie B. 1991. "The Pyramid of Corporate Social Responsibility: Toward the Moral Management of Organizational Stakeholders." *Business Horizons* July–August: 39–48.

Crouch, Colin, and Camilla Maclean, eds. 2011. *The Responsible Corporation in a Global Economy*. New York: Oxford University Press.

Dashwood, Hevina S. 2012. *The Rise of Global Corporate Social Responsibility: Mining and the Spread of Global Norms*. New York: Cambridge University Press.

Delmas, Magali. 2002. "The Diffusion of Environmental Standards in Europe and in the United States: An Institutional Perspective." *Policy Sciences* 35:91–119.

Delmas, Magali, and Ivan Montiel. 2008. "The Diffusion of Voluntary International Management Standards: Responsible Care, ISO 9000, and ISO 14001 in the Chemical Industry." *The Policy Studies Journal* 36:65–93.

Delmas, Magali, and Ann Terlaak. 2002. "Regulatory Commitment to Negotiated Agreements: Evidence from the United States, Germany, the Netherlands, and France." *Journal of Comparative Policy Analysis* 4:5–29.

DiMaggio, Paul J., and Walter W. Powell. 1983. "The Iron Cage Revisited: Institutional Isomorphism and Collective Rationality in Organizational Fields." *American Sociological Review* 48:147–160.

Esbenshade, Jill. 2004. *Monitoring Sweatshops: Workers, Consumers, and the Global Apparel Industry*. Philadelphia: Temple University Press.

Flohr, Annegret, Lothar Rieth, Sandra Schwindenhammer, and Klaus Dieter Wolf. 2010. *The Role of Business in Global Governance: Corporations as Norm-Entrepreneurs*. New York: Palgrave Macmillan.

Fransen, Luc. 2012. *Corporate Social Responsibility and Global Labor Standards: Firms and Activists in the Making of Private Regulation*. New York: Routledge.

Freeman, R. Edward. 1984. *Strategic Management: A Stakeholder Approach*. Boston: Pitman.

Freeman, R. Edward. 1994. "The Politics of Stakeholder Theory: Some Future Directions." *Business Ethics Quarterly* 4:409–421.

Freeman, R. Edward. 1999. "Divergent Stakeholder Theory." *Academy of Management Review* 24:233–236.

Galaskiewicz, Joseph. 1991. "Making Corporate Actors Accountable: Institution-Building in Minneapolis-St. Paul." Pp. 293–310 in *The New Institutionalism in Organizational Analysis*, edited by Walter W. Powell and Paul J. DiMaggio. Chicago: University of Chicago Press.

Galaskiewicz, Joseph. "An Urban Grants Economy Revisited: Corporate Charitable Contributions in the Twin Cities, 1979–81, 1987–89." *Administrative Science Quarterly* 42:445–471.

Granovetter, Mark. 1985. "Economic Action and Social Structure: The Problem of Embeddedness." *American Journal of Sociology* 91:481–93.

Greenhill, Brian, Layna Mosley, and Aseem Prakash. 2009. "Trade-Based Diffusion of Labor Rights: A Panel Study, 1986–2002." *American Political Science Review* 103:669–690.

Hall, Peter A., and David Soskice, eds. 2001. *Varieties of Capitalism: The Institutional Foundations of Comparative Advantage*. New York: Oxford University Press.

Haufler, Virginia. 2001. *Public Role for the Private Sector: Industry Self-Regulation in a Global Economy*. Washington, DC: Carnegie Endowment for International Peace.

Hirschland, Matthew J. 2006. *Corporate Social Responsibility and the Shaping of Global Public Policy*. New York: Palgrave Macmillan.

Hoffman, Andrew J. 1999. "Institutional Evolution and Change: Environmentalism and the U.S. Chemical Industry." *Academy of Management Journal* 42:351–371.

Hoffman, Andrew J. 2001. *From Heresy to Dogma: An Institutional History of Corporate Environmentalism*. Stanford, CA: Stanford University Press.

Hoffman, Andrew J., and Marc J. Ventresca, eds. 2002. *Organizations, Policy, and the Natural Environment: Institutional and Strategic Perspectives*. Stanford, CA: Stanford University Press.

Howard-Grenville, Jennifer A. 2006. "Inside the 'Black Box': How Organizational Culture and Subcultures Inform Interpretations and Actions on Environmental Issues." *Organization and Environment* 19:46–73.

Howard-Grenville, Jennifer A., and Andrew J. Hoffman. 2003. "The Importance of Cultural Framing to the Success of Social Initiatives in Business." *Academy of Management Executive* 17:70–84.

Jackson, Gregory, and Androniki Apostolakou. 2010. "Corporate Social Responsibility in Western Europe: An Institutional Mirror or Substitute?" *Journal of Business Ethics* 94:371–394.

Kell, Georg. 2005. "The Global Compact: Selected Experiences and Reflections." *Journal of Business Ethics* 59:69–79.

Kell, Georg, and David Levin. 2003. "The Global Compact Network: An Historic Experiment in Learning and Action." *Business and Society Review* 108:151–181.

Kinderman, Daniel. 2012. "'Free Us Up So We Can Be Responsible!' The Co-Evolution of Corporate Social Responsibility and Neo-Liberalism in the UK, 1977–2010." *Socio-Economic Review* 10:29–57.

Kollmam, Kelly, and Aseem Prakash. 2002. "EMS-Based Environmental Regimes as Club Goods: Examining Variations in Firm-Level Adoption of ISO 14001 and EMAS in U.K., U.S. and Germany." *Policy Sciences* 35:43–67.

Krippner, Greta R. 2001. "The Elusive Market: Embeddedness and the Paradigm of Economic Sociology." *Theory and Society* 30:775–810.

Lim, Alwyn, and Kiyoteru Tsutsui. 2012. "Globalization and Commitment in Corporate Social Responsibility: Cross-National Analyses of

Institutional and Political-Economy Effects." *American Sociological Review* 77:69–98.
Lindgreen, Adam, Philip Kotler, Joëlle Vanhamme, and François Maon, eds. 2012. *A Stakeholder Approach to Corporate Social Responsibility*. Surrey, UK: Gower Publishing.
Locke, Richard, Matthew Amengual, and Akshay Mangla. 2009. "Virtue Out of Necessity? Compliance, Commitment, and the Improvement of Labor Conditions in Global Supply Chains." *Politics and Society* 37:319–351.
Marens, Richard. 2012. "Generous in Victory? American Managerial Autonomy, Labour Relations and the Invention of Corporate Social Responsibility." *Socio-Economic Review* 10:59–84.
Margolis, Joshua D., and James P. Walsh. 2003. "Misery Loves Companies: Rethinking Social Initiatives by Business." *Administrative Science Quarterly* 48:268–305.
Marquis, Christopher, Mary Ann Glynn, and Gerald F. Davis. 2007. "Community Isomorphism and Corporate Social Action." *Academy of Management Review* 32:925–945.
Matten, Dirk, and Jeremy Moon. 2008. "Implicit and Explicit CSR: A Conceptual Framework for a Comparative Understanding of Corporate Social Responsibility." *Academy of Management Review* 33:404–424.
May, Steve, George Cheney, and Juliet Roper, eds. 2007. *The Debate over Corporate Social Responsibility*. New York: Oxford University Press.
Meyer, John W. 2000. "Globalization: Sources and Effects on National States and Societies." *International Sociology* 15:233–248.
Meyer, John W. 2010. "World Society, Institutional Theories, and the Actor." *Annual Review of Sociology* 36:1–20.
Meyer, John W., John Boli, George M. Thomas, and Francisco O. Ramirez. 1997. "World Society and the Nation-State." *American Journal of Sociology* 103:144–181.
Meyer, John W., and Brian Rowan. 1977. "Institutional Organizations: Structure as Myth and Ceremony." *American Journal of Sociology* 83:340–363.
Mosley, Layna, and Saika Uno. 2007. "Racing to the Bottom or Climbing to the Top? Economic Globalization and Collective Labor Rights." *Comparative Political Studies* 40:923–948.
Ngai, Pun 2005. *Made in China: Women Factory Workers in a Global Workplace*. Durham, NC: Duke University Press.
Pava, Moses L., and Joshua Krausz. 1995. *Corporate Social Responsibility and Financial Performance: The Paradox of Social Cost*. Westport, CT: Quorum Books.

Polanyi, Karl. 1944. *The Great Transformation: The Political and Economic Origins of Our Time.* Boston, MA: Beacon Press.

Post, James E., Lee E. Preston, and Sybille Sachs. 2002. *Redefining the Corporation: Stakeholder Management and Organizational Wealth.* Stanford, CA: Stanford University Press.

Potoski, Matthew, and Aseem Prakash. 2005. "Green Clubs and Voluntary Governance: ISO 14001 and Firms' Regulatory Compliance." *American Journal of Political Science* 49:235–248.

Potoski, Matthew, and Aseem Prakash, eds. 2009. *Voluntary Programs: A Club Theory Perspective.* Cambridge, MA: MIT Press.

Powell, Walter W., and Paul J. DiMaggio. 1991. *The New Institutionalism in Organizational Analysis.* Chicago, IL: University of Chicago Press.

Prakash, Aseem, and Matthew Potoski. 2006. "Racing to the Bottom? Trade, Environmental Governance and ISO 14001." *American Journal of Political Science* 50:350–64.

Ruggie, John G. 1982. "International Regimes, Transactions, and Change: Embedded Liberalism in the Postwar Economic Order." *International Organization* 36:379–415.

Ruggie, John G. 2003. "Taking Embedded Liberalism Global: The Corporate Connection." Pp. 93–129 in *Taming Globalization: Frontiers of Governance,* edited by D. Held and M. Koenig-Archibugi. Cambridge: Polity Press.

Sagafi-Nejad, Tagi. 2008. *The UN and Transnational Corporations: From Code of Conduct to Global Compact.* In collaboration with John H. Dunning. Bloomington: Indiana University Press.

Segerlund, Lisbeth. 2010. *Making Corporate Social Responsibility a Global Concern: Norm Construction in a Globalizing World.* Burlington, VT: Ashgate.

Sikkink, Kathryn. 1986. "Codes of Conduct for Transnational Corporations: The Case of the WHO/UNICEF Code." *International Organization* 40:815–840.

Smith, N. Craig, C. B. Bhattacharya, David Vogel, and David I. Levine, eds. 2010. *Global Challenges in Responsible Business.* Cambridge: Cambridge University Press.

Soule, Sarah A. 2009. *Contention and Corporate Social Responsibility.* New York: Cambridge University Press.

Utting, Peter, and José Carlos Marques, eds. 2010. *Corporate Social Responsibility and Regulatory Governance: Towards Inclusive Development?* Basingstoke, UK: Palgrave Macmillan.

Vogel, David. 1989. *Fluctuating Fortunes: The Political Power of Business in America.* New York: Basic Books.

Vogel, David. 2005. *The Market for Virtue: The Potential and Limits of Corporate Social Responsibility.* Washington, DC: Brookings Institution Press.

Wallerstein, Immanuel M. 1979. *The Capitalist World-Economy.* New York: Cambridge University Press.

Walsh, James P. 2005. "Taking Stock of Stakeholder Management." *Academy of Management Review* 30:426–438.

PART I
Legitimation and contestation in global corporate social responsibility

2 Legitimating the transnational corporation in a stateless world society

JOHN W. MEYER, SHAWN M. POPE, AND ANDREW ISAACSON

As seen in this volume's introductory chapter, the modern movement for corporate social responsibility (CSR) is rooted in the rise of a global society. Its norms and conceptions are supranational and explicitly appeal to very diffuse cultural principles. The corporate citizenship it espouses is global rather than national in character and is focused on matters like general human rights and universal environmental principles. In this chapter, we call attention to the global dimensions of the movement and to its origins in a world society lacking a world state and thus dependent on strong notions of the citizenship responsibilities of participating actors.

Actual and perceived globalization have generated much worldwide social structure. Economic life involves a great expansion in the numbers of transnational corporations, which come to be perceived as independent from their originating national states. These corporations are seen as both sharply self-interested (especially in recent neoliberal thought) and, in a world without a supranational state and its regulatory schemes, lacking accountability and responsibility. In response, the public has become aware of issues related to corporate responsibility, and relevant collective actors and social movements have emerged, oriented toward a more global world. These actors are fueled by and empowered to develop and articulate scandals seen as the ethical violations of supranational corporations. The social movement actors also work to incorporate the transnationals into the disciplining social structures of CSR or global

This chapter benefitted from comments received at conferences on corporate social responsibility in Ann Arbor (2010) and Tokyo (2012) and from comments from Patricia Bromley. In addition to the main funding for the CSR project, work on this paper was aided by funds from the Korean National Research Foundation project at Yonsei University.

citizenship. With institutionalization, responsibility comes to be seen as being in the interest of transnational business. In this chapter, we interpret the corporate responsibility movements as paralleling at the global level earlier systems attempting to control economic forces working beyond any organized polity. The problem is especially acute in polities granting a good deal of public standing to private self-interest. As Tocqueville (1969 [1836]) emphasized, liberal culture (as in nineteenth-century America) generates quite elaborate displays of the virtuous self as citizen. Global neoliberalism, with its celebration of economic self-interest, now produces a worldwide regime for the public certification of the global citizenship of the modern transnational corporation. Whether or not the new norms actually improve practice, they certainly tend to reinforce a "logic of confidence" that participants, although still a minor fraction of those eligible (see Chapter 3 by Peter Utting), are committed to a proper global order (Meyer and Rowan 1978).

We review the background of the issue. Then we discuss the legitimation problems posed by the rapid post-World War II expansion of transnational corporations outside the effective control of national states. Then we analyze the rise, in response, of an elaborate organizational field of CSR.[1] It is common to discuss this field as made up of and constructed by a variety of purposive actors rooted in public or private goods: moral, religious, and political leaders are involved, as are all sorts of people and organizations in the business world. There is, of course, some suspicion that these latter actors act strategically, perhaps with inclinations to cover bad practices with virtuous norms (as suggested by the term "greenwashing"). Our analysis instead focuses on the rise of an extended organizational field of CSR and, in particular, on its roots in wider cultural changes, not on claims about its

---

[1] The term *organizational field* describes the set of actors impinging on a particular social issue or arena, as well as the cultural discourse in which they are embedded (see Wooten and Hoffman 2008 for a review of the concept). For examples, see Hoffman's (2001) study of corporate environmentalism as an organizational field and Bartley's research on forest certification (2007). Some discussions see the actors as constructing the discourse (in some instances as smoke screens to hide, with manipulated frames, raw interests), whereas others see the wider discursive frames evolving to support, legitimate, and constitute the actors involved. Much of the literature on CSR takes the former view, often with skepticism about the long-term results. We take the latter view, emphasizing the causal role of cultural change without addressing the overall consequences for practice.

effectiveness in correcting the evils of corruption, environmental destruction, or the violation of human rights.

Background: social control of economic activity

Traditional human communities have strong tendencies toward closure. Economic and social activities extending beyond the socially controlled boundaries of a polity can create strong reactions. They are rewarding but also threatening to closed community control. Long-distance trade violates the stability of the community in several ways: the exchanges are often seen as asymmetric exercises of power from the point of view of any participating community, and they occur over space and time and so are implicated in investment and usury. The exchanges involve risk and require trust (Greif 2006). They often result in the stigmatization of traders and the distrust of political bodies. Problems are intensified when trading systems produce large-scale structures, seen as powerful uncontrolled conspiracies: classic accusations of witchcraft and heresy result from efforts to stigmatize and discredit what are seen as ill-gotten gains, as in Weber's term "pariah capitalism," describing inter alia Western anti-Semitism.

There are classic resolutions through which trading systems can be accounted as properly controlled, often through the direct subordination of the traders to the authority of political and/or religious elites. In the West, imperial and religious authority protected trading in exchange for economic benefits, and traders found it wise to huddle between the buttresses of the cathedral or even in its nave (for a non-Western example of the religious taxation of externally oriented economic activity seen as illicit, see Cancian 1965). The great Western trading centers were thus commonly also centers of religious wealth and power, and trading money helped build great churches.

Western social change, dramatized in the Enlightenment but with a long predecessor history, added new elements, facilitating differentiated production systems, long-distance trade, and large-scale organization (e.g., the great trading companies associated with Western expansion and the earlier schemes supporting colonial economic schemes such as Virginia). A key shift was the rise of polities built on notions of the collective economic good as a product of the activities of individuals and subgroups, so that the traders and innovators could be seen as making positive contributions to society rather than destroying stable local social goods (Eisenstadt 1968; Poggi 1983; see the review by Jepperson and Meyer 2011). Different ideologies linking self-interested actors to collective goods developed (Jepperson 2002). In most cases, legal restrictions limited the range of legitimate goals of private large-scale organizations. Only the most extreme liberal models, as in the nineteenth-century United States, permitted the widespread formation of self-interested organizations under statutes of general incorporation (Creighton 1990).

Thus, the liberal American polity, with its celebration of interested private action as the source of the public good, took the lead. But in a dialectic well analyzed by Tocqueville (1969 [1836]), the celebration of self-interest involved much institutional emphasis on the construction and control of the proper self. At the individual level, all liberal societies (the United States first and foremost) have given enormous attention to education, making it compulsory and expanding it beyond all functional reason (Meyer et al. 1979, 1992; Ramirez and Boli 1987). And, in the American case, religious mobilization of the individual self has always been central (Thomas 1989). Thus, American businessmen – classic carriers of self-interest – have famously been inclined to participate in the expansion of education, the web of participatory community organizations, and religious activity. Some built colleges and universities, like Stanford; others created a huge network of service-oriented clubs and societies. The style is celebrated by social scientists as central to a civic culture (Tocqueville 1969 [1836]; Dewey 1996 [1944]; Mead 1964; Putnam 2000) and stigmatized by humanists as self-serving, hypocritical, and altogether philistine (Lewis 1922; Mencken 1936): analysts in the tradition of Foucault (e.g., Miller and Rose 2008) tend to give an even darker interpretation, seeing invidious social control operating at distances. By all accounts, the rise of the large-scale corporation, most striking and least under the control of a weak state in nineteenth-century America (Berle and Means 1932; Bell 1956; Roe 1994), raised the quandary to a new level.

In the late nineteenth century and early twentieth century, corporations amassed much power: railroad companies dominated whole hinterlands, steel and oil trusts killed off the competition, and powerful banking structures controlled the money supply. Thus, the period reflected at the intranational level many of the same elements that now arise in more global society. And many social movements and political and cultural forces arose that have supranational parallels in

Legitimating the transnational corporation in a stateless world 31

our current world. Theories, foreshadowing current ideas, arose about how the mounting power of corporations could be checked. In a technocratic version of what we might now call stakeholder theory, management and engineering technocracies were put forward as disinterested professionalism, socialized in the rising appropriate academic institutions (Veblen 1933 [1921]; Mason 1959; Shenhav 1999). The idea was that professional managers, rooted in objective engineering knowledge, could resolve intractable conflicts between capital and labor. The parallels with the modern corporate social responsibility structures depicted later are obvious.

Another sociopolitical theory proposed that the power of the large corporation could be balanced by equally rising powers of workers, consumers, and perhaps government regulators (Galbraith 1993). Thus, it was supposed that great consumption organizations like chains of supermarkets could balance the monopoly production power of great agribusiness organizations. Again, the parallels with the social movements of our own time are clear. As importantly, a partly successful American legal theory proposed antitrust restrictions on the monopoly status of large firms (Fligstein 1990). Of course, on this point, the current world differs precisely because it has no global state and only a weak global legal system. But in the earlier period, between the world wars, all the various lines of theory found homes in one or another polity around the world.

Thus, in essentially all societies, large-scale organization in social and economic life expanded along with control efforts. Following Polanyi (1944; see Utting, this volume), one can see this as reflecting societies rising up in reaction to depredating economic power (this is the way moral social movements often present themselves). It may be more useful to follow Tocqueville and to see both growing economic organization and growing social controls over it as reflecting the same broad social and cultural processes of institutional expansion and universalization under conditions of global-level statelessness (Thomas 1989).

Expansion was going on in international society and economy, too, but more slowly by contemporary standards. A few international intergovernmental and nongovernmental associations arose with limited success in penetrating the wall of state sovereignty. And large-scale business organizations played influential international roles (e.g., the International Chamber of Commerce was formed in 1919). Much of this development went on within the boundaries of the great international empires and, as in the past, came under the legitimating control and authority of the imperial states (as in the East India companies) or, in the American case, under the umbrella of a more generalized American hegemony over its New World periphery. It was generally understood that dominant states had the right to protect the property of their firms, which could thus be seen as international but not really transnational in scope. But it was also understood – although usually very weakly enforced – that these states had obligations to assume some responsibilities, too. For example, there was much pressure to respect at least formally the principles of national sovereignty and to control some of the more extreme depredations (e.g., slavery) practiced by the firms of the core countries. Critics of large-scale capitalist firms and of their imperialist forms abounded in the world between the wars. But the critics focused mainly on the role of great firms within particular societies and the need for corrective controls: parallel criticisms of imperialism focused on the interstate domination involved, less on particular private organizations.

Postwar transnationalization

The aftermath of World War II produced a massive shift upward in actual and perceived supranational socioeconomic interdependencies. The autarkic national state was stigmatized as having created two wars, a world depression, and great violations of all sorts of human rights. International interdependencies were of overwhelming importance in a nuclear age, with a supranational Cold War and with the breakdown of a colonial system that had dominated most of the world.

A further change was in economic structure and ideology. Old European corporatist and statist models were delegitimated as having contributed to the twentieth-century disaster. The dominant world power was the liberal United States. The Americans, with the Marshall Plan and other policies, promoted international economic life as having great political and economic benefits: it would destroy the old European corporatism that had produced the disasters and lace together a newly integrated continent (Djelic 1998). And it would create economic growth in the newly independent Third World, under the new modernization theories (Inkeles and Smith 1974; classically, Kerr and Dunlop 1960; Harbison and Myers 1964). These theories, rooted in sociological functionalism, stressed the closely connected interdependencies among the modern economy, democracy, education, and cultural modernization. Expansion on any dimension would change the others. The ascendance of the liberal model of economic organizations, cast in terms of functionalism, came to depict these organizations not as a destructive force in need of control, but as carriers of social progress and economic development. Great supranational firms would both integrate Europe and overcome its corporatist and statist stagnation (Djelic 1998). General Motors, for example, was seen as an instance of progress not monopolistic competition.

The global society and economy took off, resuming the growth that had collapsed since 1914 or so. Global society took a liberal form, with American forms dominant, European forms stigmatized, Soviet structure unthinkable, and, in a global repetition of Tocqueville's America, a central state (even in Europe) not plausible (Fligstein 2008). So, world society after the war developed in the large-scale organizational forms of liberal models. Expanding and rationalized interdependencies produced a massive amount of crystallized structuration (Giddens 1984).

Thus, politically, the supranational world order came to be filled not with authoritative central structures, but with an endless array of intergovernmental organizations – a rare form before World War II, but now common (Ahrne and Brunsson 2008). The Union of International Associations (UIA; 1989 and various years) counts them, showing that the cumulative number of intergovernmental organizations skyrocketed after World War II (Boli and Thomas 1999). These associations are generally structured with the global or regional public good in mind. Most of them try to protect whales, not start wars.

Socially, the same Tocquevillian process took place. A massive set of international nongovernmental organizations (INGOs) arose to advance science, education, and peace and to devalue racism and conflict (see the analyses in Boli and Thomas 1999). Figure 2.1a reports the growth in the cumulative counts of INGOs over the years (UIA 1989). It is very difficult to see all this structure as simply a response to globalizing economic power, as per Polanyi (1944). In our view, the structuration has a Tocquevillian character, supporting and sometimes creating, as much as responding to, expanded economic organization.

Globally, a knowledge system based in science also expanded, and university enrollments soared, with most enrollments in the sciences and social sciences (Schofer and Meyer 2005, Drori and Moon 2006). Figure 2.1b charts this expansion, broken down by world region. In

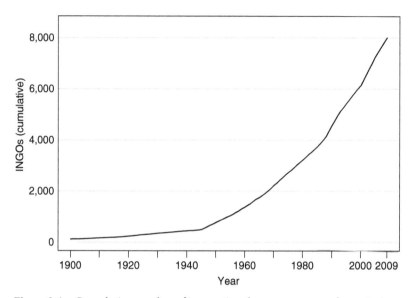

Figure 2.1a Cumulative number of international nongovernmental associations (INGOs), 1900–2009. Data prior to 1945 estimated based on founding dates from 1989 UIA Yearbook.
Source: Union of International Associations (UIA)

this period, the authority of the sciences became intertwined with the authority of the state. In 1950, practically no countries had national science ministries but now more than one hundred do (Drori et al. 2003). Similarly there was expansion in the numbers of scientific journals, societies, research papers, and so on.

A weak but globalized legal frame follows the same pattern, with the rapid expansion of efforts at international law. Of particular interest, replacing the older international order celebrating sovereign states, is the rise of human rights norms dramatizing the individual as being at the core of a global society (Lauren 2003; Stacy 2009). Elliott (2008, chap. 5; relevant data reproduced here in Figure 2.1c) reports the expanding cumulative numbers of global international human rights instruments.

On each dimension noted here, world society transcends particular national states and societies. Intergovernmental and nongovernmental associations do so explicitly and, in the latter case, are usually not even mediated by states. The expansions in science and education also have a global character. Education is defined as a human right (Chabbott

Legitimating the transnational corporation in a stateless world 35

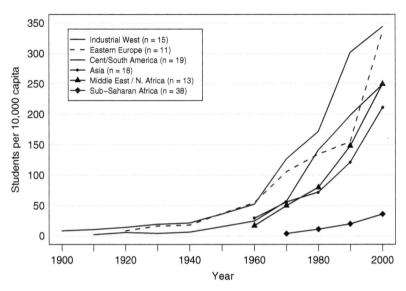

Figure 2.1b Regional averages of tertiary students per capita, 1900–2000
Source: Schofer and Meyer 2005

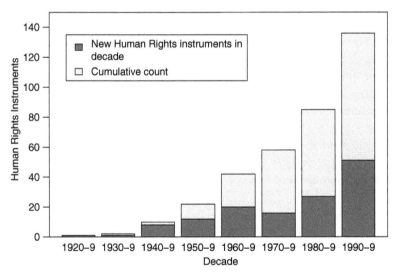

Figure 2.1c International human rights instruments: cumulative number of rights, freedoms, and entitlements declared over time
Source: Elliott 2008

2003), and curricula tend to be globally formed (Meyer et al. 1992a; Frank and Gabler 2006). Human rights principles are also global – the rights of all humans against all other humans. Thus, on each dimension just discussed, the social structures involved emphasize the global collective good rather than individual or subgroup self-interests: tones of religious-like piety pervade the system.

Economic globalization and the multinationals

Paralleling the rise of a structured world society on the dimensions just described, economic globalization was also dramatic. International trade expanded rapidly, reaching relative levels not seen since 1914. And a major portion of this trade, as well as of domestic economic production, was in the hands of multinational firms, whose numbers and power exploded (see Figure 2.2). Much of the trade, in fact, occurred within multinationals, which began direct global supply chains and the intensified extraction of profits from foreign affiliates (Markusen 1995). Overall, multinationals provided natural structure in a world society without a supranational state, exactly as with organizations in other domains.

Global expansions of science, education, and international governmental and nongovernmental organizations (NGOs) were legitimated as advancing important public goods in a global society.[2] By contrast, while the surge in multinationals might be seen in modernization theories as a source of progress for the world, their constitutional structures clearly reflected private and home-country self-interest rather than the world's public good. To legitimate these seemingly uncontrolled sources of power, two accounts were prominent in the early postwar decades and are parallel to traditional methods of legitimating long-distance trade.

---

[2] Such claims could be, and were, contested. Perhaps international organizations (whose participants commonly come from the First World) reflect dominant ideologies rather than a genuinely global good (Arnove 1982; Beckfield 2003). And perhaps expanding global education and science reflect the needs and culture of the First World, weakening Third World alternatives (Shenhav and Kamens 1991). Thus, the rising global society could be seen as carrying on imperialism in new guises. On the other hand, Third World countries, eager to incorporate scientific and educational progress, actively sought the penetrative assistance of international organizations (for the science case, see Finnemore 1996), and dominant lines of thought legitimated this.

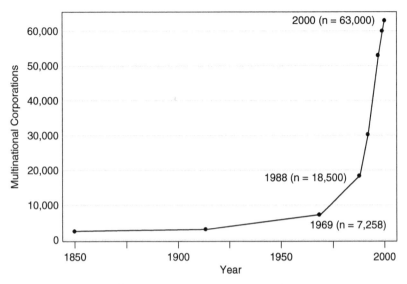

Figure 2.2 Number of multinational corporations, 1850–2000
Source: Gabel and Bruner 2003

First, the multinationals could be seen as coming under the control of their metropolitan countries and to be carriers of national interests in international society. In this case, one could criticize dominant countries for their neoimperialism or Third World states for their weakness and corruption (as in world systems thinking; see Wallerstein 1974). But, second, classic liberal theory could be invoked, and proper private interests could be seen as serving a global collective good. So development and modernization theories stressed the advantages of the improvements brought through the penetration of foreign investment, a global economy, and rationalized organizational systems (Harbison and Myers 1964; Djelic 1998). Ruggie (1982) used the term "embedded liberalism" to describe the political culture involved.[3]

---

[3] Rather than legitimating or delegitimating the changes, many discussions attempted simply to interpret them. Europeans saw the new system as providing a competitive challenge for changes in their own structures (Servan-Schreiber 1969; Djelic 1998). Americans and others saw whole new networks of power and structure as defocalizing local social structures everywhere (early on, Vernon 1977; much later Sassen 1996; Knorr Cetina and Bruegger 2002, and many others).

Scandal: the multinational as a "social problem"

The obvious inequalities of power and resources in world society and in the relation of the multinationals to most of the world led to much criticism. Even if globalized economic production and exchange were generally good things, the resulting concentrations of power seemed exploitive. In the first decades of the postwar period, criticisms attached mostly to the home states of multinational corporations. Many scandals seemed to emphasize multinational power as a type of neocolonialism. Perhaps especially influential was the 1973 coup in Chile, widely seen as reflecting ITT and copper company interests working through the CIA. Some other instances: the covert American intervention in Iran (1953), commonly partly attributed to the influence of oil multinationals; a similar intervention in Guatemala (1954), partly attributed to pressures from American corporate interests; the Vietnam War, sometimes unrealistically interpreted as resulting from oil company interests; the Anglo-French Suez invasion (1956), often given a similar cast; and Nestlé's marketing of breast milk substitutes in developing countries (1970s–1980s), understood as promoting corporate profits at the expense of the health of infants in less economically developed countries.

By the 1970s, corporate watchdog organizations such as Corporate Accountability International (1977) sought to bring covert corporate activity into the public light. The *Multinational Monitor* [1980], a bimonthly magazine founded by Ralph Nader, regularly published lists of the top scandals (leading later on to the "Ten Worst Corporations of 1997"). The earliest articles of this publication strongly emphasized the economic exploitation within the periphery by multinationals from core countries.[4] Here and in other publications, world crises were sometimes seen as reflecting the covert power of the multinationals, analogous to the witchcraft accusations against long-distance traders in many agrarian societies. But, in the decades shortly after World War II, much of the blame could be allocated to the putatively neocolonial national states from which the

---

[4] As we emphasize later, this focus on multinationals as instances of home-country powers all but disappeared in the mid-1990s (one can see this clearly by scanning the article titles in the "archived issues" section of the webpage of the *Multinational Monitor*: multinationalmonitor.org.

multinationals arose, with less blame attached to the multinationals themselves (see the review by Soule 2009).[5]

From multinationals to global corporations

In the decades following 1975, the socially embedded liberalism of the period from 1950 to 1975 was replaced by a harder edged neoliberalism that raised the principle of self-interested actorhood supported by weak collective control to very high levels. This new ideology applied to corporations, which were seen in late liberalism, both in domestic theory and at the international level, as extensions of individuals, not of the state. Indeed, the states, formerly guarantors of corporate civility in many countries, were somewhat delegitimated in ideologies of deregulation, and principles of sovereignty were subordinated to principles of property. States retained (and retain) organizational power and responsibility, but with much less of the charisma of sovereignty. The new hard-edged liberalism reached its apogee in a much-cited article from Milton Friedman (1970): "The Social Responsibility of Business Is to Increase Its Profits."[6]

---

[5] Scandal aside, a whole critique of standard modernization theories applied to the global level arose in the social sciences and in world politics. In international policy discourse, efforts to move away from the embedded liberalism of the World Bank (Ruggie 2008) toward a politically regulated New International Economic Order proliferated (Ghosh 1984). In the social sciences, a critique of the asymmetries of world power, and particularly of the economic power most visible with the multinationals, gained force. Dependency theory (e.g., Cardoso and Faletto 1967, Frank 1978) emphasized the dark side of international investment organized around the profit-making private structures of world capitalism. In sociology, world systems theory made the same points (Wallerstein 1974, Chase-Dunn 1989). Sometimes the theories involved had a Marxian flavor, stressing the inherent inequalities of capitalist production: in this picture, the multinationals are simply the visible representatives of basic economic forces. But, more often, there was a political element to the analysis: the asymmetries of power embodied in the multinationals and in world society as a whole create exploitation and inequity over and above anything inherent in capital accumulation processes. In this dramatic rendition of the theory, the organizational power of the multinationals, tending toward monopoly, is a main focus of criticism. These organizations create unfair contracts and exchanges, dominate peripheral society, and take their profits home. Organized multinationals, in other words, take precedence over disembodied economic processes in the critical analyses. The political and organizational side of world systems theory becomes completely dominant in the work of Kentor and Boswell (2003).

[6] In fact, the citations have a misleading character. Friedman was in part arguing for democratic politics, not a politics created by corporations not responsible to the public.

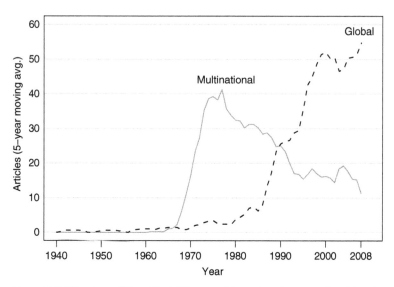

Figure 2.3 Number of *New York Times* articles using the terms "multinational company" or "global company" (five-year moving average, 1940–2008). The search included all pairings of multinational and its hyphenated form with the terms business, corporation, company, enterprise, or firm. The same pairings were used for global firms. One article in 1932 used the phrase "multinational corporation," but the next article to use the phrase is not published until 1962. To ease visual representation, the 1932 datapoint is not displayed.
Source: ProQuest Historical Newspapers: The New York Times (1851–2008)

At the same time, as Figure 2.2 shows, the number of multinational firms skyrocketed. Their expanding power and their increasing autonomy from nation-state authority meant that they could no longer be seen as creatures of their home national-states, but rather had a life of their own in a global world now seen as a society in its own right (rather than simply an interstate system; Meyer et al. 1997). As an indicator, businesses operating in several nation-states were first termed *multinational corporations* in the 1960s but are now more likely to be called *global companies*. The linguistic shift indicates the rise of a global social order above any national state. Figure 2.3 documents the shift in rhetoric from multinational to global companies in the *New York Times*. Based on the number of articles mentioning each term, the conceptualization of cross-national corporations as multinationals peaks in the 1970s. By the 1990s, they were more likely to be considered global entities. A similar shift occurs in the United Nations system when ECOSOC established the Centre on Transnational Corporations in 1974.

The shift in conception of transnational business organizations from socially regulated enterprises (at least in their home countries) to free-standing and very self-interested actors on a global stage intensified questions of legitimacy and accountability. Scandals involving multinational firms came to attach direct responsibility to the firms themselves rather than principally to the national states of their origins (see Soule 2009). Thus, the Bhopal disaster of 1984 was clearly attributed to Union Carbide, not to the American national state, and the British Petroleum oil spill of 2010 led to very little criticism of Britain itself. Similarly, the long discussion of the environmental problems produced in the 1970s and 1980s in Ecuador has led to sustained attacks on Texaco and Chevron, but only indirectly to strong criticism of their roots in the United States. The same situation describes, for the most part, the attribution of blame for massive ecological issues in Nigeria. Shell gets the blame, not the nations of its various roots. And, recently, Apple (as earlier Nike) came under strong attack for the sins of its subcontractors in Asia – the United States as a nation-state is commonly not depicted as a significant accomplice.

Accountability and responsibility questions came not only from scholars on the left and angry dependents in the periphery, but also from the core of the globalizing system itself, which began to dramatically assert the ethical responsibilities of powerful economic bodies. The overall situation is tangible in the rules of typical intergovernmental organizations linked to the UN system. In the decision-making arenas of these organizations, NGOs are commonly given participatory standing – they have identity cards, as it were, allowing them to attend meetings and represent their views. So, of course, do the scientists and educational professionals who make up much of the elite establishment of international society and all sorts of legal representatives of principles of human rights.

But the great global corporations had no such status, despite their power. They did not, in global society, have the standing as representing the collective good of this society. The self-interest that defines their status restricted their participation in the global public arena – a situation that the rise of CSR principles has tended to moderate. Analysis of the UN arena from the point of view of global tobacco companies gives a biting account of the perceived imbalances in representation in the period (Mongoven Biscoe & Duchin 1997a; 1997b). Documents produced by a consulting firm that assisted the tobacco companies in averting regulation make abundantly clear the complete inequalities between the international participatory rights of supposedly disinterested nongovernmental associations and the essential exclusion of profit-making transnationals. Thus (Mongoven Biscoe & Duchin 1997a: iii): "The [UN] committee has a definite bias in favor of more left-leaning [NGOs] or groups with a "world view," (meaning such things as UN empowerment, international regulation, world government, or international control of behaviors.)" Or (Mongoven Biscoe & Duchin 1997b: 5–6): "The power that NGOs and international organizations have gained is the result of a power shift to them from nation-states.... The growth of NGOs' power is the direct result of the growth of U.N. power. The U.N. has a built in bias in favor of NGOs."

Corporate social responsibility: transnationals as global citizens

The nineteenth-century American legitimization of business self-interest and organization generated waves of ethical ideas and organized efforts emphasizing the social citizenship of private business. If the interests of a self are to be legitimated, it becomes important to control and discipline that self. It is in the social interest to do so, but also in the interests of those claiming the rights and powers of such a self. Thus, relevant social movements grew in American areas where the new business activities were strongest (Thomas 1989). And so did ideologies, structures, and laws redefining businesses as socially responsible citizen-like actors managed by professionals oriented to the broader good (Shenhav 1999).

Paralleling the earlier expansion of intranational social control efforts in American (and other) societies, the postwar expansions of large-scale supranational business organizations gave rise to a number of exploratory social-movement-like efforts at collective social control. The modern CSR movement took shape in the 1970s when three separate internationally focused initiatives arose within a two-year period – the Organisation for Economic Cooperation and Development (OECD) Guidelines for Multinational Enterprises (1976), the Global Sullivan Principles (1977), and the International

Labour Organization (ILO) Tripartite Declaration of Principles concerning Multinational Enterprises and Social Policy (1977). Today, these organizational harbingers are little more than footnotes to history, and they underpin very little current academic research. In all three initiatives, the real foci of responsibility for proper citizenship remained with national states. The signatories of the ILO Declaration and the OECD Guidelines are not corporations but states, and even the Global Sullivan Principles, despite having corporate ratifications, were an explicit response to the policy of apartheid in the South African nation-state. The focus of these initiatives on ethical principles rather than business strategies created weak incentives for business participation. And the initiatives were thrust into an international arena that was largely empty of the CSR institutional infrastructure that plays, as we see below, such a crucial role in legitimating CSR as normal and valuable business practice. The World Economic Forum, for example, did not assume a global stance until 1987, when the name of the organization was changed from the European Management Forum.

The neoliberal breakthroughs of the later 1970s, with their hard-edged foci on self-interested profit, created a much stronger set of pressures for compensating structures of legitimating social citizenship, as did the rapidly expanding world of both multinationals and their organized international business associational community. In the same way that the rising power of centralized national states in history generated waves of social movements (Tarrow 1998, following Tilly's classic arguments), the rising power and centrality of supranational business organizations helped fuel a broad array of global social movements often reflecting ideologies paralleling Polanyi's analytic arguments about societies reacting to economic power. Public scandals and consequent ethical claims blossomed. And business interest groups grew. Even more important, ostensibly disinterested associations arose. So the relatively ineffectual idealistic efforts of the 1970s took on substance a decade or two later under changed and globalized conditions. The general term for all this new structuration has come to be "corporate social responsibility" structures. They now make up a whole institutionalized organizational field (Wooten and Hoffman 2008), and the collateral social supports and controls involved have turned the citizenship of multinationals from being an ethical ideal to more of a status as a practical business interest.

CSR is rooted in the rise of the global society and the world economy, and its standards and definitions tend to be explicitly international (Carroll 1999). Its ethical orientation, given the absence of a world state with a positive legal system, is less toward a defined conception of citizenship as in a national society and more toward very diffuse notions of a natural law sort. Strictly ethical components gave ground with time and institutionalization to more instrumental notions of the value of good business global citizenship. Thus, the "environment," the "human" characteristics of stakeholders, and broad notions of "society" are often emphasized. These are all, of course, foci of much supranational structuration in modern world society, which is grounded and legitimated in cultural notions transcending any positive legal or moral frame (Frank 1997; Meyer et al. 1997).

The history of CSR, like that of the world polity after World War II, took on a Tocquevillian character, with the institutionalization of norms occurring rapidly against the backdrop of a stateless neoliberal supranational arena. Forces especially rooted in more liberal national states (as with the United States) often took the lead. The institutionalization of a whole field of controls began to turn idealistic ethical claims into almost routine rationally motivated organizational interests and responsibilities. In this review, we emphasize the extraordinary success of the new organizational field as a normative and cultural matter: as always, practices lag far behind, and only a small fraction of business organizations operating internationally are actually directly impacted by organizational linkages. Of course, assessing the more diffuse cultural impacts on overall mentalities independent of specific organizational links is extremely difficult without detailed longitudinal data. And assessing overall impacts on practices, in any comprehensive way, would be even more difficult (and is certainly not our focus here).

Specifically, CSR associations rose to centrality in the late twentieth century and became more elaborate in their membership requirements. CSR came to stress science and rationalization, and hundreds of groups arose to measure, rank, and evaluate a variety of dimensions of corporate responsibility. CSR issues also received more attention from mass media outlets over time: more self-conscious discussion in industry-level trade journals increased as well (see Figure 2.4, taken from Soule 2009). Concurrently, professional bodies came to socialize business people in the new ways of doing business. Training programs expanded, and consulting firms

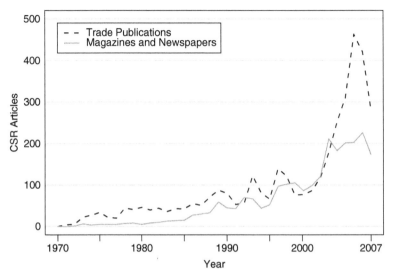

Figure 2.4 Articles referencing corporate social responsibility in trade journals and magazines/newspapers over time, 1970–2007.
Source: ProQuest ABI/INFORM global database of periodicals; Soule (2009)

came to sell assistance in meeting the business environment's demands. Eventually, substantial numbers of global corporations internalized the new system, creating within themselves professional positions and organizational units that espoused the principles of corporate responsibility. CSR became, in short, an institutionalized organizational field, supporting expanded definitions of good practice as being in the legitimated business interests of a corporation (e.g., Hoffman, 2001). We review these various dimensions in the following sections.

CSR associations

The real proliferation of CSR business associations occurred around the early 1990s, at the height of the neoliberal period and its extreme doctrines of corporate self-interest. This period in the United States, for example, witnessed the creation of the Coalition of Environmentally Responsible Companies (1989), the Business for Social Responsibility (now the BSR; 1992), and the Boston College Center for Corporate Citizenship (1985). In the same period, CSR associations arose at the global level, including the International Business Leaders Forum (1990), the World Economic Forum (1987), and the World Business Council for Sustainable Development (1995). We follow Kinderman (2011: 35) in identifying these organizations as business-led "nonprofit organizations with voluntary corporate memberships, membership dues, and mandates to advance the cause of Corporate Responsibility."

Although some researchers reasonably depict these CSR organizations as politically minded and often self-serving trade associations (Najam 1999; Albareda 2008; Kinderman 2011), we see them also as important creators, carriers, and transmitters of world-level CSR norms. Of course, the two points of view are not by any means mutually exclusive. In his monograph on the World Economic Forum, perhaps the forum that has attracted the most charges of being "a cabal of wealthy elites in business and government," Pigman (2007: 3) is careful to move away from a positivist political analysis and toward a phenomenological one. In his account, which is one of the few sustained academic treatments of a world business forum, "the Forum's story" is not only one of elite power brokering, but also "a story of the power of words, ideas, and discourse." Pigman acknowledges that deal making is in abundance at the annual conference at a posh ski resort in Davos, which attracts some 2,500 heads of state, chief executive officers, academics, and journalists. But he also paints the gathering as a discursive "global town hall," in which participants "think and talk" about such issues as environmental sustainability and poverty reduction (Pigman 2007: 4). More generally, several recent studies, building on the case studies of Galaskiewicz (1991) on the Minnesota Project on Corporate Responsibility, approach the CSR business associations from a constructivist angle, seeing them as having the ability to generate knowledge, diffuse norms, and sanction deviation (Tashman and Rivera 2010; Pope, this volume). Clearly, more than simple corporate strategic behavior is involved, whatever the immediate instrumental consequences that may reflect a "greenwashing" dimension.

Other types of CSR organizations arose later in the evolution. These include the global CSR initiatives (for an overview, Goel 2005 or Gilbert, Rasche, and Waddock 2011). They can be defined as voluntary, participatory, global organizations that promote and assess CSR standards, principles, and procedures among their corporate

Legitimating the transnational corporation in a stateless world 47

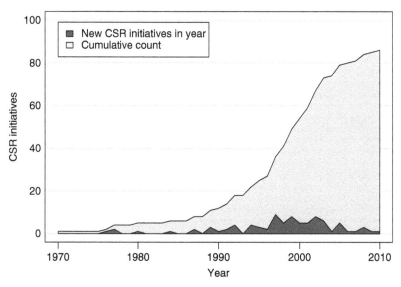

Figure 2.5 Corporate social responsibility initiatives, 1970–2010. One initiative started in 1948, but the next initiative is not established until 1976. The timeframe starts in 1970 to ease visual representation.
Source: Visser et al. 2010

membership. They include platforms through which corporations produce annual reports on CSR activities (e.g., Global Reporting Initiative, 1997), commit to universal standards of business practice (the Global Compact, 2000), disclose greenhouse gas emissions (Carbon Disclosure Project, 2003), and attain third-party certification of labor standards (the Fair Labor Association, 1999). Although forerunners to these organizations arose in the 1970s, such organizations did not take off until the turn of the millennium. Figure 2.5 shows this growth using data compiled primarily from the CSR compendium of Visser et al. (2010).[7] These CSR organizations continue to grow not only in number but also in membership. Figure 2.6 shows that by 2009 memberships were in the thousands for the Global Compact (7,600), the Global Reporting Initiative (1,300), and the European Eco-Management and Audit Scheme (4,500). The penetration has been greatest for the largest multinational corporations (Scholtens and Dam 2007; Udayasankar

---

[7] As an additional check for completeness, we checked the data against the work of Gordon (2001), Leipziger (2003), and Waddock (2008).

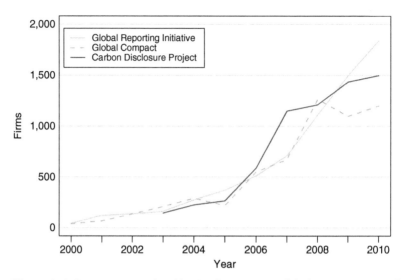

Figure 2.6 Corporate membership in three major global corporate social responsibility initiatives, 2000–2010.
Source: Websites of Global Compact, Global Reporting Initiative, and the Carbon Disclosure Project

2008). By 2008, 92 percent of the world's 250 largest companies used the guidelines of a global initiative to produce a CSR report (KPMG 2008). The proportions among smaller firms are naturally considerably lower, and the overall organizational penetration of the CSR system still reaches only a small fraction of the potential business population.

Analysts commonly see global CSR initiatives, as we do, as a response to the expansion of free market capitalism in a global arena lacking a supranational authority (Soederberg 2007; Sadler and Lloyd 2009). A common view is that the CSR initiatives are "a mechanism to fill the omnipresent governance voids which the rise of the global economy has created" (Gilbert et al. 2011: 3) and an "attempt to re-embed the economy in a wider social context, following a period of neoliberal market exposure" (Midttun et al. 2006). Our expectation, too, is that CSR initiatives are most effective in countries where economic liberalization is the strongest (Kinderman 2009).

Although the membership requirements of the CSR initiatives work, however weakly, to circumscribe corporate agency, the initiatives also raise the standing and legitimacy of the multinationals as actors in the global community. In the face of theories of the multinational corporation as a loose interorganizational network (Ghoshal and Bartlett 1990) or as a "rootless cosmopolitan" whose ties to particular stakeholders are increasingly tenuous (Davis, Whitman, and Zald 2008), the CSR initiatives work to reattach agency to their corporate members and to put them in direct contact with similarly endowed stakeholders. This asserts both the wholeness and the embeddedness of multinationals.

Structuring the field: intensification

The CSR organizations continue to elaborate their membership requirements as the field becomes an increasingly structured discursive and strategic arena. The example of the Global Compact is illustrative. At its launch in 2000, the Global Compact could rightly be called a "promotional endeavor" (Knight and Smith 2008: 2). In its early years, it "needed to maintain lax entry rules" to continue to gain adherents, according to Georg Kell, its executive director (Kell and Levin 2002). Initial participation required only that the chief executives of member companies sign a letter of support as a sort of global petition. This state of affairs began to change in 2004, when the Global Compact required companies to endorse an additional principle on corruption and bribery. Around 2005, the Global Compact began a dramatic move away from what Bremer (2008: 230) has called "a purely aspirational model that imposes no formal requirements." Then the Global Compact instituted the rule that companies could maintain membership only if they produced annual letters of progress on the implementation of the basic principles. By 2008, the Global Compact was established enough to withstand the delisting of 600 companies for failing to produce progress letters. By 2009, it had delisted another 400 companies. In 2011, the Global Compact raised the standard of participation by initiating its "Differentiation Program," which stratifies companies according to their level of disclosure, intending to "drive continuous improvement at all levels of sustainability" (unglobalcompact.org). Under the new system, laggards are easily identifiable and more readily targeted by social movement groups. Overall, in the span of a decade, the Global Compact developed from an ambitious idea to a comprehensive, consequential, and highly structured initiative.

The "ratcheting up of CSR expectations" has occurred with other initiatives, too (Bertels and Peloza 2008). The Carbon Disclosure

Project, for example, has considerably lengthened its core survey while creating additional surveys for water disclosure. In general, the CSR initiatives now require their members to produce CSR reports with increased detail and frequency. In July 2010, the largest online repository of company CSR reports, the Corporate Register (CorporateRegister.com 2010), contained some 26,515 reports from 6,592 companies, suggesting that the average company had already filed four annual CSR reports. As another indication of the intensification of membership requirements, companies now have their CSR reports certified by third parties, a practice increasing by 33 percent from 2005 to 2008 (KPMG 2008).

Linkages among CSR organizations

At the field level, the CSR organizations increasingly form a unified international CSR regime. The connectedness of the CSR field becomes apparent even from a cursory examination of the UN, a main hub in the global CSR network. The UN now backs an assortment of CSR initiatives – not only the Global Compact and Global Reporting Initiative, but also the Principles for Responsible Investing and the MBA Oath. The UN is also represented on the steering committee for the Principles for Responsible Management Education, through which nearly 400 business schools commit themselves to advancing CSR principles in the classroom. The UN has consolidated its network centrality by fostering collaboration among CSR organizations. For example, its leading initiative, the Global Compact, has signed "memos of understanding" with the European Foundation for Quality Management (in 2003), the International Organization for Standardization (ISO) 26000 Standards on Corporate Social Responsibility (2006), and the Global Reporting Initiative (2010). These memos are meant to align the Global Compact with other major initiatives, thereby increasing the coherence in the field of corporate social responsibility. Overall, the leading role that the UN plays in these and other CSR initiatives underscores the degree to which CSR has achieved legitimacy in the world polity. It also indicates the extent to which the nation-state has receded from the international stage as the UN comes to resemble a network of "United Corporations" and the nexus of a dizzying array of business-directed nonprofit organizations.

Of course, from another point of view, the CSR field remains only weakly centralized, and many structures in it lie far from any core in the

UN. Thus, other important nodes in the global CSR network are the business associations noted earlier. For example, the 1999 annual conference of the World Economic Forum was the launch pad of the Global Compact. Likewise, according to the Global Compact's Executive Director George Kell, the World Business Council for Sustainable Development and the International Business Leaders Forum provide critical "knowledge and expertise" for the management and improvement of the Global Compact (Kell and Levin 2002: 9). The density of the global CSR network is also indicated by measures of the cross-memberships in the relevant business associations. For example, in 2010, Coca-Cola was a member of at least eleven international CSR organizations of the sort considered here: the Global Compact, Global Reporting Initiative, Carbon Disclosure Project, World Business Council for Sustainable Development, Business for Social Responsibility, International Business Leaders Forum, World Economic Forum, CSR Europe, the Coalition for Environmentally Responsible Companies, Business in the Community, and the Boston College Center for Corporate Citizenship.

The increasingly dense ties and widespread cooperation among CSR-related organizations might ultimately bring to fruition the "gradual convergence of the 'Global Eight' voluntary codes of conduct" (Kell and Levin 2002), a future state of affairs in which the multinational corporations play leading roles in a much more centralized world polity.

Consulting services

CSR not only connects a sprawling field of nonprofit organizations, but also underpins a thriving for-profit industry. Driving the "commercialization of CSR into saleable services" (Windell 2007: 7) is an "emerging CSR consultancy industry" (Molina 2008: 33), which has "carried new ideas into corporations" and "transformed them into management knowledge" (Windell 2007). One of the primary tasks of CSR consultants has been to advance the "business case" for corporate social responsibility – the idea that companies profit through CSR activity (Vogel 2005). The role of CSR consultants in shifting the discussion from morals to markets has been documented in case studies in Sweden (Windell 2007), the United Kingdom (Young et al. 2003), and Mexico (Molina 2008).

The size of the CSR consultancy field is difficult to measure (Wilson and Gribben 2001). At the international level, the largest list of "CSR providers" we have found contains 5,500 organizations operating in 150 countries (CSR NEWS 2010). The largest consultants are clearly gaining much revenue. For example, the consulting division of the Business for Social Responsibility, an organization with offices on four continents and a dedicated staff of seventy professionals, has increased its revenues by an average of about 15 percent in the past four years. According to its annual report, it continues to win lucrative business from multinational corporations such as ExxonMobil and Sumitomo Trust and Banking.

In support of a business case for CSR, many studies are produced by researchers pointing to a strong consumer base for CSR products. A 2010 survey of nearly 1,000 American adults found that 70 percent asserted willingness to pay more for a $100 product made by a socially responsible company (Penn Shoen & Berland LLC 2010). Even if social desirability bias is at issue here, as in other such studies, the data can be used to indicate a high level of CSR legitimacy. As another example, with an innovative controlled experiment in which certain products in a New York City retail store were given "Fair Labor" logos, researchers found evidence that products with CSR characteristics fetch a much higher price (Hiscox and Smyth 2006). As a result of these changing consumer preferences, executives can increasingly imagine CSR activity to be a source of competitive advantage (McKinsey 2009).

The main pathway through which CFOs believe that CSR adds value is by improving company reputation and brand equity (McKinsey 2009). Currently, nearly 60 percent of leaders at private companies claim that the motivation for participating in CSR is "to manage corporate reputation" (PricewaterhouseCoopers LLC 2010). With this in mind, CSR consulting firms have arisen to build a positive CSR image among their clientele. Cause-related marketing (Varadarajan and Menon 1988) and reputation management (e.g., the Reputation Institute) have expanded immensely. Some evidence is put forward to suggest that successful CSR marketing improves financial performance. For example, studies purport to show that firms that have developed a positive CSR reputation experience smaller declines in stock price during corporate crises (Schnietz and Epstein 2005) and receive less negative publicity (Vanhamme and Grobben 2009, but see Brayden King's chapter in this volume).

Of course, a focus on CSR participation as enhancing reputation calls attention to the consequent gaps that clearly arise between commitment to public norms, on the one hand, and practices, on the other. Whether or not corporate leaders participate in CSR in very strategic bad faith, decoupling is inevitably a likely result. Our emphasis here is on the rise of the CSR organizational field and the public "logic of confidence" it supports, not on its effects on a variety of practices, which are obviously likely to be decoupled from the great global norms involved (Meyer and Rowan 1978).

CSR education

The number of venues for CSR professional development has increased rapidly in the past decade. The expansion has had a definite Tocquevillian character, producing an endless array of CSR conferences, roundtables, and seminars. By the mid-2000s, executives could participate in the Global Compact's "local networks"; they could share profiles, case studies, and best practices in the "online community" of the Boston College Center for Corporate Responsibility; and they could enroll their personnel in continuing education programs such as the Business in the Community's "Corporate Responsibility Academy," which "provides practitioners and their employers with a competency map to help them structure roles and their own professional development" (BITC 2010). In some accounts, the need for professional development takes precedence over the monitoring and enforcement of CSR standards. For example, John Ruggie, the UN Assistant Secretary General, stresses that the Global Compact is "not a regulatory arrangement" but a "learning network" of multinational corporations (Ruggie 2001). The literature offers some support for the hypothesis that professional development, in fact, fosters CSR norms. The programmatic work of Galaskiewicz (1985, 1991, 1997) suggests that executives who attend CSR seminars end up allocating more resources to community investment and that this effect persists after controlling for functional variables, such as whether a percentage of company sales are directly to consumers. Obviously, training along such dimensions helps institutionalize the field and relocate it from foci on ethical ideas to a status as an advanced business organizational model.

The proliferation of CSR training continues apace in higher education (Moon and Orlitzy 2011). We note this at four levels: universities, business schools, specific curricula, and student decisions. As for universities, the number of "academic participants" in the Global Compact grew from only 88 in 2006 to 591 in 2012. This includes universities from eighty-four countries. For business schools, the growth has been similarly strong. This is apparent from tracking the number of signatories to the UN-backed Principles for Responsible Management, a platform launched in 2007 through which schools express support for six principles of responsible management. The number of participating schools grew from 100 in 2007 to 426 in 2012. As for curricula, currently, 84.1 percent of the *Financial Times* Top 50 Global Business Schools require their students to take courses on business ethics, CSR, or sustainability (Christensen et al. 2007). In some programs, CSR comprises an entire curriculum – a growing number of universities, especially in Europe, offer master's degrees in CSR (e.g., the Nottingham University Business School, University of Saint Andrews, and Birmingham Business School). As for students, nearly 7,000 graduate students have taken the MBA Oath, a 248-word pledge to place the interests of society before the narrow pursuit of profit.

The inclusion of CSR seems to be especially strong in the elite business schools. A 2008 survey of CSR education at 142 universities worldwide found that "the greater the school's *Financial Times* ranking, the greater its commitment to CSR education" (Orlitzy and Moon 2008). The positive relationship between prestige and CSR commitment is well illustrated by Harvard University. Harvard students were the creators of the MBA Oath, the school currently offers a three-day intensive program to senior executives on CSR,[8] and Harvard is one of the limited number of schools that participate in the Responsible Endowment Coalition (among the other forty participants are such universities and colleges as Stanford, Duke, Columbia, Yale, Brown, and Dartmouth).

Rationalization and scientization of the field

The CSR field continues to undergo rapid rationalization, reinforcing the shift from an ethical orientation to institutionalized "best practice."

---

[8] http://www.exed.hbs.edu/programs/csr/Pages/default.aspx

Legitimating the transnational corporation in a stateless world 55

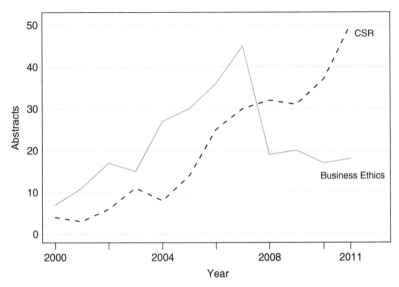

Figure 2.7 Dissertation and thesis abstracts with the phrases "corporate social responsibility" or "business ethics," 2000–2011
Source: ProQuest Dissertation and Theses Database

There is intensified rationalization in academic discourse, the popular press, and the emergent socially responsible investment industry. Within academia, a clear trend of growth in CSR theorizing is apparent. For example, increasing numbers of dissertation and thesis abstracts mention "corporate social responsibility." A search of the ProQuest Dissertation and Theses Database turned up only four such dissertations in 2000, but thirty-seven in 2010. Because dissertations take some years to complete, expansion will undoubtedly continue. In contrast, dissertation abstracts mentioning "business ethics" declined rapidly after 2005, when the topic was subsumed under the more general rubric of CSR. We chart these trends in Figure 2.7.

The rationalization of CSR continues in specialty journals, including those dedicated to environmental management (*Greener Management International, Business Strategy and the Environment, Corporate Social Responsibility,* and *Environmental Management*), business ethics (*Journal of Business Ethics, Business Ethics Quarterly, Business Ethics: A European Review*), and corporate citizenship (*Business and Society, Business and Society Review,* and *Journal of Corporate*

Citizenship).[9] Increasing scientization is evident in a meta-study entitled "A Bibliometric Analysis of 30 Years of Research and Theory on Corporate Social Responsibility" (De Bakker, Groenewegen, and Den Hond 2005). In the most recent period studied, the most common word pairs in the CSR literature (of a list of about ten) began to include such scientized concepts as "measuring" and "measurement." Undoubtedly, theoretical elaboration and conceptual specification have gained momentum in the past several years as scholars have offered a multitude of CSR constructs (Carroll 1999; Dahlsrud 2008) and a litany of CSR performance metrics (see the recent review by Wood 2010).

In the popular press, CSR rankings, another indicator of CSR scientization, fill the pages of business magazines (Waddock 2008; Scalet and Kelly 2009). As of April 2012, according to a database maintained by the Reputation Institute, there were 128 CSR-related rankings operating in thirty-nine countries, including such well-known ones as the World's Most Admired Companies, the 100 Best Corporate Citizens, and the 100 Best Companies to Work For. The intensity of the rankings field is indicated by the overlap in measurement attempts. A number of rankings, for example, stratify companies based solely on environmental sustainability (e.g., *Forbes' Magazine's* Top Ten Green Companies, the *Corporate Knight's* Global 100 Most Sustainable Companies, *Businessweek's* Most Sustainable Companies, and *Working Mother's* Best Green Companies for America's Children). Even narrow aspects of business activity are categorized, measured, and stratified. For example, three separate magazines now rank "supplier diversity" (The Top 100 Supplier Diversity Companies for Women of *Professional Women's Magazine*, the Top 10 Companies for Supplier Diversity of *DiversityInc.*, and the Top 50 Corporations for Supplier Diversity of *Hispanic Enterprise*). Another group of rankings specializes in separating the worst CSR performers from the rest (e.g., the 100 Worst Corporate Citizens of *Corporate Social Responsibility Magazine*). The expansion of CSR rankings has led some to suggest that the rankings market is now stratifying, with raters pressed both to imitate and to differentiate themselves (Chatterji, Levine, and Toeffel 2009). In Figure 2.8, with data compiled from the Reputation Institute supported by our own sweep of popular web

---

[9] Our examples of these journals are drawn from the review of Lockett, Moon, and Visser (2006).

Legitimating the transnational corporation in a stateless world   57

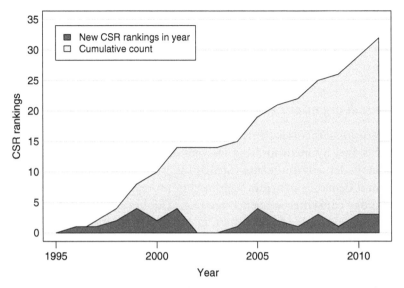

Figure 2.8 Cumulative number of corporate social responsibility rankings from 1995 to 2011.
Source: Compilation of rankings from Globescan (2012), Reputation Institute (2013), and a snowball search of the Google search engine

search engines, we show the sharp growth in global CSR rankings since the late 1990s.

Another aspect of CSR rationalization is the growth in socially responsible investment indices. These are stratification tools employing elaborate criteria to identify groups of suitable investments from a large sample of public equities. These rankings have increased with the growth of the CSR industry, and the dollar value of the assets under management in funds that attempt socially responsible investment has almost quadrupled in the past decade, from $2.6 trillion in 2002 to $10.1 trillion in 2010 (FTSE 2012). At the world level, the indices began with the creation of the Dow Jones Sustainability Index (in 1999) and the FTSE4Good Index (2001) but now include specialized ones related to emerging markets and investment-grade bonds. In the early days, the rankings focused primarily on the exclusion of "sin stocks," such as gambling casinos and tobacco companies, and involved mostly passive management strategies. Now index construction involves a complex process of assigning industry and country weightings and then ranking companies according to a growing list of

CSR concerns. The questionnaire that the DJSI Index sends to companies is more than seventy pages long and covers topics ranging from executive compensation to philanthropic donations to corporate bribery.

Internal organizational structuration, and isomorphism

Institutional theories stress the tendency of organizations to stabilize themselves by incorporating internal elements paralleling pressures from wider environments. Structural isomorphism with environmental demands provides legitimating protections, whatever actual adaptive capacities are generated (e.g., Dobbin 2009). In the case of CSR, an example of this is that, in the 2000s, multinationals began to create within themselves formal, professionally staffed CSR offices, giving rise to a "brave new breed" of executives going by titles like "Chief Sustainability Officer" (Galbraith 2009; Spinley 2010). In 2006, only six of Russell 1000 firms had such officers; less than three years later, the figure had ballooned to 208 (CRO. com 2010). Reflecting this growth, *Business Ethics Magazine* changed its name in 2006 to *Corporate Responsibility Officers Magazine* and simultaneously launched the Corporate Responsibility Officers Association.

As another indication of CSR internalization within multinationals, the largest corporations increasingly submit their employees to in-house ethics training (Valentine and Fleischman 2007) and education according to codes of conduct (Florini 2003). The CSR principles represented in these codes are increasingly instantiated within "corporate constitutions." Currently, one-half of the top 100 US retailers, according to Lee, Fairhurst, and Wesley (2009), mention CSR principles in directly separate documents or embed them in their mission statements. A particularly striking development of the degree to which CSR has stitched itself into the DNA of the modern corporation is the diffusion of the "Benefit Corporation." This new organizational form, falling somewhere between a firm and a nonprofit, has a legal mandate to advance social interests. As of December 2014, twenty-six states have passed legislation that allows such corporations, whereas another eleven states have legislation pending.[10]

---

[10] http://www.benefitcorp.net/state-by-state-legislative-status

Through these structures, policies, routines, and forms, the corporation folds CSR demands into corporate practice in cognizance of world norms that may confer legitimacy to the expansion of global capitalism.

Conclusion

The culturally expansive, liberal postwar world society, lacking its own global state structure, created a Tocquevillesque field filled with supranational organizational structures. Many of these took the forms of IGOs and INGOs claiming foci on supranational collective goods. Culturally, great scientific and educational establishments expanded and linked around the world. And, in the expanding world economy, transnational corporations provided formal structure in a context lacking in structure. They grew explosively, but posed multiple problems of legitimation because they reflected private interests and private power uncontrollable by political and legal institutions in a world society without a world state. By the 1970s, paralleling an earlier history in an American society built around a weak state, social movements arose stressing ethical responsibilities of the corporations, although with limited effectiveness. In liberal systems, responsibility as well as authority shifts from high collectives down to the legitimated participating actors, including organized ones.

The legitimation problems involved intensified greatly with the breakdown of the doctrines of "embedded liberalism" and "modernization" around 1970 and the rise of the current neoliberal regime that stresses the values of raw private interest in an unregulated environment. The self-interest of the human actor was placed at the center of things, with little ethical content, and generalized to large-scale corporate organization. As with an earlier democratic and liberal history stressing the intranational standing of the individual self, global society produced an extraordinary expansion of movements for the socialization and control of transnational corporations. A whole CSR organizational field resulted. Associations arose in great numbers, with expanding membership requirements. Ratings and evaluations became endemic. A consulting industry blossomed. Professionalization and professional training emerged and grew. Internally, transnational organizations rapidly developed professionalized offices to be isomorphic with this expanded set of structures in the whole field. By now, CSR is a substantial industry, making its own contribution to the "service sector" of the "global economy." Originally vague ethical ideals came to be institutionally supported as making business sense for the proper corporate actor.

It is difficult to make a serious normative assessment of all these changes, especially because we have limited data on the practical consequences of the new organizational field. For one thing, we do not know quite what to compare the new system to. At the macro-social level, one could compare it to a seriously regulatory and efficient world state, but that is unrealistic. At the micro- or organizational level, we can do studies to see if all these organizational changes have tangible effects – say on carbon footprints, on working conditions, on consumer benefits, or on organizational profits. This is most likely the direction that research in the field will take. Of course, such research can compare organizations that join CSR initiatives or maintain CSR policies with those that do not, looking quasi-experimentally for effects. But such studies are unlikely to capture some of the most important effects of a social movement like CSR, which reflects very diffuse cultural and normative changes operating on – and claiming to represent – global or universal values defining what it means to be a good professionalized business. A changed business culture may affect the practices of firms whether or not they have organizational links to the CSR centers. Only very sophisticated longitudinal studies can show the impact of the CSR system on the great majority of firms that have weak links to it (e.g., Prakash and Potoski 2006).

Thus, it is difficult to show empirically, at the macro or collective level, movement effects that are likely to characterize organizations in general, not simply the signatories to CSR initiatives and forms (Hafner-Burton and Tsutsui 2005; Cole 2012). As the movement intensifies over time, its whole system of normative and cognitive definitions and its conceptions of good business interests come to surround any given organization, whatever its own immediate organizational linkages. It becomes increasingly difficult for organizational leaders to avoid reporting about issues defined in terms of CSR. Both internal and external stakeholders come to expect appropriate talk and, to some extent, action, and part of the training or socialization processes for managerial positions generates inclinations and capacities to do or say the right thing.

Postscript on the future

The CSR organizational field is very dynamic, with most of its growth in the past decade. It has organizationally penetrated only a fraction of the whole business world it addresses. It will undoubtedly continue to expand, with more organizations participating in more initiatives and becoming subject to more gradings and rankings. And professionalization, in terms of training or degree programs, consulting arrangements, and specialized intraorganizational departments and offices, is likely to proceed rapidly. The Tocquevillesque forces driving the process will almost certainly also continue, with expanded global interdependence, organizational structuration, and dramatic global-level statelessness. It is very difficult to envision political or organizational closure around some sovereign authority or set of such authorities that might provide definitive lists of what are and are not organizational CSR mandates and thus constrain the overall expansion.

Conversely, social systems of this general sort generate social closure of their own around the social organization of reputation. So it seems likely that a good deal of consolidation will occur in the field. A few CSR associations will probably maintain dominance with their membership criteria and grading or ranking structures. And standardized criteria of CSR propriety can evolve, guiding both external evaluations and standard intraorganizational policies. Professionalization on a worldwide scale will assist in such matters, generating and institutionalizing frameworks claiming consensual status. Perhaps legal or administrative pressures in important national state or international associations (such as the European Union) will intensify these processes, creating CSR patterns that become, at least de facto, mandatory. In this sense, the evolution of accounting standards or of the various standards of the ISO might serve as a model.

These sorts of consolidation, as with accounting and ISO standards, are likely to press for procedural conceptions of CSR rather than substantive ones. Both organizations and their environments can stabilize themselves more effectively if the requirements are to have proper offices, inspections, reports, procedures for openly managing issues and criticisms, and policies than if mechanistic substantive requirements (e.g., reductions in carbon footprints) are central. Large American corporations operating in similarly open environments with elaborate organizational mechanisms for communicating with various publics and stakeholders might foreshadow a future global pattern. Of course, if CSR proprieties are defined in procedural rather than substantive terms, they leave open questions about the value of CSR participation and norms for practical outcome.

The CSR system has some distinctive elements that make closure and stabilization difficult to achieve in any near term and perhaps not even desirable. It is a broad canopy covering multiple dimensions, and its core claims are open-ended, having elements rooted in abstract and universalistic natural law ideas rather than positive law clarity. We may, in short, expect some continuing turbulence in the field, along with continuing rapid expansion. The expansion means that many new elements – rules and programs – are likely to occur within the field, with variable and uncertain specific or practical meaning.

References

Ahrne, Göran, and Nils Brunsson. 2008. *Meta-organizations*. Cheltenham, UK: Edward Elgar.

Albareda, Laura. 2008. "Corporate Responsibility, Governance and Accountability: From Self-regulation to Co-Regulation." *Corporate Governance* 8(4):430–439.

Arnove, Robert, ed. 1982. *Philanthropy and Cultural Imperialism: The Foundations at Home and Abroad*. Bloomington: Indiana University Press.

Bartley, T. 2007. "How Foundations Shape Social Movements: The Construction of an Organizational Field and the Rise of Forest Certification." *Social Problems* 54(3):229–255.

Beckfield, Jason. 2003. "Inequality in the World Polity: The Structure of International Organization." *American Sociological Review* 68(3): 401–424

Bell, Daniel. 1956. *Work and Its Discontents*. Boston: Beacon Press.

Berle, A. A., Jr., and Gardiner C. Means. 1932. *The Modern Corporation and Private Property*. New York: Commerce Clearing House.

Bertels, Stephanie, and John Peloza. 2008. "Running Just to Stand Still? Managing CSR Reputation in an Era of Ratcheting Expectations." *Corporate Reputation Review* 11(1):56–72.

BITC (Business in the Community). 2010. *The Corporate Responsibility (CR) Academy*. Retrieved July 25, 2010, from (http://www.bitc.org.uk/cr_academy/index.html).

Boli, John, and George M. Thomas, eds. 1999. *Constructing World Culture: International Nongovernmental Organizations since 1875*. Stanford, CA: Stanford University Press.

Bremer, Jennifer Ann. 2008. "How Global Is the Global Compact?" *Business Ethics: European Review* 17(3):227–244.

Cancian, Frank. 1965. *Economics and Prestige in a Maya Community: The Religious Cargo System in Zinacantán*. Stanford, CA: Stanford University Press.

Cardoso, Fernando H., and Enzo Faletto. 1967. *Dependencia y desarrollo en América Latina*. Lima: Instituto de Estudios Peruanos.

Carroll, A. B. 1999. "Corporate Social Responsibility: Evolution of a Definitional Construct." *Business & Society* 38(3):268–295.

Chabbott, Colette. 2003. *Constructing Education for Development: International Organizations and Education for All*. New York: RoutledgeFalmer.

Chase-Dunn, Christopher. 1989. *Global Formation: Structures of the World-Economy*. Cambridge, MA: B. Blackwell.

Chatterji, A. K., Levine, D. I., and Toffel, M. W. 2009. "How Well Do Social Ratings Actually Measure Corporate Social Responsibility?" *Journal of Economics & Management Strategy* 18(1):125–169.

Christensen, Lisa Jones, Ellen Peirce, Laura P. Hartman, W. Michael Hoffman, and Jamie Carrier. 2007. "Ethics, CSR, and Sustainability Education in the Financial Times Top 50 Global B: Baseline Data and Future Research Directions." *Journal of Business Ethics* 73:347–368.

Cole, Wade. 2012. "Human Rights as Myth and Ceremony? Reevaluating the Effectiveness of Human Rights Treaties, 1981–2007". *American Journal of Sociology* 117(4):1131–1171.

CorporateRegister.com. 2010. *Global CSR Resources*. Retrieved July 25, 2010, from http://www.corporateregister.com/.

Creighton, Andrew. 1990. The Emergence of Incorporation as a Legal Form for Organizations. Doctoral dissertation, Stanford University, California.

CRO.com. 2010. *The CRO Summits Opportunity*. Retrieved July 25, 2010, from http://www.thecro.com/files/CRO-Summit-Sponsor-Briefing-slides.pdf.

CSR NEWS. 2010. *CSR NEWS Directory*. Retrieved July 25, 2010, from http://csr-news.net/main/about/csr-directory/.

Dahlsrud, Alexander. 2008. "How Corporate Social Responsibility Is Defined: An Analysis of 37 Definitions." *Corporate Social Responsibility and Environmental Management* 15(1):1–13.

Davis, G. F., Whitman, M. V. N., and Zald, M. N. (2008). "The Responsibility Paradox." *Stanford Social Innovation Review* 6:31–37.

De Bakker, Frank, Peter Groenewegen, and Frank Den Hond. 2005. "A Bibliometric Analysis of 30 Years of Research and Theory on Corporate Social Responsibility and Corporate Social Performance." *Business & Society* 44(3):283–317.

Dewey, John. 1996 [1944]. *Democracy and Education: An Introduction to the Philosophy of Education*. New York: Free Press.

Djelic, Marie-Laure. 1998. *Exporting the American Model: The Post-War Transformation of European Business*. Oxford: Oxford University Press.

Dobbin, F. 2009. *Inventing Equal Opportunity*. Princeton, NJ: Princeton University Press.

Drori, Gili, John W. Meyer, Francisco Ramirez, and Evan Schofer. 2003. *Science in the Modern World Polity: Institutionalization and Globalization*. Stanford, CA: Stanford University Press.

Drori, Gili, and Hyeyoung Moon. 2006. "The Changing Nature of Tertiary Education: Cross-National Trends in Disciplinary Enrollment, 1965–1995." Pp. 157–186 in *The Impact of Comparative Education Research on Institutional Theory*, edited by D. Baker and A. Wiseman. Amsterdam: Elsevier Science.

Eisenstadt, S. N. 1968. "The Protestant Ethic Thesis in an Analytical and Comparative Framework." Pp. 3–45 in *The Protestant Ethic and Modernization*, edited by S. N. Eisenstadt. New York: Basic Books.

Elliott, Michael A. 2008. *A Cult of the Individual for a Global Society:* The Development and Worldwide Expansion of Human Rights Ideology. Doctoral dissertation, Emory University.

Finnemore, Martha. 1996. *National Interests in International Society*. Ithaca, NY: Cornell University Press.

Fligstein, Neil. 1990. *The Transformation of Corporate Control*. Cambridge, MA: Harvard University Press.

Fligstein, Neil. 2008. *Euroclash: The EU, European Identity, and the Future of Europe*. Oxford: Oxford University Press.

Florini, Ann. 2003. "The Growing Role of Corporate Codes of Conduct." *The Brookings Review* 21(2):4–8.

Frank, Andre Gunder. 1978. *Dependent Accumulation and Underdevelopment*. London: Macmillan.

Frank, David John. 1997. "Science, Nature, and the Globalization of the Environment, 1870–1990." *Social Forces* 76(December): 409–435.

Frank, David John, and Jay Gabler. 2006. *Reconstructing the University: Worldwide Shifts in Academia in the 20th Century*. Stanford, CA: Stanford University Press.

Friedman, Milton. 1970. "A Friedman Doctrine: The Social Responsibility of Business Is to Increase Its Profits." *New York Times Magazine*, Sept. 13.
FTSE. 2012. *FTSE Index*. London: FTSE Group.
Gabel, Menard, and Henry Bruner. 2003. *Global Inc.: An Atlas of the Multinational Corporation*. New York: New Press: Distributed by W.W. Norton.
Galaskiewicz, J. 1985. *Social Organization of an Urban Grants Economy: A Study of Business Philanthropy and Nonprofit Organizations*. Orlando, FL: Academic Press.
Galaskiewicz, J. 1991. "Making Corporate Actors Accountable: Institution-Building in Minneapolis-St. Paul." Pp. 293-310 in *The New Institutionalism in Organizational Analysis*, edited by W. W. Powell and P. J. DiMaggio. Chicago: University of Chicago Press.
Galaskiewicz, J. 1997. "An Urban Grants Economy Revisited: Corporate Charitable Contributions in the Twin Cities, 1979–81." *Administrative Science Quarterly*, 41:445–471.
Galbraith, John Kenneth. 1993. *American Capitalism: The Concept of Countervailing Power*. New Brunswick, NJ: Transaction Publishers.
Galbraith, Kate. 2009. "Companies Add Chief Sustainability Officers." *New York Times*, March, 1–13.
Ghosh, Pradip K., ed. 1984. *New International Economic Order: A Third World Perspective*. Westport, CT: Greenwood Press.
Ghoshal, Sumantra, and Chrisopher A. Bartlett. 1990. "The Multinational Corporation as an Interorganizational Network." *The Academy of Management Review* 15(4):603–625.
Giddens, Anthony. 1984. *The Constitution of Society: Introduction of the Theory of Structuration*. Berkeley: University of California Press.
Gilbert, Dirk Ulrich, Andreas Rasche, and Sandra Waddock. 2011. "Accountability in a Global Economy: The Emergence of International Accountability Standards." *Business Ethics Quarterly* 21(1):23–44.
Globescan. 2012. *Rate the Raters 2012: Polling the Experts*. Retrieved from http://www.globescan.com/component/edocman/?view=document%26id=37%26Itemid=591.
Goel, Ran. 2005. *Guide to Instruments of Corporate Responsibility: An Overview of 16 Key Tools for Labour Fund Trustees*. Toronto: Schulick/York.
Gordon, Kathryn. 2001. "The OECD Guidelines and Other Corporate Responsibility Instruments: A Comparison." *Working Papers on International Investment No. 2001/5*. Paris: OECD Directorate for Financial, Fiscal and Enterprise Affairs.

Greif, Avner. 2006. *Institutions and the Path to the Modern Economy: Lessons from Medieval Trade.* Cambridge: Cambridge University Press.

Hafner-Burton, Emilie, and Kiyoteru Tsutsui. 2005. "Human Rights in a Globalizing World: The Paradox of Empty Promises." *American Journal of Sociology* 110 (5):1373–1411.

Harbison, Frederick, and Charles A. Myers. 1964. *Education, Manpower, and Economic Growth; Strategies of Human Resource Development.* New York: McGraw-Hill.

Hiscox, M. J., and N. F. B. Smyth. 2006. "Is There Consumer Demand for Improved Labor Standards? Evidence from Field Experiments in Social Labeling." Department of Government, Harvard University.

Hoffman, Andrew J. 2001. "Linking Organizational and Field-Level Analyses: The Diffusion of Corporate Environmental Practice." *Organization & Environment* 14(2):133–156.

Inkeles, Alex, and David H. Smith. 1974. *Becoming Modern: Individual Change in Six Developing Countries.* Cambridge, MA: Harvard University Press.

Jepperson, Ronald. 2002. Political Modernities: Disentangling Two Underlying Dimensions of Institutional Differentiation. *Sociological Theory* 20(1):61–85.

Jepperson, Ronald, and John W. Meyer. 2011. "Multiple Levels of Analysis and the Limitations of Methodological Individualisms." *Sociological Theory* 29(1): 54–73.

Kell, Georg, and David Levin. 2002. "The Evolution of the Global Compact Network: An Historic Experiment in Learning and Action." Paper presented at *The Academy of Management Annual Conference.* Denver, Colorado.

Kentor, Jeffrey, and Terry Boswell. 2003. "Foreign Capital Dependence and Development: A New Direction." *American Sociological Review* 68(2):301–313.

Kerr, Clark, and John Dunlap. 1960. *Industrialism and Industrial Man: The Problems of Labor and Management in Economic Growth.* Cambridge, MA: Harvard University Press.

Kinderman, Daniel. 2009. *The Political Economy of Corporate Responsibility and the Rise of Market Liberalism Across the OECD: 1977–2007.* Discussion Paper SP2009-30, Social Science Research Center (WZB), Berlin, Germany: 1–65.

Kinderman, Daniel. 2011. "'Free Us Up So We Can Be Responsible!' The Co-evolution of Corporate Social Responsibility and Neo-liberalism in the UK, 1977–2010." *Socio-Economic Review* 10:29–57.

Knight, G., and J. Smith. 2008. "The Global Compact and its Critics: Activism, Power Relations, and Corporate Social Responsibility." Pp. 1–29 in *Discipline and Punishment in Global Politics: Illusions of Control*, edited by Jamie Leatherman. Basingstoke, UK: Palgrave Macmillan.

Knorr Cetina, Karin, and Urs Bruegger. 2002. "Global Microstructures: The Virtual Societies of Financial Markets." *American Journal of Sociology* 107(4): 905–950.

KPMG International. 2008. *KPMG Survey of International Corporate Social Responsibility Reporting*. The Netherlands: KPMG Global Services.

Lauren, Paul G. 2003. *The Evolution of International Human Rights: Visions Seen*. 2nd ed. Philadelphia: University of Pennsylvania Press.

Lee, Min-Young, Ann Fairhurst, and Scarlett Wesley. 2009. "Corporate Social Responsibility: A Review of the Top 100 US Retailers." *Corporate Reputation Review* 12(2):140–158.

Leipziger, Deborah. 2003. *The Corporate Responsibility Code Book*. Austin, TX: Greenleaf Publishing.

Lewis, Sinclair. 1922. *Babbitt*. New York: Harcourt, Brace and Company.

Lockett, Andy, Jeremy Moon and Wayne Visser. 2006. "Corporate Social Responsibility in Management Research: Focus, Nature, Salience and Sources of Influence." *Journal of Management Studies* 43(1):115–136.

Markusen, James R. 1995. "The Boundaries of Multinational Enterprises and the Theory of Trade." *The Journal of Economic Perspectives* 9 (2):169–189.

Mason, Edward S., ed. 1959. *The Corporation in Modern Society*. Cambridge, MA: Harvard University. Press.

McKinsey. 2009. "Global Survey Results: Valuing Corporate Social Responsibility." *McKinsey Quarterly* February:1–9.

Mead, George Herbert. 1964. *The Social Psychology of George Herbert Mead. Edited and with an introduction by Anselm Strauss*. Chicago: University of Chicago Press.

Mencken, H. L. 1936. *Notes on Democracy*. New York: Knopf.

Meyer, John W., John Boli, George Thomas, and Francisco Ramirez. 1997. "World Society and the Nation-State." *American Journal of Sociology* 103(1):144–181.

Meyer, John W., David Kamens, and Aaron Benavot, with Yun-Kyung Cha and Suk-Ying Wong. 1992a. *School Knowledge for the Masses: World Models and National Curricula in the Twentieth Century*. London: Falmer.

Meyer, John W., Francisco Ramirez, and Yasemin Soysal. 1992. "World Expansion of Mass Education, 1870–1970." *Sociology of Education* 65(2):128–149.

Meyer, John W., and Brian Rowan. 1978. "The Structure of Educational Organizations." Pp. 78–109 in *Environments and Organizations*, edited by M. Meyer, et al. San Francisco: Jossey-Bass.

Meyer, John W., David Tyack, Joane Nagel, and Audri Gordon. 1979. "Public Education as Nation-Building in America: Enrollments and Bureaucratization in the American States, 1870–1930." *American Journal of Sociology* 85(3):591–613.

Midttun, Atle, Kristian Gautesen, and Maria Gjølberg. 2006. "The Political Economy of CSR in Western Europe." *Corporate Governance: The International Journal of Business in Society* 6(4):369–385.

Miller, Peter, and Nikolas Rose. 2008. *Governing the Present: Administering Economic, Social and Personal Life*. Malden, MA: Polity Press.

Molina, Jorge. 2008. "The Nature of the CSR Consulting Industry in Mexico." *Ide@s CONCYTEG* 34(7):30–58.

Mongoven Biscoe & Duchin, Inc. 1997a. "An Analysis of Non-Governmental Organizations from a United Nations Perspective." In *Philip Morris. Legacy Tobacco Document Library*, edited by Mongoven BD, Inc. San Francisco: University of California. Retrieved from http://legacy.library.ucsf.edu/tid/pcj04c00.

Mongoven Biscoe & Duchin, Inc. 1997b. "An Analysis of the International Framework Convention Process." In *Philip Morris. Legacy Tobacco Document Library*, edited by Mongoven BD, Inc. San Francisco: University of California. Retrieved from http://legacy.library.ucsf.edu/tid/soq37c00.

Moon, Jeremy, and Marc Orlitzky. 2011. "Corporate Social Responsibility and Sustainability Education: A Trans-Atlantic Comparison." *Journal of Business Ethics* 17:583–603.

Najam, Adil. 1999. "World Business Council for Sustainable Development: The Greening of Business or a Greenwash?" Pp. 65–75 in *Yearbook of International Cooperation in Environment and Development 1999/2000*, edited by H. O. Bergson, G. Parmann, and O. B. Thommesen. London: Earthscan.

New York Times. 1851–2008. Accessed from ProQuest Historical Newspapers. http://www.proquest.com/products-services/pq-hit-news.

Orlitzy, Marc, and Jeremy Moon. 2008. "A Survey of CSR Education: Trends, Comparisons, Processes." Pp. 1–4 in *Academy of Management Conference*, Anaheim, CA.

Penn Schoen & Berland, LLC. 2010. *Corporate Social Responsibility Branding Survey, 2010*. New York: PSB.
Pigman, Geoffrey Allen. 2007. *The World Economic Forum: A Multi-Stakeholder Approach to Global Governance*. London: Routledge.
Poggi, Gianfranco. 1983. *Calvinism and the Capitalist Spirit*. Amherst: The University of Massachusetts Press.
Polanyi, Karl. 1944. *The Great Transformation*. New York: Farrar & Rinehart.
Pope, Shawn M. 2015; this volume. "Why Firms Participate in the Global Corporate Social Responsibility Initiatives, 2000–2010." Pp. 251–285 in *Corporate Social Responsibility in a Globalizing World*, edited by K. Tsutsui and A. Lim. New York: Cambridge University Press.
Prakash, Aseem, and Matthew Potoski. 2006. "Racing to the Bottom? Trade, Environmental Governance, and ISO 14001." *American Journal of Political Science* 50(2):350–364.
PricewaterhouseCoopers, LLC. 2010. *CSR Trends 2010*. Toronto, Canada: PwC.
ProQuest Dissertation and Theses Database. 2000–2011.
Putnam, Robert D. 2000. *Bowling Alone: The Collapse and Revival of American Community*. New York: Simon & Schuster.
Ramirez, Francisco O., and John Boli. 1987. "The Political Construction of Mass Schooling: European Origins and Worldwide Institutionalization." *Sociology of Education* 60:2–17.
Reputation Institute. 2013. *Reputation Institute – Tools & Databases*. Retrieved November 15, 2013, from http://www.reputationinstitute.com/thought-leadership/tools-databases.
Roe, Mark. 1994. *Strong Managers, Weak Owners: The Political Roots of American Corporate Finance*. Princeton, NJ: Princeton University Press.
Ruggie, John G. 1982. "International Regimes, Transactions, and Change: Embededded Liberalism in the Postwar Economic Order." *International Organization* 36(2):379–415.
Ruggie, John G. 2001. "global_governance.net: The Global Compact as Learning Network." *Global Governance* 7:371–378.
Ruggie, John G., ed. 2008. *Embedding Global Markets*. Aldershot, Hampshire: Ashgate.
Sadler, David, and Stuart Lloyd. 2009. "Neo-liberalising Corporate Social Responsibility: A Political Economy of Corporate Citizenship." *Geoforum* 40(4):613–622.
Sassen, Saskia. 1996. *Losing Control? Sovereignty in an Age of Globalization*. New York: Columbia University Press.

Scalet, Steven, and Thomas F. Kelly. 2009. "CSR Rating Agencies: What Is Their Global Impact?" *Journal of Business Ethics* 94(1):69–88.

Schnietz, Karen E., and Marc J. Epstein. 2005. "Exploring the Financial Value of a Reputation for Corporate Social Responsibility During a Crisis." *Corporate Reputation Review* 7(4):327–345.

Schofer Evan, and John W. Meyer. 2005. "The World-Wide Expansion of Higher Education in the Twentieth Century." *American Sociological Review* 70:898–920.

Scholtens, Bert, and Lammertjan Dam. 2007. "Banking on the Equator: Are Banks that Adopted the Equator Principles Different from Non-Adopters?" *World Development* 35(8):1307–1328.

Servan-Schreiber, Jean Jacques. 1969. *The American Challenge*. Translated from the French by Ronald Steel. New York: Atheneum.

Shenhav, Yehouda A. 1999. *Manufacturing Rationality: The Engineering Foundations of the Managerial Revolution*. Oxford: Oxford University Press.

Shenhav, Yehouda A., and David H. Kamens. 1991. "The 'Costs' of Institutional Isomorphism in Non-Western Countries." *Social Studies of Science* 21:527–545.

Soederberg, Susanne. 2007. "Taming Corporations or Buttressing Market-Led Development? A Critical Assessment of the Global Compact." *Globalizations* 4(4):500–513.

Soule, Sarah A. 2009. *Contention and Corporate Social Responsibility*. Cambridge: Cambridge University Press.

Spinley, K. 2010. *Sustainability Officers: A Brave New Breed. Heidrick and Struggles*. Retrieved from http://www.heidrick.com/Articles/Pages/Sustainabilityofficers.aspx.

Stacy, Helen. 2009. *Human Rights for the 21st Century*. Stanford, CA: Stanford University Press.

Tarrow, Sidney. 1998. *Power in Movement*. 2nd edition. Cambridge: Cambridge University Press

Tashman, Peter, and Jorge Rivera. 2010. "Are Members of Business for Social Responsibility More Socially Responsible?" *The Policy Studies Journal* 38(3):487–514.

Thomas, George M. 1989. *Revivalism and Cultural Change: Christianity, Nationbuilding, and the Market in the Nineteenth-Century United States*. Chicago: University of Chicago Press.

Tocqueville, Alexis de. 1969 [1836]. *Democracy in America*. J. P. Maier, ed., Trans. G. Lawrence. Garden City, NY: Anchor Books.

Udayasankar, Krishna. 2008. "Corporate Social Responsibility and Firm Size." *Journal of Business Ethics* 83(2):167–175.
Union of International Associations (UIA). 1989, and various years. *Yearbook of International Organizations*. Munich: Saur.
Utting, Peter. 2014; this volume. "Corporate Social Responsibility and the Evolving Standards Regime: Regulatory and Political Dynamics." Pp. 73–106 in *Corporate Social Responsibility in a Globalizing World*, edited by K. Tsutsui and A. Lim. New York: Cambridge University Press.
Valentine, Sean, and Gary Fleischman. 2007. "Ethics Programs, Perceived Corporate Social Responsibility and Job Satisfaction." *Journal of Business Ethics* 77(2):159–172.
Vanhamme, Joëlle, and Bas Grobben. 2009. "'Too Good to be True!' The Effectiveness of CSR History in Countering Negative Publicity." *Journal of Business Ethics* 85(S2):273–283.
Varadarajan, R., and Menon, A. 1988. "Cause-Related Marketing: A Coalignment Corporate Strategy and Corporate Philanthropy." *Journal of Marketing* 52(3):58–74.
Veblen, Thorstein. 1933 [1921]. *The Engineers and the Price System*. New York: Viking Press.
Vernon, Raymond. 1977. *Storm Over the Multinationals: The Real Issues*. Cambridge, MA: Harvard University Press.
Visser, W., D. Matten, M. Pohl, and N. Tolhurst. 2010. *The A to Z of Corporate Social Responsibility*. London: Wiley.
Waddock, Sandra. 2008. "Building a New Institutional Infrastructure for Corporate Responsibility." *Academy of Management* 22(3):87–109.
Wallerstein, Immanuel. 1974. "The Rise and Future Demise of the World Capitalist System: Concepts for Comparative Analysis." *Comparative Studies in Society and History* 16(4):387–441.
Wilson, Andrew, and Chris Gribben. 2001. "Consulting in Corporate Social Responsibility." Pp. 444–456 in *Management Consultancy: A Handbook for Best Practice*, edited by Philip Sadler. London: Kogan Page.
Windell, Karolina. 2007. "The Commercialization of CSR: Consultants Selling Responsibility." Pp. 1–29 in *Managing Corporate Social Responsibility in Action: Talking, Doing, and Measuring*, edited by Peter Neergaard. Surrey, UK: Ashgate Publishing.
Wood, Donna J. 2010. "Measuring Corporate Social Performance: A Review." *International Journal of Management Reviews* 12(1):50–84.
Wooten, Melissa, and Andrew Hoffman. 2008. "Organizational Fields." Pp. 130–148 in *The Sage Handbook of Organizational Institutionalism*,

edited by Robert Greenwood, Christine Oliver, Kerstin Sahlin, and Roy Suddaby. London: Sage.

Young, Anita Fernandez, Jeremy Moon, and Robert Young. 2003. "The UK Corporate Social Responsibility Consultancy Industry: A Phenomenological Approach." *Moon* 44(14):1–4.

3 | Corporate social responsibility and the evolving standards regime: regulatory and political dynamics

PETER UTTING

Introduction

As Karl Polanyi (1944) pointed out in his analysis of laissez-faire capitalism, processes of economic liberalization involve a "double movement": commodification and self-regulating markets prompt a societal reaction to rein in market forces and (re-)embed liberalism (Ruggie 2003). Two key political and institutional features of the double movement associated with contemporary liberalization and globalization are (i) processes of "re-regulation" (Braithwaite 2005) that create or strengthen institutions to better control environmental, social, and governance (ESG) dimensions of business and market behavior, and (ii) a "corporate accountability movement" (Broad and Cavanagh 1999) involving civil society organizations, networks, and movements that engage in diverse forms of action in an attempt to reform or transform "business-as-usual." These institutional and political dimensions of the double movement have given rise to new forms of business regulation in which international and civil society organizations are playing increasingly prominent roles.

For many years there was a tendency to describe the rise of the late twentieth-century corporate social responsibility (CSR) agenda in terms of a shift from command and control state-led regulation to

---

This chapter draws partly on analysis contained in Utting 2011 and 2012a, 2012b, 2012c. The opinions expressed in this chapter are not necessarily endorsed by the United Nations Research Institute for Social Development (UNRISD) where I work.

I would like to thank John Meyer, Virginia Haufler, Kiyoteru Tsutsui, Alwyn Lim, and other participants at the symposium "CSR in a Globalizing World" (Tokyo, July 10–12, 2012) for their constructive comments and criticisms on an earlier draft, and Hanna Sjolund and Nadine Ruprecht for research and editorial assistance.

corporate self-regulation and voluntary initiatives. For many commentators, this represented a smarter approach to business regulation. Whereas hard regulation was likely to be resisted by business interests and required significant state capacity to oversee, this softer approach could potentially have significant buy-in from both the business community (Holliday, Schmidheiny, and Watts 2002) and civil society organizations that could play their part in designing and implementing CSR standards (Heap 2000).

In the 1990s, corporate self-regulation and voluntarism took off internationally. This was reflected in the proliferation of company and industry codes, the adoption of environmental management systems, stakeholder dialogues, nongovernmental organizations (NGOs)–business partnerships, and various forms of monitoring, reporting, and verification (MRV). In a context in which many national governments were rolling back certain regulatory functions and weaknesses of the emerging CSR agenda were soon exposed, the challenge of re-regulation called forth other actors and institutions, notably multilateral and civil society or "multistakeholder" organizations (Reed et al. 2012).

Divided into three parts, this chapter examines the expanding field of business regulation associated with ESG standards. It focuses, in particular, on international business regulation via the United Nations system (in the section "Contemporary UN–business relations") and the recent rise of forms of "civil regulation" that are often referred to as multistakeholder initiatives (in the section "The expanding field of civil regulation"). The discussion questions assumptions about both the unidirectional shift from "hard" to "soft" regulation and the inherent "progressive" trajectory of CSR norms and practices in terms of more effective regulation and inclusive and sustainable development. The analysis reveals the ongoing eclectic nature of ESG regulation and significant variations in outcomes. It is argued (in the section "The politics of regulatory change") that to better understand the nature and trajectory of contemporary initiatives and their regulatory, social, and developmental implications, attention needs to focus on the political economy of regulatory change. To illustrate this aspect, the chapter looks at how different civil society actors have shaped different types of regulatory initiatives through various forms of contestation, participation, and coalitions. This analysis is applied to four very different types of multistakeholder initiative: the Roundtables on Sustainable

Palm Oil and Responsible Soy, Fairtrade International (FLO), the UN Global Compact (UNGC), and the Organisation for Economic Cooperation and Development (OECD) Guidelines for Multinational Enterprises.

Contemporary UN–business relations

Two events in 1992 marked what has come to be regarded as a turning point in UN–business relations: the closure of the UN Centre on Transnational Corporations (UNCTC), which symbolized a "harder," more confrontational, approach vis-à-vis transnational corporations (TNCs; Sagafi-Nejad 2008),[1] and the UN Conference on Environment and Development ("Earth Summit") in Rio de Janeiro, which actively promoted voluntary CSR initiatives, particularly in the field of corporate environmental responsibility.

But a timeline of contemporary UN–business regulation (see Table 3.1) indicates that numerous UN entities are active in shaping the regulatory environment and that the regulatory approaches adopted can vary considerably. Some agencies have taken a lead in promoting voluntary CSR initiatives and partnerships (e.g., the UN Children's Fund [UNICEF], the UN Development Programme [UNDP], and the UNGC). Others, such as the International Labour Organization (ILO), the UN Environment Programme (UNEP), the UN Economic Commission for Europe (UNECE), and the World Health Organization (WHO), have been active in expanding the scope of international law, both "soft" and "hard." Since the early 2000s, various UN human rights entities have assumed an active role in the field of business regulation, adopting diverse approaches.[2] In the early 2000s, the Sub-Commission on the Promotion and Protection of Human Rights oversaw the drafting of the *Norms on the Responsibilities of TNCs and Other Business Enterprises with Regard to Human Rights*. Seen as overly "hard" and divisive, the

---

[1] Certain functions of the UNCTC were relocated to the UN Conference on Trade and Development (UNCTAD), notably the analysis of the actual or potential contribution of foreign direct investment (FDI) and TNCs to developing countries.

[2] In the early and mid-2000s this included the Sub-Commission on the Promotion and Protection of Human Rights and the Commission on Human Rights; more recently, it includes the Office of the High Commissioner on Human Rights and the Human Rights Council.

Table 3.1 *Contemporary UN–business regulation (selected initiatives)*

1992	Closure of the UN Centre on Transnational Corporations
1992	TNCs engage with the UN "Earth Summit" and commit to voluntary CSR initiatives
1992	ILO creates the International Programme on the Elimination of Child Labour
1995	Entry into force of WTO treaty on food safety (SPS agreement), based on voluntary FAO/WHO Codex Alimentarius Standards
1998	ILO's Declaration on Fundamental Principles and Rights at Work
2000	Launch of the UN Global Compact, which adopts nine principles related to labor standards, environmental protection, and human rights
2001	Entry into force of UNECE "Aarhus Convention" and subsequent adoption (2003) of the first legally binding international instrument on pollutant release and transfer registers
2001	The endorsement of the Kimberley Process by the UN General Assembly, which aimed to break the link between the trade of "conflict diamonds" and armed conflict
2002	The World Summit on Sustainable Development (WSSD) promotes public–private partnerships and specific voluntary initiatives such as the Extractive Industries Transparency Initiative (EITI)
2003	Launch of the Equator Principles, based on IFC performance standards, as a banking industry framework for addressing environmental and social risks in project financing
2004	Procedural reforms to the Global Compact, known as Integrity Measures
2004	Draft UN Norms on the Responsibilities of TNCs and other Business Enterprises with Regard to Human Rights are not approved by the Commission on Human Rights
2004	Addition of a tenth principle (on anticorruption) as one of the core principles of the UN Global Compact
2005	Entry into force of the legally binding WHO Framework Convention on Tobacco Control
2006	Adoption of the Principles for Responsible Investment (PRI) via a process coordinated by UNEP's Finance Initiative and the Global Compact
2006	World Bank Group (part of the UN system) adopts and strengthens standards and policies related to the financing of large projects by financial institutions

Table 3.1 (cont.)

2008	Approval by the UN Human Rights Council of the "Protect, Respect and Remedy" Framework for business and human rights that focuses on both legal and voluntary dimensions of regulation
2009	ILO and IFC launch the Better Work Initiative aimed at improving both compliance with labor standards and competitiveness in global supply chains
2010	Launch of the Women's Empowerment Principles by the Global Compact and UNIFEM
2010	The UN Joint Inspection Unit evaluates critically the UN Global Compact, calling for substantive procedural reforms
2011	Adoption of the UN Guidelines on Business and Human Rights by the Human Rights Council
2012	Children's Rights and Business Principles developed by UNICEF, the UN Global Compact, and Save the Children

Source: Compiled by author

then Commission on Human Rights implicitly rejected the *Norms*. Subsequently, the reconstituted UN Human Rights Council and the Office of the High Commissioner for Human Rights have supported the work of the UN Secretary-General's Special Representative on Business and Human Rights who has crafted a softer, more consensual approach. UN knowledge entities, for example, UNDP's Human Development Report, UNCTAD's World Investment Report, and the UN Research Institute for Social Development (UNRISD), as well as various ILO reports, have adopted different positions on CSR and corporate accountability issues. Whereas the UNDP, for example, has generally been proactive in making the argument for engaging business in partnerships and poverty reduction,[3] research entities like the UNRISD have published far more critical assessments of CSR and public-private partnerships (PPPs) and have suggested the need for a harder regulatory environment for TNCs.[4] On occasions, the UN General Assembly, too, has served as a check on voluntarism both by

---

[3] See, for example, the 2004 report of the UNDP's Commission on the Private Sector and Development, *Unleashing Entrepreneurship: Making Business Work for the Poor*.

[4] See, for example, the UNRISD report "*Combating Poverty and Inequality,*" chapter 9 (UNRISD 2010); and Utting and Marques (2010).

calling for tighter procedures governing UN relations with business (Utting and Zammit 2006) and by questioning broader regulatory trends associated with self-regulation. Although various General Assembly resolutions have supported the Global Compact, this body has adopted a somewhat cautionary approach and certainly does not give "carte blanche" to the initiative (Fall and Zahran 2010).

Three features of regulatory dynamics associated with UN–business relations, discussed herein, illustrate the eclectic and fluid nature of international business regulation related to ESG standards. These include trends associated with voluntarism and partnership; dynamics involving both gradual ratcheting-up of standards and procedures, as well as periodic ratcheting-down; and the ongoing expansion of international law and attention to harder issues of corporate accountability.

The shift toward voluntarism and partnership

The shift toward voluntarism that was symbolized by the closure of the UNCTC and the Earth Summit process was reinforced quite dramatically by two events several years later: the establishment of the Global Compact in 2000 and the World Summit on Sustainable Development (WSSD) in 2002. The WSSD officially endorsed PPPs involving TNCs and other enterprises as one of the two types of Summit agreements to be considered (the other being conventional intergovernmental agreements).

The uptake of CSR and voluntarism within UN agencies and the content of the CSR agenda sat fairly comfortably with neoliberal thinking within both national and international policy circles. More nuanced understandings of the developmental implications of FDI had tempered the mistrust of TNCs among some UN member states and weakened the drive for 1970s-type mandatory regulation (Moran 2009). Furthermore, the rapprochement with big business within the UN reflected a new-found sense of pragmatism that had both philosophical and financial underpinnings. The failure to reach agreement on a code of conduct for TNCs after so many years of effort prompted certain change agents interested in reform to explore softer options around which a broad-based consensus could be achieved. The financial crisis that affected various UN entities in the 1990s also prompted new thinking and policy concerned with mobilizing financial and other resources for development, including those provided by TNCs and the fortunes of a new set of global philanthropists concerned with development issues (Utting and Zammit 2006).

From this context emerged the UNGC, with its aspirational and collaborative approach and its focus on cultivating shared norms and partnerships. The Global Compact quickly developed a remarkable convening power and was effective in raising awareness of CSR globally. As indicated in Table 3.1, the Global Compact has also positioned itself as a hub both to catalyze and leverage other voluntary initiatives. This is apparent through its interactions with the Principles for Responsible Investment (PRI), the Women's Empowerment Principles, the Global Reporting Initiative (GRI), ISO 26000, the OECD Guidelines for Multinational Enterprises, and the Children's Rights and Business Principles.

Although often described as "toothless," two features of the Global Compact potentially bode well from the perspective of legitimacy, regulatory authority, and corporate accountability. First, its ten principles were based on international (environmental, labor, human rights, and anticorruption) law. Second, it adopted a multistakeholder governance structure that allowed civil society to have a seat at the table, even though the dominant stakeholder was clearly business. This contrasted with the tripartite structure of the ILO, in which employer organizations and trade unions had an equal footing. But, in keeping with the ethos of voluntarism and CSR, the Global Compact was largely devoid of enforcement mechanisms. It also steered clear of certain issues and so-called critical thinking and debate about TNCs, focusing instead on raising awareness about CSR and learning about best practices (Utting and Zammit 2006).

The other "voluntary" feature of the timeline in Table 3.1 relates to the expanding arena of UN–business partnerships or PPPs. From the turn of the new millennium, many such partnerships were part of efforts to engage business more directly in poverty reduction. Developed on an ad hoc basis by numerous UN agencies, which often adopted very different standards and criteria for partner selection, PPPs were institutionalized via various initiatives. These included the Millennium Development Goals (MDGs),[5] the UN Secretary-General's Guidelines on UN–business cooperation, and the 2002 WSSD. Subsequently, the Global Compact

---

[5] In particular, Goal 8: "Develop a global partnership for development."

positioned itself as a lead entity promoting PPPs in general and UN–business partnerships in particular, and it established a UN-wide system of UN–business focal points linking multiple agencies.[6]

Incremental ratcheting-up

Another feature that emerges from the timeline relates to the gradual ratcheting-up of voluntary approaches. What begin as very soft approaches are often subsequently revised and, in the process, tend to adopt some slightly harder features. This can occur in various ways. An important mechanism for ratcheting-up involves so-called hybrid or articulated regulation (Utting 2005; McBarnet, Voiculescu, and Campbell 2007). This refers to the interface and symbiosis between voluntarism and law, including the process by which international "soft" law, which has a voluntary character, calls on governments to internalize its standards in domestic law, which is binding. This process of incorporation occurs in numerous fields; for example, in standards related to the production, use, and marketing of products such as infant formula or pesticides and international labor standards and human rights. Another variant of incorporation can be seen in the case of the International Criminal Court (ICC). Although the ICC explicitly excludes so-called legal persons such as TNCs from its jurisdiction, some national jurisdictions – where charges for international crimes can be brought against corporations – have drawn on (Ruggie 2007: 9) ICC definitions and standards.

In the case of voluntary initiatives such as the Global Compact, ratcheting-up has occurred through such measures as the introduction or tightening of rules on association and disclosure, the addition of new principles or areas of engagement, and the introduction of a mild grievance procedure to deal with complaints. The most significant measure in this regard was the attempt, discussed in the next section, to address the issue of free-riding by introducing rules on disclosure. Participating companies were required to report annually on progress. A significant proportion of companies participating in the Global Compact, however, failed to comply and, by November 2010, 1,719 companies had been delisted as Global Compact participants (UNGC 2010).

---

[6] In 2010, the UN established the web portal business.un.org as a one-stop-shop for business seeking to engage the UN.

Corporate social responsibility and the evolving standards regime

The uptake of additional principles is another aspect of ratcheting-up. This occurred, for example, with the inclusion of the tenth Global Compact principle on anticorruption in 2004 and the adoption of a set of side principles related to women's rights and empowerment in 2010. In contrast to other Global Compact principles, the latter contain some specific targets, concrete goals, and stronger language, for example: "30% or greater participation (of women) in decision-making and governance at all levels and across all business areas'; 'strive to pay a living wage to all women and men'; 'strive to offer health insurance', 'zero-tolerance' of abuse and harassment; establish benchmarks that quantify inclusion of women at all levels; measure and report on progress ... using data disaggregated by sex" (UNGC and UNIFEM 2010: 3).

.... and ratcheting-down

It is wrong to assume that regulatory dynamics involves a one-way street associated with ratcheting-up. In the case of the Global Compact, for example, ratcheting-up confronts definite limits that relate to structural, instrumental, and discursive aspects: structural, in the sense that this initiative was established to enlist and maintain the support of business and must, therefore, keep certain issues off-limits;[7] instrumental, in that business actors constitute a dominant stakeholder and voice within the initiative, thereby heavily influencing the agenda; and discursive or ideational in the sense that most of the key players involved (UN technocrats, business, academic learning networks, and NGOs) genuinely believe in this approach, with its emphasis on "principled pragmatism"[8] and social and organizational learning through dialogue and other forms of collaborative governance.

Instances of "ratcheting-down" in the field of international ESG regulation are also apparent. This often occurs when negotiations stall or fail but the fundamental issue to be resolved – and associated societal pressures – do not go away. Softer approaches are promoted usually by some coalition of interests, including, for example, governments that seek minimalist regulation and so-called change agents who

---

[7] See also Levy and Brown's (2012) discussion of the Global Reporting Initiative.
[8] The term was used by John Ruggie, in his capacity as the UN Secretary-General's Special Representative on Business and Human Rights, in his 2006 report to the Commission on Human Rights (see OHCHR 2010).

want to break the stalemate. The transition from the UN Norms on the Responsibilities of TNCs and other Business Enterprises with Regard to Human Rights, which attempted to introduce harder elements associated with monitoring, redress, and compensation, to the so-called *Ruggie process* is indicative in this regard. As noted earlier, the political tensions associated with the design of the Norms meant that they were not adopted by the UN Commission on Human Rights. But this paved the way for the appointment of John Ruggie as the UN Secretary-General's Special Representative on Business and Human Rights. He trod far more cautiously to engineer a broad-based consensus on a normative framework. Rather than calling for new institutions and regulatory instruments, the "Protect, Respect and Remedy" framework looked to existing institutions – in particular, the enforcement of national laws, corporate due diligence to apply mainstream CSR principles and instruments, and the use of existing judicial and non-judicial grievance procedure.

Ratcheting-down may also occur in terms of issue areas. As Rob van Tulder (2008) points out, issues tend to come and go, and new or renewed attention to one issue can crowd out consideration of others. The CSR agenda is prone to fads and fashions. Media and political concerns that focus attention on particular issues – currently, for example, climate change – can displace others. There are some signs that this dynamic affects the Global Compact. For example, the 2010 survey of CEOs of Global Compact companies about corporate commitment to ESG principles and future prospects reveals a significant bias in terms of environmental issues (Utting 2011) despite the fact that Global Compact principles also cover human rights, labor standards, and anticorruption.

The expanding body of international law and the turn to "effective remedy"

Although there was certainly a shift from "hard" to "soft" in the 1990s, the UN remains an eclectic institution in terms of UN–business relations and regulatory approaches. Efforts to promote corporate accountability via international and national law, as well as through grievance procedures and effective remedy, are still very much in evidence.

Where initiatives associated with international law have gained ground, they often relate to quite specific issues, products, processes, or institutions. These include, for example, the WHO Framework Convention on Tobacco Control that obliges governments to regulate tobacco companies; various multilateral environment agreements; the ongoing incorporation into national law of the International Code of Marketing of Breastmilk Substitutes; the UN Declaration on the Rights of Indigenous Peoples; and the broadening of the ILO Tripartite Declaration on Multinational Enterprises (MNEs) and Social Policy to include other ILO conventions. Within the ILO, there has also been some interest in cultivating new institutions, such as the International Framework Agreements promoted by several Global Union Federations through which global corporations agree to uphold basic labor standards and industrial relations practices throughout their core corporate structures and, in some instances, also in other parts of the supply chain (Papadakis 2008).

Furthermore, within the UN, there is growing awareness of the issue of effective remedy and the key role of grievance procedures in regulatory systems. Work sponsored by the UNRISD and the UN Non-Governmental Liaison Service (UNNGLS), which was coordinated by this author, highlighted their importance in 2001 (UN Non-Governmental Liaison Service [UNNGLS] and UNRISD 2002). This work emphasized the importance of complementing regulatory approaches centered on MRV with far more attention to a broad range of both judicial and nonjudicial complaints or grievance procedures. Grievance procedures subsequently formed one of the three main pillars of the Protect, Respect, and Remedy framework to promote business responsibility for human rights. Also relevant in this regard are efforts to periodically review complaints procedures with a view to making them more effective, as has occurred in relation to the OECD Guidelines for Multinational Enterprises, discussed in the section "The politics of regulatory change."

The expanding field of "civil regulation"

The term "civil regulation" was used by some CSR analysts in the 1990s to refer to the burgeoning role of civil society organizations and networks in standard-setting and other regulatory functions (Murphy and Bendell 1997; Zadek 2001). Important in this regard were not only formal roles in regulatory governance (e.g., in standards design and MRV) but also in diverse forms of collective action associated with protest, advocacy, lobbying, "naming and shaming," "naming and praising," critical research, and redress for actual or presumed victims of corporate irresponsibility (Utting 2012b).

The rise of civil regulation reflects not only the rise of NGOs as significant actors in governance, but also more fundamental changes in patterns of governance, state–business–society relations, and collective action in contexts of globalization and liberalization (Abbott and Snidal 2009; Mattli and Woods 2009). The field of civil regulation has evolved significantly. Early forms of engagement centered on a fairly narrow range of tactics, procedures, and relationships associated with "confrontation" or "collaboration" (Heap 2000; Bendell 2004). A key development in recent years is the increasing role of NGOs or multistakeholder entities in setting standards that have international scope.

The geographical and issue focus of multistakeholder initiatives (MSIs) varies considerably, ranging from global and multisectoral initiatives such as the GRI and SA8000 or ISO 14001 certification; through standards related to particular sectors or industries (Fair Labor Association, Forest Stewardship Council [FSC], and Marine Stewardship Council [MSC]) or particular commodities, such as the Biofuels, Soy, and Palm Oil Roundtables; to initiatives that are concerned with a specific issue such as corruption (Extractive Industries Transparency Initiative [EITI]), conflict diamonds (Kimberley Process), or child labor (Atlanta Agreement). As seen in Table 3.2, numerous MSIs have emerged since the early 1990s.

Multiple agendas, actors, and interests have come together to craft this new approach to business regulation. Key contextual factors relate to institutional and political changes associated with (i) the changing nature of the state in terms of the delegation of regulatory authority and rolling back of certain capacities (Cerny 2000; Braithwaite 2005); (ii) trends associated with deliberative democracy and "collaborative" governance, as well as with "managerialism" or "governmentality" (Gibbon and Ponte 2008), which address issues of risk, complexity, and legitimacy; (iii) changes in the nature of corporate capitalism and "the logic of capital" that demanded new and improved mechanisms of inter- and intrafirm coordination, a more streamlined and stable regulatory environment, and new approaches to protecting brand or reputational value (Zadek 2001; Jessop and Sum 2006; Palpacuer 2010); and (iv) responses and pressures related to the "double movement" and civil society contestation, advocacy, and service delivery

Table 3.2 *The expanding arena of civil regulation (selected initiatives)*

Year	Name	Focus (*)
1993	Forest Stewardship Council (FSC)	Sustainable forestry standards/certification and eco-labeling
1995	ISO 14001	Environmental management standard/certification
1997	Global Reporting Initiative (GRI)	Sustainability reporting indicators; application checks
1997	Social Accountability (SA) 8000	Labor standards/certification
1997	Marine Stewardship Council (MSC)	Sustainable fisheries; certification and eco-labeling
1997	EuropGAP/GlobalGAP	Food industry standards; certification
1997	Atlanta Agreement on Child Labour	Child labor
1997	Fairtrade International (FLO)	Fair Trade/agro-ecology; certification
1998	Ethical Trading Initiative (ETI)	Agri-food supply chain standards; reporting
1999	Fair Labor Association (FLA)	Labor standards/assessments
2000	Worker Rights Consortium (WRC)	Labor standards; investigation of complaints
2000	OECD Guidelines for MNEs revised via multistakeholder process	Global ESG standards, complaints procedure
2000	Voluntary Principles on Security and Human Rights	Standards for participating extractive industry corporations
2002	Extractive Industries Transparency Initiative (EITI)	Revenue transparency; disclosure and monitoring
2003	Common Code for the Coffee Community (CCCC)	Standards in the coffee chain
2003	The Gold Standard	Carbon mitigation standard; certification
2004	Roundtable on Sustainable Palm Oil	Standards in palm oil production; certification
2006	Roundtable on Sustainable Biofuels	Standards for biofuel production; certification

Table 3.2 (cont.)

Year	Name	Focus (*)
2006	Roundtable on Responsible Soy	Standards in soy production; certification
2007	Better Cotton Initiative	Standards in cotton production
2009	Aquaculture Stewardship Council	Standards and certification in fish farming (being designed)
2010	ISO 26 000	Guidance standard on social responsibility

* References to "certification" generally mean that the initiative promotes a certification system, rather than directly conducts audits.
Source: Compiled by author

(Utting 2012b). MSIs also emerge in the context of failed attempts to re-embed liberalism via the early CSR agenda through corporate and industry self-regulation, which centered on company codes of conduct and superficial "MRV" often associated with internal monitoring, "glossy" reporting, and "tick-box" verification.

In terms of normative and regulatory performance, MSIs have had a very mixed record. A review of some twenty initiatives (Utting 2012a) sheds light on variations in both performance and approach.

Normative and regulatory advances

From the perspective of both regulatory effectiveness and sustainable development, several areas of progress can be noted. At the normative level, multistakeholder regulation has played a key role in raising awareness of social, environmental, human rights, and governance problems associated with contemporary patterns of production, investment, trade, consumption, corporatization, and self-regulation. Some initiatives, such as the GRI and ISO 26000, have achieved considerable convening power and geographical reach, and, through numerous events and extensive global networks, they have spread the discourse and principles of CSR, as well as knowledge about specific instruments. The role of MSIs in facilitating learning via stakeholder dialogue often emerges as a key impact. Indeed, as Auld and Cashore

(2012) note in relation to the FSC, impacts related to "transparent learning processes" are often far more obvious than are those related to "problem amelioration."

At the microlevel of the enterprise or production unit, gains have been reported in certain value chains and countries in specific issue areas related to child labor, improved compliance with minimum wage legislation, improved prices for smallholders through Fair Trade schemes, anticorruption, enhanced environmental protection, and improvements in human rights situations in some conflict zones and areas of natural resource extraction. As Barrientos and Smith (2012) note in relation to the Ethical Trading Initiative (ETI), multistakeholder initiatives and participating firms have tended to pay more attention to the implementation of such "outcome standards" than to "process rights" such as freedom of association and collective bargaining. An important exception, of course, involves various initiatives whose starting point or core objective relates to worker or producer empowerment. These include, for example, the Worker Rights Consortium and International Framework Agreements signed by global union federations and TNCs, which focus on labor rights and redress, and several Fair Trade schemes, which promote not only the payment of premium prices to small producers but also their collective organization and empowerment.

Considerable regulatory dynamism is evident in the sense that many initiatives evolve, mature, and gradually raise the bar in terms of standards and procedures (Gibbon et al. 2011; Utting 2012a). This ratcheting-up is apparent in terms of adopting additional standards, as well as in strengthening specific mechanisms and procedures to enhance implementation and oversight, for example, in relation to transparency, disclosure, and complaints procedures. Several initiatives have enhanced the quality of specific tools, such as monitoring, social auditing, certification, and sustainability reporting, by addressing weaknesses that were apparent when these practices first emerged. Initiatives such as the EITI, GRI, FSC, the MSC, and SA8000 have become more inclusive of a broader range of standards, procedures, and stakeholders.

MSIs are often associated with regulation that is becoming multi-scalar (i.e., regulatory functions are carried out at global, regional, national, and local levels). They involve actors and institutions that often complement those operating at the national level by focusing on both the microlevel of the factory, mine, or farm and the global level involving international norms or agreements with corporate headquarters related to their global operations. Initiatives such as International Framework Agreements, for example, mark an initial step in crafting forms of regulatory governance adapted to globalization and that respond to the inability of national-level institutions (e.g., collective bargaining, arbitration, and mediation) to address cross-border issues.

Furthermore, some MSIs are proactively coordinating with others. The ISEAL Alliance, for example, seeks to harmonize the approaches of various standards initiatives, thus developing guidance aimed to strengthen effectiveness and impacts. Among the eleven full members are the FSC, MSC, the 4 C Association, and FLO. Formal collaborations now also exist between initiatives like the GRI, the UNGC, and the OECD Guidelines for MNEs. These initiatives are positioning themselves (or being positioned by others) as the leading global institutions in relation to particular regulatory functions, be it promotion of CSR principles and agenda setting (Global Compact), reporting indicators (GRI), or complaints mechanisms (OECD National Contact Points). Such collaboration among leading standards initiatives raises the question of whether an incipient form of transnational regulatory governance may be emerging in which a limited number of global institutions assume a key role in relation to specific regulatory functions and are coordinated and organized in an internationally networked division of (regulatory) labor.

Multistakeholder regulation has also advanced thinking and policy on the respective regulatory roles and responsibilities of public and private actors. Some initiatives are going beyond the narrow compartmentalization of "voluntary" versus "mandatory" regulation or private versus public governance by promoting hybrid forms of regulation in which voluntary standards (i) are based on international labor, environmental, human rights, and other law; (ii) serve as benchmarks for national law and public policy; (iii) involve not only business entities and civil society organizations, but also governments and intergovernmental organizations; (iv) are mandated by laws that oblige companies to report using "voluntary" standards; or (v) are promoted and scaled-up by government policy associated, for example, with organizing cross-sectoral dialogues, direct funding, and public procurement.

Limitations and dilemmas

From the perspective of effective regulation and sustainable development, five sets of constraints and contradictions seem particularly relevant. First, despite the rapid growth of certain regulatory initiatives, their base, in terms of participating companies, tends to remain limited. Around 2011–2012, labor standards certification under SA8000 involved about 3,000 entities; GRI recorded some 4,000 organizations that applied the GRI reporting indicators; FSC certification covered about 12 percent of global timber production (World Wide Fund for Nature [WWF] 2012b); whereas MSC certification covered 8 percent of global fish landings (MSC 2012). The first group of fourteen companies certified under the Roundtable on Responsible Soy production in 2011 accounted for 0.16 percent of global soy production. Such figures reveal the tremendous gap between the subuniverse of corporations and suppliers engaged with MSIs and the universe of commercial enterprise and value chains – some 100,000 TNCs, 900,000 TNC affiliates, millions of suppliers, and 1.5 billion commodity producers (UNCTAD[9]; WWF 2012a).

Second, there is often a tension between quantity, in terms of numbers of participating companies, and quality, in terms of rigorous and comprehensive standards, implementation procedures, and compliance. Whereas schemes like GlobalGAP and MSC have grown significantly, they experience significant limitations in terms of substance and scope. GlobalGAP tends to prioritize standards or issues of concern to Global North corporations and consumers, such as food safety, and pay less attention to other social and environmental issues. Focusing on commercial fisheries in the Global North, MSC has grown a $3 billion market for certified seafood but, until recently, has paid little attention to aquaculture, social issues, and small and marginalized fishers (Auld 2012).

And the reverse applies. Schemes noted for more rigorous standards and methods (e.g., the Worker Rights Consortium) engage with only a handful of companies. Furthermore, others, such as the FSC or SA8000, which over time have raised the bar, confront difficulties in scaling up. In the case of FSC, competing, less demanding certification schemes have emerged (Auld and Cashore 2012). After 2005, the rate of expansion of SA8000 certification dropped substantially (Rasche and Gilbert 2012).

---

[9] www.unctad.org/wir, accessed May 20, 2012.

Third, as in the case of some international initiatives such as the Global Compact and the OECD Guidelines for MNEs, lack of systematic review of compliance and ineffective grievance procedures and remedy emerge as key limitations in several MSIs (e.g., the GRI, SA8000, the Kimberley Process, and FLO). Processes of monitoring and verification of labor standards, which potentially could empower workers, often engage more with management than with workers. This, in turn, can create suspicion in auditors among the workforce and limit the capacity of auditing to identify issues of concern for workers. Weak transparency and disclosure associated with schemes such as the GRI and SA8000 inhibit the capacity of NGOs and trade unions to monitor and act as watchdogs. As in the case of SA8000, some social auditing and certification schemes that require the audited enterprise to pay the auditors remain compromised by conflicts of interest, lack of independence, and weak disclosure.

Fourth, multistakeholder regulation is constrained by a range of structural conditions and the fact that MSIs are nested in broader institutions and power relations associated with capitalism (Levy and Brown 2012). These include the profit motive, shareholder primacy, and consumer culture, as well as the "structural, instrumental and discursive power" of business elites (Fuchs 2005). Such conditions can impose severe limits on the scope for internalizing social and environmental costs, redistributing income and value, and lessening regulatory capture (Marques and Utting 2010). Indeed, they underpin countertrends associated with the so-called race to the bottom in labor standards and precarious employment and enhance the capacity of large corporations to transfer risks and costs related to standards' implementation along the value chain. The changing structure of global production, notably the rise of emerging market economies and their national (corporate) champions, has resulted in situations – evident in the case of the extractive industries – in which a multistakeholder initiative may seem out of step, focusing on the old guard of Western TNCs, as opposed to the new.

Both the nesting of multistakeholder regulation within broader institutional structures and the considerable influence of corporate interests in regulatory design and implementation, as well as in other policy processes, can severely constrain the potential of such initiatives to transform business practices, core product and market strategies, and patterns of corporate governance. Achievements are often not replicated in more informal and casualized segments of the value chain; indeed, standards regimes can fuel informalization as firms outsource as a means to bypass regulation and reduce costs. Within some export-manufacturing chains, women have been particularly affected by this situation (Razavi, Pearson, and Danloy 2004).

The cases of the GRI and GlobalGAP, for example, reveal that the process of enlisting support from corporate interests may involve explicit or implicit compromises that dilute some aspects of regulation or keep certain issues off limits (Kalfagianni and Fuchs 2012; Levy and Brown 2012). Similarly, the participatory process put in place to design the ISO 26000 guidance standard agreed early on to focus broadly on "organizational" rather than "corporate" social responsibility in an effort not to single out TNCs.

Finally, impacts related to economic development and the fact that there may be winners and losers within supply chains are often ignored. Indeed, limited attention to impact assessment is a widespread feature of multistakeholder regulation. Of particular concern are the cost implications of multistakeholder regulation for small suppliers and workers and the capacity of large corporations to use their market power to transfer risk and the costs of raising standards to weaker stakeholders. Productivity gains may not conform to the theory regarding "win-win" outcomes (Rasche and Gilbert 2012). Furthermore, there is a tendency for standards regimes to favor concentration at different levels of the value chain. Standards-based initiatives may facilitate market access for some enterprises and work more as a protectionist barrier to trade for others.

With some notable exceptions (e.g., the FSC) multistakeholder initiatives were generally designed in the Global North and are often perceived locally as externally driven initiatives. Global South actors and stakeholders have often played a minimal role in the design of standards, monitoring, implementation, and the governance structures of various initiatives. This has been noted in relation to ISO 14001, SA8000, GRI, ETI, FLO, and GlobalGAP. The upshot of such imbalances is that some schemes have marginalized key development issues in their respective fields; for example, aquaculture and small-scale fisheries in the case of the MSC or poverty- and conflict-related issues affecting artisanal gold miners in the case of "fair trade gold" schemes. There is sometimes limited attention paid to local solutions to specific problems.

But more equitable forms of stakeholder participation can also give rise to certain dilemmas. In the case of the FSC, for example, more inclusive participation has resulted in raising the bar in terms of standards and procedures (Auld and Cashore 2012), but this has alienated some business interests and governments and led to the growth of alternative, softer, schemes. Such tensions are also apparent in the area of fair trade, discussed next.

The politics of regulatory change

How do we explain the significant variations in regulatory approaches and outcomes noted in the preceding sections? Explanations typically found within organizational and governance literatures are clearly important in this regard. They include, for example, financial resources, professional expertise, leadership, incentives, stakeholder participation, organizational learning, and path dependence. Often, however, other factors associated with the political economy of regulatory change are sidelined or ignored. These relate to the configuration and reconfiguration of power relations; patterns of contestation both within the governance structures of regulatory initiatives and external to them; and the nature of participation, coalitions, and alliances. It is to these aspects that we now turn by examining the role of non-state actors in shaping particular regulatory initiatives.

Tensions within civil society

Voluntary initiatives that attempt to win over global corporations to the cause of CSR and achieve incremental gains in ESG performance often incur the wrath of particular civil society organizations. This reflects the heterogeneous character of civil society organizations concerned with the behavior of business and ESG issues. Although there is considerable common ground, it is possible to identify a mainstream CSR movement engaging collaboratively with business through dialogues, technical assistance, and rating and rankings of firms, and a corporate accountability movement that emphasizes the need to control and roll-back corporate power through the rule of law, the regulatory role of the state, the reconfiguration of power relations, the institutionalization of citizen's rights, and the promotion of "social economy" alternatives to corporate capitalism (Utting 2012b, 2012c, 2013).

At some point in their life span, most MSIs and some of the NGOs supporting them confront opposition from elements within the corporate accountability movement. Such has been the case, for example, with the Global Compact, the Fair Labor Association, and, more recently in the cases discussed herein, of the Roundtables established by the World Wide Fund for Nature (WWF) and others to promote responsible and sustainable commodity production.

The soy and palm oil roundtables
Drawing on the experience of the FSC and the MSC, established in 1994 and 1997, respectively, during the past decade, the WWF has established another seven standard schemes to promote more sustainable forms of production of cotton, palm oil, soy, sugarcane, biofuels, farmed salmon and shrimp, and beef. These schemes, generally called Roundtables, are part of the WWF's broader strategy that emerged in the early 2000s, which was to spread itself less thinly around the world and concentrate its efforts on protecting a relatively small number of threatened ecosystems (WWF 2012b). In these areas, environmental degradation and risks were partly, if not largely, related to the production of fifteen commodities controlled by relatively few agri-food and extractives corporations. By enlisting the participation of such corporations in the Roundtables, the WWF sought to promote more environmentally friendly production processes and consumption patterns. The strategic logic underpinning the WWF's approach was to work with a relatively small number of large companies (retailers, processors, manufacturers, and traders) that constitute the "greatest point of leverage" in the value chain in terms of their capacity to shape the choices of "7 billion consumers" and "1.5 billion producers" (WWF 2012b: 2). The WWF has prioritized some 100 companies that control about 25 percent of the supply chains of the fifteen commodities (WWF 2012a: 25).

Various civil society organizations have been highly critical of this approach, seeing it as a flawed strategy that changes relatively little in terms of production practices, ignores key development issues, and legitimizes business-as-usual. The Roundtables on Sustainable Palm Oil and Responsible Soy have been subject to intense criticism from environmental NGOs such as Greenpeace and Friends of the Earth International (Greenpeace 2012).

Discourse analysis of the soy and palm oil Roundtables conducted by Schouten et al. (2012) suggests that only certain discourses on sustainable development frame and inform internal deliberation. These are "reformist" discourses, in the sense of emphasizing the potential for achieving improvements in environmental and social performance of business activities in contexts of growth, corporate control of value, chains, and large-scale monocultures. So-called "radical" perspectives tend to be excluded, namely, those that highlight fundamental incompatibilities between such economic and production systems and sustainable development, as well as the need for harder regulation of corporate activities. Although such perspectives are prominent within deliberative processes outside the Roundtables, the findings of this research suggest that there is little transmission inward. The situation facilitates internal communication, dialogue, and agreement on standards and procedures but has major implications for the issues of scale and quality referred to earlier.

During their start-up phase, the Roundtables have been less concerned with issues of legitimacy than with "pragmatism" and the harvesting of low-hanging fruit: namely, a small number of large companies that sign up and are prepared to take at least some steps to change their production practices. But, as the earlier discussion on "ratcheting-up: suggests, reforms are likely to follow as free-riding becomes a concern not only for outsiders, but also for some internal stakeholders. This occurred, for example, with the adoption and application in 2010 of the Roundtable on Responsible Soy's "New Planting Procedure," which was in response to criticisms that some companies were not taking steps to avoid large-scale forest clearance when expanding their operations. High-profile member companies that are trying to project a global CSR image may even break corporate ranks and ally with strange bedfellows. In the case of the Roundtable on Responsible Soy, Unilever, a leading member company, dropped one of its largest Indonesian suppliers and blacklisted another in 2010 when it came under pressure from NGOs. Both suppliers were also members of the Roundtable for Responsible Soy. Unilever and Greenpeace also agreed to work together to lobby for a moratorium on deforestation associated with palm oil production. Through time, then, the balance of forces (of ideas and actors) within the governance of MSIs can change. This is seen in the case of the organization and mobilization of small farmers associated with Fairtrade, to which we now turn.

Contestation within governance structures

As noted earlier, a major concern with MSIs relates to imbalances in stakeholder participation within their governance structures, which affects their developmental orientation and regulatory approaches. The ratcheting-up and -down of standards and procedures that is a feature of regulatory dynamics associated with MSIs often reflects changes that are occurring in the balance of stakeholder interests within governance structures and evolving patterns of contestation. This is seen clearly in the case of developments in Fairtrade standards and the split within the international fair trade movement.

In late 2011, Fair Trade USA, formerly TransFair USA, left the global association of the national labeling organizations, FLO. Fair Trade USA announced unilateral plans to certify large coffee plantations, which was not allowed under FLO's global standard. The US-based United Students for Fair Trade movement promptly disassociated itself from Fair Trade USA, and the Latin American producers' organization CLAC announced plans to initiate its own fair trade label.

The pursuit of different models of development and changes in the governance of fair trade underpins these schisms (Reed 2012). Regarding the models, Fair Trade USA favors the scaling-up of the fair trade niche market by engaging large corporations and agricultural estates, facilitating market access, empowering small producers economically, and promoting corporate environmental and social responsibility – which targets not only suppliers but also agricultural workers. Several currents within FLO, and the larger movement of alternative trade organizations and advocates, promote the original ethos and principles of fair trade, which are centered on fostering solidarity, empowering small producers both economically and politically through collective organization, and promoting higher standards of agro-ecology.

Regarding governance, the voice of small producer organizations is increasingly being heard, and their vote is carrying increasing weight in FLO's governance structures, in contrast to the previous situation where the national labeling organizations controlled decision making. This development did not occur within the governance structures of Fair Trade USA. The change in the balance of social forces within FLO favored decisions to increase both the fair trade floor price and the social premiums that support various local projects (Bacon 2010).

Meanwhile, particularly in Latin America, national and regional producer associations have become stronger, gaining a more robust voice within FLO and also reframing the meaning of fair trade. This has involved broadening the focus away from merely considering how to secure premium prices in export markets. Attention has focused on how small-scale producers can capture for themselves the benefits of a growing fair trade market in their own countries and regions. This includes (i) adding value to their primary products through processing; (ii) the need to balance export-oriented commodity production with the principles and practices of "food sovereignty"; and (iii) the need for ongoing political empowerment of producers through self-supporting organization, more effective participation in both policy processes and the governance structures of intermediary organizations, and by building coalitions and alliances. This reflects a very different vision about what development means, as compared to that generally found within the mainstream CSR arena (Reed 2012).

Complementarities between insider and outsider strategies

Beyond the issue of stakeholder or actor representation, voice, and influence within the governance structures of MSIs is the issue of how insider and outsider pressures combine to facilitate both scaling-up and improved outcomes from the perspective of both sustainable development and regulation. Whereas mainstream CSR discourse often suggests that confrontation and contestation are somewhat passé and that "we are all partners now," the analysis of regulatory dynamics suggests the ongoing potency of naming and shaming, campaign advocacy, critical analysis, and other tactics of contestation. This analysis also suggests the importance of building networks and coalitions and overcoming the fragmentation associated with "NGOization" and the participation of individual civil society organizations in CSR governance.

The cases presented here are illustrative of instances in which insider and outsider tactics come together to push for reform in ways that are complementary and synergistic.

Reforming the Global Compact
Issues of credibility have plagued the Global Compact since its inception. Whereas this remains as true today as in 2000, when the initiative

began, one procedural reform introduced in 2004 attempted to address the problem of free-riding. As a result of this procedural change, some 3,123 companies were expelled from the Compact between 2005 and February 2012.[10]

This reform was part of a set of Integrity Measures that aimed to address the Global Compact's image problem. A combination of insider and outsider pressures was instrumental in driving this reform process. The Integrity Measures obliged participating companies to report on progress. Nonreporting companies were to be named publicly and persistent nonreporters delisted. The Integrity Measures also aimed at controlling the misuse of the Global Compact's name and logo and contained a mechanism for dealing with allegations of gross abuse of the Global Compact principles by companies.

Ever since it was established, the Global Compact had received considerable criticism from various NGOs and NGO networks. They were concerned that the Compact not only lacked teeth and facilitated free-riding, but also allowed for "bluewashing," whereby global corporations could use their association with the UN to project a clean image (TRAC 2000). A counter "Citizens Compact" was thus signed by several high-profile activists and civil society and other organizations. Some went on to form the Alliance for a Corporate-Free UN (Corpwatch 2001).

Simultaneously, several prominent NGOs (including Human Rights Watch, Amnesty International, and Oxfam International) formally became part of the multistakeholder governance structure of the Global Compact in an effort to reform it from within. In 2003, however, their patience ran thin. In a public letter to the UN Deputy Secretary-General, they complained of weak accountability mechanisms and limited evidence of progress and called for a series of reforms, including annual reporting by participating companies and effective stakeholder participation in national-level Compacts.

When the Global Compact held its first Leaders Summit in New York in 2004, numerous civil society organizations met nearby for the Global Compact Counter Summit. From there, they issued the Joint Civil Society Statement on the Global Compact and Corporate Accountability that accused the Compact of "reward[ing] rhetoric

---

[10] See http://www.unglobalcompact.org/news/188-02-09-2012, accessed June 10, 2012.

rather than deeds, and ... undermin[ing] our efforts to bring a measure of corporate accountability, rather than purely voluntary responsibility, into the intergovernmental arena" (NGLS 2004). Such criticisms and pressures added to the momentum for reform, which had also involved other actors. For example, the consulting firm McKinsey and Company had evaluated the effectiveness and added value of the Global Compact and made recommendations to strengthen participants' accountability (McKinsey and Co. 2004).

While some of the original civil society actors, networks, and campaigns that had contested the Global Compact withered, others emerged, notably Global Compact Critics (Gregoratti 2012) and, most recently, the End UN Corporate Capture campaign. Launched in the build-up to the Rio+20 conference on sustainable development, this campaign accused the Global Compact of "merely help[ing] businesses to boost their image and profits, instead of promoting binding obligations that would contribute to changing companies' performance."[11]

New critical voices also emerged from within the UN. The UN Joint Inspection Unit (the UN's independent evaluation body) published a report that confirmed many of the concerns about the Global Compact that various scholars and activists had been voicing for years. The report called for substantive procedural reforms to strengthen selection criteria, governance arrangements, and oversight mechanisms (Fall and Zahran 2010). What is significant in this case is the discursive influence of civil society actors and how their specific concerns about bluewashing, corporate capture, and reputational risk came to resonate within some mainstream institutional circles.

Testing and revising the OECD guidelines for MNEs

Civil society action aims not only to shape new normative frameworks (e.g., ISO26000) or add some substance to existing ones (e.g., the

---

[11] See "Ending corporate capture of the United Nations: Joint civil society statement" by Friends of the Earth International, Corporate Europe Observatory, La Via Campesina, Jubilee South/Americas, Peace and Justice in Latin America/SERPAJ-AL, Polaris Institute, The Council of Canadians, The Transnational Institute, Third World Network, World March of Women, available at http://www.foei.org/en/get-involved/take-action/pdfs/statement-un-corpcap-en/view, accessed June 10, 2012; see also Friends of the Earth International 2012. By June 10, 2012, some 360 civil society organizations had joined the campaign.

Global Compact), but also to activate or energize institutions that have remained somewhat inert. Such is the case of the OECD Guidelines for MNEs. Created in 1976, the Guidelines are nonbinding recommendations covering a wide range of issues. They are addressed by governments to TNCs operating in or from countries that adhere to the Guidelines. Against the backdrop of mounting global justice activism in the 1990s that targeted TNCs and the participation of a few NGO networks, such as Friends of the Earth, Transparency International, WWF, and the Northern Alliance for Sustainability (ANPED) in consultative processes, the Guidelines were revised in 2000, bringing on board new issue areas, such as supply chain management. The influence of NGOs complemented that of trade union representatives who, along with business and industry representatives, make up one of the two advisory committees to the OECD.

Through the grievance mechanism known as the National Contact Points, the 2000 review enhanced the potential role of NGOs in bringing complaints. There has since been a groundswell of activism centered on monitoring the application of the Guidelines and testing the complaints procedure. The implementation and effectiveness of the Guidelines has been monitored consistently by OECD Watch, a global network of more than eighty NGOs from forty-five countries. Approximately 200 cases were filed by NGOs and trade unions between 2001 and June 2010 (OECD Watch 2010). A ten-year assessment of the Guidelines concluded that they "have had a poor track record in dealing with the social, environmental and economic problems that matter most to communities and workers whose rights have been harmed by the actions of MNEs.... [T]he main impediments ... concern the confusion about their voluntary nature, their restrictive scope as well as failings with the implementation procedures and the lack of authority of most NCPs. Yet ... with their unique combination of internationally-agreed normative standards, and government oversight, [they] have the potential to make a significant contribution to improving business conduct" (OECD Watch 2010: 7–8).

In June 2010, work began on updating the Guidelines "to increase their relevance and clarify private sector responsibilities" (OECD 2011). This was in view of ongoing global industrial restructuring and the renewed attention to issues of business responsibility in the context of the financial and economic crisis and climate change. The revision was led by the OECD Investment Committee, with which OECD Watch has close interaction. The OECD Investment Committee named OECD Watch "a partner in implementing the OECD Guidelines." In addition, the Investment Committee asked for OECD Watch's advice on interpreting the Guidelines and on requests for clarification coming from the National Contact Points. Indeed, the OECD consultation note (prepared to serve as a basis for multistakeholder consultation on the update of the Guidelines and dialogues with nonadhering governments) clearly indicates that OECD Watch has become, along with the two official advisory committees representing industry and unions, the third major source of stakeholder inputs to the review process (OECD 2009).

Conclusion

The analysis in this chapter suggests that the regulatory arena associated with corporate responsibility and accountability has become far more crowded in recent years. The old regime of the 1980s and early 1990s that featured national governments and corporate self-regulation is evolving into one in which multilateral, civil society, and multistakeholder organizations figure more prominently as regulatory actors. The discussion of both eclecticism related to regulatory approaches and complex trajectories of regulatory change or reform questions simplistic assumptions about regulatory dynamics and outcomes. The very different agendas, actors, and interests involved in contemporary regulatory initiatives associated with ESG standards render broad generalizations about their normative, regulatory, and developmental potential and implications extremely difficult. Individual initiatives can yield quite different balance sheets in terms of approach, achievements, and limitations.

Different actors and institutions can bring very different logics and meanings of development to the regulatory arena. Such logics may include rationales and objectives associated with inter- and intrafirm coordination, risk management, legitimization, social and environmental justice, and regulatory efficacy. How development is conceived may range from market-led and corporate-led development paths; through "embedded liberalism," which recognizes the need for a "grand bargain" and institutions that can mitigate negative externalities; to "alter-globalization" perspectives that call for a more fundamental restructuring of production patterns and power relations and the redistribution of income and assets that favors subaltern groups (Utting 2013).

Trends associated with multistakeholder and multiscalar governance and regulation place a premium on political economy analysis that differentiates actors and their interests and factors in the question of power. To understand variations in the form and substance of regulatory initiatives and shifts in approach through time, it is important to examine the nature and evolution of power relations within governance and to recognize the heterogeneity of interests and worldviews within entities such as "the state," international organizations, business, and civil society. Yet governance and CSR literatures often conjure up the image of a new breed of regulatory entities and approaches in which multiple actors are pulling together and are doing so in ways conducive to more effective regulatory and developmental outcomes. To better understand both the nature and trajectory of contemporary initiatives and their regulatory, social, and developmental implications, this chapter has emphasized the importance of explanatory variables associated with contestation, participation, and configurations and reconfigurations of power relations, as well as with coalitions and alliances. Such a political economy lens allows us to open up the black box of regulatory governance to see how different agendas and interests are engaging, interacting, and mobilizing in efforts to shape both business behavior and development pathways.

References

Abbott, Kenneth W., and Duncan Snidal. 2009. "The Governance Triangle: Regulatory Standards Institutions and the Shadow of the State." Pp. 44–88 in *The Politics of Global Regulation*, edited by Mattli and Woods. Princeton, NJ: Princeton University Press.

Auld, Graeme. 2012. "The Marine Stewardship Council." Pp. 148–159 in *Business Regulation and Non-State Actors: Whose Standards? Whose Development?*, edited by Reed, Utting, and Mukherjee-Reed. London/Geneva: Routledge/UNRISD.

Auld, Graeme, and Benjamin Cashore. 2012. "The Forest Stewardship Council." Pp. 134–147 in *Business Regulation and Non-State Actors: Whose Standards? Whose Development?*, edited by Reed, Utting, and Mukherjee-Reed. London/Geneva: Routledge/UNRISD.

Bacon, Christopher. 2010. "Who Decides What Is Fair in Fair Trade?: The Agri-Environmental Governance of Standards, Access and Prices." *Journal of Peasant Studies* 31(1):111–147. Retrieved August 7, 2006,

from http://www.escholarship.org/uc/item/8px4f62v;jsessionid=A34F466944A02A3C254944B4B5AA1CA7page-1.
Barrientos, Stephanie, and Sally Smith. 2012. "Assessing the ETI Codes of Labour Practice." Pp. 134–147 in *Business Regulation and Non-State Actors: Whose Standards? Whose Development?*, edited by Reed, Utting, and Mukherjee-Reed. London/Geneva: Routledge/UNRISD.
Bendell, Jem. 2004. *Barricades and Boardrooms: A Contemporary History of the Corporate Accountability Movement*. Geneva: UNRISD.
Braithwaite, John. 2005. *Neoliberalism or Regulatory Capitalism*. RegNet Occasional Paper No. 5. Canberra: ANU.
Broad, Robin, and John Cavanagh. 1999. "The Corporate Accountability Movement: Lessons and Opportunities." *The Fletcher Forum of World Affairs* 23(2):151–69.
Cerny, Phillip. 2000. "Restructuring the Political Arena: Globalization and the Paradoxes of the Competition State." Pp. 117–138 in *Globalization and Its Critics*, edited by R. Germain. Basingstoke: Palgrave, Macmillan.
CorpWatch. 2001. *What Is the Alliance for a Corporate-Free UN?* Retrieved April 18, 2011, from www.corpwatch.org/article.php?id=617.
Fall, Papa Louis, and Mohamed Mounir Zahran. 2010. *United Nations Corporate Partnerships: The Role and Functioning of the Global Compact*. Geneva: United Nations Joint Inspection Unit.
Fuchs, Doris A. 2005. *Understanding Business Power in Global Governance*. Baden-Baden: Nomos.
Gibbon, Peter, and Stefano Ponte. 2008. "Global Value Chains: from Governance to Governmentality?" *Economy and Society* 37(3): 365–392.
Greenpeace. 2012. *Palm Oil*. Retrieved June 10, 2012, from www.greenpeace.org.uk/forests/palm-oil.
Gregoratti, Catia. 2012. "The United Nations Global Compact and Development." Pp. 95–108 in *Business Regulation and Non-State Actors: Whose Standards? Whose Development?*, edited by Reed, Utting, and Mukherjee-Reed. London/Geneva: Routledge/UNRISD.
Heap, Simon. 2000. *NGOs Engaging with Business: A World of Difference and a Difference to the World*. Oxford: INTRAC.
Holliday, Charles O., Stephan Schmidheiny, and Philip Watts. 2002. *Walking the Talk: The Business Case for Sustainable Development*. Sheffield: Greenleaf Publishing Limited.
Jessop, Bob, and Ngai-Ling Sum. 2006. *Beyond the Regulation Approach: Putting Capitalist Economies in their Place*. Cheltenham, UK: Edward Elgar.
Kalfagianni, Agni, and Doris Fuchs. 2012. "The Global G.A.P." Pp. 160–172 in *Business Regulation and Non-State Actors: Whose Standards? Whose*

Development?, edited by Reed, Utting, and Mukherjee-Reed. London/Geneva: Routledge/UNRISD.
Levy, David, and Halina Szejnwald Brown. 2012. "The Global Reporting Initiative: Promise and Limitations." Pp. 109–121 in *Business Regulation and Non-State Actors: Whose Standards? Whose Development?*, edited by Reed, Utting, and Mukherjee-Reed. London/Geneva: Routledge/UNRISD.
Mattli, Walter, and Ngaire Woods, eds. 2009. *The Politics of Global Regulation*. Princeton, NJ: Princeton University Press.
McBarnet, Doreen, Aurora Voiculescu, and Tom Campbell, eds. 2007. *The New Corporate Accountability: Corporate Social Responsibility and the Law*. Cambridge: Cambridge University Press.
McKinsey and Company. 2004. *Assessing the Global Compact's Impact*. Retrieved August 7, 2006, from www.unglobalcompact.org.
Moran, Theodore. 2009. "The United Nations and Transnational Corporations: A Review and a Perspective." *Transnational Corporations* 18(2):91–112.
MSC (Marine Stewardship Council). 2012. *Integrated Strategic Plan Summary Document*. Retrieved January 20, 2013, from www.msc.org/documents/institutional/strategic-plan/msc-strategic-plan-2012-2017-summary.
Murphy, David, and Jem Bendell. 1997. *Partners in Time? Business, NGOs and Sustainable Development*. UNRISD Discussion Paper No. 109. Retrieved March 20, 2009, from http://www.unrisd.org/80256B3 C005BCCF9/%28httpAuxPages%29/259BB13AD57AC8E980256 B61004F9A62/$file/dp109.pdf.
NGLS (UN Non-Governmental Liaison Service). 2004. "Joint Civil Society Statement at the Global Compact Counter-Summit, Church Center, New York, 23 June 2004." *Civil Society Observer* 1(3) June–July.
OECD (Organisation for Economic Co-operation and Development). 2009. *Consultation on an Update of the OECD Guidelines for Multinational Enterprises*. Consultation Note, 8 December 2009. Retrieved January 28, 2013, from www.oecd.org/dataoecd/32/62/44168690.pdf.
OECD (Organisation for Economic Co-operation and Development). 2011. *Updating the OECD Guidelines for Multinational Enterprises*. Retrieved February 5, 2010, from www.oecd.org/documentprint/0,3455, en_2649_34889_44086753_1_1_1_1,00.html.
OECD Watch. 2010. *Ten Years On: Assessing the Contribution of the OECD Guidelines for Multinational Enterprises to Responsible Business Conduct*. Retrieved February 5, 2010, from http://oecd watch.org/publications-en.

OHCHR (Office of the High Commissioner for Human Rights). 2010. "Principled Pragmatism: A Way Forward for Business and Human Rights." Retrieved December 5, 2014, from http://www.ohchr.org/EN/NewsEvents/Pages/PrincipledpragmatismBusinessHR.aspx.

Palpacuer, Florence. 2010. "Challenging Governance in Global Commodity Chains: The Case of Transnational Activist Campaigns for Better Work Conditions." Pp. 124–150 in *Corporate Social Responsibility and Regulatory Governance: Towards Inclusive Development?*, edited by P. Utting and J. C. Marques. Basingstoke: Palgrave Macmillan.

Papadakis, K., ed. 2008. *Cross-Border Social Dialogue and Agreements: An Emerging Global Industrial Relations Framework?* Geneva: International Labour Organization, International Institute of Labour Studies.

Polanyi, Karl. 1944. *The Great Transformation: The Political and Economic Origins of Our Time.* Boston: Beacon Press, by arrangement with Rinehart & Company, Inc.

Ponte, Stefano, Peter Gibbon, and Jakob Vestergaard. 2011. *Governing through Standards: Origins, Drivers and Limitations.* Basingstoke: Palgrave Macmillan.

Rasche, Andreas and Dirk Ulrich Gilbert. 2012. "Social Accountability 8000 and Socioeconomic Development." Pp. 68–80 in *Business Regulation and Non-State Actors: Whose Standards? Whose Development?*, edited by Reed, Utting, and Mukherjee-Reed. London/Geneva: Routledge/UNRISD.

Razavi, Shahra, Ruth Pearson, and Caroline Danloy, eds. 2004. *Globalization, Export-Oriented Employment and Social Policy: Gendered Connections.* Basingstoke/Geneva: Palgrave Macmillan/UNRISD.

Reed D., P. Utting, and A. Mukherjee-Reed, eds. 2012. *Business Regulation and Non-State Actors: Whose Standards? Whose Development?* London/Geneva: Routledge/UNRISD.

Reed, Darryl. 2012. "Fairtrade International (FLO)." Pp. 300–314 in *Business Regulation and Non-State Actors: Whose Standards? Whose Development?*, edited by Reed, Utting, and Mukherjee-Reed. London/Geneva: Routledge/UNRISD.

Ruggie, John G. 2003. "Taking Embedded Liberalism Global: The Corporate Connection." Pp. 93–129 in *Taming Globalization: Frontiers of Governance*, edited by D. Held and M. Koenig-Archibugi. Cambridge: Polity Press.

Ruggie, John G. 2007. *Business and Human Rights: Mapping International Standards of Responsibility and Accountability for Corporate Acts.* Human Rights Council (A/HRC/4/35). New York: United Nations.

Sagafi-Nejad, Tagi. 2008. *The UN and Transnational Corporations: From Code of Conduct to Global Compact.* Bloomington: Indiana University Press.

Schouten, Greetje, Pieter Leroy, and Pieter Glasbergen. 2012. *On the Deliberative Capacity of Private Multi-Stakeholder Governance: The Roundtables on Responsible Soy and Sustainable Palm Oil.* Paper presented at the 3rd International Symposium on Cross Sector Social Interactions (CSSI), May 24–25, 2012. Partnerships Resource Centre, Erasmus University, Rotterdam, The Netherlands.

TRAC (Transnational Resource and Action Center). 2000. *Tangled Up in Blue: Corporate Partnerships at the United Nations.* TRAC. Retrieved July 2011, from www.corpwatch.org/article.php?id=996.

UNDP (United Nations Development Programme) Commission on the Private Sector and Development. 2004. *Unleashing Entrepreneurship: Making Business Work for the Poor.* New York: UNDP.

UNGC (United Nations Global Compact). 2010. *A New Era of Sustainability: UN Global Compact-Accenture CEO Study 2010.* Retrieved January 19, 2012, from http://www.unglobalcompact.org/docs/news_events/8.1/UNGC_Accenture_CEO_Study_2010.pdf.

UNGC and UN Women. 2010. *Women's Empowerment Principles: Equality Means Business.* Retrieved January 30, 2013, from http://www.unglobalcompact.org/docs/issues_doc/human_rights/Resources/WEP_EMB_Booklet.pdf.

UN Non-Governmental Liaison Service (UNNGLS) and UNRISD. 2002. *Voluntary Approaches to Corporate Responsibility: Readings and a Resource Guide.* Geneva: NGLS/UNRISD.

UNRISD. 2010. *Combating Poverty and Inequality: Structural Change, Social Policy and Politics.* Geneva: UNRISD.

Utting, Peter. 2005. "Corporate Responsibility and the Movement of Business." *Development in Practice* 15(3/4):375–388.

Utting, Peter. 2011. "Promoting CSR through the United Nations: Developmental and Governance Implications." Pp. 175–202 in *The Responsible Corporation in a Global Economy*, edited by C. Crouch and C. Maclean. Oxford, UK: Oxford University Press.

Utting, Peter. 2012a. "Introduction: Multistakeholder Regulation from a Development Perspective." Pp. 1–18 in *Business Regulation and Non-State Actors: Whose Standards? Whose Development?*, Reed, Utting, and Mukherjee-Reed. London/Geneva: Routledge/UNRISD.

Utting, Peter. 2012b. "Activism, Business Regulation and Development." Pp. 38–53 in *Business Regulation and Non-State Actors: Whose*

Standards? Whose Development?, edited by Reed, Utting, and Mukherjee-Reed. London/Geneva: Routledge/UNRISD.

Utting, Peter. 2012c. *Multistakeholder Engagement in Institution Building: Arguments For and Against*. Draft paper presented at the 3rd International Symposium on Cross Sector Social Interactions, May 24–25, 2012. Partnerships Resource Centre, Erasmus University, Rotterdam, The Netherlands.

Utting, Peter. 2013. "Pathways to Sustainability in a Crisis-Rideen World." In *Reducing Inequalities: A Sustainable Development Challenge*, edited by R. Genevey, R. Pachauri, and L. Tubiana. New Delhi: TERI Press.

Utting, Peter, and José Carlos Marques, eds. 2010. *Business, Politics and Public Policy: Implications for Inclusive Development*. Basingstoke/Geneva: Palgrave Macmillan/UNRISD.

Utting, Peter, and Ann Zammit. *Beyond Pragmatism: Appraising UN-Business Partnerships*. Programme on Markets, Business and Regulation, Paper No. 1. Geneva: UNRISD.

Van Tulder, Rob. 2008. *The Role of Business in Poverty Reduction: Towards a Sustainable Corporate Story*. Retrieved April 18, 2011, from www.unrisd.org.

World Wide Fund for Nature (WWF). 2012a. *Green, Greener, Greenest: Transforming Markets*. Gland: WWF.

World Wide Fund for Nature (WWF). 2012b. *Better Production for a Living Planet*. Gland: WWF.

Zadek, Simon. 2001. *The Civil Corporation: The New Economy of Corporate Citizenship*. London: Earthscan.

4 | Explaining the rise of national corporate social responsibility: the role of global frameworks, world culture, and corporate interests

DANIEL KINDERMAN

Introduction: the significance of national corporate social responsibility in a globalizing world

In the vast literature on corporate social responsibility (CSR), CSR has become virtually synonymous with globalization and transnationality. This is problematic. Although CSR is increasingly "rooted in the rise of a global society" (Meyer, Pope, and Isaacson, this volume), CSR and globalization are not coterminous. Many CSR initiatives have domestic origins, and some of the central works of modern-day CSR focus on businesses' domestic, not their transnational or global responsibilities. Many consider Harold Bowen to be the father of contemporary CSR, and his book *Social Responsibilities of Business* (1953) is one of the most seminal in the field – but Bowen makes no reference to international or global concerns. The field's preoccupation with the international and global has led to a conspicuous omission: national-level CSR efforts have received little attention to date. The United Nations Global Compact alone has been the subject of dozens of books and hundreds of articles, and there are no signs that this interest is abating. Yet, despite their combined membership of several thousand companies and their significant role in shaping responsible business practice, there are at most a handful of treatments of the national CSR initiatives that exist in many countries across the world. National CSR associations are diverse: well-established associations have hundreds of

---

I am grateful to Lauren Balasco, Justin de Leon, and Virginia Garcia for research assistance. In addition, this chapter has greatly benefitted from input from Marlis Bärthel, Alwyn Lim, Kiyoteru Tsutsui, participants at the Institute for Sociology at the University of Jena, and other contributors to this volume. I take full responsibility for any remaining errors.

member companies and staff and annual budgets in the millions of dollars/euros. Some of the better-known examples include Brazil's Instituto Ethos, the United Kingdom's Business in the Community, and the United States' Business for Social Responsibility.

This chapter is the first systematic attempt to assess the interactions between global institutional pressure and national CSR. National CSR provides a relatively strong test of world society theory: it is not evident a priori that national responsible business organizations have anything to do with world society or global culture. Whereas world society "transcends particular national states and societies" (Meyer, Pope, and Isaacson, this volume), national CSR associations are national-level, responsible business groups. They are attuned to national culture, institutions, and social and environmental concerns. Multinational companies are often members in national CSR associations, but, in most cases, the vast majority of member companies are domestic. As a consequence, national CSR associations are domestically focused; at most, they are hybrids or institutional bridges between the global and the local. Whereas global normative pressures have fostered CSR's global diffusion and a proliferation of global CSR frameworks[1] (Lim and Tsutsui 2012), national CSR associations may be autonomous from these global processes, given their embeddedness in national traditions and institutional frameworks (on this point, see Habisch et al. 2005 Shanahan and Khagram 2005; Gjølberg 2009; Visser and Tolhurst 2010; Kinderman 2011; Grayson and Nelson 2013).

An analysis of the interactions between global institutional pressure and national CSR can help to resolve a puzzle. CSR's global rise during recent decades is commonly thought to reflect growing civil society activism and normative pressure for business conduct. The difficulty with this interpretation is that CSR-like concerns were fairly widespread by the 1970s but attempts to establish global CSR frameworks met with little success until the late 1990s. Although conventional accounts have difficulty accounting for this temporal gap, this chapter shows that dozens of national CSR associations took root during this interregnum. The first national CSR associations sprouted in the 1960s

---

[1] These frameworks include the 2011 UN Guiding Principles on Business and Human Rights; the original 1976 Organization for Economic Cooperation and Development (OECD) guidelines for Multinational Enterprises, as well as their recent update, ISO 26000; the Global Reporting Initiative; and the United Nations Global Compact.

and 1970s, and their spread accelerated in the 1980s and 1990s. By the late 1990s, when the most influential global CSR frameworks – the UN Global Compact and the Global Reporting Initiative – got off the ground, dozens of national CSR associations were in place. By 2010, according to my restrictive definition (more on this later), there were upward of seventy-two national CSR associations worldwide.[2] This chapter sets out to explore the global rise of national CSR associations and address two interrelated questions. First, given that many national organizations preceded the global frameworks, how can we explain their rise and spread across the world? Second, why were these early national efforts more successful than the initial attempts to establish global frameworks?

I use the term "national CSR" as a shorthand for business-led non-governmental organizations (NGOs) with member companies that address social and/or environmental causes at the national level. These coalitions, not all of which carry the moniker of CSR, have "the explicit and, in most cases, dedicated goal of mobilising business resources to directly tackle one or more environmental, social or governance challenges" (Grayson and Nelson 2013: 3). Grayson and Nelson call these organizations "business-led corporate responsibility coalitions" and claim that they

have been an important factor in the spread of corporate responsibility. Coalitions have conceived, created and continued to drive collaborative business action: initially mobilising business action in the community; then around responsible business practices; and now collaborative action which meets broader business and societal needs. (Grayson and Nelson 2013: xix)

Waddock refers to these organizations as "mobilizing structures," "networks of actors with similar interests in changing the way that business interact[s] with society" (Waddock 2008: 197). National CSR organizations are rooted in particular national traditions, institutions, and cultures. They arise at different times and take different forms in different countries. Their membership ranges from a few dozen companies in fledgling organizations to over a thousand in well-established ones. As important as they are, even the largest and most prominent national CSR associations only represent a minority of their country's businesses. At

---

[2] Grayson and Nelson, who use a more inclusive definition, state that there are upward of 110 (2013: 3).

the upper end, Brazil's Instituto Ethos's membership encompasses approximately 1,300 firms or one-third of Brazil's gross national product (GNP), whereas the United Kingdom's Business in the Community has approximately 850 member companies representing one-fifth of the UK's private-sector workforce. In most if not all of the other countries in my sample, the CSR associations' share of the national economy is smaller. Although I estimate the seventy-two national CSR associations in my sample to have a combined corporate membership of 4,000–5,000 companies, including many of the world's leading responsible businesses, the existence of a national CSR association implies neither the virtuousness of its member companies nor the diffusion of responsible business practices throughout a country's business community.

Each national CSR association has a distinctive, national imprint that reflects its attempts to legitimate its members and address social and environmental problems. This section surveys a few of these organizations. In 1970, in the midst of an economic and political crisis, fifty prominent business leaders founded the Philippine Business for Social Progress (PBSP). These leaders surmised that, if unchecked, their country's staggering poverty, inequalities, and social turmoil could threaten their legitimacy or their very existence: "Violent demonstrations, political assassinations, and a growing rural insurgency drove fear into the hearts of the rich and powerful Filipino business community.... In the face of the socio-political situation, big business's agenda changed from the quest for international competitiveness to self-preservation" (Tan and Bolante 1997: 5).

In response to these challenges, the PBSP and its members promoted community and social development. By the end of the 1980s, PBSP had grown to become the Philippines' largest NGO (Clarke 1988: 102). Each of the PBSP's 145 member companies committed 1 percent of their pretax net income to social development purposes. PBSP funded PHP320 million (US$8 million) of grant assistance to 1,200 social development projects, benefitting an estimated 1 million Filipinos (Garilao 1991: 1). Twenty years later, the PBSP had extended PHP7 billion (US$170 million) in grant assistance to 6,200 projects, benefitting an estimated 4.5 million beneficiaries in partnership with 3,300 organizations. PBSP now has more than 240 member companies committed to improving the lives of underprivileged groups including landless farmers, rural workers, the urban poor, and indigenous cultural minorities (http://code-ngo.org/home/membership/pbsp.html).

Since its founding at the beginning of the 1980s, Business in the Community (BITC) has grown from humble beginnings to become one of the world's leading national CSR associations. During its first decade, BITC and its member companies fostered entrepreneurship, training, and inner-city regeneration, activities that took on particular importance during Margaret Thatcher's neoliberal crusade. In 1983, BITC described its mission as one "to encourage industry and commerce to become more involved on a local basis in the economic, training, social and environmental needs of the communities in which they operate" (Kinderman 2012: 34). Enterprise agencies – which were managed by BITC and jointly funded by government and the private sector – helped create approximately one-sixth of all new jobs created in 1984 and provided training to help overcome skill shortages. Thanks to BITC, tens of thousands of employees have volunteered in their communities, and thousands of homeless people have been provided with work placements. Over time, BITC has widened its activities to encompass many different aspects of the dynamic field of CSR. BITC has recently described its mission as one "to inspire, engage, support and challenge companies on responsible business to continually improve their positive impact on society" (Kinderman 2012: 34).

Unlike British business leaders, who came together to support their newly elected government, South African business leaders came together to oppose theirs. South Africa's CSR association, the National Business Initiative, began as the Urban Foundation in 1976. The Urban Foundation opposed South Africa's apartheid regime and sought to improve the lives and rights of black South Africans, for example, by extending land tenure rights to blacks and fighting to break down barriers barring them from cities (Grayson and Nelson 2013). To be sure, the global pressure that culminated in the 1977 Sullivan Principles was also significant: the Urban Foundation emerged "at the time of intensive anti-apartheid campaigning against South African investment ... with calls for divestment and an onus on demonstrating the contribution(s) that could be made by a continued presence" (Davies 2003: 305).

The American CSR association Business for Social Responsibility was founded at the beginning of the 1990s in response to progressives' perception of a roadblock against progressive legislation by organized business in Washington. BSR's initial objective was to galvanize business support for progressive public policy initiatives. After these initiatives failed to resonate with large companies, BSR abandoned public policy to focus on supply-chain management and sustainability consulting. Unlike the aforementioned Philippine, British, and South African CSR associations, BSR's 100 staffs are not extensively engaged in on-the-ground service delivery. It is hard to generalize on the basis of this tour d'horizon. For example, although the aforementioned associations have upward of 300 member companies each, other national CSR associations have far fewer member companies. Founded in 2000, Germany's Econsense has only three dozen members – but they are among the largest publicly listed German companies, including Volkswagen, BASF, Siemens, and Deutsche Bank. What these national CSR organizations have in common is that they are a significant force in the world of CSR, not just country clubs for powerful corporations.

These examples illustrate the national roots of national CSR associations, but they do not imply the irrelevance of global institutions and processes. To return to an example from the beginning of this chapter, Harold Bowen may have been influenced by international ideas, even though they are not explicit in his work. To assess the impact of global processes on national CSR, we must attend to the way in which global CSR frameworks and global institutional pressure interact with national CSR. This chapter is concerned with one particular facet of this interaction: the timing and quantity of national CSR associations, global CSR initiatives, and countries' memberships in international NGOs (INGOs). As we will see, the success of early national efforts compared with the failure of early global frameworks and the relative autonomy of the former from the latter emerges as one finding of the analysis. I argue that we can only make sense of this by taking political economy considerations – corporate power (Utting, this volume) and interests – into account. National CSR associations are business-led, and business-led CSR is more attractive to businesspeople than are regulatory frameworks imposed on them against their will by public authorities. Yet the establishment of national CSR associations is also highly correlated with countries' participation in INGOs. These data support the power of the world society perspective (Meyer, Pope, and Isaacson, this volume). They suggest that CSR-like concerns manifested themselves first in the form of national CSR associations before percolating up into global CSR frameworks. In sum, this chapter highlights the importance of both world society and political economy perspectives for understanding CSR in a globalizing world.

The roadmap of this chapter is as follows. The second section introduces two propositions that I use to assess the data. The third section discusses the data and methods. The fourth section, "The universe of national CSR," shows the spread of national CSR across the world. The fifth section, "Global CSR frameworks and national CSR," discusses the interaction of global and national frameworks. The sixth section, "Why did early global frameworks fail and national CSR succeed?" addresses the failure of early global frameworks compared with the success of national CSR. The seventh section, "Global institutional pressure and national CSR," concentrates on the rise of INGOs and their interaction with national CSR. The eighth section concludes the chapter.

Propositions

The Global CSR Proposition

The *Global CSR Proposition* draws on the core insight of the world society approach that worldwide models and cultural scripts shape national institutions and practices and proposes that national CSR associations track global developments. It is important to emphasize that the world society approach does not deny that "the contested transnational structuration of CSR is particularistically adapted to national-sectoral settings" (Shanahan and Khagram 2006: 219). But, at its core, the Global CSR Proposition downplays local variation and sees global frameworks and institutional pressures as the driving forces of CSR at the national level. Lim and Tsutsui argue that "changes in the global normative environment have prompted many corporations to pledge commitment to CSR principles" (Lim and Tsutsui 2012: 70). Longhofer and Schofer (2010) find that "global dynamics constitute or construct local activity.... The primary impetus behind domestic ... associations may be traced to the resources and culture of world society" (Longhofer and Schofer 2010: 510, 511). As Drori has put it in an unpublished paper, the world society scholars' vision challenges the notion that "the nation-state itself can autonomously sustain more traditional organizational forms" (Drori 2004: 13). Drori argues that increasing homogeneity worldwide "suggests a common cultural source that is sweeping the intensely globalized world and breeding similar organizational formats, due to common pressures on corporations and regardless of their social locale or organizational roots" (Drori 2004: 4). According to the Global CSR Proposition, national CSR associations have limited autonomy from and tight linkages to world cultural principles.

The Autonomy of National CSR Proposition

The Autonomy of National CSR Proposition is the obverse of the Global CSR Proposition. It traces the origins of national CSR frameworks not to global CSR frameworks or broader processes in the global normative environment, but to domestic processes. This implies that the establishment of national CSR associations does not coincide with important developments at the global level. From the perspective of the Autonomy of National CSR Proposition, national CSR associations are subsystems with large degrees of autonomy or no connection at all to global frameworks and world cultural principles. Intellectually, this proposition is grounded in the work on path dependence and historical institutionalism (Steinmo, Thelen, and Longstreth 1992). Both perspectives are grounded on the assumption that social practices are strongly rooted in particular institutions in particular places at particular times. Critical junctures lock-in path-dependent trajectories that are self-reinforcing or persist in the face of external pressures (Thelen 2004). The Autonomy of National CSR Proposition does not deny the existence of isomorphic processes, but it locates the origins of these processes at the national rather than at the global level.

Data and methods

This chapter draws on a quantitative dataset compiled by the author comprising countries' membership in national CSR organizations, global CSR frameworks, and global institutional pressure. It uses the emergence of the first national CSR association to indicate the institutionalization of national CSR. If a national business-led CSR association exists in a given country in a given year, I coded that country as having CSR. If a country lacks such an organization in a given year, I coded that country as lacking CSR. Grayson and Nelson (2013: 3) define these "business-led CSR coalitions" as

Explaining the rise of national corporate social responsibility 115

Independent, non-profit membership organisations that are composed mainly or exclusively of for-profit businesses; that have a board of directors composed predominantly or only of business people; that are core-funded primarily or totally from business; and whose dedicated purpose is to promote responsible business practice. (Grayson and Nelson 2013: 3)

I coded these organizations from 1960 to 2010 for 155 countries. A full list of these organizations and their founding dates can be found in the chapter's appendix. Sources include Grayson and Nelson (2013), Kinderman (2011), and Visser and Tolhurst (2010). I went over each organization's founding documents and press releases to ensure that it conforms to the following criteria: a nonprofit organization with a for-profit corporate membership, membership fees, and a mandate to advance the cause of CSR, broadly conceived.[3] Virtually all organizations in the dataset have a voluntary dues-paying corporate membership. Only in a handful of cases did I include employers' associations engaged in well-developed CSR programs. The organization's name need not include the terms "corporate social responsibility," "corporate citizenship," or "sustainability" for it to qualify as long as responsible business, social, or environmental projects are the main focus of its activities. To varying degrees, these business-led organizations are involved in setting the agenda for responsible business, disseminating good practices among their members, building the capacity of companies, brokering partnerships with stakeholder groups, delivering on-the-ground programs, and setting standards (Grayson and Nelson 2013). Seventy-two countries in the dataset have such an organization and eighty-three do not.

Since national CSR organizations are based on a dues-paying corporate membership, their establishment says something about the currency or legitimacy of CSR among businesses in the countries in which they are based. It is worth emphasizing that national CSR associations measure the institutionalization of collective or collaborative CSR, an important yet understudied facet of CSR (Zadek 2008; Grayson and Nelson 2013). Thus, the absence of a national CSR organization does not imply the absence of responsible businesses or responsible business practices in that country.

---

[3] This includes related practices such as corporate citizenship, sustainability, and philanthropy; the underlying idea is business's voluntary engagement for social or environmental ends above legally mandated minimum standards.

Once established, national CSR associations' staff and member companies champion the cause of CSR and diffuse it within their country. Because my definition of national CSR organizations highlights their national distinctiveness, I made a conscious decision to exclude national franchises of global organizations such as the World Business Council for Sustainable Development because this could bias my findings toward the Global CSR Proposition rather than ensuring a hard test of world society theory. My definition and number of "business-led CSR coalitions" is thus more restrictive than Grayson and Nelson's (2013).

Six indicators capture the impact of global CSR at the local level and the degrees of local business's commitment to global CSR. The following can all be considered a part of world culture and world society: the UN Global Compact (UNGC), the Global Reporting Initiative (GRI), the Carbon Disclosure Project (CDP), international nongovernmental organizations (INGOs), the Organisation for Economic Cooperation and Development (OECD) Guidelines for Multinational Enterprises, and the International Labour Organization (ILO) Tripartite declaration. I begin with the most established and influential global CSR frameworks, the UNGC and the GRI. In different ways, they capture the institutionalization of CSR at the global level. Each of these global CSR frameworks has thousands of member companies and numerous associated stakeholder groups across the world.

The UNGC was established in 1999 under the leadership of then Secretary General Kofi Annan to enlist business to follow ten principles concerning human rights, labor, the environment, and corruption. Although the UNGC has recently mandated that companies periodically submit Communications on Progress on these issues or risk being delisted from the initiative, the UNGC's standards for reporting and performance remain far from stringent. This is different with the GRI, which was established in 1997; it produced its first full reporting guidelines in 2000 and recently introduced its fourth-generation reporting guidelines. The GRI provides a comprehensive and detailed reporting framework for performance on human rights, labor, environmental, anticorruption, and other issues.

To measure the institutionalization of the UNGC at the national level, I use two measures: the number of active UNGC member companies from each country in a given year and the establishment date of a country's UNGC national network. UNGC national networks are comprised of the member companies for that country and a staff that coordinates activities at the national level. Thus, it captures the impact of UNGC at the national level. Unlike the Global Compact, the GRI does not have national network offices, so I use the number of companies reporting according to GRI requirements from each country in a given year.

The CDP also deserves mention. The CDP facilitates the disclosure of greenhouse gas emissions and other environmental impacts by companies, institutional investors, and cities. The underlying idea is that this information will facilitate investors' and other stakeholders' push for a reduction of emissions because the latter represent a long-term business liability. The CDP is significant in that it operates on behalf of more than 700 institutional investors controlling more than €60 trillion in assets (www.cdp.net).

To capture the effects of global institutional pressure, I use INGOs. INGOs are nonprofit voluntary associations that link the global with the local (Boli 2012) and penetrate "even the most peripheral social spaces" (Boli and Thomas 1999: 5). INGOs are the "priests of the world polity" (Boli 1999: 284) and an important embodiment of world culture (Boli and Thomas 1999). Thus, INGOs capture embeddedness in world society and the effects of global institutional pressure. According to world society scholars, INGOs diffuse five core principles: universalism, individual rights, rational voluntarism, a rationalized view of progress, and world citizenship (Boli and Thomas 1999: 14–15). The INGO data derive from the *Yearbook of International Organizations* published by the Union of International Associations (UIA).[4] Unfortunately, due to time constraints, I was unable to input INGO data for the years prior to 1982. The INGO data in this chapter begin in 1982 and end in 2010. Therefore, it is important to stress that the lack of INGO data prior to 1982 in this chapter does not indicate the nonexistence of INGOs in this period.

The OECD Guidelines and the ILO Tripartite Declaration of principles concerning multinational enterprises and social policy are the

---

[4] Cluster I (Categories A–D) organizations from the *Yearbook of International Organizations* include federations of international organizations, universal membership organizations, intercontinental membership organizations, and limited or regionally defined membership organizations and excludes, for example, internationally oriented national organizations and inactive or dissolved organizations. As I discuss in note 13, the UIA added category F to these totals in 2002.

earliest global quasi-CSR frameworks, adopted in 1976 and 1977, respectively. Since approximately half of the countries with national CSR associations ratified these conventions, we will explore the possibility that these early global efforts, as well as the UN's failed Committee on Transnational Corporations (UNCTC), established in 1973, led to the founding of national CSR associations.

Regarding methodology, some recent work on global CSR frameworks uses sophisticated multivariate regression models (Lim and Tsutsui 2012). As the first contribution of its kind on global and national CSR, the aims of this chapter are more exploratory: to provide a first-cut assessment of the relationship between global processes and national frameworks using qualitative data and scatterplots. As such, this chapter does not advance causal arguments. In addition to quantitative data, I also interviewed some of the founding figures in national CSR associations who could speak to the influence of international institutions on the founding of their organizations. The next section provides an overview of the spread of national CSR across the world during the past three decades.

Findings: the universe of national CSR

Figure 4.1 below captures the growth of national CSR in the sample:

This figure shows that national CSR was already taking root in the 1960s and 1970s. The rise is slow until the 1980s but accelerates during the 1990s. It is unclear whether the slope has the shape of the S-curve typical of diffusion processes. A total of seventy-two national CSR organizations existed by 2010.[5] It appears that during the 1990s, CSR became "truly globalized" (Mühe 2010: 259) and underwent norm-tipping and a norm-cascade (Segerlund 2010). This finding supports Meyer, Pope, and Isaacson's claim that "The real proliferation of CSR business associations occurred around the early 1990s, at the height of the neoliberal period and its extreme doctrines of corporate self-interest" (this volume:45). Although the rate of growth of national CSR associations remained constant during the 1990s and 2000s, their

---

[5] It is likely that this chapter underestimates the true number of national CSR associations across the world. Due to language barriers, differences in terminology, and a lack of publicity and/or an extensive website presence, some national organizations may have gone uncounted.

Explaining the rise of national corporate social responsibility 119

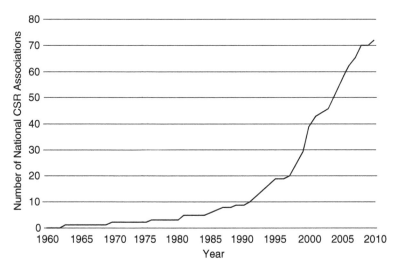

Figure 4.1 Counts of national corporate social responsibility associations, 1960–2010

absolute growth has been greatest during the past decade, which also supports Meyer et al.'s pronouncement in this volume.

Next, we examine cross-national variation in the timing of adoption of national CSR. Which countries are the early and late adopters? Table 4.1 provides an overview.

From these data, it appears that the earliest national CSR associations are not clustered geographically or temporally. As Grayson and Nelson note, a number of coalitions "were formed in the 1970s and 1980s in response to very specific national circumstances" (Grayson and Nelson 2013: 24). The countries with national CSR associations are a heterogeneous group. Although each member of the rich OECD club has a national CSR association, the first four countries to get national CSR are non-OECD countries. In fact, the majority of countries with national CSR are developing countries, and there are even some least-developed countries (such as Uganda and Bangladesh) with national CSR, which supports the claim that "the patterning of CR may well not be as core driven as extant models of global change might imply" (Shanahan and Khagram 2006: 211).

World society scholars have remarked on the isomorphism of world models to dissimilar environments irrespective of local functional requirements, and this seems to apply. Whether developing countries'

Table 4.1 Establishment dates of national corporate social responsibility associations in different countries

Year	
1960	
1961	
1962	
1963	Venezuela
1964	
1965	
1966	
1967	
1968	
1969	
1970	Philippines
1971	
1972	
1973	
1974	
1975	
1976	South Africa
1977	
1978	

Year									
1979									
1980	Paraguay								
1981		UK*							
1982									
1983									
1984									
1985	Argentina								
1986	France*								
1987	Sweden*								
1988	Mexico*								
1989	Japan*								
1990									
1991	USA*								
1992	Czech* Republic	Hungary*		United Arab Emirates					
1993	Sri Lanka	Thailand							
1994	Columbia	Peru							
1995	Canada*	Italy*							
1996									
1997	Norway*								
1998	Belgium*	Bulgaria		Brazil	India	Indonesia	New Zealand*		
1999	Spain*	Nigeria		Vietnam					
2000	Chile*	El Salvador		Ireland*	Finland*	Germany*	Greece*	Netherlands*	Portugal*	Poland*	Switzerland*
2001	Israel*	Kenya		Mexico*	Uruguay				

Table 4.1 (*cont.*)

Year						
2002	Panama					
2003	Denmark*	Hong Kong				
2004	Bolivia	Honduras	Russia			
2005	Austria*	Australia*	Bangladesh	Slovakia*	Ukraine	
2006	Estonia*	Romania	Iran	China	Nicaragua	
2007	Luxembourg*	Uganda	Jordan	Saudi Arabia	South Korea*	
2008	Croatia	Iceland*	Pakistan	Senegal	Serbia	
2009						
2010	Lebanon	Slovenia*			Singapore	Turkey*

* OECD member

Explaining the rise of national corporate social responsibility 123

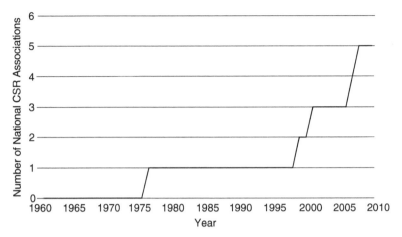

Figure 4.2 The rise of national corporate social responsibility associations in Africa

pioneering role relates to functional requirements is unclear. Social deprivation is more acute and widespread there than in OECD countries. As a comparatively powerful and well-resourced societal actor, business may face pressure to address these needs. At the very least, to save face, business should not appear to be indifferent to pressing social issues. These circumstances could help to make sense of the fact that a handful of developing countries, including Venezuela, Paraguay, and the Philippines, which in general are more norm-takers than norm-makers, established national CSR associations before rich OECD countries. The fact that these associations go by a variety of different names – the term CSR had not yet achieved widespread acceptance – suggests that global scripts were not yet powerful. This changed as more national CSR associations were established beginning in the late 1980s and 1990s. As increasingly more national CSR associations were established, national business leaders and institutional entrepreneurs sought to emulate these models and establish their own CSR associations at home. Figures 4.2–4.6 show the rise of national CSR associations on five continents.[6]

The fact that the curves are parallel across the continents may suggest a global process. Almost everywhere, the rise of national CSR

---

[6] I have opted not to provide a figure for Australia because it would contain just a single data point in 2005.

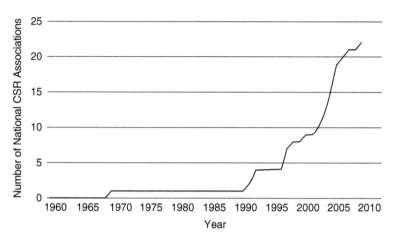

Figure 4.3 The rise of national corporate social responsibility associations in Asia

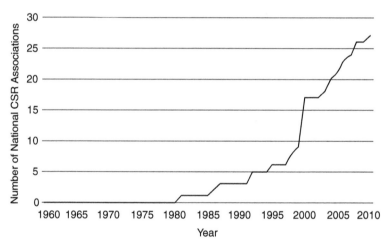

Figure 4.4 The rise of national corporate social responsibility associations in Europe

accelerated in the 1990s. Table 4.2 provides the mean establishment date of national CSR associations on each continent from earliest to latest.

Having surveyed the landscape of national CSR, the next section examines how global CSR frameworks relate to these national organizations. This will help us to determine whether national CSR is tightly connected with or autonomous from global-level developments.

Explaining the rise of national corporate social responsibility 125

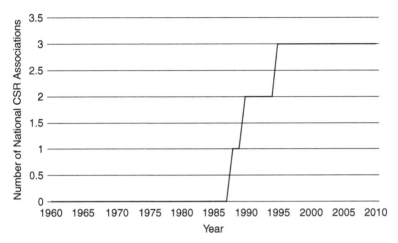

Figure 4.5 The rise of national corporate social responsibility associations in North America

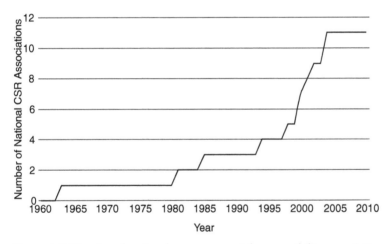

Figure 4.6 The rise of national corporate social responsibility associations in South America

Global CSR frameworks and national CSR

Figures 4.7–4.10 show the relationship between national CSR and three influential global CSR frameworks: the UNGC, the GRI, and the CDP.

Each of these figures shows that many national CSR associations predated the influential global CSR frameworks. Approximately forty

Table 4.2 *The average (mean) establishment date of national corporate social responsibility associations on six continents*

North America	1991
South America	1995
Africa	1999
Europe	1999
Asia	1999
Australia	2005

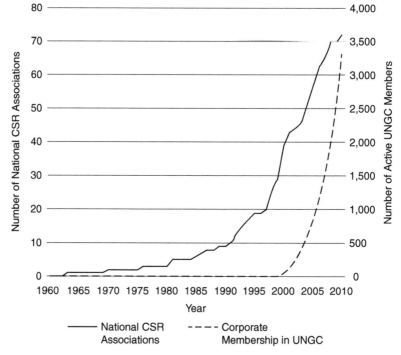

Figure 4.7 National corporate social responsibility associations and corporate membership in the United Nations Global Compact

national CSR initiatives had already been established when global CSR frameworks got off the ground. Since these national-level initiatives were in existence before the global CSR frameworks, the latter could not have caused the former. These global CSR frameworks may well

Explaining the rise of national corporate social responsibility

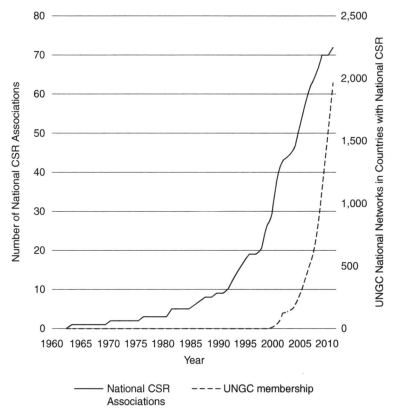

Figure 4.8 National corporate social responsibility associations and United Nations Global Compact national networks

have influenced the practices of national CSR associations post-2000, but they cannot predict the emergence of these organizations. Moreover, national CSR does not increase at a faster rate following the establishment of global CSR frameworks. These findings support the Autonomy of National CSR Proposition.

However, as I have noted earlier, the UNGC and the GRI were preceded by earlier global efforts by the UN, the OECD, and the ILO during the 1970s. The UNCTC was established in 1973. The OECD Guidelines for Multinational Enterprises were adopted in 1976, and the ILO's Tripartite Declaration of Principles concerning Multinational Enterprises and Social Policy was adopted in 1977. The fact that these global initiatives emerged before all but two

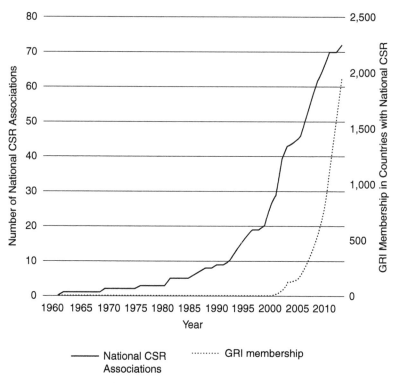

Figure 4.9 National corporate social responsibility associations and companies reporting according to the Global Reporting Initiative

national CSR associations suggests that they could have played an important role in bringing about the latter. However, an exhaustive and systematic search of the founding documents and press releases of CSR associations established within two decades after the initiation of these frameworks provides little evidence that they played an important role in the establishment of these organizations. Not a single one of the national CSR associations' founding documents or founding press releases in the 1970s, 1980s, or 1990s mentions the OECD Guidelines or the ILO Tripartite Declaration. Moreover, hardly any of my interviewees (key figures in CSR associations) say that these initiatives influenced their decision to set up a national CSR association.

David Grayson, director of the Doughty Centre for Corporate Responsibility at the Cranfield School of Management, a key figure in the UK CSR association Business in the Community, and co-author

Explaining the rise of national corporate social responsibility

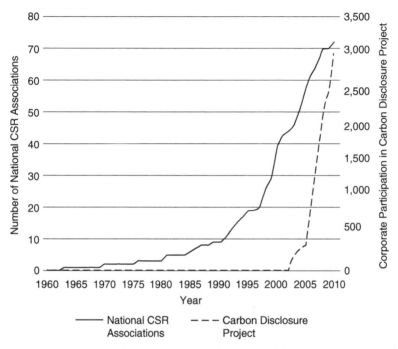

Figure 4.10 National corporate social responsibility associations and companies' participation in the Carbon Disclosure Project

of the most definitive account of national CSR associations (Grayson and Nelson 2013), remarks: "I have never had a business leader refer to the guidelines in 32 years in this field! Nor have I ever heard one talk about the guidelines in a speech ever!" (Grayson, personal communication, September 2, 2012). Anthony Pelling, founder of Business in the Community, likewise recalls that "OECD and ILO were of little consequence within UK government circles and that despite me enjoying trips to OECD in Paris to meet US counterparts" (personal communication, August 27, 2012). Laury Hammel, founder of the American CSR association Business for Social Responsibility, states that "I have never heard of these documents, and if other people were aware of them, they never mentioned them to me." Hammel recalls that he and his co-founders "weren't really into think tanks, international organizations, governmental organizations, or academia, we were entrepreneurs on the ground wanting desperately to make a difference in our world" (Laury Hammel, personal communications, September 1 and October 15, 2012).

The London Enterprise Agency (LENTA) is a London-based CSR membership organization founded in the late 1970s, around the time of the emergence of the OECD Guidelines and the ILO Tripartite Declaration. Apart from its focus on a major metropolitan region as opposed to an entire country, LENTA satisfies all the criteria for inclusion in my national CSR dataset. One might therefore wonder whether LENTA had been influenced by these global initiatives. Brian Wright, founder of LENTA, thinks that "some of the companies [involved in the founding of LENTA] were conscious of what was being said about them in august bodies such as OECD." But domestic influences, for example, corporate taxation, were paramount (personal communication, October 15, 2012). This is the strongest statement I was able to find, and it is hardly a ringing endorsement of the OECD Guidelines and ILO Tripartite Declaration's influence on national CSR. This supports Mühe's finding that the OECD Guidelines and the ILO Tripartite Declaration "did not find the resonance that CSR policy receives today" (Mühe 2010: 261) and Grayson and Nelson's observation that these early "business-led coalitions ... were established primarily as a private-sector response to socioeconomic, political or environmental crises in particular countries" (Grayson and Nelson 2013: 4).

To gain a full understanding of why these early attempts at global frameworks did not significantly influence national CSR, it is necessary to address a more general question: why did these early global attempts fail while national efforts succeeded? To answer this question, the next section examines the content of early attempts to establish legally binding global CSR frameworks in the UN, the ILO, and the OECD. Although only the UN attempt failed outright, the trajectories of these initiatives have much in common. I argue that their limited resonance, when compared with national CSR associations, can only be explained by taking corporate interests and political economy considerations into account.

Why did early global frameworks fail and national CSR succeed? Political economy considerations

In this section, I argue that national CSR associations were more appealing to business than early attempts to establish global frameworks for a very simple reason: whereas public authorities sought to use global frameworks to impose binding regulations on business, national CSR is voluntary and business-led. This explains the success of national CSR associations and the failure of the UNCTC. Founded in 1973, UNCTC began to push for a legally binding code of conduct for multinationals. One of the UNCTC's key objectives was "To secure effective international arrangements for the operation of transnational corporations designed to promote their contribution to national development goals and world economic growth while controlling and eliminating their negative effects" (MacLeod 2008: 66). These attempts to establish a binding code of conduct for multinationals eventually failed, and the UNCTC was disbanded in 1993. The UNCTC's failure was precipitated by a clash between the rich capital-exporting countries and the Group of 77 developing countries espousing a New International Economic Order. The differences between these groups were irreconcilable. Although the OECD and ILO's voluntary guidelines did not meet the same fate as the UNCTC, there is widespread agreement that their impact has been limited (Kolk and van Tudler 2005).

Meyer, Pope, and Isaacson (this volume) point out that these initiatives were "thrust into an international arena that was largely empty of the CSR institutional infrastructure that plays ... such a crucial role in legitimating CSR as normal and valuable business practice." Although this is surely correct, the failure of these 1970s efforts also has much to do with the distribution of power relations and the hard, regulatory nature of these initiatives (Utting, this volume). Recent accounts contain oblique references to these underlying conflicts:

While the group was composed of men of good intentions, certain ideologically charged views almost inevitably crept into their contributions to its work and to the tenor and content of the report. Terms such as "distributive justice" "sovereignty," and the need for a general agreement on "accountability of TNCs to the international community," while seemingly innocuous, tended to agitate and antagonize those who were against this particular exercise in the first place. (Sagafi-Negad and Dunning 2008: 86)

In an environment that saw a precipitous decline in the legitimacy of business, agreeing to legally binding codes that could entail significant liabilities and a dramatic reduction of corporate discretion was not an option for employers. Instead, capitalists and their political representatives fought against what they feared could be a slippery slope culminating in the destruction of the free enterprise system. Public support for the latter had seen a dramatic decline in liberal democracies. In 1966, 55 percent of respondents in an American public opinion poll expressed a "great deal of confidence" in the heads of large corporations. By 1975, this had declined to 15 percent (Silk and Vogel 1976: 21). As one commentator put it, "In recent years, the attack has been multipronged, concerted and severe, so that even the defenders of the citadel have begun to express doubts about the survival of the corporation" (Maheshwari 1978: 10). Many of these attacks concentrated on transnational capital:

A climate of suspicion began to surround the operations of MNEs [multinational enterprises] .... The MNE began to be described as a challenge to the nation state, a creature with no loyalties except to itself, an entity that caused economic, social and political disruption in both the host and home countries, and aimed at global dominance. The MNE had to be tamed .... during the 1960s and 1970s a significant current of opinion emerged that was critical of, if not openly hostile towards, the operation of capitalist firms .... This was an era in which the traditionally accepted benefits of free enterprise were in doubt, and in which socialism seemed to offer a viable alternative. Thus the ideological climate was receptive to the development of a critique of MNEs as the most developed symbols of capitalism. (Muchlinski 1995: 7, 8)

Since these early attempts at global CSR frameworks were seen as imposing burdensome regulations on corporate activity and possibly threatening capitalism itself, they were met with hostility by business and their political representatives.

The contrast with national CSR associations could not be starker. National CSR associations are business-led, and participation in them is voluntary. Firms are free to join and leave as they please, and national CSR associations do not seek to impose burdensome regulations on their members or on the business community more generally. On the contrary: although they seek to promote enlightened corporate self-interest, they do so on business's own terms without impinging on their entrepreneurial or managerial autonomy. Seen in this way, it is not hard to see why national CSR associations had (and have) a greater appeal for the private sector and why national business groups saw national CSR associations as a means to both legitimate themselves and further their own interests (Kinderman 2011; 2012). Furthermore, it is interesting to consider how, when successful global CSR frameworks like the UNGC did arise, they too were business-led and had weak swords and enforcement mechanisms, just like national CSR associations.

Although the UNGC and GRI have both evolved significantly over the past decade, it is useful to consider whether these initiatives embody more of a maximalist or minimalist vision of corporate responsibilities. If we follow Wallace (1982: 300) in distinguishing between a "maximalist position," which favors "legally binding, internationally enforceable rules of conduct for MNEs" and a "minimalist position," which "promotes the notion of voluntary rather than legally enforceable guidelines" (Wallace 1982: 300), then these global frameworks may in fact have greater affinities to national CSR's voluntarism than to the maximalist position. To summarize, in this section, I have argued that the world society perspective must be supplemented by a political economy approach to fully account for the success or failure of CSR initiatives at the global or national level. However, the absence of strong linkages between the early global CSR frameworks and national CSR associations does not imply the absence of world society influences. The concern about CSR may very well have spread through INGOs, which leads to the analysis in the next section.

Global institutional pressure and national CSR

Although global frameworks did not cause the rise of national CSR associations, other forms of global institutional pressure may have done so. To explore this possibility, this section uses data on countries' membership in INGOs available from the *Yearbook of International Organizations*. The Global CSR Proposition implies a strong or systematic relationship between a country's INGO memberships and its national CSR associations. The Autonomy of National CSR Proposition implies a weak or nonexistent relationship between a country's INGO membership and its CSR associations. I compiled these data for 155 countries, which allows us to compare the number of INGO memberships of countries with and without national CSR associations. Is there a systematic difference?

It turns out that countries with CSR associations have significantly more INGO memberships than do those without. Virtually all countries without national CSR associations have fewer than 1,000 INGO

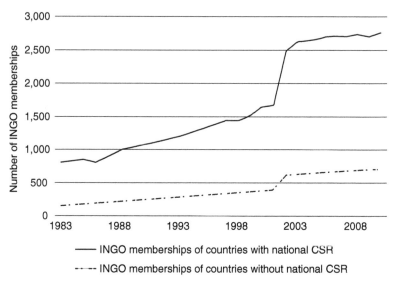

Figure 4.11 International nongovernmental organization memberships in countries with and without national corporate social responsibility associations

memberships by 2010. By contrast, virtually all countries with national CSR associations have more than 1,000 INGO memberships by that same year. Figure 4.11 presents the mean number of INGO memberships in each of these two groups between 1983 and 2010.

Although both lines show the same trend – a monotonic increase in the number of INGO memberships with a sharp rise between 2001 and 2002[7] – their values are on different scales.

On average, throughout the entire period 1983–2010, countries with national CSR associations have four times as many INGO memberships as countries without national CSR associations. Countries with large numbers of INGO memberships are likely to have a national CSR association; countries with low numbers of INGO memberships are unlikely to have a national CSR association. Countries with national CSR associations may also be more motivated to become involved in INGOs than countries without national CSR organizations. This provides strong support for the Global CSR Proposition. Figure 4.12

---

[7] The explanation for the sharp rise from 2001 to 2002 is that in 2002, the UIA included organizations of type A–D and F, whereas until 2001 the totals only included organization types A–D.

Explaining the rise of national corporate social responsibility 135

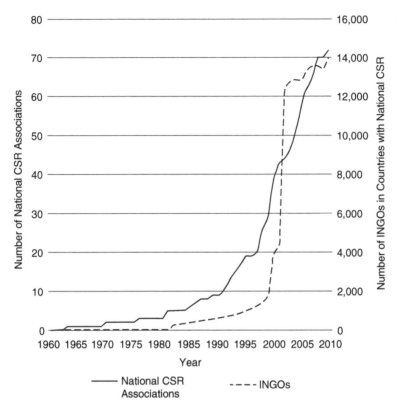

Figure 4.12 Membership in international nongovernmental organizations and national corporate social responsibility

plots the relationship between national CSR associations and the average number of INGO memberships in countries with national CSR associations.[8]

In comparing Figure 4.12 with Figures 4.7–4.10, a difference is immediately apparent. Whereas the UNGC, the GRI, and the CDP have only been around since the late 1990s or early 2000s and were preceded by national CSR associations, global institutional pressure as measured by INGOs precedes the establishment of national CSR associations and stretches back for many decades, if not centuries. (Compiling the INGO data for the 1960s and 1970s will be a priority

---

[8] The graph contains the INGO values of all countries that eventually got a national CSR association.

Table 4.3 *Correlation coefficients for national corporate social responsibility and global actors and initiatives*

Global actors and initiatives	Pearson's r correlation coefficient with national CSR
Carbon Disclosure Project	0.76
Global Reporting Initiative	0.79
UN Global Compact Corporate Membership	0.81
UN Global Compact National Networks	0.89
International nongovernmental organizations	0.95

for future research.) Although reciprocal influences cannot be ruled out, this suggests that global institutional pressure may have played an important role in bringing about national CSR associations. Table 4.3 shows that INGOs have the highest correlation with national CSR associations.

But what exactly is the link? National CSR associations seem to share INGOs' commitment to rational voluntarism, universalism, individualism, rational progress, and world citizenship. In addition, it should be noted that business and industry associations are included in UIA INGO data (Boli 2012: 1166). Thus, if it were not for national CSR association's national, as opposed to international orientation, these organizations would themselves be included in the UIA's INGO dataset. In addition, anecdotal evidence suggests that many founders and leading officials in national CSR associations have been connected to international society through international backgrounds and biographies, as well as through the multinational companies for whom they work. The following example suggests that social capital may facilitate the international diffusion of CSR (Hiss 2006).

Harry Oppenheimer, who founded the Urban Foundation, was born in South Africa to a Jewish-German family. Following his primary schooling in South Africa, Oppenheimer attended public school and studied at Oxford in the United Kingdom, before becoming chairman of the mining multinationals Anglo American and De Beers. Luzio Mazzei, president of Shell Philippines, took the initiative to found the

Philippine CSR association PBSP. A Venezuelan national himself, Mazzei modeled the PBSP after Dividendo Voluntario para la Comunidad, a business-led Venezuelan development foundation set up in 1963. The fact that both Oppenheimer and Mazzei worked for transnational or global companies likely increased their exposure to world culture and ideas about responsible business.

The linkage between INGOs and national CSR associations remains elusive. As yet, there is insufficient evidence to directly link the "propagators of world cultural principles" (Boli and Thomas 1999: 14–15) to the diffusion of national CSR. Instead, both the membership in international organizations and the diffusion of national CSR associations may be seen as an outgrowth and embodiment of an increasingly institutionalized global society (Drori and Krücken 2009). The next section summarizes this chapter's empirical findings and lays out an agenda for future research.

Conclusion

In this chapter, I asked how globalization has affected CSR at the national level. I used two propositions, the Global CSR Proposition and the Autonomy of National CSR Proposition, to assess the relationship between the global and the local. National CSR associations can be seen as a relatively hard test for world society theory and for the Global CSR Proposition, which predicts that global models shape national-level institutions. Although the chapter is exploratory, its findings could provide even stronger support for the world society thesis on global diffusion than studies of global CSR frameworks, which have a natural affinity with global scripts. How tight are the linkages between national CSR and global processes?

The results support both propositions in different ways. National CSR was institutionalized decades before the prominent and influential global CSR frameworks. By the time the UNGC and the GRI got off the ground, there were already more than forty national CSR associations across the globe. This supports the Autonomy of National CSR Proposition and suggests that recent global frameworks such as the UNGC are overstudied in comparison to national CSR associations. Moreover, since the latter predated the former, the latter could not have brought about the former. In addition to the nonexistence of CSR-specific models at the global as opposed to the national level, I have suggested that political economy factors played an important role in the success of national CSR and the failure of early attempts to establish global CSR frameworks. Whereas national CSR associations can be seen as part of the "mainstream CSR movement engaging collaboratively with business," early attempts to establish global frameworks "emphasized the need to roll-back corporate power ... and promote social economy alternatives to corporate capitalism" (Utting, this volume). CSR is corporate-led, and it is not surprising that business communities across the world have mobilized national CSR to legitimate and protect themselves against attacks by the radical corporate accountability movement. National CSR can be seen as a corporate-led response to these pressures.

However, the limited or at best indirect effects of global CSR frameworks on national CSR associations do not imply the absence of global normative pressure. As measured by memberships in INGOs, global normative pressure is strongly correlated with the establishment of national CSR associations. This chapter shows that countries with high numbers of INGO memberships are much more likely to have a national CSR association than are countries with small numbers of INGO memberships. Furthermore, countries with national CSR associations are likely to have far more INGO memberships than are countries without CSR associations. These findings support the Global CSR Proposition and a large literature that underlines the importance of INGOs (Boli and Thomas 1999; Schofer, Hironaka, Frank, and Longhofer 2012), imitation and learning in global diffusion processes (Simmons, Dobbin, and Garrett 2008), and world society theory's claim that "participation in these globalized associational networks ... is a strong predictor of rationalized actorhood" (Meyer 2000: 242). For all their national distinctiveness, national CSR associations appear to be part and parcel of world society or global culture.

This chapter raises many questions for future research. Why was CSR first a primarily domestic and then an increasingly global phenomenon? National CSR associations initially evolved in the absence of well-developed global CSR frameworks. However, these national CSR associations were facilitated and enabled by global institutional pressure and INGO linkages. Why is INGO membership such a strong predictor of national CSR? To establish causality, it will be necessary to run the analysis of INGOs and national CSR using sophisticated multivariate regression models and possibly event history analysis. Further qualitative and historical research could also help to establish the causal mechanisms at work if INGOs are "channels" or "carriers" for global pressure to adopt CSR (Lim 2012). Were national CSR associations a "second best" option for the institutional entrepreneurs who established them? If so, did costliness[9] or coordination problems prevent the prior establishment of global CSR frameworks? If it is possible to get in touch with key people or archival materials, these sources could help to answer these questions. Furthermore, it might be fruitful to probe the influence of global frameworks and institutional pressure on national associations' activities. The data in this chapter capture only the timing of the establishment of these organizations, not their actual practices. It does not seem farfetched to assume that global frameworks such as the GRI, ISO 26000, and the UN Guiding Principles on Business and Human Rights have exerted an increasing influence over the practices of national organizations during recent years.

Although my findings underline the impact of the global on the national, this does not mean that national CSR had no impact on global frameworks. The fact that a large number of national CSR associations were in existence before the establishment of the global CSR frameworks and the fact that some international CSR initiatives began at the national level makes this question worth exploring. In addition, qualitative and cross-national evidence supports the salience of domestic political-economic influences for national CSR. Contrary to the expectations of strong globalization and world society perspectives, political-economic interests and contests at the national level are consequential for the political economy of CSR. It is needless to say that, as business associations, national CSR associations are very particular NGOs. The rise of national CSR in the United Kingdom, to cite one example, underlines the importance of the voluntariness of rational voluntarism: national CSR's rose with Margaret Thatcher's neoliberal agenda of liberalization, privatization, deregulation, and dismantling of the postwar social contract (Kinderman 2012). An international branch of the national CSR organization became known as the International Business Leaders Forum, an important disseminator of CSR across China, India, and Eastern Europe. The model of CSR and capitalism propagated by these organizations is a distinctly liberal one.

[9] I am grateful to Kiyoteru Tsutsui for this point.

Further research will be needed to capture the complex interactions between national and global influences on CSR. This research will move beyond the dichotomy of global and national to develop a true synthesis of world society and political economy explanations and identify the causal pathways that link the global with the local. Since they are hybrid organizations composed of domestic as well as multi-national firms, national CSR associations can help us to understand how Tocquevillean do-gooders and hard-nosed neoliberals have jointly shaped CSR at the national and global levels.

Appendix: *national corporate social responsibility organizations*

Founding year	Country	Name of national CSR organization
1963	Venezuela	Dividendo Voluntario para la Communidad
1970	Philippines	Philippine Business for Social Progress
1976	South Africa	National Business Initiative / Urban Foundation
1981	Paraguay	ADEC Paraguay
1981	UK	Business in the Community
1985	Argentina	Instituto Argentino de Responsibilidad Social Empresaria (IARSE)
1986	France	IMS – Entreprendre pour la cite
1987	Sweden	Swedish Jobs and Society
1989	Japan	Council for Better Corporate Citizenship Nippon Keidanren
1991	USA	Business for Social Responsibility
1992	Czech Rep	Czech Business Leaders Forum
1992	Hungary	Hungarian Business Leaders Forum
1992	UAE	Emirates Environmental Group
1993	Sri Lanka	Employers' Federation of Ceylon
1993	Thailand	Thailand Business Coalition on AIDS
1994	Colombia	Colombian Centre for Social Responsibility
1994	Peru	Peru 2021
1995	Canada	Canadian Business for Social Responsibility
1995	Italy	Sodalitas
1997	Norway	Green Business Network Norway / CSR Norway

(*cont.*)

Founding year	Country	Name of national CSR organization
1998	Belgium	Belgian Business and Society
1998	Brazil	Instituto Ethos
1998	Bulgaria	Bulgarian Business Leaders Forum
1998	India	Business & Community Foundation (BCF)
1998	Indonesia	Indonesia Business Links
1998	New Zealand	New Zealand Business for Social Responsibility
1999	Nigeria	Growing Business Foundation
1999	Spain	Forética
1999	Vietnam	Vietnam Business Links
2000	Chile	Accion RSE
2000	El Salvador	Fundemas
2000	Finland	Finnish Business & Society
2000	Germany	Econsense
2000	Greece	Hellenic Network for Corporate Social Responsibility
2000	Ireland	Business in the Community Ireland
2000	Netherlands	Samenleving & Bedrij
2000	Poland	Responsible Business Forum, Poland
2000	Portugal	Grace Portugal
2000	Switzerland	Philias Foundation
2001	Israel	Maala
2001	Kenya	Ufadhili Trust
2001	Mexico	CEMEFI
2001	Uruguay	Deres – Responsabilidad Social Empresaria
2002	Panama	Sumarse a la Responsabilidad Social Empresarial
2003	Denmark	VirksomhedsNetværket
2003	Hong Kong	Community Business
2004	Bolivia	COBORSE Corporacion Boliviana de RSE
2004	Honduras	Fundación Hondureña de Responsabilidad Social Empresarial
2004	Russia	Russia Partnership for Responsible Business Practices
2004	Slovakia	Slovak Business Leaders Forum

(*cont.*)

Founding year	Country	Name of national CSR organization
2004	Ukraine	Center for CSR Development
2005	Australia	Australian Business in the Community Network
2005	Austria	RespACT
2005	Bangladesh	CSR Centre at the Bangladesh Enterprise Institute (BEI)
2005	China	Chinese Federation of Corporate Responsibility
2005	Nicaragua	uniRSE
2005	Singapore	Singapore Compact
2006	Estonia	Responsible Business Forum in Estonia
2006	Iran	CSR Iran
2006	Romania	CSR Romania
2006	Saudi Arabia	Corporate Social Responsibility Forum
2006	South Korea	Korea Institute Center for Sustainable Development
2007	Jordan	Schematt
2007	Luxembourg	CSR Luxembourg
2007	Uganda	Uganda Chapter for Corporate Social Responsibility Initiatives
2008	Croatia	Croatian Business Leaders Forum
2008	Iceland	Ethikos
2008	Pakistan	FPCCI Standing Committee on CSR
2008	Senegal	RSE Senegal
2008	Serbia	Smart Kolektiv / BLF Serbia
2010	Lebanon	CSR Lebanon
2010	Slovenia	Network for Social Responsibility of Slovenia

References

Boli, John. 1999. "Conclusion: World Authority Structures and Legitimations." Pp. 267–300 in *Constructing World Culture: International Nongovernmental Organizations Since 1875*, edited by J. Boli and G. M. Thomas. Stanford, CA: Stanford University Press.

Boli, John. 2012. "International Nongovernmental Organizations." Pp. 1161–1169 in *The Wiley-Blackwell Encyclopedia of Globalization*, edited by G. Ritzer. Chichester: Wiley-Blackwell.

Boli, John, and George M. Thomas. 1999. "INGOs and the Organization of World Culture." Pp. 13–49 in *Constructing World Culture: International Nongovernmental Organizations Since 1875*, edited by J. Boli and G. M. Thomas. Stanford, CA: Stanford University Press.

Bowen, Harold. 1953. *Social Responsibilities of the Businessman*. New York: Harper & Brothers.

Clarke, Gerald. 1988. *The Politics of NGOs in South-East Asia: Participation and Protest in the Philippines*. London and New York: Routledge.

Davies, Robert. 2003. "The Business Community: Social Responsibility and Corporate Values." Pp. 301–319 in *Making Globalization Good: The Moral Challenges of Global Capitalism*, edited by J. H. Dunning. New York: Oxford University Press.

Drori, Gili. 2004. *Doing Well and Doing Good Are Not Mutually Exclusive: Corporate Social Responsibility as an Emerging Organizational Myth of Corporate Identity*. Memo prepared for SCANCOR conference "Corporate Social Responsibility in the Era of the Transforming Welfare State" in Florence, May 7–8, 2004.

Drori, Gili, and Georg Krücken. 2009. "World Society: A Theory and a Research Program in Context." Pp. 3–35 in *World Society: The Writings of John W. Meyer*, edited by G. Drori and G. Krücken. New York: Oxford University Press.

Garilao, Ernesto. 1991. *Philippine Business for Social Progress: Can It Be Replicated?* New York: Center for the Study of Philanthropy.

Gjølberg, Maria. 2009. "The Origin of Corporate Social Responsibility: Global Forces or National Legacies?" *Socio-Economic Review* 7 (4):605–637.

Grayson, David, and Jane Nelson. 2013. *Coalitions of the Responsible: How Business Leaders Are Working Collectively to Drive Sustainable Capitalism*. Stanford, CA: Stanford Business Books.

Habisch, André, Jan Jonker, Martina Wegner, and René Schmidpeter. 2005. *Corporate Social Responsibility across Europe: Discovering National Perspectives of Corporate Citizenship*. Berlin: Springer.

Hiss, Stefanie. 2006. "Does Corporate Social Responsibility Need Social Capital?" *Journal of Corporate Citizenship* (23):81–91.

Kinderman, Daniel. 2011. "The Political Economy of Corporate Responsibility across Europe and Beyond: 1977–2007." PhD dissertation, Department of Government, Cornell University, New York.

Kinderman, Daniel. 2012. "'Free us up so we can be responsible!' The Co-evolution of Corporate Social Responsibility and Neo-liberalism in the UK, 1977–2010." *Socio-Economic Review* 10(1):29–57.

Kolk, Ans, and Rob van Tudler. 2005. "Setting New Global Rules? TNCs and Codes of Conduct." *Transnational Corporation* 14(3):1–28.

Lim, Alwyn. 2012. *The Global Expansion of Corporate Social Responsibility: Emergence, Diffusion, and Reception of Global Corporate Governance Frameworks*. PhD dissertation, Department of Sociology, University of Michigan, Ann Arbor.

Lim, Alwyn, and Kiyoteru Tsutsui. 2012. "Globalization and Commitment in Corporate Social Responsibility: Cross-National Analyses of Institutional and Political-Economy Effects." *American Sociological Review* 77(1):69–98.

Longhofer, Wesley, and Evan Schofer. 2010. "National and Global Origins of Environmental Association." *American Sociological Review* 75(4):505–533.

MacLeod, Sorcha. 2008. "The United Nations, Human Rights and Transnational Corporations: Challenging the International Legal Order." Pp. 64–84 in *Perspectives on Corporate Social Responsibility*, edited by N. Boeger, R. Murray, and C. Villiers. Cheltenham: Edward Elgar.

Maheshwari, B. L. 1978. "Future of the Corporation." *Economic and Political Weekly* XIII(47): M109–M110.

Meyer, John W. 2000. "Globalization: Sources and Effects on National States and Societies." *International Sociology* 15:233–248.

Meyer, John W. 2010. "World Society, Institutional Theories, and the Actor." *Annual Review of Sociology* 36(1):1–20.

Meyer, John W., John Boli, George M. Thomas, and Francisco O. Ramirez. 1997. "World Society and the Nation-State." *American Journal of Sociology* 103(1):144–181.

Meyer, John W., Shawn M. Pope, and Andrew Isaacson. 2015; this volume. "Legitimating the Transnational Corporation in a Stateless World Society." Pp. 27–72 in *Corporate Social Responsibility in a Globalizing World*, edited by K. Tsutsui and A. Lim. New York: Cambridge University Press.

Muchlinski, Peter. 1995. *Multinational Enterprises and the Law*. Oxford: Blackwell.

Muchlinski, Peter. 2000. "Attempts to Extend the Accountability of Transnational Corporations: The Role of UNCTAD." Pp. 97–117 in *Liability of Multinational Corporations under International Law* edited by M. T. Kamminga and S. Zia-Zarifi. The Hague: Kluwer Law International.

Mühe, Ursula. 2010. *The Politics of Corporate Social Responsibility: The Rise of a Global Business Norm*. Frankfurt: Campus.

Sagafi-Nejad, Tagi, and John Dunning. 2008. *The UN and Transnational Corporations: From Code of Conduct to Global Compact*. Foreword by Howard V. Perlmutter. Bloomington: Indiana University Press.

Schofer, Evan, Ann Hironaka, David John Frank, and Wesley Longhofer. 2012. "Sociological Institutionalism and World Society." Pp. 57–68 in *The New Blackwell Companion to Political Sociology*, edited by K. Nash, A. Scott, and E. Amenata. Oxford: Blackwell Publishing.

Segerlund, Lisbeth. 2010. *Making Corporate Social Responsibility a Global Concern: Norm Construction in a Globalizing World*. Surrey: Ashgate Publishing Company.

Shanahan, Suzanne, and Sanjeev Khagram. 2006. "Dynamics of Corporate Responsibility." Pp. 196–224 in *Globalization and Organization: World Society and Organizational Change*, edited by G. S. Drori, J. M. Meyer, and Hokyu Wang. Oxford: Oxford University Press.

Silk, Leonard, and David Vogel. 1976. *Ethics & Profits: The Crisis of Confidence in American Business*. New York: Simon & Schuster.

Simmons, Beth A., Frank Dobbin, and Geoffrey Garrett. 2008. *The Global Diffusion of Markets and Democracy*. New York: Cambridge University Press.

Steinmo, Sven, Kathleen Thelen, and Frank Longstreth, eds. 1992. *Structuring Politics: Historical Institutionalism in Comparative Analysis*. Cambridge: Cambridge University Press.

Tan, Victor E., and Maurino P. Bolante. 1997. *Philippine Business for Social Progress*. New York: The Synergos Institute.

Thelen, Kathleen. 2004. *How Institutions Evolve: The Political Economy of Skills in Germany, Britain, the United States, and Japan*. New York: Cambridge University Press.

UN Global Compact Office. 2012. *Business Participant List, 2000–2012*. New York: United Nations Global Compact.

Union of International Associations. 1982 to 2011. *Yearbook of International Organizations*. Various issues. Munchen: KG Saur Verlag.

Utting, Peter. 2015; this volume. "Corporate Social Responsibility and the Evolving Standards Regime: Regulatory and Political Dynamics." Pp. 73–106 in *Corporate Social Responsibility in a Globalizing World*, edited by K. Tsutsui and A. Lim. New York: Cambridge University Press.

Visser, Wayne, and Nick Tolhurst. 2010. *The World Guide to CSR: A Country-by-Country Analysis of Corporate Sustainability and Responsibility*. Sheffield: Greenleaf Publishing.

Waddock, Sandra. 2008. *The Difference Makers: How Social and Institutional Entrepreneurs Created the Corporate Responsibility Movement*. Sheffield: Greenleaf Publishing.

Wallace, Cynthia Day. 1982. *Legal Control of the Multinational Enterprise: National Regulatory Techniques and the Prospects for International Controls*. The Hague: Martinus Nijhoff.

Zadek, Simon. 2008. "Global Collaborative Governance: There Is No Alternative." *Corporate Governance* 8(4):374–438.

PART II

Social construction and field formation in global corporate social responsibility

5 | Corporations, conflict minerals, and corporate social responsibility

VIRGINIA HAUFLER

Introduction

Fifteen years ago the concept of "conflict commodities" did not exist, and no one demanded that corporations prevent the resources they produced or used from financing war and corruption. Precious commodities – gems, gold, drugs – had long been used by both rebels and governments to hire soldiers, buy weapons, and fund Swiss bank accounts. But, until recently, no one saw this trade as a significant contributor to conflict, and no one linked it to corporate social responsibility (CSR) or sought to regulate it as a way to promote peace and good governance. After the end of the Cold War, however, transnational activists launched successful campaigns that publicized the connection between resource wealth and civil war and promoted a regulatory agenda that spawned multiple governance initiatives in the past fifteen years that seek to ensure that the exploitation of natural resource wealth does not finance conflict.

These initiatives are some of the latest in the evolution of global CSR, reaching into areas that had previously been considered the sole responsibility of states. Issues of war and peace are the very stuff of traditional "high politics," in which powerful states establish the rules of the game. Until recently, few contemporary scholars of international relations focused their attention on corporate behavior as an independent factor in war, and still fewer identified firms as a potential instrument of peace.[1] As Meyer, Pope, and Isaacson demonstrate (this volume), transnational

---

[1] There is a rich literature on the economics of peace and war (too vast to list here), but it tends to take a macrostructural perspective on trade and investment and does not look at the microlevel of corporate behavior. For work on business and conflict, see Nelson 2000; Banfield, Lilly, and Haufler 2003; Fort and Schipani 2004; Wolf, Deitelhoff, and Engert 2007; Fort 2007; and Deitelhoff and Wolf 2010.

corporations have become subject to increased pressure over time for legitimation and accountability across a wide range of issues and problems. The perception that corporations are complicit in violence and bloodshed in areas of the world remote from their main markets has energized activists, consumers, and citizens; pushed firms to adopt new practices; and led governments to offer new regulations that respond to these demands. The regulation of conflict minerals is part of a broader effort by activists and policy makers to address conflict both as a matter for corporate responsibility and as a regulatory issue, and not one that is restricted to traditional international diplomacy among sovereign states.

Although the issues surrounding conflict minerals are interesting in themselves, what is particularly striking is the variation in how the demands for regulation and corporate responsibility have been institutionalized. The array of different initiatives includes everything from guidelines and standards to highly institutionalized international bodies, and incorporates both state and non-state actors into decision making and implementation. The first conflict minerals initiative established a single formal centralized global institution to regulate the trade in rough diamonds – the Kimberley Process Certification Scheme (KPCS), launched in 2003. The KPCS is a multistakeholder initiative, with a narrow focus on only one mineral – rough diamonds – but a broad mandate to regulate the entire market. It combines industry certification with government trade restrictions and oversight by civil society organizations. After the founding of the KPCS, different actors created a decentralized set of institutions that operate at different political levels (international, national, local) and different industry scales (firm, sector, and supply chain) for four other conflict minerals. These included a wide range of public, private, and multistakeholder systems, covering from one to all four of the minerals, some of which adopted certification and some of which did not. Within this one relatively obscure issue area, a diverse set of regulatory systems evolved in a short period of time, with growing impact on trade and investment in the mining sector.

Why this institutional variation within a single issue area? Why did the transnational regulation of conflict diamonds turn out one way whereas regulation of other conflict minerals resulted in a very different pattern of institutionalization? The successful Kimberley Process provided a powerful and persuasive model that one would think would influence the institutional design of others that followed

(DiMaggio and Powell 1983; Tolbert and Zucker 1983; Dobbin, Simmons, and Garrett 2007). Many of the same nongovernmental organizations (NGOs) that advocated action on diamonds went on to publicize the same issue regarding other conflict minerals, and, in most cases, the same consumer and producer states were involved. Despite the similarities, regulatory institutions for non-diamond conflict minerals did not follow the pattern set by the Kimberley Process. Why? This is the puzzle I explore in this chapter.

I trace the variation in institutional outcomes for conflict minerals over the course of a little over a decade, drawing out comparisons among the different results. I look in particular at four characteristics of institutional outcomes: the regulatory mechanism adopted, the level of governance, industry scale, and private sector participation. I start from the assumption that early institutional design choices influence later ones and that initiatives at one level of governance influence the design of initiatives at other levels. This highlights the fact that this issue area became progressively more "crowded" over time as new initiatives jostled up against old ones. Within this arena, the pressure to converge toward the initial model established for diamonds is modified by differences in the structure and organization of the supply chain for each of the other conflict minerals.

The institutional development of conflict minerals governance and the variation it displays is one example of the larger evolution of CSR from simple words to a multiplicity of regulatory systems that impose real constraints on firms. We know from other well-known examples, such as the textile and forestry sectors, that those constraints bite more deeply with some types of regulatory mechanisms than they do with others and that the existence of more than one regulatory system changes the character and impact of constraints (O'Rourke 2003; Cashore, Auld, and Newsom 2004; Bartley 2010). The process and evolution of governance of conflict minerals is a microcosm that illustrates the changing political dynamics of CSR and regulatory change.

State power, institutional competition, and industry structure

Interdisciplinary scholarship in international relations, sociology, and business studies identifies a number of factors that explain different institutional outcomes. Here, I look at three relevant factors identified in the literature: the power and interests of states, the dynamics of competition by both states and organizations, and strategies of transnational activism. I add to this a fourth factor that I argue is a significant explanation for variation in the conflict minerals issue area: the structure and organization of industry itself. None of these is sufficient on its own to explain the process by which this issue area produced such a range of variation in institutional outcomes, although each contributes an important insight.

The dominant explanation for regulatory outcomes in international relations scholarship is that international institutions directly reflect the interests of powerful states and of the powerful industries within them (Mearsheimer 1994; Drezner 2007). For instance, a common explanation for the relative lack of international regulation of the information sector is that the United States opposed it, largely because the information technology sector vociferously rejected government interference (Drezner 2007). These explanations based on state power may explain broad regulatory outcomes, such as whether states cooperate to impose any regulation at all, but they are not concerned with questions about institutional design, private versus public regulatory systems, or the evolution of institutions over time. Nevertheless, we can expect that powerful states will represent the interests of their industries when it comes to transnational regulatory issues and that some of the variation I seek to examine here may be explained by shifts in state power or by changes in the interests of the firms that shape state interests.

Recent scholarship has begun to address the fact that the international arena is becoming crowded with institutions and seeks to explain the dynamics of multiple regulatory systems colliding, overlapping, and competing (Orsini, Morin, and Young 2013). In international relations, the regime complex (or regime complexity) literature examines what happens when states can choose among an array of different institutions. When existing ones are not friendly toward their interests, they can choose which forum best meets their needs (Raustiala and Victor 2004; Alter and Meunier 2009; Keohane and Victor 2011; Orsini, Morin, and Young 2013). A regime complex is, at its simplest, a set of overlapping institutions within an issue area, which is what we find in the arena of conflict minerals (Keohane and Victor 2011). For instance, Keohane and Victor analyze the regime complex for climate change, which contains multiple organizations that address different aspects of the complicated issue and provide an array of choices to states looking for a congenial forum in which to negotiate. Within any regime complex, private initiatives can supplement intergovernmental ones, providing another alternative forum. Green and Auld extend the analysis of climate change to examine private initiatives as a complement to interstate agreements, for instance, through carbon disclosure mechanisms and voluntary self-regulation. They argue that state authority – the "shadow of hierarchy" – stands behind these private alternatives (Héritier and Lehmkuhl 2008, Green and Auld 2011). The literature on regime complexity points to the possibility that institutional outcomes are not a direct reflection of the interests of powerful states and their leading industries, but instead result from choices across multiple institutions.

Recent emergent literature examines interactions among transnational business governance schemes (i.e., private governance). It attempts to provide a handle on what happens when many different initiatives emerge within a particular regulatory field, as transnational regulatory systems have proliferated (Eberlein et al. 2014). Unlike the regime complex literature, this approach explicitly focuses on non-state actors, extending the literature on private authority beyond the creation of single initiatives. They note the growing number of systems designed to identify and certify firms or products that meet specified standards, for instance, in the textile and forestry sectors; the variety of corporate environmental, social, and governance (ESG) reporting systems; and the different degrees of institutionalization, from simple corporate codes to complex systems of representation, implementation, monitoring, and enforcement. Auld et al. refer to the "new" CSR (Auld, Bernstein, and Cashore 2008; see also Kitzmueller and Shimshack 2012; Lim and Tsutsui 2012).

Interactions among institutions occur over time, and new institutional models may become more widely adopted as they attain legitimacy (Tolbert and Zucker 1983). As Powell describes it, an "organizational field is a community of disparate organizations, including producers, consumers, overseers, and advisors, that engage in common activities, subject to similar reputational and regulatory pressures" (Powell 2008: 976). The participants are aware of themselves as being part of this field and reference each other and model each others' behavior. An organizational field provides a common frame of reference for the participants, generates similar pressures for conformity, and involves the participants in efforts to expand the field to incorporate other actors and issues (Bartley and Smith 2008).[2] Dingwerth and Pattberg argue that, at least on sustainability issues, "there is something akin to a standard model around which the design, rhetoric and processes of transnational rule-making organizations converge" (Dingwerth and Pattberg 2009).[3] But when there is no underlying consensus on the best way to resolve an issue, then there should be no convergence toward a single model.

The growth of transnational regulatory institutions would not have occurred without the increasing influence of transnational activists and their issue-based campaigns. Anticorporate campaigns in particular "shine the spotlight" on corporate practices, especially in the developing world and in nondemocratic closed societies (Spar 1998; Soule 2009). These activists wield material, moral, and political leverage to back up their campaigns (Prakash and Gugerty 2010). Advocacy organizations are identified with positive values, and their nonprofit status gives them legitimacy as organizations that are acting in the public interest. The influence of the moral claims of activists hinges on their ability to find a receptive audience among consumers, investors, and buyers (Vogel 2006; Bartley and Child 2014).

Campaigns can impose real costs on the firm: protests, boycotts, shareholder activism, litigation, and a range of other tactics that directly confront the firm with its violations and publicize them (Hiscox and Smyth 2011). Activists often target the firms that are the most visible – global corporations with recognizable brands, often those that have recently experienced some disaster or crisis that makes them reputationally vulnerable (e.g., the Bangladesh factory collapse and Gap, Inc.).[4] They strategically identify the weakest link in a global supply chain and mobilize attention there in order to pressure both states and firms to consent to creating a regulatory system. The variation in institutional outcomes within an issue area is in part due to the relationship between these activists and the firms they target.

---

[2] The emphasis on a "community" of organizations, however, can falsely lead one to think that political power, contestation, and difference are not part of an organizational field (Kostova, Roth, and Dacin 2008; Dingwerth and Pattberg 2009; Beckert 2010).

[3] The field of CSR as a legitimate subject of academic scholarship is still relatively new, but even mainstream economics now has a body of literature that explores it (Kitzmueller and Shimshack 2012).

[4] On the politics of branding, see King and McDonnell, this volume; Klein 1999.

Corporations, conflict minerals, and corporate social responsibility 155

This brings to the fore the importance of understanding the structure and organization of the industries themselves. Systems of regulation that span borders seek to govern transactions throughout a supply chain, even when the target is activities at one end of the global supply chain. In the case of conflict minerals, although the effort is directed literally at the ground level, where the minerals are found, the regulatory institutions span the entire supply chain from source producers to end consumers. The ease of getting a regulatory institution in place will depend in part on the structure of that supply chain – the degree of concentration, the organization of the industry as a whole, and the leverage that buyers have over the production process as a whole (Gereffi, Humphrey, and Sturgeon 2005; MacDonald 2014).

This selective review of the literature provides us with some expectations about the conditions under which we might expect different institutional outcomes, particularly the shift toward multiple institutions to resolve the same problem. The international relations literature, particularly on regime complexity, posits that the outcome hinges on the interests of powerful states and their search for a compatible institution among many options. The organizational literature looks at how reputational and regulatory pressures, along with variations in legitimacy, produce convergence in institutions. Those reputational and regulatory pressures are shaped in turn by the strategies of transnational activists who target the most vulnerable firms and industries. And the structure and organization of those industries can either facilitate or hinder institutional convergence.

Given the complexity of the literature, it makes sense to try to simplify the picture in order to make research tractable and try to limit a sprawling topic. The conflict minerals issue provides a rich but narrow source of information to trace the process by which multiple factors produced such a messy outcome – a wide range of different public, private, and mixed regulatory initiatives all addressing the same issue. The following section provides a narrative of the development of the conflict minerals field divided into two periods of time: the first one, from 1998 to 2006, is dominated by the development of a single institution, the Kimberley Process Certification Scheme; the second one, from 2006 to 2012, is characterized by the multiplicity of conflict minerals initiatives. The narrative reveals the changing dynamics of state power, transnational activism, and industry structure.

Corporate responsibility, civil conflict, and regulatory institutions

"Conflict commodities" are natural resources that finance violent conflict, including timber, oil, and other raw materials. "Conflict minerals" are a subset of commodities consisting of minerals that typically are highly valuable and small in size, making them especially convenient for illicit trade (Reno 1999; Ross 2003). Within the current discourse on conflict minerals, an even smaller group has been identified as targets for regulation: diamonds, tin, tantalum, tungsten, and gold from conflict zones in Africa, particularly from the region around the resource-rich and conflict-afflicted Democratic Republic of the Congo (DRC). The relevant actors involved in negotiations over regulating conflict minerals are the industry players throughout the supply chain, including both large firms such as DeBeers or Rio Tinto and small artisanal miners and traders; industry associations representing producers and buyers; the states most interested in the trade in minerals – as producers, consumers, or humanitarians; the United Nations and the Organisation for Economic Cooperation and Development (OECD); the International Conference on the Great Lakes Region (ICGLR)[5]; and activist NGOs concerned with the ongoing violence and bloodshed, particularly Global Witness, Partnership Africa Canada, and Enough.[6]

Conflict commodities became an issue with the rise of numerous civil wars that followed the end of the Cold War, putting to rest the idea of an immediate peace dividend. Genocide in Rwanda, endless civil war in Angola, and brutal rebellion in Sierra Leone, along with state collapse in the Balkans challenged the world community to intervene in some way to end the death and destruction. Many observers began to identify natural resources as a fuel to the fire of war, providing the financial wherewithal for rebels and warlords to hire soldiers and buy guns. Scholars and policy makers began to talk of a "resource curse" and analyzed the empirical links between natural resources and war (Karl

---

[5] The ICGLR is a regional organization established to implement peace-building in the Great Lakes region of Africa – the area of conflict for conflict minerals. It represents the interests of both producer and transit countries for the minerals trade.

[6] The primary involvement of the UN is through the Expert Committee convened by the UN Security Council to oversee sanctions on the DRC. Both it and the OECD represent the interests of the consumer countries and/or humanitarian interests.

1997; Berdal and Malone 2000; Collier 2003; Ross 2006; Humphreys, Sachs, and Stiglitz 2007). Great natural resource wealth was associated with poor development outcomes, high levels of corruption, and extremely uneven distribution of wealth. Weak governing institutions provided the conditions for resource wealth to be devastatingly mismanaged (Luong and Weinthal 2006).

The idea of a natural resource curse quickly became linked to what the World Bank and others referred to as "good governance" issues (Weiss 2000; Grindle 2007; World Bank Social Development Department 2010). Some countries were perceived to be at risk of "state failure," and donor states and intergovernmental organizations sought ways of strengthening and building government capacity to prevent instability (Esty 1998; Bates 2008). International aid organizations, particularly the World Bank and the US Agency for International Development (USAID), began to speak of a "good governance" agenda focused on the twin problems of conflict and corruption (Weiss 2000; Grindle 2007). The management of natural resources and the so-called resource curse were integrated into this agenda.

The UN sought to prevent conflict and at times promote regime change through either sanctions or direct international intervention throughout the 1990s. Although some peacekeeping interventions were successful, many were not. It became increasingly difficult over time to garner the political consensus among states needed for direct military intervention, and US support for such action disappeared following the debacle in Somalia. The UN wielded the sanctions club often throughout the decade, quickly shifting from the comprehensive sanctions imposed on Iraq to "smart" or targeted sanctions applied to succeeding conflicts. These sanctions often prohibited trade in specific commodities. From 1994 on, the UN applied sanctions to diamonds, oil, and timber in Angola, Liberia, Sierra Leone, DRC, and Côte d'Ivoire in an effort to bring an end to the violence and rebellion. These sanctions were widely seen as failing in their main aim because civil wars in Angola and Sierra Leone dragged on seemingly without end. In 2000, the UN High Level Expert Group, headed by Canadian Ambassador to the UN Robert Fowler, issued a report on its investigations of sanctions-busting in Angola – and it was a devastating indictment of the sanctions regime (Fowler 2000).

It was in this context – concern for good governance and the resource curse, the failure of intervention and sanctions, and ongoing civil war and horrific violence – that transnational activists began to highlight the role of natural resources in financing the bloodshed and began targeting corporations as complicit. Their campaigns would be facilitated by the growing discourse over CSR across a number of disparate issue areas (Utting 2005; Bendell 2009). Transnational activist organizations redefined the political dynamics surrounding conflict prevention and resolution by targeting international business as a culpable actor in the protracted civil wars of the 1990s. This ignited a controversy over greed versus grievance as causes of war and the role of the private sector within this (Berdal and Malone 2000; Collier and Hoeffler 2000; Ballentine and Sherman 2003). It was against this background that the campaign against conflict diamonds began.

The following sections look at two periods of time in the evolution of institutions to address the issue of conflict minerals: 1998–2006 and 2006 to the present. The first period covers the emergence of this as an issue area, the convergence on a single certification institution as the solution, and the establishment and early years of the Kimberley Process. The second section provides an overview of the variety of different conflict minerals initiatives that different sets of actors create as attention to different minerals fragments the process of institution-building. These two sections highlight state power, institutional competition and convergence, transnational activist strategies, and industry structure and organization.

Conflict diamonds and the Kimberley Process: 1998–2006

The label "conflict diamonds" appeared in news reports for the first time around 1997. A handful of NGOs made the link between the sale of rough diamonds and the financing of rebel violence in Angola and Sierra Leone, issuing investigative reports on the trade. Global Witness, Partnership Africa Canada, and eventually the Fatal Transactions campaign in Europe and major gatekeeping human rights NGOs picked up on the need to regulate the trade in rough diamonds in order to undermine the financing of war. In their campaigns, they utilized horrific images of child soldiers with limbs chopped off and dramatic symbolism such as diamonds dripping blood. They sought to persuade consumers and policy makers that the trade in rough diamonds should be ended and that UN sanctions had failed in this purpose. Instead, they began to target the legitimate diamond market, arguing that the industry itself was complicit in the violence. They demanded that the industry should find some way to identify rough stones from conflict-affected areas in order to prevent sales from those areas, thus separating out the "legitimate" stones.

Although they targeted the diamond industry as a whole, attention focused on DeBeers, which for more than a century used control of diamond supplies to maintain a cartel. Although DeBeers historically had been impregnable to moral appeals, by 2000, it had become more vulnerable to threats. Its market dominance was being undermined by increasing numbers of rough stones in the market that were outside its control – sold by challengers to DeBeers or released from Soviet control after communism's collapse or from the breakdown and civil war in Angola, Sierra Leone, and elsewhere in Africa. DeBeers made a strategic decision to shift from being the buyer of last resort, controlling the supply and price of rough diamonds, to becoming an active retailer of diamonds. This would make it increasingly susceptible to reputational threats that might affect its ability to sell to consumers. If it wanted to sell DeBeers branded diamonds in the United States, which is the largest market for consumer diamonds, it would need to protect and preserve the reputation of diamonds as a "girl's best friend" (United Press International 2000).

From 1998 to 2000, the campaign against "blood diamonds" began to generate concern among consumers and policy makers in the United States and Europe. By 2000, the US Congress began debating legislation to eliminate the import of conflict diamonds into the country, threatening to close off the largest consumer market for rough diamonds. Major producer countries, such as South Africa and Botswana, began to fear the impact on the diamond market – and their country's exports – if the conflict diamond campaign continued.[7] Not only DeBeers, but also the rest of the diamond industry up and down the supply chain began to recognize the fragility of the reputation upon which their market depended.

The diamond industry itself offered to develop a certification system to identify legitimate rough diamonds. It had been advising the UN sanctions committee for Angola on how to set up such a system within

---

[7] There was some effort by particular activists to ensure that the campaign did not entirely destroy the market for diamonds, which would take down a stable democracy such as Botswana, which was dependent on diamond exports for the majority of its income.

that country and was willing to devise something similar on a broader scale. The industry itself took the lead in promoting a new system to regulate the trade in conflict diamonds. The idea of an international certification system to identify stones that were not from conflict-affected areas was supported by both the UN Security Council and General Assembly, both of which called for the development of a certification system.[8] In May 2000, the South African government hosted a meeting in Kimberley of governments, industry, and activists to discuss how to devise and implement such a system. Producer governments, including South Africa, Botswana, and Namibia, all supported the construction of a certification system that would differentiate conflict diamonds from legitimate ones. Consumer governments, particularly the United States, were committed to ending civil war in Africa without direct military or peacekeeping intervention, but also wanted to find an alternative instrument to help end the bloodshed. The US and European governments looked on certification as a reasonable option. After a series of meetings and negotiations throughout 2000, consumer states and producer states, industry, and activists all supported the creation of the KPCS. Different segments of the industry jointly created the World Diamond Council to represent industry interests in negotiations over a new certification and chain-of-custody system to regulate the sector.[9] After negotiations over design and implementation, the Kimberley Process was launched officially in 2003.

The Kimberley Process is designed to remove the sale and export of rough diamonds as a source of funding for rebel armies. It defines a conflict diamond as "rough diamonds used by rebel movements or their allies to finance armed conflicts aimed at undermining legitimate governments." (www.kimberleyprocess.com/en/faq) It consists of an industry-led certification and chain-of-custody system for all rough diamonds. Member states are committed to preventing the export or import of uncertified stones and to ending all trade with nonsignatory countries. States would be the official members of the KPCS, but the

---

[8] The UN General Assembly passed General Resolution 55/56 (2000) calling for resolution of the conflict diamonds problem and, two years later, supported the idea of a certification scheme in Resolution 56/263 (2002).

[9] In 1998, industry representatives had worked with the UN sanctions committee for Angola to develop an Angolan certification system, developing some expertise and level of comfort with this option.

World Diamond Council, Global Witness, and Partnership Africa Canada would be official observers and participants.

From its implementation in 2003 to a turning point in 2006, the KPCS was the only existing international system to regulate conflict minerals. During its early years, the participants negotiated strengthened oversight of member states and instituted a monitoring system. Members were willing to punish violators by kicking them out of the scheme, as it did to Liberia and Côte d'Ivoire at different times. The creation of the Kimberley Process coincided with the winding down of conflict in Angola and Sierra Leone, and the restrictions on conflict diamonds implemented by the KPCS are often credited with playing a significant role in persuading rebel leaders to the negotiating table. Despite concerns about smuggling and corruption, the KPCS was viewed as a successful and legitimate multistakeholder regulatory institution.

Conflict minerals and the proliferation of initiatives: 2006–2012

Whereas the Kimberley Process was quickly designed and implemented, calls for similar systems for other conflict commodities went nowhere until around 2006. There was rising concern about the problem of smuggling and counterfeiting of KPCS certificates, and NGO representatives inside and outside the Kimberley Process sought to strengthen implementation and enforcement. The principles of the institution, however, were directly challenged by the violent takeover of diamond fields by one of its member governments, Zimbabwe. Activist organizations and some member states, including the US government, argued that rough stones from the Marange fields of Zimbabwe should be labeled as conflict diamonds even though the fields were government-controlled and not in rebel-held territory. They sought to extend the definition of conflict diamonds to include human rights violations by governments themselves. Fellow African governments, including South Africa, resisted this expansion of the definition as a direct challenge to state sovereignty and a violation of the basis for the creation of the KPCS in the first place. The industry was divided on this point, with some industry actors reluctant to change the scope of the KPCS and undermine the consensus upon which it was based, whereas others such as the Rapaport Group publicly stated it would not buy any Marange diamonds. The KPCS debated the issue for years, alternately banning Marange diamonds, allowing limited sales, and eventually defining them as legitimate under KP rules. Founding members Global Witness and Partnership Africa Canada withdrew in 2012 from the Kimberley Process in protest of the decision by the KPCS to recognize Zimbabwe diamonds as legitimate.[10] From 2006 to the present, the legitimacy and effectiveness of the Kimberley Process has teetered, as Western governments continued to press for change and most non-Western governments successfully resisted efforts to broaden the scope of the KPCS.

From the beginning, activists had identified other natural resources as a source of financing for war, including minerals such as coltan (columbite-tantalite) and gold. Diamonds drew attention initially because they were a significant element in financing civil wars in Angola and Sierra Leone in the 1990s. But, as the conflicts in Angola and Sierra Leone began to wind down, conflict in other areas with other natural resources drew international attention. Eventually, most attention focused on conflict-ridden regions of the DRC and neighboring countries (referred to collectively as the "DRC region)" and a set of four minerals that came to be known as the 3TG: gold, coltan, tungsten, and tin.[11]

Global Witness continued to be one of the most visible campaigners on these issues, but other new groups entered the fray, such as the NGO Enough. Based in the United States, Enough was founded in 2006 by people who were frustrated by the ineffectiveness of existing efforts to end the violence in Sudan and the DRC. Enough focused attention on conflict minerals but strategically chose to lobby the US Congress and pressure a different end of the supply chain – commercial buyers of these minerals that use them in electronics and automobiles. Whereas the diamond industry targeted by the earlier campaign worried about individual consumers and their penchant for buying diamond jewelry, the later campaign focused on a different industry entirely as a source of leverage over the supply chain for these other conflict minerals.

---

[10] The debate over this issue continues as the United States and European member states continue to press for a redefinition of what it means for a gemstone to be a "conflict diamond."

[11] Col-tan (columbite-tantalite) provides tantalum, cassiterite is needed for tin, and wolframite is a source of tungsten.

Out of this new campaign grew a range of initiatives to establish standards of "due diligence" and "responsible sourcing" in addition to continued calls for certification. These include the OECD Due Diligence Guidance for Responsible Supply Chains of Minerals from Conflict-Affected and High-Risk Areas (hereafter the OECD Due Diligence Guidance), the UN Due Diligence Guidelines of the Group of Experts on the DRC (UN Due Diligence), the Section 1502 provisions of the US Dodd-Frank Financial Reform Act, supply chain initiatives sponsored by industry groups, regional certification proposals for the Great Lakes region as a whole and within specific individual countries, and others under consideration in the European Union and elsewhere. These initiatives varied in which regulatory mechanism they adopted (certification, due diligence, responsible sourcing, transparency), the level of governance (national, regional, international), industry scale (firm, sector, supply chain), and private-sector participation (public, private, multistakeholder) (see Table 5.1).

The four conflict minerals that feature in current campaigns all have a sectoral organization that is very different from the diamond industry, which was highly structured, well organized at every stage of the production process, and dominated by a single firm. How these industries are structured affects the degree to which they are reputationally vulnerable in the face of activist campaigns. Many of them have complicated processing paths, and the supply chain is much more complex than that for gem diamonds. Coltan is a resource that is almost completely unknown among regular consumers, and the same is true for tungsten. Neither has a particularly strong industry association in place. Tin is widely used, but there are no firms that stand out recognizably for their tin production. The tin industry is in many ways the most highly organized, having until recently been organized as a cartel among both producing and consuming countries (but excluding the United States), but the cartel collapsed in 2005. The International Tin Research Institute (ITRI), a tin industry association based in London, represents the tin industry in negotiations over conflict minerals. Only gold is subject to some of the same structural and reputational dynamics as diamonds. There are a few fairly well-known corporations, such as BHP Billiton and Rio Tinto, but they are not brand-name companies recognizable to the average consumer. The World Gold Council represents the interests of the twenty-three leading gold firms and claims to be the "global authority on gold" (www.gold.org).

Table 5.1 *Primary governance institutions for conflict minerals, 2003–2013*

	KPCS	CFS	WGC	OECD	Dodd-Frank	UN GoE-DRC	ICGLR
Governance Level	International	International	International	International	National	International	Regional
Industry scale	Supply chain – diamond	Smelters/refiners – four minerals	Supply chain – gold	Supply chain – all	Supply chain – all	DRC	DRC region
Governing Actors	Multi-stakeholder	Industry	Industry	International organization, multistakeholder	US	UN Security Council	Regional governments
Mechanism	Certification, chain of custody, trade controls	Assessment, audits	CSR standards	Due diligence standards, traceability	Reporting, due diligence, traceability	Due diligence standards	Certification

KPCS, Kimberley Process Certification Scheme; CFS, Conflict-Free Smelter scheme; WGC, World Gold Council; OECD, Organisation for Economic Cooperation and Development; Dodd-Frank, Section 1502 of the US Wall Street Reform and Consumer Protection Act; UN GoE-DRC, United Nations Group of Experts for the Democratic Republic of the Congo; ICGLR, International Conference of the Great Lakes Region

The producing countries are also very different from those involved in diamonds, with the source of the minerals distributed widely. Coltan is primarily found in Brazil, which produces over three-quarters of the mineral for world markets. Relatively small amounts are produced in the DRC, but they are an important source of export revenue for the country. The main sources of gold, tin, and tungsten have shifted from Africa to China and Russia over the past decade, and these countries are now the major producers of 3TG (Research and Markets 2011; British Geological Survey 2012). These are countries that are less interested in settling resource conflicts in Africa or in regulating global production of minerals. In both industry structure and geographical distribution of production, the 3TG conflict minerals are more complicated to address than diamonds.

The regulation of the 3TG conflict minerals has gone down two main paths: voluntary industry supply chain initiatives and state and multi-stakeholder regulation of supply chains. The discussion that follows is not strictly in chronological order but instead, for reasons of clarity, focuses on each separate initiative. They were all established within the past six years, with most of them being launched in only the last two years.

The NGO Enough, through its Raise Hope for Congo campaign, specifically targeted the electronics sector instead of the minerals producers. Its partners in the campaign include both local DRC nonprofits and a number of US and international NGOs, such as Amnesty International, Oxfam, and others. The electronics sector, which includes big names such as HP, Apple, and Microsoft, was more vulnerable to criticism by this campaign than were producers of coltan or tin. When Enough labeled Apple as complicit in the conflict for sourcing their raw materials from the DRC, it targeted one of the most visible companies in the world. Apple responded initially with a commitment to clean up its supply chain, address labor issues, and participate in an industry initiative to assure that its raw materials do not come from areas of conflict (Apple 2012).

Early on, the electronics industry had responded to activist criticism on a number of issues by forming the Electronic Industry Citizenship Coalition (EICC) to develop a general code of conduct for CSR in supply chain sourcing. When the conflict minerals campaign began, the EICC partnered with the Global eSustainability Initiative (GeSI, a partnership of industry and nonprofits) to analyze the tin supply chain and identify a way to implement a conflict minerals program (Resolve 2010). It pointed to tin smelters as a choke point in the supply chain – there are relatively few smelters, they are located close to the point of production, and it would be relatively easy to identify the sources of what they processed. The EICC-GeSI partnership went on to establish a Conflict Free Smelter (CFS) program to identify conflict-free smelters. There is no certification system, but instead smelters and refiners voluntarily ask to be assessed by auditors as to whether their operations are conflict-free (Electronic Industries Citizenship Coalition 2013). The EICC and GeSI do not require their members to make use of this program, and it is completely voluntary but is available for all buyers of tin, tantalum, tungsten, and gold to use.

At the same time as the EICC-GeSI smelter program was being developed, the tin industry, through the ITRI, began to explore development of a voluntary conflict-free traceability and due diligence program, the ITRI Tin Supply Chain Initiative (referred to as the ITSCi). It basically operates from the mine to the smelter and is a "bag-and-tag" program to ensure that companies can identify the source of the minerals they buy. The ITRI also worked with the tantalum industry to develop this system. In 2012, slowly following the lead of the tin industry and pressure from other state-led initiatives, the World Gold Council (WGC) developed its own Conflict-Free Gold Standard. This is a voluntary initiative that applies to mines located in conflict-affected or high-risk areas; it requires members of the WGC to meet corporate responsibility standards and issue a statement of conformity. In addition, members must meet the due diligence requirements of the OECD Guidance (described later).

The state-led initiatives also varied greatly in terms of membership, scope, and regulatory mechanisms. In 2009, the OECD convened a series of multistakeholder meetings with the ICGLR (a regional organization) to develop guidelines on supply chain due diligence. These meetings included representatives of civil society, including activist groups such as Enough, Global Witness, and International Alert; industry players from the DRC, the minerals sector, and major mining and electronics firms; interested governments; and other international organizations. The latter included the UN Group of Experts on the DRC and the UN Stabilization Mission in the DRC (MONUSCO). Activists were generally skeptical of the OECD process, which they saw as leading to a weak lowest common denominator framework.[12] In the end, the meetings and consultations produced the OECD Guidance on Responsible Supply Chains of Minerals from Conflict-Affected and High-Risk Areas, adopted in 2011 and revised to include a gold supplement the next year. The Guidance encourages voluntary annual reporting and due diligence in supply chain management for tin, tungsten, tantalum, and gold from areas of conflict or high risk (OECD 2011). "Due diligence" refers to the responsibility to know who you do business with and the risks and circumstances surrounding your business, particularly those relating to human rights. The OECD currently is working within the DRC region on the ground to help the regional mineral sector develop supply chain management, due diligence, and reporting standards of its own (OECD 2010).

The UN Expert Group on the DRC also produced a report at the time of the OECD negotiations and recommended that the UN Security Council also adopt due diligence guidelines to complement sanctions. The report recommended that these guidelines should explicitly reference the OECD Guidance in establishing UN standards. The Security Council approved this report and established a due diligence framework for all sanctions targeting conflict minerals. In response to both the OECD Guidance and UN-sanctioned due diligence requirements, the ICGLR itself began to develop and implement its own regional certification system. It is working with the OECD, the ITRI, the nonprofit Partnership Africa Canada, and the German consultants GIZ in developing this system. Unlike the KPCS, the development of this system is clearly a state-led initiative but has the support and assistance of industry and activist organizations.

In this second wave of activism surrounding conflict minerals, the US Congress was a prominent target as activist groups such as Enough and Global Witness sought a legislative solution to the issue. They did not believe the relevant industry sectors were moving fast enough or going far enough in their proposals to end the trade in conflict minerals. The activists focused all their attention on stopping the bloodshed in the DRC. What they sought was traditional regulation, backed up by the authority of the US government, instead of the voluntary guidelines being produced by the OECD and industry initiatives. For many years, Representative Jim McDermott had

---

[12] Personal communication (2009).

proposed legislation on this issue, but it was not until 2009 that it garnered wider support. Senators Brownback, Durbin, and Feingold succeeded in attaching what became Section 1502 to the Dodd-Frank Wall Street Reform and Consumer Protection Act of 2010. It requires companies listed on the US stock exchange to identify whether any product they make depends on any of the 3TG minerals; if so, the firm must exercise due diligence in tracing the source and determining whether it is from the DRC region, and it must publish this information (PwC 2011). Trade in conflict minerals is not forbidden under the law, unlike the rules of the KPCS, but the expectation is that this transparency will reduce or eliminate the market for them. After a long public comment period and much foot dragging in the face of significant industry opposition, the Securities and Exchange Commission (SEC) produced implementation guidelines at the end of 2012.

The passage of US legislation deeply affected all other regulatory schemes for the 3TG minerals and pushed laggards to move forward with their own proposals. The EU as a whole and individual European governments are currently considering similar legislation.[13] The OECD and UN Security Council have both issued statements regarding the compatibility of their guidance with the reporting requirements of Section 1502. The World Gold Council, which had been slow to act on the issue, finally published its own corporate responsibility standards, and the London Bullion Market Association established a voluntary due diligence program for gold refiners; both of these reference the OECD Guidance and the Dodd-Frank rules. The CFS program explicitly adjusted its assurance program to fit with the Dodd-Frank rules, in addition to incorporating the OECD Guidance on due diligence (Roesen and Levin 2011).

Needless to say, business groups such as the US Chamber of Commerce and National Association of Manufacturers have condemned the regulations as intrusive and burdensome and lobbied to weaken or repeal the measure. Many citizens of the DRC itself argue that the regulations amount to an informal trade embargo that is

[13] The new UK Bribery Act, which came into effect in July 2011, is seen by some as giving the reporting requirements of the US Dodd-Frank legislation "big teeth"; the Bribery Act requires due diligence of any company doing business in the UK, with criminal consequences (http://conflictminerals.co.uk/conflict-minerals-reporting-requirements/the-bribery-act-2011/).

undermining the peaceful development of the majority of the DRC (Taylor 2012).[14] Despite the pushback, the affected firms are beginning to put in place systems to identify the source of minerals they use, report the results, audit due diligence, and address the need to ensure that resources from conflict zones do not fall into the hands of rebel forces.

This is a very brief overview of the evolution of institutions to regulate the trade in conflict minerals from 2000 to the present. This issue area is still evolving and even this short description misses some of the efforts that are still being developed. The following section discusses the differences in institutions between the two periods, highlighting institutional variation and the factors that influenced outcomes.

Variation in institutions to regulate conflict minerals

This overview of the past decade reveals the degree of contrast between the earlier and later periods – between the single institution regulating the diamond industry and the many initiatives focused on tin, tantalum, tungsten, and gold. The regulatory institutions that emerged in the second time period display a wide range of variation in governance level, industry scale, governing actors, and mechanisms (see Table 5.1). Whereas the Kimberley Process is a global initiative covering all the major producer and consumer states and the entire diamond sector supply chain, some of the later initiatives are more limited. Some are formulated by only one country (Section 1502 by the United States, certification by and for Rwanda), whereas others are truly global with regard to who makes decisions (OECD Guidance). But even something like the Dodd-Frank legislation by the US government is ultimately global in its impact because it affects international firms and their global suppliers.

These institutions differ in the roles played by states and non-state actors. The Kimberley Process was developed in a multistakeholder

---

[14] The easiest way to avoid trouble is to avoid buying anything from the DRC altogether, which undermines the economic recovery of peaceful areas of the country. USAID launched a public-private initiative to promote responsible purchasing from the DRC to counter the emergence of a de facto boycott of the country. Some companies have created "closed" pipelines from the source to their own end products.

process and is implemented through a partnership among industry, governments, and civil society. The OECD Guidance was developed through a multistakeholder consultation, but the OECD itself is an interstate organization, although implementation of the Guidance is by industry itself. The UN Security Council is also an interstate organization, with decisions and implementation by states. The ICGLR is a regional interstate organization, with decisions made by member states. In contrast, the CFS program was developed by a partnership between industry and NGOs, with no government participation. The World Gold Council, the ITRI, and the TIC are all purely private sector organizations in which the private sector negotiated its own standards and organizations.

Although the Kimberley Process only applies to the diamond sector, succeeding initiatives vary in what minerals they address. Some apply to only one mineral (the World Gold Council standards), some start with one and expand to include others (the smelter initiative began with tin smelters and grew to include smelters and refiners of all four minerals). The OECD Guidance was intended from the start for all four, but focused initially on tin, tantalum, and tungsten, only later adding a supplement for gold.

The type of regulatory mechanisms adopted in the later phase departed from the KPCS model. The KPCS is both an industry certification system and a government-run trade control regime. No later initiative copied this model in its entirety. For the other conflict minerals, a weak regional certification system is being developed by the ICGLR (and one is also being developed within Rwanda). The CFS is an assurance system that is somewhat like a certification system but without formal certifications. Smelters volunteer to be part of the CFS, and other firms choose whether or not to do business with CFS firms. The World Gold Council promotes a corporate responsibility standard. The dominant trend in the past few years is the adoption of various forms of due diligence and supply chain transparency, with the OECD Guidance becoming the global standard. Unlike the other initiatives, Section 1502 is traditional law, mandatory for any corporation listed on US stock exchanges. It requires due diligence, reporting, and auditing – but it does not actually ban the use of minerals from the DRC region.

What factors might explain this range of variation? Previously, I drew from the literature a set of factors that are commonly considered: state power, institutional competition and convergence, activist strategies, and industry structure and organization. First, we can look at the configuration of state power and interest in the two time periods and across different industry markets.

The United States is, across time and industry, the major consumer market. It is at the same time the government that is most concerned with state breakdown and violence, and the one most likely to be called upon to intervene directly in foreign conflicts. The United States provides extensive humanitarian aid and development assistance to countries in conflict and postconflict reconstruction. It is not surprising, therefore, that the United States was a key player in both periods. In the case of diamonds, the United States could support the Kimberley Process as a second-best means of addressing a humanitarian crisis in Angola and Sierra Leone without direct military intervention. It directly participated in the creation and implementation of the KPCS; there were no alternative institutions – no regime complex, no competing organizations to manipulate. After 2006, this situation changed with the proliferation of conflict minerals initiatives. The United States essentially engaged in forum-shopping when domestic political actors called for a more stringent system and passed the Dodd-Frank legislation.

The initiative for a certification scheme came from the diamond industry itself, but it was helped along by the support of the diamond producing states, led by South Africa and Botswana. They wanted to ensure the continued health of a major export market and source of employment and wealth for their country. For all of them, the certification of rough diamonds via the creation of a new international organization appeared to be the perfect solution to everyone's problems. This kind of consensus did not exist for other minerals. The major producer states for tin, tantalum, tungsten, and gold were widely dispersed around the globe and less worried about any reputational threat to the market. The DRC region itself – the target of all this activity – is not a significant producer of tin, tungsten, or tantalum, and there are many alternative sources for gold. The 3TG initiatives were driven more by consumer states than producers.

Despite the apparent institutional variation, there has been a striking effort to ensure compatibility among all these systems. This is partly because each addresses certain stages in the production process or certain steps in regulation, and, although they overlap, they do not directly compete with each other. There is nothing similar to the competition between multistakeholder and industry initiatives that we see in other issue areas (such as forestry). There has been convergence toward the OECD Guidance for due diligence by both industry and state-led programs. The most significant impact of Section 1502 legislation has been as a powerful force for rationalization of the proliferation of different institutions. Other programs rushed to ensure that their standards and processes were compatible with US law because the United States is the main consumer market and US companies the main buyers of conflict minerals. It also provided a strong incentive for industry to develop systems of implementation and to work collaboratively to develop common processes and procedures. The CFS program has developed a common reporting tool, three gold sector organizations have agreed to recognize each others' standards, the EICC-GeSI partnership offers a common template, and the auto industry is now developing its own reporting standards and template.

The structure of the diamond industry and the vulnerability of diamonds to reputational threat made it relatively simple for transnational activists to launch a successful campaign. The highly concentrated and well-organized diamond industry, one in which DeBeers was the major player but in a surprisingly vulnerable position, was able to develop a consensus supporting a certification system in response to the blood diamond campaign. No similar firm dominates any of the 3TG minerals trade, although there are some very large mining firms involved (such as BHP Billiton and Rio Tinto), and firms from China and Russia are major players today. Industry associations are relatively weak, and limited cross-industry cooperation makes it difficult to formulate a common approach.[15] The production processes for these minerals are more complex than those for diamonds, and it is the reputations of users – the electronics industry, for instance – and not producers that are at stake. In fact, it is the electronics industry that has been at the forefront in the development of regulation for the minerals trade.

Activists played a key role in establishing the very idea of conflict minerals and the need to regulate them in some fashion. But as different NGOs emerged to take on the issue, they chose to pursue different strategies, thus "partitioning" their resources and establishing their

---

[15] The International Council on Mining and Minerals (ICMM) has been active in seeking to create consensus across the different minerals sectors on the conflict minerals issue.

own niche (Soule and King 2008). The campaign regarding the 3TG minerals, led in the United States by Enough and its Raise Hope for Congo campaign, focused primarily on consumer electronics companies as the vulnerable firms, instead of producers. They identified smelting and refining as a point of leverage in the production process and supported the development of the CFS. They viewed the Kimberley Process as a flawed model and the OECD consultation as a weak alternative. In response, they sought a traditional US legislative outcome – mandatory, enforceable, and with teeth.

Each of the factors identified in the literature helps to explain the institutional variation in conflict minerals regulation, but they matter at different times and interact with each other in different ways. The power of the United States and its ability to literally change the game for everyone else through its domestic policy supports mainstream international relations theories. But the exercise of this power mattered most in the past few years and was less important to the Kimberley Process, where industry consensus mattered more. Regime complexity had no influence on the Kimberley Process when no other institutions existed, but the proliferation of initiatives for the 3TG minerals created a more complex institutional environment. Some of that proliferation was due to industry initiatives, not state-led ones. Local and regional systems initiated by some producer states tended to be a pragmatic response to the need to assure that their exports would meet evolving standards set by the OECD and the United States, and not the strategic effort to create a forum favorable to state interests envisioned by the regime complex literature. Industry structure and activist strategies clearly interacted with each other and affected the interests of producer and consumer states.

CSR in a globalizing world

This chapter started with the observation that institutional outcomes within a single, narrowly defined issue area varied in significant ways over time. The variation occurred across a number of dimensions – level of governance, scale of industry, governing actors, and regulatory mechanism. The complexity of this variation within such a small number of cases and sectors poses many challenges to the systematic exploration of outcomes. Here, I sought to provide an overview of the variation at a macro-level, comparing institution-building in two time periods. This overview identifies variables drawn from the literature that influenced the number and character of institutions and the pathways through which those variables interacted with each other.

Regulatory institutions for conflict minerals reflect the larger diffusion of CSR norms across the globe and into the most remote and even unstable areas of the world. These norms are institutionalized over time in different ways, reflecting the particular interactions among states, firms, and activists at varied times and places. This chapter highlights an issue area in which this kind of institution-building is unexpected – issues of war and peace, conflict and security are not those where we expect CSR norms to hold sway. Over the course of the past fifteen years, the idea that business has a responsibility to promote peace and security has become increasingly well established (Haufler 2010). Some even refer to the "security responsibility" of corporations instead of social responsibility (Deitelhoff and Wolf 2010).

The UN Global Compact has an entire policy stream focused on CSR for business in zones of conflict. Security issues have been one of the elements addressed in the Principles for Responsible Investment, a set of guidelines for foreign investment. Increasing numbers of governments have signed on to the Extractive Industries Transparency Initiative (EITI), which seeks to address conflict and corruption through transparency requirements for governments and extractive firms. The Principles for Human Rights and Security establishes guidelines for companies hiring private security forces or relying on government protection in unstable parts of the world. The conflict minerals issue is only one small part of this larger agenda, and the question of why we see wide variation in institutional outcomes also applies to this wider arena.

What impact have all these efforts had? We have some evidence on the KPCS since its implementation in 2003, but it is too soon to tell what the ultimate effect of the most recent programs will be. The same year that the KPCS came into existence, both Sierra Leone and Angola began serious peace negotiations, and both have maintained relative peace within their borders since that time. Since 2003, trade in legitimate diamonds has expanded, which can be attributed both to the Kimberley Process and to the settlement of civil conflicts. Since its founding, the KPCS has faced constant challenges in terms of monitoring and oversight and the undermining of the system by smuggling, corruption, and disagreement over its purpose: to address conflict or to address the broader human rights agenda.

The more recent initiatives have barely begun to be implemented, with many pilot and trial initiatives on the ground in the DRC region. Companies are beginning to implement due diligence frameworks and attempting to ensure that they have a "clean" supply chain. The US legislation has already been a powerful lever to push firms to provide more information on the source of their materials. If implemented fully, it will have a significant impact on the way in which major corporations around the world manage their business, with ripple effects throughout global supply chains.

Will due diligence, transparency, reporting, and certification undermine rebel activity and bring about a peaceful resolution of conflict? These certainly increase the cost for rebels of financing their fight through the minerals trade, but they will not eliminate conflict minerals entirely. Smuggling and corruption will remain an issue in countries with weak governments, and, in many cases, there are alternative sources of finance, including minerals not covered by existing institutions (for instance, other gemstones). However, the push for due diligence and better management of the supply chain have the potential to be a platform for capacity-building and good governance in resource-rich states.

The expansion of CSR norms to the arena of war and peace is a strong affirmation of the change in societal expectations regarding corporate behavior. As more companies reach into every corner of the world, they bring with them the spotlight of attention. Consumers are demanding more information about the materials and processes that go into the products they purchase. Companies can no longer distance themselves from what happens on the ground in the places where they operate. They find themselves subject to an increasing array of CSR programs designed to force companies to manage their global supply chains in more socially acceptable ways.

References

Alter, Karen J., and Sophie Meunier. 2009. "The Politics of International Regime Complexity." *Perspectives on Politics* 7(01):13–24.

Apple. 2012. *Apple Supplier Responsibility Report*. Retrieved from www.apple.com/supplier-responsibility.

Auld, Graeme, Steven Bernstein, and Benjamin Cashore. 2008. "The New Corporate Social Responsibility." *Annual Review of Environment and Resources* 33 (1):413–435.

Ballentine, Karen, and Jake Sherman. 2003. *The Political Economy of Armed Conflict: Beyond Greed and Grievance*. Boulder and London: Lynne Rienner.

Banfield, Jessica, Damian Lilly, and Virginia Haufler. 2003. *Transnational Corporations in Conflict-Prone Zones: Public Policy Responses and a Framework for Action*. London: International Alert.

Bartley, Tim. 2010. "Transnational Private Regulation in Practice: The Limits of Forest and Labor Standards Certification in Indonesia." *Business and Politics* 12(3): 1–34.

Bartley, Tim, and Curtis Child. 2014. "Shaming the Corporation: The Social Production of Targets and the Anti-Sweatshop Movement." *American Sociological Review* 79 (4): 653–679.

Bartley, Tim, and Shawna Smith. 2008. *Structuring Transnational Fields of Governance: Network Evolution and Boundary Setting in the World of Standards*. Working Paper. Bloomington: Indiana University.

Bates, Robert H. 2008. "State Failure." *Annual Review of Political Science* 11(1):1–12.

Beckert, Jens. 2010. "Institutional Isomorphism Revisited: Convergence and Divergence in Institutional Change." *Sociological Theory* 28(2):150–166.

Bendell, Jem. 2009. *The Corporate Responsibility Movement: Five Years of Global Corporate Responsibility Analysis from Lifeworth, 2001–2005*. Sheffield: Greenleaf.

Berdal, Mats, and David M. Malone. 2000. *Greed and Grievance: Economic Agendas in Civil Wars*. Boulder, CO: Lynne Rienner.

British Geological Survey. 2012. *World Mineral Production 2006–2010*. Nottingham, England: British Geological Survey.

Cashore, Benjamin, Graeme Auld, and Deanna Newsom. 2004. *Governing through Markets: Forest Certification and the Emergence of Non-state Authority*. New Haven, CT: Yale University Press.

Collier, Paul. 2003. "Natural Resources, Development, and Conflict: Channels of Causation and Policy Interventions." April 28. Washington, DC: World Bank, 1–13.

Collier, Paul, and Anke Hoeffler. 2000. "Greed and Grievance in Civil War." Pp. 1–44 in *World Bank Working Paper Series*. Washington, DC: World Bank.

Deitelhoff, Nicole, and Klaus Dieter Wolf. 2010. *Corporate Security Responsibility?: Corporate Governance Contributions to Peace and Security in Zones of Conflict*. Hampshire, UK: Palgrave MacMillan.

DiMaggio, Paul J., and Walter W. Powell. 1983. "The Iron Cage Revisited: Institutional Isomorphism and Collective Rationality in Organizational Fields." *American Sociological Review* 48(2):147–160.

Dingwerth, Klaus, and Philipp Pattberg. 2009. "World Politics and Organizational Fields: The Case of Transnational Sustainability Governance." *European Journal of International Relations* 15(4):707–743.

Dobbin, Frank, Beth Simmons, and Geoffrey Garrett. 2007. "The Global Diffusion of Public Policies: Social Construction, Coercion, Competition, or Learning?" *Annual Review of Sociology* 33(1):449–472.

Drezner, Daniel. 2007. *All Politics Is Global: Explaining International Regulatory Regimes*. Princeton, NJ: Princeton University Press.

Eberlein, Burkard, Kenneth W. Abbott, Julia Black, Errol Meidinger, and Stepan Wood. 2014. "Transnational Business Governance Interactions: Conceptualization and Framework for Analysis." *Regulation & Governance* 8(1):1–21.

Electronic Industries Citizenship Coalition. 2013. *Conflict-Free Smelter Program*. Retrieved May 30, 2013, from http://www.eicc.info/CFS Program.shtml.

Esty, Daniel. 1998. *State Failure Task Force Report: Phase II*. Washington, DC: State Failure Task Force.

Fort, Timothy. 2007. Business, Integrity, and Peace: Beyond Geopolitical and Disciplinary Boundaries. In *Business, Value Creation, and Society*, edited by R. Edward Freeman, Stuart L. Hart, and David Wheeler. Cambridge: Cambridge University Press.

Fort, Timothy L., and Cindy A. Schipani. 2004. *The Role of Business in Fostering Peaceful Societies*. Cambridge: Cambridge University Press.

Fowler, Robert R. 2000. *Report of the Panel of Experts on Violations of Security Council Sanctions against UNITA*. New York: United Nations Security Council.

Gereffi, Gary, John Humphrey, and Timothy Sturgeon. 2005. "The Governance of Global Value Chains." *Review of International Political Economy* 12(1):78–104.

Green, Jessica F., and Graeme Auld. 2011. "Unbundling the Regime Complex: The Effects of Private Authority."

Grindle, Merilee S. 2007. "Good Enough Governance Revisited." *Development Policy Review* 25(5):533–574.

Haufler, Virginia. 2010. "Governing Corporations in Zones of Conflict: Issues, Actors, and Institutions." Pp. 102–130 in *Who Governs the*

Globe?, edited by D. Avant, M. Finnemore, and S. Sell. Cambridge: Cambridge University Press.

Heritier, Adrienne, and Dirk Lehmkuhl. 2008. "The Shadow of Hierarchy and New Modes of Governance." *Journal of Public Policy* 28(01):1–17.

Hiscox, Michael J. and Nicholas Smyth. 2011. "Is There Consumer Demand for Fair Labor Standards? Evidence from a Field Experiment." Retrieved from http://ssrn.com/abstract=1820642.

Humphreys, Macartan, Jeffrey D. Sachs, and Joseph E. Stiglitz. 2007. *Escaping the Resource Curse*. Cambridge: Cambridge University Press.

Karl, Terry Lynn. 1997. *The Paradox of Plenty: Oil Booms and Petro-States*. Los Angeles and San Francisco: University of California Press.

Keohane, Robert O., and David G. Victor. 2011. "The Regime Complex for Climate Change." *Perspectives on Politics* 9(01):7–23.

King, Brayden G, and Mary Hunter McDonnell. 2015; this volume. "Good Firms, Good Targets: The Relationship among Corporate Social Responsibility, Reputation, and Activist Targeting." Pp. 430–454 in Corporate Social Responsibility in a Globalizing World, edited by K. Tsutsui and A. Lim. New York: Cambridge University Press.

Kitzmueller, Markus, and Jay Shimshack. 2012. "Economic Perspectives on Corporate Social Responsibility." *Journal of Economic Literature* 50(1):51–84.

Klein, Naomi. 1999. *No Logo: Taking Aim at the Brand Bullies*. New York: Picador Press.

Kostova, Tatiana, Kendall Roth, and M. Dacin. 2008. "Note: Institutional Theory in the Study of Multinational Corporations: A Critique and New Directions." *Academy of Management Review ARCHIVE* 33(4):994–1006.

Lim, Alwyn, and Kiyoteru Tsutsui. 2012. "Globalization and Commitment in Corporate Social Responsibility: Cross-National Analyses of Institutional and Political-Economy Effects." *American Sociological Review* 77(1):69–98.

Luong, Pauline Jones, and Erika Weinthal. 2006. "Rethinking the Resource Curse: Ownership Structure, Institutional Capacity, and Domestic Constraints." *Annual Review of Political Science* 9(1):241–263.

MacDonald, Kate. 2014. *The Politics of Global Supply Chains*. Cambridge and Oxford: Polity.

Mearsheimer, John. 1994. "The False Promise of International Institutions." *International Security* 15(1):5–56.

Meyer, John W., Shawn M. Pope, and Andrew Isaacson. 2015; this volume. "Legitmating the Transnational Corporation in a Stateless World

Society." Pp. 27–72 in Corporate Social Responsibility in a Globalizing World," edited by K. Tsutsui and A. Lim. New York: Cambridge University Press.

Nelson, Jane. 2000. *The Business of Peace: The Private Sector as a Partner in Conflict Prevention and Resolution*. London: Prince of Wales Business Leaders Forum.

OECD. 2011. *OECD Due Diligence Guidance for Responsible Supply Chain of Minerals from Conflict-Affected and High-Risk Areas*. Paris: OECD.

O'Rourke, Dara. 2003. "Outsourcing Regulation: Analyzing Nongovernmental Systems of Labor Standards and Monitoring." *Policy Studies Journal* 31(1):1–29.

Orsini, Amandine, Jean-Frédéric Morin, and Oran Young. 2013. "Regime Complexes: A Buzz, a Boom, or a Boost for Global Governance?" *Global Governance* 19(1):27–40.

Powell, Walter W. 2007. "The New Institutionalism." Pp. 976–980 in *The International Encyclopedia of Organization Studies*. Thousand Oaks, CA: Sage Publications.

Prakash, Aseem, and Mary Kay Gugerty. 2010. *Advocacy Organizations and Collective Action*. Cambridge: Cambridge University Press.

PwC. 2011. "The Dodd-Frank Wall Street Reform and Consumer Protection Act: Impact on Disclosures Related to the Use of 'Conflict Minerals.'" *A Closer Look* April: 1–9. Retrieved from www.pwcregulatory.com.

Raustiala, Kal, and David G. Victor. 2004. "The Regime Complex for Plant Genetic Resources." *International Organization* 58(02): 147–154.

Reno, William. 1999. *Warlord Politics and African States*. Boulder, CO: Lynne Rienner.

Research and Markets. 2011. *Global and Chinese Tantalum Industry Report 2011*. Dublin, Ireland: Research and Markets.

Resolve. 2010. *Tracing a Path Forward: A Study of the Challenges of the Supply Chain for Target Metals Used in Electronics*. Washington, DC: Resolve.

Roesen, Gisa, and Estelle Levin. 2011. *Conformance and Compatibility Analysis: CFS, iTSCi, and the OECD Due Diligence Guidance*. Cambridge: Estelle Levin.

Ross, Michael. 2003. "Oil, Drugs and Diamonds: The Varying Roles of Natural Resources in Civil War." Pp. 47–70 in *The Political Economy of Armed Conflict: Beyond Greed and Grievance*, edited by Karen Ballentine and Jake Sherman. Boulder, CO: Lynne Rienner.

2006. "A Closer Look at Oil, Diamonds, and Civil War." *Annual Review of Political Science* 9:265–300.

Soule, Sarah A. 2009. *Contention and Corporate Social Responsibility*. Cambridge: Cambridge University Press.
Soule, Sarah A., and Braydon King. 2008. "Competition and Resource Partitioning in Three Social Movements." *American Journal of Sociology* 116(6):1568–1610.
Spar, Debora L. 1998. "The Spotlight and the Bottom Line: How Multinationals Export Human Rights." *Foreign Affairs* 77(2):7–12.
Taylor, Celia. 2012. "Conflict Minerals and SEC Disclosure Regulation." *Harvard Business Law Review online* 2(1):105–120.
Tolbert, Pamela S., and Lynne G. Zucker. 1983. "Institutional Sources of Change in the Formal Structure of Organizations: The Diffusion of Civil Service Reform, 1880–1935." *Administrative Science Quarterly* 28(1):22–39.
United Press International. 2000 "DeBeers Wants Improved US Relations." *UPI Wire Service*, January 31, 2000.
Utting, Peter. 2005. "Rethinking Business Regulation: From Self-Regulation to Social Control." Pp. 1–29 in *Technology, Business and Society Programme Paper 15 September*. Geneva: UNRISD.
Vogel, David. 2006. *The Market for Virtue*. Washington, DC: Brookings Institution Press.
Weiss, Thomas. 2000. "Governance, Good Governance, and Global Governance: Conceptual and Actual Challenges." *Third World Quarterly* 21(5):795–814.
Wolf, Klaus Dieter, Nicole Dietelhoff, and Stefan Engert. 2007. "Corporate Security Responsibility: Towards a Conceptual Framework for Comparative Research." *Cooperation and Conflict* 42 (3): 294–320.
World Bank Social Development Department. 2010. *Demand for Good Governance at the World Bank: Conceptual Evolution, Frameworks and Activities*. Geneva: World Bank.

6 | *The institutionalization of supply chain corporate social responsibility: field formation in comparative context*

JENNIFER BAIR AND FLORENCE PALPACUER

On December 14, 2010, twenty-nine people perished in a factory fire in Dhaka, Bangladesh. At the time of the fire, the factory, "That's It Sportswear," was subcontracting for several well-known brands and retailers, including Gap, J.C. Penney, and Abercrombie & Fitch. In the aftermath of the tragedy, activists called on these and other leading American and European companies to address the high incidence of fire-related workplace deaths occurring annually in Bangladesh. On March 21, 2012, one of the brands that had been placing orders with the factory at the time of the fire, Philips Van Heusen (PVH), signed a contractual, two-year landmark fire safety agreement. Under this agreement, which had been negotiated with local and international nongovernmental organizations (INGOs) and trade unions, Philips Van Heusen committed to spending at least $1 million on improving worker safety via independent inspection of its Bangladeshi suppliers, disclosure and remediation of inspection results, and the creation of worker-led health and safety committees in all supplier factories. Given the lack of an equity relationship between PVH and its subcontractors, and in the absence of any legal obligation on the part of PVH toward the workers employed by its suppliers, how do we explain PVH's voluntary decision to make these commitments? The Bangladesh fire safety agreement is an outgrowth of the phenomenon analyzed in this chapter, which we call "supply chain corporate social responsibility (CSR)": the discourses and practices by which firms voluntarily pledge to guarantee labor standards in the production facilities of independent suppliers.[1]

---

[1] Although we focus on labor issues, supply chain CSR may encompass environmental standards as well.

At one level, this phenomenon is not new; since the 1960s, there have been numerous initiatives to develop voluntary schemes addressing the social and developmental implications of multinational corporations and their overseas subsidiaries, particularly in the Global South. These include the OECD Guidelines for Multinational Enterprises (1976), the International Labour Organization (ILO) Tripartite Declaration of Principles concerning Multinational Enterprises and Social Policy (1977), and the United Nations' decade-long project to draft a code of conduct for multinational corporations. Supply chain CSR differs from these earlier projects because it involves corporate commitments to ensuring basic standards – health and safety, minimum wage compliance, protection from harassment and discrimination – not just in owned and operated facilities at home and abroad, but *also in the factories of overseas subcontractors*. Like other forms of voluntary CSR, supply chain CSR is premised on the claim that powerful economic actors have obligations that extend beyond the boundaries of their own organization. What is unique about supply chain CSR, however, is the degree to which it highlights *inter*-firm dynamics and, specifically, the role that corporations play as lead firms in global production networks.

In this chapter, we explore the development and diffusion of supply chain CSR with a specific focus on the organizations and organizational practices that constitute this field-in-formation. Our analysis of field formation reveals this to be a two-phase process. During the first phase, supply chain CSR emerged on both sides of the Atlantic in response to corporate campaigns and other activist strategies that focused attention on sweatshop conditions in international supply chains for apparel and footwear products in the late 1980s and early 1990s. Within a few years, most major retailers and brands were publicly pledging to ensure that their subcontractors complied with minimum labor standards, as outlined in various codes of conduct. Yet these measures failed to mollify anti-sweatshop activists, who complained that many lead firms did not live up to their commitments. Corporate critics demanded a role for civil society groups, including NGOs and trade unions, in developing and implementing supply chain monitoring and remediation programs. These demands gave rise to multistakeholder initiatives (MSIs) as a prominent organizational form in supply chain CSR. However, sustained challenges to the social compliance model eventually led to a second phase in the field formation process during which a new generation of private-led organizations reasserted a leading role for the business community in the governance of supply chain CSR. Yet this process is far from complete: the PVH fire safety agreement and its implementation and extension to dozens of other retailers following the deadly Rana Plaza factory collapse in Bangladesh in April 2013 may signal a new phase in the formation of this field, as we explain in the concluding section of this chapter.

What is supply chain CSR, and what explains its emergence?

Supply chain CSR presents some similarities to what Davis, Whitman, and Zald define as "global CSR": the principle that firms are "responsible for actions far beyond their boundaries, including the actions of suppliers, distributors, alliance partners, and even sovereign nations" (Davis, Whitman, and Zald 2008: 32). However, as we are defining it here, supply chain CSR is a more delimited concept, referring specifically to the responsibility of a client firm to guarantee minimum conditions in the factories of its subcontractors. Most analysts argue that supply chain CSR has emerged in response to changes in the global organization of production and especially the development of commodity chains that enable lead firms to coordinate the activities of independent, offshore suppliers (Bartley 2005; Riisgaard 2009; Mayer and Gereffi 2010). This globalization of production has not, as yet, been matched by a globalization of regulation since most of the legal frameworks that govern business practices, including wages and working conditions, operate at the national level. Supply chain CSR is seen by many as the private sector's voluntarist response to the global "regulation gap" (Scherer and Palazzo 2008).

However, it is important to note that the impetus for these policies came from outside the business community. Private governance of labor standards in supply chains emerged in response to the activism of civil society groups that mobilized around the sweatshop issue in a variety of ways, including public demonstrations and economic boycotts (Bartley 2003; Rodriguez-Garavito 2005). As we note later, many of the firms that were targeted during the first wave of corporate campaigns initially rejected the central claim made by activists – namely, that the companies coordinating global production networks are responsible for the actions of geographically distant and legally independent subcontractors. But in the face of growing controversy, most of these companies reversed course in relatively short order, as denials of lead firm responsibility were replaced by assurances that companies could indeed ensure decent working conditions in their supply chains by developing codes of conduct and monitoring the compliance of subcontractors with these instruments.

To date, there is relatively little evidence that codes of conduct and factory auditing regimes have produced more than isolated and/or short-term improvements in labor conditions. The bulk of the available evidence instead suggests that supply chain CSR has failed to eradicate, or perhaps even significantly reduce, the incidence of labor violations in factories producing light manufactures such as apparel, footwear, toys, and electronics (Institute for Development Studies [IDS] 2006; Locke, Qin, and Brause 2007; Raworth and Kidder 2008; Anner 2012). The determinants of noncompliance include "local" factors, such as the limited managerial capacities and resource constraints of (particularly developing-country) suppliers or the predominance of a gender-biased managerial culture facilitating the exploitation of women workers. Another key contributor to poor supplier performance is the dynamic of buyer-driven supply chains in which lead firm sourcing practices encourage violations, primarily via downward pressure on production costs (Carr, Chen, and Tate 2000; Esbenshade 2004; Ngai 2005; Locke, Amengual, and Mangla 2009; Weil 2010; Anner, Bair, and Blasi 2013). In short, the literature on labor compliance suggests that there is a substantial degree of decoupling between the claims that are made about the ability of CSR policies to improve conditions in manufacturing facilities worldwide and the actual outcomes in these factories.

Understanding why CSR policies have not proved more effective in cleaning up supply chains is a critically important task, but it is not the one we set for ourselves in this chapter.[2] Instead, we ask what the

---

[2] By "effective," we mean policies that actually improve working conditions or ensure basic labor rights and standards in supply chains. This departs from an institutional perspective that evaluates efficacy in terms of the success of legitimation efforts, although the relationship between these two valences of effectiveness is an important area for empirical exploration and theoretical development.

disjuncture between policy and practice implies about the new organizational field of supply chain CSR. Our view is that as the limits of supply chain CSR policies become increasingly evident, the decoupling between rhetoric and reality is no longer an outcome to be explained, but rather a defining feature of the CSR landscape, and one that is itself shaping the formation of the field.

In their contribution to this volume, Meyer, Pope, and Isaacson describe CSR as a process of institutionalization that espouses a form of global "corporate citizenship" and supports "expanded definitions of good practice as being in the legitimated business interests of a corporation" (2015: 25). Supply chain CSR concretizes this otherwise underspecified notion of the good corporate citizen into a more specific set of discourses about how companies should act towards others. In so doing, it renders this process of institutionalization tractable and open to empirical investigation – not just from the sociologist or organizational theorist, but also from the corporate critic or the labor rights activist. In this sense, supply chain CSR is both a reflection of the legitimation process described by Meyer et al, and an ongoing challenge to that process because it creates a set of expectations and benchmarks for what corporations must do to be socially responsible. If companies refuse to implement supply chain CSR or fail to keep their commitments to do so, the legitimacy of corporate power in world society may be undermined as opposed to strengthened.

In addition to shedding new light on the role of decoupling in field formation, studying the development of supply chain CSR *in comparative context* addresses one of the key debates within the CSR literature: specifically, the degree to which CSR is better understood as a singular phenomenon driven by the diffusion of normative scripts and institutional models that regulate corporate power in global civil society, as Meyer et al. contend, or as a varied set of practices that emerge from and are shaped by the specific institutional contexts within which firms and their stakeholders are embedded. As recently as 2007, Campbell identified this as a neglected area of CSR research, noting "that most of the literature on corporate social responsibility does not explore whether institutional conditions affect the tendency for firms to behave in socially responsible ways" (Campbell 2007: 948). However, a spate of recent studies have contributed to the elaboration of an institutional perspective on CSR (Maignan and

Ralston 2002; Williams and Aguilera 2008; Gjølberg 2009; Kang and Moon 2012).[3]

Much of this work on the comparative dimension of CSR draws inspiration from the varieties of capitalism tradition, which categorizes political economies according to institutional configurations that produce dominant patterns of coordination and/or conflict between social groups (Hall and Soskice 2001; Casper and Whitley 2004). The classic distinction within this literature is between liberal market economies (exemplified by the United States), in which markets are the major coordinating mechanism and labor-capital relations are more openly antagonistic, and coordinated market economies, found primarily in western and northern Europe, in which corporatist institutional configurations produce more collaborative relations between stakeholders. Precisely because the rights and responsibilities of corporations differ across these types of capitalism, historical institutionalists and comparative political economists expect variation in the timing and content of the CSR policies that are developed and implemented by firms in each. For example, some of the issues addressed via CSR policies in the United States are included in the social contracts structuring European political economies, thus resulting in a more "implicit" form of CSR in Europe, where the "scope for voluntary and explicit measures by corporations may be limited" (Brammer, Jackson, and Matten 2012: 13; also Matten and Moon 2008). According to this view, the more elaborated forms of CSR found in liberal market economies function as an *institutional substitute* for the social protections that are inherent in the welfare capitalism of coordinated market economies.[4]

An alternative hypothesis predicts that CSR functions not as a substitute for corporatist institutions, but rather as an *institutional mirror* of the broader political economy (Jackson and Apostalakou 2010). When stakeholders are organized and empowered, they are more likely to effectively lobby and make demands of corporations, and the private sector, in turn, is more likely to feel compelled to respond, resulting in more CSR in coordinated market economies than in their liberal

---

[3] See, for example, an entire special issue of the journal *Socio-Economic Review* (vol. 10, 2012) devoted to this theme.

[4] Although not subscribing to the comparative institutionalist perspective on CSR, Meyer, Pope, and Isaacson also expect that "CSR initiatives are most effective in countries where economic liberalization is the strongest" (2015: 27–79).

market counterparts. For example, "strong labor unions may use their influence to pressure companies to adopt labour standards throughout their supply chain or adopt programmes supporting diversity in the workplace" (Brammer, Jackson, and Matten 2012: 13).

A third position in this debate holds that CSR developments in different countries reflect a broader process of *institutional convergence* within and across both types of capitalism. Specifically, some scholars suggest that there is a general diffusion of an American-style shareholder model of corporate governance that is leading to the increasing prevalence of "explicit" CSR even in some coordinated market economies (Hiss 2009; Kang and Moon 2012). This position is not necessarily incompatible with the institutional substitution hypothesis as an explanation for the origins of CSR in the United States, but it contends that the model is now global in scope and is being diffused across multiple countries and contexts, perhaps due to the isomorphic effect of competition within the context of an increasingly integrated world economy. For radical critics such as Sum (2009), "CSRism" is best understood as a normative tool that "helps to re-engineer consent by providing neo-liberal common sense with a soft moral spin" (2009: 12). It thereby not only legitimates corporate power as neoinstitutionalists contend, but also serves to stabilize a global neo-liberal regime.

In the analysis that follows, we evaluate these three contending hypotheses regarding the development of supply chain CSR over the course of two decades. We distinguish between two (somewhat overlapping) phases in the evolution of supply chain CSR during this period: an early phase of field emergence leading to the establishment of MSIs (1989–2000) and a later phase (2000–present) of field population and development that has been dominated by business-led CSR initiatives. To preview our conclusion, we find that the evidence regarding the institutional dynamics of supply chain CSR is somewhat mixed for the first of these two periods. On the one hand, many US companies were quicker than their European counterparts to develop and implement organizational practices such as codes of conduct and factory monitoring. Such early adoption of supply chain CSR could be interpreted as support for the "institutional substitution" hypothesis insofar as American companies had to make "explicit" the commitments that may be "implicit" in Europe's different regulatory and institutional contexts. On the other hand, European companies arguably caught up with and then surpassed their American counterparts by working more proactively with civil society stakeholders. Overall, we argue not only that the very concept of supply chain CSR was less contentious in Europe than in the United States during this early period, but also that, in both cases, the field's development during this phase reflected the institutional context shaping the role of business in society and the relationship of the private sector to other social actors – a conclusion that more closely approximates the "institutional mirror" hypothesis.

The second phase of supply chain CSR reflects growing concern on the part of civil society groups that the widespread adoption of the private governance model of supply chain CSR was occurring alongside mounting evidence that codes of conduct and factory audits were generating only modest or minimal improvement in supply chain conditions. Leading corporate actors in both the United States and Europe responded to this challenge by creating new initiatives designed both to shore up the legitimacy of supply chain CSR and to reassert private sector control over this field while still gesturing toward the principle of "multistakeholder" participation. National origins become less important during the later period, with large, publicly traded retailers taking an assertive role in both the United States and Europe. We interpret these developments as support for the "institutional convergence" hypothesis. However, we note in the conclusion that the differing responses of American and European corporations to the Rana Plaza collapse in Bangladesh again point to cross-regional differences that gesture toward the continued salience of the "institutional mirror" explanation of CSR cultures.

The primary data derive from a set of thirty-five semistructured interviews with current or former representatives of nineteen organizations active in the supply chain CSR field. Interviews were conducted over a seven-year period (2007 through 2013) in a total of seven countries (the United States, United Kingdom, the Netherlands, Belgium, France, Germany, and Switzerland).[5] Most interviews lasted between one and two hours and were carried out in person at the offices of the organization, although some were conducted by phone. Each of

---

[5] In another paper, we use these data to develop a comparative institutional analysis of transnational advocacy networks and the origins of anti-sweatshop activism in Europe and North America (Bair and Palpacuer 2012).

the interviews was transcribed, analyzed, and given an identifying code consisting of a letter and number; the letter refers to either E for Europe or US for the United States, and the number denotes the rank order of the interview among all those conducted within the relevant group. For example, E5 refers to the fifth interview carried out with one of the European-based groups in the sample. In the analysis that follows, we reference specific interviews by their identifying code and the year in which they were conducted (see Table 6.1).

Field emergence, 1989–2000

The origins of supply chain CSR lie in the corporate world's response to anti-sweatshop activism carried out and coordinated by a variety of groups, most often via transnational advocacy networks (Keck and Sikkink 1998). These campaigns emerged in response to sweatshop scandals that linked well-known corporations to cases of child labor, abusive working conditions, and other labor violations in apparel and footwear factories, mostly in Asia and Latin America. Although much of the academic literature on this so-called anti-sweatshop movement focuses on the US experience (Armbruster-Sandoval 2005; Wimberly 2009), some of the first campaigns targeting clothing brands and retailers occurred in Europe. In 1989, activists in the Netherlands burned clothes in front of a store owned by the large Dutch retailer C&A in a show of solidarity with women garment workers in the Philippines who had been fired after demanding to be paid the legal minimum wage. Although the factory at the center of this controversy was producing for C&A, it was owned by a British company, so the Dutch activists decided to coordinate protests with their British counterparts, thus giving rise to campaign actions in two different countries.

The following year, the same activists who had organized the C&A protest decided to create a European-wide anti-sweatshop organization, the Clean Clothes Campaign (CCC). From the beginning, the organization emphasized the issue of supply chain accountability: "The big retail stores subcontract the production of the clothes they sell. Very often, the subcontracting chain is long, stretching all over the world, for example, from the retail store via intermediary traders to the factory who in turn subcontracts to an illegal sweatshop and to homeworkers. In the final analysis, it is the retailers who place the orders.

Table 6.1 *Organizations interviewed*

Organization	Location of organization	# Interviews	Date of Interviews
Fair Labor Association	Washington, DC	4[a]	2007, 2008
Social Accountability International	New York	1	2012
Worldwide Responsible Accredited Production	Arlington, VA	1	2012
Business Social Compliance Initiative	Brussels	1	2012
Global Social Compliance Program	Issy-les-Moulineaux, France	1	2013
Worker Rights Consortium	Washington, DC	2	2008
Fair Wear Foundation	Amsterdam	1	2008
Ethical Trading Initiative	London	1	2007
Clean Clothes Campaign Secretariat	Amsterdam	4	2007, 2008, 2010, 2012
Clean Clothes Campaign Belgium	Brussels	1	2007
Clean Clothes Campaign Germany	Banz	1	2007
Clean Clothes Campaign UK	London	1	2007
Clean Clothes Campaign Netherlands	Amsterdam	2	2008, 2010

Clean Clothes Campaign France	Paris	1	2008
UNITE	New York	5	2008, 2010, 2012
International Labor Rights Fund	Washington, DC	1	2012
USAS	Washington, DC	1	2010
ETUF: TCL[b]	Brussels	1	2012
ITGLWF[c]	Brussels	2	2007, 2009
Unaffiliated activists[d]	Various, US and UK	3	2007, 2010
		N = 35	

[a] Includes focus group interview with eight staff.
[b] European Trade Union Federation: Textiles, Clothing and Leather Workers
[c] International Textile, Garment, and Leather Workers Federation
[d] Independent activists, including those who had previously worked for a labor rights organization.

They, in fact, determine what is produced where, for what wages and under what conditions" (CCC 1993: 2; cited in Segerlund 2010: 79; also E2 2007).

A CCC secretariat was established in Amsterdam to coordinate the activities of the national CCC coalitions that were being organized in various countries, first in France, Belgium, Germany, and the United Kingdom, and eventually in several southern European countries. When it began, CCC was primarily a campaigning group that worked with local allies in developing countries to publicize labor violations in overseas factories, mostly by organizing public demonstrations targeting the European companies linked to sweatshop conditions. In the early period, CCC's efforts focused primarily on C&A, one of Europe's largest retailers and a privately held family company. Initially, C&A rejected CCC's accusations of using Asian sweatshops, claiming that it had been singled out not because conditions in its supply chain were particularly egregious but rather because its size and degree of visibility made it an easy target for activists.

As its organizational structure took shape with the addition of new national affiliates, the CCC negotiated the transition to becoming a social movement organization, which included developing new strategies beyond the store demonstrations and other forms of activism it had used to bring the sweatshop issue to public attention. Realizing that these forms of corporate campaigning are time- and energy-intensive ways of promoting change, CCC activists soon began to explore alternative strategies that they hoped would generate sustainable improvements in global supply chains. Following lengthy internal discussions and exchanges with trade unions and NGO partners in developing countries, the CCC decided to develop a code of conduct for companies; this was released in 1998 as the Code of Labour Practices (E2 2007). In the Netherlands, the CCC also took a leading role in the creation of an MSI, the Fair Wear Foundation (FWF), to ensure the Code's meaningful implementation. With a governing board that included private-sector representatives from multiple locations in the supply chain (both retailers and suppliers) as well as trade unions and NGOs, FWF was one of the earliest and most comprehensive MSIs dedicated to supply chain monitoring.

Around the same time, British anti-sweatshop activists, including some who had been active in the 1989 C&A campaign, assembled an informal network of activist organizations in the United Kingdom that began meeting to observe and analyze the development and implementation of some of the first corporate codes of conduct. Eventually, members of this network drafted a proposal to bring private-sector actors into a conversation with civil society groups about how codes could be made meaningful instruments for supply chain monitoring (E5 2007). This effort reached fruition in 1998, when a multistakeholder organization called the Ethical Trading Initiative (ETI) was established with financial support from the British government's Department for International Development. Thus, ten years after the C&A campaign that ignited the European anti-sweatshop movement, an international (but regional) network of European NGOs successfully spearheaded the effort to create, with the participation of trade unions and the private sector, two MSIs to promote the implementation of supply chain CSR.

During this period, anti-sweatshop activism initially followed much the same trajectory in the United States. One of the first corporations targeted by US activists was Nike, which was blamed for sweatshop conditions in the Indonesian factories making its shoes. The Nike campaign was orchestrated by a US activist, Jeff Ballinger, who worked for the Asian American Free Labor Institute, a union-affiliated organization funded by the AFL-CIO, in the late 1980s. In August 1992, Ballinger published one of the earliest sweatshop exposés in *Harper's* magazine, in which he contrasted the amount Nike paid to Michael Jordan for a multiyear endorsement deal ($20 million) with the wages paid to the Indonesian workers making Nike's shoes (19 cents an hour). Ballinger also documented pervasive violations of the country's minimum wage laws by Nike's suppliers in Indonesia. Additional sweatshop scandals followed in the wake of Ballinger's campaign against Nike. The National Labor Committee, another union-related group, publicized sweatshop conditions in an El Salvadoran factory supplying the specialty retailer Gap and disclosed the presence of underage workers in a Honduran factory making the "Kathy Lee" line of clothes sold at Walmart.

In the United States, organized labor played the principal role in bringing the sweatshop issue to public attention. Many of the exposés revealing poor working conditions and labor violations in corporate supply chains were orchestrated either by unions or by union-backed organizations like the National Labor Committee, although NGOs did play an important supporting role, particularly on the West Coast

(US10 2010; US11 2010). The sweatshop issue also became more explicitly politicized in the United States in the context of debates about the implications of free trade and growing fears that economic globalization was promoting "a race to the bottom" that would negatively affect American workers. In July 1996, US President Bill Clinton announced the creation of a task force called the Apparel Industry Partnership (AIP). The goal of the AIP was to initiate a dialogue among representatives of the private sector, the NGO sector, and organized labor about how to eradicate sweatshop conditions in global supply chains. This dialogue quickly came to center on the development of an industry-wide code of conduct, but the negotiations broke down along what would prove to be enduring fault lines in the supply chain CSR field: the precise standards to be specified in the code and the methods for monitoring the compliance of suppliers with these standards.

When a final agreement was announced in November 1998, union representatives and some members of the NGO caucus refused to endorse it. They also refused to endorse the newly created Fair Labor Association (FLA), an organization that was created by several AIP participants to implement and monitor the new code (US1 2008; US14 2012). Instead, the apparel industry union, UNITE, played a leading role in creating a campus-based labor rights group called United Students Against Sweatshops (USAS). Next, UNITE worked with USAS to develop a new organization, the Worker Rights Consortium (WRC), which was established in 2000 as an alternative to the FLA.

Two conclusions emerge from this stylized history of the first decade of anti-sweatshop activism. The first is that, as a concept, the very existence of supply chain CSR emerged as a response to pressures from a diverse set of anti-sweatshop activists in Europe and North America, many of whom coordinated their actions with counterparts in the Global South. At least initially, several companies responded to reports of labor violations in their supply chains with some variation on the statement made by Nike's spokesperson, who, upon being asked about working conditions in the factories of its Indonesian suppliers, claimed "we don't make shoes" (Larimer 1998: 30). Although technically correct, as Nike neither owned nor managed the factories manufacturing its products, this kind of disavowal would soon be replaced by a commitment on the part of Nike and other leading brands to enforce basic standards in their supply chains. As a manifestation of this commitment, a number of American companies developed and adopted corporate codes of conduct, beginning with Levi Strauss in 1992. European companies soon followed. By the mid-1990s, the company at the center of Europe's anti-sweatshop movement, C&A, had also developed a code of conduct.

Having thus secured commitments from corporations to enforce basic standards in the supply chain, activists kept the pressure on by monitoring and campaigning around the effective implementation of these instruments. When Gap adopted a code of conduct in response to a sweatshop exposé, activists criticized the company's failure to ensure its meaningful implementation in supplier factories. They called for Gap to permit monitoring and verification of code compliance by local NGOs or other independent groups. In December 1995, after a year-long campaign, Gap agreed to independent third-party monitoring (Armbruster-Sandoval 2005).[6] Similarly, in 1996, C&A created its own auditing organization, called Service Organisation for Compliance Audit Management (SOCAM). Legally distinct from C&A, SOCAM's purpose is to verify that subcontractors throughout its supply chain are complying with the C&A code (Jeurissen and van der Rijst 2007). However, the formal independence of SOCAM from C&A has not protected it from critics who fault its auditing methodology for a lack of proximity to the workers who are most directly affected by supply chain conditions.[7]

Thus, the second conclusion to emerge from our analysis is that the locus of debate within this field shifted relatively quickly from the question of *whether* lead firms are responsible for conditions in their supply chain to *how* this responsibility should be exercised. Here, it is possible to distinguish between a "European" and a "North American" trajectory. In both the United States and Europe, social movement organizations, especially trade unions, were skeptical about any private governance schemes that did not provide meaningful oversight for noncorporate actors to evaluate the substance and effectiveness of CSR supply chain policies. Ultimately, though, a

---

[6] See also the website of the Institute for Global Labor and Human Rights where the NLC's GAP campaign is documented: (http://www.globallabourrights.org/campaigns?id=0043, accessed on January 15, 2013).
[7] See J. Van der Tol (2010).

number of European organizations, including trade unions, decided to accept the basic premise of supply chain CSR as a voluntary form of private sector regulation and to focus their efforts on making it as rigorous and effective as possible. For the most part, they pursued this objective by creating MSIs, which institutionalized at least some degree of voice for civil society actors in the development of the supply chain CSR field. Thus, rather than reject CSR as a fundamentally ineffective and inadequate response to the sweatshop problem, activist organizations in Europe opted for a seat at the table, hoping that they could leverage their participation into a degree of influence over the standards and procedures, such as codes of conduct and compliance monitoring, that were being developed by the private sector. Participating in these MSIs requires civil society organizations to balance a critical posture toward the private sector with a more collaborative one – a balance that some CCC organizers describe as an "oppose and propose" strategy (E1 2007). Simultaneously, the MSI model signals an acceptance by companies that other civil society actors have a legitimate role to play in this field.

In contrast, supply chain CSR has proved a more contentious concept in the United States, where the private sector and other civil society actors tend to regard each other with mutual skepticism. President Clinton's AIP served as a critical juncture in the US context; the failure of companies and unions to reach agreement on a code of conduct and the eventual departure of the unions from the initiative fractured this emergent field – a division that deepened when organized labor (and some NGO allies) created the WRC as an alternative to the FLA. American unions agreed with their European counterparts that global brands and retailers should be accountable for labor practices in their supply chain, but they were unconvinced that this could be achieved via the mechanism of private governance. One US activist we interviewed emphasized that although some US corporations were adopting various forms of supply chain self-regulation, they were primarily concerned about the perceptions of American consumers, not the well-being of developing-country workers. According to this view, supply chain CSR aims first and foremost to generate positive publicity for companies and/or avoid negative publicity that can threaten the value of brands – goals that are not necessarily congruent with the objective of improved labor standards. What makes extant models of supply chain monitoring so problematic for these critics is precisely that they are a form of

CSR – that is, a voluntary engagement with social issues that takes place on the terms of the private sector. Indeed, the term CSR was repeatedly used by our American (but not European) informants as a kind of shorthand to express the idea that a policy or program is purely cosmetic and lacks substance. One US activist explicitly claimed that the development of a CSR approach to the issue of labor standards in global supply chains "killed the [anti-sweatshop] movement" (US9 2010) because it entrenched a corporate-led, voluntarist approach to the problem that precluded other possible approaches, such as public regulation.

This voluntarist approach to supply chain CSR is aptly represented by the other two main organizations that emerged during this first phase of field formation: Worldwide Responsible Apparel Production (WRAP) and Social Accountability International (SAI). WRAP was created the same year as the FLA.[8] It grew out of a taskforce organized by the American Apparel Manufacturers' Association (AAMA) around the same time that the Clinton White House convened the AIP.[9] The AAMA played no role in AIP, preferring instead to organize a parallel but independent effort.[10] After consulting with a range of stakeholders, the task force recommended creating a separate, independent organization to certify compliance with the AAMA's newly created code of conduct, which came to be known as the *WRAP principles*. Because WRAP was the creation of a trade group, its architects realized that its legitimacy would be questioned unless it was seen as independent from the companies it was supposed to monitor and the industry association that established it. Accordingly, WRAP's articles of incorporation require that a majority of its directors be drawn from outside the apparel industry (US17 2012). Currently, its board of directors includes two individuals with academic affiliations, one CSR consultant, and one (nonlabor) NGO representative. The chairman of the WRAP board is a retired US Department of Labor inspector general. In addition to a governance structure that includes

---

[8] The "A" in WRAP now stands for "accredited," reflecting the organization's possible interest in diversifying beyond apparel.
[9] In 2000, the AAMA merged with the trade group in the footwear association, Footwear Industry America, to create the American Apparel and Footwear Association.
[10] Although the AIP counted among its members individual companies, including Nike, Liz Claiborne, and L. L. Bean, it did not have the endorsement or participation of any industry association or trade group per se.

noncorporate actors, the organization has long emphasized WRAP's financial independence from the AAMA. More than 90 percent of its revenue derives from the registration and audit fees that are assessed for the inspection and certification of a manufacturing facility.

Only manufacturing facilities can become WRAP-certified, not brands and retailers. This makes WRAP similar to Social Accountability International (SAI), another US-based group that was created during supply chain CSR's first decade. Among the organizations discussed in this chapter, SAI is most closely related to the broader domain of CSR as it is discussed elsewhere in this volume. It began as a project of the Council on Economic Priorities (CEP), a nonprofit public interest organization created in 1969 by Alice Tepper Marlin to conduct and disseminate research on the social performance of corporations. In the mid-1990s, CEP realized that it had no reliable way to assess the social performance of American companies subcontracting production to offshore factories. This discovery sparked Tepper Marlin's interest in the consequences of global supply chains for CSR and led to the creation of SAI in 1996. The organization's first major task was the creation of SA8000, an auditable social compliance standard based on the ISO9000 model. SAI developed SA8000 in consultation with numerous stakeholder groups, including ETI, CCC, and the International Textile, Garment, and Leather Workers' Federation (US15 2012). After releasing the SA8000 standard in 1997, SAI subsequently developed an extensive international program of certification training designed to teach CSR professionals, as well as civil society groups, how to evaluate and improve a factory's compliance with the standard.

By the end of its first decade, the field of supply chain CSR in Europe and the United States was populated by six main organizations. All of these organizations grew directly out of the anti-sweatshop movement. Three were closely associated with diverse civil society constituencies, including labor unions, faith-based groups, student activists, feminist groups, and development-oriented NGOs that had been mobilized by the anti-sweatshop campaigns of the early to mid-1990s. These include the FWF and ETI in Europe and the WRC in the United States. The other three organizations to emerge during this early phase of field formation were based in the United States. All were developed as standard setting and accreditation or auditing programs with closer, although varying, ties to the private sector: the FLA, SAI, and WRAP.

This latter set of organizations also emerged in response to the anti-sweatshop movement but with the primary aim of developing strategies and programs to help businesses to avoid a sweatshop scandal. As such, they played an important role in defining the practices, such as codes of conduct or standard compliance auditing, that would come to constitute the emergent field.

Field development, 2000–present

Although anti-sweatshop activism was prominent in both Europe and the United States during the 1990s, the movements that developed in the two regions differed. In Europe, supply chain CSR became institutionalized through MSIs in which business, labor groups, and other kinds of NGOs cooperated to define and pursue common goals. Disagreements and conflicts were not uncommon, but, for the most part, solutions to them were pursued within the multistakeholder framework that groups such as the FWF and ETI represented. In the United States, in contrast, the very legitimacy of supply chain CSR was called into question by civil society groups, particularly organized labor. Corporations and business groups developed supply chain CSR programs that were similar to those implemented by their European counterparts, but, for the most part, they did so without the active cooperation of activist organizations.

This distinction between the European and US approaches to supply chain CSR was eroded during the second phase of the field's development, when two new organizations arrived on the scene: the Business Social Compliance Initiative (BSCI) and the Global Social Compliance Program (GSCP). These latecomers had a less immediate relationship to the anti-sweatshop politics of the 1990s than the groups that were created before 2000. Indeed, their creation was not so much a response to anti-sweatshop campaigns or other public pressure from activists, but rather a reaction to how the supply chain CSR field had been developing during the earlier phase described in the preceding section. Both BSCI and GSCP acknowledge that multistakeholder involvement is a prerequisite for effective supply chain CSR. Yet each organization accommodates the participation of civil society groups in ways that simultaneously secure the private sector's privileged role in defining the contours of the CSR field – an approach that Egels-Zandén and Wahlqvist (2007) describe as a "post-partnership" model.

BSCI was established in 2003 by the Foreign Trade Association, an industry association comprising primarily large European retailers, to harmonize standards and promote social compliance in global supply chains. When it was created, the BSCI departed from other European initiatives in that it did not include civil society actors. For this reason, activists were highly critical of the organization, arguing that it allowed companies to appear to be "doing something" on the CSR front by giving them a business-friendly alternative to the more demanding, genuinely multistakeholder groups ETI and FWF (US13 2012; US15 2012; E14 2012). In response, the BSCI tried to cultivate a better relationship with civil society groups while continuing to advertise itself as a "business-driven" initiative (E15 2012). For example, it invited several unions and NGOs to join a newly created Stakeholders' Advisory Council. A few groups, including the US-based SAI, and one European union federation (UNI Commerce, which represents retail workers) accepted the invitation, but other unions and many NGOs, including CCC and Oxfam, refused to participate on the grounds that the Stakeholder Council has no real power to influence BSCI's policies (E14 2012; E15 2012; see also Egels-Zandén and Wahlqvist 2007; Fransen 2012). BSCI subsequently responded to this criticism, announcing that a member of the Stakeholders' Advisory Council would be given a seat on the organization's Steering Committee and granted consultative rights.

GSCP was established in 2006 under the auspices of the Consumer Goods Forum, an association of about 400 major retailers and manufacturers. It is headquartered near Paris, with branch offices in Japan and the United States. Although by the time it was launched multiple supply chain CSR initiatives already existed in Europe and the United States, GSCP attracted significant attention because it had the backing of three of the world's largest retailers: American mass discount giant Walmart, the French retailer Carrefour, and the British supermarket chain Tesco (E16 2012). As was the case with BSCI, critics dismissed GSCP as another strategic attempt to undermine MSIs by promoting a less participatory form of supply chain CSR.

In another parallel with BSCI, the governance structure of GSCP distinguishes between an Advisory Board comprising civil society representatives and an Executive Board comprising corporate members. As of 2014, the Advisory Board included two union representatives (the Head of UNI Commerce and the General Secretary of the food branch of the French union Force Ouvrière [FGTA-FO]), three (nonlabor) NGOs, a university CSR representative, and a labor relations expert who is the former Head of UNI Commerce. At the time of writing, the Executive Board was chaired by the Director of Global Social and Environmental Responsibility for Hewlett-Packard and included officers from other large corporations such as Gap, Unilever, Chiquita, and Hasbro. As the composition of its board indicates, GSCP is extending the supply chain CSR conversation far beyond the apparel and footwear industries that have dominated it historically. The group focuses its efforts on developing and refining a general reference code and audit methodology, with the goal of diffusing a set of best practices for social compliance management systems. Like BSCI, GSCP seeks to reduce audit costs and redundancies by harmonizing the diverse codes and compliance methodologies used by its members. Unlike BSCI, however, GSCP does not offer an auditing or certification process.

Table 6.2 shows the composition of the eight main organizations in the supply chain CSR field. To the extent that each includes representatives from at least three of the four civil society constituencies included in the table – business, labor, NGOs, and universities – it suggests that the participation of non-corporate actors has been institutionalized in the field of supply chain CSR. However, Table 6.2 also reveals substantial variation at the organizational level in terms of *which* stakeholders are involved. The only organizations with a shared governance structure encompassing companies, unions, and NGOs are the European groups, FWF and ETI. There is no direct US counterpart to these MSIs; the FLA includes NGOs and university representatives on its advisory board alongside companies, but lacks unions. Likewise, SAI has a tripartite advisory board with NGO participation, but minimal involvement from the trade union sector. Farthest from a tripartite structure are the other two US-based organizations created in the wake of the anti-sweatshop movement: WRAP's governing body includes neither unions nor labor-oriented NGOs, whereas the WRC does not include companies. Interestingly, although both BSCI and GSCP claim some degree of participation from NGOs and unions that can serve in an advisory or consultative capacity, these groups define themselves as "business-led" initiatives, thus underscoring a decisive and distinct role for the private sector.

Table 6.2 *Organizations in supply chain corporate social responsibility field*

	Origin	Composition			
		Companies	Unions	NGOs	Universities
Fair Wear Foundation	Dutch, 1998	Y	Y	Y	N
Ethical Trading Initiative	UK, 1998	Y	Y	Y	N
Fair Labor Association	US, 1999	Y	N	Y	Y
Worker Rights Consortium[a]	US, 2000	N	Y	Y	Y
Social Accountability Int'l.	US, 1998	Y	Y	Y	N
Worldwide Resp. Acc. Prod.[b]	US, 2000	Y	N	Y	N
Bus. Social Compliance Init.[c]	Europe, 2003	Y	Y	Y	N
Global Social Compliance Prog.[d]	Global, 2006	Y	Y	Y	N

[a] The WRC's governing board includes five universities, five members of Students Against Sweatshops, and five labor rights NGOs or independent experts.
[b] WRAP's board of directors includes scholars with academic affiliation, but who serve in an individual as opposed to institutional capacity.
[c] As noted earlier, neither anti-sweatshop groups (e.g., CCC) nor unions representing manufacturing workers have joined BSCI, although one European labor federation representing retail workers has served on the Stakeholder Council.
[d] The unions participating on GSCP's advisory board are primarily service sector-oriented in membership and do not represent manufacturing workers in labor-intensive industries such as apparel or footwear.

Differences in the composition of the groups and the level of stakeholder involvement they provide are reflected in another kind of variation among these groups: the content of the standards they advocate. Over time, the codes of all eight initiatives have evolved in two ways: first, whereas some of the first corporate codes of conduct were quite vague, the instruments developed by these organizations feature more specific standards and more precise language. Second, each code recognizes the ILO's core labor standards, including workers' rights to freedom of association and collective bargaining. However, because lead firms have suppliers in developing countries where these so-called enabling rights are not observed, codes may also include modified language appropriate to justify sourcing from countries without independent or democratic trade unions. For example, the FLA Workplace Code of Conduct states "When the right to freedom of association and collective bargaining is restricted under law, employers shall not obstruct legal alternative means of workers association." The BSCI Code of Conduct contains similar language: "In situations where the right to freedom of association and collective bargaining are restricted under law, the company shall allow workers to freely elect their own representatives."[11] The same is true of the codes developed by ETI and GSCP. The content of WRAP's instrument has changed the least over time; as a "rule of law" code, the WRAP Principles mandate compliance with local laws regarding wages, working hours, and associational rights and therefore do not outline detailed standards beyond these legal minimums.

Table 6.3 shows considerable consensus among the codes in terms of core content: all eight prohibit child labor (although the minimum age for employment varies across codes), forced labor, and discrimination; all guarantee a safe and healthy working environment; and all ensure the right to freedom of association and collective bargaining.[12] The BSCI code is unique in its inclusion of an anticorruption clause. Three of the organizations (BSCI, WRAP, and FLA) have codes addressing environmental issues, whereas the other five codes are addressed only to the labor dimension of supply chains.

---

[11] This type of language is often referred to colloquially among actors in the field as "the China clause."

[12] The information contained here reflects the content of the codes as of January 2013.

Table 6.3 *Comparison of codes*

Org.	Wages	Working Hours	Freedom of Association and Collective Bargaining	Forced/ Child Labor	Discrimination & Harassment	Health & Safety	Environment	Corruption
FWF	Living wage	48 + 12 voluntary OT	Yes	Yes	Yes	Yes	No	No
ETI	Living wage	48 + 12 voluntary OT	Yes	Yes	Yes	Yes	No	No
FLA	Legal min./prevailing + aspirational basic needs	48 regular + 12 OT[a]	Yes	Yes	Yes	Yes	Yes	No
WRC	Living wage	48; any OT must be voluntary	Yes	Yes	Yes[b]	Yes	No	No
SAI	Living wage	48 regular + 12 overtime (OT)[c]	Yes	Yes	Yes	Yes	No	No
WRAP	Legal minimum	National law	Yes	Yes	Yes	Yes	Yes	No[d]
BSCI	Legal minimum/industry standard[e]	48 regular + 12 voluntary OT	Yes	Yes	Yes	Yes	Yes	Yes
GSCP	Living wage	48 regular + 12 voluntary OT	Yes	Yes	Yes	Yes	No	No

[a] Maximum sixty-hour work week may be exceeded under "exceptional circumstances."
[b] Code also includes a specific clause addressing the rights of women workers.
[c] Mandatory OT prohibited except when required on a short-term basis and a collective bargaining agreement is in place.
[d] The eleventh and twelfth principles of WRAP's twelve-point Code deal with customs compliance and security of shipments, respectively.
[e] Code states that in situations in which the legal minimum wage and/or industry standards do not cover living expenses and provide some additional disposable income, supplier companies are further encouraged to provide their employees with adequate compensation.

The most significant variation in Table 6.3 can be found in the columns describing each code's clauses regarding wages and working hours – issues that have long been among the most controversial within the supply chain CSR field. Early codes committed lead firms only to ensuring supplier compliance with the legal minimum wage. However, many civil society activists have pushed for a stronger standard, arguing that the minimum wage is often below the level needed for subsistence. Instead, they advocate that codes mandate a living wage, defined as a wage sufficient to cover a family's basic needs (housing, health, food) and provide some discretionary income. The WRC code contains the most detailed statement regarding what the organization considers a living wage, but the ETI, FWF, SAI, and GSCP codes also include references to the standard. The FLA, WRAP, and BSCI do not require payment of a living wage. Instead, these organizations require that workers are paid either the legally mandated minimum wage or the local "prevailing" or "industry" wage. In addition, two of the three codes (FLA and BSCI) include aspirational language regarding progress toward a living wage standard.[13]

Codes also exhibit varied language regarding working hours. All eight codes establish forty-eight hours as the maximum length for the normal work week, but they differ in their regulation of overtime. The WRC, ETI, FWF, and GSCP codes all specify that any overtime work should be performed on a voluntary basis. The SAI and BSCI codes prohibit mandatory overtime except where workers are covered by a collective bargaining agreement allowing otherwise, in which case overtime is permitted on a short-term basis to meet high demand. The FLA code permits a work week in excess of sixty hours in the event of "exceptional circumstances."

Thus, on both wages and working hours, a line of demarcation can be drawn between organizations that involve activist NGOs and labor unions at the core of their governance structure (FWF, ETI, WRC), which adopted early on the most demanding standards in their codes of

---

[13] The FLA Workplace Code of Conduct states that "[w]here compensation does not meet workers' basic needs and provide some discretionary income, each employer shall work with the FLA to take appropriate actions that seek to progressively realize a level of compensation that does." Likewise, the BSCI code notes that "in situations in which the legal minimum wage and/or industry standards do not cover living expenses and provide some additional discretionary income, supplier companies are further encouraged to provide their employees with adequate compensation to meet these needs."

conduct, and those initiatives that have revised their code content over time in response to activist criticism without reaching the same level of stringency. An exception to this pattern is GCSP, a business-led initiative whose code nevertheless includes a living wage standard and stricter limits on overtime hours. This is perhaps particularly surprising since one of the architects of the GSCP, Walmart, has been widely criticized for poor working conditions, low wages, and union-suppression efforts. The content of the GCSP code may indicate a shift in the supply chain CSR field toward higher standards on these issues, particularly since the visibility of the GSCP's members could make its code the new benchmark for other retailers in the field. Yet precisely because GSCP is a benchmarking exercise as opposed to an accreditation organization, it neither monitors nor audits producers, meaning that the degree of compliance with its ambitious standards at the factory level is largely unknown.

To summarize, the second phase of supply chain CSR development that we described in this section is most notable for the creation of two major retail-driven supply chain CSR organizations. Whereas BSCI and GSCP acknowledge a limited role for civil society groups in the supply chain CSR field, both also pointedly define themselves as "business-led" and reflect the concerns of major retailers with a global presence. This international orientation is particularly pronounced in the case of GSCP. Although the three companies spearheading its creation – Tesco, Carrefour, and Walmart – are based in three different countries, they share a common structural position as lead firms in some of the world's most extensive and closely watched supply chains. They are also united by a desire to establish and maintain a dominant position for major retail corporations as key actors within an increasingly crowded CSR field. In this sense, the institutional transformation/diffusion hypothesis most closely approximates the second period in the development of the supply chain CSR field, whereby there is a process of convergence across US- and European-based organizations.

Although both BSCI and GSCP are headquartered in Europe, they depart from the fully multistakeholder governance model pioneered by FWF and ETI during the field's first phase. At the same time, the FLA, which is the product of the US government-sponsored AIP, has been pursuing an aggressive European growth strategy in recent years, and the advisory board of the US-based group SAI includes a representative from an Italian trade union. The internationalization of these groups indicates a transcontinental convergence within the supply chain CSR field whereby the policies and strategies of the leading organizations vary less by national origins than by the characteristics of their private sector constituencies. Those companies affiliated with the FLA, BSCI, and GSCP include large, publicly traded retailers and brands that want to minimize their exposure to potentially damaging allegations of sweatshop labor while also maximizing returns to their shareholders. By contrast, the WRC has a membership of universities for whom the balance between economic incentives and social responsibility is presumably different from that of corporations. Likewise, the members of FWF are predominantly medium-sized companies less subject to the maxim of shareholder value and whose focus on either niche fashion segments or work wear may enable them to concede more generous margins to suppliers (E3 2007; E8 2008). Although large corporations are more likely to have dedicated CSR departments and staff, the considerable costs required to achieve meaningful improvements throughout their far-flung supply chains and the need for publicly held companies to justify these costs to shareholders may also present unique challenges that modestly sized companies do not face.

Conclusion: whither supply chain CSR?

During the 1990s, the field of supply chain CSR emerged in Europe and North America in response to social movements linking well-known companies to incidents of sweatshop labor in overseas factories. The tactics that civil society actors used to target corporations were similar across these regions, as were the strategies that companies developed in response to this activism. As the corporate code of conduct became a standard part of the CSR toolkit for large firms, civil society groups turned their attention to strengthening these instruments. They advocated for progressively stronger codes of conduct, pushing for the inclusion of living wage clauses and clear language regarding the rights of workers to organize and bargain collectively. In light of increasing concerns about the decoupling of corporate commitments and supply chain practices, they also sought an expanded role for civil society organizations alongside the private sector. These pressures led to the institutionalization, in both Europe and the United States, of a multi-stakeholder approach, which has been critically important for the legitimation of supply chain CSR.

However, in analyzing this process of field formation, we observed some notable differences between Europe and the United States. The early period of supply chain CSR in the United States was structured largely by the division between the "labor-oriented" WRC and the "business-oriented" FLA, whereas each of the European initiatives created during the field's first decade included some degree of participation by organized labor and NGOs. As we have argued elsewhere (Bair and Palpacuer 2012), the emphasis on tripartite governance in Europe reflects the corporatist logic of many of this region's political economies (see also Walker, Chapter 10 in this volume). Although unions and other civil society groups in Europe can be highly critical of companies, they also view social dialogue as the presumptive avenue for resolving conflicts. In contrast, there is more skepticism about the value of multistakeholder approaches among US actors. This view was nicely summarized by one of our American informants when he asked, "What kind of broad change is possible when you spend all your time going to conferences, being a symbol of multi-stakeholderdom?" (US11 2010).

These findings bear on the debate among comparative institutionalists regarding the degree to which CSR functions as an institutional substitute versus the degree to which it mirrors other prevailing institutions. Arguably, American companies were quicker than their European counterparts to respond when their supply chain practices came under attack, and the model of private governance expressed in corporate codes of conduct developed earlier and became more widespread in the United States than in Europe. The fact that supply chain CSR flourished in the United States could, in this sense, be interpreted as support for the institutional substitution hypothesis. However, we see no reason to interpret supply chain CSR as a substitute for a less interventionist US state. Rather, in our view, what the early period suggests is that, *given public criticism and activist pressure regarding supply chain conditions*, actors interpreted this challenge and formulated responses within institutional contexts that made particular kinds of discursive and organizational resources available. In this sense, one could argue that the institutional mirror hypothesis more accurately describes the dynamics of supply chain CSR during the field's period of emergence and early development.

Differences between regions became less marked during the first decade of the 2000s, however, as the supply chain CSR field continued to evolve via a second generation of business-led initiatives. Both of the new arrivals on the scene, BSCI and GSCP, feature major retail and brand corporations, and their similar governance structures suggest a diffusion of the "US model" of limited stakeholder engagement to the other side of the Atlantic. With the participation of nineteen European, fifteen American, and two Asian firms, as well as one each from Australia and South Africa, GSCP is the first truly global supply chain CSR organization, breaking the pattern of regionally oriented groups that grew out of the 1990s wave of anti-sweatshop activism. In this sense, the institutional diffusion hypothesis best describes the second period in the development of the supply chain CSR field, whereby there is a process of convergence across US- and European-based organizations.

Although we would not necessarily generalize our findings regarding the formation of the supply chain CSR field to the broader domain of CSR, they do resonate with the work of Levy, Brown, and de Jong on the CSR project known as the Global Reporting Initiative. These authors describe how NGOs "have deployed the discourse of CSR to try to shift the locus of corporate governance toward civil society stakeholders" (2010: 10). In so doing, activists are attempting to create a model of "civil regulation" (Murphy and Bendell 1997) that departs from CSR as a voluntarist and unilateral business practice. This analysis of the Global Reporting Initiative is similar to the argument we have made here insofar as the efforts of unions, labor rights NGOs, and other activists to ensure meaningful forms of multistakeholder participation in labor compliance programs can also be understood as ongoing attempts to secure civil regulation in the specific area of supply chain CSR. Yet these activities are countered by corporate actors, who frequently "employ CSR strategically as a form of self-regulation that serves to accommodate external pressures, construct the corporation as a moral agent (...), deflect the threat of regulation, and marginalize more radical activists" (Levy, Brown, and de Jong 2010: 94). This is particularly true of supply chain CSR, which emerged as the private sector's response to anti-sweatshop activism.

We emphasized that the second phase of this field's formation has been marked by the reassertion of private-sector dominance. Yet field dynamics may again be shifting. Since 2010, civil society actors have grown increasingly pessimistic about the prospects for achieving meaningful improvements via supply chain CSR programs, even those that include stakeholder participation. Several major sweatshop scandals have provided ample reason for alarm. In 2012, the *New York Times* published a lengthy article revealing punishing working conditions at a factory in southern China owned by Foxconn, China's largest private sector employer and a major supplier to Apple (Duhigg and Barbosa 2012). Within days, the FLA, which Apple had recently joined, announced that it would be conducting an investigation of the factory. In its final report, the FLA report confirmed that Foxconn had repeatedly violated Apple's code of conduct and the FLA standards that Apple, as an FLA member, was supposed to observe. Furthermore, the FLA found that Foxconn had routinely violated the wages and hours provisions of Chinese labor law. The remediation plan that was announced by the FLA, Apple, and Foxconn in the aftermath of the FLA's investigation emphasized Apple's responsibility for improving conditions in the factory, thus reinforcing the principle of supply chain CSR. However, numerous civil society groups interpreted the Apple-Foxconn scandal as evidence that supply chain CSR policies have proved inadequate to the task of identifying, let alone preventing, labor violations (Barbosa and Greenhouse 2012; Bradsher and Duhigg 2012).

Later that same year, a series of deadly factory fires cast further doubt on the effectiveness of supply chain CSR. In September 2012, a fire broke out in a Pakistani factory subcontracting for Western clients, killing nearly 300 workers. In the immediate aftermath of the fire, it was revealed that auditors working for SAI had inspected the factory shortly before the fire and had certified it as consistent with the SA8000 standard. Although SAI pledged to investigate the matter, labor rights organizations, including the WRC, insisted that the tragedy provided yet more evidence of the inherent flaws in existing supply chain CSR programs (Walsh and Greenhouse 2012). Two months later, another blaze killed 112 workers in a garment factory in Bangladesh. At the time of the fire, the factory was making garments for a number of foreign retailers, including Walmart and C&A. This workplace tragedy occurred in a suburb of Dhaka, not far from the site of the 2010 factory fire at That's It Sportswear, which precipitated the fire safety agreement we described in the introduction. The continuing pattern of workplace fatalities underscored fears that supply chain CSR policies were failing to ensure even the most basic health and safety standards for workers in global subcontracting networks.

These fears were tragically confirmed by the collapse of the Rana Plaza factory in Savar, Bangladesh on April 24, 2013. The collapse of this eight-story commercial building, which housed multiple garment factories that produced apparel for European and American companies such as Primark, Benetton, Mango, and Walmart, left 1,129 dead and more than 2,500 injured. Media coverage of this event galvanized activists and reinvigorated a long-standing campaign by local and international unions and NGOs to address what was, well before this latest tragedy, a crisis in building and fire safety in Bangladesh. As the most deadly workplace disaster in the history of the garment industry, the Rana Plaza collapse was a singularly powerful indictment of the failure of supply chain CSR.

Within weeks of the event, a number of mostly European apparel brands and retailers announced a new factory safety agreement called the Accord on Building and Fire Safety in Bangladesh. The Accord grew out of the PVH Fire Safety Agreement that we described at the beginning of the chapter: despite PVH's decision to sign the agreement in 2012, and the later addition of another signatory (the German retailer, Tchibo), the Agreement had not been implemented because it required a minimum number of signatories to become operational. It was only in the context of the international pressure generated by the Rana Plaza collapse that the Accord attained the critical mass of signatories needed to trigger its implementation. In the aftermath of this tragedy, dozens of companies rushed to sign the Accord, including H&M (largest global buyer from Bangladesh), Carrefour and Tesco (the second- and third-largest retailers in the world), and Inditex (world's largest fashion retailer and owner of the Zara brand).

Under the Accord, participating companies commit to having their supplier factories inspected by independent auditors and to ensuring that any violations or hazards are remediated. Where the Accord differs from conventional supply chain CSR measures is in further obligating the brand or retailer to finance in some way the repairs or renovations that are needed to bring factories up to code. By requiring signatory companies to continue purchasing from current Bangladeshi suppliers for a minimum of two years and to pay these suppliers prices that are consistent with maintaining a safe work environment, the Accord seeks to bring a degree of stability to what are often highly volatile and extremely price-competitive sourcing networks (Anner, Bair, and Blasi 2013). Additionally, these commitments are binding, enforceable obligations.[14] To the extent that the Accord regulates aspects of lead firm business practice and creates new financial commitments for the companies orchestrating global supply chains, it points to the connection between the *social* responsibility of a corporation and its core *economic* activities.

Revealingly, the Accord on Building and Fire Safety has been a decidedly European initiative. A few US companies signed on, perhaps most notably PVH, the Accord's first signatory, but also American Eagle, Abercrombie & Fitch, and Fruit of the Loom. One year after the Rana Plaza collapse, however, the country's leading retailers, such as Walmart, Gap, J.C. Penney, and Macy's, had not joined. Instead, they created an alternative program, the Bangladesh Worker Safety Initiative (later renamed the Alliance for Bangladesh Worker Safety), which entails a similar factory inspection and remediation program – with the important exception that the US plan does not clearly obligate participating companies to pay for whatever repairs or renovations are needed. Instead, the Alliance for Bangladesh Worker Safety requests that its members contribute to a fund that will provide affordable financing to contractors so that they can access the capital needed to make repairs.

The Rana Plaza collapse and its aftermath suggest that old fault lines within the supply chain CSR model may be emerging. As alternative models of supply chain CSR, the European-led Accord and the US-led Alliance have each sought the support of civil society organizations. Each boasts some degree of participation from NGOs and labor unions. But whereas the Alliance's advisory board includes representatives of Bangladeshi unions, it lacks any formal governance role for worker representatives. In contrast, multiple labor federations are parties to the Accord. Additionally, although several large humanitarian NGOs, such as CARE, are on the advisory board of the Alliance, no

---

[14] Under the accord's dispute resolution process, disputes concerning implementation are first submitted to the seven-member oversight steering committee, composed of three representatives chosen by the trade union signatories and three representatives chosen by the company signatories, with a representative of the International Labor Organization serving as a neutral chair. Any decision of the steering committee may then, at the request of either party, be appealed to a process of binding arbitration. The arbitrator's award may be enforced in a court of law of the home country of the signatory party against whom enforcement is sought. See Anner, Bair, and Blasi (2012).

major labor rights or anti-sweatshop group is affiliated with the US group, whereas CCC, WRC, and the International Labor Rights Fund participated in the creation of the Accord.

It would be premature to predict what these contrasting responses to the Rana Plaza tragedy suggest for the future of the supply chain CSR field. This event may have been sufficiently dramatic to arrest what we described as a process of convergence that had been occurring within the field during the previous decade, as large retailers on both sides of the Atlantic sought to ensure a dominant role for the private sector in defining how and in what ways the concept of CSR should be extended along the global supply chains that corporations organize. Looking back, we may see that this kind of business-led "post-partnership" strategy was fatally compromised by the succession of factory fires, building collapses, and sweatshop scandals of the Apple-Foxconn variety – all of which underscored the shortcomings and flaws of the extant approach.

To the extent that CSR is a process of institutionalization that legitimates corporate power in world society, such highly public and visible failures would seem to pose serious challenges to this legitimation project. As such, they may well generate a search for novel strategies. Although it is too early to define what approaches will become institutionalized, it is possible that new instruments will proliferate alongside (and possibly replace) the voluntary codes of conduct and auditing protocols that dominate the current social compliance model. Narrower but more concrete agreements of the sort represented by the Accord on Building and Fire Safety may represent the frontier of the CSR field. Indeed, to the extent that new developments move supply chain CSR toward enforceable commitments and put corporate business practices – in this case, sourcing strategies in global supply chains – at the center of the CSR debate, they will dramatically redraw the very contours of the field.

References

Anner, Mark. 2012. *The Limits of Voluntary Governance Programs: Auditing Labor Rights in the Global Apparel Industry*. Project for Global Workers' Rights Working Paper 001. Retrieved from http://lser.la.psu.edu/documents/Anner_AuditingFoA_PGWRWorkingPaper001.pdf.

Anner, Mark, Jennifer Bair, and Jeremy Blasi. 2013. "Towards Joint Liability in Global Supply Chains: Addressing the Root Causes of Labor Violations in International Subcontracting Networks." *Comparative Labor Law and Policy Journal* 35(1):1–43.

Armbruster-Sandoval, Ralph. 2005. *Globalization and Cross-Border Labor Solidarity in the Americas.* New York: Routledge.

Bair, Jennifer, and Florence Palpacuer. 2012. "From Varieties of Capitalism to Varieties of Activism: The Anti-sweatshop Movement in Comparative Perspective." *Social Problems* 59(4):522–543.

Bartley, Tim. 2003. "Certifying Forests and Factories: States, Social Movements, and the Rise of Private Regulation in the Apparel and Forest Products Fields." *Politics & Society* 31(3):433–464.

Bartley, Tim. 2005. "Corporate Accountability and the Privatization of Labor Standards: Struggles over Codes of Conduct in the Apparel Industry." *Research in Political Sociology* 14:211–244.

Bradsher, Keith, and Charles Duhigg. 2012. "Signs of Change Taking Hold in Electronics Factories in China." *New York Times*, December 26, A1.

Brammer, Stephen, Gregory Jackson, and Dirk Matten. 2012. "Corporate Social Responsibility and Institutional Theory: New Perspectives on Private Governance." *Socio-Economic Review* 10:3–28.

Campbell, John. 2007. "Why Would Corporations Behave in Socially Responsible Ways: An Institutional Theory of Corporate Social Responsibility." *Academy of Management Review* 32(3):946–967.

Carr, Marilyn, Martha Alter Chen, and Jane Tate. 2000. "Globalization and Home-Based Workers." *Feminist Economics* 6(3):123–142.

Casper, Steven, and Richard Whitley. 2004. "Managing Competences in Entrepreneurial Technology Firms: A Comparative Institutional Analysis of Germany, Sweden and the UK." *Research Policy* 33:89–106.

Davis, Gerald F., Marina V. N. Whitman, and Mayer N. Zald. 2008. "The Responsibility Paradox." *Stanford Social Innovation Review* Winter: 31–37.

Duhigg, Charles, and David Barbosa. 2012. "In China, Human Costs Built into iPad." *New York Times*, January 25, A1.

Duhigg, Charles, and Steven Greenhouse. 2012. "Electronic Giant Vowing Reforms in China Plants." *New York Times*, March 29, A1.

Egels-Zandén Niklas, and Eveline Wahlqvist. 2007. "Post-Partnership Strategies for Defining Corporate Responsibility: The Business Social Compliance Initiative." *Journal of Business Ethics* 70(2):175–189.

Esbenshade, Jill. 2004. *Monitoring Sweatshops: Workers, Consumers, and the Global Apparel Industry.* Philadelphia: Temple University Press.

Fransen, Luc. 2012. "Multi-stakeholder Governance and Voluntary Program Interactions." *Socio-Economic Review* 10(1):163–192.

Gjølberg, Maria. 2009. "The Origin of Corporate Social Responsibility: Global Forces or National Legacies?" *Socio-Economic Review* 7(4):605–637.

Hall, Peter, and David Soskice. 2001. *Varieties of Capitalism: The Institutional Foundations of Comparative Advantage*. New York: Cambridge University Press.

Hiss, Stefanie. 2009. "From Implicit to Explicit Corporate Social Responsibility – Institutional Change as a Fight for Myths." *Business Ethics Quarterly* 19:433–452.

Institute for Development Studies (IDS). 2006. *The ETI Code of Labour Practice: Do Workers Really Benefit?* Sussex: Institute for Development Studies.

Jackson, Gregory, and Androniki Apostolakou. 2010. "Corporate Social Responsibility in Western Europe: An Institutional Mirror or Substitute?" *Journal of Business Ethics* 94:371–394.

Jeurissen, Ronald, and M. W. van der Rijst. 2007. *Ethics in Business*. Assen, Netherlands: VanGorcum.

Kang, Nahee, and Jeremy Moon. 2012. "Institutional Complementarity between Corporate Governance and Corporate Social Responsibility: A Comparative Institutional Analysis of Three Capitalisms." *Socio-Economic Review* 10:85–108.

Keck, Margaret E., and Kathryn A. Sikkink. 1998. *Activists Beyond Borders: Advocacy Networks in International Politics*. Ithaca, NY: Cornell University Press.

Larimer, Tim. 1998. "Sneaker Gulag: Are Asian Workers Really Exploited?" *Time International*, May 11:30–32.

Levy, David, Halina Szejnwald Brown, and Martin de Jong. 2010. "The Contested Politics of Corporate Governance: The Case of the Global Reporting Initiative." *Business & Society* 49(1): 88–115.

Locke, Richard, Matthew Amengual, and Akshay Mangla. 2009. "Virtue out of Necessity? Compliance, Commitment, and the Improvement of Labor Conditions in Global Supply Chains." *Politics & Society* 37(3):319–351.

Locke, Richard, Fei Qin, and Alberto Brause. 2007. "Does Monitoring Improve Labor Standards? Lessons from Nike." *Industrial and Labor Relations Review* 61(1):3–31.

Maignan, Isabelle, and David A. Ralston. 2002. "Corporate Social Responsibility in Europe and the U.S.: Insights from Businesses Self-Presentations." *Journal of International Business Studies* 33:497–514.

Matten, Dirk, and Jeremy Moon. 2008. "Implicit and Explicit CSR: A Conceptual Framework for a Comparative Understanding of Corporate Social Responsibility." *Academy of Management Review* 33:404–424.

Mayer, Frederick, and Gary Gereffi. 2010. "Regulation and Economic Globalization: Prospects and Limits of Private Governance." *Business and Politics* 12(3):1–25.

Meyer, John W., Shawn M. Pope, and Andrew Isaacson. 2015, this volume. "Legitimating the Transnational Corporation in a Stateless World Society." Pp. 27–72 in *Corporate Social Responsibility in a Globalizing World*, edited by K. Tsutsui and A. Lim. New York: Cambridge University Press.

Murphy, David F., and Jem Bendell. 1997. *In the Company of Partners: Business, Environmental Groups and Sustainable Development*. Bristol: Policy Press.

Ngai, Pun. 2005. *Made in China: Women Factory Workers in a Global Workplace*. Durham, NC: Duke University Press.

Raworth, Kate, and Thalia Kidder. 2008. "Mimicking 'Lean' in Global Value Chains: It's the Workers Who Get Leaned on." Pp. 165–189 in *Frontiers of Commodity Chain Research*, edited by J. Bair. Palo Alto, CA: Stanford University Press.

Riisgaard, Lone. 2009. "Global Value Chains, Labor Organization and Private Social Standards: Lessons from East African Cut Flower Industries." *World Development* 37(2):326–340.

Rodriguez-Garavito, C. 2005. "Global Governance and Labor Rights: Codes of Conduct and Anti-Sweatshop Struggles in Global Apparel Factories in Mexico and Guatemala." *Politics & Society* 33(2):203–233.

Scherer, Andreas, and Guido Palazzo. 2008. "Globalization and Corporate Social Responsibility." Pp. 413–431 in *The Oxford Handbook of Corporate Social Responsibility*, edited by A. Crane, A. McWilliams, D. Matten, J. Moon, and D. Siegel. New York: Oxford University Press.

Segerlund, Lisbeth. 2010. *Making Corporate Social Responsibility a Global Concern: Norm Construction in a Globalizing World*. London: Ashgate.

Sum, Ngai. 2009. "Wal-Martization and CSR-ization in Developing Countries." Pp. 50–74 in *Corporate Social Responsibility and Regulatory Governance*, edited by J. C. Marques and P. Utting. London and Geneva: Routledge and UNRISD.

van der Tol, Johan. 2010. "C&A: Turning a blind eye to the cost of cheap clothes?" Radio Netherlands Worldwide, September 7. Retrieved from http://www.rnw.nl/english/article/ca-turning-a-blind-eye-cost-cheap-clothes.

Walker, Edward T. 2015, this volume. "Global Corporate Resistance to Public Pressures: Corporate Stakeholder Mobilization in the United States, Norway, Germany, and France." Pp. 321–362 in *Corporate Social Responsibility in a Globalizing World*, edited by K. Tsutsui and A. Lim. New York: Cambridge University Press.

Walsh, Declan, and Steven Greenhouse. 2012. "Inspectors Certified Pakistani Factory as Safe before Disaster." *New York Times*, September 19, A6.

Weil, David. 2010. *Improving Workplace Conditions through Strategic Enforcement: A Report to the Wage and Hour Division*. Retrieved from http://www.nytimes.com/2013/01/18/arts/design/life-death-and-transformation-at-brooklyn-museum.html.

Williams, Cynthia, and Ruth Aguilera. 2008. "Corporate Social Responsibility in a Comparative Perspective." Pp. 452–472 in *The Oxford Handbook of Corporate Social Responsibility*, edited by A. Crane, A. McWilliams, D. Matten, J. Moon, and D. Siegel. New York: Oxford University Press.

Wimberley, Dale. 2009. "Setting the Stage for Cross-Border Solidarity: Movement Spillover and Early Mobilization in the Nicaragua Labor Rights Campaign." *Labor Studies Journal* 34(3):318–338.

7 Sustainability discourse and capitalist variety: a comparative institutional analysis

KLAUS WEBER AND SARA B. SODERSTROM

Introduction

The concept of corporate social responsibility (CSR) is closely tied to the rise of the public corporation as a central institution of Western capitalism. CSR promises to ameliorate the potential negative social impact of the pursuit of profit by appealing to norms of stewardship, responsibility, and charity (see, e.g., Freeman and Liedtka 1991; Jacoby 1998). The idea of CSR evolved in the specific historical context of twentieth-century North American market liberalism and, in the postwar period, became increasingly defined in relation to the rising legal doctrine and normative discourse of shareholder primacy. CSR retains the voluntaristic and contractarian premises of liberal market capitalism in that it proposes moral and normative rather than regulatory checks on corporate behavior. Notwithstanding its idiosyncratic origins, the idea of CSR has, since the 1980s, become part of an international discourse on the role of corporations in society that is promoted by global elites and other agents of world society, such as multinational corporations, nongovernmental organizations (NGOs) like the Global Reporting Initiative (GRI), intergovernmental organizations such as the Organisation for Economic Cooperation and Development (OECD) and United Nations, and civil society and social movement groups (Smith 2001; Lim and Tsutsui 2012; Zhang and Luo 2013).

An important contemporary motivator and justification for corporate CSR efforts is the concept of sustainability that was theorized in the international development community. Sustainability justifies CSR in terms of self-interest rather than on strictly normative-moral grounds. Proponents of sustainability argue that contributing to social well-being and environmental preservation is necessary for the long-term realization of economic goals (Brundtland and World Commission on Environment and Development 1987; United Nations Secretary-General's High Level Panel on Global Sustainability 2012). Sustainability as an ideological underpinning for CSR practices therefore goes beyond the moral discourse of traditional CSR to provide a theorization for CSR that draws on scientific and instrumentally rational forms of authority (Meyer, Boli, Thomas, and Ramirez 1997). Like CSR, sustainability is part of a global discourse, constructed and promoted in the public sphere by experts and international and nongovernmental organizations, and endowed with claims of universality and a focus on "transnational" problems and solutions.

However, despite these global cultural processes, understandings of sustainability at the level of practice are often still colored by the local conditions of national institutions and political economies (e.g., Campbell 2007). This view is shared by institutional scholars who see the expansion of global discourses more generally as involving local translation and interpretation rather than an unmitigated diffusion of ideas (see, e.g., Dobbin 1994; Campbell 2001; Campbell 2002; Sahlin and Wedlin 2008). The relevant differences among national political economies in capitalist societies has been elaborated most extensively by comparative institutional scholars who are often grouped together as the "varieties of capitalism (VoC) school" (Boyer 1996; Orrú, Biggart, and Hamilton 1997; Hall and Soskice 2001; Thelen 1999; Whitley 1999; Streek 2010). The VoC school provides a counterpoint to the homogenizing view of globalization associated with the world society perspective (Meyer, Boli, Thomas, and Ramirez 1997).

The main contribution of the VoC perspective has been to identify a limited plurality of capitalist systems and link observed differences to the sociopolitical organization of economies and national institutional matrices. National institutional systems are historically evolved configurations that involve varying roles of the state; distinctive organization of labor, capital, and knowledge resources into industrial production systems; and a unique organization and vibrancy of civil society actors. For example, Hall and Soskice (2001) distinguish liberal market systems mainly governed through the mechanisms of markets from coordinated market systems that are characterized by corporatist and group coordination with the participation of the state.

Such systematic institutional differences at the national level affect how the idea of sustainability is interpreted and translated even if it is universally embraced. The plurality of capitalist forms not only entails systems of material production, but also distinct policy and knowledge regimes that affect the construction of the central problems, solutions, and actors involved in achieving sustainability (Katzenstein 1977; Vogel 1996; Campbell 2001; Campbell 2002; Benson and Saguy 2005). Much of this construal is carried out in the public sphere, for example, through media discourse where varying interests and public opinion interact (Gamson and Modigliani 1989; Gamson 1992a; McCombs 1997; Fiss and Hirsch 2005; see also Walker, this volume).

In this chapter, we explore how sustainability is represented in the public discourse of six countries and link differences and similarities in discourse to the institutional diversity of national political economies. We analyze an extensive corpus of articles on sustainability that were published in 2011 in leading news sources in six countries and compare it with the 1987 UN report on "Our Common Future." Our analysis includes an inductive taxonomy of issues, a descriptive comparison between countries, and an interpretation of similarities and differences in light of institutional differences. In doing so, we offer a more nuanced understanding of how cultural and political processes interact in the configuration of CSR at the local and global levels.

Sustainability and global CSR in the VoC perspective

Although the ideas of CSR and sustainability are sometimes cast as critiques of market capitalism (Friedman 1970; Campbell 2006), they are arguably better understood as an integral (although perhaps dialectic) part of the prevalent economic ideology of capitalist societies. Both concepts directly address the question of (negative) "externalities" created by private property-based market systems. Externalities are defined by economists as costs of production, such as environmental pollution or social ills, which are not reflected in the prices of goods and services transacted in markets. These costs are instead borne by society. State regulation offers one way either to price negative externalities into market transactions (e.g., through expanded legal liability or direct prohibitions) or to tax market participants to fund the public provision of remedial services (e.g., as direct transfers or subsidies for the provisions of public goods, such as waste disposal and public safety). CSR, as a normative mandate for private enterprises, offers an alternative path, one in which corporations directly transfer resources toward providing public goods, rather than the transfer being mediated by governments.

This private allocation of resources as CSR is in many ways more compatible with (neo)liberal views of capitalism than the alternative – more extensive government regulation (see also Meyer, Pope, and Isaacson, this volume).[1] The idea of CSR reduces the role of the state and civil society associations as the sole providers of public goods and specifies appropriate mechanisms for corporations to participate in the resolution of social and environmental issues. It becomes a matter of the normative responsibility of corporations to contribute to the public good, beyond their routine business operations. Seen as normative responsibilities rather than legal requirements, the contribution and allocation of corporate resources to public causes is ultimately discretionary.

In contrast, in coordinated VoC, corporations are more deeply embedded in the political economy of social welfare. Private enterprises cooperate and negotiate directly with governments and civil society organizations over the provision of public goods, or they rely on governments with a more expansive welfare role to reduce the consequences of negative externalities from production. In corporatist systems, the "responsibility" of CSR behaviors is less discretionary but arguably also more narrow as governments and cross-sectoral groups address issues that might otherwise become the subject of voluntary corporate action (see, e.g., Campbell 2007).

The idea of sustainability, as an underpinning of global CSR, can then also be expected to take on different flavors in different institutional and ideological regimes. Sustainability has, since the 1980s, often been defined according to the UN report on sustainable development as "development that meets the needs of the present without compromising the ability of future generations to meet their own needs" (Brundtland and World Commission on Environment and Development 1987) and as requiring the reconciliation of environmental, social, and economic demands to stay within the carrying capacity of these systems. The scope of the idea of sustainability is both global in scale (the systems in question are seen as interdependent or integrated

---

[1] We acknowledge that a belief in the strong-form efficient market hypothesis would deny the existence of substantial externalities and hence the need for CSR. The same radical view would, of course, also deny the need for government intervention.

across Earth) and universal in scope (the mandate for sustainability does not hinge on historical or local contingencies). It is not surprising that actors with similar global and universalistic outlooks, such as scientists and experts located in transnational fields and global civil society organizations, have led much of the production of discourse on sustainability (e.g, Meyer, Boli, Thomas, and Ramirez 1997; Meyer, Frank, Hironaka, Schofer, and Tuma 1997; Lim and Tsutsui 2012).

From very early on, the idea of sustainability was also adopted by corporations, economists, and management scholars as a justification for corporate contributions toward the public good beyond the operation of the core business and the maximization of financial profit (Gladwin, Kennelly, and Krause 1995; Hart 1995). However, rather than casting CSR behavior as a redistribution of resources from profits toward social goods, as traditional CSR proponents did, proponents of sustainability suggest that, given sufficiently long time horizons, CSR behaviors are in the interest of corporations' permanence. Moreover, economic, social, and environmental goals can, in principle, be achieved through "win-win" solutions with few tradeoffs. As a result of this attractive framing, corporate sustainability officers, departments, and reports have, over the past two decades, proliferated, especially among multinational corporations that operate in national and transnational spheres (Bornschier and Chase-Dunn 1985; Guillén 2001a).

But the definition and emerging theory of sustainability has at the same time remained elusive and provided substantial interpretive leeway for how it may be implemented in practice (Ratner 2004). The ambiguity and breadth of the sustainability idea may well have contributed to its growing popularity. However, the ambiguous sustainability concept can also be expected to be interpreted, translated, and elaborated quite differently, in accordance with national institutional systems. For example, in a Chinese context, sustainability may take on an affinity with the values of harmony and unity (and the Communist Party's recent promotion of a "harmonious society" goal), whereas in the United States, it may become elaborated in connection with innovation and choice in a free market system. The implication may be different policy preferences, such as government planning and active industrial policy versus cap-and-trade systems and technology investments. Just as the strategies adopted in different countries for governing the early railroad industry reflected prevailing ideas of governance of their political cultures (Dobbin 1994) or how principles of market deregulation were translated into practice in different ways in liberal and coordinated political economies (Vogel 1996), so the strategies of action for sustainability may reflect national contexts.

A key insight of the VoC school, and where it diverges from the neoinstitutionalist world society perspective, is the notion of translation. "Foreign" or "global" ideas, if imported at all, are filtered, transformed, and appropriated to make sense within an institutional arrangement and corresponding cultural understandings (see Sahlin and Wedlin 2008, for a recent review). This contrasts with the processes of direct imitation or diffusion emphasized in neoinstitutional research, where ideas cross national boundaries more or less unchanged (Lee and Strang 2006; Simmons, Dobbin, and Garrett 2006; Weber, Davis, and Lounsbury 2009). Public discourse plays an important role in this translation process, but, according to comparative institutional scholars, discourse is not a purely representational activity outside the political economy of countries but an integral cultural component; it reflects and influences the interests and actions of diverse agents in an institutional system (Campbell 2007). In this regard, the VoC conception of cultural and discursive processes as integral to systems of material production differs from approaches that locate national differences in abstract value dimensions (e.g., Inglehart and Baker 2000) or that see public discourse and institutional systems as more loosely related (e.g., Schudson 1989; Gamson 1992b).

Several typologies of capitalism have been proposed, ranging from a single axis from liberal to coordinated economies, to fine-grained differences that see distinct logics at the level of almost every country (Jackson and Deeg 2006). The basis for these typologies is normally groupings of similar institutional configurations that include historically evolved systems of finance, corporate governance, industrial relations and skill creation, the organization of work and innovation, and the role of the state (Jackson and Deeg 2006). Although originally devised to point out institutional plurality within market capitalism, recent VoC research has been concerned not so much with refining static comparisons but with how such differences affect national responses to common changes (Streek 2010). More culturally oriented approaches explain such divergent paths, in part, with reference to widely held beliefs and knowledge regimes that drive the formulation of new policy and the development of authoritative knowledge (Campbell 2002; Campbell and Pedersen 2011).

For the purpose of this chapter, we draw primarily on the typology used by Campbell and Pederson (2011), which aligns political economies along two dimensions: liberal versus coordinated market economies, which captures the extent to which economic activity is governed through "free" market transactions or embedded in associational, network, and state structures; and central/closed versus decentralized/open political systems, which captures the extent to which knowledge production and policy discourse are centrally controlled. We examine one country each that corresponds to the resulting four types of market capitalism (Campbell and Pedersen 2011): the United States represents a liberal decentralized system, the United Kingdom a liberal centralized system, Germany a coordinated decentralized market system, and Japan a coordinated centralized market system. To these we add two varieties of capitalism that are only in part market-based and hence fall outside this typology: state-directed mixed economies (China) and postcolonial transition economies (Kenya). The purpose of this comparison set is not to be exhaustive but to examine if there are meaningful differences in how the idea of sustainability is represented in the public spheres of these countries. Table 7.1 profiles these countries with some stylized institutional facts.

We examine the public understanding of sustainability through the lens of articles in leading national newspapers in these six countries, using quantitative text analysis to identify dimensions and differences of sustainability discourse. To provide a reference point to the global discourse on sustainability that originated from transnational organizations and experts, we also compare these discourses to the most central document produced by the UN, the 1987 report on "Our Common Future" (Brundtland and World Commission on Environment and Development 1987).

Data and empirical method

Our first empirical goal is to describe the representation of the concept of sustainability in media discourse. The second goal is to identify similarities and differences across the six countries and interpret these differences in light of the institutional differences identified by the VoC perspective.

Since we are interested in the understandings of sustainability in public discourse, we sampled newspaper articles in each country. We

Table 7.1 Country institutional profiles[a]

Dimension	USA	UK	Germany	Japan	China	Kenya
VoC Category	Liberal – decentralized	Liberal – centralized	Coordinated – decentralized	Coordinated – centralized	State-directed mixed	Post-colonial
Population [M]	307.5	61.8	81.9	128.3	1,333.0	39.8
GNP/capita [1000 USD]	45.9	35.2	40.6	39.8	3.7	0.7
Human Development Index	0.89	0.85	0.90	0.88	0.66	0.46
Urbanization [% urban pop]	82.0	90.0	73.7	66.6	44.0	21.9
Energy use/capita [kg oil eq.]	7075	3195	3893	3713	1689	463
Political system	Federal two-party presidential, limited welfare	2–3 party parliamentary, medium welfare	Federal multiparty parliamentary, welfare state	Parliamentary, corporatist welfare state	Single party authoritarian, with large state sector	Multiparty presidential, weak state
Legal system	Common, strong rule of law	Common, strong rule of law	Civil, strong rule of law	Civil, strong rule of law	Civil based, weak rule of law	Common, weak rule of law

Table 7.1 (cont.)

Dimension	USA	UK	Germany	Japan	China	Kenya
Economy	Service and innovation oriented	Service and finance oriented	Export and manufacturing oriented	Export and manufacturing oriented	Fast growth, manufacturing, construction led	Agriculture and tourism oriented
Finance and investment	Market centered	Market centered	Bank centered	Corp. centered	State centered	Market reforms
Labor and industrial relations	High skill w low wage sector, weak unions	High skill w low wage sector, craft unions	High skill and productivity, industry unions	High skill and productivity, company unions	Large unskilled labor pool, weak representation	Mostly low skill, underemployment, weak unions
Industrial production	Market based	Market based	Mix of corporatist and market	Corporatist system with some liberalization	Mixed model (planned with/ liberal elements)	Limited industrialization, heavy regulation
Civil society	Weak environmental movement, strong civic culture	Medium environmental movement, strong civic culture	Strong environmental movement, active civic culture	Some environmental activism, civic culture	Low civic culture, movements suppressed, high migration	Tribal ties key, high urban migration, weak movements

[a] 2009 data
Sources: World Development Indicators, CIA Factbook

selected two to three leading print news sources in each country based on circulation and status. We deliberately focused on national, high-status newspapers that reach national elites as well as a large portion of the population. Public understandings, as represented in prominent newspapers, permit insights into cultural understandings and the priorities of opinion leaders in a society (Baumgartner and Jones 1991; Quinn 2005; Sonnett 2009). We used available English versions of news sources to avoid translation issues. It should be noted that the sustainability discourse observable in these sources reflects not only differences in public understandings, but also in the configurations of civil societies and the public political sphere and attention to questions of sustainability among actors participating in public debates. For example, the public media sphere in China is strongly controlled by the Communist Party, whereas newspapers in the United Kingdom are often aligned with different political ideologies and parties.

We then retrieved all articles published in these sources during the calendar year 2010 that contained the search phrase "sustainab*" in the heading or full text of the article (* indicates wildcard character). We manually screened the retrieved articles to eliminate instances where the term sustainability was used in ways unrelated to ideas around the natural environment, broader societal goals and responsibilities, or sustainable development. Most eliminated articles used sustainability in either a purely financial/fiscal context or to describe the prospective success of a strategy. Some articles referenced sustainability more than once. The final sample contains 2,372 articles, plus the UN report. Table 7.2 shows the news sources and the number of articles and mentions of phrase forms of sustainability.

To count only concepts that were closely linked to sustainability in these articles, we extracted from each article all words occurring ten words before and after the search phrase "sustainab*" and used only that co-occurrence sub-corpus to develop a category scheme of associated concepts. Effectively, our analysis therefore represents a network-associational approach to identify cultural repertoires in meaning making in that we focus on those ideas and concepts that are most proximately associated with the sustainability label (Mohr 1998; Breiger 2000; Weber 2005; Smith 2007). The conceptual associations captured by this method are agnostic to the nature of the relationship (i.e., concepts can occur in proximity to each other because they are seen as compatible, antagonistic, or similar).

Table 7.2 *Document sample*

Country	Newspaper sample	Number of articles	Number of hits (sustainab*)
China	China Daily, People's Daily	413	620
Germany	Deutsche Presseagentur, Der Spiegel	351	478
Great Britain	The Guardian, The Times, The Independent	591	986
Japan	The Daily Yomiuri, The Japan Times	96	145
Kenya	The Nation, The East African, Business Daily	101	160
United States	New York Times, Wall Street Journal, Washington Post	820	1,231
United Nations	"Our Common Futures" (full report)	1	364

Using the co-occurrence subsample, we proceeded to develop a comprehensive set of categories that capture the conceptual repertoire associated with sustainability across all countries and the UN document. The process of category development proceeded inductively, iterating between a sample of the co-occurrence text corpus, the full-text documents, and emerging classification frameworks. We seeded the analysis by extracting the 200 most frequent words and the fifty most frequent two-word phrases for each country from the co-occurrence corpus after eliminating common words and lemmatizing the corpus (see Krippendorff 2012 for an overview of standard text analysis processing). We then grouped common words thematically and elaborated the emerging category scheme with reference to the full text of the articles.

The content of public sustainability discourse

Table 7.3 shows five broad facets, thirty concept categories used, and example terms of the resulting classification scheme. The facet dimensions describe the broad domains commonly used in sustainability discourse (environmental, social, and economic concerns), the scope

Table 7.3 *Concepts frequently associated with sustainability*

Facet	Concept	Examples
Domains	Natural environment	Greening, ecosystem, biological
	Economic development	Development, growth, economy
	Social	Population, health, hunger, food,
Agents	Business	Companies, the market, business
	Government	Government, agencies, officials, international organizations
	Science	Universities, scientists, education
	People	The public, the people, humanity
Scope	Global	World, international, global
	National	National, domestic, regional
	Local	Cities, neighborhood, backyard
Problems	Energy	Power, electricity, energy
	Climate change	Carbon, greenhouse gas, global warming, fossil fuel
	Water	Water, drought
	Population	Population growth, urbanization, refugees
	Waste	Recycling, waste disposal, landfill
	Plants	Forests, plant life
	Nuclear	Nuclear, atomic
	Air	Air pollution, smog, ozone
	Land	Land use, cultivation, soil depletion, erosion
	Biodiversity	Biodiversity, extinction
	Infrastructure	Buildings, construction, transport
Solutions	Reduce	Cut, reduce, eliminate
	Conserve	Conservation, preserve
	Protect	Protect, safe-guard
	Manage	Management, control, monitor
	Goals	Target, level, objectives
	Contracts	Treaty, pact, protocol, cooperation
	Projects	Program, project, initiative, campaign, scheme
	Investment	Invest, spend
	Technology	Innovation, technology

of impacts and action (from problems seen as global in nature to being seen as concerned with local action), the agents with power to cause and resolve problems (state, business, science, and the people), problems connected with sustainability (primarily related to specific natural resources), and solutions (different management approaches to the boundaries between private and public).

Table 7.3 shows that, when aggregated across all countries, there is significant breadth in how sustainability is conceptualized in public discourse. Sustainability is complex in its focus on social, economic, and environmental issues. However, the problems connected with it are predominantly within the environmental domain, pertaining mostly to natural resources. The solutions to these problems vary from private individual-level changes, such as recycling and conservation, to large international changes, such as contracts. These concepts also highlight the often contradictory directions around sustainability – project development and investment in technology can be at conflict with conservation and protection. The breadth of the conceptual repertoires associated with sustainability in public discourses enables unique understandings of sustainability that would, in turn, prompt different strategies of action. These varied meanings can be conceptualized as different combinations of the repertoire of concepts within the facets of sustainability. Consider, for example, the following two statements constructed from the same overall conceptual repertoire: "Governments address global climate change by setting targets for energy use" versus "Businesses solve urban health issues by managing water resources."

Comparative analysis of public sustainability discourse

We use the VoC typology to explore if there are meaningful differences between the aggregate cultural register represented by Table 7.3 and how the idea of sustainability is represented in the public spheres of the focal countries. This approach draws on Swidler's (2002: 2) insight that "Differences between [the] two national cultures are best seen as different emphases and selections from repertoires with many overlapping possibilities."

We used two approaches for uncovering discursive differences across the focal countries: measuring (a) the prominence of different concepts across the countries and (b) the aggregate similarities between countries. To measure the prominence of different concepts within each country, we analyzed the 400 most frequent terms in each country (after eliminating common terms and lemmatization) and determined which concept they represented. Most natural language corpuses follow a power law distribution (Zipf's Law), which means that the top 400 terms capture a large portion of the total corpus. Table 7.4 shows the occurrence matrix at the concept level. If a specific sustainability concept was part of the public agenda, here defined as the 400 most frequent terms associated with sustainability in a country, then that concept is represented with a "1" in Table 7.4.

Substantive similarities and differences

Immediately transparent is the relatively high consensus around a small set of subcategories – the environment, business and markets, government, people, global, energy, climate change, and reduce are closely associated with sustainability in most (although not all) countries. These ideas represent a global agenda and widely shared consensus about the centrality of these concepts to sustainability. What Table 7.4 suggests is that current sustainability discourse is to some extent dominated by energy and climate change concerns regardless of country. Not surprisingly, this discursive agenda is also a central concern of organizations, NGOs, professional associations, and scientists in the international and transnational domain that world society scholars identify as agents of global cultural processes (Frank 1997; Meyer, Boli, Thomas, and Ramirez 1997). This discursive agenda is also much narrower than the set of concepts evoked in the original 1987 UN report, which supports the view that discourse in news media is more susceptible to agenda-setting processes that narrow the focus of debate (McCombs 1997). Specifically, the UN report addressed a broader set of natural resources as issues, and it included the local level as part of sustainability concerns. These differences can be explained by the desire in international agencies to be comprehensive and accommodate a large array of stakeholders. "Our Common Futures" then simply supplies a comprehensive set of ideas from which more situated discourses can draw. On the other hand, the UN report is narrower in the solutions and responses it prominently considers. For example, the report lacks extensive consideration of technological advances, investments, and private contracts. This difference is likely to reflect the participants in drafting the document,

Table 7.4 Occurrence matrix of sustainability concepts across countries

Concepts	Total	USA	UK	Japan	China	Kenya	Germany	UN
Natural environment	7	1	1	1	1	1	1	1
Economic development	5			1	1	1	1	1
Social	4		1			1	1	1
Business and markets	7	1	1	1	1	1	1	1
Government	6	1		1	1	1	1	1
Science	5	1		1	1		1	1
People	5	1	1	1	1			1
Global	7	1	1	1	1	1	1	1
National	5			1	1	1	1	1
Local	1							1
Energy	7	1	1	1	1	1	1	1
Climate change	6	1	1	1	1	1	1	
Water	5		1		1	1	1	1
Population	3				1	1		1
Waste	3				1		1	1
Plants	3	1				1	1	
Nuclear	2			1				1
Air	2				1		1	
Land	2					1	1	
Biodiversity	2			1				1

Infrastructure					1		1	1
Reduce	1		1	1	1		1	1
Conserve		1	1			1	1	
Protect	1		1	1		1	1	
Projects			1	1		1		1
Manage				1		1		1
Goals			1				1	
Contracts			1				1	
Investment				1			1	
Technology	1							
Total	**12**	**9**	**18**	**19**	**16**	**21**	**22**

which were more likely politicians and scientists than business people.

However, beyond this "global core" of sustainability discourse, countries display significant variance in their discursive agendas. To understand the extent to which countries participate in broader international discourses on sustainability versus more unique national varieties, we examined two patterns: the expansiveness of national conceptions of sustainability beyond the central core, as reflected in the total number of concepts associated with sustainability (the column totals in Table 7.4), and their agreement with the statement in the UN report (the percent agreement between the UN and each country column in Table 7.4). Expansiveness can be interpreted as connectedness to wider current agendas, whereas alignment with the UN report can be interpreted as continued adherence to canonical agendas of the transnational sphere.

The column totals in Table 7.4 indicate substantial variance in expansiveness. Public discourse is most narrow in the United Kingdom and the United States. Sustainability discourse in the United Kingdom focused heavily on the few globally shared ideas discussed earlier (nine of thirty possible concepts, all nine of which are shared by at least four other countries), with the public discourse in the United States being only slightly extensive (twelve of thirty concepts). In 2010, the US and UK public discourses did not strongly associate with sustainability concepts such as economic development; a national or local scope; problems beyond energy and climate change; or solutions around conservation, management, goals, contract, projects, or investment. By contrast, public discourse in Germany, Japan, and China is more extensive and associates a more diverse repertoire of concepts with sustainability (between 60 and 70 percent of the aggregate total). This pattern suggests that both countries in our comparison with a market-liberal capitalist system have a narrower conceptualization of sustainability than do those countries with a coordinated or state-directed system. From a VoC perspective, we can explain this pattern with the more robust and diverse participation in the public sphere by corporations, government, and civil society actors and the corresponding complexity of policy agendas. Notably, a primary difference between the market-liberal and coordinated market economies is in the solutions that are associated with sustainability: in contrast to British and US news articles, Japanese and German discourse frequently evokes conservation, goal setting, and contractual agreements as solutions to sustainability questions, in line with negotiated coordination agreements that are common in the political economy of this variety of capitalism. Table 7.5 shows illustrative quotes from the corpus we analyzed. The quotes were generated as concordances, displaying a standard window of worlds (here: ten) around a key term or set of indicator words.

In comparison to the canonical 1987 Brundtland report (UN), contemporary discourse across all countries is less consistently concerned with social issues; the local level; and a set of problems that includes biodiversity, land, air, and nuclear resources. On the other hand, climate change did not feature prominently in the report yet is today seen as central to sustainability discussions. Climate change research was not as well developed in 1987 and possibly not a central concern in the report for that reason. Of the countries in our comparison set, Kenya's public sustainability agenda is most closely aligned with the Brundtland report (67 percent category agreement), followed by China (63 percent) and Japan (60 percent). The focus of US discourse on sustainability is least similar to the UN versions, a result of its relative narrowness and more idiosyncratic problem and solution categories (e.g., technology, plant resources). The high alignment of Kenyan and official Chinese media coverage of sustainability with the concepts used in the UN report may suggest that developing and postcolonial countries are more attentive to the authority of international organizations and discourses, whereas countries at the core of the world system feel less constrained by and pay less attention to the international system and are perhaps more domestically focused (Wallerstein 1974/1980/1989). From a world society perspective, this is a surprising finding because agendas and the global are assumed to be more closely aligned with the culturally dominant nations. The observed pattern may be interpreted as evidence that world society processes are best characterized as a diffusion from the core rather than a truly encompassing and stable international sphere. Alternatively, it could be interpreted as evidence for countries having equal exposure to global discourses but responding differently due to their power and position in the world polity.

The two market-liberal countries are, on average, more distant from the UN document than the two coordinated market economies, although this effect is likely driven simply by the narrower agenda in liberal market economies compared to the comprehensive UN report.

Table 7.5 Illustrative quotes from the analyzed news sources

Country	Text illustrations		
United Nations	a profound effect upon the ability of all peoples to	*sustain*	human progress for generations to come
	Environmental protection is thus inherent in the concept of	*sustainable*	development as is a focus on the sources of environmental
	Hence the very logic of	*sustainable*	development implies an internal stimulus to Third World growth
	However a nation proceeds towards the goals of	*sustainable*	development and lower fertility levels, the two are intimately
	survival and well-being could depend on success in elevating	*sustainable*	development to a global ethic
	support activities that are economically and ecologically	*sustainable*	both in the short and longer terms.
	biological diversity and shall observe the principle of optimum	*sustainable*	yield in the use of living natural resources and ecosystems
United States	Q: Let's talk about sustainability. A:	*Sustainability*	isn't just a reference to new technology it's a rebirth
	home to a research institute focused on renewable energy and	*sustainability*	and eventually if all goes as planned to various clean-technology
	redeveloped into 28 rental apartments. Both projects are stressing	*sustainability*	by using solar power geothermal systems and recycled materials
	authorized to speak publicly on the issue. But from a	*sustainability*	perspective nuclear power makes little sense said

	The three pillars of the convention are conservation	*sustainable*	development and fair use of resources. But the argument
	plant life and legions of residents obsessed with local and	*sustainable*	food Even better it happens to be one of the
United Kingdom	need to reduce our consumption but for most people this	*sustainability*	revolution would surely have to be applied across the board
	today's postgraduates are increasingly likely to encounter	*sustainability-*	related courses during their MBA studies
	insurance companies but admits that many are offsetting their	*sustainable*	investments against large holdings in traditional companies
	rapidly increase carbon emissions and erode the environmental	*sustainability*	of biofuels In other words as the percentage of biofuel
	comfort food And yet as our interest in animal welfare	*sustainability*	and healthy eating has grown we've become increasingly
	demands of short-term shareholders and lead from the front on	*sustainability*	and climate change He told a session at Davos that
Germany	Millennium Development Goals MDGs improving the quality and	*sustainability*	of macroeconomic growth and helping to reduce carbon
	a long-term goal so that we could ensure the	*sustainability*	of fishing That would also enable future generations to eat
	is needed to deliver on EU policy goals of competitiveness	*sustainability*	and security of supply an accompanying statement said
	contribute to global warming. By promoting the conservation and	*sustainable*	management of forests we can not only mitigate climate impacts

Table 7.5 (*cont.*)

Country	Text illustrations		
	significantly lighter than conventional cars and in terms of	*sustainability*	will set a new standard across the entire value-added chain
	We will strengthen multilateral cooperation to promote external	*sustainability*	and pursue the full range of policies conducive to reducing
Japan	government bodies NGOs and businesses passed information on the	*sustainable*	use of forests protecting endangered species in Japan like the
	need to strengthen multilateral cooperation to promote external	*sustainability*	and pursue policies to reduce excessive imbalances
	Kyoto Report which focuses on efforts to secure strong	*sustainable*	and balanced growth in the region
	and supporting biodiversity is an important ingredient of	*sustainable*	economic development. A few SOS grants already have been
	information about each country's carbon dioxide emissions and self	*sustainability*	Minoru Senda a professor emeritus of the International Research
	the efforts being undertaken internationally establish a	*sustainable*	social security system capable of coping with the aging of
China	aid framework that pledges better efforts in meeting environmental	*sustainability*	social justice and boosting the country's standing in the
	We are committed to leadership in	*sustainability*	The aspiration is to harmonize economic ecologic and social
	Ernst Young has made investments in clean technology and	*sustainability*	services in India China the Middle East and Brazil
	developing economies have made growth and environmental	*sustainability*	should and can go hand-in-hand

	have been actively and continuously involved in local CSR or range of its green technologies and cooperative projects for China's	*sustainability* *sustainable*	projects since the very beginning Development. These include achieving world-class EHS
Kenya	pragmatic and makes land a valued resource in terms of	*sustainability*	productivity and efficient use of the said resource
	temperature and drought undermines people's ability to live	*sustainably*	on land they have farmed all their lives or to
	He said governments cannot talk of	*sustainable*	development when the magnitude of the population inadequately
	is unlikely that Kenya will meet the MDG on environmental	*sustainability*	water access to all by 2015 despite government's efforts to
	attractive to investors so that they can put money into	*sustainable*	charcoal production while promoting conservation and
	On renewable natural resources the bank will ensure the	*sustainability*	of agricultural infrastructure investments in the face of climate

Mapping aggregate country similarities and differences

The relative distance of countries and the question of whether countries with more similar varieties of capitalism cluster in their discursive focus can also be directly addressed by statistically analyzing aggregate repertoire similarities. The overall overlap of two countries' concept repertoires can be seen as an expression of their distance in a high-dimensional vector space, where each category represents a dimension and the difference between two countries' values on that dimension (here 0 or 1) represents their distance. A host of methods is available to reduce the dimensionality of this concept space – in our case, from thirty to one or two (Mohr 1998; Manning and Schutze 1999). We used a simple measure of overall similarity between pairs of countries, the phi coefficient of Pearson correlations, between our vectors of binary variables and converted these pair-wise distances into a country's relative position on a two-dimensional plane using nonmetric multidimensional scaling. We also used a hierarchical clustering algorithm for binary network data (UCINet 6.4) to map the countries into a tree diagram that represents local proximities. Figures 7.1 (multidimensional scaling) and 7.2 (cluster analysis) show the output of these analyses.

The figures largely confirm and clarify the descriptive patterns seen in Table 7.4. The two market-liberal countries, the United Kingdom and the United States, cluster in Figure 7.2 and are most proximately positioned in Figure 7.1. (Of course, the two countries share additional connections in addition to their economic systems.) Kenya and the UN report form a similar pairing, which confirms the impression that, as a developing country with a colonial history, the Kenyan public sphere interprets sustainability more strongly based on the ideas produced by transnational organizations and the development NGOs that are active in the country.

However, the results of these more reductionist analyses also suggest that similarities and differences cannot be reduced to one or two simple dimensions. If country differences could be reduced to the two dimensions of capitalist variety – market-liberal versus coordinated and centralized versus decentralized – we would expect the axes of the multidimensional scaling plot to reflect these dimensions. However, this is not the case. The centralization dimension in particular does not seem to affect the discourse produced. Centralization is not correlated

Sustainability discourse and capitalist variety 241

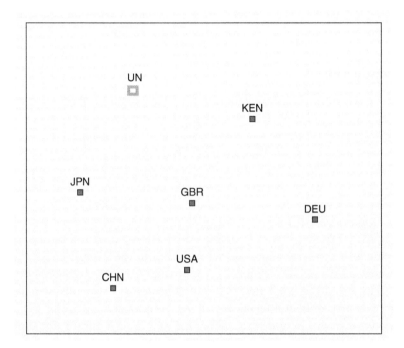

Figure 7.1 Nonmetric multidimensional scaling of country distances

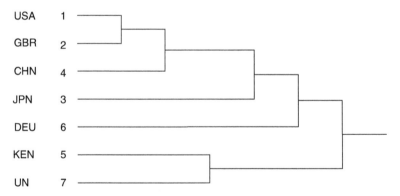

Figure 7.2 Tree diagram of country clustering

with overall discursive proximity, and, although one may reasonably expect that decentralized political economies produce a more extensive and diverse understanding of sustainability, our data do not support this expectation. Two of the more decentralized countries, the United

States and Germany, respectively display the most narrow and the most extensive conceptual repertoire around sustainability.

Conclusion

The goal of our empirical exploration was to examine how the organization of the political economies of different countries affects the local representation of the idea of sustainability as an increasingly important understanding of CSR. We contrasted the comparative tradition of the VoC school with the world society perspective, extending the limited work in the VoC tradition that integrates material and cultural dimensions in accounting for change and convergence in political economies. We found evidence for both a core global repertoire of concepts around sustainability that is widely shared and anchored in global discursive fields and extensive country-level variation in the extensiveness and content of the public meaning of sustainability. Although some of this variance could be attributed to broad dimensions of capitalist variety, notably market-liberal versus coordinated economies, much of it seems rooted in more idiosyncratic historical and contemporary domestic processes.

For example, there is no systematic pattern in sustainability discourse that could be attributed to the centralization–decentralization dimension identified by the VoC perspective. By contrast, one might speculate that the relative similarity of public discourse in Kenya and the United Kingdom is the result of the former colonial ties between these countries. Similarly, the relative similarity of public agendas in China with the United States and the United Kingdom cannot easily be attributed to institutional similarities: China is a state-run system whereas the United States and United Kingdom are both market-liberal systems and, in the case of the United States, also rather decentralized. In these cases, too, similarities may be due to (temporary) attention and aspiration dynamics.

If these explanations were in fact true, one theoretical implication is that standard and fairly static institutional parameters (as used by VoC scholars) are driving convergence and divergence less than are historical and cultural connectedness and more short-term processes of policy agenda setting. At stake is an answer to a more general question about the relationship between institutional systems and discourses that can be observed at a particular point in time. The direct link, of institutions fueling the content of discourses, may be less important than the indirect influence, via influence over broader parameters such as breadth, volatility, or heterogeneity.

The nuanced picture we found of country-level differences and commonalities and layers of global and national discourses also supports recent efforts to reconcile the continued existence and sometimes growth of national institutional differences with simultaneous changes that enlarge global spheres and influences (Guillén 2001b; Streek 2010). Although, traditionally, scholars in the VoC tradition saw national forms of capitalism as tightly integrated configurations or systems that are thus difficult to change in a piecemeal way, it may in fact be more fruitful to see national forms of capitalism as sustaining a (limited) repertoire of cultural tools to interpret, absorb, and respond to new challenges and changes. The combinatorial flexibility of these capitalist elements then becomes an empirical question, with some elements more strongly institutionalized than others and at least some amount of loose coupling. And, rather than conceiving of changes automatically as hybridization between two ideal types, with an implied incompatibility of the underlying logics (Pieterse 1995; Aguilera and Jackson 2002), incremental change can be studied as an expansion of national repertoires.

The differences and commonalities we found in national media discourses about sustainability also have implications for coordination and conflict between private and public actors in a still globalizing world. For example, governments trying to coordinate international responses to global issues such as climate change, security, and development are still strongly influenced by domestic public agendas. As a result, country differences in the representation of sustainability, for example in terms of appropriate problem agendas, solutions, or actors responsible for solving problems, may hinder policy coordination even in the face of selective consensus around a few common themes (Katzenstein 1977; Haas 1992).

At the corporate level, multinational enterprises that embrace sustainability as a guiding principle for their CSR efforts may struggle with credibly implementing and communicating their actions across diverse national contexts. The GRI sustainability reporting guidelines provide guidance to these corporations around sustainability disclosures. These guidelines are based in large part on the UN report and have a similar breadth and depth of focus as the UN report. For example, GRI requests disclosures around corporate strategy, economic sustainability, environmental sustainability, and a multifaceted approach to social sustainability including labor practices, human rights, society, and product responsibility. This pattern is perhaps not surprising given the GRI's status as an international nonprofit consortium and its objective to provide a universally applicable template for reporting.

Over time, this framework may guide multinational corporations to adopt a broader sustainability agenda, one aligned with the UN report and enshrined in standard operating procedure rather than in active management and hence less influenced by public discourses. It will be interesting to see if corporations move in this direction with their sustainability agendas, and, if so, if that movement influences national public agendas. Although emerging global reporting standards like GRI speak to the canon of issues promoted by the global elites involved in transnational discourses, corporate reputations and social evaluations by other stakeholders are still influenced by national public agendas (e.g., Banerjee 2000; Zhang and Luo 2013). Understanding this cultural heterogeneity and its embeddedness in the political economy of a country therefore remains important even with an expansion of the global public sphere.

References

Aguilera, Ruth V., and Gregory F. Jackson. 2002. "Hybridization and Homogeneity across National Models of Corporate Governance." *Economic Sociology European Newsletter* 3:17–25.

Banerjee, S. Bobby. 2000. "Whose Land Is It Anyway? National Interest, Indigenous Stakeholders and Colonial Discourses: The Case of the Jabiluka Uranium Mine." *Organization & Environment* 13:3–38.

Baumgartner, Frank R., and Bryan D. Jones. 1991. "Agenda Dynamics and Policy Subsystems." *Journal of Politics* 53:1044–1074.

Benson, Rodney, and Abigail C. Saguy. 2005. "Constructing Social Problems in an Age of Globalization: A French-American Comparison." *American Sociological Review* 70:233–259.

Bornschier, Volker, and Christopher Chase-Dunn. 1985. *Transnational Corporations and Underdevelopment*. New York: Praeger.

Boyer, Robert. 1996. "The Convergence Hypothesis Revisited: Globalization but Still the Century of Nations?" Pp. 29–59 in *National Diversity and Global Capitalism*, edited by S. Berger and R. Dore. Ithaca, NY: Cornell University Press.

Breiger, Ronald L. 2000. "A Tool Kit for Practice Theory." *Poetics* 27:91–115.
Brundtland, Gro Harlem, and World Commission on Environment and Development. 1987. *Our Common Future*, vol. 383. Oxford, UK: Oxford University Press.
Campbell, John L. 2001. "Institutional Analysis and the Role of Ideas in Political Economy." Pp. 159–189 in *The Rise of Neoliberalism and Institutional Analysis*, edited by J. L. Campbell and O. K. Pedersen. Princeton, NJ: Princeton University Press.
Campbell, John L. 2002. "Ideas, Politics, and Public Policy." *Annual Review of Sociology* 28:21–38.
Campbell, John L. 2006. "Institutional Analysis and the Paradox of Corporate Social Responsibility." *American Behavioral Scientist* 49:925–938.
Campbell, John L. 2007. "Why Would Corporations Behave in Socially Responsible Ways? An Institutional Theory of Corporate Social Responsibility." *Academy of Management Review* 32:946–967.
Campbell, John L., and Ove K. Pedersen. 2011. "Knowledge Regimes and Comparative Political Economy." Pp. 167–190 in *Ideas and Politics in Social Science Research*, edited by D. Béland and R. Cox. New York: Oxford University Press.
Dobbin, Frank. 1994. *Forging Industrial Policy: The United States, Britain, and France in the Railway Age*. London: Cambridge University Press.
Fiss, Peer C., and Paul Hirsch. 2005. "The Discourse of Globalization: Framing and Sensemaking of an Emerging Concept." *American Sociological Review* 70:25–52.
Frank, David J. 1997. "Science, Nature, and the Globalization of the Environment, 1870–1990." *Social Forces* 76:409–435.
Freeman, R. Edward, and Jeanne Liedtka. 1991. "Corporate Social Responsibility: A Critical Approach." *Business Horizons* 34:92–98.
Friedman, Milton. 1970. "The Social Responsibility of Business Is to Increase Its Profits." *The New York Times Magazine* September 13 (33):122–126.
Gamson, William A. 1992a. "Media Images and the Social Construction of Reality." *Annual Review of Sociology* 18:373–393.
Gamson, William A. 1992b. *Talking Politics*. New York: Cambridge University Press.
Gamson, William A., and Andre Modigliani. 1989. "Media Discourse and Public Opinion on Nuclear Power: A Constructionist Approach." *American Journal of Sociology* 95:1–37.
Gladwin, Thomas N., James J. Kennelly, and Tara-Shelomith Krause. 1995. "Shifting Paradigms for Sustainable Development: Implications for

Management Theory and Research." *Academy of Management Journal* 20:874–907.
Guillén, Mauro F. 2001a. "Is Globalization Civilizing, Destructive or Feeble? A Critique of Five Key Debates in the Social Science Literature." *Annual Review of Sociology* 27:235–260.
Guillén, Mauro F. 2001b. *The Limits of Convergence*. Princeton, NJ: Princeton University Press.
Haas, Peter. 1992. "Epistemic Communities and International Policy Coordination." *International Organization* 46:1–35.
Hall, Peter, and David Soskice. 2001. *Varieties of Capitalism: The Institutional Foundations of Comparative Advantage*. New York: Oxford University Press.
Hart, Stuart L. 1995. "A Natural-Resource-Based View of the Firm." *Academy of Management Review* 20:986–1014.
Inglehart, Ronald, and Wayne E. Baker. 2000. "Modernization, Cultural Change, and the Persistence of Traditional Values." *American Sociological Review* 65:19–51.
Jackson, Gregory F., and Richard Deeg. 2006. *How Many Varieties of Capitalism? Comparing Comparative Institutional Analysis of Capitalist Varieties*. MPIfG Discussion Paper 06/2.
Jacoby, Sanford. 1998. *Modern Manors: Welfare Capitalism since the New Deal*. Princeton, NJ: Princeton University Press.
Katzenstein, Peter J. 1977. "Introduction: Domestic and International Forces and Strategies of Foreign Economic Policy." *International Organization* 31:587–606.
Krippendorff, Klaus. 2012. *Content Analysis: An Introduction to Its Methodology*. Beverly Hills, CA: Sage.
Lee, Chang Kil, and David Strang. 2006. "The International Diffusion of Public-sector Downsizing: Network Emulation and Theory-driven Learning." *International Organization* 60:883–909.
Lim, Alwyn, and Kiyoteru Tsutsui. 2012. "Globalization and Commitment in Corporate Social Responsibility: Cross-national Analyses of Institutional and Political-economy Effects." *American Sociological Review* 77:69–98.
Manning, Christopher, and Hinrich Schutze. 1999. *Foundations of Statistical Natural Language Processing*. Cambridge, MA: MIT Press.
McCombs, Maxwell. 1997. "Building Consensus: The News Media's Agenda-setting Roles." *Political Communication* 14:433–443.
Meyer, John W., John Boli, George M. Thomas, and Francisco O. Ramirez. 1997. "World Society and the Nation State." *American Journal of Sociology* 103:144–181.

Meyer, John W., David J. Frank, Ann Hironaka, Evan Schofer, and Nancy Brandon Tuma. 1997. "The Structuring of a World Environmental Regime, 1870–1990." *International Organization* 51:623–651.

Meyer, John W., Shawn Pope, and Andrew Isaacson. 2015; this volume. "Legitimating the Transnational Corporation in a Stateless World Society." Pp. 27–72 in *Corporate Social Responsibility in a Globalizing World*, edited by K. Tsutsui and A. Lim. New York: Cambridge University Press.

Mohr, John W. 1998. "Measuring Meaning Structures." *Annual Review of Sociology* 24:345–370.

Orrú, Marco, Nicole Woolsey Biggart, and Gary G. Hamilton. 1997. *The Economic Organization of East Asian Capitalism*. Thousand Oaks, CA: Sage.

Pieterse, Jan Nederveen. 1995. "Globalization as Hybridization." Pp. 45–68 in *Global Modernities*, edited by M. Featherstone, S. Lash, and R. Robertson. London: Sage.

Quinn, Naomi. 2005. *Finding Culture in Talk: A Collection of Methods*. New York: Palgrave Macmillan.

Ratner, Blake D. 2004. "'Sustainability' as a Dialogue of Values: Challenges to the Sociology of Development." *Sociological Inquiry* 74:50–69.

Sahlin, Kerstin, and Linda Wedlin. 2008. "Circulating Ideas: Imitation, Translation and Editing." Pp. 218–242 in *The Sage Handbook of Organizational Institutionalism*, edited by R. Greenwood, C. Oliver, K. Sahlin, and R. Suddaby. Los Angeles: Sage.

Schudson, Michael. 1989. "How Culture Works: Perspectives from Media Studies on the Efficacy of Symbols." *Theory and Society* 18:153–180.

Simmons, Beth A., Frank Dobbin, and Geoffrey Garrett. 2006. "Introduction: The International Diffusion of Liberalism." *International Organization* 60:781–810.

Smith, Jackie. 2001. "Globalizing Resistance: The Battle of Seattle and the Future of Social Movements." *Mobilization* 6:1–19.

Smith, Tammy. 2007. "Narrative Boundaries and the Dynamics of Ethnic Conflict and Conciliation." *Poetics* 35:22–46.

Sonnett, John. 2009. "Climates of Risk: A Field Analysis of Global Climate Change in US Media Discourse, 1997–2004." *Public Understanding of Science* 19:698–716.

Streek, Wolfgang. 2010. *E Pluribus Unum? Varieties and Commonalities of Capitalism*. MPIfG Discussion Paper 10/12.

Swidler, Ann. 2002. "Cultural Repertoires and Cultural Logics: Can They Be Reconciled?" *Comparative and Historical Sociology* 14:1–6.

Thelen, Kathleen. 1999. "Historical Institutionalism in Comparative Politics." *Annual Review of Political Science* 2:369–404.
United Nations Secretary-General's High Level Panel on Global Sustainability. 2012. *Resilient People, Resilient Planet: A Future Worth Choosing.* New York: United Nations Publications.
Vogel, Steven Kent. 1996. *Freer Markets, More Rules: Regulatory Reform in Advanced Industrial Countries.* Ithaca, NY: Cornell University Press.
Walker, Edward T. 2015; this volume. "Global Corporate Resistance to Public Pressures: Corporate Stakeholder Mobilization in the United States, Australia, Germany, and France." Pp. 321–362 in *Corporate Social Responsibility in a Globalizing World*, edited by K. Tsutsui and A. Lim. New York: Cambridge University Press.
Wallerstein, Immanuel. 1974/1980/1989. *The Modern World System, vols. I–III.* San Diego, CA: Academic Press.
Weber, Klaus. 2005. "A Toolkit for Analyzing Corporate Cultural Toolkits." *Poetics* 33:227–252.
Weber, Klaus, Gerald F. Davis, and Michael Lounsbury. 2009. "Policy as Myth and Ceremony: The Global Spread of Stock Markets, 1980–2005." *Academy of Management Journal* 52:1319–1347.
Whitley, Richard. 1999. *Divergent capitalism.* Oxford, UK: Oxford University Press.
Zhang, Jianjun, and Xiaowei Rose Luo. 2013. "Dared to Care: Organizational Vulnerability, Institutional Logics and MNCs' Social Responsiveness in Emerging Markets." *Organization Science* 24 (6):1742–1764.

PART III

Corporations' reaction to global corporate social responsibility pressures

8 Why firms participate in the global corporate social responsibility initiatives, 2000–2010

SHAWN M. POPE

Why firms participate in initiatives for corporate social responsibility (CSR) is a question that has puzzled researchers. This is because CSR initiatives may be unprofitable for firms in practice or by their nature (Margolis and Walsh 2003; Vogel 2008) and thus participation may contradict a classic view of the firm as existing to maximize financial returns (Friedman 1970). Researchers have developed a recent interest, specifically, in the motives for participation in the global initiatives. These include the Global Compact (GC; Deva 2006; Bremer 2008; Knight and Smith 2008), the Global Reporting Initiative (GRI; Hedberg and von Malmborg 2003; Adams 2004; Moneva, Archel, and Correa 2006; Brown, Jong, and Lessidrenska 2009; Lim and Tsutsui 2012), and the Carbon Disclosure Project (CDP; Kim and Lyon 2007; Okereke 2007; Kolk, Levy, and Pinske 2008; Stanny and Ely 2008).

These three frameworks are important cases for the study of CSR participation motives because they are the largest in the world by corporate membership. The GC has more than 8,000 members and the GRI and CDP have more than 4,000 members apiece. The frameworks are each administered by nonprofits and require firms from many nations, in many industries, and of any ownership type to produce an annual, voluntary, publically available report of their CSR practices. Considered to be flagships of the global CSR movement – one of the more sweeping international developments of recent decades – the frameworks have come to be championed not only by the very largest multinational corporations, but also by the United Nations, World Trade Organization, International Chamber of Commerce, and many other powerful international policy groups and intergovernmental bodies.

Notwithstanding their large rosters and elite support, the global CSR frameworks are highly controversial. Much of the research on them concerns the contentious idea that, because the frameworks are voluntary and have weak membership requirements, they present corporations with a cheap means to burnish their reputations. Another core argument is that the frameworks are half-measures that corporations adopt preemptively to thwart the institution of stricter governmental regulation. Such arguments, tending to operate by rationalist and functional logics, work to recover a shareholder primacy view of the global CSR frameworks by suggesting several pathways whereby the frameworks may allow corporations to preserve or increase profits in both the short and long terms. On a more abstract level, the arguments return to an imagery of the corporation as rational, purposive, and – too often for the present case – sociopathic. For example, the claim that participation in the global CSR frameworks is a tool of "greenwash" (associated with the CDP) or "bluewash" (associated with the GC) invests corporations with a tremendous capacity to perpetuate large-scale public deceptions and to accrue rewards from such.

The thesis of this chapter is that these prevailing arguments tend to downplay the normative pressures in wider business environments that promote the adoption of global CSR frameworks. Attention to these normative pressures shifts the focus from the strategies of individual corporations to the patterns of CSR framework emergence, diffusion, and entrenchment within nations, within intercorporate networks, and, increasingly, throughout the world. The emphasis of this alternative perspective is less on utility-maximizing than on conformity, less on profits than on social acceptance and social influence. The data analysis of this chapter shows that global CSR framework participation follows not from increases in rationalistic corporate-level variables such as prior advertising expenditures, social movement pressure, or even high levels of CSR performance, but from increases in CSR networks and infrastructure within the various communities in which corporations are embedded.

Methodologically, the chapter serves to round out a literature on the global CSR initiatives that features mostly cross-sectional designs (e.g., Cetindamar and Husoy 2007), case study (e.g., Adams 2004), and cross-national comparison (e.g., Lim and Tsutsui 2012). With fixed-effect logistic regressions over a ten-year period tracking a firm-level panel of 500 of the largest multinational corporations, this chapter

Why firms participate in the global CSR initiatives 253

adds to the literature a large-scale statistical analysis of CSR adoption antecedents. Testing six hypotheses related to rational/functional explanations and three related to institutional arguments, the chapter uncovers somewhat consistent evidence that firms join the global CSR frameworks due to social ties to global, national, and intercorporate networks while offering only mixed evidence in support of corporate-level variables.

Background

Of the dozens of global CSR initiatives that have cropped up internationally since the 1970s (Leipziger 2003; Waddock 2008; Visser et al. 2010), the GC, GRI, and CDP have the most members and receive the most scholarly attention (Ruggie 2004; Goel 2005). A discussion of these frameworks as world-historical phenomena appears in this volume in the chapter by Meyer, Pope, and Isaacson; a summary of the principles advanced by these frameworks appears in the appendix to this chapter; and in-depth portraits of individual frameworks are provided in several case studies: for example, the GC (Bremer 2008), GRI (Brown and De Jong 2009), and the CDP (Kolk, Levy, and Pinske 2008).

These three frameworks represent all well-established, independent CSR frameworks with global, pan-industry, multistakeholder, and corporate membership. They are well-established in that each has been in operation since the early 2000s (GC, 2000; GRI, 2000; and CDP, 2003), a requirement that excludes newer initiatives with shorter histories such as the ISO 26000 standards (launched in 2010). They are independent in that they are not funded by firms, a criterion that excludes "world business forums" such as the World Business Council for Sustainable Development (WBCSD), World Economic Forum, and International Business Leaders Forum. The global criterion limits the analysis to frameworks with membership from many countries (all have members from more than thirty countries) and excludes nationally and regionally oriented frameworks such as the United States' Energy Star program or the European-centric Eco-Management and Audit Scheme. The pan-industry requirement excludes sector-specific frameworks such as the Fair Labor Standards (apparel industry) or the Marine Stewardship Council (fishing industry). The smaller membership of these initiatives is less suitable for large-scale multivariate analysis. The multistakeholder requirement applies only to those frameworks that foster regular dialogue among companies, nonprofits, investors, and regulators. Finally, the requirement of company-level participation excludes, for example, the ISO 14001 environmental standards, in which the members are production facilities, and the Organisation for Economic Cooperation and Development (OECD) Guidelines for Multinational Enterprises, which, similar to a treaty, has state-level ratification.

The GC, GRI, and CDP are similar in that each requires its members to produce an annual report disclosing information about corporate-level CSR practices. The report for the GC covers ten broad CSR principles related to human rights, anticorruption, labor, and the environment. GRI reports, by contrast, are similar in content but much more extensive, adhering to a 195-page manual. GRI reports may be self-declared according to several standards of stringency, with levels that may be certified also by third-party auditors. CDP reports are narrower, concerning only the disclosure of pollutants. Another commonality is that these initiatives are the most popular, with each having thousands of members (in 2010, the GC had 8,000 members; the GRI, 4,000; and the CDP, 4,000), as illustrated by Figure 8.1, which shows framework membership growth from 2000 to 2010. As recent and popular global phenomena, the frameworks attract much scholarly attention, with, for example, the GC website listing more than 200 articles on the initiative in the last twelve years. Finally, the frameworks operate with high mutual awareness. In 2006, the GC and the GRI struck a strategic alliance to ensure that the principles of each framework are mutually reinforcing. Also in 2012, the GC reached an accord with the CDP such that CDP surveys could meet the GC standards of environmental reporting. The frameworks, then, are parts of an increasingly unified global CSR regime.

Theory and hypotheses

Functional theories

Analysts of the global CSR frameworks generally try to discover their uses for meeting the business objectives of their members – most often,

Why firms participate in the global CSR initiatives 255

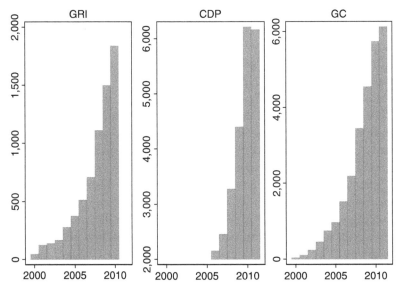

Figure 8.1 Number of worldwide members of global corporate social responsibility initiatives by year

for turning profits. The possibility of instrumental uses of membership in the frameworks seems highly plausible given that previous research on CSR, in general, finds that it may be used by companies to gain new consumers (Du, Bhattacharya, and Sen 2007), preempt regulation (Wood 2003; Delmas and Montes-Sancho 2010), limit competition (Potoski and Prakash 2005), attract better employees (Turban and Greening 1997; Bhattacharya, Sen, and Korschun 2008), obtain financial capital (Clark and Hebb 2005), bolster competitive standing (Baron 2001), improve reputation (Miles and Covin 2000), signal product quality to trade partners (Prakash and Potoski 2006), gain networking opportunities (Cetindamar and Husoy 2007), and better understand operating risks (Okereke 2007).

As an analytic framework for determining which corporations are likely to gain these benefits from participation in the global CSR frameworks, scholars often suggest a basic cost-benefit analysis (Knight and Smith 2008). The logic is often that participation in the frameworks is high because costs are generally low: the frameworks advance principles that are too abstract to entail specific changes in corporate operations (Hussey, Kirsop, and Meissen 2001) and, at any rate, the frameworks lack mechanisms to enforce breaches (Bloomfield 1999; Sagafi-nejad 2005). The thinking is that participation is high also because the benefits are presumably large: the frameworks allow firms, for example, to boost their reputation (Soederberg 2007) or build ties with the UN (Najam 1999; Alves 2009). The low costs and high benefits, some claim, engender "free-riding" (see Kell and Levin 2002; Kimbro and Cao 2007; Scholtens and Dam 2007), whereby members of the frameworks gain in reputation without having to make costly changes to their CSR practices. Low costs and high benefits may also encourage "adverse selection" (King and Lenox 2000; Williams 2004; Macve and Chen 2010), in which the returns to participation are greatest for those firms with the poorest reputations, holding participation costs constant. I explore similar rational-choice arguments in the following sections, where I discuss how participation in global CSR frameworks might enhance corporate image, increase international trade, or reduce stakeholder pressure.

Image

In a recent survey by McKinsey (2008: 3), firms themselves claim that the primary motive of CSR participation is to "Maintain a good corporate reputation." A good reputation may allow firms to produce at lower cost (Podolny 1993), send signals of product quality that are more credible (Benjamin and Podolny 1999), and attract employees of greater talent (Stigler 1962). Because good reputations are valuable, inimitable, and rare, they satisfy the definition of resources in the resource-based view of the firm (Wernerfelt 1984) and thus may drive sustained competitive advantage (Roberts and Dowling 2002). Not all firms need a good reputation to the same extent. Firms that are publically held (KPMG 2011), sell their products directly to consumers (Galaskiewicz 1997), or that are large in revenues (e.g., Udayasankar 2008) may be more dependent on a favorable public image. This chapter argues that companies that have already attained a good reputation or that spend large amounts of money on advertising to build one will join the frameworks in greater numbers so as to preserve their reputational investment.

Hypothesis 1 (H1): CSR participation increases with advertising dollars.
Hypothesis 2 (H2): CSR participation increases with public reputation.

Trade

Firms that trade internationally have higher rates of adoption of corporate governance models (Drori, Jang, and Meyer 2006), quality control standards such as ISO 9000 (e.g., Clougherty and Grajek 2008), and workforce protocols such as the fair labor standards (Greenhill, Mosley, and Prakash 2009), as well as higher rates of membership in the GC and GRI (Lim and Tsutsui 2012). In these studies, international trade disciplines companies to adopt the business practices sought by trading partners. Firms in countries with poor social and environmental regulation, for example, may adopt voluntary CSR standards to attract business from firms headquartered in nations with higher consumer expectations.

International trade may increase CSR adoption for another reason. CSR may allow firms to integrate their identities across far-flung operating divisions. This "coordination hypothesis" is at the heart of the literature on "global CSR," which asks whether "multinationals should develop centrally coordinated, 'global' CSR strategies, or whether they should stimulate decentralized, 'local' CSR strategies" (Muller 2006: 189). One position gaining ground in this literature is that multinationals should "follow a globally integrated strategy that allows them to maintain policies, processes and structures that are consistent with their expressed mission and values, across all relevant cultures" (Chaudhri 2006: 39; but also see Husted and Allen 2006; Mohan 2006; Huemer 2010). I predict here that well-articulated and ready-made CSR policies, as available through the global CSR frameworks, allow companies to strike a common chord in a globally dispersed employee and consumer base.

Hypothesis 3 (H3): CSR participation increases with a firm's overseas operations.

Pressure

Social movements can wield great influence on corporations (G. Davis et al. 2005; G. F. Davis et al. 2008). They may supply them with organizational forms (Rao, Morrill, and Zald 2000), determine the outcome of struggles for corporate control (G. F. Davis and Thompson 2007), and place corporate profits in jeopardy (B. G. King and Soule 2007; Bartley and Child 2012; Vasi and King 2012). Movements increasingly pressure companies to take up CSR (Soule 2009), using boycotts and shareholder resolutions, for example, to create adverse narratives about corporate social practices (Clark and Hebb 2005; Basu and Palazzo 2008; Soule 2009). Firms sometimes respond to these accounts with their own, more positive narratives about their CSR activity – narratives that may depart very far from the reality of their actual CSR performance (Dobers and Springett 2010; Jamali 2010; Haack, Schoeneborn, and Wickert 2012). Narrative contests affect how management perceives risk and benefit and may lead corporations to undertake dramatic actions, such as the divestment of entire business lines (Weber, Thomas, and Rao 2009; Vasi and King 2012). For these reasons, a large literature now suggests that firms may use CSR to manage movement pressure, for example, to take out an insurance policy against scandal, or engage in impression management after a major episode of corporate irresponsibility (Peloza 2005; Werther Jr. and Chandler 2005; Godfrey, Merrill, and Hansen 2009; Vanhamme and Grobben 2009; Minor and Morgan 2011). Thus:

Hypothesis 4 (H4): CSR participation increases with social movement pressure.
Hypothesis 5 (H5): CSR participation increases in the wake of a major scandal.

Performance

If one takes a cost-benefit perspective of participation in the global CSR frameworks, then it is reasonable to expect that companies with high CSR performance will have higher framework participation. This is because these companies will incur fewer costs upon joining a global CSR framework by not having to institute a host of new CSR policies and practices. Thus, by joining the global CSR frameworks, which many observers presume to be very popular with global consumer audiences, highly performing companies can improve their reputations relatively cheaply. However, one might expect that if the global CSR frameworks are subject to high levels of free-riding, then companies with high CSR performance may avoid the frameworks so as not to lend legitimacy to the insincere participation of their competitors (an outcome that has been termed the "second form of free-riding," as typified by Gunningham and Sinclair 2007). Nonetheless:

Hypothesis 6 (H6): CSR participation increases with CSR performance.

Institutional theories

Institutional arguments about the motives for CSR framework participation generally de-emphasize efficiency or profitability in favor of seeking the determinants in the very wide social environments in which CSR frameworks come to be perceived as "proper, adequate, rational, and necessary" (Meyer and Rowan 1977: 345; see also Boiral 2007). CSR frameworks appear in this line of thinking as examples of institutions – self-activating patterns of social interaction – with everyday examples being marriage, double-entry accounting, and the university system. Many institutional arguments stress that technical performance in the absence of institutional adoption is considered illegitimate or that the technical and social benefits of institutional adoption may trade off across time, with, for example, early institutional adopters doing so for technical advantage and later adopters doing so because institutional adoption becomes necessary to be perceived as legitimate (Tolbert and Zucker 1983).

In tapping institutional theory to explain the adoption of the global CSR frameworks, scholars have called attention to "how CSR is socially constructed in specific contexts" (Delmas and Toffel 2004; Wright and Rwabizambuga 2006; Campbell 2007; Dahlsrud 2008: 1; Nikolaeva and Bicho 2011; Lim and Tsutsui 2012). These scholars "go beyond grounding CSR in the voluntary behavior of companies" and seek "understanding of the larger historical and political determinants of whether and in what forms corporations take on social responsibilities" (Brammer, Jackson, and Matten 2011: 3). Identifying the relevant social contexts and social processes is the primary task for scholars who take this approach. This chapter discusses three social contexts with the potential to drive CSR adoption: business associations, nation-states, and "world society" (Meyer et al. 1997).

Business associations

Firms that interact with others in CSR-promoting forums may be more likely to undertake CSR adoption. Campbell (2007: 962), for example, writes that "Corporations will be more likely to act in socially responsible ways if they are engaged in institutionalized dialogue with unions, employees, community groups, investors, and other stakeholders."

And Bartley (2007: 233) highlights the importance of "arenas that bring a number of different actors (often with different interests, ideologies, and organizational forms) into routine contact with one another, under a common frame of reference, in pursuit of at least a common shared project."

An example of such a forum in the global CSR field is the WBCSD. Based in Geneva, Switzerland, and created in 1995 from the merger of the World Industry Council for the Environment and the Business Council for Sustainable Development, the WBCSD is a CEO-led association that attempts to promote sustainable development by brokering dialogue among leading international organizations, including governmental bodies, policy organizations, and social movement groups. It currently has 200 corporate members from thirty countries and twenty industrial sectors, including some of the largest firms worldwide, such as General Electric, Ford Motor, Siemens, and Deutsche Bank. The organization has centrality in the global CSR field, with particularly strong ties to the UN, having, for example, partnered with the UN to organize the Rio+20 conference and having signed a memorandum of understanding with the GC.

Despite its power and position, the WBCSD has not been studied extensively from an academic standpoint. When it appears in research, scholars usually probe confusions about how to perceive the organization – as an innovative CSR alliance or as a thinly veiled lobbyist organization. For example, Najam (1999: 72) takes the first position:

The public message of the World Business Council for Sustainable Development and other groups has been that business now understands and supports the goals of sustainable development and environmental protection, and business will be the leaders achieving both. At the same time, they have been working to avoid regulations of their activities, and working against agreements in the very regimes that the United Nations Conference on Environment and Development spawned, such as the Climate Convention.

The possibility of a more optimistic view of the WBCSD, however, might be built from the programmatic work of Galaskiewicz (1985, 1991, 1997). In an initial study covering the years 1979–1981 and a follow-up from 1987–1989, Galaskiewicz found that members of an elite CSR business association, the Minnesota Project on Corporate Responsibility, were more likely to have leading CSR practices. These practices, he found, could not be reduced to motives that might be perceived as more rational, such as whether firms sold directly to consumers (1991: 309). Rather, the forums fostered good social practices by subjecting firms to peer pressure and by constructing a status hierarchy around good CSR practices.

Hypothesis 7 (H7): Participation in global CSR frameworks increases with participation in a CSR-focused business association.

National institutional environment

Another social context that may affect CSR adoption is the national institutional environment. How a firm's CSR practices reflect country-specific political legacies and enduring systems of business–government relations is a perspective that has recently diverged from an older "varieties of capitalism" literature (Hall and Soskice 2001). Case studies of CSR practices in India (Gupta 2007), Switzerland (Sachs, Rühli, and Mittnacht 2005), Greece (Skouloudis, Evangelinos, and Kourmousis 2010), Italy (La Rosa and Franco 2000), and Japan (Welch, Mori, and Aoyagi-Usui 2002), as well as cross-national comparisons, for example, of the United States, the United Kingdom, Australia, and Germany (Chen and Bouvain 2008); the United States, France, and Germany (Maignan and Ferrell 2003), the United States and Spain (Vitell and Hidalgo 2006), and the United States and Europe (Doh and Guay 2006) show that CSR norms are patterned to a large extent by national contexts.

A particularly notable study here is that by Lim and Tsutsui (2012), editors of this volume, showing that membership in the GC and GRI is increased by the launch of a GC "local network" within a nation. These nationally based, officially endorsed, and professionally staffed local networks (as discussed in more detail in the methods section) attempt to "root the Global Compact within different national, cultural, and language contexts (unglobalcompact.org).

Hypothesis 8 (H8): CSR participation increases with support for CSR in the national institutional environment.

World institutional environment

A remaining social context is the world environment, increasingly analyzed through the lens of world society theory. This theory argues that global affairs are a unique, autonomous, and preeminent level of social life that contain not only politics but also specific stores of cultural material. The imagery in this theory is of world society norms diffusing from the global to the local level, where the norms present organizations with models of action already stamped with a higher legitimacy. Studies from the world society perspective have found that national ties to the global arena increase the adoption of, for example, corporate governance models, international accounting rules, and globally derived but nationally oriented environmental ministries (respectively, Drori et al. 2006; Frank, Hironake, and Schofer 2000; Jang 2006).

World society studies increasingly address CSR (Shanahan and Khagram 2006; Lim and Tsutsui 2012; Meyer, Pope, and Isaacson, this volume). In this volume, for example, Meyer et al. (this volume) trace the spread of CSR principles in the global domain, where CSR has come to be backed mostly prominently by the UN, which supports not only the GC, but also the GRI, Principles for Responsible Investing, and Principles for Responsible Management Education. Lim and Tsutsui (2012) also find that countries that are tied to the international realm through citizen-level memberships in international nongovernmental groups also have higher rates of participation in the GC and GRI. This study seeks to replicate their finding over a longer time frame and with companies as the units of analysis.

Hypothesis 9 (H9): CSR participation increases with linkages to world society.

Methods

To test the various motives for participation in the global CSR frameworks, I build an original dataset from several primary and secondary sources. The units of analysis are corporations: specifically, members of the 2010 "Global Fortune 500," a ranking by *Fortune Magazine* of the largest companies in the world by revenues, one that is common in other quantitative studies of globalization processes (Muller and

Whiteman 2008; Carroll and Sapinski 2010). *Fortune Magazine* is a monthly, US-based, popular-audience business publication with a circulation of 800,000. Companies on the 2010 Global 500 Ranking include those that are private, public, and state-owned, those from thirty-four countries, and those from all ten major industrial sectors of the Global Industrial Classification Standard.

Dependent variables

I treat CSR participation as GC membership (scored as 1 in years when a company is listed as "active" in the early years 2000–2003 and 1 in years in which the company submits a GC report to the GC offices from 2004–2010), GRI membership (1 in years when a company submits a GRI report to the online database), and as CDP membership (1 in years when a company returns a CDP survey). With multiple indicators of CSR adoption, I seek to control for their idiosyncrasies, and, by running separate models for each framework, I hope to supply a basic robustness check. As discussed earlier, the three frameworks are all well-established, independent CSR initiatives with global, pan-industry, multistakeholder, and corporate-level membership.

Functional/rational variables

The two measures of corporate image are whether the company appears in *Fortune Magazine*'s "50 Global Most Admired Companies"[1] (1 = yes) and whether it appears on *Advertising Age's* "Top 100 Global Marketers" (1 = yes). *Fortune Magazine* constructs its ranking by asking executives, directors, and other industrial analysts to rank the reputations of the 1,400 largest companies in the world by revenues. *Advertising Age* is a US-based, weekly trade magazine that uses third-party research and original surveys of advertising agencies to rank companies by worldwide media spending. The two rankings differ from one another in nature. Whereas the Most Admired list captures *attained* public image, the Top Marketer

---

[1] *Fortune* has published rankings on the top 50 companies since 2000. From 2006, *Fortune* makes information available on about the top 350 companies. I do not have these data for earlier years, however, because *Fortune* refused my request to release the 51–350 rankings in the years 2000–2005.

ranking reflects only corporate advertising expenditures. The hypotheses here are two-tailed because it is unclear from the outset whether firms use CSR participation to protect or repair their images. In the first case, companies with good images might join CSR initiatives to preserve their reputations; in the second case, companies with plummeting images may do so to save face.

Pressure to participate is a binary variable equal to 1 in a year that a company receives a shareholder resolution asking for GC or GRI participation. The source for this variable is the Ethvest database of the Interfaith Center on Corporate Responsibility, a consortium of religious groups that advance social causes through shareholder advocacy. Only companies listed on US stock exchanges can receive these shareholder resolutions because each must be approved by the US Securities and Exchange Commission (SEC).

The first of two binary measures of corporate scandal equals 1 in years when a company appears in the list of the Ten Worst Corporations (source: the watchdog group *Multinational Monitor*). Because this list ceased in 2008, for the years 2009 and 2010, I code this measure as 1 if the company was a candidate for the Corporate Hall of Shame (source: *Corporate Accountability International*).[2] These sources of scandal are similar in attempting to promote positive social change by naming and shaming those corporations with the most egregious social practices, whether it was Enron in 2001 for accounting fraud or Halliburton in 2006 for questionable lobbying activity. The second indicator of scandal equals 1 in years when a company has had a formal complaint lodged with a National Contact Point of the OECD Guidelines for Multinational Enterprises (source: online database of the watchdog group *OECD Watch*). Similar to a treaty in having nations as members rather than corporations, the OECD guidelines are nonbinding principles adhered to by forty-four mostly advanced economies, principles that reflect international standards of labor, environment, information disclosure, consumer protection, competition, taxation, human rights, bribery, and science and technology. Since 2001, the average number per year of complaints to the OECD National Contact Points has been about twelve.

---

[2] This list, too, has 8–10 candidates per year, making the lists roughly comparable in size.

CSR performance

I measure CSR performance as inclusion (1 = yes) in the Dow Jones Sustainability Index. Produced since 1999 from annual company surveys disseminated and compiled by Dow Jones in consultation with the research firm Sustainable Asset Management, the index is constructed by reducing the 2,500 largest companies by market capitalization to the top 10–20 percent in terms of assessed CSR performance according to dozens of indicators of social, financial, and environmental responsibility. One primary use of the index is by socially responsible investors to determine which companies are suitable for inclusion in investment portfolios managed for both financial and social returns.

A final indicator of rational-choice CSR participation is financial internationality, captured by inclusion in the list of the 1,000 Largest Transnational Companies, produced by the UN Conference on Trade and Development by ranking companies according to the average across three categories: the percentage of revenues that come from abroad, overseas employees, and overseas assets. If companies on this list have greater participation in the global CSR frameworks, one could infer that CSR participation results from the imperatives of international trade. This measure of financial internationality contrasts with a measure of social internationality that appears in the following section: specifically, the number of linkages of the headquarter nation to the world polity through memberships in international nongovernmental organizations.

Institutional variables

The first of four measures of embeddedness in CSR-promoting institutional environments is membership in the WBCSD, a measure that I gather from rosters on the WBCSD website and past annual reports. The WBCSD resembles the "CSR associations" of Kinderman (2009: 17), being a "non-profit organization with a voluntary corporate membership, membership dues, and a mandate to advance the cause of Corporate Responsibility." Although the WBCSD functions partly as a lobbyist organization, it also attempts to increase the legitimacy of its lobbying activities by promoting good CSR practices among its corporate membership.

The second measure of CSR support in the national institutional environment is the number of firms in the headquarter country that are GC members (divided by the country's number of publicly listed companies). The number of GC participants is a good proxy of national CSR support for several reasons. Because the GC has lax membership requirements, its membership is less likely to skew toward large multinational corporations from developed nations that can make expensive outlays on CSR reporting infrastructure. The framework, in fact, has lax membership requirements by design. George Kell, executive director of the GC, notes that the framework has "neither the mandate nor the capacity to become a regulatory force" (Kell 2002: 25) and needs to "maintain lax entry rules" (25) to foster an atmosphere of "inclusivity" (2). Given that its mission is to drum up support for the CSR movement, the extent to which the GC takes hold in a particular nation is probably a good indicator of CSR receptivity there. Another strength of this measure is that participants in the GC are highly international (as of 2012, they came from more than 140 countries), thus allowing for a good deal of national-level variation.

The third measure of national CSR support is whether the country has a GC "local network" (source: UNGlobalCompact.org), a measure that appears for the same purpose in Lim and Tsutsui (2012: 92). Local networks are administered by members of the GC for the goal of exchanging ideas, developing CSR best practices, and increasing GC outreach. All networks must hold an annual meeting chaired by the Global Compact Offices (unglobalcompact.org). By 2011, more than 100 countries had an active local network.

The fourth and final measure is the number of memberships in the headquarter nation in international nongovernmental organizations, which has become a conventional measure of linkages to the world polity (source: Union of International Associations [UIA]). This measure includes memberships in all organizations that the UIA classifies as Cluster I, including federations of international organizations, universal membership organizations, intercontinental membership organizations, regionally defined membership organizations, and a catch-all category for organizations having a special form with high equivalency to more conventional international organizations. These organizations are bodies that, for example, try to protect whales, advance the sport of table tennis, or increase knowledge in the scientific field of entomology, serving as a diffuse indicator of national-level ties to the global cultural, scientific, and political core.

Control variables

Other studies find that CSR adoption increases with company size (Lepoutre and Aimé 2006; Udayasankar 2008), which I code as year-end, US dollar, logged corporate revenues. I replace missing values (18 percent) with multiple imputation, using the technique developed by Royston (2004) and available in Stata 10 through the "ice" command.

Models

I estimate three multivariate, panel, logistic regressions of membership in the three separate CSR frameworks. Multivariate regressions allow one to assess how single variables affect an outcome while controlling for the effects of other variables. Panel techniques allow one to assess how an outcome is affected by time trends or how an outcome changes relative to the average expected outcome of a particular corporation during the window of analysis. Logistic regressions are the standard choice for the analysis of dichotomous outcomes; here, whether a corporation is a member of a global CSR framework or not. All regressions have firm-level fixed effects on the basis of the Hausman test, which calls for the rejection of the hypothesis of equality of the fixed and random effects coefficients ($p > .05$). An advantage of using firm-level fixed effects is that it allows one to control for all time-invariant heterogeneity across firms even if the heterogeneity cannot be measured or observed. All variables in all models are time-varying by year and lagged by one year as a basic guard against endogeneity. The window of observation is 2000–2010, all years from the inception of the first framework to the most recent period with available company-level data on all measures. The regressions have bootstrap-corrected standard errors clustered by company as an additional robustness check. Revenues and national GC participants are logged to reduce skewness. Correlations and univariate statistics appear in Tables 8.1 and 8.2, respectively.

Table 8.1 *Univariate statistics*

Variable	Mean	Std.	Min	Max
10 Worst Companies	0.01	0.09	0	1
100 Largest Transnationals	0.20	0.40	0	1
100 Most Admired Companies	0.06	0.24	0	1
100 Top Global Marketers	0.10	0.30	0	1
CDP Member	0.39	0.49	0	1
GC Member	0.18	0.39	0	1
GRI Member	0.17	0.38	0	1
International Nongovernmental Orgs.	2,689.35	995.89	235	4,317
Listed Companies	2,253.97	2,067.54	12	7,524
Local Network	0.43	0.50	0	1
National GC Participants	51.84	87.89	0	673
OECD Complaint	0.01	0.08	0	2
Revenue (mm)	26,287.82	36,347.15	0	458,361.0
Shareholder Resolution	0.01	0.08	0	1
WBCSD Member	0.12	0.32	0	1

Results

Regression results for institutional variables appear toward the top of Table 8.3 and rationalist variables toward the bottom. Coefficients represent the change in the log odds of participation in a global CSR framework for a given change across time in a dependent variable, controlling for other variables. Exponentiating the coefficients produces odds ratios, the likelihood of participation divided by the likelihood of nonparticipation.

The broadest pattern to emerge from the results table is that nearly all institutional-type variables associate positively and significantly with CSR participation in at least one of (and sometimes all of) the global CSR frameworks (p <.05). None of the functional variables, by contrast, associates positively and significantly with participation in more than one global CSR framework. Moreover, the direction of the signs of these coefficients reverses across many models, a further suggestion that these variables do not have consistent effects.

Table 8.2 Univariate statistics and correlation matrix

Mean	Std. Dev.	Min	Max	No.	Variables	1	2	3	4	5	6	7	8	9	10	11	12	13	14	15	16
0.01	0.11	0.00	1.00	1	10 Worst Companies	1.00															
0.22	0.42	0.00	1.00	2	100 Transnationals	0.09	1.00														
0.49	0.29	0.06	1.00	3	100 Most Admired	-0.07	-0.13	1.00													
0.13	0.34	0.00	1.00	4	100 Global Marketers	0.07	0.28	-0.10	1.00												
0.78	0.42	0.00	1.00	5	CDP Member	0.03	0.22	-0.10	0.10	1.00											
0.24	0.42	0.00	1.00	6	DJSI	0.04	0.32	-0.14	0.18	0.32	1.00										
0.22	0.41	0.00	1.00	7	GC Member	0.01	0.23	0.01	0.11	0.26	0.30	1.00									
0.26	0.44	0.00	1.00	8	GRI Member	0.02	0.24	-0.06	0.22	0.25	0.32	0.42	1.00								
3011.62	838.18	717.00	4317.00	9	INGOs	0.03	0.22	-0.09	0.09	0.26	0.25	0.27	0.17	1.00							
2712.03	2191.76	33.00	7651.00	10	Listed Companies	0.08	-0.10	-0.31	0.01	-0.15	-0.11	-0.20	-0.07	-0.07	1.00						
0.46	0.50	0.00	1.00	11	Local Network	-0.02	0.08	0.02	0.06	0.28	0.19	0.30	0.28	0.40	-0.12	1.00					
56.72	91.95	0.00	673.00	12	National GC Members	0.01	0.06	0.07	0.03	0.16	0.10	0.36	0.25	0.38	-0.02	0.51	1.00				
0.01	0.09	0.00	2.00	13	OECD Complaint	-0.01	0.08	-0.04	0.00	0.05	0.05	0.06	0.07	0.05	-0.02	0.02	-0.01	1.00			
37192.68	41654.98	0.00	470171.00	14	Revenue (mm)	0.19	0.31	-0.18	0.28	0.11	0.12	0.17	0.21	0.14	0.08	0.17	0.16	1.00	1.00		
0.01	0.10	0.00	1.00	15	Shareholder Resolution	0.04	-0.03	-0.05	0.02	0.00	-0.03	-0.05	-0.02	0.02	0.15	-0.03	0.00	-0.01	0.05	1.00	
0.14	0.35	0.00	1.00	16	WBCSD Member	0.05	0.28	-0.15	0.19	0.18	0.28	0.23	0.25	0.10	-0.06	0.10	0.04	0.10	0.25	0.00	1.00

Table 8.3 *Fixed effects logistic regressions of participation in the Global Compact, Global Reporting Initiative, and Carbon Disclosure Project, 2000–2010*

	GC	GRI	CDP
Intercorporate networks			
World Business Council for Sustainable Development	0.63 (0.41)	0.43 (0.29)	1.87* (0.82)
Global Compact "local network"	0.85** (0.27)	0.43* (0.18)	1.39*** (0.26)
National Institutional Environment			
National GC members/listed companies	25.23*** (3.32)	7.10*** (1.07)	0.94 (1.20)
INGO memberships in headquarter nation	13.81*** (2.96)	27.87*** (2.18)	30.21*** (4.50)
Geographical Financial Spread			
"Top Transnational" (1 = yes)	0.35 (0.27)	0.38 (0.20)	0.97** (0.37)
Stakeholder Pressure			
CSR-related shareholder resolution	0.14 (1.87)	−0.70 (0.58)	0.37 (0.60)
OECD complaint	−0.73 (0.64)	−0.94 (0.67)	−1.49 (1.14)
Ten Worst Companies	0.13 (0.69)	0.95* (0.47)	2.01 (1.13)
Corporate Image			
Most Admired Company	−1.58 (0.52)	0.37 (0.31)	0.13 (0.47)
Top Global Marketer	−0.07 (0.47)	−0.50 (0.34)	0.69 (0.82)
CSR Performance			
DJSI index	0.08 (0.30)	−0.16 (0.22)	−0.23 (0.45)
Control			
Revenues (logged)	0.59* (0.24)	0.18 (0.10)	0.47 (0.34)
Log-likelihood	−381.94	−761.76	−302.06
N company years	1930	2922	1169
Years under analysis	2001–2010	2001–2010	2003–2010

Standard errors in parentheses; *$p<0.05$, **$p<0.01$, ***$p<0.001$; all dependent variables are lagged by one year.

In terms of supported individual hypotheses, there is evidence in favor of H3 that the Top 100 Transnationals, which have a large percentage of overseas revenues, employees, and assets, are more likely to participate in the CDP ($p < .05$; log odds of $2.63 = e \wedge 0.97$), but not more likely to participation in the GC or GRI. There is also evidence in favor of H5 that corporations experiencing a major scandal (the "Ten Worst Companies") are more likely to participate in the GRI ($p < .05$), although this effect does not obtain for the other initiatives and does not replicate when scandal is measured by complaints submitted to the National Contact Points of the OECD Guidelines for Multinational Enterprises. Perhaps the most surprising nonfinding related to the corporate-level variables is that CSR performance does not correspond with participation in any initiative – surprising because companies with high CSR performance could reasonably be expected to obtain the benefits of framework participation at lower cost.

By contrast, the coefficients corresponding with CSR-directed intercorporate networks and CSR-promoting national institutional environments have generally positive effects. At the national level, for example, growth in international nongovernmental organizations (INGO) memberships and the presence of a GC network promotes participation in all global CSR frameworks (H8; $p < .05$). Similarly, growth in GC signatories within nations increases the log odds that a company in those nations will join the GC and GRI (H8 and H9; $p < .05$). Finally, joining the WBCSD increases the log odds of participation in the CDP (H7; $p < .05$). These consistent results underscore the importance of the business and social environment while shifting the emphasis from corporate-level determinants.

Conclusion

Academics have become interested in why firms join the global CSR frameworks, a puzzling phenomenon given that many previous studies fail to find strong, consistent links between CSR activity and profitability. Much of the scholarship that has resulted from this interest can be grouped according to claims that firms join the global CSR frameworks either for financial/reputational rewards or because of institutional pressures within nations or at the level of world society. The current study tested numerous hypotheses grouped according to these theoretical buckets. Panel regressions of 500 multinational corporations tended to support the claims that institutional effects are important while weakening the claims in favor of rationalist explanations. The analysis suggested that the influence of corporate-level variables such as marketing expenditures, corporate scandal, size, and CSR performance have been overstated in recent research, which has presented an account of corporate CSR activity that is overly rationalist and somewhat undersocialized.

Indeed, there is growing support for the importance of the institutional drivers of CSR participation; for example, in this volume's chapter by Miura and Kurusu, whose interviews find that corporate leaders join the GC partly because of a "logic of appropriateness." Institutional drivers of CSR appear also in cross-national methods (Lim and Tsutsui 2012) and national case studies (Boiral 2007). Functional drivers of CSR participation, by contrast, receive little support in much previous scholarship. Several meta-studies, for example, conclude that the relationship between CSR and profits is mixed, small, weak, or nonexistent (e.g., Margolis and Walsh 2003). The jury is still out, to be sure, on whether other variables mediate the relationship between CSR and financial performance. More recent work suggests that CSR is profitable only in certain circumstances. One topical example is whether a corporate scandal provides the opportunity for firms to use CSR as a loss-limiting strategy (Minor and Morgan 2011). This effect is not observed in the current analysis, although it is probably best witnessed through detailed case study.

The current study, to be sure, has several limitations. Many relate to representativeness. The study covers only 2000–2010, leaving out the decades from the 1970s to 2000, when some claim the modern CSR movement came into strength (Lim and Tsutsui 2012: 71). The study deals with only three frameworks, leaving out the dozens that are industry-specific or have participation from nations, not corporations. The study skews toward multinational corporations, overlooking hundreds of smaller companies that participate in the global CSR frameworks. Nearly 20 percent of GC members, for example, are "small and medium enterprises" that have fewer than 250 employees. Another limitation, not to be overlooked, is that the study relies on many metrics with little variation. For example, the study captures corporate scandal by membership in the list of the Ten Worst Companies of the Multinational Monitor. At best, only 10 of the

650 companies could make the list in a given year – less than 2 percent of the sample – although this problem is mitigated to some extent because the study covers an eleven-year time frame, thus increasing the degrees of freedom. Measures with little variation may produce large standard errors and thus insignificant results. Overall, the limitations of the current study reflect the nature of the primary method – longitudinal, large-N regressions. Although this method tends to produce results that have better prospects for generalization across social contexts, the method requires researchers to instantiate abstract concepts in concrete variables. For the present study, the difficulty lay in finding variables that are publicly available, measured annually, and applicable to a large sample of companies from many nations. Such variables are rare.

As a final remark, the current study is highly consonant with a growing body of research on the global CSR frameworks that calls into question whether the public is even aware of them or considers them in purchasing decisions. For example, a recent article in the *Harvard Business Review* calls the CDP "The Most Powerful NGO You've Never Heard Of" (Winston 2010). Likewise, other studies have shown that the GC has limited recognition even among international MBA students, particularly those in developing nations (Morikawa and Morrison 2007; Haski-Leventhal 2013). These studies, similar to the present one, cast doubt on the common notion that the global CSR frameworks are strategic tools to improve consumer relations.

Appendix *Global Compact, Global Reporting Initiative, and Carbon Disclosure Project principles*

Global Compact	***Human Rights***
	1. Businesses should support and respect the protection of internationally proclaimed human rights;
	2. Make sure that they are not complicit in human rights abuses.
	Labor
	3. Businesses should uphold the freedom of association and the effective recognition of the right to collective bargaining;

Appendix *(cont.)*

	4. the elimination of all forms of forced and compulsory labor; 5. the effective abolition of child labor; and 6. the elimination of discrimination in respect of employment and occupation. ***Environment*** 7. Businesses should support a precautionary approach to environmental challenges; 8. undertake initiatives to promote greater environmental responsibility; and 9. encourage the development and diffusion of environmentally friendly technologies. ***Anticorruption*** 10. Businesses should work to eliminate corruption in all its forms, including extortion and bribery.
Global Reporting Initiative	***Materials*** e.g., Percent of materials used that are recycled input materials ***Energy*** e.g., Direct energy consumption by primary energy source ***Water*** e.g., Total water withdrawal by source ***Biodiversity*** e.g., Location and size of land ... [near] areas of high biodiversity ... ***Emissions, Effluents, Waste*** e.g., Total direct and indirect greenhouse gas emissions by weight ***Products and Services*** e.g., Percent of products sold and their packaging materials that are reclaimed by category

Appendix (cont.)

	Compliance
	e.g., Monetary value of significant fines ... for non-compliance with environmental laws ...
	Transport
	e.g., Significant environmental impacts of transporting products and other goods ...
	Overall
	e.g., Total environmental protection expenditures and investments by type
Carbon Disclosure Project	*Management*
	1. Governance
	2. Strategy
	3. Targets and Initiatives
	4. Communications
	5. Climate Change Risk
	Risks and Opportunities
	6. Climate Change Opportunities
	Emissions
	7. Emissions Methodology
	8. Emissions Data
	9. Scope 1 Emissions
	10. Scope 2 Emissions
	11. Scope 2 Contractual Emissions
	12. Energy
	13. Emissions Performance
	14. Emissions Trading
	15. Scope 3 Emissions

References

Adams, Carol A. 2004. "The Ethical, Social and Environmental Reporting-Performance Portrayal Gap." *Accounting, Auditing & Accountability Journal* 17(5):731–57.

Alves, Igor M. 2009. "Green Spin Everywhere: How Greenwashing Reveals the Limits of the CSR Paradigm." *Governance An International Journal of Policy and Administration* 11(1):1–26.

Baron, David P. 2001. "Private Politics, Corporate Social Responsibility, and Integrated Strategy." *Journal of Economics & Management Strategy* 10(1):7–45. Retrieved from http://www.catchword.com/cgi-bin/cgi?body=linker%26ini=xref%26reqdoi=10.1162/105864001300122548.

Bartley, Tim. 2007. "How Foundations Shape Social Movements: The Construction of an Organizational Field and the Rise of Forest Certification." *Social Problems* 54(3):229–55.

Bartley, Tim, and C. Child. 2012. "Movements, Markets, and Fields: The Effects of Anti-Sweatshop Campaigns on U.S. Firms, 1993–2000." *Social Forces*. Retrieved from http://sf.oxfordjournals.org/cgi/doi/10.1093/sf/sor010.

Basu, Kunal, and Guido Palazzo. 2008. "Corporate Social Responsibility: A Process Model of Sensemaking." *Academy of Management Review* 33(1):122–36.

Benjamin, B. A., and Podolny, J. M. 1999. "Status, Quality, and Social Order in the California Wine Industry." *Administrative Science Quarterly* 44(3): 563–589.

Bhattacharya, C. B., Sankar Sen, and Daniel Korschun. 2008. "Using Corporate Social Responsibility to Win the War for Talent." *MIT Sloan Management Review* 42(2):37–44.

Bloomfield, Heidi S. 1999. "'Sweating' the International Garment Industry: A Critique of the Presidential Task Force's Workplace Codes of Conduct and Monitoring System." *Hastings International & Comparative Law Review* 22:567–595.

Boiral, Oliver. 2007. "Corporate Greening through ISO 14001: A Rational Myth?" *Organization Science* 18(1):127–146. Retrieved February 12, 2012, from http://orgsci.journal.informs.org/cgi/doi/10.1287/orsc.1060.0224.

Brammer, S., G. Jackson, and D. Matten. 2011. "Corporate Social Responsibility and Institutional Theory: New Perspectives on Private Governance." *Socio-Economic Review* 10(1):3–28. Retrieved July 17, 2012, from http://ser.oxfordjournals.org/cgi/doi/10.1093/ser/mwr030.

Bremer, Jennifer Ann. 2008. "How Global Is the Global Compact?" *Business Ethics: A European Review* 17(3):227–244.

Brown, Halina Szejnwald, Martin De Jong and Teodorina Lessidrenska. 2009. "The Rise of the Global Reporting Initiative: A Case of Institutional Entrepreneurship." *Environmental Politics* 18(2):182–200.

Campbell, John L. 2007. "Why Would Corporations Behave in Socially Responsible Ways? An Institutional Theory of Corporate Social Responsibility." *Academy of Management Review* 32(3):946–467. Retrieved from http://connection.ebscohost.com/an/25275684.

Carroll, W. K., and J. P. Sapinski. 2010. "The Global Corporate Elite and the Transnational Policy-Planning Network, 1996–2006: A Structural Analysis." *International Sociology* 25(4):501–538. Retrieved February 17, 2012, from http://iss.sagepub.com/cgi/doi/10.1177/0268580909351326.

Cetindamar, Delik, and Kristoffer Husoy. 2007. "Corporate Social Responsibility Practices and Environmentally Responsible Behavior: The Case of the United Nations Global Compact." *Journal of Business Ethics* 76(2):163–176.

Chaudhri, Vidhi A. 2006. "Organising Global CSR." *Journal of Corporate Citizenship* 23:39–51.

Chen, Stephen, and Petra Bouvain. 2008. "Is Corporate Responsibility Converging? A Comparison of Corporate Responsibility Reporting in the USA, UK, Australia, and Germany." *Journal of Business Ethics* 87:299–317. Retrieved July 19, 2011, from http://www.springerlink.com/index/10.1007/s10551-008-9794-0.

Clark, Gordon L., and Tessa Hebb. 2005. "Why Should They Care? The Role of Institutional Investors in the Market for Corporate Global Responsibility." *Environment and Planning A* 37(11):2015–2031. Retrieved January 5, 2012, from http://www.envplan.com/abstract.cgi?id=a38116.

Clougherty, Joseph A., and M. Grajek. 2008. "The Impact of ISO 9000 Diffusion on Trade and FDI: A New Institutional Analysis." *Journal of International Business Studies* 39(4):613–633.

Dahlsrud, Alexander. 2008. "How Corporate Social Responsibility Is Defined: An Analysis of 37 Definitions." *Corporate Social Responsibility and Environmental Management* 15(1):1–13.

Davis, G., D. McAdam, Richard W. Scott, and M. N. Zald, eds. 2005. *Social Movements and Organization Theory*. New York: Cambridge University Press.

Davis, Gerald F., Calvin Morrill, Hagreeva Rao, and Sarah A. Soule. 2008. "Introduction: Social Movements in Organizations and Markets." *Administrative Science Quarterly* 53:389–394.

Davis, Gerald F., and Tracy A. Thompson. 2007. "A Social Movement Perspective of Corporate Control." *Administrative Science Quarterly* 39(1):141–173.

Delmas, Magali, and Maria J. Montes-Sancho. 2010. "Voluntary Agreements to Improve Environmental Quality: Symbolic and Substantive Cooperation." *Strategic Management Journal* 31:575–601.

Delmas, Magali, and Michael W. Toffel. 2004. "Stakeholders and Environmental Management Practices: An Institutional

Framework." *Business Strategy and the Environment* 13:209–222. Retrieved July 12, 2011, from http://doi.wiley.com/10.1002/bse.409.

Deva, Surya. 2006. "A Critique of the U.N.'s 'Public-Private' Partnership for Promoting Corporate Citizenship." *Syracuse Journal of International Law & Commerce* 34:107–151.

Dobers, Peter, and Delyse Springett. 2010. "Corporate Social Responsibility: Discourse, Narratives and Communication." *Corporate Social Responsibility and Environmental Management* 17:63–69.

Doh, Jonathan P., and Terrence R. Guay. 2006. "Corporate Social Responsibility, Public Policy, and NGO Activism in Europe and the United States: An Institutional-Stakeholder Perspective." *Journal of Management Studies* 43(1):47–73.

Drori, Gili S., Yong Suk Jang, and John W. Meyer. 2006. "Sources of Rationalized Governance: Cross-National Longitudinal Analyses, 1985–2002." *Administrative Science Quarterly* 51:205–229. Retrieved November 26, 2011, from http://asq.sagepub.com/lookup/doi/10.2189/asqu.51.2.205.

Du, Shuili, C. B. Bhattacharya, and Sankar Sen. 2007. "Reaping Relational Rewards from Corporate Social Responsibility: The Role of Competitive Positioning." *Research in Marketing* 24:224–241.

Frank, David John, Ann Hironaka, and Evan Schofer. 2000. "The Nation-State and the Natural Environment over the Twentieth Century." *American Sociological Review* 65(1):96–116.

Friedman, Milton. 1970. "The Social Responsibility of Business Is to Increase Its Profits." *The New York Times Magazine (September)*:32–33, 122, 124, 126.

Galaskiewicz, Joseph. 1985. *Social Organization of an Urban Grants Economy: A Study of Business Philanthropy and Nonprofit Organizations*. Orlando, FL: Academic Press.

Galaskiewicz, Joseph. 1991. "Making Corporate Actors Accountable: Institution-Building in Minneapolis-St. Paul." Pp. 293–310 in *The New Institutionalism in Organizational Analysis*, edited by W. W. Powell and P. J. DiMaggio. Chicago: University of Chicago Press.

Galaskiewicz, Joseph. 1997. "An Urban Grants Economy Revisited: Corporate Charitable Contributions in the Twin Cities, 1979–81, 1987–89." *Administrative Science Quarterly* 41:445–471.

Godfrey, Paul C., Craig B. Merrill, and Jared M. Hansen. 2009. "The Relationship between Corporate Social Responsibility and Shareholder Value: An Empirical Test of the Risk Management Hypothesis." *Strategic Management Journal* 30:425–445.

Goel, Ran. 2005. *Guide to Instruments of Corporate Responsibility: An Overview of 16 Key Tools for Labour Fund Trustees*. Retrieved from http://business-humanrights.org/en/pdf-guide-to-instruments-of-cor porate-responsibility-an-overview-of-16-key-tools-for-labour-fund-trustees

Greenhill, Brian, Layna Mosley, and Aseem Prakash. 2009. "Trade-Based Diffusion of Labor Rights: A Panel Study, 1986–2002." *American Political Science Review* 103(04):669. Retrieved July 25, 2012, from http://www.journals.cambridge.org/abstract_S0003055409990116.

Gunningham, N., and Sinclair, D. 2007. *Leaders & Laggards: Next Generation Environmental Regulation*. Sheffield, England: Greenleaf.

Gupta, Aruna Das. 2007. "Social Responsibility in India towards Global Compact Approach." *International Journal of Social Economics* 34(9):637–663. Retrieved March 27, 2012, from http://www.emeraldin sight.com/10.1108/03068290710778642.

Haack, Patrick, Dennis Schoeneborn, and Christopher Wickert. 2012. "Talking the Talk, Moral Entrapment, Creeping Commitment? Exploring Narrative Dynamics in Corporate Responsibility Standardization." *Organization Studies* 33(5):815–845.

Hall, P. A., and D. Soskice. 2001. "An Introduction to Varieties of Capitalism." Pp. 1–69 in *Varieties of Capitalism: The Institutional Foundations of Comparative Advantage*, edited by Peter A. Hall and David Soskice. New York: Oxford University Press. Retrieved February 26, 2012, from http://books.google.com/books?hl=en&l r=&id=EPeDRYilckUC&oi=fnd&pg=PA21&dq=An+Introduction+to+ Varieties+of+Capitalism&ots=rSu7aitCZ1&sig=QRKpKAJhDlMw AdYvtcVzC8emU9 c.

Haski-Leventhal, Debbie. 2013. *MBA Students Around the World and Their Attitudes towards Responsible Management*. Retrieved from http://www.unprme.org/resource-docs/MGSMPRMEMBAStudentStu dy2013.pdf.

Hedberg, Carl-johan, and Fredrik von Malmborg. 2003. "The Global Reporting Initiative and Corporate Sustainability Reporting in Swedish Companies." *Corporate Social Responsibility and Environmental Management* 10:153–164.

Huemer, Lars. 2010. "Corporate Social Responsibility and Multinational Corporation Identity: Norwegian Strategies in the Chilean Aquaculture Industry." *Journal of Business Ethics* 91:265–277.

Hussey, Dennis M., Patrick L. Kirsop, and Ronald E. Meissen. 2001. "Global Reporting Initiative Analysis: An Evaluation of Sustainable Development Metrics for Industry." *Environmental Quality Management* 11(1):143–162.

Husted, Bryan W., and David B. Allen. 2006. "Corporate Social Responsibility in the Multinational Enterprise: Strategic and

Institutional Approaches." *Journal of International Business Studies* 37:838–849.
Jamali, Dima. 2010. "MNCs and International Accountability Standards through an Institutional Lens: Evidence of Symbolic Conformity or Decoupling." *Journal of Business Ethics* 95(4):617–640. Retrieved March 27, 2012, from http://www.springerlink.com/index/10.1007/s10 551-010-0443-z.
Jang, Y. S. 2006. "Transparent Accounting as a World Societal Rule." Pp. 167–196 in *Globalization and Organization*, edited by G. S. Drori, J. W. Meyer, and Hokyu Hwang. New York: New York University Press.
Kell, Georg, and David Levin, D. 2002. "The Evolution of the Global Compact Network: An Historic Experiment in Learning and Action." *The Academy of Management Annual Conference*: 1–41.
Kim, Eun-hee, and Thomas P. Lyon. 2007. "When Does Institutional Investor Activism Pay? The Carbon Disclosure Project." *B.E. Journal of Economic Analysis & Policy* 11(1): 1–26. Retrieved from http://webuser.bus.umich.edu/tplyon/PDF/Published%20Papers/The %20Carbon%20Disclosure%20Project%20and%20Shareholder%2 0Value.pdf
Kimbro, Marinilka Barros, and Zhiyan Cao. 2007. "Does Voluntary Corporate Citizenship Pay? An Examination of the UN Global Compact." *International Journal of Accounting and Information Management* 19(3):288–303.
Kinderman, Daniel. 2009. *The Political Economy of Corporate Responsibility and the Rise of Market Liberalism across the OECD: 1977–2007*. Retrieved from http://www.econstor.eu/bitstream/10419/ 49636/1/614778352.pdf
King, Andrew A., and Michael J. Lenox. 2000. "Industry Self-Regulation without Sanctions: The Chemical Industry's Responsible Care Program." *Academy of Management Journal* 43(4):698–716.
King, Brayden G., and Sarah A. Soule. 2007. "Social Movements as Extra-Institutional Entrepreneurs: The Effect of Protests on Stock Price." *Administrative Science Quarterly* 52(3):413–442.
Knight, G., and Jackie Smith. 2008. "The Global Compact and Its Critics: Activism, Power Relations, and Corporate Social Responsibility." Pp. 1–29 in *Discipline and Punishment in Global Politics: Illusions of Control*, edited by J. Leatherman. New York: Palgrave Macmillan.
Kolk, Ans, David Levy, and Jonatan Pinske. 2008. "Corporate Responses in an Emerging Climate Regime: The Institutionalization and Commensuration of Carbon Disclosure." *European Accounting Review* 17(4):719–745.

KPMG. 2011. Fortune *International Survey of Corporate Responsibility Reporting 2011*. Retrieved from http://www.kpmg.com/global/en/issue sandinsights/articlespublications/corporate-responsibility/pages/2011-survey.aspx

Leipziger, Deborah. 2003. *The Corporate Responsibility Code Book*. Sheffield, UK: Greenleaf.

Lepoutre, Jan, and Heene Aimé. 2006. "Review the Impact of Firm Size on Small Business Social Responsibility: A Critical Review." *Journal of Business Ethics* 67(3):257–273.

Lim, Alwyn, and Kiyoteru Tsutsui. 2012. "Globalization and Commitment in Corporate Social Responsibility: Cross-National Analyses of Institutional and Political-Economy Effects." *American Sociological Review* 77(1):69–98. Retrieved February 1, 2012, from http://asr.sage pub.com/cgi/doi/10.1177/0003122411432701.

Macve, Richard, and Xiaoli Chen. 2010. "The 'Equator Principles': A Success for Voluntary Codes?" *Accounting, Auditing & Accountability Journal* 23(7):890–919. Retrieved February 17, 2012, from http://www.emer aldinsight.com/10.1108/09513571011080171.

Maignan, Isabelle, and O. C. Ferrell. 2003. "Nature of Corporate Responsibilities Perspectives from American, French, and German Consumers." *Journal of Business Research* 56:55–67.

Margolis, Joshua D., and James R. Walsh. 2003. "Misery Loves Rethinking Companies: Social Initiatives by Business." *Administrative Science Quarterly* 48(2):268–305.

McKinsey. 2008. *Global Survey Results: Valuing Corporate Social Responsibility*. Retrieved from http://www.mckinsey.com/insights/corpor ate_finance/valuing_corporate_social_responsibility_mckinsey_global_survey_results

Meyer, John W., John Boli, George M. Thomas, and Francisco O. Ramirez. 1997. "World Society and the Nation-State." *American Journal of Sociology* 103(1):144–181.

Meyer, John W., Shawn M. Pope, and Andrew Isaacson. 2015; this volume. "Legitimating the Transnational Corporation in a Stateless World Society." Pp. 27–72 in *Corporate Social Responsibility in a Globalizing World*, edited by K. Tsutsui and A. Lim. New York: Cambridge University Press.

Meyer, John W., and Brian Rowan. 1977. "Institutionalized Organizations: Formal Structure as Myth and Ceremony." *American Journal of Sociology* 83(2):340–363.

Miles, Morgan P., and Jeffrey G. Covin. 2000. "Environmental Marketing: A Source of Reputational, Competitive, and Financial Advantage." *Journal of Business Ethics* 23(3):299–311.

Minor, Dylan, and John Morgan. 2011. "CSR as Reputation Insurance: Primum Non Nocere." *California Management Review* 53(3):40–60.

Miura, Satoshi, and Kaoru Kurusu. 2015; this volume. "Why Do Companies Join the United Nations Global Compact? The Case of Japanese Signatories." Pp. 286–320 in *Corporate Social Responsibility in a Globalizing World*, edited by K. Tsutsui and A. Lim. New York: Cambridge University Press.

Mohan, Anupama. 2006. "Global Corporate Social Responsibilities Management in MNC." *Journal of Business Ethics* 32(1):9–32.

Moneva, Jose M., Pablo Archel, and Carmen Correa. 2006. "GRI and the Camouflaging of Corporate Sustainability." *Accounting Forum* 30(2):121–137.

Morikawa, Mari, and Jason Morrison. 2007. *Results of Survey on the Current and Future CSR Landscape*. Oakland, CA: Pacific Institute for Studies in Development, Environment, and Security. Retrieved from http://www.pacinst.org/inni/CSR_Landscape_Survey_Result_Summary final Jan 2007.pdf.

Muller, Alan. 2006. "Global Versus Local CSR Strategies." *European Management Journal* 24(2–3):189–198.

Muller, Alan, and Gail Whiteman. 2008. "Exploring the Geography of Corporate Philanthropic Disaster Response: A Study of Fortune Global 500 Firms." *Journal of Business Ethics* 84(4):589–603. Retrieved February 21, 2014, from http://link.springer.com/10.1007/s10551-008-9710-7.

Najam, Adil. 1999. "World Business Council for Sustainable Development: The Greening of Business or a Greenwash?" Pp. 65–76 in *Yearbook of International Cooperation in Environment and Development 1999/2000*, edited by H. O. Bergson, G. Parmann, and O. B. Thommesen. London: Earthscan.

Nikolaeva, Ralitza, and Marta Bicho. 2011. "The Role of Institutional and Reputational Factors in the Voluntary Adoption of Corporate Social Responsibility Reporting Standards." *Journal of the Academy of Marketing Science* 39(1):136–157. Retrieved April 16, 2012, from http://www.springerlink.com/index/10.1007/s11747-010-0214-5.

Okereke, C. 2007. "An Exploration of Motivations, Drivers and Barriers to Carbon Management: The UK FTSE 100." *European Management Journal* 25(6):475–486. Retrieved October 16, 2011, from http://linkinghub.elsevier.com/retrieve/pii/S0263237307000849.

Peloza, John. (2006). "Using Corporate Social Responsibility as Insurance for Financial Performance." *California Management Review* 48(2):

52–72. Retrieved from http://www.nbs.net/wp-content/uploads/RI-Strategic-CSR-acts-as-insurance-for-reputation-which-improves-financial-performance.pdf

Podolny, Joel M. 1993. "A Status-Based Model of Market Competition." *American Journal of Sociology* 98(4): 829–872.

Potoski, Matthew, and Aseem Prakash. 2005. "Green Clubs and Voluntary Governance: ISO Regulatory Compliance." *American Journal of Political Science* 49(2):235–248.

Prakash, Aseem, and Matthew Potoski. 2006. "Racing to the Bottom? Trade, Environmental Governance, and ISO 14001." *American Journal of Political Science* 50(2):350–364.

Rao, Hayagreeva, Calvin Morrill, and Mayer N. Zald. 2000. "Power Plays: How Social Movements and Collective Action Create New Organizational Forms." *Research in Organizational Behavior* 22:239–282. Retrieved from http://linkinghub.elsevier.com/retrieve/pii/S0191308500220078.

Roberts, Peter W., and Grahame R. Dowling. 2002. "Corporate Reputation and Sustained Superior Financial Performance." *Strategic Management Journal* 23(12): 1077–1093. doi:10.1002/smj.274

La Rosa, Salvatore, and Eva Lo Franco. 2000. "Corporate Social Responsibility: A Survey of the Italian SA8000 Certified Companies." *Asian Journal on Quality* 63(3):132–152.

Royston, Patrick. 2004. "Multiple Imputation of Missing Values." *Stata Journal* 4(3):227–241.

Ruggie, J. G. 2004. "Reconstituting the Global Public Domain – Issues, Actors, and Practices." *European Journal of International Relations* 10(4):499–531. Retrieved October 8, 2012, from http://ejt.sagepub.com/cgi/doi/10.1177/1354066104047847.

Sachs, Sybille, Edwin Rühli, and Veronika Mittnacht. 2005. "A CSR Framework Due to Multiculturalism: The Swiss Re Case." *Corporate Governance* 5(3):52–60.

Sagafi-nejad, Tagi. 2005. "Should Global Rules Have Legal Teeth? Policing (WHO Framework Convention on Tobacco Control) vs. Good Citizenship (UN Global Compact)." *International Journal of Business* 10(4):363–382.

Scholtens, Bert, and Lammertjan Dam. 2007. "Banking on the Equator: Are Banks that Adopted the Equator Principles Different from Non-Adopters?" *World Development* 35(8):1307–1328. Retrieved February 17, 2012, from http://linkinghub.elsevier.com/retrieve/pii/S0305750X07000897.

Shanahan, S., and S. Khagram. 2006. "Dynamics of Corporate Responsibility." Pp. 196–224 in *Globalization and Organization:*

World Society and Organizational Change, edited by G. S. Drori, J. W. Meyer, and H. Hwang. Oxford, UK: Oxford University Press.

Skouloudis, Antonis, Konstantinos Evangelinos, and Fotis Kourmousis. 2010. "Assessing Non-Financial Reports according to the Global Reporting Initiative Guidelines: Evidence from Greece." *Journal of Cleaner Production* 18:426–438. Retrieved February 16, 2012, from http://linkinghub.elsevier.com/retrieve/pii/S0959652609003904.

Soederberg, Susanne. 2007. "Taming Corporations or Buttressing Market-Led Development? A Critical Assessment of the Global Compact." *Globalizations* 4(4):500–513. Retrieved January 3, 2012, from http://www.tandfonline.com/doi/abs/10.1080/14747730701695760.

Soule, Sarah A. 2009. *Contention and Corporate Social Responsibility*. Cambridge: Cambridge University Press.

Stanny, Elizabeth, and Kirsten Ely. 2008. "Corporate Environmental Disclosures about the Effects of Climate Change." *Corporate Social Responsibility and Environmental Management* 15:338–348.

Stigler, George J. 1962. "Information in the Labor Market Author." *Journal of Political Economy* 70(5): 94–105.

Tolbert, Pamela S., and Lynne G. Zucker. 1983. "Institutional Sources of in the Formal Change Structure of Organizations: The Diffusion of Civil Service Reform." *Administrative Science Quarterly* 28(1):22–39.

Turban, Daniel B., and Daniel W. Greening. 1997. "Corporate Social Performance and Organizational Attractiveness to Prospective Employees." *Academy of Management Journal* 40(3):658–672.

Udayasankar, Krishna. 2008. "Corporate Social Responsibility and Firm Size." *Journal of Business Ethics* 83(2):167–175. Retrieved March 1, 2012, from http://www.springerlink.com/index/10.1007/s10551-007-9609-8.

Wernerfelt, Birger. 1984. "A Resource-Based View of the Firm." *Strategic Management Journal* 5(2): 171–180.

Vanhamme, Joëlle, and Bas Grobben. 2009. "'Too Good to Be True!' The Effectiveness of CSR History in Countering Negative Publicity." *Journal of Business Ethics* 85(S2):273–283. Retrieved April 4, 2012, from http://www.springerlink.com/index/10.1007/s10551-008-9731-2.

Vasi, I. B., and B. G. King. 2012. "Social Movements, Risk Perceptions, and Economic Outcomes: The Effect of Primary and Secondary Stakeholder Activism on Firms' Perceived Environmental Risk and Financial Performance." *American Sociological Review* 77(4):573–596. Retrieved July 13, 2012, from http://asr.sagepub.com/cgi/doi/10.1177/0003122412448796.

Visser, Wayne, Dirk Matten, Manfred Pohl, and Nick Tolhurst. 2010. *The A to Z of Corporate Social Responsibility*. West Sussex, UK: Wiley.
Vitell, Scott J., and Encarnación Ramos Hidalgo. 2006. "The Impact of Corporate Ethical Values and Enforcement of Ethical Codes on the Perceived Importance of Ethics in Business: A Comparison of U.S. and Spanish Managers." *Journal of Business Ethics* 64(1):31–43.
Vogel, David. 2008. "CSR Doesn't Pay." *Forbes*. Retrieved from http://www.forbes.com/2008/10/16/csr-doesnt-pay-lead-corprespons08-.
Waddock, Sandra. 2008. "Building a New Institutional Infrastructure for Corporate Responsibility." *Academy of Management* 22(3):87–109.
Weber, Klaus, L. G. Thomas, and Hayagreeva Rao. 2009. "Firms from Streets to Suites: How the Anti-Biotech Movement Affected German Firms." *American Sociological Review* 74(1):106–127.
Welch, Eric W., Yasuhumi Mori, and Midori Aoyagi-Usui. 2002. "Voluntary Adoption of ISO 14001 in Japan: Mechanisms, Stages and Effects." *Business Strategy and the Environment* 11:43–62. Retrieved February 18, 2012, from http://doi.wiley.com/10.1002/bse.318.
Werther Jr., William B., and David Chandler. 2005. "Strategic Corporate Social Responsibility as Global Brand Insurance." *Business Horizons* 48(4):317–324. Retrieved March 14, 2012, from http://linkinghub.elsevier.com/retrieve/pii/S000768130400134X.
Williams, Oliver F. 2004. "The UN Global Compact: The Challenge and the Promise." *Business Ethics Quarterly* 14(4):755–774.
Winston, A. 2010. The Most Powerful Green NGO You've Never Heard Of. *Harvard Business Review Blog Network*. Retrieved from http://blogs.hbr.org/winston/2010/10/the-most-powerful-green-ngo.html
Wood, Stepan. 2003. "Green Revolution or Greenwash? Voluntary Environmental Standards, Public Law, and Private Authority in Canada." Pp. 123–165 in *New Perspectives on the Public–Private Divide*, edited by Law Commission of Canada. Vancouver: UBC Press.
Wright, Christopher, and Alexis Rwabizambuga. 2006. "Institutional Pressures, Corporate Reputation, and Voluntary Codes of Conduct: An Examination of the Equator Principles." *Business and Society Review* 111(1):89–117.

9 Why do companies join the United Nations Global Compact? The case of Japanese signatories

SATOSHI MIURA AND KAORU KURUSU

Introduction

Over the past years, we have witnessed the development of a variety of voluntary transnational corporate social responsibility (CSR) initiatives at various levels. As other chapters in this volume have documented, many companies have joined these initiatives. This chapter focuses on the following question: why do companies decide to join them? To answer this question, we take up the case of the largest initiative among them, the United Nations Global Compact (UNGC), and investigate its corporate signatories in Japan.

Spearheaded by then UN Secretary-General Kofi Annan, the UNGC was launched in July 2000. It can be depicted as a mechanism to disseminate an idea of global corporate citizenship and to encourage companies to voluntarily implement principles in the fields of human rights, labor, environment, and anticorruption through learning processes. The UNGC is based on the "leadership model," which means that only the signature of top management and support from the corporate board are required for a company to become a signatory.

The number of UNGC participants has increased steadily over the past years from about fifty to more than 10,000, including more than 7,000 companies. There have been discussions on why companies join the UNGC and what impacts, if any, its membership might have on them. Earlier critics of the UNGC, for example, argued that its signatories were merely "bluewashing" (i.e., wrapping their wrongdoings

---

The authors thank the UN Information Center in Tokyo for giving us relevant information. Our gratitude also goes out to all the interviewees for sharing their views. Both authors acknowledge financial support by the Japanese Society for the Promotion of Science: Grant in Aid for Young Scientists (B) and Grant in Aid (C) for Miura, and Grant in Aid (C) for Kurusu.

Why do companies join the United Nations Global Compact? 287

with the UN blue flag and enhancing their reputation) and that, lacking the necessary "teeth" to punish noncompliance, UNGC membership would not affect their behavior in any way (Bruno and Karliner 2000; for a summary of arguments against the UNGC, see Rasche 2012). Proponents of the UNGC, on the other hand, have argued that the UNGC is "a necessary supplement" to legal regulations and that its membership will encourage learning and collective action (Rasche 2009; see also Kell 2013). Despite the heated discussion by both practitioners and academics on this topic, they have mostly based their arguments on *assumed* motives of companies. It is therefore worth scrutinizing the *actual* motives and factors behind corporate participation in the UNGC.

Why do companies join the UNGC? Why and how is it important and significant for corporate signatories? To answer these questions, we examine the case of the corporate signatories in Japan. Our research is based on interviews with thirty-three companies conducted in 2004, 2011, and 2012. By using a coding method, we generated hundreds of observations indicating that companies had a wide variety of motives and reasons for joining the UNGC. In this chapter, we categorize these observations according to two dimensions: inward-outward orientation and reactive-proactive response.

In the next section, we review the existing research on corporate motives to join the UNGC to demonstrate that, although many studies have emerged on this topic, much remains to be done to understand why corporations *actually* decided to participate in the UNGC and the meanings they attached in so doing. The third section briefly discusses the methods of our research. The fourth section outlines the development and diffusion of the UNGC in Japan with an aim to identifying characteristics of Japanese signatories and UNGC local network in Japan. The fifth section presents our findings by utilizing a framework with the two dimensions outlined earlier. We conclude by discussing the theoretical and practical implications of our research.

Literature review

Why do companies join the UNGC? The official website of the UNGC enumerates the following "benefits of participation" or reasons companies should join the initiative: "adopting an established and globally recognized policy framework," sharing "best and emerging practices," advancing "sustainability solutions with ... stakeholders," having "access to the UN's ... knowledge ... and experience," and "utilizing Global Compact management tools and resources, and [engaging] in specialized workstreams" (UN Global Compact Office n.d.). This list suggests that the supposed benefits come down to learning and action: that is, learning from the experience of other participants and the UN and advancing individual and/ or collaborative action by employing tools developed by the UNGC or by engaging with stakeholders.

UN Global Compact Office, the secretariat of the UNGC, has published several reports inquiring into corporate motives for joining the UNGC. *United Nations Global Compact Annual Review 2010* (UN Global Compact Office 2011a: 12), for example, cites eight "top reasons for engagement in the Global Compact" (percentages in parentheses indicate the results of an annual Global Compact Implementation Survey): "increase trust in company" (74 percent), "integration of sustainability issues" (71 percent), "universal nature of principles" (66 percent), "networking with other organizations" (39 percent), "address humanitarian concerns" (37 percent), "expanded business opportunities/risks" (37 percent), "attract, motivate and retain employees" (33 percent), and "improve operational efficiency" (33 percent). Although "signing on to" and "engaging in" the UNGC are not necessarily identical, the data are still suggestive. Earlier, in a report commissioned by the UN Global Compact Office, McKinsey & Company (2004: 5) inquired into the reasons companies joined the UNGC. When asking "Why [do] companies sign on to the Global Compact?", the questionnaire had nine options: "address humanitarian concerns" (55 percent), "acquire practical know-how" (50 percent), "network with other organizations" (49 percent), "become (more) familiar with CSR" (46 percent), "CEO or senior leadership passion" (37 percent), "establish links with the UN" (32 percent), "improve public relations" (26 percent), "improve market access" (16 percent), and "other" (9 percent).

Although demonstrating interesting data regarding corporate motives, these reports fall short in two ways. First, the choices in their questionnaires fail to list wider corporate motives, thereby creating an impression that firms strategically join the UNGC mostly for positive instrumental values. Our study, by contrast, reveals that some companies sign on to the UNGC partly in response to pressures exerted by their external stakeholders. Second, the reports do not provide an analytical structure; in order to better understand corporate motives, however, we need frameworks for analyzing and categorizing them in a more systematic and comprehensive fashion.

For their part, scholars have discussed various variables that arguably explain why firms engage in socially responsible activities. Haufler (2001), for example, distills three factors that drive industry self-regulation: political and economic risks, reputation, and learning. Major risks include new or stricter government regulation, civil society activism, and market competition. Corporate reputation refers to that of being a good corporate citizen. Learning concerns "the spread of knowledge, information, and ideas within the business community regarding the relative costs and benefits of voluntary initiatives" (Haufler 2001: 27). Alternatively, Campbell (2007) enumerates a larger number of factors that are likely to affect socially responsible corporate behaviors: corporate financial performance, market competition, state regulations, industrial self-regulations, watchdogs (such as nongovernmental organizations [NGOs], institutional investors, and the press), and social environment or trade associations that have institutionalized CSR. Most research centers on institutional factors such as regulatory, market, or social pressures, and there are also studies that regard economic rationales for firms such as eco-labeling and green marketing as important factors. Others emphasize moral motives anchored in the idea that business has an ethical duty to contribute to society.

In line with the focus of this chapter, recent years have witnessed an emerging literature on participation in the UNGC, mainly by scholars employing large-N statistical analyses, which examines factors that influence corporate adoption. In this vein, Lim and Tsutsui (2012) conducted systematic and sophisticated statistical analyses to sort out variables that affect the likelihood of participation. Their findings show that conditions positively influencing such a probability include institutional factors at the national level (government endorsement for the UNGC as measured by the national launch of Global Compact Local Networks) and international level (the number of international NGO memberships), as well as political-economy factors at the international level (i.e., a large volume of exports to countries with large numbers of UNGC signatories).

In an earlier study of corporate participation in the UNGC, Bennie et al. (2007) found that its determinants include market factors such as larger firm size, UN vendorship (whether a company is a supplier to the UN), and higher cost of exit (as in the case of companies in extractive industries), as well as a political factor (i.e., a national political environment where commitment to the UN is high). Similarly, Perez-Batres et al. (2011) examine factors related to coercive, normative, and mimetic mechanisms of institutionalization using a sample of some 400 firms in Western European and Latin American countries. They demonstrate that the number of local universities and a listing on the New York Stock Exchange (NYSE) – variables arguably constitutive of normative and mimetic mechanisms, respectively – exert significant pressures on corporations to register for the UNGC.[1] Furthermore, Drezner and Lu (2009) analyze why certain firms in Pacific-Rim developing countries commit to the UNGC, ISO 14001, and/or the Free Burma campaign. Based on descriptive statistics, they reason that those firms with high brand-consciousness are most likely to do so, and they concluded that such factors as a transparent governance system and the degree of civil society strength also matter.

Although these works have their own merits, they all too often assume that specific factors pressure or encourage companies to join the UNGC. In those studies, a company or country is measured by certain properties it has, such as size, economic openness, and embeddedness within international society. Although such macrolevel studies can reveal some general and interesting cross-country patterns, what they actually show is correlations between participation in the UNGC and certain properties, whether of firms or their external environments. They thus stop short of revealing exactly why particular firms decide to participate in the UNGC, especially what making such a commitment means for corporate decision makers. Therefore, we need more research on why firms decide to join the UNGC, particularly by inquiring into their actual motives and reasons.

In this regard, Cetindamar and Husoy (2007) provide a rare academic study of UNGC signatories by inquiring into their reasons for joining the UNGC. Based on a multiple-choice questionnaire they conducted in

---

[1] As for coercive mechanisms, they assume that companies in Western Europe are all subject to government regulation whereas those in Latin America are not. They also posit the number of local NGOs as another agent of a normative mechanism.

2004, they find that "to be part of sustainable development efforts" is the most important motive and "to improve corporate image," "to distinguish your firm," and "to be good citizen" are the second most important motives. These results show, they argue, that the respondents regard both "ethical" and "economic" reasons as important: "Companies have more than one reason, including both ethical and economic ones, and they vary a lot" (Cetindamar and Husoy 2007: 172).

Although we concur with their assertion, their method offers little insight into the reasoning made by the signatories in their deliberation on whether to join the UNGC. First, they fail to reveal what the decision meant to the companies. For example, it is not obvious what "to be part of sustainable development efforts" meant to the respondents themselves; it might have been based on either the "ethical" reasoning that a corporation should help solve environmental problems or on "economic" reasoning that it should enhance its own competitiveness by adapting to a new market trend. Second, it is unclear why the respondents chose to join the UNGC rather than (or in addition to) other voluntary initiatives because the "motives" most choices arguably represent can apply to other initiatives as well. Third, multiple-choice questionnaires tend to square the circle by forcing respondents to choose from stylized "motives" that are predetermined by researchers. Fourth, the method can fail to capture actual corporate motives if the choices either are too general or do not reflect a whole range of possible reasons. For example, a choice in their questionnaire, "pressure of stakeholders," is too general to specify which stakeholders mattered to the respondents and why – crucial questions for both theoretical and practical reasons.

Because participation in the UNGC can be regarded as a case of corporate adoption of voluntary CSR initiatives, a burgeoning literature in this strand should also be pertinent to our research.[2] Particularly relevant are studies on the adoption of ISO 14001, some of which point to the importance of legitimacy and timing. Jiang and Bansal (2003: 1063–1064), for example, conduct interviews with managers of sixteen companies in the Canadian pulp and paper industry, explicitly shed light on reasons why firms certify to ISO 14001, and find that corporate consideration of "external recognition, credibility, and procedural

---

[2] We thank Shawn Pope for bringing to their attention this strand of research and the relevant literature.

legitimacy" matters. Furthermore, other scholars astutely point to the importance of timing and thus the need for analytically distinguishing between early and late adopters. Based on the data gathered from survey questionnaires, Welch et al. (2002) perform statistical analyses to examine what factors contributed to the adoption of ISO 14001 by Japanese facilities. They make an important observation that early and late adopters differ in size, resources, and decision-making structure and face different degrees of external pressure. Our study confirms that these two factors, legitimacy and timing, also matter for Japanese signatories to the UNGC.

In summary, many scholars have inquired into what factors contribute to corporate adoption of voluntary CSR initiatives, including the UNGC. Although quantitative research is good at specifying variables that influence its probability across countries, qualitative research is better at illuminating the motives and reasons behind particular companies' choices of certain initiatives. Although both types of studies can contribute in their own ways and can complement each other, this brief review revealed a dearth of qualitative research on UNGC participants, particularly that based on interviews.

Method

The preceding discussion shows that most of the existing research has focused on finding general patterns of corporate participation in the UNGC. Although we do not deny the importance of such large-N quantitative studies at the macrolevel, our research runs counter to this trend. First, our method is decidedly qualitative: understanding and analyzing the reasons corporate participants had for joining. Drawing extensively on interviews with UNGC signatories, we attempt to illuminate what lay behind the decision; that is, the actual logics of corporate action (Kornprobst 2011).

Second, our research is also distinguished by a within-country analysis focusing on Japanese corporations, in contrast to many quantitative studies interested in finding cross-national variations. As discussed in the next section, the case of Japanese UNGC signatories is more or less anomalous and important in its own right, and thus it merits close scrutiny. Third, we used abductive reasoning in our analysis (Friedrichs and Kratochwil 2009). We did not have any particular hypotheses in mind when we did interviews, at least during the first round; rather, driven by questions rather than by theories, we created, modified, rejected, and refined analytical frameworks, concepts, categories, and hypotheses as we proceeded by going back and forth between the data gathered from our interviews and the relevant literature. Even the range of "relevant literature" expanded during the process; we started from the discipline of International Relations (political science) and ventured into those of management and economic sociology.

We conducted interviews and their analyses in the following fashion. We interviewed contact persons, mostly managers and general managers, of thirty-three Japanese UNGC signatories (see Appendix 1). In July and August 2004, we interviewed fourteen of the then seventeen Japanese UNGC signatories (Miura and Kurusu 2005). We conducted interviews again in May through June 2011 with nine companies and in February 2012 with ten companies. Most of them signed on to the UNGC after 2009, but we also interviewed seven companies that became UNGC members between 2005 and 2008. Thus, if we divide the years between 2001 and 2011 into three periods, our sample consists of thirteen "early adopters" (2001–2004), seven "middle adopters" (2005–2008), and ten "late adopters" (2009–2011). Although the largest time lag between a firm's signature and our interview was around seven years (we conducted interviews in 2012 with representatives of firms that joined the UNGC in 2005), our interviewees had either stayed involved with CSR during the entire period or were well-informed about the discussion around the time of the participation because their predecessors either told them or left them written notes about the process.

In each interview, we posed three broad sets of questions to the interviewees: (1) "Why did your company decide to join the UNGC?" (2) "What impact, if any, has the participation had upon your company?" and (3) "What are the CSR activities of your company?"[3] Although their answers to the second and third questions are quite revealing in their own right, this chapter focuses on their answers to the first question. In asking the first question, we saw to it that our interviewees told stories about the time of the decision. This

---

[3] In preparing for each interview, we read all online CSR reports from each company so that we could both expect answers beforehand and ask further questions if we thought actual answers were not enough in light of the facts covered in the reports.

consideration led us to break up the broad question into several smaller questions: "Who came to know the UNGC from whom and around when?" "Who proposed joining the UNGC, at what time, and with what thoughts?" "How did the top management decide to approve it, with what arguments and procedures?" "Who or what division was most influential in the process?" "What motivated your company to join the UNGC at that particular time?" and "Why did your company choose the UNGC instead of others?" These questions allowed us to hear stories, sometimes spanning more than a few years, of why and how their companies had begun, gone through, and completed discussions on UNGC participation and to contextualize and weave together various factors that initiated, facilitated, strongly influenced, or even hindered that decision.

Each interview was audio recorded and transcribed word-for-word. Each author then separately coded every transcription by adding short explanatory comments where necessary. When there were differences between us as to how and where to code, we discussed the issue until we reached a single evaluation. Then we "meta-coded"; that is, we coded the already created codes with a few key concepts. Finally, we created a spreadsheet consisting of key dimensions that enabled us to make a "structured, focused comparison" among all the interviews (George and Bennett 2005). These processes facilitated our gradual movement from the particular and concrete to the more general and abstract. We then constructed more general categories of reasons and motives for joining the UNGC by both drawing on existing theoretical frameworks and moving back and forth between the transcriptions, codes, meta-codes, and categories. Throughout this process, we created a framework that helped us map and classify these categories. This abductive reasoning allowed us, first, to provide empirically grounded categories and frameworks that would help us better understand and explicate why firms join the UNGC and, second, to derive some hypotheses from the analysis.

However, we need to carefully distinguish between "real motives" at the moment of corporate participation from post hoc explanation, justification, and rationalization that (representatives of) corporations may make out of their organizational or personal interests. We cannot deny that the stories our interviewees told us might consist partially of the latter. Nevertheless, although we do not claim to have uncovered the "real motives" of the Japanese signatories we interviewed, we think it would be safe to assume that our interviews enabled us to demonstrate "stated reasons" for joining the UNGC. Moreover, we would argue that stated reasons are good proxies for corporate motives, and the former can take us closer to unveiling the latter.

The UNGC in Japan

A distinctive characteristic of the UNGC is that it is both "global and local" (UN Global Compact Office 2008b). As of April 2014, it has Local Networks in 101 countries. A Local Network in Japan, the Global Compact Japan Network (hereafter GC-JN), was launched in 2003 with the UN Information Center Japan as its secretariat. In February 2008, the member corporations took the initiative to reorganize it as a "CEO-led network" and fee-based organization (UN Global Compact Office 2008a). Since then, the GC-JN has significantly expanded its membership and activities. In this section, we put Japanese UNGC signatories in context by analyzing data on Japanese corporate membership in both the UNGC and GC-JN, which helps shed light on how the UNGC has been adopted in Japan.

First, the GC-JN has been a business-led network driven in particular by larger corporations. Since the first Japanese company joined the UNGC in 2001, the number of its corporate signatories, after years of relative stagnation, has increased steadily – and more conspicuously after the reorganization of the GC-JN in 2008 – to reach 100 in 2010. As we can observe in Figure 9.1, however, the number grew rapidly in 2011 when some forty small and medium-sized enterprises (SMEs) joined the UNGC because of an active campaign led by a group from the Junior Chamber International (JCI) Japan. Despite this increase in the number of SME signatories, larger companies still account for some 84 percent of corporate GC-JN members because many SME signatories have not joined the Network.[4] Out of 217 Japanese organizations that had signed on to the UNGC by the end of 2013, 149 firms, 21 SMEs, and 8 nonbusiness organizations have also participated in the GC-JN. The composition of the GC-JN shows that it is predominantly a business organization.

---

[4] We follow the UNGC in defining SMEs as "[c]ompanies with less than 250 employees" (UN Global Compact Office 2012a: 2).

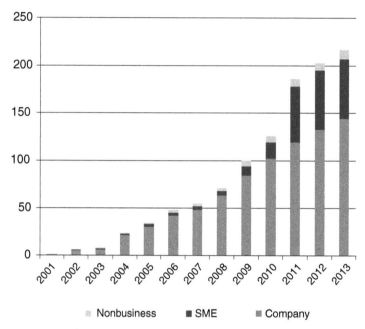

Figure 9.1 The number of United Nations Global Compact signatories in Japan, 2001–2013

Second, the GC-JN has been quite dynamic and lively in its local activities, at least since its reorganization in 2008. It had as many as thirteen thematic Working Groups in 2011 (Global Compact Japan Network 2011: 12), and the Network as a whole held 101 activities in 2010, which made it by far the most active Local Network in the world.[5] The purposes of their activities are mostly to encourage either learning or policy dialogues – respectively accounting for 50 percent and 23 percent of their overall activities – which indicates that the GC-JN is primarily oriented toward knowledge-based activities (UN Global Compact Office 2011b: 65).

Third, individual Japanese signatories have performed quite well in the UNGC, at least in terms of compliance with its procedural rules.

---

[5] The French Network ranked the second with seventy activities, followed by the Spanish Network with fifty-four activities. Featuring the information on sixty-two Local Networks, the report shows that the global average in the number of yearly Local Network activities in 2010 was 9.3 (UN Global Compact Office 2011b).

For example, the number of delisted UNGC signatories is remarkably low in Japan when compared with that in other countries; a UNGC participant database shows that, as of April 2014, only three Japanese companies have been expelled from the initiative due to their failure to submit an annual Communication on Progress (COP) – a mandatory requirement for all corporate UNGC signatories.[6] In addition, out of 935 "Advanced level" COPs[7] as of April 2014, 65 have been submitted by Japanese signatories, second only to their Spanish (170 COPs) and French (66 COPs) counterparts. This number is all the more notable if we take into account that the number of signatories, and thus of corporate participants required to submit a COP, in each country differs greatly.[8] These pieces of evidence from the database testify that both Japanese signatories, especially GC-JN members, and the GC-JN are on the most advanced end of UNGC signatories and Local Networks. Moreover, these numbers suggest that there is relatively little "decoupling" – a gap in declared norms and actual practice – in the case of Japanese firms.

Fourth and finally, the case of Japan is unique in that the GC-JN has grown into such a vibrant network despite little support from the Japanese government. The launch of the Japan Network in 2003 was initiated by the UN Information Center in Tokyo, and its reorganization was led predominantly by its corporate participants, whereas the Japanese government played virtually no role in both instances. This is in contrast to a trend among UNGC's Local Networks toward "greater multi-stakeholder involvement in network governance structures" (UN Global Compact Office 2012b: 29). Thus, we can regard the case of Japan as an anomaly that merits close examination. All in all, these characteristics make a study of UNGC signatories in Japan a unique contribution to research on the UNGC and its participants.

---

[6] Two among them are SMEs. Expelled participants account for 4,426 as of April 27, 2014. The database can be accessed at "Expelled Participants," http://www.unglobalcompact.org/COP/analyzing_progress/expelled_participants.html

[7] The UNGC differentiates its signatories into three levels, "learner," "active," and "advanced." A signatory can declare its COP as "advanced" when it "submits a COP meeting the advanced criteria (based on self-assessment)" (UN Global Compact Office 2012a: 8).

[8] As a rough estimate of the differences between Japan on the one hand and Spain and France on the other, the number of business participants, as of April 27, 2014, in the former is 215 while that of the latter two is 1,269 and 904, respectively.

Why do companies join the UNGC?

As discussed earlier, existing research has revealed various factors and reasons why companies adopt voluntary initiatives in general and the UNGC in particular. In this chapter, we propose a two-dimensional framework to map the reasons for joining the UNGC: inward-outward orientation and reactive-proactive response.[9] The first dimension of our framework captures an orientation, either inward or outward, of a company when it decides to join the UNGC. In other words, we categorize an act of signing on to the UNGC as directed either to the company itself, including its subsidiaries and employees as internal stakeholders, or to something else (i.e., external stakeholders). On the one hand, we regard a signatory as oriented inward when participation is either a response to requests and demands from its internal stakeholders or simply a recognition and affirmation of its corporate mission and vision. On the other hand, a company is oriented outward when it takes into account its external stakeholders, which include, inter alia, governments, intergovernmental organizations (such as the United Nations), NGOs, local communities, suppliers, business associations, investors, and index makers.

The second dimension echoes what Carroll (1979) termed "philosophy of responsiveness." For the sake of simplicity and parsimony, we categorize corporate social responsiveness as either reactive or proactive. A company is reactive when it reacts or responds to the demands, criticisms, and/or regulations of its internal or external stakeholders.[10] Alternatively, a company is proactive when it attempts either to preempt possible actions from its stakeholders, especially external ones, or to make gains by either collaborating with them or taking a unilateral

---

[9] We created this framework inductively through iterative processes of coding and meta-coding our interviews, by which we aimed at generalizing our findings as much as possible. Only after having come up with an idea of featuring the two dimensions and of creating a framework thereof did we search online for the relevant literature by using combinations of the four keywords: inward, outward, proactive, and reactive. The inquiry enabled us to ascertain that our framework resonated well with some existing works that we cite herein.

[10] Here, we assume that the top management and (to a lesser degree) middle management in charge of CSR at the headquarters of a corporation are the locus of decision making when it comes to participation in the UNGC. If other actors in a corporation, such as internal stakeholders, push or request them to join the UNGC, and the main actors respond to the request, then we regard the corporation as "inward-reactive."

Table 9.1 *Framework of corporate motives and reasons for adopting voluntary initiatives*

Response orientation	Reactive	Proactive
Inward/Self	Responding to internal pressures/demands; Signaling	Organizational change; Affirming/ reconstructing an identity; Signaling
Outward/Other	Responding to external requests/pressures/ regulations; Signaling	Preempting and preventing pressures/ regulations; Branding; Engagement; Signaling

action to forestall its competitors. The former is motivated by loss aversion, whereas the latter is driven by gain seeking. A company can also act proactively by implementing its vision and mission without taking into account its external stakeholders, in which case it is oriented inward rather than outward. As discussed in more detail later, reactive motives come down to signaling stakeholders, whereas proactive motives are more diverse.

Combining the two dimensions yields a simple framework, presented in Table 9.1, containing four kinds of motives and reasons for joining the UNGC (or voluntary initiatives more generally): inward-reactive, inward-proactive, outward-reactive, and outward-proactive.[11] These distinctions help us create a useful categorization of corporate motives. For example, Cao and Prakash (2011: 114) suggest the objectives of a voluntary initiative, ISO 9000, as follows:

The objectives of this certification program [read corporate motives for seeking certification] are twofold. Internally, it seeks to improve the organization's quality management practices; externally, it seeks to provide the organization with a mechanism to signal to its external stakeholders (who

---

[11] Aguilera et al. (2007: 838) allude to the four elements of our framework as follows: "One premise in our analysis is that, in either case (reactive or proactive CSR initiatives) corporations are being pressured by internal and external actors to engage in CSR actions to meet rapidly changing expectations about business and its social responsibilities." They stopped short, however, of drawing implications from this statement; neither did they turn it into a framework for classifying various corporate motives.

cannot fully observe what the organization is doing internally) its commitment to quality assurance.

By adding the reactive-proactive dimension, our framework further differentiates each objective, regarding the former objective as "inward-proactive" and the latter as either "external-reactive" or "external-proactive." It also helps us ask if signaling can be directed to internal or external stakeholders of a firm. We regard signaling, an act of communication intended to send certain information about oneself, as a general motive encompassing four categories: it can be either reactive or proactive, and inward- or outward-oriented.

In sum, our two-dimensional framework allows us to systematically classify various corporate motives and reasons for adopting voluntary initiatives as discussed in the literature. Employing this framework, we next analyze corporate motives for joining the UNGC in turn and illustrate them with the stated reasons raised by our interviewees.

Signature as signaling

For the interviewed companies, communicating their commitment to CSR was one of the most frequently stated reasons for deciding to join the UNGC. Signing on to the UNGC can provide a certain signal (Bennie et al. 2007; Janney, Dess, and Forlani 2009) either internally to its employees; to its external stakeholders such as investors, index makers, and suppliers; or to both. In addition, the act of signature as signaling can either be reactive or proactive and thus covers the four cells. It should be noted, however, that we did not find any remarks in our interviews that can be meaningfully categorized as inward-reactive signaling. In this section, we first discuss in turn signaling effects of participation in the UNGC that falls within the other three categories of our framework. Then, we consider if the signatories regarded the signature (*qua* signaling) as cheap talk that critics of the UNGC have claimed it to be. Last, we consider why firms choose the UNGC rather than (or in addition to) other CSR initiatives as a signaling device.

Based on our interviews, we argue that some companies join the UNGC in order to send either of four types of signals: intention, identity, status, or legitimacy. We discuss each function of signaling in turn. Inwardly and proactively, a few companies saw that the signature would inform their employees of top management *intention*. For example, as an interviewed firm attempted to integrate sustainability and CSR into the heart of its corporate culture, the top management expected that participation in the UNGC would demonstrate to employees its determination to implement CSR policy, which they hoped would help drive cultural change within the organization (Interview 10).[12] Similarly, another company decided to join the UNGC partly because the executives wanted to inform employees of their intention that the company would integrate CSR into their business operations with the aim of adding value to society and that each and every employee would need to work with this spirit as the company was attempting to go global (Interview 19). Alternatively, the top management of yet another corporation hoped to raise awareness of its employees abroad by signing on to the UNGC, which they expected would make them understand that theirs was a global corporation – a corporate *identity* (Interview 9).

For a larger number of interviewed companies, however, sending a signal to their external stakeholders was a more important reason for joining the UNGC. Some conceived of external stakeholders in general terms, whereas others had more specific ones in mind. Especially in the earlier years of the UNGC in Japan, self-proclaimed industry-leading corporations had an incentive to be the first to join and declare UNGC membership and to make use of the first mover advantage, thereby advancing and further solidifying their sustainability leadership, a social *status*, in their respective industries. Whereas the intention of these early adopters was to demonstrate their commitment to corporate citizenship, to their competitors in particular, and to the market in general (Interviews 5, 10, 11, 13, and 26), late adopters needed to signal their commitment to more specific issues like human rights (Interview 17) and anticorruption (Interview 29) to more specific market actors such as index makers (Interviews 17, 18, and 29), socially responsible investors (Interviews 18, 28, and 31), and suppliers

---

[12] To provide some information on the company of each interviewee, we assign a number that corresponds with that shown in Appendix 1. For example, "Interview 10" means that the interview is conducted with a representative of the company listed as 10 in Appendix 1. On another note, in referring to our interviewees and the persons they mentioned and in quoting the remarks of the former, we use "he/she" to preserve anonymity.

(Interviews 18 and 28) – all of them operating in Europe as well. We categorize the earlier move as outward-proactive and the more recent one as outward-reactive, to which we turn our attention now.

As discussed in the Introduction, critics of the UNGC have claimed that signatories attempt to "bluewash" their wrongdoings, apparently assuming that participation is akin to "cheap talk." In other words, firms may abuse their participation in the UNGC in order to signal their *legitimacy* to their stakeholders (Mundlak and Rosen-Zvi 2011).[13] In such cases, a credible signal needs to be costly to the sender, a UNGC signatory; that is, a commitment should be accompanied by some actions that involve some costs to the participant. The remarks of our interviewees reveal that both firms and their external stakeholders indeed conceive of participation as a costly signal. On the one hand, some firms had feared the impact of committing to the UNGC and thus being subject to a higher probability of public scrutiny and criticism, which caused discussions on whether to take part in the initiative to drag on for years. On the other hand, certain market actors do not regard corporate support for the UNGC as cheap talk. Instead, they use UNGC membership as a good indicator of corporate commitment to CSR. A story of one company is quite telling in this regard (Interview 18). The top and middle management of this company deliberated on the cost and benefit of joining or not joining the UNGC. That is, they surmised that participation would enable the company to send a good signal to investors, suppliers, and index makers abroad, but that, at the same time, it might expose itself to a higher risk of attracting criticism, especially on their labor practices abroad. By contrast, inaction (i.e., not sending any signal) would risk losing their credibility while avoiding a perceived higher risk of increased public exposure. After years of internal deliberation and especially after more pressure from external stakeholders, the company finally concluded that the risk of inaction was higher and so decided to join the UNGC, which we regard as an outward-reactive move.

Next, why do companies choose to join the UNGC, rather than other initiatives, to signal their CSR commitment to their stakeholders? Our

---

[13] We follow Suchman (1995: 574) in defining legitimacy as "a general perception or assumption that the actions of an entity are desirable, proper, or appropriate within some socially constructed system of norms, values, beliefs, and definitions."

interviews reveal that UNGC membership has come to be regarded – at least among certain European firms and investors and especially by European sustainability index makers such as FTSE4Good – as a convenient and globally valid tag for "socially responsible" and "sustainable" companies. In some cases, the membership speaks more eloquently than any words. As one interviewee put it:

> Saying that we comply with [the company's] Way had not been persuasive enough for [the index maker].... When we do business globally and say that we put so much effort on CSR globally, referring to our [UNGC] membership makes us more easily understood. (Interview 22)

Comprehensibility, as Suchman (1995) points out, is an important element of cognitive legitimacy, and the affiliation with the UNGC can provide firms with precisely such legitimacy. Judgment about what acts might be appropriate and legitimate is socially constructed, in this case by sustainability index makers and in other cases by institutional investors and other UNGC companies (as private regulators of their own supply chains). In any case, we regard joining the UNGC in response to external pressures as an act of reactive legitimation.

Indeed, for some firms in Japan, these external stakeholders, especially FTSE4Good, are a "significant other" to whom they seek to signal legitimacy. For instance, an interviewee confessed that a strong initial reason for advocating for UNGC membership within the company had been its fall from the FTSE4Good index, which could affect the company's financial outlook. As the interviewee recalled:

> Our company had been once delisted from a FTSE4Good list. When we asked a person in charge [of the index] about the reasons, [he/she] replied: "Because your company did not disclose information on your policy on bribery and corruption." We did believe we had done everything we could, but [he/she] told us that we had not disclosed the relevant information in English. When we then asked how we would be listed again, [he/she] answered: "Joining the UNGC is one of the factors." From that moment, we started to think seriously about doing so. (Interview 29)

It should be noted that, in order to be relisted by the index, the company was not necessarily asked to disclose more information; they were simply asked to provide the same information in English and were advised to join the UNGC as a signal for being a transparent and socially responsible company. Thus, a firm can make it look as if it were appropriately sustainable by, *inter alia*, joining the UNGC.

Proactive moves: inward and outward

Companies join the UNGC for reasons other than signaling, as we discuss in this section. Many of the interviewed corporations decided to become UNGC signatories without being pressured to do so from their stakeholders, and there are a variety of motives for doing so. As discussed earlier, proactive moves can be either inward- or outward-oriented. As for inward proactive responses, our interviews reveal two main reasons for joining the UNGC: to drive organizational change and to either affirm or reconstruct corporate identity. As for outward proactive responses, some companies signed on to the UNGC expecting that the signature would either enhance their corporate brand and reputation, give them access to various platforms provided by the UNGC, or both.

Organizational change

Some firms decided to join the UNGC in order to start, facilitate, or accelerate organizational changes such as applying the Plan-Do-Check-Action (PDCA) cycle for their CSR activities, setting and clarifying priorities regarding such activities, and enhancing their risk management capability (for a similar argument in the case of ISO 14001, see Cao and Prakash 2011). An interviewed company utilized the signaling function of the signature discussed earlier to help accelerate the PDCA cycle for the continuous improvement of its CSR activities (Interview 5). More directly, another firm joined the UNGC in order to "bolster the PDCA management system" regarding their CSR activities. As the interviewee put it:

We joined the UNGC in order to help set priorities among our [CSR] activities by using external indices such as those of the Millennium Development Goals (MDGs). As we reflected on our past activities, we realized that we have done too many different things at once. In order to improve that, we needed to have certain goals or indices. Thus, joining the UNGC was not a goal in itself but rather a means to plan and then implement strategies for [CSR] activities. (Interview 20)

As for enhancing risk management capability, another company expected that joining the UNGC would provide it with a "global common language and guidelines" while helping it identify and proactively mitigate risks, especially those of human rights and labor rights violations, which can arise from having to make different responses depending on the local laws of host countries. For that company, actions aligned with the UNGC would "protect [itself] globally from global risks" (Interview 16).[14]

Identity affirmation/reconstruction

Some companies joined the UNGC to either affirm or reconstruct their organizational identity. When learning about the UNGC, especially its principles, the top management of a corporation might first recognize its identity, possibly almost automatically and unreflectively; then compare its own beliefs with UNGC principles; recognize the match between them; and say to themselves "a company like us should join it." In such a case, the assumed "cultural match" (Checkel 1999) between UNGC principles and corporate culture facilitates the adoption of the former. Thus, by deciding to join the UNGC, a company affirms itself and recognizes its organizational identity.

Indeed, about half of our interviewees pointed out that their firms had decided to join the UNGC because top management saw a match between UNGC principles and their corporate mission, culture, policy, and/or practice. Many of them described UNGC principles as *atarimae*, or natural, proper, normal, and being a matter of course. For a few corporations, this perception was enough, as one interviewee noted: "It is natural for a company trying to do business globally to sign on to the UNGC; otherwise, I assume that people will raise doubts." He/she also recalled as follows: "Our CEO at the time decided to join the UNGC because [he/she] did not see anything in its principles that went against our corporate mission." The company's top management, the interviewee added, "did not contemplate on the benefits and costs [of the signature]" (Interview 25). Thus, in recognizing the affinity between the corporate mission and UNGC principles, the company paid attention to itself, not to others. Similarly, another interviewee recalled what the CEO told him/her when deliberating on participation in the UNGC: "As our company

---

[14] This expectation echoes a point made by rational institutionalism in international relations that international institutions reduce transaction costs by providing common rules and that this motive is a primary reason why states create and join international institutions. For a seminal discussion, see Keohane (1984).

has kept saying since its foundation that 'company is a public institution in society,' there is nothing in us that contradicts with the ten principles of the Global Compact. Rather, they are good things" (Interview 23). This reasoning indeed overrode opposition from the company's US branch that had expressed concerns about joining the UNGC because of the anticipated legal risks. In both cases, top management perceived the congruence between UNGC principles and their corporate mission and culture and reasoned that committing to the UNGC was natural for their companies.

The "cultural match" argument indicates that the UNGC has a strong appeal to firms that have already integrated within their organization those elements that resonate with UNGC principles, in which case they do not feel the need to change their practice. In such an instance, the act of joining the UNGC is more of affirming an existing self than of reconstructing it, which implies that the UNGC may find it difficult to attract corporations that perceive the need for dramatic changes in practice. An irony here is that those corporations are precisely the most-wanted targets for such an initiative. This is called a *problem of endogeneity*: actors are most likely to adopt norms and rules that are easier to follow, which enhances their compliance rate (Downs, Rocke, and Barsoom 1996).[15] Thus, we can hypothesize that those companies that first find the cultural match and then join the UNGC may not change their activities much after participation because they have practiced CSR well before their signature.

By way of contrast, a few corporations decided to join the UNGC in order to strategically reconstruct, rather than to affirm, their organizational identity within a global context. As one interviewee put it, "In seeking to integrate our entire corporate group not with norms of Japanese origin but with global norms, we created our corporate group codes of conduct by utilizing the UNGC [principles]" (Interview 17). The intention was to "create a new image of the corporate group by endowing it with a sense of globalism," which the company hoped would help it diffuse the new codes throughout its affiliated organizations worldwide.[16]

---

[15] We owe this point to Virginia Haufler.
[16] In attempting to "globalize" its identity, the company did not copy UNGC principles, but built upon the existing codes, expanded them to cover its entire corporate group, and inserted into the preamble a sentence declaring its support for the UNGC.

Most of the interviewed companies reckoned that UNGC principles would provide them with a base and/or a proper language to speak and act as legitimate corporate citizens, especially in the eyes of their stakeholders overseas. Although they have arguably practiced socially responsible activities for years, decades, or even more than a century, they perceived a need to have "a global common language" (Interviews 16 and 18) and "global guidelines" (Interview 22) and to adapt their practice to "global standards" (Interviews 28 and 31). Thus, they saw value not only in UNGC membership, but also in UNGC *principles* because they expected that endorsing and *actually following* them would give them the identity of a global corporate citizen able to talk about and practice sustainability in an appropriate and competent manner, which they assumed would make their commitment and practice more easily understood globally. As mentioned earlier, comprehensibility constitutes a cognitive dimension of legitimacy. In contrast with reactive legitimation discussed therein, some companies join the UNGC, even without facing external pressures, in order to enhance their legitimacy by utilizing and following UNGC principles as an act of proactive legitimation (O'Dwyer 2002; Samkin and Schneider 2010).[17]

Building a brand and reputation
Although building a brand and reputation is frequently mentioned by scholars and critics alike as a major reason that companies join the UNGC (Drezner and Lu 2009), we did not find strong evidence for that. True, six of our interviewees raised this as a motive, but for none of them was it a major reason. Four of them are "early movers" that joined the UNGC before or in 2004 when participation made them the first UNGC signatories in their respective industries. For an interviewee from a later participant, participation in itself did not enhance its corporate brand; it was just a driver for building it by practicing continuous improvement (Interview 19).

Engagement
Some firms expected that the UNGC would serve as a platform for networking, learning, dialogue, and/or advocacy. Although only two

[17] Bansal and Roth (2000: 726) define legitimation as "the desire of a firm to improve the appropriateness of its actions within an established set of regulations, norms, values, or beliefs." We argue that legitimation is not only a desire but also an act.

companies pointed out either dialogue or advocacy as a reason for joining the UNGC, many signatories named networking and learning as such. Networking was, in fact, the most frequently mentioned reason among the interviewed companies. Some firms conceived of networking in general terms without identifying particular stakeholders, whereas others had specific stakeholders in mind when they referred to it: UN agencies and UNGC member corporations, either foreign or Japanese, or both.

One company stands out in that its interviewee emphasized that engagement in developing "good global community relations" had been an important reason for the company to sign on to the UNGC:

> We think that the Global Compact is quite useful as guidance in developing global business operations.... We want to do business with integrity, and that will contribute to risk management as well. So we did not join the Global Compact in order to say "We are a good company"; rather, we want to build good global community relations. (Interview 22)

An interviewee from a different corporation pointed out four reasons for joining the UNGC. In addition to "enhancing competitiveness" and "demonstrating leadership in corporate citizenship" – discussed earlier as inward-proactive and outward-proactive orientation, respectively (with the latter pertaining to signaling status) – UNGC membership would enable the corporation to "get opportunities to share experience and lessons with like-minded companies and organizations" and to "build partnerships and relations with other companies, the United Nations, international organizations, and civil society organizations" (Interview 5). An interviewee from yet another company explained that the decision to join the UNGC had been a culmination of a set of actions the corporation had taken. As he/she explained:

> We [in CSR department] had started to strengthen our global operations since 2007.... We had either CSR divisions or managers in our group companies [around the world] and collaborated with them to advance our activities.... [In so doing] we realized that we could get information on global trends [on CSR] much faster via our global network than we could from think tanks and consultants in Japan.... Then we recognized that, unless we would not get involved more actively with the world, we could not demonstrate our leadership. At the time, we set it as our goal both to join the leading sustainable companies in the world and to demonstrate CSR leadership in the world. We

Why do companies join the United Nations Global Compact? 309

thought that we would remain a follower if we would remain in Japan. (Interview 16)

Thus, for these firms, joining the UNGC was one avenue to actively engaging in a community of leading CSR companies in the world. These companies have been seeking to enhance their legitimacy not just by signing on to the UNGC and then implementing UNGC principles, but also by *engaging in* the UNGC. Indeed, these corporations have become very active members of both the UNGC and the GC-JN.

Trends over time

We now shift our unit of analysis from reasons that companies gave to companies that gave reasons; that is, we now classify companies, not reasons, according to the two-dimensional framework. Our interviews revealed that, in choosing to become a UNGC signatory, most companies had a variety of reasons, both inward- and outward-oriented and both proactive and reactive. We rarely find a case where a single reason dominated and drove a company; most had diverse reasons when they deliberated upon whether or not to join the initiative. Be that as it may, we can still classify each of the newcomers according to "types": whether a company is more or less inward- or outward-oriented and reactive or proactive when it chooses to sign on to the UNGC.

Based on the transcripts of our interviews, we coded the reasons each company had in deciding to join the UNGC, which enabled us to then classify each company as either "inward," "outward," or "balanced," on the one hand, and as either "reactive," "proactive," or "balanced," on the other.[18] Of course, a type is of relative, not

---

[18] The coding proceeded as follows: we read the transcript of each interview, identified all the reasons an interviewee gave us, and examined if there was a main reason for the decision. If we judged that he/she had explicitly mentioned such a reason, we regarded it as expressive of that company's basic orientation. In cases where we did not find a main reason, we counted and coded every reason according to the two dimensions, internal-external and reactive-proactive. For example, consider a case where an interviewee gave us three reasons for his/her firm's decision to join the UNGC. If we coded them as one "internal" and two "external" reasons and one "reactive" and two "proactive" reasons, then we categorized the firm as "external-proactive." In cases where the reasons for a company canceled each other out (as in the case of four reasons, with two "internal" and two "external"), we coded the company as "balanced." Each author did the coding; if the results differed, we had discussions to resolve the difference.

Table 9.2 *The basic orientations of United Nations Global Compact signatories in Japan*

	Inward	Balanced	Outward	Total
Reactive	2 (2, 0, 0)	0	8 (1, 1, 6)	10 (3, 1, 6)
Balanced	1 (0, 1, 0)	3 (2, 1, 0)	0	4 (2, 2, 0)
Proactive	3 (2, 0, 1)	2 (1, 0, 1)	11 (5, 4, 2)	16 (8, 4, 4)
total	6 (4, 1, 1)	5 (3, 1, 1)	19 (6, 5, 8)	30 (13, 7, 10)

Note: The three numbers in each cell (e.g., [1, 3, 3]) indicate the number of new signatories during the period 2001–2004 (thirteen signatories), 2005–2008 (seven signatories), and 2009–2011 (ten signatories), respectively.

absolute, character, and the differences among them are only in degree, not in kind. Nevertheless, the resulting data help us uncover some tendencies and trends regarding the basic orientation of Japanese UNGC signatories. We created a matrix by combining the two dimensions, each with three categories, which generated nine "types" as presented in Table 9.2. Each cell indicates the number of companies, with the three numbers in parentheses indicating the number of the new signatories in three periods.[19]

First, the data show that, overall, the number of "outward" companies (nineteen) far outweighs that of "inward" companies (six). The breakdown data, however, reveal that the gap was not so wide during the first period, from 2001 to 2004, when the percentages of "inward" and "outward" companies were 30.8 and 46.2 percent, respectively. It has dramatically widened during the second and third periods, when the percentages of "inward" and "outward" companies were 14.3 and 71.4 percent, and 10.0 and 80.0 percent, respectively. Thus, we observe a trend toward the dominance of "outward" companies among the new signatories.

Second, regarding the reactive-proactive dimension, the total number of "proactive" companies (sixteen) exceeds that of "reactive" ones (ten), along with four "balanced" ones. Although we cannot

---

[19] We created this periodization for the analytical purpose of comparing the orientations of Japanese UNGC participants according to the timing of their participation. We do not thereby suggest that the years dividing each period constitute "critical junctures."

observe any linear trend regarding "reactive" new signatories, the percentage rose sharply from 23.1 and 14.3 percent in the first and second period, respectively, to 60.0 percent in the third. The percentage of "proactive" signatories, on the other hand, has decreased gradually from 61.5 to 57.1 and then to 40 percent. Thus, the third period has witnessed a shift in the majority of the new signatories from "proactive" to "reactive" ones.

Third, comparisons between individual cells show that "outward-proactive" companies constitute the largest group, whereas "outward-reactive" companies are the second largest. Within the "outward-proactive" category, the percentage has fluctuated over the three periods from 38.5 to 57.1 percent, and then to 20.0 percent. Among the "outward-reactive" companies, only 7.7 percent belonged to this category in the first period, but the percentage increased to 14.3 percent in the second period and then rose steeply to 60.0 percent in the third period. To be more specific, among eight companies that alluded to networking through the UNGC, an "outward-proactive" reason, five are "early movers" that joined the UNGC in the first period. Turning to learning, which six companies referred to as a reason, we can observe a similar tendency: four are early movers.

Fourth, regarding variance among corporate "types," we can discern an increasing concentration. That is, the ratio of the largest cluster of all the nine cells as described in Table 9.2 – "outward-proactive" during the first two periods and "outward-reactive" during the third period – has increased from 38.5 to 57.1 percent and then to 60.0 percent. This trend suggests that, despite the difference in the largest type between the second and third periods, new signatories have been converging toward a particular type over the years. We can hypothesize that the shift in the main type from "outward-proactive" to "outward-reactive" is a result of stronger external pressures against UNGC non-signatory companies.

What do these observations imply? We can infer from both the qualitative and quantitative data gathered from our interviews that more Japanese companies have felt increasing external pressures from various actors that have encouraged and, in some cases even pushed, Japanese companies to join the UNGC. We would further argue that, perhaps during the third period, an organizational field centering around the UNGC has been institutionalized whose main constituents include the UN Global Compact Office, Local Networks, corporate signatories (especially as private regulators through their supply chain networks and as members of Local Networks), sustainability index makers, and institutional investors (especially the signatories of UNGC's spinoff initiative, the UN Principles for Responsible Investment), to name a few.[20] These players in the assumed organizational field, by working either independently or collaboratively, have begun to exert more pressure on the nonsignatories in the third period starting in 2009. Or, it might be that the field had emerged before 2009 but its influence reached Japanese companies later, in or after 2009. Of course, these are still hypotheses at this stage, and we need further research on this topic to probe their plausibility.

Conclusion

We demonstrated the complex nature of corporate motivations in deciding to join the UNGC while providing a two-dimensional framework to make sense of such complexity. This chapter contributes to the discussion on participation in the UNGC by drawing a picture of corporate rationales that is at once theoretically more integrated, empirically more plausible, and practically more relevant.

Our findings have theoretical and practical implications. First, our interviews demonstrated that companies participate in the UNGC not only proactively, but also reactively; indeed, our analysis hints at the possibility that reactive motives have become more important over time and that such market actors as sustainability index makers and institutional investors are emerging as important external stakeholders that encourage and urge certain companies, especially those aiming at a global market, to join the UNGC. By way of contrast, most existing research on corporate participation in the UNGC restricts itself to considering motives that are mostly proactive (McKinsey & Company 2004; Cetindamar and Husoy 2007; UN Global Compact Office 2011a). Another strand of research employing statistical

---

[20] For a study of the emergence of the "transnational sustainability governance" organizational field, see Dingwerth and Pattberg (2009). We follow Tolbert and Zucker (1983: 25) in defining institutionalization as "the process through which components of formal structure become widely accepted, as both appropriate and necessary, and serve to legitimate organizations."

analyses tends to consider properties and forces at macrolevels and thus fails to specify agents and mechanisms that lead corporations to join the UNGC (Bennie et al. 2007; Perez-Batres et al. 2011; Lim and Tsutsui 2012). In this context, this chapter fills these gaps by drawing on interviews to specify which actors and mechanisms are instrumental in encouraging companies to join the UNGC. We hasten to add, however, that our research has limitations that come from our interviewed companies: they are all Japanese UNGC signatories (not nonsignatories) and are mostly large companies.

Second, our research also reveals motives that are discussed in existing research but largely absent in our interviews. One of them is what is called "investment in political capital," with the UNGC serving as "a mechanism to engage with a range of relevant environmental, labor, and human rights actors who seek to influence media and governments on issues of concern to firms" (Bernhagen and Mitchell 2010: 1177).[21] Relatedly, no interviewees mentioned forestalling government regulation as a motive for signing on to the UNGC, although this is a frequently mentioned motive in the literature on CSR (Haufler 2001). In addition, very few interviewees mentioned pressures from NGOs, except as partners in concrete CSR activities. The near absence of a political dimension may be peculiar to our interviewed companies or to Japanese signatories. Assuming that this is the case, we surmise that this might be caused by the relatively weak political pressures on Japanese firms from NGOs. Or, it might be a reflection of a more general tendency of companies worldwide that prefer to free-ride on others' efforts to prevent tighter legal regulation. Either way, we can hypothesize that, at least for companies in some countries, pressures from market actors – such as index makers, institutional investors, and suppliers – are more effective in recruiting firms to join the UNGC than are those from NGOs. Should that be the case, those interested in expanding the number of UNGC signatories, or any other voluntary corporate initiatives for that matter, will fare better if they enroll market actors, especially sustainability index makers, to create a synergetic force for the initiative. We need to keep in mind, however, that although market forces may help increase the quantity of UNGC

---

[21] Only one interviewee mentioned anything that can be meaningfully related to "political capital" argument. The company joined the UNGC with a view to using the platform to advocate for a specific agenda on CSR (Interview 21).

Appendix 1 *List of interviewees*

	Sector	Category (size)	Date of interview	Position and department	Duration
1	Manufacturing	Company	2004/7/16	General Manager (CSR)	40 min.
2	Manufacturing	Company	2004/8/12	General Manager and Manager (Environment and Social Relations)	90 min.
3	Others	Company	2004/8/13	General Manager and Staff Member (CSR)	80 min.
4	Manufacturing	Company	2004/8/17	General Manager and Manager (Management Planning)	60 min.
5	Manufacturing	Company	2004/8/17	Group Manager and Staff Member (Environmental Management and CSR)	90 min.
6	Others	SME	2004/8/19	Executive and Manager	135 min.
7	Others	SME	2004/8/20	Executive and Manager	60 min.
8	Others	Company	2004/8/20	Executive	60 min.
9	Manufacturing	Company	2004/8/20	General Manager (CSR)	60 min.
10	Others	Company	2004/8/23	General Manager (Management Planning)	70 min.
11	Manufacturing	Company	2004/8/23	General Manager (Environment and CSR)	75 min.
12	Others	SME	2004/8/23	General Manager and Staff Member (CSR)	60 min.
13	Others	Company	2004/8/25	Group Manager (General Affairs)	80 min.
14	Others	Company	2004/8/25	General Manager and Manager (Environment)	60 min.
15	Manufacturing	SME	2011/5/19	Manager (Management Planning)	70 min.
16	Manufacturing	Company	2011/5/27	General Manager (CSR)	80 min.

17	Manufacturing	Company	2011/6/2	General Manager (CSR)	60 min.
18	Others	Company	2011/6/2	Director and Manager (CSR)	75 min.
19	Others	Company	2011/6/2	General Manager and Manager (CSR)	75 min.
20	Others	Company	2011/6/3	Staff Member (Planning)	60 min.
21	Others	SME	2011/6/16	Executive	60 min.
22	Manufacturing	Company	2011/6/23	Senior Director (CSR)	100 min.
23	Manufacturing	Company	2011/6/24	General Manager (CSR)	70 min.
24	Others	Company	2012/2/20	Manager (CSR)	70 min.
25	Manufacturing	Company	2012/2/22	Two General Managers (Corporate Strategy)	70 min.
26	Manufacturing	Company	2012/2/22	General Manager and Senior Manager (CSR)	70 min.
27	Others	Company	2012/2/22	Senior Manager (CSR)	65 min.
28	Others	Company	2012/2/23	Manager (CSR)	60 min.
29	Manufacturing	Company	2012/2/23	Director (CSR)	45 min.
30	Manufacturing	Company	2012/2/23	Manager and Staff Member (CSR)	70 min.
31	Manufacturing	Company	2012/2/24	General Manager and Manager (CSR)	50 min.
32	Others	SME	2012/2/27	Executive	55 min.
33	Others	SME	2012/2/27	Executive	55 min.

Appendix 2 *Exemplary quotations from our interviews*

Motivation	Exemplary quotes
Inward-reactive	"We did not have a specific awareness about the UNGC, but there were some requests from overseas affiliates to sign the principles. At least we had no problem with the GC principles and so decided to sign the Compact."
Outward-reactive	"We realized that SRI surveys asking companies if they support the UNGC were on the increase, and that suppliers which had already introduced CSR procurement measures were requesting us to take human rights into greater consideration in our corporate activities. We also paid attention to the fact that ISO 26000, which was said to include items quite similar to UNGC principles, was in the process of codification."
Inward-proactive	"Our company was recently formed by a merger. In creating a new company, we intended to build a new corporate culture. A task force consisting of young employees also demanded that CSR should be placed at the center of corporate culture. So we had to demonstrate clearly to our employees that our company is serious about CSR."
	"We joined the UNGC in order to help set priorities among our [CSR] activities by using external indices such as the MDGs. As we reflected on our past activities, we realized that we have done too many different things at once. In order to improve that, we needed to have certain goals or indices. Thus, joining the UNGC was not a goal in itself but rather a means to plan and then implement strategies for [CSR] activities."
Outward-proactive	"We have been promoting our corporate brand since our company was listed on the stock exchange. We found the following aspects especially beneficial in this regard. That is, showing our leadership role in our industrial sector; gaining lessons and know-how in CSR from member companies; and building positive relations with international organizations, governmental organizations, labor organizations, and NGOs."
	"We have a long history of cooperation with international organizations such as the UN, the UNICEF, and the WTO in the field of the MDGs, which we believe had been evaluated quite highly by them. Our strongest motive was to involve ourselves further in such activities by joining the UNGC, a cooperative body of the UN and corporations."

signatories, they may not contribute to enhancing the quality of the UNGC. There is even a possibility that those "reactive" companies that are more or less pushed to join it by external pressures may have less incentive to improve their performance than their "proactive" counterparts. Thus, we need further research on how corporate motives relate to corporate performance once firms join the UNGC.

References

Aguilera, Ruth V., Deborah E. Rupp, Cynthia A. Williams, and Jyoti Ganapathi. 2007. "Putting the S Back in Corporate Social Responsibility: A Multi-Level Theory of Social Change in Organizations." *Academy of Management Review* 32(3): 836–863.

Bansal, Pratima, and Kendall Roth. 2000. "Why Companies Go Green: A Model of Ecological Responsiveness." *Academy of Management Journal* 43(4):717–736.

Bennie, Lynn, Patrick Bernhagen, and Neil J. Mitchell. 2007. "The Logic of Transnational Action: The Good Corporation and the Global Compact." *Political Studies* 55(4):733–753.

Bernhagen, Patrick, and Neil J. Mitchell. 2010. "The Private Provision of Public Goods: Corporate Commitments and the United Nations Global Compact." *International Studies Quarterly* 54(4):1175–1187.

Bruno, Kenny, and Joshua Karliner. 2000. *Tangled Up in Blue: Corporate Partnerships at the United Nations*. San Francisco: TRAC-Transnational Resource & Action Center. Retrieved November 12, 2012, from http://s3.amazonaws.com/corpwatch.org/downloads/tangled.pdf.

Campbell, John L. 2007. "Why Would Corporations Behave in Socially Responsible Ways: An Institutional Theory of Corporate Social Responsibility." *Academy of Management Review* 32(3):946–967.

Cao, Xun, and Aseem Prakash. 2011. "Growing Exports by Signaling Product Quality: Trade Competition and the Cross-National Diffusion of ISO 9000 Quality Standards." *Journal of Policy Analysis and Management* 30(1):111–135.

Carroll, Archie B. 1979. "A Three-Dimensional Conceptual Model of Corporate Performance." *Academy of Management Review* 4(4):497–505.

Cetindamar, Dilek, and Kristoffer Husoy. 2007. "Corporate Social Responsibility Practices and Environmentally Responsible Behavior: The Case of the United Nations Global Compact." *Journal of Business Ethics* 76(2):163–176.

Checkel, Jeffrey T. 1999. "Norms, Institutions, and National Identity in Contemporary Europe." *International Studies Quarterly* 43(1):83–114.

Dingwerth, Klaus, and Philipp Pattberg. 2009. "World Politics and Organizational Fields: The Case of Transnational Sustainability Governance." *European Journal of International Relations* 15(4):707–744.

Downs, George W., David M. Rocke, and Peter N. Barsoom. 1996. "Is the Good News about Compliance Good News about Cooperation?" *International Organization* 50(3):379–406.

Drezner, Daniel W., and Mimi Lu. 2009. "How Universal Are Club Standards? Emerging Markets and Volunteerism." Pp. 181–206 in *Voluntary Programs: A Club Theory Perspective*, edited by M. Potoski and A. Prakash. Cambridge, MA: MIT Press.

Friedrichs, Jörg, and Friedrich Kratochwil. 2009. "On Acting and Knowing: How Pragmatism Can Advance International Relations Research and Methodology." *International Organization* 63(3):701–731.

George, Alexander L., and Andrew Bennett. 2005. *Case Studies and Theory Development in the Social Sciences*. Cambridge, MA: MIT Press.

Global Compact Japan Network. 2011. *Activity Report 2010–2011*. Tokyo: Global Compact Japan Network.

Haufler, Virginia. 2001. *A Public Role for the Private Sector: Industry Self-Regulation in a Global Economy*. Washington, DC: Carnegie Endowment for International Peace.

Janney, Jay J., Greg Dess, and Victor Forlani. 2009. "Glass Houses: Market Reactions to Firms Joining the UN Global Compact." *Journal of Business Ethics* 90(3):407–423.

Jiang, Ruihua Joy, and Pratima Bansal. 2003. "Seeing the Need for ISO 14001." *Journal of Management Studies* 40(4):1047–1067.

Kell, Georg. 2013. "12 Years Later: Reflections on the Growth of the UN Global Compact." *Business & Society* 52(1):31–52.

Keohane, Robert O. 1984. *After Hegemony: Cooperation and Discord in the World Political Economy*. Princeton, NJ: Princeton University Press.

Kornprobst, Markus. 2011. "The *Agent's* Logics of Action: Defining and Mapping Political Judgement." *International Theory* 3(1):70–104.

Lim, Alwyn, and Kiyoteru Tsutsui. 2012. "Globalization and Commitment in Corporate Social Responsibility: Cross-National Analyses of Institutional and Political-Economy Effects." *American Sociological Review* 77(1):69–98.

McKinsey & Company. 2004. *Assessing the Global Compact's Impact*. Retrieved December 1, 2012, from http://www.unglobalcompact.org/docs/news_events/9.1_news_archives/2004_06_09/imp_ass.pdf.

Miura, Satoshi, and Kaoru Kurusu. 2005. "How to Activate a Global Compact Local Network: Present State and Prospect of Japan Network." In *Bridging the Gap: Sustainable Environment. The First UN Global Compact Academic Conference* (CD-ROM).

Mundlak, Guy, and Issi Rosen-Zvi. 2011. "Signaling Virtue? A Comparison of Corporate Codes in the Fields of Labor and Environment." *Theoretical Inquiries in Law* 12(2):603–663.

O'Dwyer, Brendan. 2002. "Managerial Perceptions of Corporate Social Disclosure: An Irish Story." *Accounting, Auditing & Accountability Journal* 15(3):406–436.

Perez-Batres, Luis A., Van V. Miller, and Michael J. Pisani. 2011. "Institutionalizing Sustainability: An Empirical Study of Corporate Registration and Commitment to the United Nations Global Compact Guidelines." *Journal of Cleaner Production* 19(8):843–851.

Rasche, Andreas. 2009. "'A Necessary Supplement': What the United Nations Global Compact Is and Is Not." *Business & Society* 48(4):511–537.

Rasche, Andreas. 2012. "The United Nations and Transnational Corporations: How the UN Global Compact Has Changed the Debate." Pp. 33–49 in *Globally Responsible Leadership: Managing According to the UN Global Compact*, edited by J. T. Lawrence and P. W. Beamish. Thousand Oaks, CA: Sage.

Samkin, Grant, and Annika Schneider. 2010. "Accountability, Narrative Reporting and Legitimation: The Case of a New Zealand Public Benefit Entity." *Accounting, Auditing & Accountability Journal* 23(2):256–289.

Suchman, Mark C. 1995. "Managing Legitimacy: Strategic and Institutional Approaches." *Academy of Management Review* 20(3):571–610.

Tolbert, Pamela S., and Lynne G. Zucker. 1983. "Institutional Sources of Change in the Formal Structure of Organizations: The Diffusion of Civil Service Reform, 1880–1935." *Administrative Science Quarterly* 28(1):22–39.

UN Global Compact Office. 2008a. "Global Compact Japan Transitioning to CEO-led Network." New York: UN Global Compact Office. Retrieved December 20, 2012, from http://www.unglobalcompact.org/NewsAndEvents/news_archives/2008_02_27.html.

UN Global Compact Office. 2008b. *United Nations Global Compact: Corporate Citizenship in the World Economy.* New York: UN Global Compact Office. Retrieved 20 December, 2012, from http://www.unglobalcompact.org/docs/news_events/8.1/GC_brochure_FINAL.pdf.

UN Global Compact Office. 2011a. *United Nations Global Compact Annual Review 2010*. New York: UN Global Compact Office. Retrieved December 20, 2012, from http://www.unglobalcompact.org/docs/news_events/8.1/UN_Global_Compact_Annual_Review_2010.pdf.

UN Global Compact Office. 2011b. *United Nations Global Compact Local Network Report 2010*. New York: UN Global Compact Office. Retrieved December 20, 2012, from http://www.unglobalcompact.org/docs/networks_around_world_doc/Annual_LN_2010.pdf.

UN Global Compact Office. 2012a. *2011 Global Compact Implementation Survey: Annual Review of Business Policies and Actions to Advance Sustainability*. New York: UN Global Compact Office. Retrieved December 1, 2012, from http://www.unglobalcompact.org/docs/news_events/8.1/2011_Global_Compact_Implementation_Survey.pdf.

UN Global Compact Office. 2012b. *United Nations Global Compact Local Network Report 2011*. New York: UN Global Compact Office. Retrieved December 20, 2012, from http://www.unglobalcompact.org/docs/networks_around_world_doc/2011_Annual_Local_Network_Report.pdf.

UN Global Compact Office. n.d. "Business Participation." New York: UN Global Compact Office. Retrieved December 1, 2012, from http://www.unglobalcompact.org/HowToParticipate/Business_Participation/index.html.

Welch, Eric W., Yasuhumi Mori, and Midori Aoyagi-Usui. 2002. "Voluntary Adoption of ISO 14001 in Japan: Mechanisms, Stages and Effects." *Business Strategy and the Environment* 11(1):43–62.

10 | Global corporate resistance to public pressures: corporate stakeholder mobilization in the United States, Norway, Germany, and France

EDWARD T. WALKER

Introduction

Recent decades have witnessed considerable growth in nongovernmental organizations (NGOs) across the globe, in what some have called a "global associational revolution" (Salamon 1994). These organizations have accompanied democratization and the spread of aid programs directed at developing nations (Schofer and Longhofer 2011) and are both a force for social globalization "from below" and a response to economic globalization "from above" (Smith and Johnston 2002; Tarrow 2005). Civil society has been revalorized as a space for the development of citizen governance and as a means of correcting for democratic deficits in the governance of complex institutions (Fung and Wright 2003; Sirianni and Friedland 2001).

As civic and economic globalization has continued apace, new institutions have emerged to regulate the behavior of firms and industries (Bartley 2007; Vogel 2008, 2010). Pressures for greater corporate social responsibility (CSR) among multinational firms have mounted, with initiatives for a more accountable business sector emerging in response to the concerns of citizen groups, firms' industry peers, and national governments (Soule 2009; Lim and Tsutsui 2012). Although the "business case for CSR" is relatively limited and uneven

---

For assistance with data sources on the four nations in the study, thanks are due to Frank Baumgartner, Wesley Longhofer, Sabine Saurugger, Evan Schofer, and Cornelia Woll. I thank the participants and organizers of the CSR in a Globalizing World conference for feedback, and especially John Meyer for his careful and detailed comments on the study.

(Vogel 2005), the operating belief that CSR benefits both firms and their stakeholders is very real in its consequences. Thus, it appears to many that public pressures are indeed leading to changes in business practices – or at least to the symbolic appearance that they are (Lim and Tsutsui 2012).

But we also know that economic globalization has not necessarily made the firm any less a political creature. If anything, firms have become more political in nature because they need to adapt to a broader variety of public affairs environments in diverse global settings (Boddewyn 2007; A. Barron 2010, 2011; Johnson et al., forthcoming; Moss et al. 2012).[1] Indeed, a variety of analyses now show that even when firms adopt CSR practices with the best of intentions, CSR is not unrelated to a firm's need to manage its political environment (Walker 2014; Walker and Rea 2014). Consider that firms often engage in forms of "strategic philanthropy" in which the broader political and market interests of the firm are aligned with a company's efforts to be seen as a valued corporate citizen (Porter and Kramer 2002); evidence of this can be found, for instance, in the substantial funds that pharmaceutical companies donate to patient advocacy groups such as the National Alliance on Mental Illness (Rothman et al. 2011). Companies also often see their CSR efforts not only as a source of protection or a "buffer" against negative information that could harm the firm's market position during a crisis (see King and Hunter-McDonnell, this volume), but they also see it as helpful in managing political or regulatory issues facing the company during similarly challenging circumstances. Alternatively, companies often turn to grassroots mobilization strategies instead of an exclusive CSR approach when they are in a weak reputational position and face crisis, protest, or controversy (Walker 2014).

This chapter investigates one aspect of the contentious relationship between firms and publics that has otherwise gone largely unrecognized by scholars of social movements, organizations, and international politics: the mobilization of pro-corporate public activism in response to pressures emerging from NGOs and governments for businesses to change their practices. Although earlier work has explored

[1] Furthermore, domestic laws, such as the Foreign Corrupt Practices Act of 1977 in the United States and the Corruption of Foreign Public Officials Act of 1999 in Canada, require that firms not engage in bribery and other illicit political practices in their overseas operations.

Global corporate resistance to public pressures 323

this relationship (Rao 2008: 131–135; Walker 2009, 2010, 2012, 2014), such scholarship focuses on the United States and neglects addressing how cross-national variation in the structures of the state, as well as the state-civil society relationship, affects the prevalence of pro-corporate mobilization and its character. Although these corporate-driven grassroots practices appear to be most common in the United States, the public affairs practitioner and journalistic literatures provide a range of examples of such campaigns in settings well beyond the United States (e.g., Rowell 1996; Grefe 2000, 2009; Fleisher 2005). In addition, although certain practitioners suggest that "global [corporate] grassroots is a reality" (Grefe 2000), there has been little attempt made to examine cross-national variation in corporate grassroots practices in a more detailed fashion.[2]

An advantage of this study's focus on the influence of the state-civil society interface on corporate political practices is that it holds greater analytic utility than alternative approaches, which might emphasize the relative risk of corporate practices in certain nations, the prevalence of corporate scandals, or other firm-level factors that might invite public controversy. In fact, what this study shows is that even in contexts where firms engage in highly controversial practices that draw substantial resistance from civil society groups, these firms' capacity for response is conditioned on the state–civil society interface.

Comparing the United States, Norway, Germany, and France, this study offers an initial analysis of how national characteristics shape the prevalence and character of corporate grassroots campaigns. I begin by considering the role of the state in corporate politics, then I continue by describing expectations for how the state–civil society interface should shape efforts to mobilize public support for the political preferences of business. Next, I compare the degree of corporate political mobilization, public affairs practices, scale of the interest group sector, and cultural factors present in the American, Norwegian, German, and French political systems. I find that the

---

[2] Public affairs as practiced today, in which firms seek to go beyond advertising and public relations by mobilizing mass support in the company's issue environment, is used widely in a variety of global settings, with new evidence suggesting that the public affairs function of the firm is increasingly being deployed in Asia (Burns 2011), Africa (Rensburg 2011), Latin America (Hogenboom et al. forthcoming), and developing democracies in general (Thomas and Hrebenar 2008).

French system, as a strong statist polity without corporatist bargaining, tends to have the least corporate mobilization of public participation, whereas the US context features an exceptional amount of such activity. Norway, a corporatist system with a relatively active associational field, has a moderate amount of corporate grassroots campaigning. Germany, with its statism and legacy of corporatist bargaining, features a low to moderate amount of corporate campaigning, but such activities are carried out mainly by trade groups rather than individual firms. I conclude by considering the implications of these findings for how scholars should best understand the role of the state in shaping corporate politics and stakeholder relations.

State mediation in the politics of the corporation

The globalization of business and the neoliberal policy environment has encouraged civil society groups, including social movement organizations, grassroots advocacy groups, and NGOs, to target the internal polity of the corporation as a site for broader policy change. This has been referred to by some as the expansion of a regime of "private politics," in which firms are targeted directly for change instead of appealing to the state for coercive change in business practices (D. Baron 2003; Reid and Toffel 2009; Werner 2012). Consistent with the assumptions of neoinstitutional theory, the vast majority of research on corporate responses to public contention has emphasized efforts by firms – to some extent independent of the demands of the state – to address directly the concerns raised by contentious challengers. From these studies, we know, for instance, that pressure by employee groups can facilitate the institutionalization of contentious practices within firms (Briscoe and Safford 2008), that social movements help to legitimate new market categories (e.g., Rao 2008; Sine and Lee 2009), and that civil society groups encourage firms to engage in new forms of self-regulation beyond that demanded by the state (e.g., Potoski and Prakash 2005; Bartley 2007). Corporate-targeted protests may also generate negative media attention to firms' activities and limit their access to key resources, thus facilitating corporate concessions to the demands of protest groups (King 2011). Neoinstitutional theory is often invoked in understanding how stakeholders can encourage companies to deinstitutionalize undesirable practices, often with the implication that social movement campaigns that target leading firms can lead to isomorphic change in lower status firms. In place of these largely mimetic processes, however, the coercive power of the state through regulation, court decisions, and/or legislative actions nonetheless remains an extraordinary force in generating endogenous change in organizational fields (Edelman, Uggen, and Erlanger 1999; Dobbin and Kelly 2007).

Yet it is also clear that public contention over corporate practices has not made companies any less political creatures; if anything, there are strong reasons to expect that popular contention has made companies even more aware of the importance of their government and public affairs functions. The corporate polity is one that is capable not only of granting challenging groups their wishes, ignoring them, or coopting them by granting symbolic access to positions of organizational authority; like the state, corporate polities are also capable of organizing resistance to collective challenges or engaging in repression, despite the fact that the state holds a monopoly on the legitimate use of force. Companies may fire striking employees, launch countermobilization efforts (Useem and Zald 1982), or even file strategic lawsuits against activist groups (Pring and Canan 1996).[3]

It should, then, be acknowledged that the interface of state and civil society conditions the ability of companies and industry groups to engage in strategic responses to challenges in the company's external environment. Although certain political systems are quite receptive to the notion that business should have a say in lobbying government and have some influence in civil society, other systems foreclose the possibility of substantial business political influence. Of course, it is also true that the state shapes challenging groups' interest in targeting corporations directly. In state-led market economies, as in France, for example, the nationalization of many industries means that the very notion of "private politics" outside the state may not be quite as meaningful as in liberal market economies, as in the United States and United Kingdom, although activism targeting multinationals

---

[3] Such strategies may be even more likely in developing world contexts where media monitoring is less pervasive and state regulations are less encompassing for firms, although "boomerang effects" (Keck and Sikkink, 1998) may be possible. The case of Shell's controversial actions in Nigeria represent one such instance (Bob, 2002).

such as McDonalds (that are not as well-rooted in the domestic state) may nonetheless be common. Thus, the state plays a role in mediating corporate contention in two senses beyond shaping the very formation of advocacy groups: (i) in making corporations a more (or less) desirable direct target for advocacy groups, and (ii) in expanding (or limiting) the options available to firms and trade associations as they weigh their options for how best to respond to contentious claims brought against them.

The topic of how the state shapes firms' options for responding strategically to external issues is relevant not only for those interested in the politics of the corporation, but also for those interested in understanding how societies and states encourage companies to be more responsible to their stakeholders and broader publics. The expansion of a discourse and organizational field surrounding CSR has taken place alongside the globalization of business and the concerns of civil society groups about the role of firms' labor, environmental, and social practices. States, as recent work has pointed out (Seidman 2007; Lim and Tsutsui 2012), should be seen as highly influential in encouraging companies to adopt more responsible practices and to become more transparent. Although some have linked CSR to the disembedding of the market from society alongside declining labor unions, retrenchment of the welfare state, and weaker regulation of corporate activity (Kinderman 2010: 8), it is nonetheless clear that nations vary substantially in their encouragement of CSR practices. A nation's CSR practices and the political role of the companies that operate within it should be linked, in that those states that tend to do the most to encourage firms to be more socially responsible are more likely to allow for a substantial voice for business in the political domain.[4]

---

[4] On a political level, these factors are more directly linked in that firms often describe their CSR efforts as strategic in nature, opening up not only opportunities for reputational development but also new avenues of political influence for the firm. In addition, as Kinderman (2010: 28) suggests, "the fact that Britain and the United States have played leading roles in [CSR] advocacy, suggests that high liberalism, with its cultural scripts and the interest-driven politics of [CSR] and political-economic reforms, are associated with each other. The cultural traditions and scripts of liberalism are used to legitimate political-economic reforms driven by employers' material interests."

The state–civil society interface

Which particular characteristics of the state, then, should be most influential in making possible strategic efforts by corporations to resist sociopolitical pressures? I expect that certain models of the state–society interface, based upon historical legacies and path-dependent political trajectories (Clemens and Cook 1999), should be especially significant in shaping both the necessity and the appropriateness of corporate mobilization of public participation. I examine this question not, as certain important analyses have, with reference to the issue of "state formation" (Tilly 1992; Mann 1993). Instead, I seek to understand how polity characteristics shape contemporary political formations in isomorphic fashion. A central statement of such state influences is found in Jepperson (2002), from which the following discussion builds.

First, a dichotomy can be established between systems that operate under more state-centric forms of organizing authority ("statist") and those that privilege civil society in the political realm ("societal") (Badie and Birnbaum 1983; Jepperson 2002). As explained by Jepperson (2002: 66), "*statist* visions locate collective authority in a differentiated, insulated, and charismatic organizational center – in the modern period, in a unified state apparatus. In contrast, more *societal* visions locate purpose and authority in society at large, with government seen more as an instrument and expression of society" (emphasis added). Statist systems include a strong bureaucratic elite and tend to privilege expertise. Statist systems also tend toward the belief that the state is the central arbiter of society's moral order and that civil society is the less legitimated realm of particularity (Jepperson 2002: 67); societal systems, by contrast, allow for a greater degree of interest representation and authority in an independent public, and government is seen as "an instrument wielded by society, [which] thus has less independent legitimation and standing" (67). The integration of business into the political system can also be understood along these lines: statist systems tend to circumscribe the role of market actors (Hall and Soskice 2001), whereas business has more of a capacity to represent itself as just another interest group (Hart 2004) in systems organized around societal authority.

Strong statist systems should discourage both the development of a substantial interest group sector and also discourage business efforts to mobilize public participation through it. As Schofer and Fourcade (2001: 812) argue, statist systems tend to remove associations from the centers of power, as is evident in the French treatment of minority group identities as factional and in conflict with the universalism of the state. In non-statist systems, particularly Anglo-American states like Britain and the United States, civic participation is actively encouraged by the state and promoted as a protective boundary between the public and private spheres (for a recent treatment, see Clemens and Guthrie 2011).

Second, an additional dichotomy exists between systems that adopt more corporate forms of group incorporation ("corporatist") and those that organize groups through noncorporate means ("associational"). This distinction is often conflated with the previous in that corporate systems are treated as if they are inherently statist, which is often not the case (consider corporatist-societal systems like Norway, which I describe in greater depth later). Corporatism is defined by Jepperson as a system in which "society is imagined as a communal order, with subsidiary elements – often collectivities themselves – carrying out explicitly imagined and differentiated public roles or functions" (2002: 66). In associational orders, by contrast, "society is imagined more as a fellowship of highly socialized and coordinated members taking public action together" (2002: 66). Corporatist societies have legacies in which modernization meant the incorporation of preexisting estates, guilds, classes, elites, and other traditional corporate structures, whereas associational societies tended to deinstitutionalize the previous order through either revolution (e.g., France, the United States) or other transformations in the social order (e.g., the United Kingdom, Netherlands).

These factors should influence the ability and interest of contemporary business groups to engage in the public sphere by shaping the development of the interest group system and also expectations about the normative political role of business. Corporate efforts to mobilize public participation, although often derided by critics as merely "Astroturf" or "fake" grassroots participation, build upon and work within the existing structures of civil society in its relation to the state (Walker 2009, 2010, 2014). The power of organized civil society both makes possible forms of corporate participation in public life and also places a limit on it due to the countervailing pressures of social movements, advocacy organizations, and public opinion about the issues relevant to corporate political action. Given these considerations, the strength of organized civil society should have particularly strong influences on a company's interest in (and capacity for) mobilizing participation in the public sphere.

In particular, the statist-societal distinction just described should play a considerable role in structuring industry interventions in the public sphere. Strong statist systems like France privilege expertise and place actors who are well connected to the elite bureaucracy in a strong position for having their voice heard, while they also delegitimize lay participation in government (and they associate lobbying of all sorts with unsavory and perhaps even corrupt practices; see Safran 2003; Knapp and Wright 2006). Societal systems, by contrast, promote civic action and the open exchange of ideas in spaces outside the state; they also tend to have much larger associational sectors and have different public understandings of the legitimacy of lobbying. Societal systems are also much less likely to nationalize industries or to engage in other forms of state-based market coordination (Hall and Soskice 2001).

I also expect that, independent of a nation's degree of statism, the level of corporatism has an impact on business engagement in politics. Although corporatist systems are likely to encourage greater overall levels of public participation because "they promote collective, inclusive forms of political incorporation" (Schofer and Fourcade 2001: 815), they should see higher levels of public engagement but fewer overall associations. Associational activity in corporatist systems tends to be encompassing and involve large numbers of individuals in employer associations and trade unions, but these systems tend to be dominated by a relatively small number of "peak" associations (Jepperson 2002). They therefore tend to encourage a certain level of public participation through well-established routes to influence and bargaining within the state but have smaller overall interest group sectors. Businesses are given an inherent voice within the state through corporatist systems, thus reducing the interest of companies in mobilizing public participation more broadly as a lobbying mechanism. This tendency, however, works against the feature of corporatist systems that valorizes group participation and encourages citizens to view society in more collective or class-based terms.

It is also reasonable to expect that these state–civil society structures will have synergistic effects, in that a nation's degree of statism and corporatism combine to endogenously produce and reinforce political cultures and processes of political engagement (Schofer and Fourcade 2001; Jepperson 2002: 68; Schofer and Longhofer 2011). The statist-associational form, most closely associated with France, features both a very strong state and relatively little state incorporation of labor unions or employer associations. The statist-corporatist form, most closely associated with Germany (although the corporatist tradition has weakened in the past half century), continues to privilege peak associations and empowers them in public life. The social-associational (liberal) form, most closely associated with Anglo-American systems, should see the greatest amount of business political mobilization of the public because of the strong independent role of business and the well-developed interest group system.[5] Last, the social-corporatist form, seen mainly in Scandinavian countries like Norway, should see a moderate amount of business mobilization. As suggested earlier, many of these same factors that encourage business mobilization in political life should also encourage corporate efforts to promote an image of social responsibility independent of the coercive power of the state.

Although a variety of other factors are likely to also be at play in facilitating business efforts to mobilize public participation in cross-national contexts – including the capacity of the media to serve as a tool for mass mobilization (Mahoney 2008: 150), whether the state has a federal or unitary structure, the system of party competition, and the type of corporate governance system in place[6] – previous research has suggested that the practices of corporate mobilization of public participation have more to do with the development of the field of advocacy organizations and the mobilization of business in public life (Walker 2009; see also, e.g., Vogel 1989).

---

[5] Australia, which features partial corporatism and a relatively small interest group sector with a liberal market economy, features substantial business mobilization but falls short of the very high levels found in the US system.

[6] For example, consider the distinction between shareholder-based systems and those based on blockholder ownership (see Gourevitch and Shinn 2007). Although contentious claims brought by shareholders are common in those systems (Thompson and Davis 2002), it seems reasonable to expect that blockholder systems would bring a more restricted set of claims and through less contentious means.

Table 10.1 *Corporate grassroots practices in four nations*

Variable	U.S.	Norway	Germany	France
Extent of corporate grassroots mobilization	High	Moderate	Low	Very low
Predominant actor in corporate grassroots	Firms & Trade Assns.	Firms & Trade Assns.	Trade Assns.	None
Interest group system (per 100k capita)	9	2.7	0.7	1.1
Statist	No	No	Yes	Yes
Corporatist	No	Yes	Yes	No
Business political mobilization	High	Moderate	Moderate-Low	Low

This study therefore compares four nations that vary in the development of their interest group system and the extensiveness of business engagement in politics – both of which are shaped by a polity's degree of statism and corporatism – with the expectation that both of these factors should be significant in shaping the interest and appropriateness of business in mobilizing public participation. Table 10.1 describes the four nations compared in this study: the United States, Norway, Germany, and France.

The United States: a fully formed grassroots industry

The US context

The system of government in the United States, with its inherent separation of powers, decentralized federal organization, and antistatist cultural sentiments (Quadagno 2004), has made for a nearly ideal environment for the political mobilization of industry in the public sphere. The American political system has a long tradition of valorizing public participation that emerges from civil society actors independent of the state, and the state actively promotes the formation of civic associations through offering funding, tax deductions, contracts, and moral support to associations (Jenkins 2006). Although bargaining between labor groups and employers has been a regular feature of the US system in the postwar years, no system of corporatist bargaining among unions, employers, and the state exists in a fashion similar to Germany or the Scandinavian states; the state has, in fact, stepped back even further in such arrangements in that the National Labor Relations Board is now seen by many labor unions as an unsympathetic venue, leading many labor groups to target firms directly (Manheim 2001; Martin 2008).

Consistent with the weak American state and its lack of corporatism, the United States has a very high associational density of some nine associations per 100,000 capita; this puts the United States above all other major industrialized nations, although Ireland and the United Kingdom are not very far behind. Thus, consistent with the expectations of Schofer and Longhofer (2011), liberal, nonstatist systems tend to have very high associational density. That high associational density means that the United States has a competitive interest group field, such that the influence of business in politics is partially held in check on issues that elicit strong popular opinions, such as taxation or business regulation (Smith 2000).

The ability of business to influence the political process in the United States is restrained by the variety of countervailing groups pressuring government for change, but the US legislative process allows for groups to have the power to influence (or derail) a bill at all stages from agenda-setting to implementation. By contrast, group influence in the policy process in most parliamentary settings is restricted to the precaucus stage, such that a lobbying group's goal should be to "have backbenchers advocating one's position during the deliberations in caucus" (Grefe 2009: 446). Such systems tend to be more collaborative and stand in stark contrast to the more confrontational and adversarial style associated with advocacy in the US political process (Grefe 2009: 446).

Corporate grassroots campaigns in the United States

Grassroots campaigns by firms in the United States have been described in a number of systematic scholarly accounts (Kollman 1998; Goldstein 1999; Mahoney 2008; Walker 2009, 2010, 2012, 2014) and in a broad practitioner literature (Wittenberg and

Wittenberg 1989; Grefe and Linsky 1995; Heath, Douglas, and Russell 1995; Grefe 2000, 2009; Lord 2000a, 2000b; Lerbinger 2006). A common refrain in this literature is that a company's decision about whether to mobilize a grassroots campaign – based on the US context – tends to follow a logic similar to the one outlined in Schattschneider's (1960) well-known theory of conflict expansion. As Baumgartner (2005b: 45) explains concisely, "losers expand a conflict by portraying issues in a more politically-charged manner. They hope that this will attract the attention of non-specialists. Those whose views appear to be prevailing within the policy community, by contrast, portray issues in the most arcane and technically complicated manner possible in order to ensure that no one else will become interested." Smith's (2000) account of corporate conflict expansion practices provides further evidence in support of this claim. A grassroots campaign is a "costly signaling" (Kollman 1998) strategy typically adopted by an actor possessed by a genuine fear of losing in a policy battle, and this presumes both (a) that an issue of interest to the firm can effectively be contested through corporate political action and (b) that organized constituencies exist that are aligned against the firm. The changing regulatory environment of the United States since the late 1960s has encouraged more corporate mobilization in public life not only because of the presence of contestable issues and opposing constituencies, but also because business found it necessary to frame its claims as expressing a general public interest in the post-Nader era (e.g., Vogel 1989; Walker 2009). This contrasts rather sharply with the political claims made by business elites in prior eras, such as during the New Deal; these were more plainly framed in terms of the self-interest of business and its social benefits (Phillips-Fein 2009).

Since the 1970s, the corporate public affairs function has expanded in a dramatic fashion (Marcus and Irion 1987; Meznar and Nigh 1995). The Public Affairs Council, a peak association for corporate and trade association public affairs staff and leaders, states that the concept can be defined as "an organization's efforts to monitor and manage its business environment. It combines government relations, communications, issues management and corporate citizenship strategies to influence public policy, build a strong reputation, and find common ground with stakeholders" (Public Affairs Council 2010; see also Meznar and Nigh 1995; Griffin and Dunn 2004).

Grassroots mobilization, lobbying, and public issues management are all central to these tasks (Public Affairs Council 1998).

Public affairs practices are rooted in earlier campaigns that were organized to address corporate challenges in the 1950s and 1960s, during which organized labor remained strong and new regulatory regimes expanded at an unprecedented pace (Public Affairs Council 1998). Grassroots mobilization practices became more widespread as a commercialized practice, in which public affairs consultants were often hired by firms to help them address and respond to contentious claims made by labor activists, policy makers, and other stakeholder groups (Walker 2009, 2014). Firms use them for campaigns that engage in letter writing and coordinated op-ed publications and to facilitate public events and rallies and more, and these campaigns are targeted at legislatures, regulatory agencies, other organizations, or the general public. Constituency building may be a powerful political strategy for firms (Baysinger, Keim, and Zeithaml 1985; Heath et al. 1995; Hillman and Hitt 1999; Lord 2000a, 2000b, 2003; Meznar and Nigh 1995). In addition, new technologies have lowered the costs of collective action for pro-corporate mobilization, ranging from the direct mail campaigns of the 1980s to Facebook and Twitter today (Lord 2000a, 2000b; Walker 2009, 2014).

The public affairs industry in the United States is remarkably well developed by a variety of metrics. Most significantly, a census of the professional consulting firms that companies can hire in support of their grassroots mobilization efforts showed that there were more than 700 such specialized organizations active during the mid-1990s to early 2000s (Walker 2009) providing services including grassroots coalition building, patch-through phone calling, targeted advocacy advertisements, speaker training, and help with staffing and infrastructure-building for corporate "third-party" advocacy organizations. In addition, the Public Affairs Council, which includes as members the public affairs officers of leading US corporations, currently has 509 organizational members (Public Affairs Council 2012). My 2010 investigation found that nearly 40 percent of the *Fortune* 500 appear on the client lists of at least one public affairs consulting firm (Walker 2014).

Having briefly sketched the US context, we now consider what such practices look like beyond American borders.

Grassroots in Norway: some emerging trends

The Norwegian context

Although in many ways a polar opposite to the United States – consider its relatively limited income inequality, unitary state structure, generous welfare state, and population of less than 5 million (e.g., Dahl et al. 2006) – Norway is closer to the United States in the vibrancy of its associational field than is France or Germany. In fact, as shown in Table 10.1, Norway features an interest group system that, although still tiny compared to the American and British systems, nonetheless (at 2.7 associations per 100,000 capita) is more than twice the size of the population-adjusted interest group sector of France and nearly four times that of Germany. Consistent with the categorization of Norway as a system with a notable degree of associationalism, the nation's political culture promotes the formation of associations and encourages such groups to play an important role in the policy process.

Norway's political structure is one that features a (largely symbolic) constitutional monarchy with a structure of parliamentary representative democracy. The parliament, known as the *Storting*, is unicameral and involves competition among multiple and diverse parties (consistent with party-list proportional representation; see Shaffer 1998). The executive branch features a prime minister and cabinet charged with managing some eighteen government ministries. The Norwegian system prides itself on openness, transparency, and inclusiveness, in which these executive ministries often invite public consultation in proposed agency rules, and legislators also have routinized channels of contact with organized publics (Ihlen and Rakkenes 2009: 440).

In fact, processes of government consultation with advocacy groups are so active here that some commentators have noted that Norway hosts a relatively limited range of social movement organizations in domains such as environmentalism: "organization into the state has meant playing by a common set of rules and integration into a unified system. There has been no space in civil society for oppositional formations to develop their own rules of engagement ... [such as in the] United States environmental justice movement" (Dryzek et al. 2003: 128). Similarly, Martin and Gabay (2013) find that Norway tends to have among the lowest size-adjusted rates of protest surrounding fiscal issues among developed countries; one interpretation of this finding is that the

Norwegian state may be quite effective at incorporating the concerns of challenging groups into either the associational system or the process of corporatist bargaining, thus making outside protest a much less appealing (or even unnecessary) option. John Dryzek and colleagues suggest that this is one reason why, despite the notably contentious practices employed by Norway's sizable whaling industry, relatively few protest groups challenge it (Dryzek et al. 2003: 76).

Norway's structures of corporatist bargaining also shape the advocacy environment for firms. Although some argue that Norway's associational field (its degree of "lobbyism") has, in some respects, come to eclipse the nation's corporatist features, it remains true that corporatist boards, committees, and councils have continued to play a powerful role in Norwegian politics and society (Christiansen and Rommetvedt 1999). The postwar development of corporatist organizations and their incorporation into the policy making of the executive branch had evolved to such an extent that, by the 1960s, one observer found that parliament began playing a subservient role to administrators (Kvavik 1976; Christiansen and Rommetvedt 1999: 199). Like Austria and Sweden, corporatism in Norway revolves around a peak labor confederation (Siaroff 1999: 179) in addition to employer associations; the combination of these structures allows the country to focus on the joint goals of both groups, such as full employment (Glyn and Rowthorn 1988: 198).

Corporate grassroots in Norway

The practice of grassroots issues management and popular mobilization on behalf of corporate interests is somewhat well developed in Norway although still in its infancy relative to the United States. In the United States, the ranks of grassroots political consultants swelled in the 1970s and 1980s in a context of a vastly expanding interest group sector and more politically mobilized business, buttressed by the convergence of lobbying, public relations (PR), and political consulting practices (Walker 2014). Norway, by comparison, has a limited (but growing) sector of political consultants, which are more often brought on as in-house staff to the political parties rather than serving as "outside" experts that help particular candidates or causes (as in the United States; see Karlsen 2010: 203). Still, corporate lobbying in Norway has been described as having a prominent role for PR managers; one study argues that such actors play a more active role in corporate lobbying than do CEOs (Haug and Koppang 1997). Furthermore, in another study of lobbying in Norway, Rommetvedt (2005:754) found that a large majority of private business organizations in the country were active in lobbying the parliament, political leadership of the executive ministries, and also civil servants working in the ministries; looking more deeply at the targeted lobbying of particular members of parliament, the study also found that business groups were substantially more active in lobbying than were trade unions, environmental groups, or other civic associations (Rommetvedt 2005: 759). Trade associations are also influential collective actors in Norwegian politics and civic life (Bowman 1998).

Lobbying by corporations in Norway is often delegated in a fashion designed to maximize grassroots influence on legislators, such that for firms with local branches, the leaders of those subunits will often be delegated the task of seeking influence with local policy elites (Haug and Koppang 1997: 239). As a small society with a relatively vibrant associational field, companies mobilize their grassroots social capital and network ties to policy makers (Haug and Koppang 1997; Rommetvedt 2005) rather than relying simply on the (perhaps overly formalistic and impersonal) influence of paid lobbyists. Companies are often deeply rooted in local communities, and this combines with the corporatist-associational culture of Norway to facilitate grassroots activism by business actors as players in the broader interest group system. Lobbying by business is overall quite common, with one study reporting that approximately 40 percent of Norwegian managers have contacted their Member of Parliament multiple times, and 63 percent have made multiple contacts to other government departments (Alt et al. 1999: 106).

Consistent with these observations, the practice of corporate PR is relatively well developed in Norway and is, to some extent, integrated into corporate lobbying efforts. Estimates of how many PR practitioners are at work in Norway have ranged from 3,000 to 5,000, and the Norwegian Communications Association (NCA) reported approximately 2,600 of these professionals as members as of 2007 (Ihlen and Rakkenes 2009: 432). The growing demand for PR services in Norway has picked up to such an extent that the industry has had trouble maintaining staff to provide needed services (Ihlen and Rakkenes 2009: 433). And, given the ability of powerful elites to purchase PR services to promote their point of view, industry growth has led to a broader popular discussion about the place of PR firms in distorting democratic representation in the country (Ihlen and Rakkenes 2009: 434).

As Horsle (2004: 286) contends, one of the key functions of PR in Norway is to serve a "managerial" function, in which the consultant works to "develop plans to communicate and maintain relationships with public groups in order to gain public trust and/or mutual understanding," as well as "operational" in that they "help the organization formulate its communication."[7] These managerial functions in particular mesh with corporate strategies of gaining public and political influence. As Horsle (2004: 288) elaborates, PR strategies are increasingly integrated with issues management, lobbying, and the use of new communications technologies for engaging the public and policy makers.

Overall, the institutional design of the state–civil society interface in Norway combines to create a particular context for firms as they seek to manage their public affairs environment. Although not as active as the grassroots engagement by US firms, Norwegian companies nonetheless employ these strategies in a manner consistent with the corporatist-associational context in which they operate. Osborne and Huston (2009), for example, describe a campaign in Norway organized against nuclear firm Sellafield in 2001, in which environmental NGOs raised critical concerns about discharges of radioactive nuclear materials into coastal waters. In response, the company engaged in a campaign to build social consensus around the firm's practices by engaging in dialogues with government ministers, politicians, local communities, and regulators (Osborne and Huston 2009: 201). The goals of these negotiations were to identify all relevant stakeholders, seek to understand their interests, reach an agreement about how to go forward with the dialogue, develop trust, and share all information (even that which was deemed "confidential and sensitive"; Osborne and Huston 2009: 203). This process of searching for consensus was set up along the lines of the corporatist system in that meetings focused on dialogues in which "trade unionist met with trade unionist, fisherman with fisherman, councilors with councilors, and so on. This produced a greater knowledge of each others' needs and concerns engendering greater trust and some personal bonding

---

[7] They also, Horsle (2004) argues, help organizations to reflect on the fit of their values with broader society, as well as for managers to communicate effectively with internal stakeholders.

between individuals" (Osborne and Huston 2009: 205). This case seems to suggest that corporate grassroots efforts in Norway tend to have a more subtle influence on public debate than the more aggressive approaches taken in the United States by certain firms such as Walmart (Walker 2014).

Grassroots in Germany: limited engagement

The German context

The German system of government is a parliamentary federation, which includes a multiparty system and a federal organization. This system is also known for its corporatist design and practices that formally incorporate the interests of employers (especially trade associations), labor groups, and certain other recognized constituencies. However, as Dryzek and colleagues (2002: 660) point out, the German system is best described as "passively exclusive" in that "once labor and business have been organized into the state, other interests are left out. Exclusion is passive because the state simply leaves those interests alone, providing few channels of influence but otherwise doing nothing to undermine them. Parliament is often inconsequential, so public policy does not respond to election results."

Consistent with a statist-corporatist system, the estimates used by Schofer and Longhofer (2011) illustrate that Germany has a relatively small field of associations, with only 0.7 associations per 100,000 capita. This puts Germany in roughly the same category as the highly statist French system, which has 1.12 associations per 100,000. However, the nation's legacy of corporatism tends to concentrate power in the associational field toward established labor and employer associations.

But even without a strong associational field, there is a substantial amount of business and public interest group lobbying that takes place in Germany. However, given the relatively undeveloped nature of the field, lobbying regulations are somewhat uneven in Germany. West Germany first implemented its lobbyist registry in 1951, but registration is not compulsory, and many groups fail to register (Holman and Luneburg 2012: 86). In fact, the German system today is "primarily a registration system for issuing passes to enter the parliamentary buildings" and includes only organizations and not individuals (Holman and Luneburg 2012: 89). Furthermore, it does not include financial information, details about whom the lobbyist is representing, or the issues in question; instead, registration was meant as a means to further institutionalize corporatist representation of trade associations and labor unions (Holman and Luneburg 2012). Indeed, although the concepts of "public relations" or *Öffentlichkeitsarbeit* are both well-known in Germany, the English term "lobbying" is unknown to almost half of Germans (Lederer, Lomba, and Scheucher 2005). Yet the public acceptance of the legitimacy of lobbying practices is also linked to the statist-corporatist German system; citizens accept business lobbying on the condition that it be transparent, honest, and not overwhelming of other groups or overly distorting of political representation (Bentele and Seidenglanz 2003).

The lack of a strong and well-developed interest group system in Germany limits the ability of firms or industry groups to mobilize public campaigns that benefit industry interests, and the formal incorporation of industry groups into the German system of corporatist bargaining limits business's ability to cast itself as firmly in opposition to unwelcome regulatory or legislative developments. As Streeck (1983: 272) argued, "the higher one gets in the multi-layered hierarchy of German business transactions, the more institutionalized associations tend to be in the realm of public policy, and the more both their organizations and the substantive interests they represent tend to be linked into the machinery of the modern state." Still, there is evidence that corporate-driven advocacy campaigns do take place in Germany.

Although some argue that the practice of corporate public affairs in Germany is "still in its infancy" (Lederer et al. 2005: 361) and that the "need to do something political" has not translated into a specific demand for public affairs services (Behrens 2002), there is evidence that the companies have increased the amount of lobbying they do, both on behalf of their own firm and also through trade groups (Sebaldt 1997). Associated with this expansion, and consistent with the findings of research on the United States (Walker 2009, 2014), the expansion of the trade association field has made possible the development of new consultancies that provide political support to firms and industries (Schönborn 2002). The field of public affairs consultant firms in Germany has now become sufficiently dense to support a division of labor among consultancies into four major types: "individual consultants, public affairs departments of international agency associations, individually owned national agencies, and full-service agencies" (Lederer et al. 2005: 363; see also Lianos and Simon 2003).

Further evidence that the German system is seeing a greater influence of corporations in mobilizing public support lies in the founding of the German Association of Political Consulting (DeGePol) in 2002, which requires all of its members to sign on to a code of conduct regulating their transparency and honesty both to the public and to their clients (DeGePol 2003). The development of this association occurred around the same time as a major scandal in Germany surrounding a consultant named Moritz Hunzinger who was found to have been engaging in political bribery (Wassermann 2002); the scandal triggered a national debate about the role of PR and lobbying in the German political system. The DeGePol requires of its 120 current members[8] that they maintain the confidentiality of their clients; not engage in bribery or other illegal contributions; not engage in racist, sexist, or religiously offensive communications; separate their activities from other political offices; avoid activities that damage the standing of the consultant profession; and more (Lederer et al. 2005: 368).

Unlike in the United States, the United Kingdom, Australia, or Canada, expertise and abstract knowledge of politics is more valued in Germany than is having a practical knowledge of the operations of politics and PR. One study of lobbying over accounting rules in Germany suggests that the influence of lobbyists in Germany tends to involve considerable expertise and to be narrowly targeted at specific regulations and subregulations (McLeay, Ordelheide, and Young 2000: 81). Associated with this, PR and lobbying practitioners in Germany tend to focus on insider methods requiring technical knowledge of the law, mass communications, and journalism. PR training in German universities tends to neglect questions of political organization (Lederer et al. 2005).

Corporate grassroots in Germany

Given this background, as might be expected, practices of pro-corporate grassroots organizing are relatively rare in Germany. Only

---

[8] http://www.degepol.de/eng/become_a_member/

10 percent of German trade groups engage in at least some grassroots practices (Irmisch 2011), compared to more than 90 percent of their US counterparts (Kollman 1998). The statist context of the country favors expertise over lay participation, and this is also reflected in the low presence of advocacy organizations in the political system. The structure of corporatist bargaining also encourages lobbying through well-established channels of negotiation among the state, trade groups, and labor unions, thus obviating a substantial amount of what would become lobbying or protest efforts in other national contexts. Still, such efforts do exist.

Irmisch (2011) describes a number of cases in Germany of industry-driven public advocacy, arguing that this is a relatively new strategy in the country. Consistent with work on the US context of industry advocacy (Walker 2010, 2014), Irmisch argues that the boundary between authentic "grassroots" participation and inauthentic "Astroturf" participation is problematic. Many grassroots organizations rely on the strong organizational support of key patrons, and many corporate campaigns will not be seen as legitimate without support from public opinion. Nonetheless, there is a new recognition that mass public participation beyond established corporatist mechanisms may be politically effective in modern Germany, and this has meant that this new form of *"gesellschaftlich erweitertes Lobbying* [socially enhanced lobbying]" is now playing more of a role among a limited subset of actors.

Irmisch (2011) describes a number of key examples of pro-industry campaigns that attempt to channel the political interests of industry through advocacy groups:

- Coalition for Patient Information [*Koalition Pro Patienteninformation*] was an organization active in Germany in 2009 claiming to represent a network of patient organizations and individuals (Grill 2007; Irmisch 2011). The organization targeted a proposed new European Union (EU) regulation that would ban direct advertising of pharmaceuticals, arguing that the advertising ban would limit patient access to information about drugs relevant to treating a variety of conditions. In Germany, drug advertising is allowed only for cough syrup, nasal spray, and certain homeopathic remedies; consumer advocates feared that direct pharmaceutical advertising artificially boosts demand and harms the patient (Grill 2007). The

consultant in charge of the campaign would neither confirm nor deny whether a pharmaceutical trade association was funding the initiative, leading to a reprimand from the German Council for Public Relations (DRPR). It also led to the campaign's leader, Jan Burdinski, being ousted from DeGePol (Banse 2008). The coalition's members, including self-help organizations for sufferers of osteoporosis, claimed to have only met the coalition's leaders once in Cologne (Grill 2007), and, in fact, opposed the Coalition's lobbying efforts in Brussels.
- Citizens for Technology (CFT) [*Bürger für Technik*] is an organization with a small membership run by Ludwig Lindner (Banse 2008), a leader of a variety of trade groups representing nuclear power plants, genetic engineering interests, and chemical industries. Lindner and CFT are both very active in lobbying about the benefits of PVC and other chemicals. As of 2012, CFT continues to be very active, especially in the domain of promoting the safety of nuclear power. Their website claims that nuclear power is a necessary component of Germany's energy needs alongside traditional sources such as coal and natural gas; wind and solar sources will not be sufficient (Bürger für Technik 2012). Furthermore, the campaign claims that solar and wind energy are more costly and that policies supporting alternative energy will make energy less affordable to the poor (Bürger für Technik 2012). The organization focuses on writing letters to the editor in order to support the position of industry in public discourse.
- Society for Road and Transportation Planning [*Gesellschaft zur Förderung umweltgerechter Straßen- und Verkehrsplanung (GSV)*] was founded in 1980 by trade associations in the road construction and automotive industries. The primary task of the association was to advise and coordinate 250 citizens' groups and to link these groups with mayors, public officials, and road builders. The association continues to be headquartered in the former German capital of Bonn. Linked directly to the CSR efforts of auto companies and construction firms, the association seeks to engage in planning efforts to manage traffic congestion and to promote environmental protection and pollution mitigation. Irmisch (2011) argues that this case in particular demonstrates that it is often very difficult to distinguish between genuine citizen initiatives and industry-driven campaigns,

although the role of industry in the association remains less than fully transparent.

These rare examples show that such strategies are generally not considered legitimate in Germany and gain relatively little traction when they take place. They are also likely to involve trade associations rather than individual corporations, consistent with the political recognition of established corporatist actors. Grassroots mobilization of the general public by business is also limited in a sense by law; whereas in the United States corporate advocacy campaigns can easily purchase lists of voting records and/or identified consumer data on individuals, German law restricts such uses of private data on the political and market activities of individuals (Althaus 2009: 310).

Relatedly, the development of the field of PR in Germany provides some interesting and relevant insights. Prior to the 1960s, PR practices were understood as fundamentally about advertising in order to establish trust between businesses and consumers (Bentele and Wehmeier 2009: 411). But starting in the 1970s, "an understanding of public relations as [a] dialogue with different target groups started to develop ... [due to] the appearance of environmental activism [which] turned customers into demanding groups with whom dialogue needed to be established" (Bentele and Wehmeier 2009: 411). Indeed, the very notion of "public relations" in German is linked to the notion of a mediated public sphere ("*Öffentlichkeit*") (Habermas 1991); employment in the PR sector is typically referred to as *Öffentlichkeitsarbeit* ("public sphere work"). Still, this corporate work in the public sphere is typically not associated with efforts to mobilize public participation.

Grassroots in France: the restrictions of a strong state

The French context

The French system, which is renowned for its overwhelming statism and also its lack of corporatist bargaining (Jepperson 2002), has a quite small interest group system (Safran 2003; Knapp and Wright 2006; Schofer and Longhofer 2011). The power of the French state privileges forms of technical expertise and discourages lay political participation.

Given these considerations, the term "lobbying" has generally very unsavory connotations in France. Schmidt (1996), for example, suggests that this distaste for influence peddling also played out at the EU level, leaving French interests underrepresented in Brussels in the past. Although the French are famous for their engagement in contentious protest politics (Tilly 1989; Traugott 1993), forms of influence through the state tend to be quite seriously restricted when compared with the United States, United Kingdom, Australia, Norway, or even Germany. As Jepperson (2002: 73) puts it, French "state institutions have continued to limit participation and representation, redirecting popular forces into protest efforts." French interest groups are more dependent on allies within the state than are groups in the United States, yet those associations that do exist in France tend to be stronger organizationally because of this very independence (Baumgartner 2005a). As Knapp and Wright (2006: 312) put it, "the political culture of Jacobinism, as inherited from the French Revolution, has even less use for interest groups than for parties ... [they] opposed the narrow, 'particular' (and inevitably selfish) interests represented by the groups to the 'general interest' which only the state could incarnate."

The political situation of business in France is also much different from systems that incorporate corporatist bargaining (such as Germany, Austria, Japan, and many of the Scandinavian countries) in that powerful, recognized labor unions and integrated employer associations are not a standard element of the French system; this has consequences for the employment and training systems used in French workplaces (Hall and Soskice 2001: 324). In the absence of corporatist bargaining, employers and labor unions are both in a position to lobby for their interests through mobilizing direct contacts with affiliates in government (Schmidt 1996) rather than through efforts to mobilize mass civic participation. The channels that exist through "peak associations" in Germany and Scandinavia are generally closed off in Paris, and many of the most influential firms in the primary French employers' association (the *Conseil national du patronat francais* [CNPF] or National Council of French Employers) are nationalized (Knapp and Wright 2006: 314).

The role of that employers' association (CNPF) warrants further comment. CNPF is an umbrella organization of approximately 900,000 French employers in a variety of industrial, commercial, and banking sectors (Safran 2003: 152). The association was founded in 1946, during a period in which the business community in France was widely discredited for collaboration with the Vichy regime (Safran 2003: 152). As the memory of the war began to fade, the transition into the Fifth Republic in 1958 brought with it closer ties between business organizations and the state bureaucracy. This period saw major expansions of industry, declines in farming, and the modernization of French business; CNPF was generally in favor of the protectionism and subsidies offered by the *dirigisme* regime (Knapp and Wright 2006: 21). In the late 1990s, CNPF became the *Mouvement des Entreprises de France* (MEDEF, or Movement of the French Enterprises), an organization that became more politically active under new leadership (Safran 2003: 153). Although this association and other trade groups for small and medium-sized enterprises, such as the *Confédération Générale des Petites et Moyennes Entreprises* (CGPME), involve a substantial number of organizations, their routes to political influence have been modest because of the weakness of the centrist parties they have traditionally supported (Safran 2003: 153). The business community in France tends toward fragmentation, and mass mobilization of membership on behalf of interests is quite rare in a culture that tends to favor "impersonal, highly formalized, distant and hierarchical rules imposed from above," which are seen as more impartial and less arbitrary (Knapp and Wright 2006: 315).

More generally, the French system limits public participation in policy making through a variety of means. For example, although antinuclear advocates were able to generate substantial policy change in Germany and a retreat from nuclear power (Kitschelt 1986: 74), the French legal system did not allow public contestation of the siting of nuclear facilities, thus shutting off opportunities for generating change in this domain (Touraine 1980). The French educational system involves a substantial amount of advocacy and interorganizational conflict, but much of this conflict is mediated by the party system rather than directly by advocacy groups as in more pluralist systems (Baumgartner 2005b: 47–49). Similarly, a comparison of policy making over the promotion of electric vehicles and environmentalist efforts to reduce urban air pollution in France and California showed that whereas the Californian process called for a broad-based participatory process involving the public, the media, advocacy groups, and academics, the French process involved relatively little public participation and resulted in a state-based project with weak industry involvement (Calef and Goble 2007: 28).

In 2010, France instituted a voluntary lobbyist registration system that covers the legislature but not the executive branch (Holman and Luneburg 2012: 95); those who register are granted easier access to both the National Assembly and the Senate in exchange for having the lobbyist and her clients listed in public disclosures (Holman and Luneburg 2012: 90). Given its voluntary nature and limited financial disclosure requirements, the French lobbyist registry system is quite weak.

Corporate grassroots in France

In the strong statist system of France, in which firms are deeply rooted in the state and do not mobilize on an issue-by-issue basis as in the United States, United Kingdom, and Australia (Barron 2011: 321), cultural traditions and the institutional design of the state strongly condition the style and narrow the scope of corporate political engagement. As Wilson put it more than twenty years ago (1987: 168), "there is no French parallel to the development in the United States of professional public-relations firms or specialized law offices to represent interest groups or corporate clients in their dealings with government. Instead, group politics remains a home industry for each group, based on the activities of their own, often untrained and non-professional staff." Similarly, a more recent account (Carayol 2004: 143) finds from a survey of the leading consultancies in France that only 6 percent report engaging in "communications with public authorities" on behalf of their clients. Leading scholars of the French interest group system were also hard-pressed to identify any noteworthy cases of corporate mobilization of public participation or scholarly literature documenting such a presence in the country (personal communications).

Accordingly, the PR profession in France, unlike in the United States, United Kingdom, Australia, or Germany, does not feature a strong "public affairs" tradition in which firms seek to manage public challenges to corporate reputations. The most dominant PR firms in France tend to be those that are French-owned independent firms or are a subunit of French-owned advertising agencies (Pritchard, Ahles, and Bardin 2005: 424). Given the relatively weak voluntary and philanthropic sectors in France, the clients of PR firms are almost never nonprofit groups (Pritchard et al. 2005: 424), whereas in the United States major nonprofit groups and foundations engage in a significant amount of paid PR activity. Related to this, although US-based firms regularly partner with nonprofit and civic groups on voluntary initiatives, partnerships between firms and external stakeholders are much less common in France (Antal and Sobczak 2007: 26). This is consistent with the unique history of the discourse of CSR in the French context (Antal and Sobczak 2007: 26).

French PR firms specialize in such areas as crisis communications, investor or financial communications, and, to some extent, issues management and lobbying (Josephs and Josephs 1993). However, unlike in the US and UK contexts where consultants are often central to the development of corporate campaign strategies, French consultants are more often seen as "technicians" rather than comprehensive strategists (Pritchard et al. 2005).

In addition, a firm's interest in engaging in constituency-building efforts relates to its cultural understanding of which policy makers are authorized to make decisions. In strong statist systems like France, business elites may be likely to assume that decisions are made by "ruling elites of likeminded politicians, civil servants and businessmen who attended the same prestigious education establishments" (Barron 2011: 324), whereas both more corporatist systems like Germany and pluralist systems like the United States tend to involve greater public consultation, whether by peak associations in the former or in a variety of public lobbying efforts in the latter. The French system of lobbying involves a heavy degree of influence cultivated through personal connections to elites in the state bureaucracy. Given these concerns, constituency-based lobbying efforts in France are relatively rare compared to those in countries that have either a more pluralist or a more corporatist design.

There is, however, one exception to this expectation, in that some have shown that the French have become considerably more active in lobbying at the EU level (Lory 2002) despite a tradition of being relatively inactive in lobbying their own domestic government. Mahoney (2008: 147–165) shows that although outside lobbying strategies are considerably less common when targeting Brussels compared to Washington, such strategies are nonetheless still employed. However, there is evidence that, even when seeking influence at the

EU level, French cultural traditions are manifest in that French business lobbyists are notably more likely to request direct meetings; British business lobbying in the EU, by comparison, involves more PR, constituency mobilization, and work through the media (Lory 2002).

Conclusion

Through an examination of practices of corporate mobilization of grassroots participation in the United States, Norway, Germany, and France, this study illustrates that the interface between state and civil society is central to making possible forms of corporate political influence mediated by citizen activism. Two key characteristics of a polity appear to be quite influential in shaping this practice: its degree of statism and its degree of corporatism. Statist systems privilege expertise, discourage lay political participation, and reduce the size of the interest group system. They also tend to engage in more coordination and regulation of the marketplace, thus limiting the autonomy of business to press for its political interests. Corporatist systems empower peak associations of employers and labor unions and generally feature more civic participation at the individual level, even if through fewer associations. Thus, the effect of a polity's corporatism on the empowerment of corporations in mobilizing the public incorporates two countervailing tendencies: on the one hand, corporatism decreases the number of associations by channeling activity into peak associations in a position to bargain with the state, but, on the other hand, corporatist systems give additional powers to those formally recognized associations. This recognition may serve as a force for organizing support in civil society albeit under a more limited set of circumstances. Consistent with these expectations, I found that corporate grassroots mobilization practices are most widespread and advanced in liberal states (nonstatist systems without corporatist bargaining as in the United States), moderately developed in a system that is associational and corporatist (Norway), rarely used but only done by trade groups in a statist-corporatist polity (Germany), and extremely rare in a strong state without corporatism (France).

These findings are consequential for those seeking to understand business practices in a context of economic globalization and private politics, especially with respect to the mediating role of the state. Just as states are critical actors in making possible a more responsible and ethical corporation (e.g., Seidman 2007), states also make available opportunities for firms and industries to engage in forms of counter-mobilization to resist pressures they face in their external environments. In the United States, an unintended consequence of the expansion of citizen mobilization in the 1970s and 1980s was the increase of corporate mobilization of participation in civil society (Walker 2009). In a cross-national context, this study shows that polities that encourage the formation of interest groups outside the state also make possible corporate efforts to facilitate mass participation in pro-business campaigns.

Importantly, this study also shows that firms' relations with stakeholders serve not only to reinforce or supplement a firm's CSR programs and broader efforts at reputational management, but also that maintaining these relations may be a useful political force when the firm faces protest, controversy, or crisis. In a sense, then, CSR and grassroots campaigning by firms and industries represent complementary sources of social and political stakeholder management for firms. However, as I have argued throughout this chapter, these relationships are conditioned on the institutional design of the state in its interaction with civil society and cannot be understood simply as a universal corporate strategy taken in response to controversy or negative claims.

To further illustrate this point, consider the following example. Grefe (2000) provides an interesting illustration of a corporate grassroots campaign organized in Australia in the 1980s, which was "one of the first times" a corporate grassroots approach was attempted on a large scale in Australia. The Australian Soft Drink Association expressed concerns about a proposition to "add a mandatory deposit on every soft drink sold" (Grefe 2000: 267). The industry claimed that such a deposit would lead to fewer sales and force reductions in employment within their member firms. The campaign first sought the support of employees in the industry, and, as campaigns often do in the United States (Walker 2014), matched employees' home addresses to legislative (parliamentary) districts. The campaign then undertook a full evaluation of all the firm's political allies, which members of parliament could be considered vulnerable to losing the next election, and how best to activate the social capital and network ties of the member firms (Grefe 2000: 267). The campaign was successful in defeating the proposed measure (Grefe 2000). Importantly, the campaign illustrates one of the many ways that corporate grassroots campaigns and CSR are linked: the campaign focused on the message emphasizing that consumers should "Do The Right Thing" and voluntarily return bottles and cans to recycling centers, thus averting the apparent need for regulatory action. Thus, in this case (and in many others), CSR efforts serve an important political function for businesses as they navigate their institutional environment.

Furthermore, some firms see grassroots engagement as a form of corporate citizenship (Walker 2014); another study showed that Walmart makes significantly higher contributions to charity in areas where it has faced controversies over opening new stores (Ingram, Yue, and Hayagreeve 2010: 77–81). In the United States, the consultants that companies hire to mobilize such campaigns often report that a firm's CSR efforts provide a crucial foundation for corporate public affairs campaigns by generating good will among both consumers and would-be pro-corporate activists.

Combined, these findings call for a broader understanding of the political uses of CSR and how it is linked to the political challenges that firms face in a context of globalization and increased popular contention targeted against corporations.

References

Alt, James E., Fredrik Carlsen, Per Heum, and Kåre Johansen. 1999. "Asset Specificity and the Political Behavior of Firms: Lobbying for Subsidies in Norway." *International Organization* 53(1):99–116.

Althaus, Marco. 2009. "Discovering our (Corporate) Grassroots: European Advocacy 2.0." Pp. 477–494 in *Routledge Handbook of Political Management*, edited by D. W. Johnson. New York: Routledge.

Antal, Ariane Berthoin, and André Sobczak. 2007. "Corporate Social Responsibility in France: A Mix of National Traditions and International Influences." *Business & Society* 46(1):9–32.

Badie, Bertrand, and Pierre Birnbaum. 1983. *The Sociology of the State*. Chicago: University of Chicago Press.

Banse, Philip. 2008. "Lobbyismus gut getarnt: Wie Firmen verdeckt die öffentliche Meinung beeinflussen." *D Radio*, November 22. Retrieved from http://www.dradio.de/dlf/sendungen/hintergrundpolitik/880660/.

Baron, David P. 2003. "Private Politics." *Journal of Economics & Management Strategy* 12(1):31–66.

Barron, Andrew. 2010. "Unlocking the Mindsets of Government Affairs Managers: Cultural Dimensions of Corporate Political Activity." *Cross Cultural Management* 17(2):101–117.

Barron, Andrew. 2011. "Exploring National Culture's Consequences on International Business Lobbying." *Journal of World Business* 46(3):320–327.

Bartley, Tim. 2007. "Institutional Emergence in an Era of Globalization: The Rise of Transnational Private Regulation of Labor and Environmental Conditions." *American Journal of Sociology* 113(2):297–351.

Baumgartner, Frank R. 2005a. "Independent and Politicized Policy Communities: Education and Nuclear Energy in France and in the United States." *Governance* 2(1):42–66.

Baumgartner, Frank R. 2005b. "Public Interest Groups in France and the United States." *Governance* 9(1):1–22.

Baysinger, Barry D., Gerald D. Keim, and Carl P. Zeithaml. 1985. "An Empirical Evaluation of the Potential for Including Shareholders in Corporate Constituency Programs." *Academy of Management Journal* 28:180–200.

Behrens, Peter-Alberto. 2002. "Germany: Public Affairs Reinvented." *Journal of Public Affairs* 2(3):173–176.

Bentele, Günther, and Rene Seidenglanz. 2003. *PR-Images in Germany: Population Poll and Journalist Survey*. Leipzig: Institut für Kommunikations- und Medienwissenschaft, Universität Leipzig.

Bentele, Günther and Stefan Wehmeier. 2009. "From Literary Bureaus to a Modern Profession: The Development and Current Structure of Public Relations in Germany." Pp. 407–429 in *The Global Public Relations Handbook*, edited by K. Sriramesh and D. Vercic. New York: Routledge.

Bob, Clifford. 2002. "Political Process Theory and Transnational Movements: Dialectics of Protest among Nigeria's Ogoni Minority." *Social Problems* 49(3):395–415.

Boddewyn, Jean J. 2007. "The Internationalization of the Public-Affairs Function in U.S. Multinational Enterprises Organization and Management." *Business & Society* 46(2):136–173.

Bowman, John R. 1998. "Achieving Capitalist Solidarity: Collective Action among Norwegian Employers." *Politics & Society* 26(3):303–336.

Briscoe, Forrest, and Sean Safford. 2008. "The Nixon-in-China Effect: Activism, Imitation, and the Institutionalization of Contentious Practices." *Administrative Science Quarterly* 53(3):460–491.

Bürger für Technik. 2012. "Bürger für Technik." Retrieved from http://www.buerger-fuer-technik.de/.
Burns, Wayne. 2011. "The Three Waves of Corporate Public Affairs Development in Asia." *Journal of Public Affairs* 12(1):81–85.
Calef, David, and Robert Goble. 2007. "The Allure of Technology: How France and California Promoted Electric and Hybrid Vehicles to Reduce Urban Air Pollution." *Policy Sciences* 40(1):1–34.
Carayol, Valerie. 2004. "[Public Relations in] France." Pp. 135–151 in *Public Relations and Communication Management in Europe*, edited by B. van Ruler and D. Vercic. Berlin: Mouton de Gruyter.
Christiansen, Peter M., and Hilmar Rommetvedt. 1999. "From Corporatism to Lobbyism? – Parliaments, Executives, and Organized Interests in Denmark and Norway." *Scandinavian Political Studies* 22(3):195–220.
Clemens, Elisabeth S., and James M. Cook. 1999. "Politics and Institutionalism: Explaining Durability and Change." *Annual Review of Sociology* 25:441–466.
Clemens, Elisabeth S., and Doug Guthrie, eds. 2011. *Politics and Partnerships*. Chicago: University of Chicago Press.
Dahl, Espen, Jon Ivar Elstad, Dag Hofoss, and Melissa Martin-Mollard. 2006. "For Whom is Income Inequality Most Harmful? A Multi-Level Analysis of Income Inequality and Mortality in Norway." *Social Science & Medicine* 63(10): 2562–2574.
DeGePol. 2003. *Was ist Politikberatung?* Berlin: Deutsche Gesellschaft für Politikberatung.
Dobbin, Frank, and Erin L. Kelly. 2007. "How to Stop Harassment: Professional Construction of Legal Compliance in Organizations." *American Journal of Sociology* 112(4):1203–1243.
Dryzek, John S., David Downes, Christian Hunold, David Schlosberg, and Hans-Kristian Hernes. 2003. *Green States and Social Movements: Environmentalism in the United States, United Kingdom, Germany, and Norway*. New York: Oxford University Press.
Dryzek, John S., Christian Hunold, David Schlosberg, David Downes, and Hans-Kristian Hernes. 2002. "Environmental Transformation of the State: The USA, Norway, Germany and the UK." *Political Studies* 50(4):659–682.
Edelman, Lauren B., Christopher Uggen, and Howard S. Erlanger. 1999. "The Endogeneity of Legal Regulation: Grievance Procedures as Rational Myth." *American Journal of Sociology* 105(2):406–454.
Fleisher, Craig S. 2005. "The Global Development of Public Affairs." Pp. 5–30 in *The Handbook of Public Affairs*, edited by P. Harris and C. S. Fleisher. Thousand Oaks, CA: Sage.

Fung, Archon, and Erik Olin Wright, eds. 2003. *Deepening Democracy*. London: Verso.

Glyn, Andrew, and Bob Rowthorn. 1988. "West European Unemployment: Corporatism and Structural Change." *American Economic Review* 78(2):194–199.

Goldstein, Kenneth M. 1999. *Interest Groups, Lobbying, and Participation in America*. New York: Cambridge University Press.

Gourevitch, Peter A., and James Shinn. 2007. *Political Power and Corporate Control: The New Global Politics of Corporate Governance*. Princeton, NJ: Princeton University Press.

Grefe, Edward. 2000. "Global Grassroots is a Reality." Pp. 265–275 in *Winning at the Grassroots*, edited by T. Kramer. Washington, DC: Public Affairs Council.

Grefe, Edward. 2009. "Building Constituencies for Advocacy in the United States and other Democracies." Pp. 433–449 in *Routledge Handbook of Political Management*, edited by D. W. Johnson. New York: Routledge.

Grefe, E. A., and M. Linsky. 1995. *The New Corporate Activism: Harnessing the Power of Grassroots Tactics for Your Organization*. New York: McGraw-Hill Companies.

Griffin, Jennifer J., and Paul Dunn. 2004. "Corporate Public Affairs: Commitment, Resources, and Structure." *Business & Society* 43:196–220.

Grill, Markus. 2007. "Zweifelhafte PR: Scheinbar im Namen der Patienten – Wirtschaft." *Stern*. Retrieved from http://www.stern.de/605158.html.

Habermas, Jürgen. 1991. *The Structural Transformation of the Public Sphere: An Inquiry into a Category of Bourgeois Society*. Cambridge, MA: MIT Press.

Hall, Peter A., and David W. Soskice. 2001. *Varieties of Capitalism: The Institutional Foundations of Comparative Advantage*. New York: Oxford University Press.

Hart, David M. 2004. "'Business' Is Not an Interest Group: On the Study of companies in American National Politics." *Annual Review of Political Science* 7: 47–69.

Haug, Magne, and Haavard Koppang. 1997. "Lobbying and Public Relations in a European Context." *Public Relations Review* 23(3):233–247.

Heath, Robert L., William Douglas, and Michael Russell. 1995. "Constituency Building: Determining Employees' Willingness To Participate in Corporate Political Activities." *Journal of Public Relations Research* 7:273–288.

Hillman, Amy J., and Michael A. Hitt. 1999. "Corporate Political Strategy Formulation: A Model of Approach, Participation, and Strategy Decisions." *Academy of Management Review* 24:825–842.

Hogenboom, Barbara, Fernández Jilberto, and Alex E. Forthcoming. "Neoliberalism, Big Business and the Evolution of Interest Group Activity in Latin America." *Journal of Public Affairs*.

Holman, Craig, and William Luneburg. 2012. "Lobbying and Transparency: A Comparative Analysis of Regulatory Reform." *Interest Groups & Advocacy* 1(1):75–104.

Horsle, Pål. 2004. "Norway." Pp. 277–290 in *Public Relations and Communication Management in Europe*, edited by B. van Ruler and D. Vercic. Berlin and New York: Mouton de Gruyter.

Ihlen, Oyvind, and Kjell S. Rakkenes. 2009. "Public Relations in Norway: Communication in a Small Welfare State." Pp. 430–448 in *The Global Public Relations Handbook*, edited by S. Krishnamurthy and D. Vercic. London: Routledge.

Ingram, Paul, Lori Yue, and Hayagreeva Rao. 2010. "Trouble in Store: Probes, Protests, and Store Openings by Wal-Mart, 1998–2007." *American Journal of Sociology* 116(1):53–92.

Irmisch, Anna. 2011. *Astroturf: Eine Neue Lobbyingstrategie in Deutschland?* Wiesbaden: VS Verlag für Sozialwissenschaften.

Jenkins, Craig. 2006. "Nonprofit Organizations and Political Advocacy." Pp. 307–332 in *The Nonprofit Sector: A Research Handbook*, edited by W. W. Powell and R. Steinberg. New Haven, CT: Yale University Press.

Jepperson, Ronald L. 2002. "Political Modernities: Disentangling Two Underlying Dimensions of Institutional Differentiation." *Sociological Theory* 20(1):61–85.

Johnson, Julius H., Dinesh A. Mirchandani, and Martin B. Meznar. Forthcoming. "The Impact of Internationalization of U.S. Multinationals on Public Affairs Strategy and Performance: A Comparison at 1993 and 2003." *Business & Society*.

Josephs, Ray, and Juanita W. Josephs. 1993. "Public Relations in France." *Public Relations Journal* 49(7):20.

Karlsen, Rune. 2010. "Fear of the Political Consultant Campaign Professionals and New Technology in Norwegian Electoral Politics." *Party Politics* 16(2):193–214.

Keck, Margaret E., and Kathryn Sikkink. 1998. *Activists beyond Borders: Advocacy Networks in International Politics*. New York: Cambridge University Press.

Kinderman, Daniel. 2010. "The Rise of Corporate Responsibility and Market Liberalism, 1977–2009." Unpublished manuscript, University of Delaware.

King, Brayden G. 2011. "The Tactical Disruptiveness of Social Movements: Sources of Market and Mediated Disruption in Corporate Boycotts." *Social Problems* 58(4):491–517.

King, Brayden G, and Mary Hunter-McDonnell. 2015; this volume. "Good Firms, Good Targets: The Relationship Among Corporate Social Responsibility, Reputation, and Activist Targeting." Pp. 430–454 in *Corporate Social Responsibility in a Globalizing World*, edited by K. Tsutsui and A. Lim. New York: Cambridge University Press.

Kitschelt, Herbert P. 1986. "Political Opportunity Structures and Political Protest: Anti-Nuclear Movements in Four Democracies." *British Journal of Political Science* 16(1):57–85.

Knapp, Andrew, and Vincent Wright. 2006. *The Government and Politics of France*. London and New York : Routledge.

Kollman, Ken. 1998. *Outside Lobbying: Public Opinion and Interest Group Strategies*. Princeton, NJ: Princeton University Press.

Kvavik, Robert B. 1976. *Interest Groups in Norwegian Politics*. Oslo, Norway: Universitetsforlaget Oslo.

Lederer, Andreas, Niombo Lomba, and Christian Scheucher. 2005. "Emerging Markets: Public Affairs in Germany and Austria." Pp. 361–378 in *The Handbook of Public Affairs*, edited by P. Harris and C. S. Fleisher. Thousand Oaks, CA: Sage.

Lerbinger, Otto. 2006. *Corporate Public Affairs: Interacting With Interest Groups, Media, and Government*. Mahwah, NJ: LEA Associates.

Lianos, Manuel, and Stephanie Simon. 2003. "Politikkongress und Politikaward: Ein Blick hinter die Bühnen." *Politik und Kommunikationen*, December.

Lim, Alwyn, and Kiyoteru Tsutsui. 2012. "Globalization and Commitment in Corporate Social Responsibility Cross-National Analyses of Institutional and Political-Economy Effects." *American Sociological Review* 77(1):69–98.

Lord, Michael D. 2000a. "Constituency-Based Lobbying as Corporate Political Strategy: Testing An Agency Theory Perspective." *Business and Politics* 2:289–308.

Lord, Michael D. 2000b. "Corporate Political Strategy and Legislative Decision Making." *Business & Society* 39:76–93.

Lord, Michael D. 2003. "Constituency Building as the Foundation for Corporate Political Strategy." *Academy of Management Executive* 17:112–124.

Lory, S. (2002). "Les entreprises font-elles la loi à Bruxelles?" *Alternatives Economiques*, June 1.

Mahoney, Christine. 2008. *Brussels Versus the Beltway: Advocacy in the United States and the European Union*. Washington, DC: Georgetown University Press.

Manheim, Jarol B. 2001. *The Death of a Thousand Cuts*. Mahwah, NJ: Lawrence Erlbaum.

Mann, Michael. 1993. "Nation-States in Europe and Other Continents: Diversifying, Developing, Not Dying." *Daedalus* 122(3):115–140.

Marcus, Alfred A., and Mark S. Irion. 1987. "The Continued Growth of the Corporate Public Affairs Function." *Academy of Management Executive* 1:247–250.

Martin, Andrew W. 2008. "The Institutional Logic of Union Organizing and the Effectiveness of Social Movement Repertoires." *American Journal of Sociology* 113(4):1067–1103.

Martin, Isaac W., and Nadav Gabay. 2013. "Fiscal Protest in Thirteen Welfare States." *Socio-Economic Review* 11 (1): 107–130.

McLeay, Stuart, Dieter Ordelheide, and Steven Young. 2000. "Constituent Lobbying and Its Impact on the Development of Financial Reporting Regulations: Evidence from Germany." *Accounting, Organizations and Society* 25(1):79–98.

Meznar, Martin B., and Douglas Nigh. 1995. "Buffer or Bridge? Environmental and Organizational Determinants of Public Affairs Activities in American Firms." *Academy of Management Journal* 38:975–996.

Moss, Danny, Conor McGrath, Jane Tonge, and Phil Harris. 2012. "Exploring the Management of the Corporate Public Affairs Function in a Dynamic Global Environment." *Journal of Public Affairs* 12(1):47–60.

Osborne, Peter, and Robbie Huston. 2009. "Taking the Time To Listen, Learn and Act – an Example of Complex International Dialogue." *Journal of Public Affairs* 9(3): 201–209.

Phillips-Fein, Kim. 2009. *Invisible Hands*. New York: W.W. Norton.

Porter, Michael E., and Mark R. Kramer. 2002. "The Competitive Advantage of Corporate Philanthropy." *Harvard Business Review* 80(12):56–68.

Potoski, Matthew, and Aseem Prakash. 2005. "Green Clubs and Voluntary Governance: ISO 14001 and Firms' Regulatory Compliance." *American Journal of Political Science* 49(2):235–248.

Pring, George, and Penelope Canan. 1996. *SLAPPs: Getting Sued for Speaking Out*. Temple University Press.

Pritchard, Betty J., Catherine B. Ahles, and Nathalie Bardin. 2005. "Public Relations Practice in France Compared to The United States." Unpublished manuscript, Institute for Public Relations.

Public Affairs Council. 1998. "Public Affairs: Its Origin, Its Present, and Its Trends." Retrieved July 22, 2010, from http://web.archive.org/web/19980111071443/pac.org/whatis/index.htm.

Public Affairs Council. 2008. *Grassroots Benchmarking Report.* Washington, DC: Public Affairs Council.

Public Affairs Council. 2010. "Frequently Asked Questions." Retrieved from http://pac.org/faq.

Public Affairs Council. 2012. "Membership Directory." Retrieved from http://pac.org/content/membership-directory-industry.

Quadagno, Jill. 2004. "Why the United States Has No National Health Insurance: Stakeholder Mobilization against the Welfare State, 1945–1996." *Journal of Health and Social Behavior* 45:25–44.

Rao, Hayagreeva. 2008. *Market Rebels: How Activists Make or Break Radical Innovations.* Princeton, NJ: Princeton University Press.

Reid, Erin M., and Michael W. Toffel. 2009. "Responding to Public and Private Politics: Corporate Disclosure of Climate Change Strategies." *Strategic Management Journal* 30(11):1157–1178.

Rensburg, Ronél. 2011. "Aspects of Public Relations, Communication Management and Sustainable Development: African Reflections." *Journal of Public Affairs* 11(4):189–194.

Rommetvedt, Hilmar. 2005. "Norway: Resources Count, but Votes Decide? From Neo-Corporatist Representation to Neo-Pluralist Parliamentarism." *West European Politics* 28(4):740–763.

Rothman, Sheila M., Victoria H. Raveis, Anne Friedman, and David J. Rothman. 2011. "Health Advocacy Organizations and the Pharmaceutical Industry: An Analysis of Disclosure Practices." *American Journal of Public Health* 101(4):602–609.

Rowell, Andrew. 1996. *Green Backlash: Global Subversion of the Environmental Movement.* London & New York: Routledge.

Safran, William. 2003. *The French Polity.* New York: Longman.

Salamon, Lester M. 1994. "The Rise of the Nonprofit Sector." *Foreign Affairs* 73:109–122.

Schattschneider, E. E. 1960. *The Semisovereign People.* New York: Holt & Winston.

Schmidt, Vivien Ann. 1996. *From State to Market? The Transformation of French Business and Government.* New York: Cambridge University Press.

Schofer, Evan, and Marion Fourcade-Gourinchas. 2001. "The Structural Contexts of Civic Engagement: Voluntary Association Membership in Comparative Perspective." *American Sociological Review* 66(6):806–828.

Schofer, Evan, and Wesley Longhofer. 2011. "The Structural Sources of Association." *American Journal of Sociology* 117(2):539–585.

Schönborn, Gregor, ed. 2002. *Public Affairs Agenda*. Berlin: Luchterhand Verlag.

Sebaldt, Martin. 1997. *Organisierter Pluralismus in Deutschland*. Opladen: Westdeutscher Verlag.

Seidman, Gay. 2007. *Beyond the Boycott*. New York: Sage.

Shaffer, William R. 1998. *Politics, Parties, and Parliaments: Political Change in Norway*. Columbus: Ohio State University Press.

Siaroff, Alan. 1999. "Corporatism in 24 Industrial Democracies: Meaning and Measurement." *European Journal of Political Research* 36(2):175–205.

Sine, Wesley D., and Brandon H. Lee. 2009. "Tilting at Windmills? The Environmental Movement and the Emergence of the U.S. Wind Energy Sector." *Administrative Science Quarterly* 54(1):123–155.

Sirianni, Carmen, and Lewis Friedland. 2001. *Civic Innovation in America: Community Empowerment*, Public Policy, and the Movement for Civic Renewal. Berkeley: University of California Press.

Smith, Jackie, and Hank Johnston. 2002. Globalization and Resistance: Transnational Dimensions of Social Movements. Lanham, MD: Rowman & Littlefield.

Smith, Mark Alan. 2000. *American Business and Political Power: Public Opinion, Elections, and Democracy*. Chicago: University of Chicago Press.

Soule, Sarah A. 2009. *Contention and Corporate Social Responsibility*. New York: Cambridge University Press.

Streeck, Wolfgang. 1983. "Between Pluralism and Corporatism German Business Associations and the State." *Journal of Public Policy* 3(03):265–283.

Tarrow, Sidney. 2005. *The New Transnational Activism*. Cambridge and New York: Cambridge University Press.

Thomas, Clive S., and Ronald J. Hrebenar. 2008. "Understanding Interest Groups, Lobbying and Lobbyists in Developing Democracies." *Journal of Public Affairs* 8(1–2):1–14.

Thompson, Tracy A., and Gerald F. Davis. 2002. "The Politics of Corporate Control and the Future of Shareholder Activism in the United States." *Corporate Governance* 5(3):152–159.

Tilly, Charles. 1989. *The Contentious French*. Cambridge, MA: Harvard University Press.

Tilly, Charles. 1992. *Coercion, Capital, and European States, AD 990–1992*. New York: Blackwell.

Touraine, Alaine. 1980. *La Prophétie Anti-Nucléaire*. Paris: Seuil.

Traugott, Mark. 1993. "Barricades as Repertoire: Continuities and Discontinuities in the History of French Contention." *Social Science History* 17(2):309–323.

Useem, Bert, and Mayer N. Zald. 1982. "From Pressure Group to Social Movement: Organizational Dilemmas of the Effort to Promote Nuclear Power." *Social Problems*. 30:144–156.

Vogel, David. 1989. *Fluctuating Fortunes: The Political Power of Business in America*. New York: Basic Books.

Vogel, David. 2005. *The Market for Virtue*. Washington, DC: Brookings Institution Press.

Vogel, David. 2008. "Private Global Business Regulation." *Annual Review of Political Science* 11(1):261–282.

Vogel, David. 2010. "The Private Regulation of Global Corporate Conduct: Achievements and Limitations." *Business & Society* 49(1):68–87.

Walker, Edward T. 2009. "Privatizing Participation: Civic Change and the Organizational Dynamics of Grassroots Lobbying Firms." *American Sociological Review* 74(1):83–105.

Walker, Edward T. 2010. "Industry-Driven Activism." *Contexts* 9(2):44–49.

Walker, Edward T. 2012. "Putting a Face on the Issue: Corporate Stakeholder Mobilization in Professional Grassroots Lobbying Campaigns." *Business & Society* 51(4):561–601.

Walker, Edward T. 2014. *Grassroots for Hire: Public Affairs Consultants in American Democracy*. Cambridge and New York: Cambridge University Press.

Walker, Edward T., and Christopher M. Rea. 2014. "The Political Mobilization of Firms and Industries." *Annual Review of Sociology* 40:281–304.

Wasserman, Andreas. 2002. "*Bisschen viel wind.*" Der Spiegel, July 29. Retrieved from http://www.spiegel.de/spiegel/print/d-23685470.html.

Werner, Timothy. 2012. *Public Forces and Private Politics in American Big Business*. New York: Cambridge University Press.

Wilson, Frank Lee. 1987. *Interest-Group Politics in France.* New York: Cambridge University Press.

Wittenberg, Ernest, and Elisabeth Wittenberg. 1989. *How to Win in Washington: Very Practical Advice about Lobbying, the Grassroots, and the Media.* Cambridge, MA: B. Blackwell.

PART IV

The impact of global corporate social responsibility pressures on corporate social responsibility outcomes

11 Is greenness in the eye of the beholder? Corporate social responsibility frameworks and the environmental performance of US firms

ION BOGDAN VASI

Introduction

Reporting corporate social responsibility (CSR) initiatives has become standard practice among large corporations in recent times. Worldwide, the number of top 250 companies that issued CSR reports has increased from 45 percent in 2002 to nearly 80 percent in 2008. In the United States, the number of top-100 companies that publish a sustainability report increased from 36 in 2002 to 78 in 2008.[1] Many of the sustainability reports conform to the guidelines created by nonprofit organizations such as the United Nations Global Compact (UNGC), the Global Reporting Initiative (GRI), or the World Business Council on Sustainable Development (WBCSD). Indeed, the number of US companies that publish sustainability reports that conform to the GRI's guidelines increased from 24 in 2003 to 183 in 2010.[2]

Academic studies on CSR have also proliferated during the last two decades (Hart and Ahuja 1996; Russo and Fouts 1997; Dowell, Hart,

---

[1] See KPMG International Survey of Corporate Sustainability Reporting 2002, accessed online March 2012 at http://www.gppi.net/fileadmin/gppi/KPMG2002.pdf
  See also KPMG International Survey of Corporate Sustainability Reporting 2008, accessed online March 2012 at
    http://www.kpmg.com/global/en/issuesandinsights/articlespublications/pages/sustainability-corporate-responsibility-reporting-2008.aspx
[2] See the GRI's website, accessed online March 2012 at https://www.globalreporting.org/network/regional-networks/gri-focal-points/focal-point-usa/Pages/default.aspx

and Yeung 1999; Andersson and Bateman 2000; Bansal and Roth 2000; Konar and Cohen 2001; Jiang and Bansal 2003; Kanter 2003; Porter and Kramer 2003; Toffel 2005; Potosky and Prakash 2005; Vogel 2006; Bullis and Ie 2007; Cetindamar and Husoy 2007; Etzion 2007; Delmas and Montiel 2008; Janney, Dess, and Forlani 2009; Runhaar and Lafferty 2009; Chen and Delmas 2011; Delmas and Montes-Sancho 2011). Many of these studies focus on firms' environmental performance (EP) because, as Vogel (2006: 133) points out, "no dimension of corporate social responsibility has attracted as much attention from the business community as environmental protection. Since the mid-1990s, hundreds of corporations, both large and small, have initiated or expanded programs and policies to reduce their environmental impact and made 'sustainability' part of their professed business mission." Numerous studies examine the relationship between environmental and financial corporate performance and argue that doing the right thing for the environment provides a competitive advantage (Hart and Ahuja 1996; Russo and Fouts 1997; Dowell, Hart, and Yeung 1999; Konar and Cohen 2001; Porter and Kramer 2003; Margolis and Walsh 2003). Some studies also show that companies may become greener in response to existing legislation or in anticipation of future legislation (Lawrence and Morell 1995; Delmas and Montes-Sancho 2011), because of company values (Wood 1991; Lawrence and Morell 1995; Buchholz 1998), or due to the pressure from stakeholders such as environmental nonprofits (Berry and Rondinelli 1998; Vasi 2011; Vasi and King 2012).

Despite this growing body of literature on CSR, only a handful of studies have examined the relationship between CSR frameworks and EP (King and Lenox 2000; Potoski and Prakash 2005). Although CSR frameworks vary depending on whether they sanction noncompliance and require public disclosure and third-party audits, current research does not examine the EP of firms that adopt CSR frameworks requiring self-certification (first-party audits) and public disclosure. This is a significant knowledge gap because many firms participate in programs that require public disclosure and self-certification, such as the aforementioned UNGC, GRI, or WBCSD. Moreover, existing research does not analyze both the actual and perceived EP of companies that adopt various CSR frameworks. Although it is assumed that a major reason why companies adopt programs such as ISO 14001 is to improve their image and "send a credible signal of superior management practices" (Toffel 2005: 1), no studies have examined whether this signal is actually received by stakeholders.

This research advances the literature on CSR in three ways. First, it examines whether US firms' adoption of CSR frameworks that require only first-party audits and public disclosure is associated with superior actual EP. Second, it analyzes whether the adoption of those frameworks is associated with perceived superior EP. Third, it examines whether the adoption of multiple CSR frameworks has a cumulative effect on both actual and perceived EP of US firms. The study examines both international programs that aim to address a variety of sustainability issues (e.g., the UNGC, GRI, WBCSD) and US-specific programs that focus only on the global climate change problem, such as the Pew Center's Business Environmental Leadership Council (BELC) and the Environmental Protection Agency's Climate Leaders (CL). Results from a quantitative analysis based on an original dataset of Fortune 500 corporations show that the adoption of only two CSR frameworks is associated with both actual and perceived high-level EP. The analysis also shows that the adoption of multiple CSR frameworks has a cumulative effect, but this effect exists only for perceived EP. The discussion highlights the study's contribution to the literature on CSR and environmental risk management.

Corporate social responsibility: theory and hypotheses

The concept of CSR dates back to the 1950s but became important in the business strategies of companies only during the 1990s (Caroll 1999; van Marrewijk 2003; also see Chapter 1 of this volume). Although there are no universally accepted definitions of CSR, most authors agree that CSR includes those actions of companies that address social and environmental concerns beyond what is required by law (Runhaar and Lafferty 2009). Most academic studies of CSR focus on the relationship between firms' social and financial performance, seeking to provide evidence for the argument that CSR initiatives offer a competitive advantage to adopters (Kanter 2003; Porter and Kramer 2003). A review of studies published between 1972 and 2002 finds that corporate social performance predicts financial performance in 54 out of 109 studies, whereas only twenty-eight studies report that the association between the two variables is not significant, and seven studies report that the association is significant but negative.

The review also finds that some studies have attempted to determine which factors shape companies' decision to adopt practices that address social problems: of twenty-two such studies, sixteen report that financial performance contributed to the adoption of CSR practices (Margolis and Walsh 2003: 274).

Corporate EP is frequently used as a proxy measure for corporate social performance not only because the natural environment is an important issue for management but also because quantitative measurements of pollution – for example, the toxic release inventory – are readily available. Consequently, numerous studies examine the relationship between financial performance and various dimensions of EP, and many find positive and significant associations (Hart and Ahuja 1996; Russo and Fouts 1997; Dowell, Hart, and Yeung 1999; Konar and Cohen 2001; Toffel 2005; Potoski and Prakash 2005). Some authors, however, question the causality between environmental expenditures and firm profitability, arguing that "various omitted variables affecting both environmental and financial performance are responsible for the apparent statistical relationship" (Vogel 2006: 30).

Studies also analyze how different company attributes contribute to their EP. For example, some studies focus on cultural or nonmaterial factors such as workforce values and attitudes, organizational culture, or reputation (Wood 1991; Lawrence and Morell 1995; Russo and Fouts 1997; Buchholz 1998; Bansal 2003; 2005). Others focus on material factors such as research and development (R&D) activities or organizational size (Florida 1996; Bowen 2000; Christman 2000; King and Lenox 2002; Jiang and Bansal 2003).

Furthermore, current research recognizes that companies' decisions to become greener are shaped by their organizational environment. Some studies suggest that regulators exert a strong influence on firms' environmental approach because regulation can create economic frameworks for redistributing environmental costs and benefits, specify environmental targets that must be achieved, or improve information flow by mandating disclosure of pollution (Lawrence and Morell 1995; Konar and Cohen 1997; Hoffman and Ventresca 2002; Delmas and Montiel 2008; Delmas and Montes-Sancho 2011). Other studies suggest that, at least in the US context, regulatory pressures have little or no influence on companies' EP (Kassinis and Vafeas 2002). Still others argue that stakeholders such as activists are very important in the environmental arena because they can influence companies' actions by developing either conflicting or collaborating relationships (Lawrence and Morell 1995; Turcotte 1995; Berry and Rondinelli 1998; Doh and Guay 2006; Hendry 2006; Vasi 2011; Vasi and King 2012).

Notwithstanding the burgeoning literature on CSR, relatively little is known about how specific CSR frameworks affect firms' EP. Research has shown that firms that adopt certain CSR frameworks – those that require both third-party audits and public disclosure, such as the 33/50 program, and those that require only third-party audits, such as the ISO 14001 program – are likely to have better EP than are firms that do not adopt these frameworks (Khanna and Damon 1999; Potoski and Prakash 2005; Toffel 2005). Firms that adopt programs without third-party audits and public disclosure, such as the Responsible Care program, are not more likely to have better EP than are other firms (King and Lenox 2000; Lenox and Nash 2003). Yet no research has examined the EP of firms that adopt CSR frameworks requiring first-party audits (self-certification) and public disclosure, such as the UNGC or GRI.[3] Additionally, although it is assumed that most companies adopt CSR frameworks to improve their image and send a signal to their stakeholders, it is not known whether firms that adopt CSR frameworks are actually perceived to be greener.

This study examines the effect of adopting CSR frameworks that require only first-party audits and public disclosure on firms' actual and perceived EP. Two types of CSR frameworks are examined: *wide* frameworks (UNGC, GRI, WBCSD) that are global in scope and attempt to improve firms' social and environmental performance and *narrow* frameworks (BELC and CL) that are specific to the United States and address only global climate change.

Founded in 2000, the UNGC is "a strategic policy initiative for businesses that are committed to aligning their operations and strategies with ten universally accepted principles in the areas of human rights, labour, environment and anti-corruption." Its main objectives are to "mainstream the ten principles in business activities around the world and catalyze actions in support of broader UN goals, including

---

[3] Research on the UNGC framework, for example, has examined either how markets respond to firms' decision to join UNGC (Janney, Des, and Forlani 2009) or the factors that contribute to firms' decision to join UNGC (Cetindamar and Husoy 2007; Runhaar and Lafferty 2009).

the Millennium Development Goals."[4] GRI was founded in 1997 by the Coalition for Environmentally Responsible Economies (CERES) in partnership with the UN Environment Program (UNEP); it defines itself as "a network-based organization that has pioneered the development of the world's most widely used sustainability reporting framework and is committed to its continuous improvement and application worldwide."[5] The WBCSD was founded on the eve of the 1992 Rio Earth Summit "to involve business in sustainability issues and give it a voice in the forum. [It] provides a platform for companies to explore sustainable development, share knowledge, experiences and best practices, and to advocate business positions on these issues in a variety of forums, working with governments, non-governmental and intergovernmental organizations."[6] BELC was created in 1998 "with the belief that business engagement is critical for developing efficient, effective solutions to the climate problem. ... [It] is now the largest U.S.-based association of corporations focused on addressing the challenges of climate change and supporting mandatory climate policy."[7] Finally, CL is "an EPA industry-government partnership that works with companies to develop comprehensive climate change strategies. Partner companies commit to reducing their impact on the global environment by completing a corporate-wide inventory of their greenhouse gas emissions based on a quality management system, setting aggressive reduction goals, and annually reporting their progress to EPA."[8]

The study addresses a number of questions. First, is the adoption of CSR frameworks that require only first-party audits and public disclosure associated with superior *actual* EP? Some studies have found that firms that adopt CSR frameworks without requirements for third-party audits, such as Responsible Care, are more likely to have an inferior EP (King and Lenox 2002; Lenox and Nash 2003). Other

---

[4] See the UNGC's website, accessed online July 2010 at http://www.unglobalcompact.org/AboutTheGC/index.html

[5] See the GRI's website, accessed online July 2010 at http://www.globalreporting.org/AboutGRI/WhatIsGRI/

[6] See the WBCSD's website, accessed online July 2010 at
http://www.wbcsd.org/templates/TemplateWBCSD2/layout.asp?type=p&MenuId=NDEx&doOpen=1&ClickMenu=LeftMenu

[7] See the BELC's website, accessed online July 2010 at http://www.pewclimate.org/business/belc

[8] See the EPA Climate Leaders' website, accessed online July 2010 at http://www.epa.gov/climateleaders/

studies have found that the adoption of CSR frameworks that require third-party audits and public disclosure, such as Sustainable Forestry or ISO 14001, is associated with superior EP (Lenox and Nash 2003; Potoski and Prakash 2005; Toffel 2005). CSR frameworks that require public disclosure may attract firms with above-average EP that seek recognition for their investments in environmental protection. Moreover, firms' actual EP could improve after they adopt a CSR framework due to normative pressures – in other words, because adopters are likely to feel pressured to keep up with other "green club" members. Therefore, the first two hypotheses state:

Hypothesis 1 (H1): Firms that adopt a CSR program that require only first-party audits and public disclosure will demonstrate high actual EP.

Hypothesis 2 (H2): Firms that adopt a CSR program that require only first-party audits and public disclosure will improve their actual EP.

The second question addressed is: are firms that adopt CSR frameworks that require first-party audits and public disclosure perceived to have better EP than nonadopting firms? Because CSR frameworks such as UNGC, GRI, WBCSD, BELC, and CL require public disclosure, adopting firms will be perceived by relevant stakeholders to be proactive in environmental protection and, consequently, greener than nonadopting firms. Indeed, some of the most important reasons for reporting CSR initiatives are to improve their brands and reputation and to manage and reduce risks. For example, 55 percent of the largest 250 global companies have identified improving brand and reputation as the main driver for reporting CSR practices, whereas 35 percent of those companies have identified risk management and reduction as the main driver.[9] Therefore, the third hypothesis states:

Hypothesis 3 (H3): Firms that adopt a CSR program that require only first-party audits and public disclosure will be perceived as having better EP than will nonadopters.

Finally, the last question addressed is: do firms that adopt multiple CSR frameworks have better actual as well as perceived EP than those that adopt only one framework? If a CSR framework that requires

---

[9] See KPMG International Survey of Corporate Sustainability Reporting 2008, accessed online March 2012 at
http://www.kpmg.com/global/en/issuesandinsights/articlespublications/pages/sustainability-corporate-responsibility-reporting-2008.aspx

public disclosure attracts firms with above-average EP, and if the adoption of such a framework results in the greening of the corporate image, then the adoption of multiple frameworks should have a cumulative effect on both actual and perceived EP. In other words, it is likely that firms that adopt multiple CSR frameworks that require public disclosure are more likely to have above-average EP and to be perceived as greener than nonadopter firms. Hence, the fourth and fifth hypotheses:

Hypothesis 4 (H4): The more CSR programs a firm adopts, the better its actual EP.

Hypothesis 5 (H5): The more CSR programs a firm adopts, the better its perceived EP.

Methods and data

Dependent variables

These hypotheses are tested using regression analyses. The dataset is composed of all US companies listed in Fortune 500 in 2007 – the most recent year for which dependent variables were available. The dependent variables are actual and perceived EP. The actual EP is measured using the toxic score data from the Political Economy Research Institute (PERI). The toxic score range is calculated as "the population health risk from air releases and incineration transfers reported to the US Environmental Protection Agency's Toxics Release Inventory (TRI) for the 2007 Reporting Year, as computed by the US EPA's Risk-Screening Environmental Indicators from quantity released, toxicity of chemicals, and population exposure." According to PERI, "The Toxics Release Inventory (TRI), compiled by the U.S. Environmental Protection Agency (EPA) in accordance with the Emergency Planning and Community Right-to-Know Act of 1986, annually reports the weight (in pounds) of each of approximately 600 toxic chemicals released into the environment by major industrial facilities in the United States. The EPA Office of Pollution Prevention and Toxics processes the raw TRI reports to create the Risk Screening Environmental Indicators. The EPA combines three variables to assess the human health risks posed by toxic releases: fate and transport, or how the chemical spreads from the point of release to the surrounding area; toxicity, or how dangerous the chemical is on a per-pound basis; and population, or how many people live in the affected areas."[10] The variable has the minimum 0 – no significant population health risk – and the maximum 189,649 – the highest population health risk. This variable is transformed with the natural logarithm to reduce skewness.

To calculate improvement in actual EP, the toxic score for 2002 was used in addition to the score for 2005. Although PERI has also calculated toxic scores for 2006 and 2007, only 2002 and 2005 can be compared because they use the same methodology for plume modeling and toxicity weights.

Perceived EP is measured using data from the iRatings (former Innovest) database, which ranks companies according to their eco-value score in 2007 – the most recent year for which data were available. The eco-value score has a minimum of 23 – the least green – and a maximum of 1,781 – the greenest. This score is based on a number of dimensions: board and executive oversight, risk management systems, disclosure/verification, process efficiencies, health and safety, new product development, and environmental risk assessment.[11]

Independent variables

Membership in CSR frameworks is measured using information from the UNGC, GRI, WBCSD, the Pew Center's BELC, and EPA's CL programs. These variables are coded as dummies, with the value 1 if the company became a member of one of those CSR frameworks prior to 2007 and 0 otherwise. A sum of CSR framework variables is also created: the cumulative membership variable is coded as an ordinal variable, with the minimum of 0 if the company is not a member of any CSR frameworks and 5 if the company is a member of all CSR frameworks.

Three alternative measures were also used: the number of years since a firm has been a member of the UNGC, the number of years since a firm has been a member of the GRI, and the number of years since a

---

[10] For more information on the toxic score, see PERI's website, accessed online June 2012 at http://www.peri.umass.edu/tech_notes/

[11] For more information on the iRatings/Innovest methodology, see the RiskMetrics website accessed online June 2009 at http://www.iratings.innovestgroup.com/index.php?option=com_content&task=view&id=4247&Itemid=86

firm has been a member of the WBCSD. These measures were transformed with the natural logarithm to reduce skewness. The exact number of years since a firm joined BELC and the EPA's CL could not be obtained.

Controls

The control variables include company size, R&D activities, reputation, governance type, and industry sector. Company size is measured as the natural logarithm of firm's assets; this variable is coded using information from the Compustat database; the year 2000 is used as a baseline. R&D activities were measured using information from KLD Research and Analytics – the year 2000 is used as a baseline (KLD Research and Analytics 2007). The variable is coded as a dummy variable, with the value 1 if the company is considered a leader in its industry for research and development and 0 otherwise. Reputation is measured as an ordinal variable using information from *Fortune Magazine*'s list of the most admired companies from 2000. The variable has the value 2 if the company was in the top 100 list, the value 1 if the company was ranked between 101 and 200, and 0 if the company was not among the top 200 most admired companies. Corporate governance is measured using the Governance Index data developed by Gompers, Ishii, and Metrick (2003). High values indicate that companies are in the "dictatorship portfolio," which means they have the highest management power or the weakest shareholder rights; low values indicate companies are in the "democracy portfolio," which means they have the lowest management power or the strongest shareholder rights. Finally, dummy variables for industry sectors are also included – for simplicity in presentation, the industry sector dummies are not included in the tables of results.

Estimation

PERI ranks only the worst 100 polluters out of all Fortune 500 companies. Therefore, the data are left-censored at 0 for many companies. To deal with this issue, the analysis of actual environmental pollution uses Tobit regression for left-censored data. The analysis of improvement in actual environmental pollution uses panel Tobit regression for left-censored data. The panel includes 2002 and 2005, for which

Is greenness in the eye of the beholder? 375

Table 11.1 *Means, standard deviations, and sources of variables used in the regression analyses*

Variable name	Mean	Standard deviation	Source
Pollution score (Ln)	6.148	3.269	Political Economy Research Institute (2007)
Green score	874.630	304.585	iRatings (2007)
Assets (Ln)	9.213	1.477	Compustat (2000)
R&D	.030	.171	KLD Research and Analytics (2007)
Reputation	.473	.754	*Fortune* (2000)
Governance	9.616	.132	Gompers, Ishii, and Metrick (2003)
Mining sector	.039	.195	Compustat (2000)
Utilities sector	.062	.242	Compustat (2000)
Finance sector	.175	.380	Compustat (2000)
Construction sector	.015	.122	Compustat (2000)
Trade sector	.088	.284	Compustat (2000)
Transportation sector	.022	.149	Compustat (2000)
Services sector	.031	.172	Compustat (2000)
UNGC	.023	.149	United Nations Global Compact (2000–2006)
GRI	.031	.173	CERES (1997–2006)
WBCSD	.050	.218	World Business Council for Sustainable Development (1995–2006)
BELC	.033	.180	Pew Center on Global Climate Change (1998–2006)
CL	.060	.242	Environmental Protection Agency's Climate Leaders (2002–2006)
Sum of CSR	.200	.600	UNGC, CERES, WBCSD, BELC, CL

comparable toxic scores are available. The iRatings eco-value score for perceived EP is a continuous variable. Therefore, ordinary least squares regression is used for the analysis of perceived EP. Descriptive statistics are presented in Table 11.1.

Results

Table 11.2 presents results of estimates of actual pollution in terms of nine models. The first eight models estimate the effect of membership in each of the CSR initiatives (including alternative measures); the ninth model estimates the cumulative effect of membership in different CSR initiatives on actual environmental pollution. Results show that only membership in the UNGC framework has a significant negative effect on firms' actual environmental pollution; in other words, firms that are members of UNGC are likely to have a better EP. Firms that are members of the UNGC score 6.7 points below firms that are not members of this framework on the toxic score logarithmic scale. The alternative measure for UNGC also has significant effects: an increase of 1 in the logarithmic scale of the variable number of years since the firm joined UNGC is associated with a decrease of approximately 4 points on the toxic score logarithmic scale.

In contrast, results show that membership in the WBCSD has a significant positive effect. In other words, adoption of the WBCSD frameworks is associated with a 4.1 increase in the toxic score logarithmic scale. The alternative measure for WBCSD – the number of years since adoption – also has a significant ($p<.05$) effect. The adoption of BELC and CL does not have a significant effect, and the cumulative effect of all of these frameworks is not significant. Results from this table also show that firms are significantly more likely to pollute if they are large but that governance style, reputation, and R&D activities do not have significant effects.

Results of estimates of improvements in actual EP are presented in Table 11.3. The adoption of the UNGC and GRI frameworks is associated with a decrease in the toxic score, but only the adoption of the GRI framework is associated with a significant ($p<.05$) decrease. However, the adoption of the WBCSD framework is associated with a significant ($p<.001$) increase in the toxic score. The alternative measure of WBCSD – the number of years since adoption – is also associated with a significant ($p<.001$) increase in the toxic score, but the alternative measure of GRI is not associated with a significant decrease in the toxic score. Similarly, the adoption of BELC and CL does not have a significant effect on actual environmental pollution. Thus, results from Tables 11.2 and 11.3 suggest that CSR frameworks can have opposite effects: while the adoption of GRI is associated with decreasing levels

Table 11.2 Corporate social responsibility initiatives and actual environmental pollution: toxic scores, 2007 (Tobit regressions)

	Model 1	Model 2	Model 3	Model 4	Model 5	Model 6	Model 7	Model 8	Model 9
Assets (Ln)	3.088***	3.108***	3.177***	2.503***	2.500***	2.192***	2.696***	2.878***	2.778***
	(.566)	(.567)	(.573)	(.639)	(.578)	(.624)	(.590)	(.577)	(.609)
R&D activities	3.038	2.846	1.820	.425	1.220	.235	1.094	.487	.925
	(2.601)	(2.589)	(2.555)	(2.976)	(2.531)	(2.918)	(2.593)	(2.751)	(2.692)
Reputation	−1.073	−1.074	−1.211*	−1.205	−1.393*	−1.458*	−1.319*	−1.268*	−1.250*
	(.604)	(.604)	(.606)	(.698)	(.607)	(.693)	(.619)	(.621)	(.623)
Governance	.360	.360	.391*	.466*	.385*	.426*	.351	.376	.377
	(.193)	(.193)	(.194)	(.218)	(.192)	(.214)	(.196)	(.196)	(.196)
Sectors	included	included	included	included	included	included	included	included	included
UNGC (1st measure)	−6.765**	—	—	—	—	—	—	—	—
	(2.570)								
UNGC (2nd measure)		−3.991**	—	—	—	—	—	—	—
		(1.542)							
GRI (1st measure)			−3.696	—	—	—	—	—	—
			(1.946)						
GRI (2nd measure)				.715 (.966)	—	—	—	—	—
WBCSD (1st measure)					4.106**	—	—	—	—
					(1.517)				
WBCSD (2nd measure)						2.734*	—	—	—
						(1.098)			

Table 11.2 (*cont.*)

	Model 1	Model 2	Model 3	Model 4	Model 5	Model 6	Model 7	Model 8	Model 9
BELC							3.059	–	–
							(1.702)		
CL								1.801	–
								(1.452)	
Sum of CSR									.634
									(.641)
Constant	-26.307***	-26.517***	-27.430***	-23.626***	-21.500***	-20.202**	-22.810***	-24.874***	-23.967***
	(6.107)	(6.115)	(6.171)	(6.850)	(6.174)	(6.751)	(6.359)	(6.216)	(6.462)
Log likelihood	-569.62	-569.71	-571.42	-557.86	-569.68	-555.09	-571.63	-572.48	-572.76
Nr. of comp.	334	334	334	334	334	334	334	334	334

* $p<0.05$; ** $p<0.01$; *** $p<0.001$

Table 11.3 Corporate social responsibility initiatives and change in actual environmental pollution: toxic scores change, 2002–2005 (Tobit regressions)

	Model 1	Model 2	Model 3	Model 4	Model 5	Model 6	Model 7	Model 8	Model 9
Assets (Ln)	5.300***	5.298***	5.652***	4.832***	3.695**	3.988***	4.850***	4.957***	4.697***
	(1.261)	(1.263)	(1.273)	(1.279)	(1.258)	(1.240)	(1.272)	(1.258)	(1.319)
R&D activities	−12.537	−12.851	−14.171	−14.805*	−16.056*	−18.263*	−14.646*	−15.711*	−15.592*
	(7.613)	(7.560)	(7.357)	(7.269)	(7.857)	(8.777)	(7.282)	(7.556)	(7.499)
Reputation	−1.408	−1.440	−2.005	−1.642	−2.285	−2.530	−1.751	−1.682	−1.749
	(1.377)	(1.377)	(1.381)	(1.378)	(1.367)	(1.396)	(1.398)	(1.388)	(1.397)
Governance	.754 (.444)	.765 (.446)	.801 (.442)	.806 (.446)	.814 (.434)	.692 (.434)	.767 (.447)	.789 (.447)	.792 (.446)
Sectors	included	included	included	included	included	included	included	included	included
UNGC (1st measure)	−13.223 (7.310)	—	—	—	—	—	—	—	—
UNGC (2nd measure)	—	−6.793 (4.211)	—	—	—	—	—	—	—
GRI (1st measure)	—	—	−12.231* (5.242)	—	—	—	—	—	—
GRI (2nd measure)	—	—	—	−1.514 (1.789)	—	—	—	—	—
WBCSD (1st measure)	—	—	—	—	9.781*** (3.054)	—	—	—	—

Table 11.3 (*cont.*)

	Model 1	Model 2	Model 3	Model 4	Model 5	Model 6	Model 7	Model 8	Model 9
WBCSD (2nd measure)						6.109*** (1.924)			
BELC							3.304 (3.634)		
CL								2.508 (3.068)	
Sum of CSR									1.214 (1.366)
Constant	-64.757*** (14.216)	-64.905*** (14.250)	-67.915*** (14.279)	-61.492*** (14.311)	-50.832*** (13.973)	-51.821*** (13.934)	-61.015*** (14.379)	-62.419*** (14.219)	-60.094*** (14.631)
Log likelihood	-565.39	-565.88	-564.32	-567.13	-562.29	-562.26	-567.08	-567.16	-567.10
Nr. of obs.	668	668	668	668	668	668	668	668	668

* $p<0.05$; ** $p<0.01$; *** $p<0.001$

of pollution between 2002 and 2005 and the adoption of UNGC is associated with lower levels of pollution in 2007, the adoption of WBCSD is associated with higher *and* increasing levels of pollution. Overall, participation in multiple CSR frameworks does not improve a firm's EP.

Table 11.4 presents results of estimates of perceived EP – as measured by iRatings' eco-value score – in terms of nine models. The first eight models estimate the effect of membership in each of the initiatives, and the ninth model estimates the cumulative effect of membership in CSR initiatives on perceived performance. Results show that membership in UNGC, GRI, WBCSD, BELC, and CL has significant effects – all of these effects are positive and significant. The alternative measure of membership in UNGC and GRI also has significant effects, but the alternative measure of membership in WBCSD does not. Moreover, results show that the sum of CSR frameworks has a significant ($p<.001$) effect. The adoption of an extra CSR framework corresponds to an increase of more than 136 points on the scale of perceived EP. Put differently, a firm that adopted all five CSR frameworks would score more than 680 points (about 33 percent) more on this scale than a firm that did not adopt any CSR frameworks, even after controlling for actual environmental pollution (as measured by the toxic scores). Perceived greenness is also significantly and positively associated with company size, R&D activities, and reputation, but not with governance style or actual EP.

Taken together, results from Tables 11.2–11.4 support the third and fifth hypotheses. Firms that adopt a CSR program will be perceived as having superior EP, and firms that adopt multiple CSR programs are more likely to be perceived as having superior EP. These results, however, only partially support the first and second hypotheses, and they do not support the fourth hypothesis. Firms that adopt the UNGC framework are more likely than other firms to demonstrate high actual EP, and firms that adopt the GRI framework are more likely to improve their performance over time. Yet firms that adopt WBCSD frameworks are less likely than other firms to demonstrate high actual EP, and adoption of more CSR frameworks does not lead to better EP. Possible interpretations for these findings are offered in the discussion section.

Table 11.4 *Corporate social responsibility initiatives and perceived EP: iRatings eco-value scores, 2007 (OLS regressions)*

	Model 1	Model 2	Model 3	Model 4	Model 5	Model 6	Model 7	Model 8	Model 9
Assets (Ln)	55.690***	54.993***	45.027**	41.403*	47.048**	56.179**	45.954**	52.676***	32.520*
	(16.353)	(16.287)	(16.336)	(16.785)	(16.511)	(17.690)	(16.455)	(16.350)	(16.096)
R&D activities	315.010***	316.794***	362.688***	363.191***	342.956***	388.407***	320.812***	280.346**	221.318*
	(96.071)	(94.938)	(92.452)	(101.222)	(93.546)	(106.905)	(93.740)	(97.796)	(92.623)
Reputation	65.260***	65.021***	71.802***	59.538**	59.093**	68.230**	56.489**	59.202**	46.778*
	(20.321)	(20.224)	(19.952)	(20.368)	(20.327)	(21.782)	(20.322)	(20.440)	(19.663)
Governance	7.983	8.274	6.666	9.358	8.300	7.811	6.109	7.400	7.998
	(6.541)	(6.515)	(6.423)	(6.470)	(6.493)	(6.828)	(6.465)	(6.506)	(6.233)
Pollution score	4.785	4.869	5.485	-.894	-.666	1.914	.534	.820	-.829
	(4.941)	(4.911)	(4.850)	(4.968)	(5.001)	(5.334)	(4.902)	(4.947)	(4.721)
Sectors	included	included	included	included	included	included	included	included	included
UNGC (1st measure)	212.017*	–	–	–	–	–	–	–	–
	(84.767)								
UNGC (2nd measure)	–	156.050**	–	–	–	–	–	–	–
		(51.752)							
GRI (1st measure)	–	–	269.800***	–	–	–	–	–	–
			(64.572)						
GRI (2nd measure)	–	–	–	186.729***	–	–	–	–	–
				(31.768)					
WBCSD (1st measure)	–	–	–	–	197.154***	–	–	–	–
					(59.031)				

WBCSD (2nd measure)					24.181 (41.704)		
BELC						246.004*** (66.833)	—	—
CL							159.747** (53.591)	—
Sum of CSR								136.214*** (21.970)
Constant	277.760 (177.062)	279.648 (176.282)	378.927* (175.514)	383.908* (178.087)	373.441* (177.699)	289.141 (189.346)	410.219* (178.356)	324.630 (176.824)	491.585** (172.152)
Adjusted R-sq. Nr. of comp.	0.201 334	.208 334	0.228 334	0.257 334	0.213 334	0.207 334	0.219 334	0.208 334	0.273 334

* $p<0.05$; ** $p<0.01$; *** $p<0.001$

Conclusion

The environmental movement has had a significant impact on Americans' attitudes and opinions. Between 2000 and 2010, more than 61 percent of Americans have been involved in or sympathetic toward the environmental movement, and more than 70 percent have bought products specifically because they were better for the environment than were competing products.[12] The movement has also succeeded in creating the perception that corporations need to do more to protect the environment: a 2005 survey found, for example, that 71 percent of respondents believed that large corporations were doing less than their share to help reduce environmental problems.[13] Moreover, the environmental movement has frequently pressured corporations through both primary and secondary stakeholder activism, particularly during the last decade (Vasi and King 2012).

Corporations have responded in a number of ways. Some have adopted green practices (Lenox and Eesley 2009), and many have stepped up their green marketing. For example, green marketing has increased from approximately $9 billion in 1995 to approximately $30 billion in 2000 (Ongkrutraksa 2007). A growing number of companies have also reported CSR initiatives that conform to the guidelines created by various nonprofits: the UNGC, GRI, or WBCSD. Indeed, as pointed out in the introduction to this chapter, the number of companies that publish sustainability reports has increased significantly during the past decade.

This study has sought to contribute to the debate over CSR by examining whether the adoption of CSR frameworks that require only first-party audits and public disclosure is associated with superior actual and perceived EP. The main finding is that, although the adoption of these frameworks is not usually associated with lower actual pollution, it is often associated with higher perceived EP. Two cases stand out. First, the adoption of GRI and UNGC is associated with a superior EP, both actual and perceived. Because the adoption of the GRI framework is associated with lower pollution, this framework has

---

[12] See "At 40, Environmental Movement Endures, with Less Consensus," by Riley E. Dunlap. Accessed May 2012 at http://www.gallup.com/poll/127487/environmental-movement-endures-less-consensus.aspx

[13] See The Harris Poll, August 9–16, 2005; accessed July 2011 at http://www.pollingreport.com/enviro2.htm

an effect similar to that of programs that require third-party audits, such as ISO 14001 and 33/50 (Khanna and Damon 1999; Potoski and Prakash 2005; Toffel 2005). Second, the adoption of WBCSD is associated with lower actual EP. Thus, the WBCSD framework's effect is similar to that of Responsible Care: it seems to attract a disproportionately large number of firms with inferior EP (King and Lenox 2000).

Why is the adoption of the GRI framework associated with improving actual EP? One explanation may be related to the unique nature of the organization that promotes this framework: CERES. This organization has three advantages over other organizations that launched CSR frameworks. First, it is older – it was founded in 1989 – and it includes a broad coalition of companies, investor groups, and environmental and public interest groups. For example, the list of environmental and public groups that are CERES members includes many large, well-known environmental organizations – Environmental Defense, Friends of the Earth, The World Wildlife Fund, Natural Resources Defense Council, Union of Concerned Scientists, and Sierra Club – as well as major human rights and labor associations such as Oxfam and AFL-CIO. Being older and larger than any other organization that promotes CSR programs, CERES has the resources to "advance its vision by bringing investors, environmental groups and other stakeholders together to encourage companies and capital markets to incorporate environmental and social challenges into their day-to-day decision-making."[14]

Second, CERES's practice of carefully selecting companies that can join it is likely to attract mainly companies that have above-average EP and commitment to further improve their performance. Indeed, companies interested in joining CERES are expected to do much more than pay an annual fee, which ranges from $2,000 to $40,000. They are required to develop a plan on priorities for sustainability disclosure and action with help from CERES. They are also required to present the plan to CERES's board of directors for a review of the company's executive-level commitment to sustainability. If the company is accepted as a member, it is expected to engage in an ongoing basis with stakeholders and to respond to input from them. Because of these conditions, only companies that are already committed to

---

[14] See CERES's website, accessed online July 2010 at http://www.ceres.org/Page.aspx?pid=415

sustainability and are taking significant steps to reduce their pollution are likely to be accepted as CERES members.

Third, CERES's practices are likely to result in an improvement in the actual EP of companies after they become members of this organization. Although CERES does not provide a third-party audit of sustainability reports, it provides a number of important services to companies that adopted the GRI framework. For example, CERES offers "stakeholder team support on reporting including report development advice and report review by CERES staff and coalition members." It also offers "monthly consultation and/or advice as required; incident response advice, including correspondence with coalition members and contacts if required; communications service – company link on CERES website, electronic newsletter, press referrals, advance notice of CERES publications and events; participation at CERES board meetings; and participation at CERES annual conference and other CERES events."[15] Having access to these services, CERES companies are likely not only to be perceived as being greener but also to *become* greener than other companies.

It is also likely that the adoption of UNGC frameworks is associated with higher actual EP because it includes a broad coalition of global and local nongovernmental organizations (NGOs), foundations, and companies – even though the number of environmental NGOs involved in the UNGC is smaller than the number of environmental groups that are members of CERES. In addition, the UNGC includes a number of academic institutions – primarily business schools – because, as UNGC argues, "through research and educational resources, this sector can increase knowledge and understanding of corporate citizenship."

Companies that join the UNGC are also required to develop a plan for continuously improving their performance in implementing the Global Compact principles. The UNGC classifies its members into three categories. First, companies in the Learner group – who submitted a timely communication of progress (COP) report but did not meet all minimum content requirements – are given a twelve-month grace period from the date of submission of their report to submit a new report that meets all minimum requirements. Companies in the Learner group receive special support and assistance from the Global

---

[15] See CERES's website, accessed online July 2010 at http://www.ceres.org/Page.aspx?pid=425

Compact office. Second, companies in the Active group – who fulfilled all minimum COP content requirements – are encouraged to fulfill their commitment to implement all ten UNGC principles and publicly disclose their progress. Third, companies in the Advanced level – those who report on a range of best practices in sustainability governance and management – receive recognition for their leadership.

But, why is the adoption of WBCSD associated with lower actual EP? One interpretation is that the WBCSD attracts companies with lower actual EP that want to project a green image without taking major steps to reduce pollution. Indeed, although the WBCSD contains a partnership of companies, investor groups, and environmental nonprofits, the number of partners is significantly smaller than in the case of CERES. Moreover, unlike in the case of CERES, the WBCSD does not include US environmental organizations (e.g., Environmental Defense, Natural Resources Defense Council, Union of Concerned Scientists, and Sierra Club), which makes it less capable of influencing and monitoring corporations' behavior. Another, although less likely, interpretation is that WBCSD has a different standard for EP. For example, instead of emphasizing reduction of pollution locally, the WBCSD could emphasize reduction of pollution globally, which, in the case of greenhouse gases, may be achieved by investing in carbon offsets in a different country.

Similarly, why is the adoption of the BELC and CL frameworks positively associated only with perceived greenness? One possibility is that these frameworks are competing with the GRI for firms' resources. Companies may consider that it is redundant to adopt multiple sustainability frameworks and may choose the GRI initiative because it is more widely used. Another reason may be that these frameworks seek reductions in greenhouse gases rather than toxic chemicals. Thus, companies may get "green points" for investing in renewable energy rather than for reducing their levels of toxic chemicals. Yet another explanation is that the organizations that promote these frameworks do not have the capacity to attract companies with superior performance and to significantly change companies' environmental practices. The Pew Center on Global Climate Change (PCGCC) or the US EPA are very important organizations that offer significant resources to companies that adopt their sustainability frameworks. For example, the EPA "provides publicly available tools for developing and managing greenhouse gas inventories [and] free technical assistance to each partner as they develop and document their inventory management plan and complete their base year inventory."[16] These resources help adopting companies improve their environmental management record and send signals to stakeholders that they take environmental protection seriously. But, unlike CERES, the PCGCC and the EPA do not include wide coalitions of companies, investor groups, and environmental and public interest groups that constantly challenge companies to do more for environmental protection.

This study contributes not only to the existing debate over CSR but also to the literature on risk management. Theorists of risk society (Giddens 1991; Beck 1992) point out that risk construction is a widespread practice in contemporary societies. Giddens (1991:124), for example, argues that "thinking in terms of risk and risk assessment is a more or less ever-present exercise, of a partly imponderable character." Recent research showed that environmental activism against a firm affects its perceived environmental risk, which subsequently has a negative effect on the firm's financial performance (Vasi and King 2012). This study shows that firms can manage the perception of environmental risks through the adoption of CSR frameworks. It is worth emphasizing that the adoption of most CSR frameworks is strongly associated with the perception of superior EP even after controlling for pollution. (The framework with the weakest effect is the UNGC, but this is most likely due to the fact that UNGC focuses not only on EP but also on human rights, labor, and anticorruption.)

The study has a number of limitations. One is that it cannot show that the adoption of CSR frameworks *causes* an improvement in actual or perceived EP. As more data on companies' actual and perceived EP become available, future studies could use more sophisticated methods to move beyond associations and tease out the causal effects of CSR framework adoption. Another limitation is that it uses only one measure of environmental pollution – the toxic scores. Future studies could use other measures, such as greenhouse gas emission, to examine if reductions of toxic chemicals are perceived as more important than reductions of greenhouse gases or vice versa. Finally, this study cannot identify those factors that trigger the adoption of CSR frameworks. It is not known, for example, if the global forces that lead to the adoption

---

[16] See the EPA's website, accessed online July 2010 at http://www.epa.gov/climateleaders/partners/benefits.html

of environmental state policies (Frank, Hironaka, and Schofer 2000) or the development of environmental associations (Longhofer and Evan Schofer 2010) also lead to CSR reporting. To develop a comprehensive understanding of this issue, it is necessary to conduct further research that examines companies' motivation to join CSR frameworks.

References

Andersson, Lynne M., and Thomas S. Bateman. 2000. "Individual Environmental Initiatives: Championing Natural Environmental Issues in U.S. Business Organizations." *Academy of Management Journal* 43:548–570.

Bansal, Pratima. 2003. "From Issues to Actions: The Importance of Individual Concerns and Organizational Values in Responding to Natural Environment Issues." *Organization Science* 14:510–527.

Bansal, Pratima. 2005. "Evolving Sustainably: A Longitudinal Study of Corporate Sustainable Development." *Strategic Management Journal* 26:197–218.

Bansal, Pratima, and Kendall Roth. 2000. "Why Companies Go Green: A Model of Ecological Responsiveness." *In Academy of Management Journal* 43(4):717–736.

Beck, Ulrich. 1992. *Risk Society: Towards a New Modernity*. New Delhi: Sage.

Berry, Michael, and Dennis Rondinelli. 1998. "Proactive Corporate Environmental Management: A New Industrial Revolution." *Academy of Management Executive* 12(2):1–13.

Bowen, Frances E. 2000. "Environmental Visibility: A Trigger of Green Organizational Response?" *Business Strategy and the Environment* 9:92–107.

Buchholz, Rogene A. 1998. *Principles of Environmental Management: The Greening of Business*. New York: Prentice Hall College Div; 2 Subedition.

Bullis, Connie, and Fumiko Ie. 2007. "Corporate Environmentalism." Pp. 321–336 in *The Debate over Corporate Social Responsibility*, edited by S. May, G. Cheney, and J. Roper. New York: Oxford University Press.

Caroll, Archie B. 1999. "Corporate Social Responsibility, Evolution of a Definitional Construct." *Business and Society* 38(3):268–295.

Cetindamar, Dilek, and Kristoffer Husoy. 2007. "Corporate Social Responsibility Practices and Environmentally Responsible Behavior: The Case of the United Nations Global Compact." *Journal of Business Ethics* 76(2):163–176.

Chen, Chien-Ming, and Magali Delmas. 2011. "Measuring Corporate Social Responsibility: An Efficiency Perspective." *Production and Operations Management* 20(6):789–804.

Christmann, Petra. 2000. "Effects of 'Best Practices' of Environmental Management on Cost Competitiveness: The Role of Complementary Assets." *Academy of Management Journal* 43:663–680.

Delmas, Magali, and Ivan Montiel. 2008. "The Diffusion of Voluntary International Management Standards: Responsible Care, ISO 9000 and ISO 14001 in the Chemical Industry." *Policy Studies Journal* 36(1):65–93.

Delmas, Magali, and Maria Montes-Sancho. 2011. "An Institutional Perspective on the Diffusion of International Accountability Standards: The Case of the Environmental Management Standard ISO 14001." *Business Ethics Quarterly* 21(1):1052–1081.

Doh, Jonathan, and Terrence R. Guay. 2006. "Corporate Social Responsibility, Public Policy, and NGO Activism in Europe and the United States: An Institutional-Stakeholder Perspective." *Journal of Management Studies* 43:47–73.

Dowell, Glen, Stuart Hart, and Bernard Yeoung. 1999. "Do Corporate Global Environmental Standards Create or Destroy Market Value?" *Management Science* 46(8):1059–1074.

Etzion, Dror. 2007. "Research on Organizations and the Natural Environment, 1992-Present: A Review." *Journal of Management* 33:637–664.

Florida, Richard. 1996. "Lean and Green: The Move to Environmentally Conscious Manufacturing." *California Management Review* 39:80–105.

Frank, David J., Ann Hironaka, and Evan Schofer. 2000. "The Nation-State and the Natural Environment over the Twentieth Century." *American Sociological Review* 65:96–116.

Giddens, Anthony. 1991. *Modernity and Self-Identity: Self and Society in the Late Modern Age*. Cambridge, UK: Polity.

Gompers, Paul, Joy Ishii, and Andrew Metrick. 2003. "Corporate Governance and Equity Prices." *Quarterly Journal of Economics* 118:107–155.

Hart, Stuart, and Gautam Ahuja. 1996. "Does It Pay to Be Green?" *Business Strategy and the Environment* 5(1):30–37.

Hendry, Jamie R. 2006. "Taking Aim at Business. What Factors Lead Environmental Non-Governmental Organizations to Target Particular Firms?" *Business and Society* 45:47–86.

Hoffman, Andrew, and Marc Ventresca., eds. 2002. *Organizations, Policy, and the Natural Environment. Institutional and Strategic Perspectives*. Stanford, CA: Stanford University Press.

Janney, Jay, Greg Dess, and Victor Forlani. 2009. "Glass Houses? Market Reactions to Firms Joining the UN Global Compact" *Journal of Business Ethics* 90(3):407–423.

Jiang, Ruihua, and Pratima Bansal. 2003. "Seeing the Need for ISO 14001." *Journal of Management Studies* 40:1047–1067.

Kanter, Rosabeth M. 2003. "From Spare Change to Real Change: The Social Sector as Beta Site for Business Innovation." Pp. 189–214 in *Harvard Business Review on Corporate Social Responsibility*. Boston: Harvard Business School Publishing.

Kassinis, George, and Nikos Vafeas. 2002. "Corporate Boards and Outside Stakeholders as Determinants of Environmental Litigation." *Strategic Management Journal* 23:399–415.

Khanna, Madhu, and Lisa Damon. 1999. "EPA's Voluntary 33/50 Program: Impact on Toxic Releases and Economic Performance of Firms." *Journal of Environmental Economics and Management* 37:1–25.

King, Andrew, and Michael Lenox. 2002. "Exploring the Locus of Profitable Pollution Reduction." *Management Science* 48:289–299.

KLD Research and Analytics. 2007. "Getting Started with KLD Stats and KLD's Ratings Definitions." *KLD Research and Analytics Inc.* Document accessed through Wharton Research Data Services.

Konar, Shameek, and Mark Cohen. 2001. "Does the Market Value Environmental Performance?" *Review of Economics and Statistics* 83(2):281–289.

Lawrence, Anne, and David Morell. 1995. "Leading-Edge Environmental Management: Motivation, Opportunity, Resources and Processes." Pp. 99–127 in *Research in Corporate Social Performance and Policy*, edited by D. Collins and M. Starik. Jai Press.

Lenox, Michael and Jennifer Nash. 2003. "Industry Self-Regulation and Adverse Selection: A Comparison Across Four Trade Association Programs." *Business Strategy and Environment*, 12(6): 343–356.

Lenox, Michael, and Charles Eesley. 2009. "Private Environmental Activism and the Selection and Response of Firm Targets." *Journal of Economics and Management Strategy* 18:45–73.

Longhofer, Wesley, and Evan Schofer. 2010. "National and Global Origins of Environmental Association." *American Sociological Review* 75:505–533.

Margolis, Joshua, and James Walsh. 2003. "Misery Loves Companies: Rethinking Social Initiatives by Business." *Administrative Science Quarterly* 48:268–305.

Ongkrutraksa, Worawan Y. 2007. "Green Marketing and Advertising." Pp. 365–378 in *The Debate Over Corporate Social Responsibility*,

edited by S. May, G. Cheney, and J. Roper. New York: Oxford University Press.
Porter, Michael, and Mark Kramer. 2003. "The Competitive Advantage of Corporate Philanthropy." Pp. 27–64 in *Harvard Business Review on Corporate Social Responsibility*. Boston: Harvard Business Press.
Potoski, Matthew, and Aseem Prakash. 2005. "Covenants with Weak Swords: ISO 14001 and Facilities' Environmental Performance." *Journal of Policy Analysis and Management* 24(4):745–769.
Runhaar, Hens, and Helene Lafferty. 2009. "Governing Corporate Social Responsibility: An Assessment of the Contribution of the UN Global Compact to CSR Strategies in the Telecommunications Industry." *Journal of Business Ethics* 84(4):479–495.
Russo, Michael V., and Paul A. Fouts. 1997. "A Resource-Based Perspective on Corporate Environmental Performance." *Academy of Management Journal* 40(3):534–559.
Toffel, Michael W. 2005. "Resolving Information Asymmetries in Markets: The Role of Certified Management Programs." *Center for Responsible Business, Working Paper Series*, University of California, Berkeley.
Turcotte, Marie-France. 1995. "Conflict and Collaboration: The Interfaces between Environmental Organizations and Business Firms." Pp. 195–229 in *Research in Corporate Social Performance and Policy. Sustaining the Natural Environment. Empirical Studies on the Interface between Nature and Organizations*, edited by D. Collins and M. Starik. JAI Press.
van Marrewijk, Marcel. 2003. "Concepts and Definitions of CSR and Corporate Sustainability: Between Agency and Communion." *Journal of Business Ethics* 44(2–3):95–104.
Vasi, Ion B. 2011. *Winds of Change. The Environmental Movement and the Global Development of the Wind Energy Industry*. New York: Oxford University Press.
Vasi, Ion B., and Brayden King. 2012. "Social Movements, Risk Perceptions, and Economic Outcomes: The Effect of Primary and Secondary Stakeholder Activism on Firms' Perceived Environmental Risk and Financial Performance." *American Sociological Review* 77(4): 573–596.
Vogel, David. 2006. *The Market for Virtue. The Potential and Limits of Corporate Social Responsibility*. Washington, DC: Brookings Institution Press.
Wood, Donna. 1991. "Corporate Social Performance Revisited." *Academy of Management Review* 16:691–718.

12 | The mobility of industries and the limits of corporate social responsibility: labor codes of conduct in Indonesian factories

TIM BARTLEY AND DOUG KINCAID

Introduction: Contradictions of corporate social responsibility

The discourse and practice of corporate social responsibility (CSR) have become standard features of consumer products industries in affluent countries. Mega-retailers and brands from Apple to Ikea to Zara have developed voluntary standards, ethical sourcing guidelines, and benchmarking systems for the social and environmental impacts of their supply chains. New forms of auditing have been developed to provide assurances that can be included in "sustainability reports" or communicated through certification and labeling. Numerous voluntary programs seek to oversee and guide the CSR practices of firms and add credibility to their assurances. Many of these initiatives first gained traction in the apparel and footwear industry, where responses to anti-sweatshop activism in the 1990s made "codes of conduct" and factory monitoring nearly ubiquitous among large, branded firms. As these activities have expanded and spread to other industries

---

For comments on a previous version of this chapter, we thank Ion Bogdan Vasi, Shawn Pope, Kiyo Tsutsui, Alwyn Lim, Jennifer Bair, and the other participants in the Workshop on Corporate Social Responsibility in a Globalizing World, Tokyo, July 2012. We thank Jamie Davis and colleagues at the American Center for International Labor Solidarity office in Jakarta for the use of their survey data. They bear no responsibility for any shortcomings of our analysis or argument, and their lending of the data should not be taken as endorsement of our work. We also thank Niklas Zandén for his collaborative fieldwork and numerous scholars of Indonesian labor, especially Teri Caraway and Hari Nugroho, for guidance in the field. Partial funding for the research was provided by a grant from the American Sociological Association's Fund for the Advancement of the Discipline.

393

(e.g., electronics, home furnishings), their limitations have also become clearer: labor-related CSR initiatives have failed to transform "low road" models of global production or even to greatly reduce allegations of sweatshops and labor rights abuses.

The list of reasons for this is long and, by now, well-known: auditing is often done poorly and falls prey to falsification by resistant factory managers and coached responses from workers (Pun 2005; Ethical Trading Initiative 2006; Frank 2008; China Labor Watch 2009). Even when imperfect auditing turns up significant problems, business often goes on as usual, since compliance ratings are only loosely coupled with sourcing decisions (Egels-Zanden 2007; Locke, Amengual, and Mangla 2009). Improvements tend to be marginal and fail to shift fundamental power dynamics within firms or within the industry (Esbenshade 2004; Mamic 2004; Barrientos and Smith 2007). More broadly, voluntary CSR commitments and programs lack the capacity – and often the willingness – to force change upon recalcitrant actors. Many CSR programs are little more than "fairwash," and this problem is made worse by the proliferation of programs and subsequent confusion among consumers (Seidman 2007).

These critiques are important, but they can only take scholars and practitioners so far. In some instances, firms do seem willing to engage in meaningful monitoring and remediation, especially when disciplined by active watchdogs, credible voluntary programs, and demanding consumer and investor audiences (e.g., O'Rourke 2005; Rodríguez-Garavito 2005; Malets 2011). Most existing critiques overlook a more fundamental limitation to the current practice of labor-related CSR: put simply, CSR commitments fail to problematize features of the production process that undermine lasting improvements in working conditions. One such silence in CSR practice revolves around the stability – or rather the instability – of production. Although scholars and activists have often argued that retailers' and brands' demands for quick turnaround times and rapid adaptation to design changes, coupled with intense price pressure, are root causes of labor rights abuses (Bonacich and Appelbaum 2000), codes of conduct fail to engage with this issue except to note that busy production seasons might require exceptions to rules about maximum working hours. Neither do codes of conduct explicitly address the shifting of orders from one factory – or one country – to another, even when this clearly undermines improvements or involves a move from stronger to weaker labor laws. Many of the practices that have been institutionalized in CSR fields are about making stepwise (or "continuous") improvements in whatever facilities brands and retailers choose to use, rather than encouraging more respectable sourcing decisions in the first place. Most importantly, because CSR commitments focus almost completely on what occurs within the factory walls rather than on the supply chain or the sociopolitical context in which the factory is located, their implications for labor conditions are severely constrained.

In this chapter, we develop this perspective on CSR by exploring the relationship between CSR and the instability of firms and jobs in the Indonesian textile, footwear, and apparel (TFA) sector. This sector was the source of some of the earliest sweatshop scandals involving Nike in the early 1990s (Spar and LaMure 2003), and it continues to be a rich site for examining the unruly character of the industry and the contested nature of CSR. We examine the sector's instability, the consequences of this instability, and ask whether CSR commitments mitigate this unruliness in meaningful and discernible ways. Finding that they do not, we suggest an alternative conception of CSR. CSR fields might be more meaningful if they demanded (and rewarded) more patient forms of sourcing behavior. If "responsible capitalism" were operationalized as stable, patient capitalism, this might allow improvements in working conditions to develop over time rather than undermining them.

We begin by discussing how attention to industry mobility challenges existing work on the diffusion of standards. We then turn to the Indonesian context, documenting instability in the TFA sector in the 2000s. Next, we use two different quantitative datasets to explore whether export markets and codes of conduct have implications for the stability of business and employment in this sector. We then use case-based evidence to consider how instability has undermined potential improvements at the factory level and how these events have generated new debates about the extent of retailers' and brands' responsibilities. In a concluding section, we consider the limitations of current CSR models and the promise of a "patient capital" version of CSR.

This chapter demonstrates the importance of paying attention to the often black-boxed local consequences of global CSR.

Whereas many analyses of CSR focus on the global level or on the institutional environments of corporations in the United States and Europe, there is much to be gained from careful attention to CSR at the point of production. Most fundamentally, it allows us to understand CSR not just as an overarching discourse but also as a set of locally situated practices. These practices are both varied and contested. Overarching nods to fairness, sustainability, and respect for rights can mean very different things in, say, an oil palm plantation in Brazil, an oil field in Nigeria, or an electronics factory in China. In any of these settings, as one looks more closely at implementation, the cracks in the CSR discourse become clearer as actors struggle over the material and legal consequences of corporate responsibility, for instance (Bartley 2005). Local struggles can feed into the evolution of the global model of CSR (Halliday and Carruthers 2009), generating new debates, new rule-making projects, and new assurances of credibility and trustworthiness (Djelic and Sahlin-Andersson 2006).

Focusing on concrete CSR practices in particular places also pushes scholars to move beyond a reliance on "decoupling" as an explanation for the muted impacts of global scripts. Starting with analyses of the widespread diffusion of norms and scripts, scholars often use decoupling as a residual, catch-all concept to explain the limited behavioral impact of those norms and scripts. But this obscures other, more proximate (and often more telling) processes. These include countervailing forces (i.e., trends that coincide with the rise of CSR but push in the direction of diminished responsibility) – in this chapter, a destabilization of industries and employment. Furthermore, writing off noncompliance to decoupling may overlook a kind of "looseness" in the very notion of CSR, making it so adaptable as to be nearly meaningless. The bracketing of certain issues may be a *reason* for the popularity of CSR discourse, not merely a function of its imperfect implementation. At the same time, activists and nongovernmental organizations (NGOs) sometimes seek to "tighten" the definition of CSR and push firms to accept particular obligations. This struggle is of both substantive and theoretical importance. Like attempts to promote a more "inhabited institutionalism" (Hallett 2010), this research seeks to make "loose coupling," "decoupling," and "recoupling" a focus of empirical inquiry rather than just a theoretical trope.

The mobility of investment and orders

Reconceptualizing capital mobility

"Globalization" has been a project to enhance the mobility of capital. Capital mobility is traditionally defined as the degree to which investment can move across national borders, whether in the form of direct investment (such as purchasing part or all of a company) or portfolio investment (such as more passive forms of stock ownership). Economists view the phenomenon with reference to an imagined state of perfect capital mobility, in which the free flow of investment equalizes rates of return across jurisdictions (Frankel 1992). Although scholars have often debated the influence of capital mobility on the nation-state (Garrett 1995; Evans 1997), it also has serious implications for labor, with actual or threatened mobility often spurring layoffs and undermining unions (Cowie 1999; Bronfenbrenner 2000).

Traditional conceptions of capital mobility need to be expanded in order to consider how the movement of firms and jobs shapes CSR in contemporary consumer products industries. A growing number of consumer products industries are taking the form of "buyer-driven commodity chains," in which lead firms (retailers and brands) do not own production facilities in other countries but instead "source" from a network of suppliers (Gereffi 2005). Apparel and footwear brands were pioneers of this model, which has since led even traditional apparel manufacturers to shed their factories; and its variants have also taken hold in consumer electronics, home furnishings, and agro-food industries (Gereffi, Humphrey, and Sturgeon 2005). In this type of industry structure, mobility of investment is only part of the story. In the TFA sector, the firms that own factories – often of Taiwanese or South Korean origin – do shift their investments (i.e., move their factories) across countries to take advantage of changes in wages, infrastructure, or trade agreements. But even if these investments remain fairly stable, brands and retailers may shift their *orders* across suppliers and across countries in search of low prices, high quality, and quick delivery times. Attention to the mobility of direct investment must increasingly be accompanied by attention to the mobility of *orders* from lead firms. Factory owners are still relevant, but their decisions are often dependent on buyers' preferences for particular locations. Methodologically, the volume of orders can partially be picked up by measuring international trade (imports and exports) rather than just foreign direct investment (Mosley and Uno 2007), although it remains difficult to reconstruct a global supply chain from such data (see Bair and Mahutga 2012). Although our goal in this chapter is not to systematically measure the mobility of orders, we argue that volatility in foreign orders has had noticeable effects on firms and workers in the Indonesian TFA sector. Secondarily, our analyses also provide some evidence about how foreign ownership might matter for the implementation of CSR principles.

Ours is certainly not the first examination of capital mobility in Indonesia. For Winters (1996), "power is manifested in the motion of capital itself, into and out of a community or region or country" (x). He examined the pendulum swings in Indonesian policy from the mid-1960s to mid-1990s as the state shifted from high to low and back to high degrees of responsiveness to mobile "capital controllers" – that is, the actors that direct the flow of investors' money, including development banks, pension funds, and private investors themselves. Capital flight destabilized the Indonesian economy in the lead-up to the 1997 Asian financial crisis and disciplined the country's reforms in the post-Suharto era (Robison and Hadiz 2006). Given its history and position in the international division of labor, it is perhaps not surprising that Indonesia continues to serve as a powerful example of the structuring power of firms' mobility through both investment and orders – in this case on the effectiveness of CSR.

Mobility and standards: could codes of conduct make a difference?

Codes of conduct – like many other CSR instruments – were designed specifically for a world of buyer-driven commodity chains with production dispersed and highly mobile across different countries. Global industries required global standards, the reasoning went, especially standards that would travel along with a brand or retailer's shifting mix of production locations (Gereffi, Garcia-Johnson, and Sasser 2001; O'Rourke 2003). With intergovernmental regulation proving politically difficult (as seen in the refusal of the World Trade Organization [WTO] to address labor rights, for instance), many actors saw private, voluntary standards as a potentially useful solution, albeit a partial and contested one (Bartley 2007). In this sense, there is a strong affinity between geographically mobile industries and labor codes of conduct.

But paying closer attention to the dynamics of mobility complicates the ways in which scholars have conceptualized linkages between globalization and labor rights/standards. For instance, scholars have shown that trade flows – as well as other types of global connection – facilitate the diffusion of CSR norms (Lim and Tsutsui 2012) and of labor law (Greenhill, Mosley, and Prakash 2009). Contrary to fears of a race to the bottom, scholars have shown that international trade can, in some conditions at least, bolster labor standards. But, at the same time, trade flows can destabilize sectors and economies in ways that are contrary to the application of these standards. The gap between CSR principles and performance may not simply be a case of ceremonial commitment but may also reflect countervailing pressures – for speed and flexibility, for instance – that undermine the lengthy struggles and learning processes that generate durable, substantive change.

Apparel and footwear production are especially mobile industries due to their low level of capital intensity and minimal skill requirements. The industry became highly globalized in the 1990s, not only because of the movement of factories from high-wage to low-wage countries but also because existing trade agreements (the Multi-Fibre Agreement [MFA]) set maximum quotas for apparel exports from particular countries. In effect, this kept the industry geographically dispersed and fostered the growth of garment factories in Lesotho, Mauritius, and other hinterland locations that had enough infrastructure to take advantage of their quota allotments. China's entry into the WTO in 2001 paved the way for even more rapid growth in its TFA industries. With the phase-out of the MFA in 2005, the industry has become more geographically concentrated, with China taking a dominant role, and with growth in Vietnam, Bangladesh, and India.

Labor costs alone do not determine the location of apparel production. Infrastructure and delivery times matter a great deal, and productivity gains may sometimes offset higher per-unit labor costs. Nevertheless, among a handful of directly competing industrializing economies in the Global South, the cost and docility of labor can often be an important factor (Chan and Ross 2003). Changes in wages and labor disruption are often discussed by actors within the apparel and footwear industry as shaping whether orders go to companies in China, Vietnam, Indonesia, India, or a few other possibilities. In the language of the industry, orders are shaped by expectations of quality, delivery, and price. The rise of CSR has added "compliance" to that list, but, as one representative of an international brand put it, "we both know that's bullshit" (interview with compliance official, Shenzhen, October 15, 2010).

For the most part, CSR initiatives have bracketed the mobility of investment and orders, the instability of industries, and the contingency/flexibility of work arrangements. Although brands face negative attention if they quickly "cut and run" from a problematic factory rather than trying to improve it, this kind of scrutiny is only activated when there are clear and publicized violations in a particular factory. The more routine and systemic movements of orders are not restricted by codes of conduct, by industry standards bodies (e.g., the Fair Labor Association, Business Social Compliance Initiative), by factory certification programs (e.g., Social Accountability International), or by CSR rating bodies (e.g., KLD). We argue that this is a significant weakness in the CSR model. Yet it is not beyond the pale to expect CSR to address the mobility, instability, and contingency of production networks. In fact, a closer look reveals several ways in which CSR projects promise – often implicitly or indirectly – to address these issues.

First, for some initiatives and some scholars, CSR is about building relationships between companies and their "stakeholders" around the world. Although many CSR initiatives trumpet stakeholders without really addressing the nature of those relationships, there are at least a few initiatives that do emphasize embedding markets in more durable relationships. Fair Trade certification is the clearest example. Fair Trade claims to foster "sustainable trade partnerships between producers and their buyers, which enable producers to have long-term access to markets under viable conditions" (Fairtrade International 2011: 12). This goal is not present in CSR initiatives and codes of conduct in the apparel and footwear industry; nevertheless, some scholars have argued that leading brands in this industry have developed a "commitment approach" to implementing their codes of conduct, which involves more stable relationships with core suppliers (Frenkel and Scott 2002; Locke et al. 2009).

Second, some scholars and practitioners have also argued that CSR can not only provide competitive advantages for brands and retailers (Porter and Kramer 2006) but also that CSR compliance can enhance the competitive positions of suppliers (Prakash and Potoski 2006b; Center for International Private Enterprise and Social Accountability International 2009), thus potentially improving prices, market access, or buffering them from shocks. If true, this could be an important stabilizing force, given that suppliers in the apparel industry have often faced declining prices and shorter lead times even as their productivity has increased (Schrank 2004). The idea that an ethical niche could help smaller exporting countries to cope with competition from China was one of the foundations of the International Labor Organization's "Better Factories" program in Cambodia (Polaski 2006). In an analysis of apparel factories participating in this program, Oka (2012) finds that compliance with labor standards has little to no effect on attracting business from reputation-sensitive buyers but that some forms of compliance are linked to a higher likelihood of retaining orders from these buyers. Oka argues that "better compliance does not automatically translate to more business" but nevertheless that "if suppliers look to upgrade their competencies and seek to attract such buyers, improving labour standard compliance is a necessity" (22). Our research examines the related issue of whether CSR commitments have implications for the stability of suppliers' business.

Finally, a few codes of conduct and related CSR initiatives do speak to the stability of employment, namely, by limiting suppliers' ability to use contingent workers and labor dispatch agencies to shirk their legal and ethical obligations. Nike's code of conduct bans "excessive use of temporary production workers or short-term contracts" such as a situation in which "more than 15% of production line workers are temporary workers or on short-term contract" (Nike 2010: 1). Both the Ethical Trading Initiative's Base Code and the SA8000 standard for certification of decent factories say that companies cannot use "labour-only contracting," multiple short-term contracts, or phony "apprenticeship" programs to avoid legal obligations to workers (Ethical Trading Initiative 1998; Social Accountability International 2008). Recent versions of the Fair Labor Association's compliance benchmarks move in a similar direction, allowing short-term contract and temporary workers only when the type or volume of production outstrips the capacities of the permanent workforce (FLA Workplace Code of Conduct and Compliance Benchmarks, Revised October 5, 2011). Moreover, nearly all codes of conduct call for basic legal compliance so that, to the extent that contingent work conflicts with domestic labor law, codes of conduct indirectly restrict it. A discursive emphasis on legal compliance is widespread, from Limited Brands ("full compliance with all laws, rules, and regulations ... ") to Carrefour ("strict observance of legality") to Walmart ("must fully comply with all applicable national and/or local laws and regulations"). Legal compliance is the first principle in the Worldwide Responsible Accredited Production program, which was developed by the American Apparel and Footwear Association, and in the Business Social Compliance Initiative, which was developed by retailers in Europe. For many scholars, CSR is defined as "beyond compliance" activities, yet, as will become clear in the analyses herein, basic legal compliance should not be taken for granted.

Instability in the Indonesian TFA industries

Given these suggestions that CSR might have some bearing on stability, albeit in the midst of a larger silence on this issue, what are the actual relationships between CSR and the stability of firms and employment? In the sections that follow, we use several different types of data to address this question. Here, we start by describing instability in the Indonesian TFA footwear industries, which we argue has hindered any serious attempt to implement CSR principles there.

Production and employment in the Indonesian TFA sector expanded greatly in the late 1980s and 1990s (Harrison and Scorse 2010). This was fueled especially by export-oriented production, such that a majority of the apparel produced in Indonesia in the 1980s and 1990s was exported, primarily to the United States and Europe (Dicken and Hassler 2000; Hill 2000). Movement into the country by Korean, Taiwanese, and Hong Kong-based investors was especially important in expanding the textile and footwear industries and, to a lesser extent, the garment industry, where domestic ownership was also common. These investors shifted to Indonesia both because of rising labor and production costs at home and because of the Suharto government's export-promotion policies (Thee 2009). Several foreign buyers developed strong linkages to apparel factories in Indonesia, who became "full package" producers, capable of taking on all the tasks of producing to a buyer's specifications. Yet the industry soon faced rising competition from other low-wage sites like Vietnam, China, India, and Bangladesh (Thee 2009). By the time of the MFA phase-out in 2005, the global competitiveness of Indonesian apparel factories had declined. Wages remained low, however, so as China and Vietnam began to experience rising wages and increased work disruption around 2007, some orders began to return to Indonesia. At a conference in 2009, the sourcing director for US apparel company VF reported that the company would more than triple its sourcing from Indonesia in the next four years because "labor costs and living standards are growing so fast in China and Vietnam" (presentation at WRAP conference, Jakarta, July 2, 2009). Yet VF, like many other companies, has also moved aggressively into Bangladesh, where wages are lower than in Indonesia.

Figure 12.1 shows significant instability in textile and garment exports from Indonesia between 1995 and 2010. Large declines in the value of exports occurred from 1996 to 1997, 2000 to 2002, and 2008 to 2009. The first of these may be linked in part to the Asian

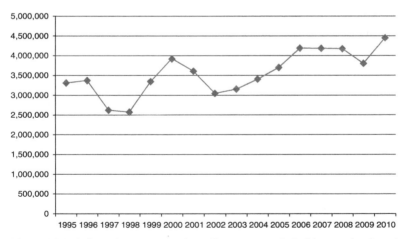

Figure 12.1 Indonesian exports of textiles, yarn, and clothing to developed countries, in thousands of 1990 dollars
Source: UNCTADstat, with US dollar amounts adjusted using CPI (1990 = 100)

financial crisis of 1997. The second may reflect an industry shift toward China around the time of its entry into the WTO in 2001. The third dip in export values, from 2008 to 2009, likely reflected the onset of the global financial crisis.

The TFA sector had grown in the 1990s to take its place among the leading sources of manufacturing employment in Indonesia. But employment contracted thereafter. Based on data from the Indonesian Statistics Bureau's (Badan Pusat Statistik [BPS]) annual manufacturing surveys (in 2000, 2004, and 2008), the total number of production workers in this sector decreased by 15 percent from 2000 to 2004, with the largest declines occurring in the textile and footwear industries. Employment in these two industries continued to decline between 2004 and 2008, while apparel industry employment grew, combining for a slight aggregate decline of around 1 percent for the TFA sector as a whole. In the textile and footwear industries, total employment in 2008 was lower than it had been in 1996.

More important than overall levels of employment are the shifting forms of employment. In the 2000s, Indonesia underwent a partial and highly contested liberalization of labor market regulations. Labor Law 13 (Manpower Act) of 2003 allowed short-term contract work, temporary/probationary work, and outsourcing but also put limits on their use. For instance, only "non-core" work activities can be outsourced, fixed-term contracts can only be used for up to three years, and temporary/probationary status can last for no more than three months. Even with these limits, these provisions represented a chipping away of the status of "permanent" workers who cannot be laid off without paying sizeable severance packages. For some observers, this began a slippery slope of flexibilization, especially given loopholes and poor enforcement of those aspects of the law that limit flexibility (Tjandraningsih and Nugroho 2008). For other observers, the law represents a surprisingly limited form of flexibilization, given trends in other countries and the weakness of Indonesian unions, who successfully defended limits on contingency (Caraway 2004). For neoclassical economists and international financial institutions, the law illustrates the continuing rigidity of Indonesian labor markets and the need for further reform (Manning and Roesad 2007; World Bank 2010).

Regardless of one's ideal level of flexibility of Indonesian labor markets, there are several key features of this setting. First, there has been a partial flexibilization of employment, even if more in practice

Table 12.1 *Employment of textile, apparel, and footwear production workers across provinces, 2000–2008*

Province	2000	2004	2008	% change 2000–2004	% change 2004–2008	% change 2000–2008
West Java (incl. Banten)	746,283	641,259	609,666	−14.07	−4.93	−18.31
Central Java	194,229	180,053	214,096	−7.30	18.91	10.23
Jakarta	152,003	127,091	94,933	−16.39	−25.30	−37.55
East Java	128,711	87,471	94,717	−32.04	8.28	−26.41
Yogyakarta	16,442	17,007	18,675	3.44	9.81	13.58

than in policy. Second, given the lack of unemployment insurance and a minimal social safety net, severance pay is an important device for compensating unemployed workers, but employers are often unable or unwilling to pay the legally required amount. Third, in some sense, Indonesian workers may be getting the worst of both worlds (i.e., of both flexibility and rigidity). It is plausible that the rigidity of labor market regulations has impeded job growth, even as flexibility has fostered insecure employment. But the potential benefits for workers of more rigid/less flexible labor markets have rarely materialized: unions are weak and fragmented (Caraway 2006; Ford 2009; Juliawan 2011), and severance pay is rarely given in full (Brusentsev, Newhouse, and Vroman 2012) especially when investors flee the country.

In addition to shifting investment and orders across countries, there has been a high degree of mobility and instability within the Indonesian TFA sector in the 2000s. Table 12.1 shows the number of production workers in the top five provinces for TFA production (based on BPS data). Employment in Jakarta declined dramatically, with a 38 percent drop from 2000 to 2008. The nearby province of West Java (including industry clusters in Tangerang, Bogor, and Bandung) also saw large declines in employment, especially between 2000 and 2004. The other province experiencing large declines was East Java, where employment fell by 32 percent between 2000 and 2004, although it rebounded with 8 percent growth from 2004 to 2008. One province with net growth from 2000 to 2008 was Central

Java, where a 19 percent increase occurred from 2004 to 2008. Although smaller in employment, Yogyakarta's employment rate also grew from 2000 to 2008. This pattern at least partly reflects differences in the cost of labor in different parts of the country. Of these five major areas, Jakarta has the highest minimum wages, followed by East Java, both of which saw large declines in employment. Central Java, a site of industry growth, has the lowest minimum wage in this group. This pattern has led some labor activists to argue that a "race to the bottom within Indonesia" has combined with the flexibilization of labor markets to significantly undermine labor rights (interview with labor rights activist, Jakarta, June 28, 2008).

Overall, the Indonesian TFA sector is an important but volatile component of global commodity chains and of the Indonesian economy. Long deemed a "sunset industry" by much of the Indonesian business community, the apparel industry has risen and fallen several times while also migrating to different parts of the country. Foreign and domestically owned apparel factories have sought orders from large American and European buyers, and although these brands and retailers have not abandoned Indonesia (or have returned), neither have they committed to it. Both factory owners – at least those without the capability to move – and Indonesian workers must cope with this volatility. As discussed earlier, although codes of conduct largely fail to address these issues head-on, some framings of CSR imply that it should strengthen the relationships between brands and their stakeholders (such as the workers in their supply chain).

Export-oriented production, CSR, and the stability of employment

The contours of business failures

To examine if CSR makes global commodity chains less unruly, we look at which types of employers are most and least likely to fail. The failure of a company has obvious implications for the livelihoods of workers, especially in a setting where unemployment benefits are dependent on legally mandated (but often unpaid) severance payments from the failing firm itself. Could CSR commitments influence this process? If one takes seriously the language of deepened corporate commitment to "stakeholders," including currently employed workers, then perhaps the answer is yes. Furthermore, if one believes that engaging with ethically sensitive markets can help to buffer firms or states from competition, then there may be a link between CSR and the viability of supplier firms.

To examine the contours of business failure in the TFA sector, we use data from the Indonesian Statistics Bureau's (BPS) annual manufacturing surveys in 2000, 2004, and 2008. This was a turbulent period in these industries, even though it was prior to the onset of the global financial crisis of late 2008. We limit our analyses to firms with at least fifty employees to avoid counting as failures firms that shrank below the limit of at least twenty employees for inclusion in the dataset. The BPS data allows only for an indirect assessment of the influence of CSR, by way of comparisons in the aggregate rate of failure in different segments of the market. Specifically, because CSR commitments are rooted in international trade (Lim and Tsutsui 2012) and because only exporting firms are subject to CSR commitments, we compare firms that produce only for the domestic market to those that export at least some of their products. (Unfortunately, the BPS data does not include information on the destination of the exports.)

Overall, there was a high rate of failure in the Indonesian TFA sector during this period. Fewer than half of the firms that existed in 2000 survived until 2008. Approximately 25 percent of firms that existed in 2000 had failed by 2004. Around 26 percent of those that existed in 2004 had failed by 2008. In both periods, footwear manufacturers were most likely to fail, followed by apparel manufacturers and then textile makers. Of course, these exits were balanced to some extent by new entrants. Eighteen percent of firms operating in 2004 and 31 percent of those operating in 2008 had entered the market sometime in the previous four years. Yet failures were often common here as well, with 35 percent of those founded between 2001 and 2004 having failed by 2008. (Overall, there was a net increase in the number of firms from 2000 to 2008, but this was mostly due to increasing numbers of small firms.)

Table 12.2 shows some simple logistic regression analyses of the types of firms that were more or less likely to fail in each of the two periods (2000 to 2004, 2004 to 2008). In the first period, footwear

Table 12.2 *Logistic regression analysis of failure of Indonesian textile, apparel, and footwear firms, 2000–2008*

	Failure 2000–2004	Failure 2004–2008
Textile	.8096945	.8052442
	(−1.42)	(−0.92)
Footwear	1.604501*	1.139391
	(2.35)	(0.40)
Exporter	1.348552+	1.564714+
	(1.82)	(1.89)
Exporter * Textile	.758574	.5905605
	(−1.11)	(−1.56)
Exporter * Footwear	.5290441+	1.203002
	(−1.87)	(0.41)
Constant	.3002915***	.2331288
	(−10.71)	(−8.08)
N	1961	1118
Log likelihood	−1055.8152	−543.17607

Omitted category: Apparel + p<0.10, *p<0.05, **p<0.01, ***p<0.001
Likelihood ratios shown, z-statistics in parentheses

manufacturers producing for the domestic market were most likely to fail overall, with exporting footwear producers somewhat less likely to fail. But the story is different for apparel firms. Apparel exporters were more likely to fail than were their domestically oriented counterparts (the reference category). In the second period, exporting apparel firms continued to be more likely to fail than were apparel firms producing for the domestic market. (Because these differences do not quite reach the conventional .05 level of statistical significance, they may be considered suggestive.) No other patterns are apparent in the second period.

Overall, the enhanced rate of failure among apparel exporters suggests the same industry segments that were likely to be subject to codes of conduct and CSR standards of foreign buyers were also likely to be unstable. Although the growth of Chinese imports into Indonesia posed challenges for the domestically oriented apparel industry (AKATIGA Center for Social Analysis 2007), our analyses show that failure rates were higher in the export-oriented segments of the industry (at least when focusing on firms with at least fifty workers). The same does not appear to be true for textile or footwear manufacturers, however, perhaps due to the higher barriers to entry (and thus lower levels of competition) in these industries. Although these findings are highly aggregated and cannot discern firm-specific linkages to ethically sensitive markets, they point toward a gap in the CSR model: CSR commitments in importing markets were not sufficient to stabilize the tumultuous Indonesian apparel industry. Going further, these analyses suggest that market segments where codes of conduct are in force might also be those where stability is most difficult to achieve.

Codes of conduct and employment stability

A second source of data allows us to measure firm-level CSR linkages more precisely by examining the possible effects of codes of conduct among unionized firms in the TFA industries. We can thus ask if manufacturers that are subject to a foreign buyer's code of conduct perform differently than others. In 2009, the Jakarta office of the AFL-CIO's American Center for International Labor Solidarity (ACILS or the Solidarity Center) commissioned a survey of unionized firms in Indonesia. The survey was conducted by an Indonesian research firm (JRI Research, which conducts many surveys for international organizations), which administered questionnaires to union leaders in 658 firms in eight major industrial cities. Our analyses are restricted to firms that were manufacturers of apparel, textiles, or footwear (137 total). Although it is possible that survey responses would reflect biases in union leaders' knowledge and relationship with the company, most of the survey asks respondents to report on specific activities, not to provide their own judgments. In addition, we think it is fair to assume that any biases in responses are distributed broadly and are not systematically associated with the key variables in our analyses.

In addition to measuring a variety of factory characteristics and indicators of labor rights, the survey asked whether there is "a code of conduct [kode etik, or "code of conduct"] in your company that has been required by one or more foreign brands that buy your products to be sold abroad " This allows us to examine possible differences among three types of firms – those that produce only for the domestic market (24 percent), those that export and are subject to a buyer's code of conduct (55 percent), and those that export but are not subject to a code of conduct (19 percent). Although the data do not include measure of the extent to which buyers seek to monitor compliance with the code of conduct, it provides a rare opportunity to make basic comparisons and examine the implications of CSR on the shop floor. Most researchers have focused on the content or negotiation of codes of conduct or their adoption by brands and retailers in affluent countries (O'Rourke 2003; Fransen 2011; Wetterberg 2011). Those who have examined them at the factory level have usually relied either on case studies of a small number of factories (Frenkel and Kim 2004; Pun 2005) or on data collected by CSR auditors themselves (Locke, Qin, and Brause 2007; but see Kim 2010 for a different approach). The current data provide a rare opportunity to move beyond small numbers of cases without relying on information provided by companies.[1]

The models in Table 12.3 examine the correlates of several measures of instability in this sample of Indonesian factories. Although our interest is primarily in comparing domestic producers, exporters, and exporters subject to buyers' codes of conduct, we also include a number of other potentially salient factory characteristics. In particular, we control for industry (apparel/textiles vs. footwear/leather), company size (log of the number of workers), composition of the workforce (by gender and nonpermanent employment status), the existence of a collective bargaining agreement (CBA, which exists in 61 percent of the factories in our sample), and whether the factory has been visited by a government labor inspector in the past two years (true of 67 percent of these factories). We also examine the nationality of the owners, comparing factories owned by Indonesian investors (73 percent of our sample), Japanese investors (4 percent), investors from newly industrialized East Asian countries (19 percent, mainly from South Korea and Taiwan), and investors from other countries (4 percent, the United States and India).

---

[1] This can also be complicated, of course. In our case, we identified seventeen factories where the respondent indicated that a code of conduct was present but where the factory's profile of products and export destinations made that highly unlikely. To avoid having false positives that could obscure the influence of codes of conduct, we dropped these firms from our analyses. Our effective sample size is thus 120 firms. Analyses with these false positives included and marked by a dummy variable produce substantively identical results.

Table 12.3 starts by using logistic regression to look at the likelihood that a factory had layoffs in the previous two years (which occurred in 20 percent of the cases in our sample). Model 1a shows that layoffs were less likely to occur in factories producing for the domestic market than in those producing for export. This is consistent with a view of export markets as less stable than domestic markets. In addition, ownership seems to be related to instability: factories owned by investors from East Asian newly industrialized countries (NICs) were more likely to have layoffs than those owned by Indonesian investors (and Japanese investors); factories owned by other foreigners also seem more likely to have layoffs (although this result only reaches the .10 level of significance). Layoffs were more likely at apparel/textile factories than at footwear factories. None of our other measures is significantly associated with the likelihood of layoffs.

Model 1b allows us to see if codes of conduct mitigate exporters' higher likelihood of laying off workers. Scholars have sometimes hoped that codes of conduct might help to build more durable supply chain relationships, but we find no evidence of this in the present context. Exporters subject to codes of conduct are no different from other exporters in their likelihood of layoffs. Domestic producers remain less likely than either type of exporter to have layoffs. The pattern of other associations remains quite similar as in model 1a.

Models 2a and 2b take a similar approach, this time through an ordinary least squares (OLS) regression of the proportion of nonpermanent workers in the factory. Despite fairly strict limits on contingent work set by both Indonesian labor law (and some codes of conduct), the factories in our sample had an average of 29.5 percent of their workforces composed of nonpermanent employees. In nearly 20 percent of the factories, nonpermanent employees were a majority of the workforce. The extent of reliance on nonpermanent workers, though, does not seem to be related to whether companies produce for domestic or export markets (as shown in model 2a) or whether they are subject to buyers' codes of conduct (as shown in model 2b). We do find some patterns, though. Factories with a collective bargaining agreement in place have lower levels of reliance on nonpermanent employees – a possible indication of the ability of more capable unions resisting the flexibilization of work. Indeed, factories with CBAs have average levels of nonpermanent employment that are around 13 percentage points lower than others. East Asian-owned factories have higher levels of

Table 12.3 Regression analyses of unstable/contingent employment in unionized textile, apparel, and footwear firms in Indonesia

	Layoffs in the past two years (logistic)		Proportion of nonpermanent workers (OLS)		Illegal situations w/ contract workers (NB reg)	
	1a	1b	2a	2b	3a	3b
Group:						
Domestic Prod.	−1.870*	−2.035*	−0.00742	0.0179	−0.185	−0.254
	(−2.04)	(−2.13)	(−0.14)	(0.27)	(−1.08)	(−1.31)
Exporter w/ codes		−0.387		0.0459		−0.133
		(−0.55)		(0.72)		(−0.72)
Ind: Footwear	−2.291+	−2.175+	0.0636	0.0640	0.00165	−0.000913
	(−1.78)	(−1.71)	(1.00)	(1.01)	(0.01)	(−0.00)
Log #workers	−0.233	−0.176	0.0404+	0.0350	−0.0640	−0.0489
	(−0.79)	(−0.57)	(1.74)	(1.44)	(−0.85)	(−0.63)
Proportion female	−0.230	−0.0964	0.0378	0.0252	0.219	0.235
	(−0.22)	(−0.09)	(0.42)	(0.27)	(0.76)	(0.82)
Proportion Nonpermanent	0.895	0.935			0.577+	0.584+
	(0.78)	(0.81)			(1.89)	(1.92)
CBA	−0.672	−0.625	−0.127*	−0.129*	−0.0595	−0.0565
	(−1.02)	(−0.94)	(−2.40)	(−2.42)	(−0.35)	(−0.33)

Gov't. inspections	-0.863	-0.833	-0.0897+	-0.0899+	-0.197	-0.187
	(-1.42)	(-1.36)	(-1.82)	(-1.82)	(-1.36)	(-1.28)
Owners: E. Asian	1.772**	1.729**	0.148*	0.151*	0.000594	-0.00133
	(2.82)	(2.72)	(2.43)	(2.48)	(0.00)	(-0.01)
Owners: Japanese	-0.0249	0.00127	0.0323	0.0313	0.489	0.470
	(-0.02)	(0.00)	(0.27)	(0.26)	(1.29)	(1.24)
Owners: Other	1.875+	1.866+	0.00684	0.00368	0.248	0.261
	(1.70)	(1.69)	(0.06)	(0.03)	(0.76)	(0.79)
Constant	-0.172	-0.163	0.299***	0.286**	0.909**	0.948**
	(-0.17)	(-0.16)	(3.43)	(3.22)	(3.03)	(3.12)
Lnalpha						
Constant					-30.21	-30.21
N	120	120	120	120	89	89

t statistics in parentheses
Omitted Categories:
Group: (a) All exporters, (b) Exporters not subject to codes of conduct
Industry: Textile/Apparel
Ownership: Indonesian + $p<0.10$, * $p<0.05$, ** $p<0.01$, *** $p<0.001$

reliance on nonpermanent employees. There are suggestive effects of firm size and government labor inspection on the use of nonpermanent workers as well.

Finally, a third set of models examines the extent to which short-term contract workers are employed in ways that conflict with Indonesian labor law. In factories that utilized contract workers (81 percent of the total in our sample), interviewers asked respondents whether the factory engaged in five different practices – using contract workers for routine/permanent work (not just in exceptional circumstances), hiring them for longer than three years, extending the contract multiple times, transferring them to related companies, and dismissing and then rehiring contract workers. All of these are illegal under Indonesian labor law, which requires longer term, more regular employees to be classified as permanent workers, entitling them to certain benefits. Yet 93 percent of the factories were reported as engaging in at least one of these practices, 54 percent had at least three such violations, and 4 percent had all five. This is a substantial rate of noncompliance with domestic law. It is perhaps not surprising in light of employers' opposition (albeit unsuccessful) to the 2003 Manpower Act that restricts these practices (Caraway 2004). On the other hand, nearly all codes of conduct call for compliance with domestic labor law. If strict legal compliance (or beyond compliance practices) is strongly demanded by buyers, we would expect to find evidence of this at the factory level.

Models 3a and 3b assess whether exporters, or exporters subject to codes of conduct, engaged in lower levels of legal noncompliance than did other factories. Here, we use negative binomial regression models to explain differences in the number of violations. We find no evidence that exporters were more legally compliant than domestic producers (model 3a). Nor were exporters subject to codes of conduct more legally compliant than other exporters (model 3b). Not surprisingly, the greater a factory's dependence on nonpermanent workers, the higher the number of illegal situations involving their use (although these coefficients are significant at the .10 level only). None of the other measured factors appears to shape the extent of illegal situations with contract workers. Overall, this suggests that noncompliance with the labor contract law is widely diffused among different types of factories, including those subject to codes of conduct that call for domestic legal compliance.

Patterns of instability

Taken together, our analyses portray export-oriented production as often unstable and codes of conduct as ineffectual in shaping the contingency of work or respect for legal mandates on this topic. This should not be taken as a glorification of domestically oriented production, though, or as an assumption that there are no differences between exporters and domestic producers. Existing evidence suggests that export-oriented firms generally pay more on average than their domestically oriented counterparts (Bernard and Jensen 1997) and that moving into export markets can be a way for domestically oriented firms to "upgrade" their capacities, capture higher returns, and potentially pass some of those gains on to workers (Bair and Gereffi 2001). In Indonesia, Harrison and Scorse (2010) found that export-oriented TFA manufacturers in the 1990s paid higher wages than domestically oriented factories in this sector, although these wages were nevertheless significantly lower than wages in other manufacturing industries (even controlling for skill differences). Export-oriented workplaces may also be more formalized, partially as a result of management standards demanded by foreign buyers (Guthrie 2002; Gallagher 2005; Prakash and Potoski 2006a). But there are tradeoffs. Exporters may offer higher wages but less secure employment. Formalized labor relations may also be flexibilized, contingent labor relations. Our point is not that exporters are "worse" than domestic producers in any general sense, but only that there is substantial (often more) instability in export-oriented production and that CSR commitments do not meaningfully intervene in this issue. It is also important to remember that the domestic producers in our sample (like all firms in our sample) are unionized factories, so they most likely do not represent the more informal segments of domestic producers, where work may be highly uncertain and conditions harsh. Our comparisons are within the more formalized segments of the industry, not between large, rationalized exporters and small home-based production shops.

It is also not our intent to suggest that factories subject to codes of conduct are no different from others. Whereas our analyses show that they are no different when it comes to the stability and contingency of employment, this does not mean there are no differences at all. Existing research shows that codes of conduct are almost never implemented fully and that auditing of compliance is rarely trustworthy (Sum and

Pun 2005; Egels-Zanden 2007; Locke et al. 2009), but there is also evidence that CSR commitments can sometimes be associated with improvements in health and safety, working hours, and compliance with minimum wage laws (Barrientos and Smith 2006). For instance, attention from footwear brands with codes of conduct helped to phase out certain dangerous chemicals in footwear production (Brown 2003). Certification of workplaces in China has been plagued by corruption and lax auditing but nevertheless seems to mark increased managerial interest in rationalized human resource management systems (Bartley and Zhang, forthcoming). Indeed, in our own data on Indonesian factories, there is some initial evidence that codes of conduct may matter for health and safety and the formalization of employment relationships. Still, the silences in CSR commitments are deafening, and the gaps in their implementation are wide. As our analyses suggest, they fail to impact fundamental issues of job security, industry stability, and respect for domestic law restricting the flexibility of labor markets.

Activist campaigns and factory closures

Industry instability is hard to ignore if one looks at anti-sweatshop activism focused on Indonesian factories. The Indonesian apparel and footwear industry is a rich and important site for examining activists' attempts to hold international brands and retailers to their CSR commitments. To an alarming extent, anti-sweatshop and international solidarity campaigns here have had to address factory closures. Factory closures have abruptly ended attempts by activists and brands to improve conditions in some factories. In other cases, closures have spurred campaigns seeking justice for displaced workers. Furthermore, these campaigns have raised new questions about the extent to which brands and retailers are responsible for keeping factories in business or covering workers' severance pay when factory owners flee the country or go bankrupt.

In this section, we draw on interviews with representatives of local labor unions, NGOs, and brands operating in Indonesia (conducted from 2008 to 2010) and on other documentary evidence to examine several cases in which industry instability has intertwined with social movement campaigns and attempts to "leverage" brands' CSR commitments into concrete improvements on the ground (see also

Egels-Zandén and Bartley 2012). These brief case studies illustrate both how industry instability matters for the improvement of working conditions and how this issue has mostly been defined out of brands' CSR commitments. They also shed light on the question of whether organized pressure makes brands' CSR commitments more meaningful. To some degree, it does. But even brands with heavy investments in CSR have been, at worst, reckless in their exits from particular factories and, at best, hesitant to accept any obligation to displaced Indonesian workers. Several recent attempts to expand brands' responsibilities in this area are intriguing and important.

Factory closure and the undermining of improvements: PT Kolon Langgeng

The case of the PT Kolon Langgeng garment factory, a Nike supplier in Jakarta, illustrates how codes of conduct can sometimes help local activists carve out space for union organizing but also how these can be quickly undermined by instability and factory closure. In 2002, workers from this factory filed a complaint with the US-based Worker Rights Consortium (WRC), which investigates labor rights abuses in collegiate apparel production. The subsequent WRC investigation turned up a variety of code of conduct violations, including forced overtime, verbal abuse, arbitrary firings, and especially a lack of respect for workers' freedom of association. The existing *Serikat Pekerja Seluruh Indonesia* (SPSI; All-Indonesia Workers Union) union consisted of just one supervisor, referred to as the union chairman by management but disavowed by regional and national SPSI officials (Worker Rights Consortium 2003). After urging from the WRC, factory management agreed to negotiate with other worker representatives when the current contract expired but as that time approached, and with a group of workers having registered as affiliates of the activist-oriented Gabungan Serikat Buruh Indonesia (GSBI; Joint Trade Unions), management began constructing a company union, which the WRC argued was illegitimate. A meeting of representatives from the WRC, Nike, and PT Kolon Langgeng management ultimately led to a plan whereby factory management would convey its respect for freedom of association and allow an election. The WRC reported that "in the view of the Assessment Team, intervention by Nike and its broker, particularly during

[this] meeting ..., played a central role in achieving this result" (Worker Rights Consortium 2003: 10). The pressure did not come solely from outside, though. According to union activists, an alliance of unions in the export processing zone told management that it would come with an "army of workers" unless they agreed to meet with the GSBI-affiliated organizers (interview with union official, Jakarta, September 26, 2010).

To this point, the case of PT Kolon Langgeng appeared to be a success, and Nike had helped to support freedom of association, much as it had two years earlier at the Kukdong factory in Mexico (Ross 2006). Despite some internal conflict, the GSBI-affiliated union received a majority of worker support and began preparing for collective bargaining negotiations (interview with labor activists, Jakarta, October 1, 2010). Responding to other WRC findings, the factory agreed to reinstate several workers who had been capriciously dismissed. Overall, although the WRC reported a few serious remaining problems, it stated that the factory "has made important progress on several fronts" (Worker Rights Consortium 2003: 35). When the WRC developed its Designated Suppliers Program in 2005, PT Kolon Langgeng was one of a handful of candidates listed.

But, around this time and for reasons that are hard to uncover, the factory lost its direct orders from Nike and several other brands, was reorganized under new ownership, and was renamed PT Kwangduk Langgeng (Worker Rights Consortium 2011). Unions have described this as a bankruptcy that involved a temporary factory closure (interview with union official, Jakarta, September 26, 2010), although the exact nature of this reorganization is unknown. In any case, within a few years, PT Kwangduk was itself failing. In 2009, the company pressured permanent workers to agree to be rehired as contract workers, locked out union members, and sought to blacklist them from other jobs in the export processing zone; by early 2010, the factory had closed (Worker Rights Consortium 2011). The WRC described this as a case in which "a factory, for several years, made good faith efforts to comply with university and buyer codes of conduct, yet experienced a continuing loss of orders from buyers" (Worker Rights Consortium 2011: 5). Another company, PT BTS, reopened the factory with new management and new workers in 2010 – finally fully nullifying any previous gains (interview with former worker, November 2010).

This is certainly not the only case in which the instability of a factory undermined durable change in labor standards. Within Indonesia, similar processes have occurred at PT Dae Joo, which produced for Adidas and VF before its owners shut the factory and shifted production to China, and recently at PT Dong One, where the local union had experienced some success in leveraging Nike's code of conduct until the factory owner fled the country in 2011 (Egels-Zandén and Bartley 2012).

Factory closure spurring anti-sweatshop campaigns: PT Spotec

In other cases, it is factory closings themselves that have spurred international campaigns and debates about brands' responsibilities for severance pay and re-employment. The PT Spotec factory in Tangerang shut down in 2007 after Adidas pulled its orders. The reason for the brand's exit from the factory has been the topic of much debate. According to the brand, the problem was "purely financial," having to do with the factory's ability to pay its bills, but activists have argued that Adidas imposed new costs on the factory and drove down prices to a point that the factory could not survive (interviews with brand representative, July 10, 2008; NGO activists June 29, July 8, 2008). The factory was purchased by Ching Luh, a Taiwan-based transnational corporation perceived by activists as strongly anti-union (interview with NGO activist, Jakarta, July 7, 2008), and it reopened to produce, once again, for Adidas. Oxfam led an international campaign pressuring Adidas to help ex-Spotec workers get jobs in the new factory. Amid complaints that Adidas was dragging its heels on this and factory management was imposing unreasonable barriers to hiring, around 900 of the roughly 4,500 ex-Spotec workers gained employment in the new factory, but the majority were effectively abandoned (interview with NGO activist, Jakarta, July 7, 2008). Nike was the target of similar calls for re-employment or severance pay after the closures of the PT Hasa/PT Nasi, PT Doson, and PT Dong One factories. These stories are by no means unique to Indonesia; similar processes have occurred in factories in Thailand, the Dominican Republic, El Salvador, and Honduras (see, e.g., Armbruster-Sandoval 2005).

These factory closures have spurred new debates about the extent and limits of brands' responsibilities for their supplier's obligations. To be sure, most companies have strongly resisted any implication of financial or legal responsibility for code of conduct or human rights violations in their supply chains (Shamir 2004; Bartley 2005). Yet some firms have faced intense pressure to compensate workers for legally required severance pay when factory owners flee or go bankrupt, and, in a few cases, firms have agreed to do so to some degree. In 2010, Nike agreed to contribute $1.5 million to a fund for workers displaced by two suppliers' plant closings in Honduras. The next year, Nike did something similar in Indonesia, contributing nearly $1.2 million toward severance payments for displaced workers from PT Dong One and PT Kizone. Adidas, which also used the factories, initially refused to provide monetary compensation, proposing an insurance fund to cover severance payments and supermarket vouchers as substitutes (United Students against Sweatshops 2012). Under further pressure, Adidas later agreed to contribute some compensation, but another buyer, Silver Star Merchandising (affiliated with the Dallas Cowboys football team) has refused any contribution. This is evolving and highly contested terrain, which pushes the limits of firms' CSR commitments. But moves toward tighter links between CSR commitments and job stability are clearly at the margins: as our findings show, in practice, most CSR efforts bracket the stability of jobs and industries in spite of (or perhaps because of) the fact that markets in which CSR initiatives are common among brands are also markets that are highly volatile for production firms and workers.

Conclusion: CSR and (im)patient capital

A close look at practices "on the ground" is necessary to appreciate the significance and limits of the CSR model. This should not simply mean invoking "decoupling" to explain away divergences from the global CSR discourse. Instead, it is worth considering whether some of the same processes that give rise to CSR make meaningful implementation of CSR highly unlikely. In the apparel and footwear industries, the rise of CSR has occurred in the midst of production dynamics that frustrate the very sorts of improvement and "capacity building" that CSR advocates claim to foster. Industry mobility and instability pose serious challenges for the achievement of decent work. But CSR commitments have largely bracketed these issues, and "responsible" brands and retailers have ignored (or undermined) the social conditions that might allow their codes of conduct to be meaningful. Niches and firms with codes of conduct are no more stable – and sometimes less so – than those that fall outside the reach of CSR. To be sure, there are a few nascent countertrends, such as some brands' interest in forging more collaborative relationships with key suppliers (Gereffi et al. 2005; Sabel 2007; Locke et al. 2009) and the expansion of the ILO-IFC "Better Work" programs, which seek to couple compliance and competitiveness, to more countries (Indonesia, Nicaragua, Vietnam, and others). But unless they deal with the industry's underlying tendency toward cutthroat competition and high mobility, these projects will remain limited.

Theoretically, scholars should acknowledge and grapple with the fact that CSR commitments coexist with a variety of countervailing pressures that may undermine improvements. In the case of labor conditions in consumer products industries, the rise of CSR has happened along with a race to countries that severely restrict labor rights (especially China and Vietnam, where independent unions are banned), attraction to destinations with low wages and lax safety standards (e.g., Bangladesh and Pakistan), and a high degree of volatility in orders from places where labor standards seemed to be improving (to some degree, Indonesia and some parts of Central America and the Caribbean). The rise of CSR has also occurred along with the persistence of intense competitive pressures on suppliers (meaning demand for low prices and quick delivery times) and political projects to liberalize/flexibilize labor markets in developing countries, which can hinder labor organization. Even when brands and retailers monitor their suppliers' factories and push for improved conditions, their desire for factories able and willing to meet short deadlines at low costs nullifies actual and potential improvements. Such contradictory tendencies are not unique to the study of CSR. In studies of global governance, some scholars have begun to take account of the countervailing (and often contradictory) forces emanating from the diffusion of cultural scripts and projects of NGOs on one hand and the dynamics of trade and investment on the other (Jorgenson, Dick, and Shandra 2011; Shorette 2012) but far more theoretical and empirical attention to this is needed.

Practically, a different approach to CSR might produce more meaningful results. Instead of equating corporate responsibility with "fairness," "sustainability," or especially "risk management," activists and firms could make responsible capitalism synonymous with stable, patient capitalism. Scholars of comparative political economy have used the concept of "patient capital" to explain why some sectors and countries have been more fertile ground for the development of working class political power and "high road" industries (see, e.g., Thelen 2004). Whereas discussions of patient capital in this literature primarily refer to firms' access to finance (Hall and Soskice 2001), an application of this concept to global commodity chains requires that it refer to patience not only in investment but in orders. "Patient sourcing" could be more productive than "ethical sourcing" as currently practiced. It takes time and collective struggle to improve working conditions, yet current production logics value speed, flexibility, and mobility. Of course, patience on its own is not sufficient. A model of patient sourcing would need to involve commitments to sociopolitical contexts where meaningful collective action is possible, to stabilizing orders with well-performing suppliers in these settings, and to bearing temporary upswings in cost in order to reap future rewards in productivity or price premiums. The current view of CSR as risk management for brands does almost the opposite. One compliance specialist for a brand with an active CSR program described union activism in some countries as "another risk for us, since protest and strikes will affect production" (interview with brand representative, Hong Kong, December 2010). In this model, brands have an incentive to avoid the very sites where significant improvements are possible, and, given their ability to quickly move production to other suppliers, they often have the capacity to avoid disruptive sites as well. The emphasis within the world of CSR of "minimizing risk" may be its most vexing contradiction. If one wants to take CSR seriously, then concerned consumers, investors, and other stakeholders should be pressuring and rewarding firms to prefer national and local settings where collective gains are politically possible and to be patient as those struggles occur. Of course, companies are unlikely to prefer a model of CSR that reduces their autonomy and flexibility. But nascent trends toward more "relational" supply chains and investments in national structures of compliance may provide openings for this kind of rethinking of CSR. Furthermore, it is concerted pressure by activists and NGOs – and their occasional ability to institutionalize new forms of scrutiny and new conceptions of ethical behavior – that has forced companies to at least discursively accept new obligations, and it is to this kind of pressure and field-building that we should look if we want CSR to become more meaningful.

References

AKATIGA Center for Social Analysis. 2007. "ATC Phase-Out and Indonesian Textile and Clothing Industry: Where Do We Stand?" AKATIGA – Center for Social Analysis, Bandung and Friedrich Ebert Stiftung, Jakarta.

Armbruster-Sandoval, Ralph. 2005. *Globalization and Cross-Border Labor Solidarity in the Americas: The Anti-Sweatshop Movement and the Struggle for Social Justice*. New York: Routledge.

Baccaro, Lucio, and Chris Howell. 2011. "A Common Neoliberal Trajectory: The Transformation of Industrial Relations in Advanced Capitalism." *Politics & Society* 39(4):521–563.

Bair, Jennifer, and Gary Gereffi. 2001. "Local Clusters in Global Chains: The Causes and Consequences of Export Dynamism in Torreon's Blue Jeans Industry." *World Development* 29(11):1885–1903.

Bair, Jennifer, and Matthew C. Mahutga. 2012. "Varieties of Offshoring? Spatial Fragmentation and the Organization of Production in Twenty-First Century Capitalism." Pp. 270–298 in *Capitalisms and Capitalism in the Twenty-First Century*, edited by G. Morgan and R. Whitley. Oxford: Oxford University Press.

Barrientos, Stephanie, and S. Smith. 2006. "Ethical Trading Initiative Impact Assessment Report." London: Ethical Trading Initiative. Retrieved from http://www.ethicaltrade.org/resources/key-eti-resources/eti-impact-assessment-report-summary.

Barrientos, Stephanie, and Sally Smith. 2007. "Do Workers Benefit from Ethical Trade? Assessing Codes of Labour Practice in Global Production Systems." *Third World Quarterly* 28(4):713–729.

Bartley, Tim. 2005. "Corporate Accountability and the Privatization of Labor Standards: Struggles over Codes of Conduct in the Apparel Industry." *Research in Political Sociology* 12:211–244.

Bartley, Tim. 2007. "Institutional Emergence in an Era of Globalization: The Rise of Transnational Private Regulation of Labor and Environmental Conditions." *American Journal of Sociology* 113(2):297–351.

Bartley, Tim, and Lu Zhang. Forthcoming. "China and Global Labor Standards: Making Sense of Factory Certification." In *The Dragon's Learning Curve: Global Governance and China*, edited by S. Kennedy. New York: Routledge.

Bernard, Andrew, and J. Bradford Jensen. 1997. "Exporters, Skill-upgrading, and the Wage Gap." *Journal of International Economics* 42(1–2):3–31.

Bonacich, Edna, and Richard P. Appelbaum. 2000. *Behind the Label: Inequality in the Los Angeles Apparel Industry*. Berkeley: University of California Press.

Bronfenbrenner, Kate. 2000. "Uneasy Terrain: The Impact of Capital Mobility on Workers, Wages, and Union Organizing." Submitted to the U.S. Trade Deficit Review Commission. Retrieved from http://digitalcommons.ilr.cornell.edu/reports/3/.

Brown, Garrett D. 2003. "China's Factory Floors: An Industrial Hygienist's View." *International Journal of Occupational and Environmental Health* 9(4):326–339.

Brusentsev, Vera, David Newhouse, and Wayne Vroman. 2012. *Severance Pay Compliance in Indonesia*. World Bank Policy Research Working Paper 5933.

Caraway, T. L. 2006. "Freedom of Association: Battering Ram or Trojan Horse?" *Review of International Political Economy* 13(2):210–232.

Caraway, Teri L. 2004. "Protective Repression, International Pressure, and Institutional Design: Explaining Labor Reform in Indonesia." *Studies in Comparative International Development* 39(3):28–49.

Center for International Private Enterprise and Social Accountability International. 2009. "From Words to Action: A Business Case for Implementing Workplace Standards." Retrieved from http://www.cipe.org/publications/papers/pdf/SAI.pdf.

Chan, Anita, and Robert J. S. Ross. 2003. "Racing to the Bottom: International Trade without a Social Clause." *Third World Quarterly* 24:1011–1028.

China Labor Watch. 2009. "Corrupt Audits Damage Worker Rights: A Case Analysis of Corruption in Bureau Veritas Factory Audits." Retrieved from www.chinalaborwatch.org.

Cowie, Jefferson. 1999. *Capital Moves: RCA's Seventy-Year Quest for Cheap Labor*. New York: The New Press.

Dicken, Peter, and Markus Hassler. 2000. "Organizing the Indonesian Clothing Industry in the Global Economy: The Role of Business Networks." *Environment and Planning A* 32:263–280.

Djelic, Marie-Laure, and Kerstin Sahlin-Andersson. 2006. "Introduction: A World of Governance: The Rise of Transnational Regulation." Pp. 1–28 in *Transnational Governance: Institutional Dynamics of Regulation*, edited by M. -L. Djelic and K. Sahlin-Andersson. New York: Cambridge University Press.

Egels-Zanden, Niklas. 2007. "Suppliers' Compliance with MNCs' Codes of Conduct: Behind the Scenes at Chinese Toy Suppliers." *Journal of Business Ethics* 74: 45–62.

Egels-Zandén, Niklas, and Tim Bartley. 2012. *Local Challenges to Global Production Networks: "Going to the Brands in the Indonesian Apparel Industry*. Working paper presented at the annual conference of the Society for the Advancement of Socio-Economics, June 2012.

Esbenshade, J. 2004. *Monitoring Sweatshops: Workers, Consumers, and the Global Apparel Industry*. Philadelphia: Temple University Press.

Ethical Trading Initiative. 1998. "Base Code of Conduct." London: Ethical Trading Initiative. Retrieved from http://www1.umn.edu/humanrts/lin ks/eticode.html.

Ethical Trading Initiative. 2006. "Getting Smarter at Auditing: Tackling the Growing Crisis in Ethical Trade Auditing." London: Ethical Trading Initiative. Retrieved from www.eti2.org.uk/Z/lib/2006/11/smart-audit/ eti-smarter-auditing-2006.pdf.

Evans, Peter. 1997. "The Eclipse of the State? Reflections on Stateness in an Era of Globalization." *World Politics* 50:62–87.

Fairtrade International. 2011. "Generic Fairtrade Trade Standard." *version* 01.05.2011.

Ford, Michele. 2009. *Workers and Intellectuals: NGOs, Trade Unions and the Indonesian Labour Movement*. Honolulu: University of Hawaii Press.

Frank, T. A. 2008. "Confessions of a Sweatshop Inspector." *Washington Monthly* April: 34.

Frankel, Jeffrey A. 1992. "Measuring International Capital Mobility: A Review." *The American Economic Review* 82(2):197–202.

Fransen, Luc. 2011. "Why Do Private Governance Organizations Not Converge? A Political–Institutional Analysis of Transnational Labor Standards Regulation." *Governance* 24(2):359–387.

Frenkel, Stephen J., and Seongsu Kim. 2004. "Corporate Codes of Labour Practice and Employment Relations in Sports Shoe Contractor Factories in South Korea." *Asia Pacific Journal of Human Resources* 42(1):6–31.

Frenkel, Stephen J., and Duncan Scott. 2002. "Compliance, Collaboration, and Codes of Labor Practice: The Adidas Connection." *California Management Review* 45(1):29–49.

Gallagher, Mary Elizabeth. 2005. *Contagious Capitalism: Globalization and the Politics of Labor in China.* Princeton, NJ: Princeton University Press.

Garrett, Geoffrey. 1995. "Capital Mobility, Trade, and the Domestic Politics of Economic Policy." *International Organization* 49(4):657–687.

Gereffi, Gary. 2005. "The Global Economy: Organization, Governance, and Development." Pp. 160–182 in *The Handbook of Economic Sociology*, edited by N. J. Smelser and R. Swedberg. Princeton, NJ: Princeton University Press.

Gereffi, Gary, Ronie Garcia-Johnson, and Erika Sasser. 2001. "The NGO-Industrial Complex." *Foreign Policy* July/August:56–65.

Gereffi, Gary, John Humphrey, and Timothy Sturgeon. 2005. "The Governance of Global Value Chains." *Review of International Political Economy* 12(1):78–104.

Greenhill, Brian, Layna Mosley, and Aseem Prakash. 2009. "Trade-based Diffusion of Labor Rights: A Panel Study." *American Political Science Review* 103(4):169–190.

Guthrie, Doug. 2002. "The Transformation of Labor Relations in China's Emerging Market Economy." *Research in Social Stratification and Mobility* 19:139–170.

Hall, Peter A., and David Soskice. 2001. "An Introduction to Varieties of Capitalism." Pp. 1–68 in *Varieties of Capitalism: The Institutional Foundations of Comparative Advantage*, edited by P. A. Hall and D. Soskice. New York: Oxford University Press.

Hallett, Tim. 2010. "The Myth Incarnate: Recoupling Processes, Turmoil, and Inhabited Institutions in an Urban Elementary School." *American Sociological Review* 75(1):52–74.

Halliday, Terence C., and Bruce G. Carruthers. 2009. *Bankrupt: Global Lawmaking and Systemic Financial Crisis.* Stanford, CA: Stanford University Press.

Harrison, Ann, and Jason Scorse. 2010. "Multinationals and Anti-Sweatshop Activism." *American Economic Review* 100(1):247–273.

Hill, Hal. 2000. "Export Success against the Odds: A Vietnamese Case Study." *World Development* 28(2):283–300.

Jorgenson, Andrew K., Christopher Dick, and John M. Shandra. 2011. "World Economy, World Society, and Environmental Harms in Less-Developed Countries." *Sociological Inquiry* 81(1):53–87.

Juliawan, Benny Hari. 2011. "Street-level Politics: Labour Protests in Post-authoritarian Indonesia." *Journal of Contemporary Asia* 41(3):349–370.

Kim, Jee Young. 2010. *Villains, Dummies, and Victims? The Role of Local Actors in Transnational Private Labor Regulation in Vietnam.* Paper

presented at the 22nd Annual Meeting of the Society for the Advancement of Socio-Economics, Philadelphia.
Lim, Alwyn, and Kiyoteru Tsutsui. 2012. "Globalization and Commitment in Corporate Social Responsibility." *American Sociological Review* 77(1):69–98.
Locke, Richard, Matthew Amengual, and Akshay Mangla. 2009. "Virtue out of Necessity?: Compliance, Commitment and the Improvement of Labor Conditions in Global Supply Chains." *Politics & Society* 37(3):319–351.
Locke, Richard, Fei Qin, and Alberto Brause. 2007. "Does Monitoring Improve Labor Standards? Lessons from Nike." *Industrial & Labor Relations Review* 61(1):3–31.
Malets, Olga. 2011. *From Transnational Voluntary Standards to Local Practices: A Case Study of Forest Certification in Russia*. Max-Planck-Institut für Gesellschaftsforschung, MPIfG Discussion Paper 11/7.
Mamic, Ivanka. 2004. *Implementing Codes of Conduct: How Businesses Manage Social Performance in Global Supply Chains*. Sheffield, UK: Greenleaf.
Manning, Chris, and Kurnya Roesad. 2007. "The Manpower Law of 2003 and Its Implementing Regulations: Genesis, Key Articles and Potential Impact." *Bulletin of Indonesian Economic Studies* 43(1):59–86.
Mosley, Layna, and Saika Uno. 2007. "Racing to the Bottom or Climbing to the Top?" *Comparative Political Studies* 40(8):923–948.
Nike. 2010. "Code Leadership Standard." Retrieved from http://www.nikeresponsibility.com/report/uploads/files/COC_CLS_-_Regular_Employment.pdf.
Oka, Chikako. 2012. *Does Better Labour Standard Compliance Pay? Linking Labour Standard Compliance and Supplier Competitiveness*. Better Work Discussion Paper Series: No. 5. Geneva: International Labor Organization.
O'Rourke, Dara. 2003. "Outsourcing Regulation: Analyzing Non-Governmental Systems of Labor Standards and Monitoring." *Policy Studies Journal* 31:1–29.
O'Rourke, Dara. 2005. "Market Movements: Nongovernmental Organization Strategies to Influence Global Production and Consumption." *Journal of Industrial Ecology* 9:115–128.
Polaski, Sandra. 2006. "Combining Global and Local Forces: The Case of Labor Rights in Cambodia." *World Development* 34(5):919–932.
Porter, Michael E., and Mark R. Kramer. 2006. "Strategy and Society: The Link Between Competitive Advantage and Corporate Social Responsibility." *Harvard Business Review* December 2006:1–13.

Prakash, Aseem, and Matthew Potoski. 2006a. "Racing to the Bottom? Trade, Environmental Governance, and ISO 14001." *American Journal of Political Science* 50(2):350–364.

Prakash, Aseem, and Matthew Potoski. 2006b. *The Voluntary Environmentalists: Green Clubs, ISO 140001, and Voluntary Environmental Regulations.* New York: Cambridge University Press.

Pun, Ngai. 2005. "Global Production, Company Codes of Conduct, and Labor Conditions in China: A Case Study of Two Factories." *The China Journal* 54:101–113.

Robison, Richard, and Vedi R. Hadiz. 2006. "Indonesia: Crisis, Oligarchy, and Reform." Pp. 109–136 in *The Political Economy of South-East Asia: Markets, Power, and Contestation*, edited by G. Rodan, K. Hewison, and R. Robison. Oxford: Oxford University Press.

Rodríguez-Garavito, César A. 2005. "Global Governance and Labor Rights: Codes of Conduct and Anti-Sweatshop Struggles in Global Apparel Factories in Mexico and Guatemala." *Politics and Society* 33(2):203–233.

Ross, Robert J. S. 2006. "A Tale of Two Factories: Successful Resistance to Sweatshops and the Limits of Firefighting." *Labor Studies Journal* 30(4):65–85.

Sabel, Charles. 2007. "Rolling Rule Labor Standards: Why Their Time Has Come, and Why We Should Be Glad of It." Pp. 257–273 in *Protecting Labour Rights as Human Rights: Present and Future of International Supervision (conference proceedings)*, edited by G. P. Politakis. Geneva: ILO.

Schrank, Andrew. 2004. "Ready-to-Wear Development? Foreign Investment, Technology Transfer, and Learning by Watching in the Apparel Trade." *Social Forces* 83(1):123–156.

Seidman, Gay. 2007. *Beyond the Boycott: Labor Rights, Human Rights and Transnational Activism.* New York: Sage/ASA Rose Series.

Shamir, Ronen. 2004. "Between Self-Regulation and the Alien Tort Claims Act: On the Contested Concept of Corporate Social Responsibility." *Law & Society Review* 38(4):635–664.

Shorette, Kristen. 2012. "Outcomes of Global Environmentalism: Longitudinal and Cross-National Trends in Chemical Fertilizer and Pesticide Use." *Social Forces* 91(1):299–325.

Social Accountability International. 2008. "Social Accountability 8000 Standard, SA8000:2008." New York: Social Accountability International. Retrieved from http://www.sa-intl.org/index.cfm?fuseaction=Page.ViewPage&PageID=937

Spar, Debra L., and Lane T. LaMure. 2003. "The Power of Activism: Assessing the Impact of NGOs on Global Business." *California Management Review* 45(3):78–101.

Sum, Ngai-Ling, and Ngai Pun. 2005. "Globalization and Paradoxes of Ethical Transnational Production: Code of Conduct in a Chinese Workplace." *Competition and Change* 9(2):181–200.

Thee, Kian Wie. 2009. "The Development of Labour-intensive Garment Manufacturing in Indonesia." *Journal of Contemporary Asia* 39(4):562–578.

Thelen, Kathleen. 2004. *How Institutions Evolve: The Political Economy of Skills in Germany, Britain, the United States, and Japan.* New York: Cambridge University Press.

Tjandraningsih, Indrasari, and Hari Nugroho. 2008. "The Flexibility Regime and Organised Labour in Indonesia." *Labour and Management in Development* 9:1–14.

United Students against Sweatshops. 2012. "On Eve of Alpine Summit, PT Kizone and Hermosa Workers Lambast Adidas' Efforts to Shirk Responsibility." Retrieved from http://usas.org/2012/10/22/on-eve-of-alpine-summit-pt-kizone-and-hermosa-workers-lambast-adidas%E2%80%99-efforts-to-shirk-responsibility/.

Wetterberg, Anna. 2011. "Public–Private Partnership in Labor Standards Governance: Better Factories Cambodia." *Public Administration and Development* 31(1):64–73.

Winters, Jeffrey A. 1996. *Power in Motion: Capital Mobility and the Indonesian State* Ithaca, NY: Cornell University Press.

Worker Rights Consortium. 2003. *Assessment re Pt Kolon Langgeng (Indonesia).* Washington, DC: Worker Rights Consortium.

Worker Rights Consortium. 2011. Factory Update: Kwangduk Langgeng (Indonesia) (formerly, Kolon Langgeng). Washington, DC: WRC, March 9, 2011.

World Bank. 2010. *Indonesia Jobs Report: Towards Better Jobs and Security for All.* Washington, DC: World Bank.

13 | Good firms, good targets: the relationship among corporate social responsibility, reputation, and activist targeting

BRAYDEN G KING AND MARY-HUNTER MCDONNELL

Much research on social movements and organizations contends that there is an empirical link between activists' contentious activity and corporate social responsibility (CSR; e.g., Bartley 2007; Campbell 2007; Soule 2009). Typically, we assume that activists influence firms' CSR practices directly. Activists target corporations in order to pursue their social change agendas, hoping to influence those companies to change their policies or practices (King and Pearce 2010). Targeting corporations gives activists a way to directly address their grievances and influence a firm to amend an undesirable practice (King and Soule 2007; Walker, Martin, and McCarthy 2008; Lenox and Eesley 2009). For example, if a retail firm regularly sources its products from manufacturers that employ sweatshop labor, activists may raise concerns about this inflammatory practice by protesting the firm or boycotting it. Getting in the activists' spotlight puts public pressure on firms to change their practices, especially inasmuch as movement tactics draw unwanted negative attention from the media that could influence the public's perceptions about a firm's level of social responsibility (King 2008, 2011; Bartley and Child 2011).

Another way that activists shape CSR is by encouraging corporations to engage in prosocial actions as protective measures against potential activist campaigns. Fearing that they will become protest, lawsuit, or boycott targets, firms seek to build their reputation as

We would like to thank John McCarthy, Kiyoteru Tsutsui, Alwyn Lim, and participants in the Global CSR conference for providing feedback to an earlier version of this manuscript.

"virtuous" firms with the belief that activists will go after the most grievous violators of social and ethical norms. Proactive social responsibility is thought to deter activists from opportunistically launching campaigns against a company (Maxwell, Lyon, and Hackett 2000; Baron and Diermeier 2007; Godfrey, Merrill, and Hansen 2009). Used in this way, CSR practices and prosocial claims are both reputation-building activities and deterrents of future activism.

Although we have a growing body of evidence indicating that direct pressure from social movements influences firms to adopt prosocial practices, we have less evidence that firms are successful in using CSR to deter future activism. The relationship between past CSR, a firm's reputation, and future activist targeting is unclear. In fact, despite strong arguments made to the contrary, there are good reasons to think that "doing well by doing good" and creating a positive firm reputation may actually attract unwanted activist attention. If activists see their goal as not only to coerce firms into dropping bad policies and practices but also to increase general awareness about a social issue, then activists have incentives to go after firms that will maximize the likelihood of garnering attention and outrage. High-status firms with identities grounded in prosocial behavior should attract more attention for perceived normative violations than firms that are not seen in an equally positive light. For this reason, activists may be *more* likely, not less, to target firms that have committed themselves to CSR and have built a positive reputation.

The purpose of this chapter is to assess these two competing arguments about why firms are chosen as targets. Assuming that activists' grievances against firms are widespread, why do activists target some firms over others? To what extent does a firm's reputation and past prosocial claims affect the likelihood of its being targeted? On the one hand, making prosocial claims and building a positive reputation may deter activists from taking actions because it creates goodwill for the firm. On the other hand, a firm's past prosocial claims and positive reputation may attract activists who seek a high-profile target to generate attention for their issue in the public limelight.

Using data on corporate boycotts, we find empirical evidence that firms' past prosocial claims and a positive reputation increase the likelihood of a firm being targeted. This evidence suggests that, for all of their positive benefits, attempts to enhance CSR and reputation may have an unintentional negative side effect: they amplify a firm's attractiveness as an activist target. We discuss the implications of this finding for the literature on social responsibility and social movement activism.

Two competing views of corporate social responsibility and reputation

In their worst moments, the corporate drive to maximize wealth causes firms to take actions that harm the environment, abuse their workers, and sell products that are dangerous for consumers. Outraged by this corporate insolence, activists publicly "name and shame" the offenders. In recent years, corporations have proved vulnerable to activist influence, succumbing to their demands when threatened by lawsuits, protests, or boycotts (Hendry 2006; King 2008; Lennox and Eesley 2009; Reid and Toffel 2009). Corporations have proved to be highly sensitive to activists' demands, perhaps even more open to policy innovation than are elected representatives of the state. As Chatterji and Listokin observed, "A generation of activists has been raised on the idea of corporate social responsibility (CSR) – that large corporations can be cajoled into paying employees better, being more environmentally responsible, improving labor conditions in developing countries, retaining more American workers, embracing diversity, and donating money to fix inner-city schools. Where firms cannot be enticed, the strategy goes, they can be bullied" (2007: 53).

By pressuring companies to alter their practices, activists have changed corporations' outward attitude toward CSR (Soule 2009). The fear of being targeted by activists appears to be an even more direct cause of the adoption of CSR than is financial performance. Although the research seeking to find an empirical link between CSR and financial performance is voluminous, there is very little evidence that "doing good" really does improve a firm's profitability or market value. In a meta-analysis of 127 such studies, Margolis and Walsh (2003) concluded that the relationship is tenuous at best and is likely limited to very specific conditions. Marquis, Glynn, and Davis (2007) suggest that social dynamics, such as community-level normative pressures, are more likely instigators of corporate social actions (for more evidence about community pressures to adopt CSR practices see Galaskiewicz 1991, 1997).

Corporations do not seem to adopt prosocial practices because they are good for the bottom line, at least not in the short term, but rather because they are good for the firm's relationships with other actors in their community or because they appeal to global norms or institutional pressures (Lim and Tsutsui 2012). Understanding this rationale, activists do their best to frustrate the lives of corporations that do not live up to ethical or social standards. Firms accommodate activists because they wish to avoid becoming future targets. They seek to develop reputations as socially and morally appropriate actors by engaging in prosocial actions and thereby deter future activist targeting.

The prevalence of CSR practices has, in part, increased with the rise of corporate reputation rankings as quantified measures of corporate quality and prestige (Fombrun 2007) and the simultaneous spread of CSR frameworks that attempt to hold multinational corporations accountable to emerging standards of conduct (Meyer, Pope, and Isaacson, this volume). As reputational dynamics have come to be seen as more integral to corporate strategy, firms have sought increasingly sophisticated ways to differentiate themselves from their peers. Building a reputation is about being able to distinguish one's position in the global corporate field by excelling according to ever-higher social and economic performance standards (Haufler, this volume). As activist groups have built a complex framework of CSR standards and norms that prescribe certain practices and policies, thereby defining what it means to be "good," firms increasingly seek to build their reputations not only through product quality but also by affiliating themselves with these prestige-enhancing CSR practices. In this light, CSR practices are a tool of impression management that firms use to build positive reputations and gain the support of stakeholders, including activists.

But does "doing good" and reputation-building help firms avoid becoming activist targets? Two competing views exist. Certainly, many managers believe that by building a positive overall reputation and engaging in prosocial activities they are buffering themselves from the threat of future activist targeting. Many reputation scholars similarly believe that a positive reputation will protect a firm from stakeholder criticisms. We refer to this view as the *reputational halo effect*. But an alternative perspective suggests that activists are more likely to target firms that distinguish themselves through prosocial actions and that have created a positive reputation. Firms in this position garner more attention, making them salient targets for activists who crave the public limelight (and need it for their success). We refer to this view as the *reputational liability effect*. We discuss each perspective herein.

The reputational halo effect

In 1996, the anti-sweatshop movement coalesced as various human rights groups and labor organizations, such as the National Labor Committee, began organizing activists to draw media attention to manufacturers that employed sweatshop laborers. The movement gained momentum when it was revealed that Kathie Lee Gifford's clothing brand was made by teenage girls in Honduras who worked 16-hour days. Quickly, the issue of sweatshop labor made it into the national spotlight (Bullert 2000; Bernstein 2004; Soule 2009). A 1989 survey conducted by Asian American Free Labor Institute discovered that factory employees in Indonesia were paid, on average, 14 cents per hour (Bullert 2000). Nike was a glaring contributor to the low wage problem by keeping its employees at training-level wages for months. Despite employee strikes, the wages did not improve throughout the early 1990s.

Activists went looking for a vulnerable target, and Nike was on the top of their list. Rather than target a number of retailers that used sweatshops – any number of manufacturers, including Nike's competitor Reebok, could have just as easily have been targeted – the human rights group Global Exchange decided to focus its efforts squarely on Nike. Nike had done little to build relationships with activists; in fact, their CEO Phil Knight had actively derided critics of the firm who suggested that Nike ought to be more concerned with its image as a world citizen. When asked by Michael Moore if it bothered him that 14-year-olds worked in Indonesian factories with sweatshop conditions, Knight decisively answered "no."[1] The incident reinforced the larger reputational problem that Nike had in the 1990s, making them an attractive target for anti-sweatshop activists.

The media campaign alerted activists across the globe of the inhumane conditions of Nike's factories, initiating a series of protests of Nike stores and boycotts of their products. Student protestors began demanding that their universities end their business relationships with Nike. The protests and boycotts created a storm of negative media

---

[1] The interview can be heard on Moore's website at http://www.dogeatdogfilms.com/mikenike.html

attention. Although Nike's CEO defended the company throughout most of the 1990s, by the 2000s, Knight succumbed to pressure and began instituting employment practices that would raise the minimum age of employees, increase employees' wages, and improve working conditions.

In addition to taking care to eliminate concerns about sweatshop employment, Nike changed its antagonistic relationship with activists and has sought to build a more prosocial image. The company now proudly touts its commitment to environmental responsibility, implementing environment-friendly policies that caused the Dow Jones Sustainability Index to include the firm (Beder 2002). Conscious of the value of its reputation, Nike has poured money into marketing and branding, seeking to make consumers forget that they were the company that was, in Phil Knight's words, "synonymous with slave wages, forced overtime and arbitrary abuse" (Beder 2002: 27).

Nike's reputation-building strategy is not unlike many other firms that seek to avoid being targeted by activists. Movement protests and boycotts inflict reputational damage on firms, which increases the costs of doing business and hurts market value (King and Soule 2007; King 2008b, 2011; Bartley and Child 2011). Recognizing that failing to abide by moral and ethical standards puts their reputation at risk motivates firms to take preemptive action and engage in more prosocial behavior.

Some have argued that taking preemptive action by instituting socially responsible practices makes firms less attractive targets (Klein and Harford 2004). Inasmuch as firms are willing to publicly make prosocial commitments, they signal that they are doing the right things and living up to environmental and social standards. Activists therefore have more trust in them and will be less critical of them in the future. Furthermore, because these organizations have demonstrated a commitment to abiding by norms of social responsibility, activists are more likely to work directly with them rather than publicly antagonize them if they have a problem with a firm policy or practice. Companies that engage in more philanthropic behavior, for example, tend to have closer relationships with nonprofit organizations (Galaskiewicz 1997). As companies do more prosocial activities, they enhance their credibility with actors in the nonprofit world and create alliance relationships, rather than conflicting relationships, with activist groups (Bansal and Roth 2000).

The idea that "doing good" enhances firms' relationships with activist groups is consistent with scholarship that argues that CSR practices have "insurance-like" properties (Godfrey, Merrill, and Hansen 2009). "CSR activities create a form of goodwill or moral capital for the firm that acts as 'insurance-like' protection" from attacks or negative assessments following crisis situations (Godfrey et al. 2009: 426; see also Gardberg and Fombrun 2006). Having "purchased" this insurance by adopting CSR practices in the past, firms will be given more benefit of the doubt by activist groups in the future. One implication of the insurance effect may be that activists are simply less likely to notice grievous behavior by companies that engage in CSR. Because they see those companies as more trustworthy and credible, they monitor them less frequently and therefore are less likely to uncover reasons to target them with future boycotts. Activist groups may also be more likely to forgive these firms should bad practices be discovered. Or, more likely, rather than publicly humiliate them, activist groups will approach them privately and seek to work out potential issues before they escalate and move to a public stage. Companies that are not actively engaged in CSR, in contrast, do not have those relationships of trust and have not built up the moral capital needed to avoid public shaming.

Similarly, companies that have created positive reputations, more generally, should benefit from a "halo effect" that buffers them from criticism and unwanted negative attention (Fombrun and Shanley 1990; Roberts and Dowling 2002; Sine, Shane, and Di Gregorio 2003). The more admired a company is, the more likely it is to be viewed favorably by all of its stakeholders. The effect of being a prestigious firm may be especially strong when its reputation is quantified as a ranking, such as *Fortune*'s reputation index. Rankings inform stakeholders about the quality and value of a company, thereby positively biasing evaluations of a company's behavior (Espeland and Sauder 2007; Sauder 2008). Thus, being highly ranked in a reputation index should discourage a firm from being investigated and having negative attention focused on it.

Based on this argument, we should expect the following:

Hypothesis 1 (H1): Firms that engage in more prosocial activities are less likely to be activist targets than are firms that do not engage in prosocial activities.

Hypothesis 2 (H2): Firms that are ranked highly in a reputation index are less likely to be activist targets than are firms that have weaker overall reputations.

The reputational liability effect

Seen from the perspective of activists, however, reputation-building through CSR practices may have the opposite effect. If one motivation of activists is to use tactics that will generate public attention for their cause, then they should target firms that maximize their visibility (Bartley and Child 2014). Furthermore, firms that have made commitments to CSR and have developed positive reputations should be associated with greater expectations to abide by social norms, which, when violated, may lead to greater outrage and sanctioning (Rhee and Haunschild 2006). Inasmuch as CSR and reputation-building have become critical tools that corporations use to build consumer and stakeholder support, activists may use a firm's reputation or brand against them in their efforts to instigate broader social changes (Klein 1999; Bartley 2007; Seidman 2007; Vogel 2010).

For example, Starbucks Coffee has frequently found itself in the activists' spotlight despite trying to consciously build a reputation for being a socially responsible company (Linn 2001). In 2001, community activists concerned about the increasing corporate presence in their neighborhoods targeted Starbucks specifically despite it being just one of several large companies to set up shop. In that same year, organic food activists called for a boycott of Starbucks even though the company had already agreed to stop using milk that contained an artificial growth hormone. Both protesters and corporate representatives believed that the firm was targeted *because of*, not despite, its CSR practices. As an activist leader in the anti-growth hormone boycott expressed, "We believe that Starbucks is the weakest link in the chain because their customer base cares about the environment and cares about social justice and cares about their health" (Linn 2001). Having committed the company to cultivating a "socially conscious image," Starbucks drew the attention of activists who wanted to draw more attention to their cause and vilify a potentially high-profile corporation. One Starbucks representative noted that being the target of activists was "the price of being so visible" (Linn 2001).

Firms that make prosocial claims and develop positive reputations are more visible and salient to activists. By proclaiming their dedication to prosocial values, they put themselves in a spotlight, drawing the attention of socially conscious consumers and investors. Attracting the attention of the public is, of course, one purpose of this tool of impression management. Firms embrace CSR practices in order to increase their visibility in the field, drawing greater attention to reputation-enhancing characteristics (Udayasankar 2008) and positively differentiating themselves from their competitors (Mackey, Mackey, and Barney 2007). Although this increased visibility may increase customers' and suppliers' commitment to the firm, a negative side effect is that it also exposes the firm to activists' attention. Social movement activists become more critical of a firm's practices when they become aware of its claims to decency and moral excellence.

In a similar way, having a positive overall reputation makes a firm more visible in the public eye (Brammer and Millington 2005). This increased visibility makes activists more likely to focus on an organization's actions and thereby more likely to notice when they do something controversial. This increased visibility also makes the firm a more attractive target because news media and the public will pay more attention to activists' grievances when they make claims about the firm's poor behavior (King 2011). The public expects more from reputable companies and will react more negatively to exposed faults than they would to companies that they are unfamiliar with or that have negative reputations. For example, a company like Starbucks, which is one of the most reputable companies in the United States, must be more careful in monitoring its behavior because any mistakes are magnified due to its high reputation. Activists, who realize that their leverage over firms comes from their ability to mobilize public retaliation via negative media attention (King 2008, 2011; Bartley and Child 2011), may see Starbucks's reputation as a resource they can draw on to generate attention for their cause.

Another reason that reputation-building through CSR activities may make a firm a more vulnerable activist target is because it exposes a firm to potential internal contradictions in behavior that may create stakeholder discontent. A number of scholars have argued that when a firm commits to CSR, it becomes obligated to uphold values and ethics that stakeholders, including employees and activists, view as important (Joyner and Payne 2002; Brammer, Millington, and Rayton 2007).

Firms that take public prosocial orientations foster enhanced expectations among their critical stakeholders, who expect them to live up to their claims. Inevitably, firms that set high standards for their conduct face dilemmas in which they must choose between maximizing profitability and holding their behavior accountable to those standards. When reputable organizations fail to "put their money where their mouth is" by violating their stakeholders' expectations, jilted stakeholders may be especially angered, perceiving such actions as evidence of "organizational hypocrisy" (Holzer 2010) or "organizational sacrilege" (Harrison, Ashforth, and Corley 2009).

Once a firm makes a prosocial claim about its behavior, even if it is only for impression management purposes, activists now have a weapon to use against that firm should it prove to engage in some other harmful behavior. Some proponents of CSR worry that by embracing prosocial practices, firms have unintentionally created unrealistic expectations. Bryan Cress, a global CSR adviser, has said, "CSR has been hijacked by NGOs [nongovernmental organizations], so that businesses are expected to do things they just can't do.... There are limits to what business can do" (*The Guardian* 2003). Firms that engage in more prosocial activities become more vulnerable to activism because they have already publicly committed to many of the goals espoused by the movement.

Therefore, we should expect:

Hypothesis 3 (H3): Firms that engage in more prosocial activities are more likely to be activist targets than are firms that do not engage in prosocial activities.

Hypothesis 4 (H4): Firms that are ranked highly in a reputation index are more likely to be activist targets than are firms that have weaker overall reputations.

Methods

In our analysis, we assess the effects of prosocial activities and reputation on the likelihood of being targeted by an activist boycott. To build our sample of boycotted firms, we collected information on all US boycotts targeting publicly traded companies that were covered by top national newspapers from 1990 to 2005. To limit the potential for regional bias in our sample, we searched for boycotts across five regionally diverse newspapers: the *New York Times, Washington Post, Wall Street Journal, Chicago Tribune,* and *Los Angeles Times*. Research assistants searched Factiva, ProQuest, and Lexis-Nexis databases for all articles in these newspapers that contained the word "boycott" in the article's text. To control for firm characteristics, we only included boycott targets in our final dataset that were publicly traded because of the availability of financial data for these firms. In total, coders identified 133 distinct boycotts waged against 189 target firms. Next, we matched each boycotted company with company-specific financial data from COMPUSTAT. Full financial data were not available for twenty-eight of the targeted firms. Four additional firms were excluded because the companies were acquired in the year of the boycott, reducing the final sample to 157 target firms.

Next, we sought to create a set of matched firms that were also at high risk of being boycotted. Given that prior research has found that a company's size increases its likelihood of being boycotted (King 2008), we created this initial matched set by randomly pairing each boycotted firm with three firms from a sample of the 500 largest publicly traded firms in the year of the boycott (by asset value). This resulted in a total set of 471 matched firms, bringing the total number of firms in our analysis to 628.

To test Hypotheses 1 and 3, we used the online database Factiva to search the two largest press release outlets – PR Newswire and Business Wire – for all prosocial action–related press releases issued by each boycotted and nonboycotted company in the six months prior to the date of the boycott's announcement. Identified claims span a wide array of topics including social justice and diversity initiatives, disaster relief, environmental protection programs, promotion of education, and support of the arts. Our search yielded a total of 548 press releases in which targeted companies made prosocial claims. In the models, we included a count variable capturing the number of each firm's prosocial claims released in public relations (PR) press releases (*CSR PR*) in the six months prior to a boycott event. Because the raw count variable is skewed to the right, we transformed this variable by adding 0.5 (so as not to lose "0" observations) and then took the natural log of the variable.

To assess Hypotheses 2 and 4, we coded each firm's *reputation* using *Fortune's Most Admirable Companies* index. This list is regularly employed in organizational scholarship as a reliable indicator of a company's overall reputation (McGuire, Sundgren, and Schneeweis 1988; Fombrun and Shanley 1990; Staw and Epstein 2000; Roberts and Dowling 2002; King 2008, 2011). *Fortune's* reputation scores, which range from 0 to 10, are derived from surveys capturing the perceptions of the executives of peer firms. The variable used in our initial model represents an ordinal transformation of the raw reputation scores. Past research of organizational reputations suggests that firms are more concerned with their relative reputation than their absolute reputation (e.g., Elsbach and Kramer 1996; Philippe and Durand 2011). Thus, we opted for an ordinal transformation based on each firms' relative position within the *Fortune* rankings. Companies not included in *Fortune's* ranking received a value of 0. A score of 1 was given to companies in the lowest third of *Fortune's* annual index within a given year; companies in the middle tier of the rankings in their year received a value of 2, and the highest value, 3, was allotted to all companies in the top third of the rankings.

As an additional robustness check of this categorical measure, we ran a second model in which we only included firms that were ranked in the *Fortune* rankings (n = 332). The measure of *reputation* in this model is the firm's raw reputation score.

Control variables

We include a number of control variables to account for other reasons that a firm might be targeted. To control for a firm's general level of PR activity, we include variables capturing each firm's (boycotted and nonboycotted) total number of non-prosocial PR releases in the six months prior to (*Other PR Before*) a boycott. To address a skew in this variable, we use its logged transformation in the models after adding 0.5 so as not to lose observations with 0 values. As a proxy for each firm's size, we control for its *logged assets*. We also control for financial performance, using return-on-assets (*roa*) in the year prior to the boycott to capture differences in firms' performance.

We also control for the past social performance of the firms in our sample. It is possible that firms engage in more prosocial behavior and attract more activist attention because they have previously exhibited poor social performance. In this sense, they engage in prosocial actions and become activist targets because they are known for their bad behavior. To capture a firm's prior social performance, we include a measure of social responsibility derived from the KLD Research and Analytics database. The KLD provides annual assessments of firms' strengths and weaknesses across seven separate dimensions – community, environment, diversity, employee relations, corporate governance, product, and human rights. In the model, we include three different binary controls to capture firms' KLD scores. First, *In KLD* is included as a binary variable coded 1 if a firm was covered by the KLD rankings in a given year and 0 otherwise. *KLD Positive* is coded as 1 if the number of a firm's strengths across the seven dimensions exceeded its weaknesses in a given year and 0 otherwise. *KLD Negative* is coded as 1 if the total number of a firm's weaknesses across the seven dimensions exceeded its strengths in a given year. The reference category includes those firms that are not in the KLD index at all and are thus not publicly known as violators of CSR norms.

Because a target firm's industry may affect its general propensity to engage in CSR initiatives (e.g., Delmas and Toffel 2004; Chen and Bouvain 2009), we included a separate fixed effect for each of the four most common industries in our sample (by two-digit SIC code): *Transportation, Petro, Chemicals,* and *Food*.

We also included a binary variable to capture whether the firm was boycotted in the prior year (*firm boycotted in prior year*) because firms that are chronically targeted might behave differently than first-time targets. Controlling for this tendency ensures that we are accounting for those firms that are already in the activist spotlight. And, finally, to account for temporal or seasonal factors that could affect a firm's PR activity, we included fixed effects for the *year* and the *month* in which the boycott was announced. Descriptive statistics for independent and dependent controls are included in Table 13.1.

The dependent variable we employ is a binary variable capturing whether a firm was the target of a *boycott* during the observed time period, 1990–2005. This variable is coded 1 for all boycotted firms and 0 for all of the matched firms in our sample. The data are cross-sectional, rather than longitudinal, so that we can measure the effects of CSR in the time window before the boycott event. To test our hypotheses, we employ a series of probit models. The probit model is a specialized case of generalized linear regression that is appropriate for use with a binary dependent variable. Here, the probit models allow us to measure the association between all independent and control variables and the likelihood of being boycotted.

Table 13.1 *Descriptive statistics and correlation matrix*

Variable	N	Mean	Std. Dev.	Min	Max
1. Reputation	628	1.19	1.28	0	3
2. Logged CSR PR Releases	628	0.093	1.02	−0.69	3.86
3. Logged Other PR	628	2.90	2.00	−4.60	7.17
4. Firm Boycotted in Prior Year	628	0.062	0.24	0	1
5. Industry Boycotts in Prev Year	628	13.62	6.37	3	25
6. ROA	628	0.037	0.047	−0.28	0.40
7. Logged Assets	628	9.58	1.47	2.07	14.04
8. KLD Positive	628	0.15	0.36	0	1
9. KLD Negative	628	0.15	0.35	0	1
10. Firm Included in KLD	628	0.33	0.47	0	1

Table 13.1 (*cont.*)

Variable	1	2	3	4	5	6	7	8	9	10	11
1. Boycott	1.0000										
2. Reputation	0.1713	1.0000									
3. Logged CSR PR	0.3247	0.2195	1.0000								
4. Logged Other PR	0.1350	0.2275	0.3657	1.0000							
5. Firm Boy. Prev Year	0.3500	0.2074	0.1221	0.0542	1.0000						
6. Ind. Boy. Prev Year	0.0034	-0.1014	0.0812	-0.0473	-0.0156	1.0000					
7. ROA	0.1199	0.1071	0.0343	0.0192	0.0486	0.0471	1.0000				
8. Logged Assets	0.0276	0.2447	0.2966	0.2758	0.0522	0.0000	-0.2221	1.0000			
9. KLD Positive	0.0832	0.2218	0.0752	0.1207	0.0344	-0.0879	0.0971	0.0919	1.0000		
10. KLD Negative	-0.0342	0.1895	0.0941	0.0760	-0.0150	-0.1335	-0.0098	0.1361	-0.1694	1.0000	
11. Firm in KLD	0.0209	0.3487	0.1156	0.1450	0.0013	-0.1822	0.0870	0.1689	0.6127	0.6019	1.0000

Results

Results for all models are shown in Table 13.2.

Several interesting relationships emerge among our control variables. We find a significant negative relationship between a firm's size (in terms of logged assets) and its likelihood of being targeted. We argue that this contradictory finding derives primarily from our matching scheme because all of the matched sets of untargeted firms were selected from among the largest US firms. If we had included firms of varying size in the sample, we likely would have found size to have a positive effect (e.g., King 2008). Across both models, we find that the number of times that a firm has been targeted in the past five years is highly positively related to its likelihood of being targeted, suggesting that some firms may be singled out and serially targeted. Also, in model 1, we find that a firm's total amount of non-CSR PR activity is positively related to its likelihood of being targeted. Non-CSR PR is a good proxy for a firm's media engagement and indicates the firm's overall visibility in the public. This finding suggests that firms that are more active in their communications with the public are more likely to be singled out by activists. Activist groups may assume that their contentious tactics will receive more public exposure and media attention if they target these more conspicuous and publicly active firms. Surprisingly, we do not find that either being in the KLD index or the net valence of a firm's social performance in the index has an effect on the likelihood of being targeted by a boycott. This result suggests that the most grievous violators of CSR norms are no more likely to be the targets of boycotts than are firms that have not attracted the public's attention as norm violators.

We now turn to our hypotheses. In model 1, we find that the likelihood of being targeted for firms in the bottom or middle tier of the reputation rankings does not differ significantly from unranked firms. However, firms in the highest tier of the reputation rankings – that is, the most reputable firms – are significantly more likely to be targeted. Firms in the highest reputation category are 5.85 percent more likely to be targeted than are firms not listed in the reputation rankings at all. In model 2, where we limit the model to include only those firms that were included in the reputation index and compare their raw scores, we again find a significant and positive relationship between firm reputation and the likelihood of being targeted by a boycott. For each

Table 13.2 *Probit regressions predicting the likelihood of being boycotted, 1990–2005*

	(Model 1)	(Model 2)
	All firms	Firms in Fortune's Most Admired Index
Independent Variables		
Rep: Bottom Third	0.0536	
	(0.20)	
Rep: Middle Third	–0.138	
	(0.20)	
Rep: Highest Third	0.360*	
	(0.17)	
Reputation: Raw Score		0.218*
		(0.11)
Logged CSR PR	0.425***	0.537***
	(0.07)	(0.08)
Control Variables		
Logged Other PR	0.043	0.042
	(0.03)	(0.05)
ROA	2.005	2.179
	(1.40)	(2.79)
Logged Assets	–0.128*	0.0266
	(0.05)	(0.09)
Prev. Industry Boycotts	–0.006	0.040
	(0.02)	(0.03)
Prev. Firm Boycott	1.636***	2.040***
	(0.33)	(3.93)
KLD Positive	0.592	–0.103
	(0.40)	(0.42)
KLD Negative	0.063	–0.286
	(0.38)	(0.40)
In KLD	–0.287	0.122
	(0.41)	(0.12)
Constant	0.053	–3.622**
	(0.80)	(1.32)
Industry Controls	YES	YES
Yearly Fixed Effects	YES	YES
Quarterly Fixed Effects	YES	YES
N	628	332
Log Pseudo-likelihood	–262.16	–127.39

Robust standard errors, clustered by firm, are in parentheses.
* $p<0.05$, ** $p<0.01$, *** $p<0.001$

standard deviation change in a firm's reputation, the predicted probability of being targeted increases by 4.5 percent. Thus, with regard to activists' selection of targets for boycotts, our results support the predictions of the reputation as liability effect over the perspective about reputation's halo effect. However, the results in model 1 suggest that this liability may only attach to the most reputable firms, which are the most visible and whose audiences' expectations are likely to be highest.

Lending further support to the predictions of the reputation as liability approach, we find a positive and highly significant relationship between the amount of a firm's prosocial activity (in terms of its CSR PR releases) and its likelihood of being targeted. For each standard deviation change in a firm's logged prosocial PR, the predicted probability of being targeted increases by 10.35 percent. This finding holds across both models. Rather than buffering a firm from being targeted, these results suggest that a firm's prosocial activity may make it more vulnerable to being targeted because activists may seek to impugn the organization's claims of being socially responsible. Firms that actively engage in prosocial activities and implicitly make claims about being socially responsible appear to synchronously be making themselves more shameable.

Thus, we find strong support for the reputation as liability approach. Both a firm's standing in the *Fortune* reputation index and its previous levels of prosocial activities, as advertised by itself, make a firm a more attractive target to activists. Notably, the effect of reputation and prosocial activities is net of a firm's actual social performance rating in the KLD index, and the latter does not even have a statistically significant effect. The findings, then, indicate that activists tend to target firms that have high reputational standing and firms that promote their prosocial activities more than they do firms that have become known for poor social performance.

Conclusion

The global market has created a complex political environment for corporations. On the one hand, they seem less beholden to state control; on the other hand, they have become more concerned with brand, image, and reputation as assets used to gain customer loyalty, stakeholder support, and regulatory freedom (Meyer et al., this volume; Klein 1999). Their reliance on reputation as an asset means that they have become more committed to impression management tactics, such as philanthropic activity and improving firm environmental standards, to gain the approval of the stakeholders that matter most.

Although having a good reputation has numerous positive consequences for firms, this study suggests that it also creates certain liabilities. Belonging to the top tier of most-reputable firms and engaging in reputation-building actions (such as announcing prosocial activities) exposes a firm to activist attention, making it a more likely target of boycotts. Activists, ever eager for media coverage and the agenda-setting influence attached to it, use firms' reputation-seeking as a weapon against them. By targeting firms that are already committed to reputation-building, they put those firms in positions where they must react by conceding or by doing more CSR activities if they wish to maintain their lofty status in the field. Our findings suggest that scholars who have asserted that CSR and other reputation-building activities have insurance-like properties that protect a firm from future activist challenges may be partially wrong. Rather than serving as a form of insurance against future criticism, CSR may in fact make firms more attractive targets. Insofar as activists are eager to target companies that the media and other stakeholders will notice, companies that built reputations for being socially conscious are certainly on their radar. Such companies offer a visible stage for activists.

The irony of our finding is that firms believe reputations will protect them, and, in a sense, they are correct in this assessment. Past research suggests that boycotted firms are initially protected from negative investor reaction (King 2011). Investors seem to believe that high-reputation firms will be able to better deal with the consequences of the boycott than will firms with weaker reputations. But a firm's positive reputation also creates critical liabilities. Firms with positive reputations also receive more negative media attention following a boycott, and, for every additional day of boycott media coverage a corporate target experiences, greater damage to its market value. The implication of this is that firms with a positive reputation have a greater incentive to quickly concede to activists' demands. Failing to do so can damage their reputation and lead to a decline in their value.

Firms that become boycott targets are also more likely to increase the amount of prosocial activities they do in the public (McDonnell and King 2013). Fearing the reputational threat represented by the boycott, they do more philanthropy, more community outreach, and engage in other CSR activities, hoping that their audiences will give more weight to these positive actions than they will to the negative claims made by boycotters. The results of this study suggest, however, that by increasing the amount of prosocial activities they do, these firms also expose themselves to the threat of future activist targeting.

The implication of these various studies is that the increasing focus on reputation building only makes firms more vulnerable to activist attacks. Reputation, in this sense, has become an important liability for firms. Once a firm develops a positive reputation, it is obligated to maintain it. From the activist perspective, there is much to gain by forcing firms to defend their reputations. Not only do they generate more attention to their cause by targeting high-reputation firms (King 2011), but the net social impact is also positive. As these firms do more prosocial activities to renovate their image after the boycott, they subsequently dedicate more resources and strategic focus on CSR. A virtuous circle – at least from the perspective of the activist – follows. More CSR practices lead to an improved (or at least maintained) reputation, which causes the firm to continue to be a target of activism, the consequence of which is more commitment to CSR. From the point of view of the company, having a good reputation can be a double-edged sword or at least a potential liability when facing activists who seek the public limelight (Rhee and Haunschild 2006).

Of course, another implication of this pattern is that activist focus is almost exclusively on the upper tier of reputable firms. Corporations that are in the lower tier of the reputation index or that are not ranked at all receive considerably less attention from activists; therefore, those same firms have fewer incentives to engage in prosocial activities and may fly under the radar of activists no matter how irresponsible their practices. Inasmuch as they are ignored by social movement activists, they have fewer reasons to engage in CSR activities and are freer to deviate from norms of moral and social appropriateness. Thus, even as prestigious firms are doing their best to improve their standards and become more socially conscious citizens, firms that fly under the radar because of their weak reputations are able to get away with irresponsible behavior. The net social impact of activists ignoring these less-reputable firms is almost surely negative. Scholars and activists who put a great deal of hope in private or voluntary regulation as a way to rid society of corporations' negative influences will surely be disappointed, especially if they believe that reputation management is the primary motivation for a sustainable system of private regulation (King 2013).

Future research ought to focus on the behaviors of firms that are not targeted by activists and assess the consequences of failing to engage these firms. In addition, we need to develop a better understanding of how firms and activists negotiate settlements, such as those observed by Bartley (2007), in which activist targeting is curtailed in favor of setting up certification systems or active partnerships between firms and social movement groups. Our research suggests that firms with positive reputations have good reasons to set up such partnerships, inasmuch as it would allow them to escape future activist targeting while also benefiting from the glow of prosocial actions.

References

Bansal, Pratima, and Kendall Roth. 2000. "Why Companies Go Green: A Model of Ecological Responsiveness." *Academy of Management Journal* 43:717–736.

Baron, David P., and Daniel Diermeier. 2007. "Strategic Activism and Nonmarket Strategy." *Journal of Economics and Management Strategy* 16:599–634.

Bartley, T., and C. Child. 2011. "Movements, Markets and Fields: The Effects of Anti-Sweatshop Campaigns on U.S. Firms, 1993–2000." *Social Forces* 90:425–451.

Bartley, Tim. 2007. "Institutional Emergence in an Era of Globalization: The Rise of Transnational Private Regulation of Labor and Environmental Conditions." *American Journal of Sociology* 113:297–351.

Bartley, Tim, and Curtis Child. 2014. "Shaming the Corporation: The Social Production of Targets and the Anti-Sweatshop Movement." *American Sociological Review*. 79: 653–679.

Beder, Sharon. 2002. "Putting the Boot In." *The Ecologist* 32:24–28.

Bernstein, Aaron 2004. "Nike's New Game Plan for Sweatshops" *Businessweek Online*, September 20, 2004. Retrieved from http://www.businessweek.com/stories/2004-09-19/online-extra-nikes-new-game-plan-for-sweatshops

Brammer, S., A. Millington, and B. Rayton. 2007. "The contribution of corporate social responsibility to organizational commitment." *International Journal of Human Resource Management* 18:1701–1719.

Brammer, Stephen, and Andrew Millington. 2005. "Corporate Reputation and Philanthropy: An Empirical Analysis." *Journal of Business Ethics* 61:29–44.

Bullert, B. J. 2000. "Strategic Public Relations, Sweatshops, and the Making of a Global Movement." Working paper no. 14, *Joan Shorenstein Center on the Press, Politics, and Public Policy*. Seattle: University of Washington.

Campbell, J. L. 2007. "Why Would Corporations Behave in Socially Responsible Ways? An Institutional Theory of Corporate Social Responsibility." *Academy of Management Review* 32:946–967.

Chatterji, Aaron, and Siona Listokin. 2007. "Corporate Social Irresponsibility." *Democracy: A Journal of Ideas* Winter:52–63.

Chen, S., and P. Bouvain. 2009. "Is Corporate Responsibility Converging? A Comparison of Corporate Responsibility Reporting in the USA, UK, Australia, and Germany." *Journal of Business Ethics* 87:299–317.

Delmas, M. A., and M. W. Toffel. 2004. "Institutional Pressure and Environmental Management Practices." Pp. 230–245 in *Stakeholders, the Environment and Society*, edited by S. Sharma and M. Starik. Cheltenham, UK: Edward-Elgar.

Elsbach, Kimberly D., and Roderick M. Kramer. 1996. "Members' Responses to Organizational Identity Threats: Encountering and Countering the Business Week Rankings." *Administrative Science Quarterly* 41:442–476.

Espeland, Wendy Nelson, and Michael Sauder. 2007. "Rankings and Reactivity: How Public Measures Recreate Social Worlds." *American Journal of Sociology* 113:1–40.

Fombrun, Charles J., and Mark Shanley. 1990. "What's in a Name? Reputation Building and Corporate Strategy." *Academy of Management Journal* 33:233–258.

Galaskiewicz, J. 1997. "An Urban Grants Economy Revisited: Corporate Charitable Contributions in the Twin Cities, 1979–81, 1987–89." *Administrative Science Quarterly* 42:445–471.

Galaskiewicz, Joseph. 1991. "Making Corporate Actors Accountable: Institution Building in Minneapolis-St. Paul." Pp. 293–310 in *The New Institutionalism in Organizational Analysis*, edited by W. W. Powell and P. J. DiMaggio. Chicago: University of Chicago Press.

Gardberg, N. A., and C. J. Fombrun. 2006. "Corporate Citizenship: Creating Intangible Assets across Institutional Environments." *Academy of Management Review* 31:329–346.

Gardberg, Naomi A., and William Newburry. 2010. "Who Boycotts Whom? Marginalization, Company Knowledge, and Strategic Issues." *Business & Society*. 52: 318–357.

Godfrey, P. C., C. B. Merrill, and J. M. Hansen. 2009. "The Relationship between Corporate Social Responsibility and Shareholder Value: An

Empirical Test of the Risk Management Hypothesis." *Strategic Management Journal* 30:425–445.

Harrison, S. H., B. E. Ashforth, and K. G. Corley. 2009. "Organizational Sacralization and Sacrilege." *Research in Organizational Behavior* 29: 225–254.

Haufler, Virginia. 2015; this volume. "Corporations, Conflict Minerals, and Corporate Social Responsibility." Pp. 149–180 in *Corporate Social Responsibility in a Globalizing World*, edited by K. Tsutsui and A. Lim. New York: Cambridge University Press.

Hendry, Jamie. 2006. "Taking Aim at Business: What Factors Lead Environmental Non-governmental Organizations to Target Particular Firms?" *Business & Society* 45:47–86.

Holzer, Boris. 2010. *Moralizing the Corporation: Transnational Activism and Corporate Accountability*. Cheltenham, UK/Northampton, MA: Edward Elgar.

Joyner, B. E., and D. Payne. 2002. "Evolution and Implementation: A Study of Values, Business Ethics and Corporate Social Responsibility." *Journal of Business Ethics* 41:297–311.

King, Brayden G. 2008. "A Political Mediation Model of Corporate Response to Social Movement Activism." *Administrative Science Quarterly* 53:395–421.

King, Brayden G. 2011. "The Tactical Disruptiveness of Social Movements: Sources of Market and Mediated Disruption in Corporate Boycotts." *Social Problems*. 58: 491–517.

King, Brayden G. 2013. "Reputational Dynamics of Private Regulation." *Socio-economic Review* 12:200–206.

King, Brayden G., and Nicholas Pearce. 2010. "The Contentiousness of Markets: Politics, Social Movements and Institutional Change in Markets." *Annual Review of Sociology* 36:249–267.

King, Brayden G., and Sarah A. Soule. 2007. "Social Movements as Extra-institutional Entrepreneurs: The Effect of Protest on Stock Price Returns." *Administrative Science Quarterly* 52:413–442.

Klein, Michael, and Tim Harford. 2004. "Corporate Responsibility: When Will Voluntary Reputation Building Improve Standards?" Note Number 271, *Public Policy for the Private Sector*. Washington DC: World Bank.

Klein, Naomi. 1999. *No Logo: Taking Aim at the Brand Bullies*. New York: Picador.

Lenox, M. J., and C. E. Eesley. 2009. "Private Environmental Activism and the Selection and Response of Firm Targets." *Journal of Economics & Management Strategy* 18:45–73.

Lim, Alwyn, and Kiyoteru Tsutsui. 2012. "Globalization and Commitment in Corporate Social Responsibility: Cross-National Analyses of Institutional and Political-Economy Effects." *American Sociological Review*. 77: 69–98.

Linn, Allison. 2001. "When Protesters Really Want Attention, They Zero in on Starbucks." *Associated Press*. Retrieved from http://www.highbeam.com/doc/1P2-23480812.html

Mackey, A., T. B. Mackey, and J. B. Barney. 2007. "Corporate Social Responsibility and Firm Performance: Investor Preferences and Corporate Strategies." *Academy of Management Review* 32:817–835.

Margolis, J. D., H. A. Elfenbein, and J. P. Walsh. 2008. "Do Well by Doing Good? Don't Count on It." *Harvard Business Review* 86:19.

Margolis, J. D., and J. P. Walsh. 2003. "Misery Loves Companies: Rethinking Social Initiatives by Business." *Administrative Science Quarterly* 48:268–305.

Marquis, C., M. A. Glynn, and G. F. Davis. 2007. "Community Isomorphism and Corporate Social Action." *Academy of Management Review* 32:925–945.

Maxwell, J. W., T. P. Lyon, and S. C. Hackett. 2000. "Self-regulation and Social Welfare: The Political Economy of Corporate Environmentalism." *Journal of Law & Economics* 43:583–617.

McDonnell, Mary-Hunter, and Brayden King. 2013. "Keeping up Appearances Reputational Threat and Impression Management after Social Movement Boycotts." *Administrative Science Quarterly* 58(3):387–419.

McGuire, Jean B., Alison Sundgren, and Thomas Schneeweis. 1988. "Corporate Social Responsibility and Firm Financial Performance." *Academy of Management Journal* 31:854–872.

Meyer, John W., Shawn M. Pope, and Andrew Isaacson. 2015; this volume. "Legitimating the Transnational Corporation in a Stateless World Society." Pp. 27–72 in *Corporate Social Responsibility in a Globalizing World*, edited by K. Tsutsui and A. Lim. New York: Cambridge University Press.

Philippe, Déborah, and Rodolphe Durand. 2011. "The Impact of Norm-Conforming Behaviors on Firm Reputation." *Strategic Management Journal* 32:969–993.

Reid, E. M., and M. W. Toffel. 2009. "Responding to Public and Private Politics: Corporate Disclosure of Climate Change Strategies." *Strategic Management Journal* 30:1157–1178.

Rhee, M., and P. R. Haunschild. 2006. "The Liability of Good Reputation: A Study of Product Recalls in the US Automobile Industry." *Organization Science* 17:101–117.

Roberts, Peter W., and Grahame R. Dowling. 2002. "Corporate Reputation and Sustained Superior Financial Performance." *Strategic Management Journal* 23:1077–1093.

Sauder, Michael. 2008. "Interlopers and Field Change: The Entry of U.S. News into the Field of Legal Education." *Administrative Science Quarterly* 53:209–234.

Seidman, Gay W. 2007. *Beyond the Boycott: Labor Rights, Human Rights, and Transnational Activism*. New York: Sage.

Sine, Wesley D., Scott Shane, and Dante Di Gregorio. 2003. "The Halo Effect and Technology Licensing: The Influence of Institutional Prestige on the Licensing of University Inventions." *Management Science* 49:478–496.

Soule, Sarah A. 2009. *Contentious and Private Politics and Corporate Social Responsibility*. Cambridge: Cambridge University Press.

Staw, Barry M., and Lisa D. Epstein. 2000. "What Bandwagons Bring: Effects of Popular Management Techniques on Corporate Performance, Reputation and CEO Pay." *Administrative Science Quarterly* 45:523–556.

Udayasankar, K. 2008. "Corporate Social Responsibility and Firm Size." *Journal of Business Ethics* 83:167–175.

Vogel, David. 2010. "The Private Regulation of Global Corporate Conduct: Achievements and Limitations." *Business & Society* 49:68–87.

Walker, Edward T., Andrew W. Martin, and John D. McCarthy. 2008. "Confronting the State, the Corporation, and the Academy: The Influence of Institutional Targets on Social Movement Repertoires." *American Journal of Sociology* 114:35–76.

14 Conclusion: corporate social responsibility as social regulation

ASEEM PRAKASH

The subject of corporate social responsibility (CSR) continues to fascinate social scientists. The core issue is: do corporations have responsibilities toward stakeholders beyond shareholders (Carroll 1979)? The CSR norm suggests that instead of focusing on maximizing shareholders' wealth, corporations should recognize their responsibilities to a larger set of actors and therefore invest a portion of these rents for their welfare. Yet CSR is not limited to the voluntary redistribution of corporate rents; it raises fundamental issues about corporate responsibilities in contemporary societies beyond their usual legal obligations. Because the limited liability corporation was created to serve a social purpose, CSR proponents believe it to be fair to expect that corporations will consider themselves as social actors, embedded in social interactions and responding to societal expectations and concerns.

CSR invariably entails that corporations devote a portion of their rents to stakeholders other than shareholders. Hence, CSR is fundamentally a political issue. Following Lasswell (1958), we can conceive politics as a struggle about who gets what, when, and how. Arguably, along with costs, CSR also has a payoff for firms and, eventually, therefore for shareholders: it bestows legitimacy and provides the firm with the "social license to operate" (Gunningham, Kagan, and Thornton 2004). In the long run, this is expected to translate into improved access to resources required for firms' operations and eventual profitability. Yet, the division of rents that CSR entails remains an important source of concern. It opens a Pandora's box of related issues: what portion of rents should be earmarked for nonshareholders? Even among these stakeholders, whose preferences should take precedence? Should the firms invest in labor issues, environmental issues, or community issues, given that the firm cannot satisfy every constituency?

CSR has its share of critics, both conservatives and liberals. The conservative critics view CSR as reflecting "agency conflict": managers (as agents) are expected to maximize profits and distribute them to shareholders (their principals) instead of deciding how these profits might be spent by the corporation on charity. According to Milton Friedman:[1]

> The discussions of the social responsibilities of "business" are notable for their analytical looseness and lack of rigor. What does it mean to say that "business" has responsibilities? Only people can have responsibilities. A corporation is an artificial person and in this sense may have artificial responsibilities, but "business" as a whole cannot be said to have responsibilities, even in this vague sense. ... The executive is exercising a distinct "social responsibility," rather than serving as an agent of the stockholders or the customers or the employees, only if he spends the money in a different way than they would have spent it. ... But if he does this, he is in effect imposing taxes, on the one hand, and deciding how the tax proceeds shall be spent, on the other.

Left-wing critics recognize CSR as an attempt toward social regulation but dislike its voluntary character. For them, CSR is a corporate ruse to preempt governmental regulations (Maxwell, Lyon, and Hackett 2000; Manzini and Mariotti 2003), the assumption being that governments are not captured and enact regulations to serve the public purpose. According to these critics, CSR dampens the demand for new regulation because concerned stakeholders might be led to believe that firms are self-motivated to address social, environmental, or labor issues. However, these critics believe that businesses do not have incentives to credibly self-regulate because doing so would hurt profits. In particular, they are suspicious of those CSR programs sponsored by industry associations. They point to the spectacular failures of self-regulation, for example, in Enron and Deepwater Horizon. Whereas tax dodging by Apple does not speak directly to CSR issues, it contributes to the perception that firms will seek to dodge regulations and their obligations, public or private, to protect profits.

Definitional issues aside, the empirical literature reports conflicting findings on whether CSR improves firms' environmental, labor, and social performance (Vogel 2005; Morgenstern and Pizer 2007). Hence,

---

[1] http://www.colorado.edu/studentgroups/libertarians/issues/friedman-soc-resp-business.html.

it is difficult to assess claims about the efficacy or inefficacy of CSR as a category of social regulation. Arguably, one should look at specific programs – given the low entry barriers to establish CSR programs, which leads to considerable heterogeneity regarding the types and stringency of obligations they impose on their participants – and the mechanisms they incorporate to ensure that these obligations are fulfilled (Prakash and Potoski 2006).

In sum, although CSR has emerged as a global concern, it is a contested norm. Its usefulness is challenged by critics, both conservatives and liberals. CSR discourse is inherently political, involving multitudes of actors with varying preferences. This volume enters this fascinating debate at the appropriate time and with an excellent lineup of leading scholars. As I discuss herein, the chapters move forward our understanding of CSR, both its potential and limitations. Instead of accepting that CSR is a global solution to a global problem, this volume recognizes the considerable heterogeneity in types and scales of these programs, as well as firms' responses to them. The chapters explain the cross-national and cross-sectoral variations in the emergence and forms of CSR and how global and domestic, as well as political-economic and socio-institutional, forces work together to explain these trends.

CSR emergence and field formation

Why, when, where, and in what form did CSR emerge as a global norm for social regulation? Corporations have engaged in charity prior to the emergence of the CSR norm. Carnegie devoted his wealth to a variety of social causes; his Gospel of Wealth is a remarkable essay on how the rich should deploy their wealth.[2] Ford is said to have paid wages much above the market rate (Raff and Summers 1987). In developing countries such as India, industrialists established hospitals, educational institutions, and lodges for travelers. Given a considerable history of charitable giving by business leaders who recognized the social obligations of their firms, it is important to understand when and why CSR became accepted as a norm of social regulation and took on a meaning beyond the narrow confines of corporate or personal charity.

For Meyer, Pope, and Isaacson (Chapter 2), CSR is a corrective to a structural problem in the contemporary global system: whereas cross-

---

[2] http://www.fordham.edu/halsall/mod/1889carnegie.asp

national interactions have increased over the past several decades, especially economic interactions, there is no supranational regulator to oversee these transactions in ways that minimize their negative consequences. This has led to a global governance gap. Furthermore, the key global economic actor, the multinational corporation (MNC), does not inspire confidence among many that its actions serve the public interest. The MNCs' legitimacy gap is structurally rooted in the global governance gap. The legitimacy gap has become salient in ways that constrain MNCs' functioning. With the globalization of media and the spread of informational democracy, MNCs are subjected to close scrutiny. Human rights violations in the Niger Delta are a global issue, and MNCs engaged in oil exploration in that region are tainted by the human rights abuses that take place in that region. Similarly, the tragic collapse of garment factories and the death of workers in Bangladesh create an international uproar. This compels MNCs to respond in ways that demonstrate that they are undertaking due diligence to ensure that such tragedies are not repeated in the future. The global reality is that MNCs cannot contain local problems, especially if they are newsworthy (Prakash 2002). Thus, the global economic structure, which has been beneficial for the growth of MNCs, also creates new legitimacy challenges for them. MNCs therefore seek to provide evidence that they are good global citizens, not merely profitable companies.

Given this structural context, CSR has emerged as a corporate response to its legitimation problems and the rise of the global society that challenges MNCs' actions. Even when MNCs are not actively sponsoring CSR programs, they show some willingness to participate in them. CSR is an attempt to secure the social license to operate because it allows these firms to proclaim their global citizenship commitments. This point is also made by Utting in Chapter 3. Invoking Polanyi (1944), Utting suggests that CSR, along with re-regulation, is a part of the "double movement" in response to globalization and liberalization. Utting goes a step further and sees that active United Nations sponsorship of CSR initiatives suggests that the UN seeks a rapprochement with the business sector. It has evolved from being a votary (and a hostile actor) of mandatory business regulation to a cheerleader of business-friendly voluntary social regulation. Both Meyer et al. and Utting see CSR as a global-level response to a global problem. Whereas the "world society" school that Meyer has founded sees a secular

Conclusion: corporate social responsibility as social regulation   459

increase in the reach of global society actors (of which the UN is a critical part) and other actors seeking to adopt the norms these social actors propound, Utting sees accommodation on the part of the UN, perhaps even a retreat, in the context of how the "world society" relates to global business. The contest and cooperation between the world society actors and world business actors and how this shapes the trajectory of social regulation is a promising area for future research.

Whereas the idea of a "governance gap leading to CSR" is reiterated by Daniel Kinderman in Chapter 4, for him, CSR is predominantly a domestic response to a domestic problem, although indirectly influenced by global factors. He documents that CSR associations and programs emerged in the 1960s. CSR rapidly spread worldwide in the 1980s, in part because it was a corporate response to deregulatory policies. As the state withdrew, corporations had to step in. This is consistent with the "double movement" argument that Utting invokes, but at the domestic level. However, this was a double movement on terms that were agreeable to corporations. Whereas Meyer et al. speak specifically to the legitimacy problems of global flows without global regulations guiding CSR, Kinderman suggests CSR as a conscious national-level policy response of corporations to minimize or contain backlash to deregulation or, more broadly, to seek legitimacy. Thus, national-level CSR associations developed autonomous of the global CSR frameworks and the "world society," reflecting the priority firms attached to their domestic political-economic environment. This is an interesting debate because for Meyer et al. the structural changes in the global economy and global society are somewhat exogenous to MNCs. Although MNCs might support such changes, they also bear the consequences. In Kinderman's perspective, CSR is predominantly a national-level phenomenon; it began as a national-level response to domestic imperatives. Kinderman does point out that the role of transnational nongovernmental organizations (NGOs) was important even in these domestic CSR developments. Thus, global society played an important role, albeit an indirect one, in fostering the national-level evolution of CSR.

Domestic roots of CSR are also emphasized by Weber and Soderstrom in Chapter 7. Environmental stewardship or sustainability is an important component of the CSR norm. Yet how the environmental sustainability discourse is articulated varies across countries. The authors link these variations in the discourse articulation to variations in institutional environments of specific countries. Arguably, what types of CSR initiatives emerge and how firms respond to them should also reflect this institutional diversity and, therefore, variations in the sustainability discourse. There is much debate in the political communications literature on this subject. Scholars find variations in discourse even across states in the United States, although the institutional structures are remarkably similar (Dolšak and Houston, forthcoming). Future work should examine factors explaining variations in CSR discourses beyond institutional differences and how these variations influence the density and design of CSR programs.

If CSR has indeed emerged as an important social regulation instrument since the 1960s, how have CSR instruments evolved? Over time, have the CSR programs become more stringent in terms of the obligations they impose on their participants, reflecting their maturation as policy tools? Have they moved from industry-sponsored to multistakeholder initiatives that arguably would constitute a more compelling social license to operate? Utting (Chapter 3) challenges the notion that there have been consistent shifts in any one way. He suggests that the CSR programs and the obligations they impose can only be understood by taking into account factors associated with the political economy of regulatory change. Thus, CSR variations over time reflect changing power relationships. Furthermore, Utting points out that although CSR may be portrayed as a global norm, only a subset of global MNCs actually subscribe to these initiatives. In this way, Utting and Kinderman challenge Meyer et al.'s narrative of the globality of CSR. Utting also points to the tension among civil society actors regarding different facets of CSR. This again challenges the notion of a homogenous global civil society with congruent preferences. Taken together, these chapters compel us to think about the notion of citizenship and how CSR might fulfill them. Future work needs to explore how firms working in several jurisdictions think of their citizenship obligations, broadly defined, and how they seek to reconcile the conflicts between these obligations. In some ways, global citizenship without recognition of varying domestic citizenship obligations is a vacuous concept. On the other hand, the idea of a global citizen must provide some value to the society that is greater than the sum of its domestic parts. What exactly this value is, and how CSR might create it is an area for future work.

Conclusion: corporate social responsibility as social regulation 461

Building on Utting's call for microlevel analysis of CSR programs, the volume includes chapters that examine CSR evolution in three specific areas: conflict minerals, supply-chain CSR, and sustainability. Conflict minerals, especially blood diamonds, have generated significant interest in the civil war literature. Collier and Hoeffler (2000) introduced the notion of "greed versus grievance" drivers of civil wars, pointing to the availability of valuable resources in fueling civil conflicts. This cohered very well with the emerging concern about the "resource curse" thesis (Auty 1993), which suggests that countries blessed with significant natural resources tend to fare poorly on economic development and political development. The argument was that availability of resources leads governments to cut their accountability bonds with the citizens: instead of taxing them, they can raise revenue for their organizational sustenance through resource sale.

The greed versus grievance debate took resource-curse concerns to new levels of policy attention: resources were no longer related to arrested economic and political development; they are causal factors for civil wars. Indeed, if the contest to control valuable resources leads to conflict, then actors involved in trade in these resources bear a partial burden for this human suffering. MNCs entered this controversy as accessories to this crime. Haufler (Chapter 5) traces the evolution of the CSR field in this sector. Her chapter raises questions as to why governments did not sign international treaties to curb trade in conflict minerals. The choice of the voluntary regulation route reflects the nature of the actors involved, sector characteristics, and the global normative environment. Civil wars tend to break out in failing states that have virtually no regulatory capacity. Furthermore, the diamond industry, the first one in this sector to adopt a CSR program, reflected unique characteristics. Diamond is a reputational product; the romanticism that the advertising industry has developed around it could easily be tarred by conflict, an issue that NGOs exploited. Plus, the virtual monopoly of DeBeers facilitated collective action. CSR was, therefore, an obvious route for regulation that also cohered with the emerging global normative environment.

Haufler documents how CSR efforts to regulate trade in conflict material have shifted from a single framework to multiple initiatives, especially as new minerals were included in the ambit of conflict commodities. This is an interesting phenomenon because no single actor has the monopoly of power or monopoly of legitimacy to impose

CSR solutions in these commodities; with different institutional interests and preferences, different regulatory initiatives have emerged. Whereas the domination of DeBeers in the diamond industry facilitated the emergence of a single dominant initiative, the Kimberly Process, the fragmented nature of industry in other minerals has led to multiple initiatives emerging. Haufler's chapter raises an interesting question: would this multiplicity of CSR program lead to a race to the bottom, given the potential that regulatees can venue shop and look for the least costly and least cumbersome alternative? Or, would it lead to mimetic isomorphism, with different initiatives adopting the best features of others, given the close scrutiny of civil society actors on these issues?

Although Hauler finds that CSR initiatives have evolved from single, industry-dominated initiatives to several initiatives sponsored by different actors, Bair and Palpacuer (Chapter 6) suggest the opposite in the context of MNCs' supply chain CSR initiatives. Although agreeing with the "governance gap" narrative in explaining the emergence of CSR, they find that, during the 1980s and 1990s, CSR programs manifested primarily as multistakeholder initiatives. However, in the past decade, these programs have taken the form of corporate-sponsored CSR. It is interesting that the authors find that civil society concerns about CSR did not lead to strengthening of multistakeholder initiatives; instead, it created incentives for corporations to develop business-led CSR to assert their control over an emerging aspect of their institutional environment (Sasser et al. 2006). This is an important issue that might suggest diminishing returns to civil society activism; after some time, corporations may not be willing to cede regulatory authority to NGOs. Ed Walker (Chapter 10) takes this argument a step further by documenting how firms themselves are creating civil society actors to exercise greater control over the CSR discourse. A study of business – civil society interactions is an exciting area for future work because these interactions influence CSR emergence, form, and efficacy. These interactions also remind us that CSR is inherently a political issue. It is also malleable, and different actors seek to capture it in order to interpret it in light of their own interests and preferences.

Firms' response to CSR

Several factors have shaped the emergence, design, and configuration of CSR initiatives. As Lim and Tsutsui lay out in their introductory chapter, these can be located in global as well as domestic arenas, as well as in the socio-institutional and the political-economic environment. The emerging web of CSR initiatives has altered the institutional environments that firms face, and firms have actively worked to shape these environments, as several chapters document.

If CSR has emerged as an important type of social regulation, why do we find some firms actively embracing it, some grudgingly accepting it, and others resisting it? Why this variation in the response to an arguably global norm? Second, having embraced it, has it altered firms' CSR behaviors? Do they pollute less and treat their workers better? Several chapters offer interesting accounts of firm-level responses that help us understand the promise and limitations of CSR as social regulation.

Human action can be guided by instrumental as well as normative considerations, which may arise from inward and outward factors. March and Olsen (1989) identify two competing logics to guide human behavior. Political economists view action as being guided by the logic of instrumentality. For them, actors calculate benefits and costs of action and undertake actions if benefits exceed costs. In this perspective, firms are expected to focus on the payoffs of participating in CSR programs, such as reputational benefit. In contrast, sociological explanations suggest that actors undertake actions based on the logic of appropriateness. That is, actors seek to understand the legitimacy of the proposed actions, not their net benefits, and they undertake actions if they are deemed legitimate. Shawn M. Pope (Chapter 8) suggests that the world's largest MNCs adopt CSR primarily guided by the logic of appropriateness. Whereas Pope offers a test between logic of appropriateness and consequentiality, Satoshi Miura and Kaoru Kurusu (Chapter 9) offer a test between inward and outward motivation to join global CSR programs. They examine the response of Japanese companies to the UN Global Compact (UNGC); they find that new participants are guided primarily by external motivations, and these are reactive in nature. Taken together, these chapters raise important issues as to where we should look for CSR drivers and the extent to which they can be influenced by policy interventions. Arguably, the institutional environments that shape the persuasiveness of the two competing logics of human action can be structured by policy interventions. Some interventions, such as the UNGC (Lim and Tsutsui 2012), are explicitly designed to appeal to the logic of appropriateness. If CSR is a portfolio of different types of policies, then CSR designers must correctly understand their target population and the context in which these firms function. Export-oriented firms in Bangladesh are likely to respond well to a CSR initiative that has a strong labor component, given the recent tragedy in Rana Plaza and the trade sanction imposed by the United States. My intuition is that efforts to persuade Bangladeshi firms to sign on to environmentally focused CSR will not bear significant results. Thus, instead of looking at CSR as a global norm that appeals to some global idea, it is more helpful to understand specific dimensions of CSR programs and how they might help firms to address specific concerns. This would also allow scholars to recognize that CSR programs involve tradeoffs, with different constituencies favoring different subsets of CSR – the issue of the political aspect of CSR addressed earlier.

Furthermore, issues such as business cycles and industry profitability may also bear on the efficacy of different logics to persuade firms to sign on to CSR initiatives. For example, firms with considerable "organizational slack" might be more willing to be persuaded by the logic of appropriateness. Firms that are doing poorly and are under constant pressure from the stock market to show economic results might be more persuaded by the logic of instrumentality.

Thus, the framing of the CSR program and the logics of behaviors it seeks to evoke might influence firms' participation decisions. Future work needs to probe deeper to understand what sorts of framing strategies are best suited for different types of audiences and how this might vary across CSR program types.

Beyond participating and not-participating, firms can also decide to resist CSR by seeking to undermine forces that seek to encourage CSR per se or to promote specific types of CSR. If the pressure civil society brings to bear is an important factor in encouraging (and sometimes goading) corporations to join CSR, then a countermovement might dilute its influence and allow corporations to shape this pressure in ways that serve their interests. In Chapter 10, Walker points out that political systems shape what sorts of corporate grassroots mobilization might be permitted. Specifically, liberal/pluralist systems (as in the United States) facilitate countermobilization, statist but noncorporatist systems (as in France) do not, and statist-corporatist systems (as in Germany) facilitate moderate corporate countermobilization. Thus, for Walker, demand for CSR has an agentic component; it is not an inexorable global force that sweeps away the corporation. Rather, CSR

Conclusion: corporate social responsibility as social regulation 465

is a political demand for sharing of rents. Those who oppose this redistribution may seek to oppose it, and certain political systems offer the political space for countermobilization.

Does participation in CSR initiatives lead firms to improve their CSR performance? This issue has generated considerable debate, with some focusing on program design. Although CSR programs do fail (Morgenstern and Pizer 2007), in other instances, those CSR programs requiring their participants to adopt more extensive, specific, and demanding requirements should show higher levels of performance (Anton, Deltas, and Khanna 2004; Darnall and Kim 2012).

In addition to the physical measures of CSR efficacy, one can also think of perception-based measures. In Chapter 11, Ion Bogdan Vasi examines how industry analysts perceive the impact of CSR participation on the environmental performance of US-based firms. He finds that analysts do not view all CSR programs to be identical. They seek cues about the efficacy of various programs by looking at both program features, such as reporting requirements, as well as at links to stakeholders that have incentives to hold firms accountable to certain levels of CSR performance (Prakash and Potoski 2011). Thus, CSR programs such as the UNGC and the Global Reporting Initiative carry more credibility with analysts. This is an important finding because it shows that the CSR field is becoming differentiated. Merely claiming that a firm is participating in a CSR program does not purchase it the goodwill or the social license to operate. Informed observers are expected to inquire about which sorts of CSR programs this firm has joined. This is a welcome development because it sorts firms' CSR intentions by the types of CSR programs in which they seek to participate. The implication is that instead of expecting a uniform improvement or deterioration in firms' CSR performance, one can expect to see different CSR performance clusters emerging, and these clusters are associated with programs that share certain types of characteristics. This is a positive development for both scholars and practitioners because it will allow us to outgrow debates such as whether CSR works or does not.

Along with environmental concerns, labor rights are perhaps the most important other dimension of CSR. In Chapter 12, Tim Bartley and Doug Kincaid examine the labor dimension of CSR performance in the apparel, textile, and footwear industries in Indonesia. They find that CSR programs do not deliver in practice what they promise on paper, a finding consistent with other work on this subject (Greenhill, Mosley, and Prakash 2009). Instead of finding fault with the design of CSR programs or attributing poor CSR performance to suppliers' dishonest intentions, they emphasize the structural problems that suppliers face in supply chain relationships. As long as buyers who exercise strong influence on labor practices in the supply chain emphasize speed and flexibility over CSR, suppliers have neither the incentives nor the capacity to act upon their CSR commitments. Thus, Bartley and Kincaid remind us that CSR is much more than a social regulation program that a company signs on to and creates an internal bureaucracy to administer. CSR requires a fundamental shift in how firms think of their relationships with their supply chains and the investments they are willing to make to ensure that their subcontractors have the resources to enforce CSR codes. CSR requires that buyers adopt a position that casts a long shadow on the future; internalizing CSR practices and inculcating a CSR culture takes time. If suppliers are constantly faced with cost pressures and tight delivery schedules, they simply will not have the resources to implement CSR in their facilities. Bartley and Kincaid therefore challenge both the political economy and sociological perspectives on CSR performance. For them, CSR does not depend on the logic of instrumentality or appropriateness; it depends on the logic of patience and shared risk management.

CSR reflects the corporate quest for social legitimacy. It outlines good deeds and good practices for firms to follow. But conservative critics of social activism sometimes believe that no good deed goes unpunished: if companies undertake CSR, they will invite more scrutiny and criticisms from activist groups. For these critics, the politically sensible course is for firms to resist CSR, perhaps via strategies that Edward Walker lays out. In Chapter 13, Brayden King and Mary Hunter-McDonnell provide evidence that good deeds indeed get punished. Instead of shielding corporations from criticism and purchasing them the social license to operate, participation in CSR makes these firms more vulnerable to consumer boycotts. Arguably, this is because CSR participation raises the expectations of consumer activists about firms' CSR policies and invites additional scrutiny. This eventually leads activists to target these firms. Future research should examine if specific types of programs lead to greater scrutiny and criticism from activists. For example, are activist groups more likely to target firms if they join industry-sponsored programs as opposed to multistakeholder initiatives? Similarly, do activists target firms that join weak CSR programs instead of stronger ones? Or, do activists target firms that join global CSR programs as opposed to national ones? These issues will allow us to understand the usefulness of CSR not only as a tool of corporate citizenship but also as a tool to manage firms' nonmarket environment.

Conclusion

CSR programs should be viewed as institutions or rule structures. As the scholarship on and the practice of CSR mature, we will have a better understanding of its strengths and limitations as a tool for social regulation. In assessing the usefulness of CSR, it is important not to set impossibly high standards for its performance. Like any institution, CSR is an imperfect tool. Like any other institution, it will sometimes fail: governments fail, markets fail, and CSR also fails. We live in a world of pervasive institutional failures. Yet we do not discard the state or the market; we try to reform them. Arguably, CSR should be treated similarly. Although it is not a panacea for our governance gap problems, CSR makes useful contributions to our regulatory tool kit, which we deploy to govern an increasingly complex society. The speed of technological change, as well as the changing expectations of citizens, can make regulatory institutions obsolete in a short span of time. Thus, the regulatory tool kit needs to be regularly revisited and examined. Some tools need to be discarded and others updated. What works today might not do so tomorrow, and what works in one context might fail in another. As long as we retain intellectual flexibility and appreciate the limitations of all regulatory instruments, we will be able to avoid dysfunctional debates such as the one focused on states versus markets. Like state-building and market-building, CSR was a political project. From the reflexive law perspective (Teubner 1983), CSR responds to challenges of modernity as well as to a quest for autonomy. Although this may be so, CSR also speaks to basic power relationships and reorders social relationships. As the field and scholarship progress, we must bear in mind CSR's social purpose.

Taken together, this volume makes an important contribution to our understanding of CSR as a tool of social regulation. CSR includes a remarkably diverse set of practices and institutions united by a few core ideas. These pertain to the responsibility of the firm beyond the objective of shareholder wealth maximization or of adhering to legal obligations. CSR seeks to remind us of the original justification for the public limited company outlined in various statutes, such as the United Kingdom's Joint Stock Companies Act of 1844 and the Limited Liability Act of 1855. It also reminds us of the possibility of social response to market excesses, as outlined in Polanyi's (1944) "double movement" thesis, and the more deliberately negotiated compact between labor and capital, as outlined in Ruggie's (1982) notion of "embedded liberalism."

This volume underlines the inherently political nature of the CSR concept and how it is open to capture by different actors. Consequently, from a scholarly perspective, it is difficult to provide a unidimensional assessment of whether CSR is effective or ineffective. For example, it might be effective for labor issues but not for environmental issues.

In addition to emphasizing different CSR dimensions, CSR programs vary along the types of obligations they impose on their participants and program features they have in place to ensure participants' compliance with these obligations. In addition, firms have different incentives, motivations, and capacities to fulfill their CSR obligations. Hence, we can expect to see the emergence of different CSR "performance clusters."

In terms of firms' responses to CSR, this volume emphasizes that there are different logics (instrumental, appropriateness, patience) that might persuade or compel firms to participate in CSR initiatives. The effectiveness of these logics is shaped by firm-level characteristics, as well as by program features. Thus, instead of debating the universal supremacy of a given logic of action over others, a more productive pursuit might be to recognize that firms are able to work with different logics of action and then to identify specific conditions under which different logics can be expected to dominate decision-making processes.

Finally, the volume reminds us that CSR is a global norm. It is a global response to a global governance gap problem. CSR is both a product of and a response to globalization pressures. However, the globality of CSR does not deny its domestic foundations. Instead of domestic versus global debates, perhaps scholars can begin to think of nested CSR fields in which domestic and sectoral CSR fields become nested within the global CSR field. This approach should allow us to explain the considerable domestic, sectoral, and programmatic diversity and yet capture the broader structural trajectory across countries toward a new system of social regulation.

Like any outstanding collection, this volume raises several questions and outlines ideas for new research. It takes stock of our considerable scholarly output on the subject of CSR, and it channels the core themes in a disciplined way. Its multidisciplinary approach provides a refreshing contrast to somewhat silo-based tendencies that begin to appear as any field matures. This volume weaves together insights from several disciplines to further our understanding of the limitations and promises of CSR as a mode of social regulation.

References

Anton, Wilma, George Deltas, and Madhu Khanna. 2004. "Incentives for Environmental Self-Regulation and Implications for Environmental Performance." *Journal of Environmental Economics and Management* 48:632–654.

Auty, Richard. 1993. *Sustaining Development in Mineral Economies: The Resource Curse Thesis*. London: Routledge.

Bair, Jennifer, and Florence Palpacuer. 2015; this volume. "The Institutionalization of Supply Chain Corporate Social Responsibility: Field Formation in Comparative Context." Pp. 181–217 in *Corporate Social Responsibility in a Globalizing World*, edited by K. Tsutsui and A. Lim. New York: Cambridge University Press.

Bartley, Tim, and Doug Kincaid. 2015; this volume. "The Mobility of Industries and the Limits of Corporate Social Responsibility: Labor Codes of Conduct in Indonesian Factories." Pp. 393–429 in *Corporate Social Responsibility in a Globalizing World*, edited by K. Tsutsui and A. Lim. New York: Cambridge University Press.

Carroll Archie. 1979. "A Three-Dimensional Conceptual Model of Corporate Performance." *The Academy of Management Review* 4(4): 497–505.

Collier, Paul, and Anke Hoeffler. 2000. *Greed and Grievance in Civil War*. Washington, DC: The World Bank Policy Research Working Paper 2355.

Darnall, Nicole, and Kim Younsung. 2012. "Which Types of Environmental Management Systems are Related to Greater Environmental Improvements?" *Public Administration Review* 72:351–365.

Dolšak, Nives, and Kristen Houston. Forthcoming. "Global Climate Change and the Media: Newspaper Coverage and Climate Change Legislative Activity across U.S. States." *Global Policy*.

Greenhill, Brian, Layna Mosley, and Aseem Prakash. 2009. "Trade and Labor Rights: A Panel Study, 1986–2002." *American Political Science Review* 103(4):669–690.

Gunningham, Neil, Robert Kagan, and Dorothy Thornton. 2004. "Social License and Environmental Protection: Why Businesses Go beyond Compliance." *Law and Social Inquiry* 29(2):307–341.

Haufler, Virginia. 2015; this volume. "Corporations, Conflict Minerals, and Corporate Social Responsibility." Pp. 149–180 in *Corporate Social Responsibility in a Globalizing World*, edited by K. Tsutsui and A. Lim. New York: Cambridge University Press.

Kinderman, Daniel. 2015; this volume. "Explaining the Rise of National Corporate Social Responsibility: The Role of Global Frameworks, World Culture, and Corporate Interests." Pp. 107–146 in *Corporate Social Responsibility in a Globalizing World*, edited by K. Tsutsui and A. Lim. New York: Cambridge University Press.

King, Andrew, and Michael Lenox. 2000. "Industry Self-Regulation without Sanctions: The Chemical Industry's Responsible Care Program." *Academy of Management Journal* 43:698–716.

King, Brayden G, and Mary Hunter-McDonnell. 2015; this volume. "Good Firms, Good Targets: The Relationship among Corporate Social Responsibility, Reputation, and Activist Targeting." Pp. 430–454 in *Corporate Social Responsibility in a Globalizing World*, edited by K. Tsutsui and A. Lim. New York: Cambridge University Press.

Lasswell, Harold. 1958. *Politics: Who Gets What, When, How*. New York: Meridian Books.

Lim, Alwyn, and Kiyoteru Tsutsui. 2012. "Globalization and Commitment in Corporate Social Responsibility: Cross-National Analyses of Institutional and Political-Economy Effects." *American Sociological Review* 77:69–98.

Manzini, Paola, and Marco Mariotti. 2003. "A Bargaining Model of Voluntary Environmental Agreements." *Journal Public Economics* 87:755–767.

March, James, and Johan Olsen. 1989. *Rediscovering Institutions*. New York: Free Press.

Maxwell, John, Thomas Lyon, and Steven Hackett. 2000. "Self-Regulation and Social Welfare." *Journal of Law and Economics* 43:583–617.

Meyer, John W., Shawn M. Pope, and Andrew Isaacson. 2015; this volume. "Legitimating the Transnational Corporation in a Stateless World Society." Pp. 27–72 in *Corporate Social Responsibility in a Globalizing World*, edited by K. Tsutsui and A. Lim. New York: Cambridge University Press.

Morgenstern, Richard, and William Pizer, eds. 2007. *Reality Check: The Nature and Performance of Voluntary Environmental Programs in the United States, Europe, and Japan*. Washington, DC: RRF Press.

Polanyi, Karl. 1944. *The Great Transformation: The Political and Economic Origins of Our Time*. Boston: Beacon Press/Rinehart & Company.

Prakash, Aseem. 2002. "Beyond Seattle: Globalization, the Non-Market Environment, and Business Strategy." *Review of International Political Economy* 9(3):513–537.

Prakash, Aseem, and Matthew Potoski. 2006. *The Voluntary Environmentalists*. Cambridge: Cambridge University Press.

Prakash, Aseem, and Matthew Potoski. 2011. "Voluntary Environmental Programs: A Comparative Perspective." *Journal of Policy Analysis and Management* 31(1):123–138.

Raff, Daniel, and Lawrence Summers. 1987. "Did Henry Ford Pay Efficiency Wages?" *Journal of Labor Economics* 5(4):S57–S86.

Ruggie, John. 1982. "International Regimes, Transactions and Change: Embedded Liberalism in the Postwar Economic Order." *International Organization* 36:379–415.

Sasser, Erica, Aseem Prakash, Benjamin Cashore, and Graeme Auld. 2006. "Direct Targeting as NGO Political Strategy: Examining Private Authority Regimes in the Forestry Sector." *Business and Politics* 8(3):1–32.

Teubner, Gunther. 1983. "Substantive and Reflexive Elements in Modern Law." *Law & Society Review* 17:239–285.

Utting, Peter. 2015; this volume. "Corporate Social Responsibility and the Evolving Standards Regime: Regulatory and Political Dynamics." Pp. 73–106 in *Corporate Social Responsibility in a Globalizing World*, edited by K. Tsutsui and A. Lim. New York: Cambridge University Press.

Vasi, Ion Bogdan. 2015; this volume. "Is Greenness in the Eye of the Beholder? Corporate Social Responsibility Frameworks and the Environmental Performance of US Firms." Pp. 365–392 in *Corporate Social Responsibility in a Globalizing World*, edited by K. Tsutsui and A. Lim. New York: Cambridge University Press.

Vogel, David. 2005. *The Market for Virtue*. Washington, DC: The Brookings Press.

Walker, Edward T. 2015; this volume. "Global Corporate Resistance to Public Pressures: Corporate Stakeholder Mobilization in the United States, Norway, Germany, and France." Pp. 321–362 in *Corporate Social Responsibility in a Globalizing World*, edited by K. Tsutsui and A. Lim. New York: Cambridge University Press.

Weber, Klaus, and Sara B. Soderstrom. 2015; this volume. "Sustainability Discourse and Capitalist Variety: A Comparative Institutional Analysis." Pp. 218–248 in *Corporate Social Responsibility in a Globalizing World*, edited by K. Tsutsui and A. Lim. New York: Cambridge University Press.

Index

AAMA. *See* American Apparel Manufacturers' Association (AAMA)
Accord on Building and Fire Safety, 211–212, 213
accountability, 41, 73, 82, 100, 433
activist movements, 17, 154, *See also* social movements
  anti-sweatshop, 77, 182, 183, 189–199, 207, 395, 416–420
  conflict minerals and, 166, 167, 172
  critics of, 466
  CSR and, 430–444, 466
adverse selection, 255
advocacy groups, 325, 328, 334, 335, 342, 346, *See also specific organizations*
agency conflict, 456
Alliance for a Corporate-Free UN, 97
alter-globalization perspective, 100
American Apparel Manufacturers' Association (AAMA), 197
American hegemony, 31, 32
Angola, 156, 157, 158, 159, 162, 171, 174
Annan, Kofi, 116, 286
anti-corporate campaigns, 154
anti-corruption, 81, 84, 87
antinuclear movement, 346
anti-sweatshop movement, 77, 182, 189–199, 207, 395, 416–420
anti-trust laws, 30
apartheid, 42
apparel industry, 8, 393, 397, *See also* textile, footwear, and apparel (TFA) sector
Apparel Industry Partnership (AIP), 193, 196, 197, 206
Apple, 41, 165, 209, 213, 393

articulated regulation, 80–81
Asian financial crisis, 403
Atlanta Agreement, 84
auditing, 90, 369, 370–372, 393, 394
Australia, 330, 350
auto industry, 171
autonomy of national CSR proposition, 114, 137

Balkans, 156
Ballinger, Jeff, 193
Bangladesh, 119, 181, 182, 211, 421, 457
Bangladesh Worker Safety Initiative, 211
banking sector, 30
BELC. *See* Business Environmental Leadership Council (BELC)
Benefit Corporation, 58
Better Work Initiative, 76
Bhopal disaster, 41
bilateral trade linkages, 8
BITC. *See* Business in the Community
blood diamonds, 158–161, 461
bluewashing, 97, 252, 286, 302
Boston College Center for Corporate Citizenship, 45, 53
Botswana, 159
Bowen, Harold, 107, 112
boycotts, 17, 257, 431, 437, 439, 448–449, 466
BP oil spill, 41
brand equity, 52, 307
Brazil, 165
Bribery Act (UK), 168
Britain. *See* United Kingdom
Brundtland report, 235
BSCI. *See* Business Social Compliance Initiative (BSCI)

473

business associations, 50, 139, 259–261, *See also specific organizations*
business cycles, 464
Business Environmental Leadership Council (BELC), 367, 369, 373
 environmental performance and, 376, 387
business ethics, 54
business failures, 406–411
Business for Social Responsibility, 45, 52, 107, 111
Business in the Community (BITC), 9, 53, 107, 109, 111, 128
business industry associations, 136, *See also specific organizations*
business interest groups, 43
business regulation. *See* regulatory environment
business schools, 54
Business Social Compliance Initiative (BSCI), 199–200, 202, 203, 206–207, 208
business-led CSR coalitions, 112, 114–117, 130–133, 206, 462
buyer-driven commodity chains, 397, 398

C&A, 192, 194, 195, 210
Cambodia, 401
capital flight, 398
capital mobility, 16, 397–402
 standards and, 398–402
capitalism, 139
 corporate, 84, 137
 free market, 48, 218, 224
 laissez-faire, 73
 pariah, 29
 power relations and, 90
 varieties of, 186, 219–225, 234, 242–244, 261
Carbon Disclosure Project (CDP), 46, 48, 49, 116, 129, 135, 401
 background on, 253–254
 membership in, 251, 254
 motivations for participation in, 251–269
Carnegie, Andrew, 457
Carrefour, 200, 206, 211
cause-related marketing, 52

CDP. *See* Carbon Disclosure Project (CDP)
Centre on Transnational Corporations, 40, 127
CERES. *See* Coalition for Environmentally Responsible Economies (CERES)
change agents, 81
charity, 457
chemical industry, 6, 8
Chevron, 41
Chief Sustainability Officer, 58
child labor, 84, 193, 203
Children's Rights and Business Principles, 79
Chile, 38
China, 209, 224, 234, 235, 242, 395, 399, 401, 415, 421
Citizens Compact, 97
Citizens for Technology, 343
civil culture, 30
civil regulation, 74, 83–102
civil society, 13, 79, 182, 187, 321, 324, 326, 328, 464, *See also* nongovernmental organizations (NGOs), *See also* social movements, *specific organizations*
 in France, 344–347
 in Germany, 339–341
 in Norway, 335–336
 in US, 331–332, 349
 naming-and-shaming by, 2, 83, 96, 432
 role of, in regulation, 73, 83–102
 state-civil society interface, 323–324, 327–331, 338
 supply chain CSR and, 188
 tensions within, 92–93
civil wars, 156, 157, 162, 461
Clean Clothes Campaign (CCC), 189–193, 212
climate change, 235
Climate Leaders (CL), 367, 369, 373
 environmental performance and, 376, 387
Clinton, Bill, 193, 196
Coalition for Environmentally Responsible Economies (CERES), 385–386
Coalition for Patient Information, 342

Index

Coalition of Environmentally Responsible Companies, 45
Coca-Cola, 50
Code of Conduct for Transnational Corporations, 2
Code of Labour Practices, 192
codes of conduct, 58, 78, 183–184, 188, 203, 204, 393, 394, 398–402, 409–444
Cold War, 32
collaboration, 88
collaborative governance, 84
colonialism, 32
coltan, 162, 163, 165
Committee on Transnational Corporations, 117
commodity chains, 183
  buyer-driven, 397, 398
company reputation, 256
competitive advantage, 365, 367, 401
compliance, 89
conflict commodities, 13, 149–150, 156, 461
conflict minerals, 149–178, 461
  civil wars and, 156, 162
  coltan, 162, 163, 165
  diamonds, 150–151, 158–161, 162, 171, 172, 174, 461,
  global supply chains and, 154–155
  gold, 156, 162, 163
  governance of, 151
  institutional variation in regulation of, 169–178
  proliferation of initiatives and, 161–169
  regime complex in, 152
  regulation of, 156, 165–178
  state power and, 152–153
  tin, 156, 162, 163, 165–166
  tungsten, 156, 162, 163
Conflict-Free Smelter program, 165, 168, 170
constituency building, 334
consulting services, 51–53
consumer boycotts. *See* boycotts
consumer culture, 90
Consumer Goods Forum, 200
consumer movements, 17, *See also* activist movements, *See also* social movements

consumer preferences, 52
coordinated economies, 9, 186, 223, 224, 234, 240, 242–243
coordination hypothesis, 257
Corporate Accountability International, 38
corporate citizenship, 185, 308, 351, 460
corporate constitutions, 58
corporate governance, 187, 374
corporate grassroots mobilization, 15, 321–353
  in Australia, 350
  in France, 331, 344–349
  in Germany, 331, 339–344
  in Norway, 331, 335–339
  in US, 331–334
corporate identity, 305–307
corporate lobbying, 337–338, 339, 340, 341, 344, 347
corporate mission, 305
corporate philanthropy, 457
corporate politics, 331
  state mediation in, 324–326, 349
corporate rankings, 56
Corporate Register, 49
corporate reputation, 52–53, 61, 256, 263, 289, 307
  activist targeting and, 430–444
  CSR and, 430–444
  rankings, 56, 433
  reputational halo effect, 434–437, 445
  reputational liability effect, 437–439, 447
corporate resistance, 15
Corporate Responsibility Officers Association, 58
corporate scandals, 38–39, 41, 43, 257, 264, 271, 323
corporate social responsibility (CSR), 1, 185, 218, 367
  activist targeting and, 430–444, 466
  as social regulation of economy, 2–5, 7, 17–18, 455–457
  business case for, 321
  business-led, 112, 114–117, 130–133, 206, 462
  comparative analysis of, 185–188
  conflict minerals and, 149–178

consulting services, 51–53
contradictions of, 393–396
corporate resistance to, 15
critics of, 456
education, 53–54
effectiveness of, 465
employment stability and, 406–444
environmental performance and, 365–380
evolution of, 460
field of, 28, 43, 49–50, 54–58, 59, 60–62, 457–462
financial performance and, 432
firm stability and, 402–412
firms' response to, 1, 3, 14–15, 251–269, 462–467
future of, 61–62
global framework for. *See* global CSR frameworks
global nature of, 1
globalization and, 173–175
history and development of, 3, 11, 42–59, 73, 457–462
impact of, 16–17
in developing countries, 6, 10
institutional contexts, 5–8, 185
insurance effect of, 436
intensification of field of, 49–50
maximalist position, 133
minimalist position, 133
motivations for participation in, 251–269, 286–315
national, 9, 12, 107–204, 459
organizations/nitiatives, 44–51, 60
patient capital and, 76–80
performance and, 265, 456, 465
politics of, 455
production factories and, 395–444
rationalization and scientization of, 54–58
reports, 49
reputation and, 430–444
research on, 17, 54, 365, 367
social movement pressure and, 27
spread of, 109
standards regime and, 73–120
sub-fields of, 13–14
supply chain, 13, 181–204, 462
sustainability discourse and, 218–225

transnational, 6
varieties of capitalism perspective on, 219–225
corporate social responsiveness, 298, 300
corporations, 29, 218, *See also* transnational corporations
economic contexts for, 5, 8, 9
financial performance of, 3
green, 16
institutional contexts for, 5, 6, 8
motivations for joining Global Compact, 286–315
public confidence in, 131–132
reactions of, to CSR, 1, 3, 8, 14–15, 462–467
reasons for participation in global CSR initiatives by, 251–269
resistance by, to public pressures, 321–353
rise of, 30–32, 218
role of, in society, 218, 221
security responsibility of, 174
corporatism, 32, 328, 329–330, 331, 349, 464
in Germany, 339
in Norway, 336
corruption, 81, 84, 87, 175
cost-benefit analysis, 14
Cote d'Ivoire, 157
Council on Economic Priorities (CEP), 198
counterfeiting, 161
credibility signaling, 302–304
CSR organizations\initiatives, 60, *See also specific organizations*
global. *See* global CSR frameworks
internal structure, 58
linkages among, 50–51
CSR products, 52

Davos conference, 46
DeBeers, 156, 159, 172, 461
decoupling, 185
Deepwater Horizon, 456
deliberative democracy, 84
Democratic Republic of Congo (DRC), 156, 157, 162, 165, 166, 167, 168, 171
dependency theory, 38

Index

deregulation, 39, 459
developed countries, CSR in, 6
developing countries, 119, 130
  CSR in, 6, 10
  economic growth in, 32
  labor rights in, 8
  motivations for joining Global Compact in, 290
  NGOs in, 321
development theories, 37
Dhaka, Bangladesh, 181
diamonds/diamond industry, 13, 150–151, 156, 158–161, 162, 163, 171, 172, 174, 461,
Dodd-Frank Financial Reform Act, 163, 167, 169, 171, 175
domestic level, 5
domestically oriented production, 415
Dow Jones Sustainability Index, 57, 265, 435
due diligence, 20, 163, 166–167, 168, 457

Earth Summit, 75, 76
Eco-Management and Audit Scheme, 253
economic contexts, 5, 8, 9
economic development, 91
economic globalization. *See* globalization
economy
  growth of, in post-war period, 33
  social regulation of, 1–5, 29–32, 455–457
Econsense, 111
education, 30, 33, 34, 35, 36
  CSR, 53–54
  ethics, 58
'effective remedy', 82–83
Electronic Industry Citizenship Coalition (EICC), 165–166
electronics industry, 165–166, 172, 397
embedded liberalism, 37, 39, 59, 100
Emergency Planning and Community Right-to-Know Act, 372
emerging markets, 90
employer organizations, 79
employers' associations, 345–346
employment stability, 16, 401
  codes of conduct and, 409–444

CSR and, 406–444
  in Indonesian factories, 402–412
  patterns of instability, 415–416
enabling rights, 203
End UN Corporate Capture campaign, 98
Energy Star program, 253
engagement, 307–309
Enlightenment, 29
Enough, 156, 162, 165, 166, 167, 172
Enron, 456
Environmental Management and Audit Scheme, 8
environmental movement, 346, 384, 388
environmental organizations, 338, 385, 387
environmental performance, 365–380, 465
  auditing of, 370–372, 384
  company attributes and, 368
  perceived, 381–413
  public disclosure of, 370–372, 384
  regulatory environment and, 368
environmental protection, 87, 93–94
Environmental Protection Agency (EPA), 372, 387
environmental sustainability, 459, *See also* sustainability
environmental, social and governance (ESG) standards, 19, 73–120
environmentalism, 16
Equador, 41
Equator Principles, 76
Ethical Trading Initiative (ETI), 87, 192, 198, 201, 202, 401
ethics training, 58
European Eco-Management and Audit Scheme, 46
European Foundation for Quality Management, 50
European Management Forum, 42
European Union (EU), 8, 168
  CSR in, 186, 187
  supply chain CSR in, 195, 198, 199–204, 208–213
export-oriented production, 406–411, 415–416
external environment, 5, 14, 368
external stakeholders, 289

externalities, 220
Extractive Industries Transparency Initiative (EITI), 84, 174

factory audits, 188
factory closures, 416–420
factory fires, 181, 210
factory monitoring, 393
Fair Labor Association (FLA), 46, 93, 194, 198, 201, 202, 205, 206, 208, 209, 401
Fair Labor Standards, 253
Fair Trade, 87, 95–96
Fair Trade certification, 400
Fair Trade USA, 94–96
Fair Wear Foundation (FWF), 192, 198, 201, 202
Fairtrade International (FLO), 95–96
Fatal Transactions, 158
Fiedman, Milton, 39
financial internationality, 265
financial performance, 3, 265, 365, 367, 432
fire safety, 181
fire-related workplace deaths, 210
first-party audits, 366, 369, 370–372, 384
FLA. *See* Fair Labor Association (FLA)
footwear industry, 393, 397, *See also* textile, footwear, and apparel (TFA) sector
forced labor, 203
Ford, Henry, 457
foreign direct investment (FDI), 75
Foreign Trade Association, 200
Forest Stewardship Council (FSC), 86, 89
forestry industry, 8, 171
Fortune Magazine, 263, 374, 436, 440
Fowler, Robert, 157
Foxconn, 209, 213
France, 8, 325
  civil society in, 344–347
  corporate grassroots practices in, 331, 344–349
  CSR in, 15
  minority groups in, 327
  politics in, 344–347
  statist system in, 330
free market capitalism, 48, 218, 224

free market liberalism, 9
free-riding, 80, 94, 255
Friedman, Milton, 456
Friends of the Earth International, 93
FTSE4Good Index, 57
functional theories, of corporation motivations for CSR, 254–256, 263
functionalism, 32
FWF. *See* Fair Wear Foundation (FWF)

Gap, 193, 195
General Motors, 32
Germany, 8
  as coordinated economy, 224, 240
  civil society in, 339–341
  corporate grassroots practices in, 331, 339–344
  corporatism in, 330
  CSR in, 111
  political system in, 339, 341
  sustainability discourse in, 234
Germany Society for Political Consulting, 341
Gifford, Kathie Lee, 434
global citizenship
  concept of, 44
  transnationals and, 42–59
Global Compact. *See* United Nations Global Compact (UNGC)
Global Compact Counter Summit, 97
Global Compact Critics, 98
Global Compact Japan Network, 295–297
global corporations. *See* transnational corporations
global CSR frameworks, 2, 5, 6, 12, 87, 183, 322, 349
  background on, 253–254
  benefits of participation in, 254–256
  controversial nature of, 252
  corporate reactions to, 14–15
  failure of early, 130–133
  impact of, 16–17
  motivations for participation in, 286–315
  national CSR and, 116–118, 125–130, 137–140
  political economy considerations, 130–133

Index 479

reasons for firm participation in, 251–269
research on, 118
varieties of capitalism perspective and, 219–225
global CSR proposition, 113, 137
global culture, 117, 138
global economy, 44
Global eSustainability Initiative (GeSI), 165
Global Exchange, 434
global institutional pressure, 138, 262
national CSR and, 133–141
global norms, 17, 27, 396, 399, 460, 463
global public policy, 6
Global Reporting Initiative (GRI), 1, 46, 50, 79, 84, 86, 89, 91, 108, 116, 135, 209, 218, 365, 369, 465
background on, 253–254
environmental performance and, 376, 384–386
membership in, 251, 254, 373
motivations for participation in, 251–269
national CSR associations and, 128
objectives of, 369
sustainability discourse and, 243
global scripts, 396
Global Social Compliance Program (GSCP), 199, 200–201, 202, 205, 206–207, 208
global society, 27, 30, 33, 34–36, 41, 44, 107, 113, 116, 117, 133, 458, 459
Global Sullivan Principles, 2, 42
global supply chains, 8, 16, 36, 154–155, 397
Global Witness, 156, 158, 161, 162, 166, 167
GlobalG.A.P., 89, 91
globalization, 8, 27, 73, 84, 107, 321, 324, 326, 397, 458
CSR and, 173–175
multinationals and, 36–37
gold, 156, 162, 163
governance, 95–96
collaborative, 84
corporate, 187, 374
for conflict minerals, 169–178
gap, 459

good, 157
good governance, 157
multistakeholder, 79
government actions, 4, 5
government regulation, 9, 15, 73, 84
CSR and, 456
of conflict minerals, 167–169
governmental organizations, 36
governmentality, 84
grassroots mobilization. *See* corporate grassroots mobilization
Grayson, David, 128
green corporations, 16
green marketing, 384
Greenpeace, 93, 94
greenwashing, 28, 46, 252
GRI. *See* Global Reporting Initiative (GRI)
grievance procedures, 83
Group of 77, 130
GSCP. *See* Global Social Compliance Program (GSCP)
Guatemala, 38

halo effect, 17, 433, 434–437, 445
Hammel, Laury, 128
hard regulation, 74, 75
Harvard University, 54
higher education, 54
Human Development Report, 75
human rights, 32, 34, 75, 87, 457
Hunzinger, Moritz, 341
hybrid regulation, 80–81

identity, 305–307
Ikea, 393
ILO Tripartite Declaration, 2, 42, 116, 117, 127, 130, 182
image, 256, 263
impact assessment, 91
incorporation, 80
Indonesia
anti-sweatshop activism in, 416–420
capital mobility i n, 398–402
exports, 403
factory closures in, 416–420
labor markets, 404–405
textile, footwear, and apparel (TFA) sector in, 395–444, 465
wages in, 434

industry mobility, 395
information technology sector, 152
institution substitution hypothesis, 187
institutional competition, 152–154
institutional contexts, 5, 6, 8, 185, 261–262, 264, 266, 272
institutional convergence, 155, 187, 188
institutional mirror hypothesis, 187, 188
institutional theories, 58, 258–259
institutional variation, in regulation of conflict minerals, 169–178
Instituto Ethos, 107, 109
instrumentality, 463
insurance, CSR as, 436
Integrity Measures (Global Compact), 76, 97–98
interest groups, 67–69, 328, 331, 335, 344, *See also* civil society
inter-firm dynamics, 182
intergovernmental organizations, 11, 31, 218
  in post-war period, 33
  UN system, 41
international aid organizations, 157
International Alert, 166
International Business Leaders Forum, 45, 50, 139, 253
International Conference on the Great Lakes Region (ICGLR), 156, 166, 169, 170
International Criminal Court (ICC), 80
International Framework Agreements, 82, 87
International Labor Organization (ILO), 79, 82, 116, 401
International Labor Rights Fund, 212
international law, 34
  expansion of, 82–83
international nongovernmental organizations (INGOS), 112, 117, 138, 266, 271, *See also specific organizations*
  national CSR and, 133–141
  rise of, 33, 36
international relations, 152–153, 155
International Tin Research Institute (ITRI), 163
international trade, 36
investment, socially responsible, 57

Iran, 38
Iraq, sanctions on, 157
iRatings database, 373, 381
ISEAL Alliance, 88
ISO 140001 standards, 6, 8, 84, 290, 366
ISO 26000 Standards on Corporate Social Responsibility, 50, 79, 86, 91
ISO 9000 standards, 257
isomorphism, 58
issue-based campaigns, 154
ITRI Ton Supply Chain Initiative (ITSCi), 166

Japan, 224, 234, 235
Japanese corporations, UN Global Compact and, 15, 286–315, 463
journals, 55, 56

Kell, George, 49, 50
Kenya, 224, 235, 240, 242
Kimberley Process Certification Scheme (KPCS), 76, 84, 150–151, 158–161, 169, 170, 171, 172, 173, 174
Knight, Phil, 434
KPCS. *See* Kimberley Process Certification Scheme (KPCS)

labor issues, 16, 193
  capital mobility and, 397–402
  child labor, 84, 193, 203
labor rights, 8, 465
labor standards, 82, 87, 89, 90, 182, 184, 189, 192, 196, 203, 204, 207, 394, 399, 401, 409, 418, 421, 465
labor unions, 9, 79, 186, 203, 205, 208, 326, 331, 339, 345, 404, 417, 422
labor-capital relations, 186
laissez-faire capitalism, 73
law, international, 34, 82–83
legal compliance, 401
Levi Strauss, 194
liability effect, 17
liberal economies, 9, 29–30, 33, 44, 186, 218, 223, 224, 234, 235, 240, 242–243
liberal theory, 37

Index 481

liberalization, 73, 84
Limited Brands, 401
Lindner, Ludwig, 343
lobbying, 337–338, 339, 340, 341, 344, 347
logic of appropriateness, 463
'logic of capital', 84
London Bullion Market Association, 168
London Enterprise Agency (LENTA), 130

management standards
  stakeholder perspective in, 30
  voluntary, 6
management studies, stakeholder perspective in, 4
managerialism, 84
Marange diamonds, 161
Marine Stewardship Council, 253
market economies, 186, 218, 223, 224, 234, 235, 240, 242–243, 325
marketing, cause-related, 52
Marshall Plan, 32
maximalist position, 133
Mazzei, Luzio, 136
MBA Oath, 50
McDermott, Jim, 167
McDonalds, 325
Millennium Development Goals (MDGs), 79, 369
minimalist position, 133
minimum wage, 205
Minnesota Project on Corporate Responsibility, 46
modernization theories, 32, 36, 37, 38, 59
monitoring, reporting and verification (MRV), 73
monopoly, 38
Most Admirable Companies index, 440
MSIs. *See* multistakeholder initiatives (MSIs)
Multi-Fibre Agreement (MFA), 399
multinational corporations. *See also* transnational corporations
  accountability of, 433
  as social problem, 38–39
  globalization and, 36–37
  number of, 1850-2000, 37
  public confidence in, 131–132, 457
  shift to transnationals, 39–42
Multinational Monitor, 38
multistakeholder governance, 79
multistakeholder initiatives (MSIs), 12, 74, 84–102
  in supply chain CSR, 182, 187, 188, 192, 195, 199
  insider and outsider strategies, 96–100
  limitations, 90–92
  tensions within, 92–93
multistakeholder organizations, 73

Namibia, 159
naming and shaming, 2, 83, 96, 432
National Alliance on Mental Illness, 322
National Association of Manufacturers, 168
national boundaries, 5
National Business Initiative, 111
National Contacts Points, 99
national corporate social responsibility, 107–204, 459
  autonomy of, 114
  cross-national variation in adoption of, 119–204
  data and analysis of, 114–118
  future research on, 138–140
  global CSR frameworks and, 113, 116–118, 125–130, 137–140
  global pressure and, 108, 133–141
  growth of, 118–119
  national CSR associations and, 108–112
  political economy considerations, 130–133
  significance of, 107–113
National Council of French Employers (CNPF), 345–346
national CSR associations, 12, 108–112, 142
  business-led, 112, 114–117, 130–133
  data and analysis of, 114–118
  establishment of, 119–204
  growth of, 118–119
  INGOs and, 133–141
national institutional environment, 261, 266

national interests, 37
National Labor Committee, 193, 434
National Labor Relations Board, 331
national sovereignty. *See* state sovereignty
natural law, 44
natural resources, 231
  exploitation of, 149, *See also* conflict minerals
  resource curse and, 156–157, 461
negative externalities, 221
neo-colonialism, 38
neo-institutional theory, 223, 324
neoliberalism, 9, 27, 39, 43, 45, 59, 78, 221, 324
Nestlé, 38
Netherlands, 8
new institutional approach, 4
New International Economic Order, 38, 130
New York Stock Exchange, 290
NGOs. *See* nongovernmental organizations (NGOs)
Niger, 457
Nigeria, 41
Nike, 193, 194, 395, 401, 418, 420, 434–435
nongovernmental organizations (NGOs), 6, 11, 12, 31, 218, 266, 324, *See also specific organizations*
  civil regulation and, 83–102
  environmental, 338
  Global Compact and, 97
  growth of, 321
  international, 33, 36
  UN and, 41
normative pressures, for participation in global CSR initiatives, ,5, 8, 17, 27, 74, 81, 174, 396, 399, 433, 460, 463
norms, 75, 81
Norms on Responsibilities of TNCs and Other Business Enterprises with Regard to Human Rights, 323, 330
Norway, 331, 335–339
  corporate grassroots practices in, 336
  corporatism in, 335
  political system in, 337

Norwegian Communications Association (NCA), 163

OECD Due Diligence Guidance, 166, 169, 171
OECD Guidance on Responsible Supply Chain of Minerals from Conflict-Affected and High-Risk Areas, 2, 42, 79, 83, 90, 98–100, 116, 117, 127, 130, 171, 182, 253, 271
OECD Guidelines for Multinational Enterprises, 99
OECD Investment Committee, 99
OECD Watch, 75
Office of the High Commissioner for Human Rights, 136
Oppenheimer, Harry, 156, 166, 168, 169
Organization for Economic Cooperation and Development (OECD), 304–305
organizational change, 19, 28
organizational field, 305–307
organizational identity, 5
organizational institutionalism, 4
organizations
  external pressures on, 4
  sociological research on, 199, 466
organized labor, 220, 224, 231
Our Common Future report, 13
overseas subsidiaries, 421

Pakistan, 119
Paraguay, 29
pariah capitalism, 156, 158, 161, 167
Partnership Africa Canada, 16, 76–80, 395
patient capital, 422
patient sourcing, 304
PDCA (Plan-Do-Check-Action) cycle, 157
peacekeeping interventions, 128
Pelling, Anthony, 258, 265
performance, 265, 456, 465
  CSR and, 365–380, 465
  environmental, 3, 265, 365, 367, 432
  financial, 368
  social, 387

Pew Center on Global Climate Change (PCGCC), 322, 342
pharmaceutical industry, 110, 136
Philippine Business for Social Progress (PBSP), 119
Philippines, 181, 200, 211, 213
Philips Van Heusen (PVH), 73
Polanyi, Karl, 4
political actions, 8
political conflict, 74, 130–133, 186, 221, 465
political economy, 372, 373
Political Economy Research Institute (PERI), 5, 8, 9, 12, 186
political-economic factors, 331
politics
  corporate, 455
  CSR and, 149
  high, 344–347
  in France, 339, 341
  in Germany, 335
  in Norway, 92–100
  of regulatory change, 324–326, 349
  of the corporation, state mediation in, 324, 325, 349
  private, 331
  US, 368
pollution
  disclosure of, 376–380, 384
  levels of, and CSR frameworks, 368
  measures of, 224
post-colonial transition economies, 42, 59
post-war period, 32–36
  transnationalization in, 79
poverty reduction, 90, 92
power relations, 81
principled pragmatism, 174
Principles for Human Rights and Security, 50
Principles for Responsible Investing, 76, 79, 174
Principles for Responsible Investing (PRI), 50, 54
Principles for Responsible Management Education, 324, 325, 349
private politics, 430, 435
proactive social responsibility, 394, 395
production stability\instability, 53–54
professional development, 30, 61

professionalization, 464
profitability, 90, See also financial performance
proft motive, 437–439, 447
prosocial claims, 430–444
  activist targeting and, 81, 83
Protect, Respect, and Remedy framework, 91, 345
protectionist barriers, 417–419
PT Kolon Langgeng, 419–420
PT Spotec, 333, 334
Public Affairs Council, 221
public goods, 256, 263
public image, 337–338, 344, 347–348, See also corporate reputation
public pressure. See social pressure
public relations (PR), 79
public-private partnerships (PPPs), 90, 193, 399

race to the bottom, 30
railroad companies, 172
Raise Hope for Congo campaign, 211, 212, 213, 463
Rana Plaza factory, 54–58
rationalization, of CSR, 434
Reebok, 152, 173
regime complexity, 12, 73–120
regulatory environment, 74, 83–102
  civil regulation, 151, 165–178
  conflict minerals, 95–96
  contestation within governance structures, 368
  environmental performance and, 9, 15, 73, 84
  government regulation, 80–81
  hybrid regulation, 96–100
  insider and outsider strategies, 89–92
  limitations and dilemmas in, 84–102
  multistakeholder initiatives, 86–88
  normative and regulatory advances, 74
  political economy of, 92–100
  politics and, 81–82
  ratcheting-down in, 80–81, 87
  ratcheting-up in, 73
  re-regulation, 73, 75
  self-regulation, 152–153
  state power and, 74, 75–76, 83

United Nations and, 154
regulatory institutions, 29, 30
religion, 56
Reputation Institute, 14, 52–53, 252, 255, 307, 430–444
reputation management, 434–437, 445
  reputational halo effect, 437–439, 447
  reputational liability effect, 433, 434–437, 445
reputational halo effect, 433, 437–439, 447
reputational liability effect, 73, 458
re-regulation, 374
research & development (R&D), 156–157, 461
resource curse, 369, 370
Responsible Care program, 54
Responsible Endowment Coalition, 156
Rio Tinto, 388, 422
risk management, 372
Risk-Screening Environmental Indicators, 150–151, 158–161
rough diamonds, 93–94
Roundtable on Responsible Soy, 93–94
Roundtable on Sustainable Palm Oil (RSPO), 81
Ruggie process, 81
Ruggie, John, 156
Rwandan genocide, 84, 89, 90, 210, 401

SA8000 standard, 157
SAI. *See* Social Accountability International (SAI)
sanctions, 33, 34, 36, 44
science, 54–58
scientization, of CSR, 163, 167, 171
Section 1502 legislation, 174
security responsibility, 366, 369, 370–372
self-certification, 29, 30, 34, 36, 39, 41, 42, 43, 45, 59, 132, 218
self-interest, 73, 75, 456
self-regulation, 195
Service Organisation for Compliance Audit Management (SOCAM), 90, 187, 252
shareholder primacy, 257
shareholder resolutions, 41
Shell, 156, 157, 158, 159, 162, 171, 174

Sierra Leone, 300–304
signaling, as reason for joining UNGC, 57
sin stocks, 161, 175
smuggling, 197, 198, 200, 201, 202, 210
Social Accountability International (SAI), 321
social globalization, 265
social internationality, 466
social legitimacy, 27, 30, 154, 324
social movements, 466, *See also* activist movements
  critics of, 43
  global, 335
  in Norway, 257–259
  influence of, 42
  nineteenth-century, 42
  post-war period, 368
social performance, 2, 11, 14, 257–259
social pressure, 321–353
  corporate resistance to, 1–5, 29–32
social regulation of economy, 2–5, 7, 17–18, 455–457
  CSR as, 57
socially responsible investment indices, 327, 329, 330
societal systems, 343
Society for Road and Transportation Planning, 5, 6, 8
socio-institutional factors, 4
sociological research, 74, 75, 80–81
soft regulation, 157
Somalia, 42, 111, 159, 161
South Africa, 39
sovereignty, 93–94
Soy and Palm Oil Roundtables, 9, 92, 96
stakeholder participation, 4
stakeholder perspective, 30
stakeholder theory, 350
stakeholders, 289
  external, 400, 406
  relationships with, 200
Stakeholders' Advisory Council, 398–402
standards. *See also* regulatory environment
  capital mobility and, 398–402
  codes of conduct, 82, 87, 89, 90, 182, 184, 189, 192, 196, 203, 204, 207, 394, 399, 401, 418, 421, 465

labor, 81–82
ratcheting-down of, 80–81, 87
ratcheting-up of, 437, 438
voluntary. *See* voluntary standards/voluntarism
Starbucks Coffee, 327
state formation, 152–153, 170–171, 173
state power, 31, 34, 39, 161
state regulation. *See* government regulation
state sovereignty, 323–324, 327–331, 338, 349
state-civil society interface, 224
state-directed economies, 15, 327–328, 329, 331, 344, 349, 464
statist systems, 322
strategic philanthropy, 58
structural isomorphism, 75
Sub-Commission on the Promotion and Protection of Human Rights, 13, 16, 181–182, 183, 189
subcontractors, 162
Sudan, 38
Suez Canal, 111
Sullivan Principles, 13, 181–204, 462
supply chain CSR, 183–189
  about, 187, 199–204
  development of, 183–184, 189–199, 208–213
  emergence of, 182, 208–213
  field formation, 213
  future of, 182, 187, 188, 192, 195, 199
  multistakeholder initiatives in, 199–204
  organizations in field of, 182
  origins of, 208–213
  regional differences in, 196, 209
  self-regulation in, 165
supply chains, 163, 166–167, 168, 175
  due diligence in, 8, 16, 36, 154–155, 397
  global, 422
  relational, 165–178
  sourcing, CSR in, 14, 74, 218
supra-national corporations. *See* transnational corporations
sustainability, 228–237
  concepts associated with, 221–223
  definition of, 365, 384, 393
  reports, 218–225, 459
sustainability discourse, 230–237
  comparative analysis of, 228–237
  concept of public, 224–229
  data and empirical method for, 224–229, 235
  in media, 219–225, 242–244
  varieties of capitalism perspective and, 370
Sustainable Forestry, 77, 182, 183, 189–199, 209, 395
sweatshops, 156

T3 G conflict minerals. *See* conflict minerals
tantalum, 198
Tepper Marlin, Alice, 200, 206, 211
Tesco, 41
Texaco, 416–420
textile, footwear, and apparel (TFA) sector
  activist campaigns and, 406–411
  business failures in, 397–402
  capital moblility and, 409–444
  codes of conduct in, 405
  employment in, 416–420
  factory closures in, 399
  globalization and, 395–444, 465
  in Indonesia, 402–412
  instability in, 399–400
  location decisions in, 181, 210
That's It Sportwear, 369, 370–372, 384
Third World. *See* developing countries
third-party audits, 156, 162, 163, 165–166
tin, 41
tobacco companies, 27, 30, 31
Tocqueville, Alexis de, 372
Toxics Release Inventory (TRI), 29, 36, 257, 461
trade, 8
trade relations, 95
trade unions. *See* labor unions
TransFair USA, 223
translation, 265
transnational corporations, 42–59, *See also* corporations, multinational corporations
  as global citizens, 149, 157

conflicts and, 41
criticism of, 27, 39–42
growth and expansion of, 11, 27–62, 185, 302–304, 457–459
legitimation of, 32–36
post-war period, 75
UN and, 78–80
voluntarism and, 107
trans-nationality, 87, 167, 174
transparency, 156, 162, 163
tungsten, 119

Uganda, 406
unemployment benefits, 200
UNI Commerce, 94
Unilever, 41
Union Carbide, 33
Union of International Associations, 194
UNITE, 8
United Kingdom, 192
  anti-sweatshop activism in, 224, 240
  as liberal economy, 9, 111, 139
  CSR in, 234, 242
  sustainability discourse in, 2, 41, 50, 74, 156, 262
United Nations (UN), 75–76, 97–98
  business relations, 83
  effective remedy and, 157
  peacekeeping interventions by, 74, 75–76, 83
  regulatory environment and, 157
  sanctions, 167, 168, 169
  Security Council, 40, 75, 76, 127, 130
United Nations Centre on Transnational Corporations (UNCTC), 75
United Nations Commission on Human Rights, 75
United Nations Conference on Environment and Development, 75
United Nations Conference on Trade and Development (UNCTAD), 75
United Nations Development Programme (UNDP), 163
United Nations Due Diligence, 167
United Nations Expert Group on the DRC, 1, 6, 15, 16, 46, 48, 49, 50, 53, 54, 75, 90, 107, 108, 116, 135, 365, 369, 463, 465

United Nations Global Compact (UNGC), 253–254, 286
  background on, 174
  conflict zones and, 82
  environmental issues and, 376, 381, 384, 386–387
  environmental performance and, 78, 79, 116
  establishment of, 79
  features of, 116
  impact at national level, 295–315
  in Japan, 76, 97–98
  Integrity Measures, 266, 289, 295–297
  local networks, 251, 254, 266, 286, 373
  membership in, 251–269, 286–315, 463
  motivations for participation in, 126, 137
  national CSR and, 369
  objectives of, 93
  opposition to, 305–307
  principles of, 81
  ratcheting-down of, 80
  ratcheting-up of, 96–98
  reform of, 98
United Nations Joint Inspection Unit, 83
United Nations Non-Governmental Liaison Service (UNNGLS), 2
United Nations Norms on the Responsibilities of Transnational Corporations, 75, 83
United Nations Research Institute for Social Development (UNRISD), 8
United States, 193–194
  anti-sweatshop activism in, 224, 240
  as liberal economy, 349
  civil society in, 167
  conflict minerals legislation in, 17
  consumer boycotts in, 331–334
  corporate grassroots practices in, 9, 15, 111, 186, 187, 196
  CSR in, 365–380
  environmental performance of firms in, 31, 32
  hegemony of, 171, 173
  intervention by, 29–30
  liberal model in, 38

Index

neo-colonialism and, 331
political system in, 196–204, 208–213
supply chain CSR in, 234, 235, 242
sustainability discourse in, 194
United Students Against Sweatshops (USAS), 95
United Students for Fair Trade, 54, 290
universities, 33
university enrollment, 111, 136
Urban Foundation, 157
US Agency for International Development (USAID), 168
US Chamber of Commerce, 186, 219–225, 234, 242–244, 261
varieties of capitalism (VoC), 395, 421

Vietnam, 38
Vietnam War, 6, 8, 73, 75, 88, 132–133, 139, 393, 456
voluntary standards/voluntarism, 168
 conflict minerals and, 16
 labor standards, 80–81
 ratcheting-up of, 78–80
 shift toward, 181–204
 supply chain CSR and, 205, 395, 399, 415, 434

wages, 200, 205, 206, 210, 351, 401
Walmart, 149, 162, 174, 175
war, 38
watchdog organizations, 326
welfare state, 82
WHO Framework Convention on Tobacco Control, 184
women workers, 79
Women's Empowerment Principles, 81

women's rights, 87, 89, 194, 196, 198, 201, 208, 212, 417, 418
Worker Rights Consortium (WRC), 181, 203
worker safety, 203, 207, 465
workers' rights, 205,
working hours, 157
World Bank, 45, 50, 116, 253, 260, 264, 365
World Business Council for Sustainable Development (WBCSD), 376, 387
 environmental performance and, 373
 membership in, 369
 objectives of, 42, 45, 46, 253
World Economic Forum, 163, 166, 168, 169, 170
world economy. *See* global economy
World Gold Council (WGC), 262
world institutional environment, 75
World Investment Report, 5, 138, 262, 458
world society theory, 76, 78, 79
World Summit on Sustainable Development (WSSD), 5, 38
world systems theory, 93–94
World Wide Fund for Nature (WWF), 197–198, 201, 203, 401
Worldwide Responsible Apparel Production (WRAP), 130
Wright, Brian, 117

Yearbook of International Organizations, 393

Zara, 161
Zimbabwe, 161

For EU product safety concerns, contact us at Calle de José Abascal, 56–1°, 28003 Madrid, Spain or eugpsr@cambridge.org.

www.ingramcontent.com/pod-product-compliance
Ingram Content Group UK Ltd.
Pitfield, Milton Keynes, MK11 3LW, UK
UKHW020451090825
461507UK00007B/180